A EUROPEAN SOCIAL UNION AFTER THE CRISIS

Today, many people agree that the EU lacks solidarity and needs a social dimension. The debate is not new, but until now the notion of a 'social Europe' remained vague and elusive. To make progress, we need a coherent conception of the reasons behind, and the agenda for, not a 'social Europe', but a new idea: a European Social Union. We must motivate, define, and demarcate an appropriate notion of European solidarity. We must also understand the legal and political obstacles, and how these can be tackled. In short, we need unequivocal answers to questions of why, what, and how: on that basis, we can define a clear-cut normative and institutional concept. That is the remit of this book: it provides an in-depth interdisciplinary examination of the rationale and the feasibility of a European Social Union. Outstanding scholars and top-level practitioners reflect on obstacles and solutions, from an economic, social, philosophical, legal, and political perspective.

FRANK VANDENBROUCKE studied economics in Leuven and Cambridge (UK) and received his DPhil in Oxford. He was member of the Belgian and Flemish parliament and Minister of social affairs, employment, pensions, and education. Vandenbroucke was closely involved with the launching of the EU Lisbon Strategy in 2000, notably with the development of its social dimension. He was professor at the University of Leuven (2011–15). In 2015, he was appointed as University Professor at the University of Amsterdam. His research focuses on the social impact of the European Union. He also holds a chair at the University of Antwerp.

CATHERINE BARNARD, MA (Cantab), LLM (EUI), PhD (Cantab) is Professor in European Union Law and Employment Law at the University of Cambridge, and senior tutor and fellow of Trinity College. She specialises in EU law and employment law. She is author of *EU Employment Law* (2016, 5th edn), *The Substantive Law of the EU: The Four Freedoms* (2016, 5th edn), and (with Peers ed.), *European Union Law* (2014). Currently, Catherine is a Senior Fellow in the ESRC's UK in a Changing Europe project where she is looking at various issues connected with Brexit.

GEERT DE BAERE, cand. iur., lic. iur. (Antwerp), LLM, PhD (Cantab) is Legal Secretary at the Court of Justice of the EU and Associate Professor of EU Law and International Law at the University of Leuven. He has been nominated judge at the General Court of the EU from October 2017. His research interests include EU constitutional law and theory, particularly regarding EU external action, and (the theory of) international law. His publications include *Constitutional Principles of EU External Relations* (2008); with E. Cloots and S. Sottiaux, *Federalism in the EU* (2012), and with J. Wouters, *The Contribution of International and Supranational Courts to the Rule of Law* (2015).

A European Social Union after the Crisis

Edited by

FRANK VANDENBROUCKE

University of Amsterdam

CATHERINE BARNARD

University of Cambridge

GEERT DE BAERE

University of Leuven

CAMBRIDGE
UNIVERSITY PRESS

CAMBRIDGE
UNIVERSITY PRESS

University Printing House, Cambridge CB2 8BS, United Kingdom

One Liberty Plaza, 20th Floor, New York, NY 10006, USA

477 Williamstown Road, Port Melbourne, VIC 3207, Australia

4843/24, 2nd Floor, Ansari Road, Daryaganj, Delhi – 110002, India

79 Anson Road, #06-04/06, Singapore 079906

Cambridge University Press is part of the University of Cambridge.

It furthers the University's mission by disseminating knowledge in the pursuit of
education, learning, and research at the highest international levels of excellence.

www.cambridge.org
Information on this title: www.cambridge.org/9781108415781
DOI: 10.1017/9781108235174

First published 2017

Printed in the United Kingdom by Clays, St Ives plc

A catalogue record for this publication is available from the British Library.

Library of Congress Cataloging-in-Publication Data
Names: Vandenbroucke, Frank, 1955– editor. | Barnard, Catherine, editor. |
Baere, G. de, editor.
Title: A European social union after the crisis / edited by Frank Vandenbroucke,
University of Amsterdam, Catherine Barnard, University of Cambridge,
Geert De Baere, Katholieke Universiteit Leuven, Belgium.
Description: Cambridge, United Kingdom; New York, NY: Cambridge University Press, 2017. |
Includes bibliographical references and index.
Identifiers: LCCN 2017011181 | ISBN 9781108415781 (hardback : alk. paper)
Subjects: LCSH: European Union. | European Union countries–
Social conditions–21st century. | European Union countries–Social policy–21st century.
Classification: LCC HN373.5 .E835 2017 | DDC 306.094–dc23
LC record available at https://lccn.loc.gov/2017011181

ISBN 978-1-108-41578-1 Hardback

Contents

Figures

Tables

Contributors

László Andor

László Andor is Head of Department of Economic Policy at Corvinus University (Budapest) and Senior Research Fellow at IMK (Hans Böckler Stiftung). He was EU Commissioner for Employment, Social Affairs and Inclusion in the Barroso II Commission (2010–14). Beforehand, he was a member of the Board of Directors of the EBRD. Since 2015, he has been lecturing at Hertie School of Governance (Berlin), ULB (Brussels) and Sciences Po (Paris) and became member in various think tanks (IZA, EPC, RAND Europe, Friends of Europe, Notre Europe). He was awarded Doctor Honoris Causa at Sofia University of National and World Economy and the Legion of Honour by the French President in 2014.

Geert De Baere

Geert De Baere, cand. iur., lic. iur. (Antwerp), LLM, PhD (Cantab) is Legal Secretary at the Court of Justice of the EU and Associate Professor of EU Law and International Law at the University of Leuven. His research interests include EU constitutional law and theory, particularly regarding EU external action, and (the theory of) international law. His publications include *Constitutional Principles of EU External Relations* (2008), with E. Cloots and S. Sottiaux, *Federalism in the EU* (2012), and with J. Wouters, *The Contribution of International and Supranational Courts to the Rule of Law* (2015).

Catherine Barnard

Catherine Barnard MA (Cantab), LLM (EUI), PhD (Cantab) is Professor in European Union Law and Employment Law at the University of Cambridge, and senior tutor and fellow of Trinity College. She specialises in EU law and employment law. She is author of *EU Employment Law* (2016), *The Substantive Law of the EU: The Four Freedoms* (2016), and with S. Peers *European Union*

Law (2014). Currently, Catherine is a Senior Fellow in the ESRC's UK in a Changing Europe project where she is working with Dr Amy Ludlow on a project entitled: '"Honeypot Britain?" The Lived experience of working as an EU migrant in the UK'.

Sonja Bekker

Dr Sonja Bekker is an associate professor of European Governance and Social Policy at the ReflecT labour-market institute of Tilburg University, the Netherlands. Her research deals with the evolving EU socioeconomic governance within the European Semester. It includes research on vulnerable groups, such as youth, NEETs, and people who have atypical employment contracts. She coordinates the master Labour Law and Employment Relations, which offers students an international and multidisciplinary view on employment. Between 2010 and 2015 she was the Dutch labour-market correspondent for the European Employment Policy Observatory of the European Commission.

Philippe de Buck

Philippe de Buck is Senior Advisor at Hill & Knowlton Strategies and is a member of the employers group of the European Economic and Social Committee. From 2002 to 2012 he was Director General of BusinessEurope, the leading business group and the main employer's social partner at EU level. Previously he had led Agoria, which regroups the Belgian technology industry, dealing with social dialogue at sector and company level. He holds a law degree from the University of Leuven. During his professional life he has been involved in industrial relations and in economic and international trade matters. He is visiting professor at the College of Europe in Bruges.

Christophe Degryse

Christophe Degryse is a senior researcher at the European Trade Union Institute (ETUI), in charge of the Foresight Unit. His most recent area of research includes the European social dialogue (cross-industry and sectoral level), the 'new' European economic governance, and the social impacts of the digitisation of the economy.

Maxime Cerutti

Maxime Cerutti was appointed as BusinessEurope's Social Affairs Director in January 2012. He is responsible for a diverse portfolio of social affairs and labour-market policy issues, including BusinessEurope's engagement as social partner as part of the European social dialogue. Prior to joining BusinessEurope as social affairs adviser in 2007, Maxime started his career at the European Youth

Forum in Brussels. He graduated in political science in Sciences Po Paris and also holds a double law degree from the Universities of Bordeaux and Canterbury, and took part in a summer session at the University of Berkeley.

Helder de Schutter

Helder de Schutter is Associate Professor in Social and Political Philosophy at the University of Leuven and directs the research group RIPPLE (Research in Political Philosophy Leuven). He works on linguistic justice, federalism, and nationalism. He was previously affiliated to Princeton University, the University of Oxford (Nuffield College), and the Facultés Universitaires Saint-Louis (Brussels). Publications have appeared in journals such as the *British Journal of Political Science, Inquiry, Journal of Political Philosophy, Journal of Applied Philosophy, Metaphilosophy*, and *Politics, Philosophy, and Economics*.

Simon Deakin

Simon Deakin is Professor of Law and Director of the Centre for Business Research at the University of Cambridge, where he teaches labour law, private law, and the economics of law. He has been contributing to the debate over European social policy since the late 1980s, when his paper with Ulrich Mückenberger, 'From Deregulation to a European Floor of Rights', was published in the *Zeitschrift für ausländisches und internationales Arbeits- und Sozialrecht* (1989). In subsequent work he developed the concept of 'Labour Law as Market Regulation' in *Liber Amicorum Bill Wedderburn* (1996) and an economic critique of the *Laval* judgment, 'Regulatory Competition after *Laval*' in the *Cambridge Yearbook of European Legal Studies* (2008). He is a member of the ETUI's Transnational Trade Union Rights group and in that capacity has commented extensively on social policy aspects of the Eurozone crisis.

Sjoerd Feenstra

Sjoerd Feenstra is a legal advisor in the Directorate General Employment, Social Affairs and Inclusion of the European Commission. He is currently working on employment policies and labour-market issues, such as employment protection legislation, labour-market segmentation, wage-setting mechanisms, and labour mobility, in the context of the economic governance and socioeconomic policy coordination in the EU (the European Semester). He was, on behalf of the European Commission, one of the main negotiators of the legislative initiative on the enforcement of the Posting of Workers Directive. He joined the European Commission in 1998 after having worked as senior manager/consultant for Ernst & Young and PriceWaterhouse Coopers.

Maurizio Ferrera

Maurizio Ferrera holds a Laurea degree in Philosophy (University of Turin), an MA in Political Science (Stanford University), and a PhD in Social and Political Sciences (European University Institute). He is Professor of Political Science at the University of Milan. He has been serving on various Advisory Commissions at national and EU levels as well as on several editorial boards of academic journals and publishers. His academic work focuses on comparative welfare states, European integration, and political theory. Since 2003 he is an editorialist for *Il Corriere della Sera*. His last book in English is *The Boundaries of Welfare* (2005); in Italian he has recently published *Rotta di collisione. Euro contro welfare?* (2016). In 2013 he was awarded an ERC Advanced Grant for a five-year project on Reconciling Economic and Social Europe: ideas, values, and consensus (www.resceu.eu).

Paul De Grauwe

Paul De Grauwe is John Paulson Professor at the London School of Economics, He was a member of the Belgian parliament from 1991 to 2003. He is honorary doctor of the University of Sankt Gallen (Switzerland), the University of Turku (Finland), the University of Genoa, the University of Valencia, and Maastricht University. He was a visiting professor at various universities: Paris, Amsterdam, Berlin, Kiel, Milan, Pennsylvania, and Michigan. He obtained his PhD from the Johns Hopkins University in 1974. He is a research fellow at the Centre for European Policy Studies in Brussels and CEPR fellow in London. His research interests are in the economics of monetary unions and behavioural macroeconomics. His book publications include: *The Limits of the Market* (2017), *The Economics of Monetary Union* (2016), and *Lectures on Behavioral Macroeconomics* (2012).

Jose A. Gutiérrez-Fons

Jose A. Gutiérrez-Fons is Legal Secretary in the Chambers of President Koen Lenaerts at the Court of Justice of the European Union, since 2009. He holds a degree in Law from the University of Madrid (Universidad Autónoma de Madrid), an LLM in European Law from the College of Europe, and a PhD in Law from Queen Mary and Westfield College, University of London.

Kathleen Gutman

Kathleen Gutman is Legal Secretary at the Court of Justice of the European Union and Visiting Professor and Senior Affiliated Researcher at the Institute for European Law, University of Leuven. Her main research interests include EU constitutional, procedural, and private law. She holds a PhD in Law and an MA in European Studies from the University of Leuven and a JD and LLM in International and Comparative Law from the Duke University School of Law.

Marc Hooghe

Marc Hooghe is a professor of political science at the University of Leuven (Belgium), where he directs the Centre for Citizenship and Democracy. He holds an ERC Advanced Grant to investigate the democratic linkage between citizens and the state in Europe. He has been a visiting professor in France, Germany, the Netherlands, Finland, and Canada. He has published mainly on political participation, political trust, and comparative political research. He has edited or written some 20 books, in Dutch and English, and he regularly contributes to the public debate in Belgian newspapers.

Yuemei Ji

Yuemei Ji is a lecturer in Economics at the University College London. She obtained her PhD in economics from the University of Leuven. She was a visiting fellow at the European Institute at LSE, the Centre for European Policy Studies (CEPS) in Brussels and the National Bank of Belgium. She gives lectures on European Macroeconomics and International Macroeconomics. Her research interests cover international macroeconomics in general and the European Monetary Union during the post-crisis period in particular. She has done intensive research on the causes of Eurozone debt crisis and its impact on the austerity policies in the Eurozone.

Christian Joerges

Christian Joerges is Professor of Law and Society at the Hertie School of Governance in Berlin. His research focuses on economic ordering through law at the national level and in the processes of European integration and globalisation. The focus of current projects is on the European crisis, and transnational risk regulation and trade governance. He is also a Co-Director of the Centre of European Law and Politics at the University of Bremen. Until 2007, he held the chair for European Economic Law at the European University Institute Florence. He was a Visiting Professor at the law faculties of the Universities of Trento, Toronto, NYU; Columbia and the Birkbeck College of Law in London. He has been a fellow at the Institutes for Advanced Study in Berlin and Wassenaar, NL. In 2009, he was awarded an honorary doctorate from the University Freiburg i.Ue. His most noted book is *Darker Legacies of Law in Europe* (2003).

Alexander Kornezov

Alexander Kornezov graduated in law from St Kliment Ohridski University, Sofia (2002), and obtained a Master of Laws in European law from the College of Europe (Bruges, 2004). He became Doctor of Laws in 2008. He was a lawyer at the Brussels Bar (2004–06), as well as Senior Lecturer in EU procedural law at the University of National and World Economy, Sofia (2008–12), and St Kliment Ohridski University, Sofia (2010–13). He is Associate Professor of EU Law and International Private Law at the Bulgarian Academy of Sciences (since 2014), and has been a guest lecturer at the University of Cambridge and at the University of Leuven. He was Legal Secretary at the Court of Justice of the European Union (2007–16). He is a founding member and member of the board of directors of the Bulgarian Association for European Law, and editor-in-chief of the European law journal *Evropeiski praven pregled*. He is the author of numerous publications in the field of European law. He was Judge at the Civil Service Tribunal from 13 April 2016 to 31 August 2016, and has been Judge at the General Court since 19 September 2016.

Koen Lenaerts

Koen Lenaerts, lic. iuris, PhD in Law (University of Leuven), graduated as a Master of Laws (1978) and Master in Public Administration (1979) from Harvard University. He was Lecturer (1979–83) and subsequently Professor of European Law at the Katholieke Universiteit Leuven (since 1983). Following this he was Legal Secretary at the Court of Justice (1984–85); Professor at the College of Europe, Bruges (1984–89); member of the Brussels Bar (1986–89); Visiting Professor at the Harvard Law School (1989); and Judge at the Court of First Instance of the European Communities from 25 September 1989 to 6 October 2003. He has been Judge at the Court of Justice since 7 October 2003; Vice-President of the Court of Justice from 9 October 2012 to 8 October 2015; and President of the Court of Justice since 8 October 2015.

Philippe Pochet

Philippe Pochet, political scientist, is currently General Director of the European Trade Union Institute (ETUI). He is Professor at the Catholic University of Louvain (Belgium), invited lecturer at the Faculté Universitaire Saint Louis. His main research fields are: social impacts of the monetary union, social dimension of the European Union and social dialogue at sectoral and cross-sectoral levels, the open method of coordination and the new modes of governance, the social challenges of the globalisation process and of climate change.

Dorte Sindbjerg Martinsen

Dorte Sindbjerg Martinsen is Professor at University of Copenhagen, Department of Political Science. Her research focuses on EU welfare policies, investigating integration, national implementation of and compliance with EU social policies, including health care. Her recent work examines the interaction between legal integration and legislative politics in the European Union, published in the book *An Ever More Powerful Court? The Political Constraints of Legal Integration in the European Union* and in the article in *Comparative Political Studies* (2015), 'Judicial Influence on Policy Outputs? The Political Constraints of Legal Integration in the European Union' (2015). She acts as a national expert in the EU Commission's FreSsco (Free movement of workers and Social security coordination) network as well as sitting as expert on the Danish government's council for implementation of EU law.

Frank Vandenbroucke

Frank Vandenbroucke studied economics in Leuven and Cambridge (UK) and received his DPhil in Oxford. He has held several political offices in Belgium, including member of the Belgian parliament and minister (both at the federal and the Flemish levels). Vandenbroucke was closely involved with the launching of the EU Lisbon Strategy in 2000, notably with the development of its social dimension. He was Professor at the University of Leuven (2011–15). In 2015 he was appointed as Professor at the University of Amsterdam. As a professor his research focuses on the social role of the European Union.

Gerhard van der Schyff

Gerhard van der Schyff PhD (Leiden) PhD (Antwerp) LLM (RAU, Johannesburg) is an associate professor in the Department of Public Law, Jurisprudence and Legal History at Tilburg Law School in the Netherlands. His research focuses on European and comparative constitutional law. He is a Member of the International Association of Constitutional Law and an editor of the *European Constitutional Law Review* (published by Cambridge University Press). In 2016 he held a Humboldt Foundation Fellowship for Experienced Researchers at the Chair of Professor Christian Calliess at the Law Faculty of the Free University of Berlin where he conducted research into the interaction between EU and Member State law.

Soetkin Verhaegen

Soetkin Verhaegen is a postdoctoral researcher at the department of Political Science at the University of Stockholm and is affiliated to the Centre for Political Science at the University of Leuven. She is part of the LegGov research programme funded by Riksbankens Jubileumfond. Here she studies sources of legitimacy of global and regional governance institutions among citizens and elites. Additionally, Soetkin's research inquires into the relationship between European identity and public opinion and behaviour towards the EU. In 2015 Soetkin obtained a doctoral degree for her dissertation about the development of European identity among adolescents and adults at the Centre for Political Science at the University of Leuven.

Rumiana Yotova

Rumiana Yotova is a Lecturer and Director of Studies in Law at Lucy Cavendish College, University of Cambridge, and an Affiliated Lecturer at the Faculty of Law. Her research interests are in the areas of sources of international law, international dispute settlement, investment law, and the interaction between different legal regimes within international law. Rumiana practises international law as Door Tenant at Thomas More Chambers. She completed her PhD in Cambridge. She gained practical experience in international law during her two years of work as Research Associate to Professor James Crawford and at the Secretariat of the Permanent Court of Arbitration. She also spent time with the European Commission in Brussels.

Preface

For over fifty years we have been debating whether European integration requires an active social dimension. The number of publications describing the weaknesses of 'Social Europe' has reached the size of a small mountain. All too often, these writings were merely lamentations of the unattainable. Nevertheless, the experience of the succession of economic, social, and political crises hitting the European Union since 2008 creates an opportunity to put the social dimension firmly back on the agenda. Rather than a lamentation, what is needed now is a coherent conception of the reasons behind, the agenda for, and the governance of, a European Social Union. In short, we need an unequivocal answer to questions of *why*, *what*, and *how*. On that basis we have to define a clear-cut normative and institutional concept. This explains our title, 'A European Social Union after the Crisis'.

We deliberately use the expression 'European Social Union', rather than the elusive notion of 'a Social Europe'. Our core idea – explained and developed in Chapter 1 – can be summarised as follows: a Social Union would create a holding environment that enables Member States to be flourishing welfare states. Therefore, a Social Union would support national welfare states on a systemic level in some of their key functions (such as stabilisation when economic shocks occur). As a corollary to this systemic support, a Social Union would guide the development of national welfare states by establishing general social standards and objectives. The ways and means to implement social policy would be left to Member States, with due respect to their different historical legacies and institutions. The argument motivating this book is not that the EU should become a welfare state itself.

The idea of a 'union of welfare states' that is *not* a federal state leads us into uncharted territory. There is no historical template to follow and important issues have to be clarified. Therefore, we have discussed this idea in two conferences, one organised by the *Euroforum*[1] of the University of Leuven in September 2014, another organised in Cambridge, UK, in September 2015. Our aim was to confront our concept of a European Social Union with state-of-the-art legal scholarship, normative philosophy, political science, and economic analysis. This book is the outcome of that critical, interdisciplinary process. The analysis presented here is not meant to be exhaustive, but rather it reflects ongoing debate, with sometimes conflicting views. It should be read as a plea for rigorous and clear thinking on key issues that have to be settled, if we are serious about having a meaningful, functioning social dimension to the EU.

Our discussion of the *why* question (why is a Social Union needed?) emphasises the Eurozone problematic and the 'legacy of unresolved tensions' between economic principles and free movement on one hand and the scope for domestic social regulation on the other hand. The *what* question (what should be on the agenda of a European Social Union?) is examined first through the lens of normative political theory: we cannot set out an operational agenda for a European Social Union, without clarification of the nature and purpose of 'European solidarity'.

Our discussion of the *how* question focuses predominantly on the legal constellation of the EU and its impact on the actual feasibility of a Social Union; but it also covers the role of social dialogue, the flexibility of social and employment governance in the European Semester, and the EU's investment agreements; it also explores the politics of legislative action.

Obviously, political developments did not stop in 2015 when our second conference finished. In September 2015, Brexit was a faint possibility; in June 2016 it became a reality. In March 2016, the European Commission launched the idea of a 'European Pillar of Social Rights'. These recent developments are taken on board in different chapters, but they are also elaborated upon in two specific contributions.

The book is divided into four parts. The first part sets out the main guiding ideas of a European Social Union, with a strong focus on notions of solidarity, justice, and legitimacy. The second part focuses on specific policy topics and the third part discusses legal challenges. Finally, a short but important fourth part returns to the politics of European social policy and European integration.

[1] Euroforum was created by Metaforum, an initiative of the University of Leuven to stimulate interdisciplinary debate on socially relevant issues; see www.kuleuven.be/metaforum (accessed 13 March 2017). We are grateful for the financial support offered by Metaforum to make these conferences possible. We also thank the Centre for European Legal Studies, Law Faculty Cambridge, and Trinity College, Cambridge, the main sponsors of the second conference.

In the first chapter of Part I, Frank Vandenbroucke introduces and explains the idea of a European Social Union and considers the relationship between this concept and the other contributions in the book. He then focuses on normative questions, notably the definition and demarcation of 'European solidarity'. Thus, Chapter 1 engages extensively with the following two chapters, one by Maurizio Ferrera (who tackles the ambiguous notion of 'Social Europe') and one by Helder De Schutter (who presents arguments in favour of European integration based on distributive justice). With Ferrera and De Schutter the book juxtaposes two approaches in normative political philosophy, a 'realist' and an 'idealist' one. In Chapter 4, Christian Joerges emphasises the distinction between justice 'within' and justice 'between' Member States and the respect for diversity within the union, on the backdrop of long-standing debates among legal scholars. With the final chapter of Part I, by Marc Hooghe and Soetkin Verhaegen, we turn from normative theory to the empirical study of public support for social policy at the EU level.

The first policy topic examined in Part II of the book concerns the governance of the Eurozone, which is a key issue in the argument for a European Social Union. László Andor describes the impact of Eurozone governance on welfare state stability in Chapter 6: he calls for a substantial reconstruction of the monetary union and discusses the potential of a European unemployment benefit scheme. In Chapter 7, Paul De Grauwe and Yuemei Ji elaborate upon the same problem and question the traditional textbook treatment of shocks in a monetary union. They argue that when shocks are the result of business-cycle movements, the way to deal with them is by stabilisation efforts, not by structural reforms for more flexibility. In his discussion of the 'European Pillar of Social Rights', Simon Deakin (Chapter 8) develops a congenial argument with regard to the monetary union, but from a very different academic perspective: coordinated wage bargaining and adequate protection of workers can be assets in a monetary union rather than liabilities; in that respect, the Pillar initiative merits a cautious welcome. The next two chapters consider the role of social dialogue at EU level: what is its future? In Chapter 9, an employers' perspective is presented by Philippe de Buck and Maxime Cerutti; in Chapter 10, a trade union perspective is developed by Philippe Pochet and Christophe Degryse. Chapter 11, by Sonja Bekker, examines the actual governance of unemployment, wage-setting and pension schemes in the European Semester, notably its adaptability and the leeway it grants to Member States. Finally, Part II adds a trade and investment dimension to the idea of a European Social Union in Chapter 12: Rumiana Yotova examines how economic objectives and social considerations are balanced in the new EU investment agreements, a salient legal and political issue in today's Europe.

Part III of the book discusses legal challenges for the development of a European Social Union. In Chapter 13, Sjoerd Feenstra revisits the controversies created by the *Viking* and *Laval* judgments by the European Court of Justice and their implications for collective standard-setting and the balancing of economic freedoms and fundamental social rights. He adds nuance to the debate and discusses legal solutions. In Chapter 14, Geert de Baere and Kathleen Gutman address one of the key challenges of this book's project head-on: does the legal constellation of the EU admit progress towards a European Social Union, and if so, on what basis? However, the difficulty is not just in the nature of the European Treaties, but also in the legal constellations of the Member States, as Gerhard van der Schyff points out in Chapter 15, which compares Member States' constitutional controls on EU social policy developments. In Chapter 16, Alexander Kornezov formulates a sobering analysis with regard to the potential of the Charter of Fundamental Rights of the EU to become the constitutional foundation of the European Social Model. He concludes that the ideal of a more social Europe has been put into a legal straitjacket in the Charter: it is there, but it can hardly move. Koen Lenaerts and José A. Gutiérrez-Fons examine two questions in Chapter 17: first, the scope of application of EU social law – in particular, that of the Charter – in situations where a Member State is the recipient of financial assistance; and second, the horizontal application and justiciability of primary EU social law, once a national measure falls within the scope of EU law. The upshot of their analysis is more upbeat than Kornezov's account, which may testify to the fact that we are in new and hence uncharted territory.

In Part IV of the book, we venture into the political. In Chapter 18, Dorte Martinsen analyses the politics of legislative action in the EU in the social domain. She revisits thorny issues discussed in preceding chapters (from a normative and legal perspective), such as posting of workers, and underscores the importance of legislative politics. For a European Social Union to turn into reality, she argues it needs a political mandate and political ownership. The final chapter of the book is permeated with the harsh reality of politics: looking back on the developments that led to Brexit, Catherine Barnard reflects on the role of social policy in a post-Brexit Europe.

Given the importance of some legal cases discussed by legal scholars in this book, we provide a Table of Cases and brief summaries of the essence of the most important (in the context of this book) judgments by the European Court of Justice.

Compiling this book was a demanding project: establishing a real dialogue between scholars from different disciplines, and pairing deep-felt commitment to sober analysis are two notoriously difficult tasks. As editors, we are grateful to our co-authors that they made this journey together with us. But we would not have been able to deliver without the permanent and highly efficient management and editorial support by Chris Luigjes (UvA). We are also grateful to Veerle Achten (Metaforum, University of Leuven), for her organisational support at the two conferences, and to Ad-Willem Dashorst (UvA) for additional support in the final editing process and the compilation of the Table of Cases.

Table of Cases

Table of Cases

EUROPEAN COURT OF HUMAN RIGHTS

EUROPEAN COMMITTEE OF SOCIAL RIGHTS

EFTA COURT

INTERNATIONAL COURT OF JUSTICE

Summaries of Key Court Cases

For those readers without a legal background, the following summary of the key cases discussed in this book may be of assistance.

AMS (c-176/12)

Private parties (in this case, a French trade union and employer) could not rely on Article 27 of the Charter of Fundamental Rights, in which the right of workers to information and consultation was enshrined, to challenge a national provision that was incompatible with this right. The more specific expression of that right in provisions of EU law or national law did not in any way alter that assessment.

Cassis de Dijon (c-120/78)

National regulation requiring the alteration of an imported physical product before it could be sold, even if addressed equally to domestic products, was incompatible with the free movement of goods. Member States were obliged to accept products that were lawfully produced and marketed in another Member State, unless there were good and proportionate reasons why not.

Commission v *Luxembourg* (c-319/06)

In the absence of 'public policy' justifications, national regulation establishing working conditions that went beyond those stipulated in the Posting of Workers Directive was incompatible with the free provision of services.

This section draws, unless stated otherwise, on the ECJ's press releases, which are available at: curia.europa.eu/jcms/jcms/Jo2_16799 (accessed 12 December 2016).

Defrenne (C-43/75)

The prohibition on pay discrimination between men and women, found in Article 157 TFEU, could be directly invoked in national courts in disputes between private parties, and not solely in disputes between a private party and a national government.

Dano (C-333/13)

EU citizens who were economically inactive and travelled to another Member State with the sole purpose of obtaining social assistance in this Member State could be lawfully denied access to certain benefits.

Laval (C-341/05)

Collective action by a trade union in the form of a blockade of sites, carried out with a view to forcing a foreign employer using posted workers to enter into negotiations on remuneration and to comply with the host state's collective agreement, constituted a restriction on the free provision of services. Such a restriction could be legitimate if it was necessary and proportionate with a view to protecting workers, providing the terms of the Posted Workers Directive were respected. The collective action *in casu* did not meet these requirements and was therefore incompatible with EU law.

Ledra (C-8 TO 10/15 P)

An action for annulment of a memorandum of understanding signed between a Member State and the European Stability Mechanism, represented by the Commission, could be dismissed, since such a memorandum could not be attributed to an institution of the EU and the acts of the European Stability Mechanism did not fall under the scope of EU law. At the same time, the involvement of the Commission in the European Stability Mechanism did not alter the Commission's role as guardian of the Treaties. As such, the Commission was to safeguard the conformity with the Charter of Fundamental Rights of such a memorandum and could be liable for any failures to do so.

Gauweiler (C-62/14)

The ECB's programme to purchase the sovereign debt of Member States on the secondary market did not constitute a breach of the powers of the ECB and did not violate the prohibition on monetary financing of Member States. Therefore, the programme was compatible with EU law.

Pringle (c-370/12)

The ratification of the treaty establishing the European Stability Mechanism by the Member States that had adopted the euro as their currency was compatible with EU law.

Rüffert (c-346/06)

The Directive on the Posting of Workers could prohibit national regulation applicable to public contracts and bringing about a requirement for a foreign employer using posted workers to pay these workers the remuneration set out in a national collective agreement, if the collective agreement and its provisions were not determined in accordance with the rules set out in the Directive and did not meet the objective of protecting workers.

Rush Portuguesa (c-113/89)

During the transitional period following the accession of Portugal to the European Communities as part of which the free movement of Portuguese workers was limited, a Portuguese firm could use Portuguese workers in its operations in France, under the rules on the freedom of services. The French authorities were not allowed to obstruct this process by means of requiring working permits or the employment of domestic workers. The French authorities could, however, lawfully verify whether the Portuguese firm was circumventing the temporal limitation of the free movement of workers by exercising the right to freely provide services throughout the EU. The French government was also not precluded from extending its legislation concerning working conditions, or collective labour agreements between French employers and employees, to any person employed, even temporarily, on French territory, and enforcing this in an appropriate manner.

Viking (c-438/05)

Collective action in the form of strikes was liable to prevent the foreign firm from exercising its right to establish itself in another Member State of the EU. It therefore constituted a restriction on the right of freedom of establishment.

A restriction of this sort might be legitimate if it was necessary and proportionate with a view to protecting workers. In contrast to *Laval*, the ECJ did
not itself decide on whether these conditions were met in the case at hand
and left this for the national court to decide (the concrete *Viking* case was
subsequently settled).

PART I

Solidarity and Legitimacy

1

The Idea of a European Social Union:
A Normative Introduction

Frank Vandenbroucke

1.1 INTRODUCTION

The European Union is a union of countries that aspire to be welfare states. In all Member States, whatever their social policy tradition or level of development, there is large support for core ambitions of a modern welfare state: promoting general prosperity, sustaining social cohesion, protecting vulnerable individuals and supporting education. However different European welfare states are, their national tax and benefit systems have created, to varying degrees and with varying success, a capacity for social and economic stabilisation in periods of economic stress. These automatic stabilisers are intrinsically linked with the protection of vulnerable individuals.

The founding fathers of the European project were convinced that European economic integration would contribute to the development of prosperous national welfare states, whilst leaving social policy concerns essentially at the national level. History did not prove them wrong, at least until the mid-2000s. Yet, the experience of the protracted crisis that has hit Europe forces us to reconsider the question: how can the EU be a successful union of flourishing welfare states? Both on the left and the right of the political spectrum, despite conflicting views on the exact policy mix that is needed, many would argue that the crux is to implement the right kind of economic, financial and monetary governance at EU level. This book is inspired by a different position: yes, economic, financial, and monetary policies are crucial, but they cannot be isolated from the longer-term imperative to develop a social policy concept for the EU, that is, a basic consensus on the role the EU should play and the role it should not play in the domain of social policy. The argument

I thank Robert Jan van der Veen, Helder De Schutter, Catherine Barnard, Geert De Baere, Erik Schokkaert, Chris Luigjes, Ad-Willem Dashorst, Maurizio Ferrera, and Erik De Bom for comments and criticism. The usual disclaimer applies.

presented in this chapter is not that the EU should become a welfare state itself. However, restoring the social sovereignty of the Member States, with the EU strictly confining its role to economic, financial, and monetary policy, is also not an option. We need a coherent conception of a 'European Social Union'. The project that led to the publication of this book started on the basis of this idea, which is not to say that all the contributors agree with the way I develop it here.

I use the notion 'Social Union' deliberately, for three reasons. First, it invites us to propose a clear-cut concept, in contrast to the rather vague notion of 'a Social Europe', which often surfaces in discussions on the EU. Second, it indicates that we should go beyond the conventional call for 'a social dimension' to the EU. It would be wrong to assert that the EU has no social dimension today. The coordination of social security rights for mobile workers, standards for health and safety in the workplace, and some directives on workers' rights, constitute a non-trivial acquis of 50 years of piecemeal progress. The EU also developed a solid legal foundation for enforcing non-discrimination among EU citizens. The notion of a European Social Union is not premised on a denial of that positive acquis. The next steps can build on that acquis. However, the next stage of development must respond to a new challenge, which is about more than 'adding a social dimension'. Third, the emphasis on a Social *Union* is not a coincidence. A European Social Union is not a European Welfare State: it is a union of national welfare states, with different historical legacies and institutions. As explained below, a union of national welfare states requires more tangible solidarity between those welfare states as collective entities. But its primary purpose is not to organise interpersonal redistribution between individual European citizens across national borders; the main mechanisms of solidarity that the EU now needs to develop are between Member States; they should refer to insurance logics rather than to redistribution, and to support for social investment strategies. I will touch upon specific aspects of social policy for which we may have to rethink the practical application of the subsidiarity principle, both within Member States and at the level of the EU. Yet, a 'union of welfare states' would apply subsidiarity as a fundamental organising principle. Solidarity between Member States necessitates a degree of convergence, but convergence is not the same as harmonisation. More generally, the practice of a Social Union should be far removed from a top–down, one-size-fits-all approach to social policy-making in the Member States.

The core idea of this introductory chapter can be summarised as follows: a Social Union would support national welfare states *on a systemic level* in some of their key functions and guide the *substantive development* of national welfare states – via general social standards and objectives, leaving ways and means of social policy to the Member States – on the basis of an operational definition of 'the European Social Model'. In other words, European countries would cooperate in a union with an explicit social purpose – hence, the expression European Social Union.

A Social Union, so conceived, is not only desirable but necessary – unless we would drop the idea that the integration project concerns welfare states with at least some shared aspirations. To make that analysis is not to say it leads to only one definitive version of a European Social Union: depending on the normative judgements that are brought to bear, a Social Union may be a more ambitious or a less ambitious project; it can be based on different conceptions of social justice. Nor is it to say that an operational concept of a European Social Union is already on the table. We are in uncharted territory: important issues have to be clarified. An exercise in clarification has to start from three sets of basic questions. *Why* would a Social Union become an existential necessity for the European project, if that was not the case 60 years ago? *What* does it add to the agenda of the EU? And *how* would that agenda be implemented?

Sections 1.2 and 1.3 focus on the *why* question, bringing together the contributions by Deakin, De Grauwe and Ji, Andor, Feenstra and Barnard in this volume combined with arguments which I have developed elsewhere in more detail.[1] In his contribution to this volume, Deakin returns to the Single European Act of 1986: the deepening of the internal market implied a step change in levels of labour and capital mobility. To prevent a regression in social standards, a pan-European floor of social rights would have been a logical corollary, but such a floor of rights did not emerge in the 1990s, except for health and safety at work. My emphasis in this chapter is on two successive developments, which clearly *necessitate* a basic consensus on the European Social Model today, whatever reservations there might have been at the time of the Single European Act: on the one hand, the consequences of monetary unification (notably the need for stabilisation, as explained in Section 1.2), on the other hand, the consequences of enlargement (notably the need to reconcile free movement and domestic social cohesion across a heterogeneous set of Member States, as explained in Section 1.3). My argument, at this point, is not that these developments force upon the Member States a unique,

---

[1] See F. Vandenbroucke, 'The Case for a European Social Union. From Muddling Through to a Sense of Common Purpose', in B. Marin (ed.), *The Future of Welfare in a Global Europe* (Ashgate, 2015); F. Vandenbroucke, *Structural Convergence versus System Competition: Limits to the Diversity of Labour Market Policies in the European Monetary Union*. Paper submitted for the DG ECFIN Fellowship Initiative 2016–2017 (2017, forthcoming).

well-defined conception of social justice. To put it more bluntly, a basic consensus on the European Social Model may well be a consensus that does not correspond to my personal conception of social justice. The argument is that the debate about the future of our social model has now inevitably shifted, in part, to the European level, for functional reasons. However, that debate is not totally open-ended if we reconnect with the original inspiration of the founding fathers of the European project: the ambition to reconcile upward convergence in prosperity across the Member States with internal social cohesion in each of the Member States (my rendering of the founding fathers' belief), delineates the contours of the debate.

In Section 1.4, I argue that we need a 'theory of justice for the European Union', that is, a conception of justice that is based on a specific understanding of the point and purpose of the Union as a multi-tiered polity. Therefore, we must revisit the original inspiration of the founding fathers and the political legitimacy that was intrinsic to the European project. I believe these political legitimacy arguments are compelling and should appeal to people with a variety of political opinions. But it would be intellectually incorrect and politically counterproductive to consider the founding fathers' inspiration as dogma or to present arguments on political legitimacy as hard science. We must justify a return to ideas of the founding fathers and examine whether their ideas can be sustained or need amendment. We should not deny that we enter the realm of political choices.

Thus, the discussion of the *why* question starts with functional observations, indicates issues that must be addressed at the European level, and then ventures into the political. The answer to the *what* question – what is the agenda of a European Social Union? – definitely implies political choices. A key normative issue informing our political choices is how we define and demarcate 'European solidarity': defining and demarcating solidarity sets the agenda for a European Social Union. I explain this in Section 1.4. Section 1.4 does not provide definitive answers; it explores the issues at hand with reference to contemporary theories of distributive justice that offer a useful framework to conceptualise solidarity, insurance, and redistribution. Section 1.4 connects with the contributions by De Schutter and Ferrera in this volume. In order to focus on the underlying normative debate, my discussion of De Schutter's position takes it for granted that economic integration results in upward convergence of prosperity across Member States (which means that the optimistic hypothesis of the founding fathers is at least partially vindicated). I add a short Section 1.5, in which I briefly qualify that hypothesis. I conclude in Section 1.6.

This introductory chapter focuses on the why question and on the normative foundations of the what question. It does not elaborate upon the *how* question, but different chapters in this volume touch upon the how question (Deakin, Martinsen, Bekker, de Buck and Cerutti, Pochet and Degryse, and, from a legal perspective, Feenstra, De Baere and Gutman, Kornezov, Lenaerts and Guttiérrez-Fons). The emphasis on the legal constellation is not happenstance: a fundamental difficulty for a 'European Social Constitution' (using Ferrera's expression, in his description of the different components of a European Social Union in this volume) resides in the legal legacy of the initial division of labour created by the founding fathers: the Union's competences had to serve the purpose of economic integration, whilst leaving social policy concerns to the national level. However, as the reader will see, the assessment of the current legal constellation differs among the scholars who contributed to this book, with some being more optimistic than others (compare, for instance, the contribution by Kornezov with the one by and Lenaerts and Guttiérez-Fons). However, the difficulty is not just in the nature of the European Treaties, but also in the legal constellations of the Member States, as van der Schyff points out in his contribution.

Since this chapter is about normative foundations, it does not develop policy proposals.[2]

1.2 THE INCOMPLETE MONETARY UNION

1.2.1 *Traditional Textbook Analysis Revisited*

A Social Union is not only desirable but necessary, unless we drop the idea that the integration project concerns welfare states with at least some shared aspirations. The 'necessity' argument is partly based on the *functional* implications of a monetary union. These functional implications are twofold. First, a monetary union requires systemic support for the Member States, in the form of a fiscal stabilisation capacity. Second (but related), there is a limit to the

---

[2] Policy proposals are discussed in some of the chapters that follow. See also F. Vandenbroucke with B. Vanhercke, A *European Social Union. 10 Tough Nuts to Crack* (Friends of Europe, Brussels, 2014), available at: www.friendsofeurope.org/quality-europe/10-tough-nuts-to-crack/ (accessed 15 December 2016); F. Vandenbroucke and D. Rinaldi, 'Social Inequalities in Europe – The Challenge of Convergence and Cohesion', in Vision Europe Summit Consortium (eds), *Redesigning European Welfare States – Ways Forward* (Gütersloh, 2015), available at: www.delorsinstitute.eu/011-22215-Social-inequalities-in-Europe-the-challenge-of-convergence-and-cohesion.html/ (accessed 15 December 2016); F. Vandenbroucke, 'Automatic Stabilisers for the Euro Area and the European Social Model', *Tribune*, Notre Europe Jacques Delors Institute, 22 September 2016, available at: www.delorsinstitute.eu/011-23652-Automatic-stabilizersfor-the-Euro-area-and-the-European-social-model.html (accessed 12 December 2016); Vandenbroucke, *Structural Convergence versus System Competition*, n. 1 in this chapter.

diversity of national social systems that can be accommodated in a monetary union; therefore, monetary unification implies guidance with regard to the substantive developments of national welfare states in some specific domains. On the national level, stabilisation is a key feature of welfare states; stabilisation is generated by tax-and-benefit systems, in particular by unemployment insurance. Hence, there is an intrinsic link between our conception of automatic stabilisers at the Eurozone level and our conception of the EU's role in social policy. This link necessitates a careful discussion, which goes beyond the brief of this chapter; here, I focus on some essential insights.

Well-known economic theory explains the benefits and drawbacks of monetary unification in terms of trade-offs. Members of a currency area are confronted with a trade-off between symmetry and flexibility. Symmetry refers to movements in output, wages, and prices. Asymmetry may arise because of differences in productivity growth, or differences in inflation rates, which both may lead to asymmetry in the evolution of competitiveness. Asymmetry may also be the consequence of different patterns of industrial specialisation, which makes some countries more vulnerable to specific structural changes in the world economy than other countries ('asymmetric shocks'). Flexibility relates to wage flexibility and interregional and international labour mobility, which determine a country's internal adjustment capacity in case of an asymmetric development. Less symmetry necessitates more flexibility: the less symmetry there is between the countries of a single currency area, the greater the required capacity for internal adaptability in order for the monetary union to be beneficial. In this traditional textbook analysis 'adaptability' is understood mainly in terms of labour mobility and/or wage flexibility. There is a second trade-off: if asymmetric shocks can be absorbed through fiscal transfers between the Member States, then the need for internal flexibility is reduced. Fiscal transfers make it possible to alleviate the plight of countries hit by a negative shock. Obviously, fiscal transfers, even if they are not permanent but only temporary and reversible, require a readiness to organise solidarity among the members of the monetary union.

De Grauwe and Ji add two important qualifications to the traditional textbook analysis in their contribution to this volume. First, they argue that EMU should not only be equipped with a capacity to mitigate asymmetric shocks, but also with a capacity for intertemporal stabilisation, i.e. a capacity to smooth economic volatility over time, rather than only between countries. Smoothing business cycles over time requires the possibility to increase public debt in downturns, and decrease public debt in boom periods. In short, EMU needs to be equipped with a budgetary union that can also issue common bonds. Second, they argue that the trade-off between what budgetary union can achieve and what flexibility (or, 'structural reform' to increase flexibility, in the EU's jargon) can achieve depends crucially on the nature of the economic shocks. De Grauwe and Ji argue that when shocks are the result of business-cycle movements, the way to deal with them is by stabilisation efforts, not by structural reforms for more flexibility. They also provide evidence suggesting that the biggest shocks in the Eurozone were the result of business-cycle movements.

1.2.2 *Automatic Stabilisers in a Multi-Tiered Polity*

Analytically, the case for a euro area stabilisation capacity is compelling; politically it is an uphill battle in today's Europe. We therefore need a comprehensive exploration of different scenarios and a thorough understanding of how they can fit into the broader challenge of developing a European Social Union. In this volume, Andor presents arguments in favour of a European unemployment benefit scheme. I elaborate on this particular proposal, because it highlights issues of social convergence and issues of solidarity that are important to my overall argument in this chapter. One should note that the basic proposal comes in different variants: a European unemployment benefit scheme could either be a 'genuine' European unemployment insurance or a system of 're-insurance'. The difference between a genuine European unemployment insurance and re-insurance is twofold. First, in a genuine European scheme, individual citizens who are short-term unemployed receive an individual benefit from a European fund, whilst a model of re-insurance would operate with lump sum budgetary transfers between a European fund and Member States. Second, in a model of re-insurance, Member States would receive transfers on the basis of a trigger (based on the deviation of current short-term unemployment in the Member State from its past trajectory in that same Member State); in a genuine European unemployment scheme, there would be no trigger for the scheme to start disbursing money (any short-term unemployed individual in a participating Member State receives a benefit, independent of the level or growth rate of short-term unemployment in that Member State).

Unemployment insurance raises well-known issues of moral hazard. In essence, moral hazard occurs when a person (or an institution) takes more risks because someone else (or another institution) bears the costs of those risks. Moral hazard means that the insured individual can manipulate the liability that the insurer incurs, by influencing the frequency and/or the importance of the insured risk. In other words, the risk is influenced by behaviour and choice – or, in the case of institutional actors, influenced by deliberate policies – rather than being purely exogenous and beyond control.

Moral hazard can be reduced by a careful design of the insurance policy, but it can never be totally excluded: it is inevitable, to some extent, in any context of insurance. The possibility for Member States that benefit from a European unemployment benefit scheme (whether it takes the form of a genuine European unemployment insurance or re-insurance) to become lax with regard to the activation of the unemployed and (re)employment policies at large, generates an obvious risk of institutional moral hazard; this risk cannot be dismissed out of hand. Therefore, the quality of national activation policies is a matter of common concern in a group of countries organising a common unemployment scheme in one or other way. This caveat about institutional moral hazard is important for our thinking about fiscal stabilisation at the European level, but we should be aware that moral hazard is, in any system of insurance, a price to pay to obtain risk pooling and stabilisation. Hence, the objective is to mitigate the trade-off between stabilisation capacity and institutional moral hazard: for desirable levels of stabilisation capacity, institutional moral should be minimised.

In this respect, we can draw lessons from the experience with unemployment insurance and activation policies in existing multi-tiered polities, such as the United States, Canada, Germany, Switzerland, Austria, or Belgium.[3] Studying multi-tiered systems leads to interesting conclusions with regard to institutional moral hazard in an eventual European unemployment benefit scheme. First, such a scheme should incorporate financial mechanisms to avoid permanent transfers and minimise the possibility for any country to be, on average, a net beneficiary of the scheme. Second, in addition to such financial mechanisms, in order to fight different forms of institutional moral hazard when unemployment risks are pooled at the European level, Member States should comply with minimum requirements with regard to both the 'activation quality' and the 'stabilisation quality'[4] of their unemployment benefit system. That is the reason why a European unemployment benefit scheme requires a significant degree of convergence in the national

---

[3] F. Vandenbroucke and C. Luijges, *Institutional Moral Hazard in the Multi-tiered Regulation of Unemployment and Social Assistance Benefits and Activation. A Summary of Eight Country Case Studies* (Centre for European Policy Studies, 2016), available at: www.ceps.eu/system/files/SR%20No%20137%20Moral%20hazard%20in%20multi-tiered%20reg%20of%20UB.pdf (accessed 15 December 2016).

[4] The extent to which incomes are smoothed when an unemployment shock occurs determines the stabilisation quality of unemployment insurance; the generosity of short-term unemployment benefits and the coverage of the system are key parameters in this respect. Segmented labour markets, in which a significant part of the labour force is poorly insured against unemployment, reduce the stabilisation quality; Deakin underscores the problem of labour market segmentation in his analysis of the Eurozone's problems.

regulation of unemployment, both in the genuine model and the re-insurance model. However, the governance method and the flexibility with which convergence is pursued in these models are very different, and the way in which they can respond to the challenge of institutional moral hazard also differs.[5] Re-insurance not only allows more flexibility and offers more scope to mitigate the risk of institutional moral hazard, it also seems a less complicated option. Politically, the re-insurance option may be more true to the idea that a European Social Union should be a 'union of welfare states', rather than a European welfare state.

It is by now generally accepted that design failures of EMU made it unstable and fragile: it lacked not only a banking union, but also a mechanism for fiscal stabilisation, as recognised by the Five Presidents' report on *Completing Europe's Economic and Monetary Union*.[6] Both with regard to banking union and fiscal stabilisation, the Five Presidents' Report signals an acute awareness that the EU needs to organise more solidarity in the Eurozone. The organisation of solidarity requires mutual trust. Solidarity on the basis of mutual insurance is a rational option, but even the most rational individuals will not engage in mutual insurance if they do not trust each other sufficiently. In the context of a European unemployment benefit scheme the 'minimum requirements' mentioned in the previous paragraph are key to create trust. But European solidarity requires mutual trust with regard to the quality of the social fabric in the Member States in a more general sense, including with regard to their capacity to deliver on competitiveness and sound public finances. Exposure to market forces has not in itself produced 'discipline' in the monetary union with respect to competitiveness and public finance. On the contrary, we witnessed asymmetrical developments and divergence, rather than symmetry and convergence. Relative competitiveness deteriorated significantly in some countries and improved in other countries, thus creating huge economic imbalances in the Eurozone. Since the invisible hand of the market does not deliver, EMU needs a visible hand that pursues symmetry, notably with regard to wage increases. Moreover, Member States need labour-market institutions that can coordinate wage increases: the visible hand must be effective.

---

[5] See Vandenbroucke, 'Automatic Stabilisers', n. 2 in this chapter.
[6] The report, published in June 2015, was drafted by the Presidents of five major EU Institutions: the European commission, The European Council, the European Central Bank, the Eurogroup, and the European Parliament. See J.C. Juncker, 'The Five Presidents' Report: Completing Europe's Economic and Monetary Union, Report in Close Cooperation D. Tusk, J. Dijsselbloem, M. Draghi and M. Schulz' (2015), available at: ec.europa.eu/priorities/sites/beta-political/files/5-presidents-report_en.pdf (accessed 30 March 2016).

1.2.3 *Wage Coordination and the Social Model*

Arguing that a visible hand is necessary does not mark a departure from current EU *principles*, but rather from current *practice*. The Six-Pack and the Macroeconomic Imbalance Procedure[7] are deliberate attempts to strengthen the visible hand of European policy makers. But current practice has put a one-sided emphasis on adjustment in Member States with current account deficits and has not addressed the role of Member States with surpluses. Symmetry should be organised instead around a common benchmark, for instance, a 'golden rule' linking national wage increases to national productivity increases. Such a golden rule would avoid both excessive wage moderation in some countries and excessive pay increases in other countries. A further desirable departure from current practice is to acknowledge the positive results from coordinated wage bargaining within Member States, as Deakin emphasises in his contribution to this book. Instead of encouraging the decentralisation of collective bargaining, the EU should take steps to encourage and facilitate bargaining coordination; this presupposes a positive stance vis-à-vis social dialogue at large, one which has been little in evidence in recent years (on social dialogue in the EU, see the chapters by de Buck and Cerutti and by Pochet and Degryse in this volume).

Bearing in mind these observations on the importance of adequate unemployment insurance and the positive role of coordinated bargaining and social dialogue within Member States and across the Eurozone, we can now return to the long-term trade-off between symmetry and flexibility that is seen as essential to the sustainability of a monetary union. De Grauwe and Ji argue

---

[7] The Six-Pack is a set of European legislative measures, bundled into a 'six pack' of regulations introduced in 2010–11, to introduce greater macroeconomic surveillance. The Macroeconomic Imbalance Procedure was part of the Six-Pack; it is a specific surveillance mechanism that aims to identify potential risks early on, prevent the emergence of harmful macroeconomic imbalances and correct the imbalances that are already in place. For the legal basis of the Six-Pack, see: Regulation 1173/2011 of the European Parliament and of the Council of 16 November 2011 on the effective enforcement of budgetary surveillance in the euro area, [2011] OJ L 306/1; Regulation 1174/2011 of the European Parliament and of the Council of 16 November 2011 on enforcement measures to correct excessive macroeconomic imbalances in the euro area, [2011] OJ L 306/8; Regulation 1175/2011 of the European Parliament and of the Council of 16 November 2011 amending Council Regulation (EC) No 1466/97 on the strengthening of the surveillance of budgetary positions and the surveillance and coordination of economic policies, [2011] OJ L 306/12; Regulation 1176/2011 of the European Parliament and of the Council of 16 November 2011 on the prevention and correction of macroeconomic imbalances, [2011] OJ L 306/25; Council Regulation 1177/2011 of 8 November 2011 amending Regulation (EC) No 1467/97 on speeding up and clarifying the implementation of the excessive deficit procedure, [2011] OJ L 306/33; and Council Directive 2011/85/EU of 8 November 2011 on requirements for budgetary frameworks of the Member States, [2011] OJ L 306/41.

that flexibility is not the right answer to business-cycle shocks affecting the monetary union; nevertheless, flexibility of labour markets is important to deal with permanent shocks of an exogenous nature. Even if they have been less prominent in recent times, according to De Grauwe and Ji's data, permanent shocks cannot be excluded. What kind of flexibility is needed then, to facilitate the necessary reallocation of labour and capital? Flexibility is a container concept. A 'high road' to labour-market flexibility can be placed in opposition to a 'low road' to labour-market flexibility. The high road is based on a highly skilled and versatile labour force, adequate unemployment insurance and activation and training policies that facilitate transitions. The low road is based on mere labour-market deregulation and easy hiring and firing. At first sight, it might be thought irrelevant which of these flexibility models are adopted as pillars of a sustainable monetary union: i.e. they can be seen as functionally equivalent models as long as the outcome is economic adaptability. However, apart from the social costs that are attached to certain types of flexibility, not all systems of labour-market regulation deliver equally well with regard to wage coordination and the quality of unemployment insurance. The members of the monetary union should perform well in each of these dimensions of labour-market regulation. The way in which labour-market flexibility, wage coordination and unemployment insurance are combined in national labour-market institutions is a matter of common concern in a monetary union: these choices cannot be relegated totally to the national domain. That does not mean that the EU should counsel Member States in detail on the organisation of their labour markets. But there is a limit to the social diversity that can be accommodated in a monetary union, not with regard to the institutional details of labour markets, but with regard to their basic features. This is not to say that the EU can *impose* limits to national diversity; the degree of convergence that is desirable can be promoted by more or less flexible approaches to governance (this is a domain in which the EU is acquiring considerable experience; see Bekker's contribution in this volume on the flexibility of the actual European Semester in the governance of unemployment, wage-setting and pensions).

Whatever the governance method, neither flexibility nor fiscal transfers, nor systems of wage coordination or unemployment insurance, are socially neutral choices. Hence, the long-term trade-offs implied by monetary unification force upon the participating countries a consensus on the social order on which the monetary union is based. Although its proposals remain rather vague and timid in this respect, the Five Presidents' report illustrates a growing recognition of this fact. The report refers, for instance, to the need for European 'standards for labour markets', which should combine security and flexibility. In March 2016, the Commission emphasised the need for social convergence, when it launched the 'European Pillar of Social Rights'. The initiative was specifically linked to the Eurozone: the Commission communication noted that 'the Pillar is conceived to be established within the euro area, but would also be open for other Member States to join on a voluntary basis'.[8] The *First Preliminary Outline of the European Pillar of Social Rights* mentions, for example, the role of unemployment benefits in economic stabilisation, next to the role of benefits in fighting poverty and creating security. The *Outline* observes that '[i]n some cases the coverage of unemployment benefits is very low due to strict eligibility requirements. The duration of benefits in some Member States, as well as the enforcement of conditions for job search and participation in active support are a concern.' The *Outline* proposes the following principle: 'Action to support the unemployed shall include the requirement for active job search and participation in active support combined with adequate unemployment benefits. The duration of benefits shall allow sufficient time for job search whilst preserving incentives for a quick return to employment.' Obviously, this statement is very general. Minimum requirements with regard to the stabilisation quality of national unemployment benefits would need to be more precise in terms of the minimum coverage that is required and the generosity of benefits for short-term unemployed. However, the debate on the European Pillar of Social Rights provides an opportunity to elaborate upon this theme; well-formulated general principles with regard to unemployment benefits should be linked with incisive benchmarking of Member States' performance in this domain.

In his contribution to this volume, Deakin gives the Pillar a cautious welcome: 'As a restatement of social rights it is less than adequate, but this is not its main purpose. It should be understood as a much overdue attempt to reintegrate social policy into the evolving process of economic and monetary union'.[9] He notes that the Pillar is, as yet, unclear with regard to the relationship between means and ends. I agree and I would add that the expression 'rights' creates expectations: if the perception is that the Pillar is merely a replay of earlier initiatives based on soft coordination, without tangible consequences, the initiative will frustrate expectations and create a backlash. Hence, the European Commission should clarify how the Pillar will feed into the European Semester on one hand, and its legislative agenda on the other hand.

[8] COM(2016)127 *Launching a Consultation on a European Pillar of Social Rights* (Strasbourg, 8 March 2016). This chapter was written before the new Commission Communication, establishing the Pillar of Social Rights, of 26 April 2017.
[9] S. Deakin, 'What Follows Austerity? From Social Pillar to New Deal', Chapter 8 in this volume.

1.2.4 Preliminary Conclusions

In this section, I have presented arguments for a degree of social convergence across the welfare states that belong to the European Union, in particular among the members of the monetary union and with regard to some key features of their social systems. To state that there are limits to the social diversity that can be accommodated in a monetary union implies – as the other side of the coin – that social diversity is not per se in contradiction with monetary and economic integration. In his contribution to this volume, Joerges emphasises this other side of the coin: the European project should not only recognise the legitimate diversity of the members' social systems, but that diversity can be beneficial. In Joerges' view, '[t]he threefold commitment of the Union to respect the democratic autonomy of its Member States, to strive for a curtailment of external effects of their policies and to further targeted fair co-operative problem-solving would in all likelihood be more favourable to the generation of solidarity in the Union than the kind of "we-pay-and-you-obey" strategy which the European crisis management has established and legalised'.[10] The idea of a European Social Union indeed rejects the notion of a one-size-fits-all supranational welfare state model. However, if there are limits to the diversity in social systems that can be accommodated in a monetary union, there is no escape from the conclusion that a basic consensus on our social model is necessary: a consensus on the convergence that is needed on one hand, and the diversity that is legitimate and possibly beneficial on the other hand. Only playing the sovereignty card is trading in illusions, as Crouch explains well in the context of a more general debate on the future of our social model and the role of social and political actors.[11] Obviously, establishing such a basic consensus necessitates a degree of 'political union' and democratic accountability, a point also emphasised by De Grauwe and Ji in their discussion of the stabilisation problem. This is by no means an easy goal.

1.3 INTEGRATION AND SOCIAL REGULATION IN THE EU28: A BALANCING ACT

Some arguments in favour of an active social dimension to the EU transcend the Eurozone problematic, as they apply to the EU as a whole. A well-known argument holds that economic integration without social harmonisation induces downward pressure on social development in the most advanced

[10] C. Joerges, 'Social Justice in an Ever More Diverse Union', Chapter 4 in this volume.
[11] C. Crouch, *Making Capitalism Fit for Society* (Polity Press, 2013).

Member States. Although in the past the spectre of large-scale social dumping
has never materialised, in the enlarged EU of today blatant cases of illegal
working conditions and exploitation do occur, resulting from the interplay of
lacunae in the domestic implementation of social and employment protection
in the Member States, reduced legal sovereignty of the Member States, and
the absence of common social standards in a very heterogeneous entity. Fears
of social dumping, but also welfare tourism, are causing considerable social
and political tensions with regard to labour migration. These discussions will
not be easily resolved, but a crucial condition for European public opinion to
accept migration is that cross-border mobility should fit into a regulated social
order; it must not undermine that social order.

1.3.1 *Free Movement and the Spectre of Social Dumping*

The question of to what extent Member States can uphold social standards
in a context of free movement is particularly relevant with regard to minimum wages. In Member States such as Germany and Sweden, trade unions
traditionally resisted state regulation of minimum wages: they considered
that to be the domain of collective bargaining and a no-go area for public
authorities. Thus, they applied a domestic principle of subsidiarity. The *Laval*
judgment by the European Court of Justice[12] suggests that that traditional position may be unsustainable: the Court argues that only *predictable* systems of
minimum wage protection can be imposed on foreign companies that post[13]
workers: Member States must create a legal context in which only generally
applicable minimum wage protection has to be respected by foreign service
providers. This means that social partners should reconsider traditional positions on subsidiarity within welfare states, which means that they should
reconsider the respective roles of social partners and public authorities, or,
reconsider the relation between nationwide collective bargaining and local
bargaining. The actual responses in Sweden and Denmark to the *Laval* case
reaffirm the autonomy of collective bargaining, but introduce conditions for
the exercise of collective action: collective agreements can be enforced only

[12] ECJ, judgment of 18 December 2007 in *Laval un Partneri*, C-341/05, EU:C:2007:809.
[13] A 'posted worker' is an employee who is sent by his employer to carry out a service in another
EU Member State on a temporary basis. Posted workers are different from EU mobile workers
in that they remain in the host Member State temporarily and do not integrate in its labour
market, as they maintain an employment contract with an employer in their home ('sending')
country. In contrast to posted workers, EU mobile citizens who work in another Member State
and have an employment contract with an employer in the latter Member State are entitled to
full equal treatment with nationals in access to employment, working conditions and all other
social and tax conditions.

through collective action against foreign service providers if they correspond to existing nationwide collective agreements and do not define conditions beyond the hard core of the Posting of Workers Directive.[14] Hence, the Swedish and Danish domestic responses also change the rules of the game in terms of the subsidiarity of the national versus the local level. Politically, the upshot of such developments might be that the case for a pan-European framework with regard to the concept and regulation of minimum wages becomes more plausible too: both at the domestic and the European level, we might have to reconsider the application of subsidiarity principles.

Together with the *Viking* judgment[15] (which did not concern the free movement of services, as in *Laval*, but the freedom of establishment), the *Laval* judgment however raises a more fundamental problem than merely the requirement of 'predictability' of minimum provisions. Prior to these decisions, the Court had attempted to respect the original settlement contained in the Treaty of Rome that social policy was largely a matter for domestic law. It had deployed a number of techniques to protect national social policy from the application of the (hierarchically superior) economic provisions on the internal market. However, in *Viking* and *Laval* the Court applied its internal market case law with full vigour. The moment collective action was found to be a 'restriction' and thus in breach of EU law, the social interests were on the back foot, having to defend themselves from the economic rights of free movement. The Court has made it difficult to defend the social interests due to its strict approach to justification and proportionality. Moreover, because the Court applied the freedoms to an area expressly excluded from EU competence (strikes) it created a legislative vacuum. It potentially struck down the national rules but the EU could not deal with the problem created by the Court, given the absence of express competence for the EU to act. This is one aspect of the so-called social deficit in the EU, as Barnard and De Baere put it.[16] It is not impossible to solve this problem; Barnard discusses different solutions, of which a reform of the proportionality principle seems the most promising one.[17]

---

[14] M. Blauberger, 'With Luxembourg in Mind ... The Remaking of National Policies in the Face of ECJ Jurisprudence' (2012) 19 *Journal of European Public Policy* 109.

[15] ECJ, judgment of 11 December 2007 in *International Transport Workers' Federation and Finnish Seamen's Union* ('Viking'), C-438/05, EU:C:2007:772.

[16] C. Barnard and G. De Baere, 'Towards a European Social Union. Achievements and Possibilities under the Current EU Constitutional Framework' (2014) *Euroforum Policy Paper*, 14.

[17] C. Barnard, 'Free Movement and Labour Rights: Squaring the Circle?' (2013) *University of Cambridge Faculty of Law Legal Studies Research Paper*, 23/2013.

Feenstra returns to the *Viking/Laval* conundrum in his contribution to this volume. He argues that the *Laval* regulatory conundrum is not as big as some have argued (but, see the importance attached to these judgments in the contributions by Deakin and Martinsen). However, there is one matter that gives pause for concern in Feenstra's review. Articles 49 and 56 TFEU are directly effective and apply both to Member States and trade unions, but the Posting of Workers Directive leaves considerable regulatory margin to the Member States on matters concerning public policy provisions. Trade unions cannot avail themselves of that same public policy derogation. According to Feenstra, '[t]he approach of the Court imposing on trade unions the same limits the Court imposes on Member States' authorities while refusing to entrust trade unions with the task of determining the nature of the public social order appears at odds with the different regulatory instruments (including the implementation of Directives by social partners) used in Member States to attain public policy objectives'.[18] Unlike *Laval*'s regulatory conundrum, the question of how to balance economic freedoms and fundamental social rights (the *Viking* conundrum) appears far from resolved. Feenstra argues that the proportionality principle is, in principle, an appropriate tool to balance between the economic and social rights of the EU, provided the EU follows a different, alternative approach than the very strict application of proportionality in *Viking*.

1.3.2 *Reconciling Openness and Domestic Cohesion*

Fundamentally, the challenge is to preserve the regulatory capacity of national governments and social partners, whilst allowing labour migration and the cross-border delivery of services. Space forbids discussion of the issue of 'welfare tourism' and the comprehensive analyses by Scharpf and Höpner and Schäfer on the impact of the four freedoms and mobility on European welfare states. Unlike these authors, I do not believe that the institutional architecture and the internal heterogeneity of the EU lead systematically and *irresistibly* to greater economic liberalisation, unchecked mobility and the erosion of solidarity. Reconciling mobility and the four freedoms on the one hand with the internal cohesion of national welfare states and industrial relations on the other hand is a complex challenge, but it is not an insurmountable one. It requires a 'balancing act', which is feasible. In other words, there is room for politics in the EU arena. A less pessimistic assessment of the potential

---

[18] S. Feenstra, 'How Can the Viking/Laval Conundrum Be Resolved? Balancing the Economic and the Social: One Bed for Two Dreams?', Chapter 13 in this volume.

for such a balancing act is probably associated with a different understanding of the social meaning of cross-border mobility. In contrast with Scharpf, Höpner, and Schäfer, Caporaso and Tarrow[19] argue that the Court of Justice has attempted to embed the transnational market in Polanyi's terms within its (the Court's) understanding of legitimate social purposes, by acting as a regulatory arbiter between international openness and domestic social cohesion. Both international openness (under certain conditions) and domestic social cohesion can be understood in terms of social justice. In the same spirit, De Witte[20] develops a subtle account of 'transnational solidarity' in the EU. On the basis of a broad notion of reciprocity De Witte aims to accommodate cross-border mobility and domestic social cohesion within welfare states; I briefly return to this in the next section. In this view, the balancing act is between different dimensions of social justice.[21] That is not to say that *Viking* and *Laval* are satisfactory examples of such a balancing act; the challenge is to make the balancing act satisfactory.

Ferrera formulates the difference between the approach inspiring this book and the scholarly tradition set by Scharpf as follows: our approach would allow for 'a fruitful re-framing of some classical issues that in the last two decades have dominated debates on the "social deficit" of the EU as an institutional and political construct, such as the asymmetry between negative and positive integration, market-making and market-correcting, EU (economic and legal) powers and national social sovereignty. If Social Europe is a composite construct that cannot be reduced to a single component and thus has to live with inherent tensions, there is no single "asymmetry" or "deficit" to which weaknesses can be imputed. Likewise, there is no single instrument or solution that can remedy such weaknesses.'[22]

In the final chapter of this book, Barnard offers a sobering analysis of the Brexit vote in the UK. She confronts us with two discomforting questions: what might have made a difference, and what would have made no difference? Barnard calls for a balancing act between openness and domestic cohesion that is much broader than merely regulating the rights of employees in cross-border situations and remedying the *Viking/Laval* conundrum and

[19] J. Caporaso and S. Tarrow, 'Supranational Institutions and the Transnational Embedding of Markets' (2009) 63 *International Organization* 593.
[20] F. De Witte, *Justice in the EU. The Emergence of Transnational Solidarity* (Oxford University Press, 2015).
[21] Despite all the problems with these judgments, especially with the *Viking* judgment, it should be recognized that by opening up cross-border provision of services greater employment opportunities are created for workers from Eastern European countries.
[22] M. Ferrera, 'The European Social Union: A Missing but Necessary "Political Good"', Chapter 2 in this volume.

related issues. Migration has put pressure on the social fabric of the UK, not only in precarious segments of the labour market but also because of shortages in the provision of public services. In short, 'EU migration created pressure on domestic provision. Domestic policy let down the local population; EU social policy could not respond.'[23] Obviously, the imbalance has been generated by UK domestic policies, and not by EU policies per se: the decision not to apply a transition period for intra-EU migration after 2004, the lacunae in public services, the choice for austerity in a non-Eurozone country … were all *made in the UK*. However, Barnard's point is that those who would have wanted to call upon the EU to prevent or remedy such a situation could not find resources at the EU level: the EU was a promoter of the austerity idea; the EU did not put pressure on Member States with regard to the adequacy of public services; the EU lacked the competences to translate nice principles on inclusive labour markets into practical rights. With regard to the latter – a broad approach to fairness in employment regulation – Barnard wryly concludes that 'the emperor had no clothes'.[24] In other words, even if one might think (as I do) that domestic UK policies were to blame for the Brexit vote, the EU's policy stance and discourse did not offer tangible support for the Remain case: the EU's current framework is guilty by passive neglect, so to speak. The conclusion that follows is twofold. First, the EU should be guided by principles that guarantee a balance between domestic social cohesion – broadly understood – on the one hand and freedom of movement on the other hand; balancing principles of free movement and social principles underpinning welfare states should be part and parcel of the basic social consensus guiding the EU as a Union of welfare states. Second, the EU cannot afford a delivery gap with regard to those principles: the emperor needs clothes, that is, effective governance and the necessary competences to translate principles in practice.

1.4 THE FOUNDING FATHERS' INSPIRATION AND THE MEANING OF JUSTICE AND SOLIDARITY

The foregoing discussion shows that we have to combine two perspectives on the meaning of justice in Europe: a pan-European notion of justice and justice within welfare states. Given the increasing role of migration and mobility, entertaining a purely domestic view on social justice and solidarity is increasingly anachronistic in today's Europe. We need a theory of justice for the

[23] C. Barnard, '(B)Remains of the Day: Brexit and EU Social Policy', Chapter 19 in this volume.
[24] Ibid.

European Union. My thesis is not, merely, that the EU's initiatives and actions should be informed by consistent concerns about social justice: that is obviously the case. The argument I want to submit is more specific: we need a conception of justice that is based on a specific understanding of the point and purpose of the European Union as a multi-tiered polity, with at least three sets of principles: principles to be applied between Member States as collective actors (common) principles to be applied within Member States, and principles for regulating the mobility of citizens across Member States. This argument also resonates in the contributions by Joerges and Ferrera to this volume,[25] which is not to say that I would agree with their take on it. Developing such a tiered conception of justice is indeed far from self-evident and leads us into uncharted territory, as I hope to illustrate in this section (without being exhaustive or pretending to give any definitive answers).

The present section consists of four subsections. The first subsection sets the scene by sketching in a summary and relatively benign way what we might consider – with hindsight – the social inspiration of the founding fathers of the European project. The second subsection connects with contemporary political philosophy and defines some key concepts (solidarity, insurance, redistribution). The third subsection sets out questions and difficulties one encounters when one tries to relate the founding fathers' inspiration, the role of subsidiarity and free movement on one hand, to a notion of supranational distributive justice, as discussed in contemporary political philosophy, on the other hand. The fourth subsection sketches a more fundamental normative puzzle that emerges from this brief exploration.

The reader should note that I do not want to conflate 'justice' and 'solidarity': solidarity is a specific dimension (one might say, a component) of justice. Solidarity is also a multifaceted notion. For the purpose of this chapter, I propose to define solidarity rather narrowly as follows: solidarity is a readiness to share resources, with the aim to compensate individuals for (disadvantageous) circumstances for which we do not hold them responsible. I need a slight

---

[25] Andrea Sangiovanni has developed a thought-provoking understanding of solidarity in the European Union which also explicitly distinguishes principles applying within Member States from principles applying between Member States, and introduces a notion of 'reciprocity'. See A. Sangiovanni, 'Solidarity in the European Union' (2013) 36 *Oxford Journal of Legal Studies* 1. There is a congeniality between my approach and Sangiovanni's deliberately 'realist' approach (I also borrow the expression 'point and purpose' from him), but there are also differences. Space forbids to pursue this here. In short, I attempt to develop bridges with theories of justice that Sangiovanni might consider as 'idealist' and thus not fit for purpose. Sangiovanni's subtle account of solidarity in the EU seems premised on a notion of 'cooperative justice', whilst I think the normative foundation should be in conceptions of distributive justice. I also think the reference to a Dworkinian insurance device has less purchase in the context of constraints on Member States, created by the EU, than Sangiovanni seems to assume.

detour in the realm of theories of justice to situate that definition in well-rehearsed conceptions of justice. What follows focuses on matters of distributive justice, and thus is incomplete: I am fully aware of the fact that important debates, such as on European citizenship or on the way in which conceptions of justice would shape our view on employment relations, are not integrated in my exploratory exercise in this section.

1.4.1 *Setting the Scene: The Founding Fathers' Social Inspiration*

The European integration project has been described as a 'convergence machine'. Convergence was not just a result, it was also a pre-condition for continuing European integration: its 'output legitimacy' was based on the simultaneous pursuit of *economic progress*, on the one hand, and of *social progress and cohesion*, on the other hand, both *within* countries (through the gradual development of welfare states) and *between* countries (through upward convergence across the Union). Since 2008 we observe exactly the opposite: growing inequalities within a significant number of Member States and divergence across the Eurozone. Europe is becoming more unequal, both within and between Member States.

   The founding fathers of the European project who prepared the Treaty of Rome optimistically assumed that growing cohesion both between and within countries could be reached by supranational economic cooperation, together with some specific instruments for raising the standard of living across the Member States (which were later brought together in the EU's economic, social, and territorial cohesion policy). Economic integration was to be organised at the EU level, and would boost economic growth and create upward convergence; domestic social policies were to redistribute the fruits of economic progress, while remaining a national prerogative. The specific social dimension of the EU would, in essence, be confined to the coordination of social security rights for mobile citizens and to the gradual development of anti-discrimination legislation. Admittedly, after sixty years of piecemeal developments, the European social acquis encompasses other important policy areas that were shifted from the national to the EU level, such as health and safety standards at work. But redistributive policies, education policies and the development of social security remained – at least in theory – firmly anchored at the national level.

   With hindsight (and in a slightly benign interpretation), one may say that the founding fathers of the European project created two perspectives on social cohesion: a pan-European perspective and a national perspective. How would we understand this 'dual perspective'? Can we understand it in terms of solidarity (or different solidarities)? Solidarity within national welfare states is well-known territory. It refers to social insurance, income redistribution, and the underlying balance of social rights and obligations. As already indicated, the founding fathers did not believe that integration would diminish the potential for national solidarity, so conceived. On the contrary, they were confident that welfare state actors and institutions would redistribute the produce of economic integration, that is to say more economic growth, fairly within the Member States, in tune with social preferences in each state. Their belief was the exact opposite of the idea that international openness – or globalisation – is doomed to create not only winners, but also losers. On the basis of this (benign) interpretation, it is normatively relevant to revisit the founding fathers' inspiration: can the EU be a model of cooperation that contradicts an overly pessimistic view on the consequences of international openness, and, if so, how?

The founding fathers wanted upward economic convergence and cohesion on a European scale. They also wanted to give individual Europeans the right to improve their own lives by working in a Member State other than the one of which they are nationals, with no discrimination on the basis of nationality. Gradually, patients acquired the right to benefit, under certain conditions, from medical care in other Member States than their state of residence. How should we qualify this vision? Apart from redistributive aspects of the common agricultural policy, and a limited degree of cross-country redistribution in favour of less-developed regions through structural funds in the context of the so-called cohesion policy, the founding fathers' approach was not redistributive. Nor was it about the mutual insurance of risks. In other words, they did not envisage the organisation of solidarity as we normally understand it, which implies mixtures of redistribution and insurance (I define these concepts in the next subsection). Historically, the founding fathers' approach predominantly implied *fair access to opportunities*: trade and investment opportunities for countries joining the EU and personal opportunities for all their citizens wanting or needing to be mobile. One might also say that, in pursuing cohesion, it was motivated by *inclusion* on a pan-European scale.

However, the consequences of monetary unification force upon the Union a classic notion of solidarity in coping with *shared risks*. Whatever the solutions that are proposed to a variety of problems besetting the monetary union (a banking union; a more efficient organisation of the European Stability Mechanism (ESM) and pre-established rules with regard to sovereign default and debt restructuring; a fiscal capacity at the Eurozone level, possibly associated with a re-insurance of national unemployment insurance schemes or a genuine EU unemployment insurance scheme), these solutions always entail the ex ante organisation of solidarity mechanisms.[26] In short, a polity that initially emerged as an 'opportunity structure', motivated by the aspiration of growing cohesion, is in need of mutual insurance and effective solidarity. Thus, a dual perspective on solidarity, national, and pan-European, seems the logical consequence of developments that started more than sixty years ago. In fact, one might consider such a dual perspective on solidarity to be the defining normative feature of the European Social Model of the future: the European Social Model is not simply a summary description of a set of co-existing national social models; it also describes the way these national welfare states interact with each other – or are supposed to interact with each other – in Europe.

This dual perspective on solidarity is inherently complex and multifaceted. Monetary unification necessitates forms of solidarity which have been, so far, a no-go area in European politics, such as a Eurozone stabilisation capacity and fiscal transfers. Simultaneously, enlargement to the east created significantly more tension between the goals of upward convergence and domestic cohesion: what is seen by the new Member States as 'the dynamics of upward convergence' is seen as social dumping by others. In addition, the principle of non-discriminatory access to social benefits and services in all Member States for mobile citizens has become increasingly controversial.

Given the complexity of this dual perspective on solidarity, superficial rhetorical references to European solidarity will not suffice to revamp the European project's political legitimacy. We have to able to explain what European solidarity means, in terms that are both understandable to ordinary citizens and embedded in sound normative principles.

1.4.2 *Normative Foundations in Contemporary Theories of Justice*

The rigorous definition of sound normative principles has been the point and purpose of academic theories of justice. Is it possible to build bridges between, on one hand, the original inspiration of the pioneers of the European project, and, on the other hand, the vast academic debate on social justice as it has developed since the 1970s?

According to the pioneers, European integration would promote the simultaneous pursuit of social cohesion both within countries and between countries. In practical terms, the upshot would be the reduction of *inequalities*

---

[26] In the context of the Eurozone crisis management since 2008, we witnessed successive episodes of ex post solidarity, which came about most often after protracted and difficult negotiations. For that reason and for other reasons, ex post solidarity is less efficient than the establishment of ex ante solidarity mechanisms.

between and within Member States. Therefore, I start from the premise that promising academic resources for our purpose are to be found in the realm of what is called 'distributive justice'. Loosely put, theories of distributive justice typically focus on the distribution of entitlements to economic goods; obviously, the ultimate objective is not the distribution of economic goods per se, but the well-being of citizens. In democratic societies, any plausible conception of distributive justice reflects the idea that the members of a society should regard each other as equals and therefore owe each other a justification by which they can, as equals, accept any inequality in the entitlements which their societies define. This general statement about equal concern obviously needs elaboration. In the development of egalitarian theories of distributive justice, two debates have attracted considerable attention: first, what is the role of responsibility?; second, what are the boundaries of the society to which the principles of distributive justice apply and should we entertain a domestic or a supranational perspective on distributive justice?[27]

What role should personal responsibility play in our normative evaluation of inequalities in outcomes? Are we in favour of 'equality of opportunity' or 'equality of outcome'? Philosophical proponents of equality of opportunity argue that one should make a distinction between circumstances for which we do not hold people responsible (for instance, their family background, innate talents) and choices for which we hold them responsible (for instance, the effort with which they put their talents to work). Issues of responsibility dominate many political debates. To what extent are individuals responsible for their individual social situation, and to what extent should they be able to rely on solidarity? To what extent are Member States responsible for their nation's social situation, and to what extent can they count on pan-European solidarity? To structure our thinking on these thorny issues, we can build on 'responsibility-sensitive egalitarianism', an approach developed in the 1980s and 1990s in the slipstream of debates on Rawls's Theory of Justice.[28]

---

[27] Another crucial issue, which has attracted considerable attention concerns the metric of well-being ('equality of what?'): I do not address this here.

[28] Some classic philosophical references on equality of opportunity, responsibility-sensitive egalitarianism and 'luck egalitarianism' are R. Dworkin, 'What is Equality? Part 2: Equality of Resources' (1981) 10 *Philosophy and Public Affairs* 283; R. Arneson, 'Equality and Equal Opportunity for Welfare' (1989) 56 *Philosophical Studies* 77; G. Cohen, 'On the Currency of Egalitarian Justice' (1989) 99 *Ethics* 906 – and for an influential critical position: E. Anderson, 'What is the Point of Equality?' (1999) 109 *Ethics* 287. Important monographs with a more economic perspective are J. Roemer, *Equality of Opportunity* (Harvard University Press, 1998); and M. Fleurbaey, *Fairness, Responsibility and Welfare* (Oxford University Press, 2008). A recent survey of the literature can be found in J. Roemer and A. Trannoy, 'Equality of Opportunity', in A. Atkinson and F. Bourguignon (eds), *Handbook of Income Distribution* (Elsevier, Volume 2A, 2015).

1.4.2.1 Responsibility, Insurance, and Distribution

Responsibility-sensitive egalitarian justice[29] provides a framework for defining normative benchmarks to assess whether a given distribution is 'just' or 'unjust'.[30] That framework is flexible since it can capture different normative perspectives, depending on where one locates the 'responsibility cut', i.e. the threshold that determines for which factors individuals are held responsible and for which factors there is compensation. Traditionally, social security schemes apply an explicit responsibility cut: unemployment or sickness benefits are granted on the basis of people not being responsible for their economic inactivity. However, responsibility-sensitive egalitarianism also applies to dimensions of the social contract outside of traditional social risks covered by social security. For instance, we may hold each other responsible for the effort we deploy in our working life, but not for what we achieve (or fail to achieve) due to innate intelligence, socioeconomic background, gender, or origin. A social contract based on such a definition of the responsibility cut will not compensate people for differences in working hours or career length, but it will try to neutralise the impact of socioeconomic background and innate talent (and, obviously, fight disadvantage on the basis of gender or origin). Both childcare and education policies as well as income redistribution will be at play, but, ideally, income redistribution should not compensate for differences in hours worked. In contrast, if the social contract holds people responsible for their innate talent, there is no *principled* reason for income redistribution if socioeconomic background conditions would be fully neutralised due to child care, education, etc. (which is, obviously, an important 'if'). If we do not hold individuals responsible for anything or if we think that policy makers do not have the tools to identify personal responsibility, we are simply back in a straightforward equality-of-outcomes approach. The more characteristics one includes in the set of responsibility variables, the further one moves away from equality of outcomes.

---

[29] One should note that I use the 'equality of opportunity approach' and 'responsibility-sensitive egalitarian justice' as synonyms. Hence, in my usage, the equality of opportunity approach is also a normative framework with a flexible character.

[30] I do not want to say that responsibility-sensitive egalitarian justice suffices as a normative basis for social policy-making. In fact, I believe social policy needs a combination of responsibility-sensitive egalitarian justice and compassion (F. Vandenbroucke and K. Lievens, 'Wederkerigheid: niet vanzelfsprekend, wel hard nodig', in P. Janssens (ed.), *Voor wat hoort wat. Naar een nieuw sociaal contract* (De Bezige Bij, 2011); F. Vandenbroucke, 'De actieve welvaartsstaat. Een Europees perspectief', Den Uyl Lecture, Amsterdam, 13 December 1999, available at: www.canonsociaalwerk.eu/1999_actieve_welvaartstaat/1999Vandenbrouckeactievewelvaartstaat.pdf (accessed 12 December 2016)).

The responsibility-sensitive egalitarian framework can therefore be seen as an intellectual device that makes it possible to bring together these different perspectives under one coherent structure. It must not be confused with one single perspective.[31] The responsibility cut is often seen as drawing a line between unchosen circumstances and individual choice. If the framework is predicated on a notion of choice that presupposes freedom of will, it obviously becomes liable to the objection that with such notions one ventures into unending philosophical disputes, with no agreement in sight. However, the location of the responsibility cut, or what we *hold* people responsible for, is not a metaphysical question in this context but an unavoidable subject matter of the social contract: we cannot interact as human beings without holding each other responsible for at least something. This holds for relations between individuals, but also for relations between collective actors, like nation-states.

In Section 1.2 I argued that the EU is in need of more solidarity and I referred to proposals for mutual insurance at the Eurozone level, without providing clear-cut definitions of these concepts. The responsibility-sensitive egalitarian strand in contemporary political philosophy is interesting for our purpose, because it allows us to fit in notions of solidarity, insurance, and redistribution in a coherent normative framework. In that framework,[32] solidarity means that we share resources, with the aim of compensating individuals for (disadvantageous) circumstances for which we do not hold them responsible. Depending on the circumstances for which we do not hold individuals responsible, two different types of solidarity can be conceptually distinguished: *insurance* and *redistribution*. Pure insurance means that we compensate individuals for risks

---

[31] Often, equality of opportunity is defined as follows: individuals are not responsible for their socioeconomic background, but are responsible for everything else (including their innate intelligence); 'equal opportunities', *so conceived*, implies that we are satisfied when socioeconomic background has as little influence as possible on later life outcomes of individuals. This is not *the* theory of equality of opportunity; it is only a specific instance that fits into the theoretical framework on the basis of a specific responsibility cut. In yet other words, a low degree of intergenerational mobility suggests that 'equal opportunities', *so conceived*, are not realised; however, a high degree of intergenerational mobility is not in itself sufficient to conclude that more demanding notions of equality of opportunity are satisfied. When developing practical policies, we also have to take on board the following observation: achieving greater equality of opportunities without tackling inequalities in outcomes can be very difficult. This holds specifically in the family context: equality in outcomes among parent generations can be of instrumental importance for achieving equality of opportunities in the generation of the children, see A.B. Atkinson, *Inequality. What Can Be Done?* (Oxford University Press, 2015); OECD, *In It Together: Why Less Inequality Benefits All* (OECD Publishing, 2015). This raises complex normative questions: to what extent is equality of outcomes needed and, hence, legitimate, as an instrument to achieve equality of opportunity, even if 'on first principles' our interpretation of equality of opportunity does not lead to full equality of outcomes?

[32] I do not wish to say that this is the only possible definition of solidarity.

that cannot be foreseen at the level of the individual, but can reasonably be calculated at the level of a homogeneous group (a group of individuals with identical risk profiles). In practical terms, since individual risk profiles are identical, the expected net present value of benefits cashed in by a pure insurance mechanism is, for all individuals, equal to the net present value of their contribution to the scheme. Insurance is, by definition, about future risks.

Redistribution occurs when individuals are different with regard to the circumstances for which we do not hold them responsible. The prime example of redistribution is progressive taxation, which redistributes (inter alia) from economically talented individuals to economically less-talented individuals: progressive taxation compensates (in part) the disadvantage of having less economic talent; redistribution follows from the fact that individuals differ with regard to talent.[33] In terms of the motivation and disposition of the participating individuals, redistribution is seen as a more 'demanding' form of solidarity than insurance. Well-organised insurance can readily be understood as a matter of enlightened self-interest: the expectation is that, in the end, everybody wins. So conceived, redistribution is, prima facie, not a matter of enlightened self-interest. In practice, insurance and redistribution very often get mixed up, and this creates the true cement of national welfare states. For instance, sickness benefits are redistributive across individuals when some individuals have a higher risk of sickness than others. In addition, sickness benefits might be redistributive because of minima and maxima that apply to the benefits, whilst contributions are proportional to income. Given differences in skill levels, unemployment insurance normally embodies redistribution from the high-skilled to the low-skilled. A presumption (which, admittedly, has not been tested empirically, and which I do not elaborate upon) of the analysis that follows is that it is probably easier to persuade European citizens about cross-border insurance mechanisms than about cross-border redistribution (Hooghe and Verhaegen refer to this assumption at the end of their chapter in this book).

These definitions can be extended to relationships between public authorities: we can use 'inter-institutional solidarity' for mechanisms that imply transfers between public authorities (say, governments of nation-states); the transfers are triggered by circumstances defined at the level of those nation-states. In contrast, 'interpersonal solidarity' specifically focuses on mechanisms of insurance or redistribution that imply transfers of resources between individuals; the transfers are triggered by individual circumstances.

---

[33] Progressive taxation also compensates income differences that follow from 'bad luck', and thus incorporates an insurance dimension too.

1.4.2.2 The Boundaries of Justice

We can now turn to the second debate that has exercised academic theorising on justice: what are the boundaries of justice? This question is well rehearsed in the literature on global justice. The logic of responsibility-sensitive egalitarian justice implies that it has no national boundaries: if an individual is worse-off than other individuals because of the place where he is born and lives – say, a very poor country – this fact is certainly a circumstance rather than a choice. From that perspective, it is prima facie very hard *not* to apply principles of egalitarian justice on a global level. Nevertheless, whether or not principles of egalitarian justice apply on a global level has been the subject of intense debate in contemporary political philosophy. Just as with responsibility-sensitive egalitarianism, the debate on 'international distributive justice' also developed, to a considerable extent, in reaction to (in defence of, or against) Rawls.[34] Fundamentally, international distributive justice is about the boundaries of the solidarity circle: who are the members of 'our' solidarity circle?

In a survey paper on international distributive justice, Van Parijs argues that the mere existence of national borders is a sufficient condition for the demands of egalitarian justice to kick in on a global level. Prima facie, this is a convincing argument. Borders imply that people are being prevented, by virtue of where they happen to be born, from taking advantage of opportunities open to people born elsewhere. These coercive rules have a major effect on people's lives. Thus, the existence of national borders creates a constraining 'global basic structure', which – just as is the case for the 'basic structure' of national societies in Rawls's theory – must be the subject matter of a conception of justice. Subsequently, Van Parijs argues that national welfare states should be 'demoted from the framework' (of our normative thinking) 'to the toolbox':

> Suppose we adopt such a minimalist conception of what is necessary and sufficient for the demands of egalitarian justice to kick in. Under present conditions – with a global basic structure that has become the subject of a global conversation – global distributive justice should then evidently be given logical priority over domestic distributive justice. It would not follow

---

[34] The literature on international distributive justice is large, with important early contributions by Barry, Rawls, Beitz, Pogge, Nagel, and others. I understand this domain of philosophical debate as Van Parijs defines and discusses it, and as it is also discussed in the Stanford Encyclopedia of Philosophy. See: Van Parijs, 'International Distributive Justice', in R.E. Goodin, P. Pettit, and T. Pogge (eds), *A Companion to Contemporary Political Philosophy* (Blackwell, Volume 2, 2007); Stanford Encyclopedia of Philosophy, International distributive justice, entry available at: plato.stanford.edu/entries/international-justice (accessed 12 December 2016).

that states and nations ought to vanish, that borders ought to be erased or peoples dissolved. *But they must all be demoted from the framework to the toolbox.* Instead of seizing them in a desperate attempt to halt the irresistible globalisation of our sense of justice, we must urgently think about how they can best be constrained, reconfigured and empowered in the service of distributive justice for a global society of equals.[35]

If we accept that argument, it obviously also holds for the EU, which must be part of the toolbox rather than of the framework. In this view, both national welfare states and the EU are merely an instrument to implement international distributive justice, the ultimate aim of which is a global society of equals. However, given the difficulty of implementing truly *global* justice, we might conceive of the EU as a 'laboratory' for the implementation of international distributive justice. I will adopt this view (which is basically Van Parijs's view, and also inspires De Schutter's contribution in this volume) as a starting position for the next subsection, to explore some of the challenges with which this view is confronted.

1.4.3 *Supranational Justice, Subsidiarity and Openness*

In this subsection, I take it that the EU would be a laboratory for international distributive justice and that principles of distributive justice would apply between citizens at the EU level. Below, I will use the expression 'supranational justice' as a short-cut for this laboratory idea.

1.4.3.1 Two Observations on Global Justice and the Organisation of Interpersonal Solidarity

Contrary to what is sometimes thought, global justice does not imply that interpersonal solidarity – resource sharing between individuals – must always be organised at the highest possible level, without a specific role for nation-states. There are two different reasons why this is not the case. Both reasons can be seen as applications of a specific subsidiarity principle: you should do at the lower level what can be done at the lower level without loss of efficiency.[36] First, there is, to some extent, scope for subsidiarity in the *practical implementation* of global justice[37]: global justice can be organised by a mix

---

[35] Van Parijs, 'International Distributive Justice', n. 34 in this chapter, p. 652 (emphasis added).

[36] There is not a unique definition of subsidiarity; this is one definition among others.

[37] My emphasis, here, is on the implementation of policies, not on the definition of policy objectives.

of interpersonal solidarity within nation-states on the one hand and inter-institutional solidarity between nation-states on the other hand, without any 'loss' in terms of ideal global justice. Second, whether we need to organise solidarity at the highest possible level, from the point of view of global justice, depends on background conditions: prima facie, it seems that global justice requires global solidarity mechanisms only if nation-states are *different from each other* in a relevant sense. In contrast, if that is not the case, no inter-institutional solidarity is needed; interpersonal solidarity at the nation-state level suffices, at least prima facie (I will qualify this argument below).[38]

In the domain of pure insurance, we find the most straightforward application of the first observation (there may be scope for subsidiarity in the implementation of global justice): any efficient sharing of risks among a (sufficiently large) group of individuals can be implemented in either one or two stages, with the same final outcome for every individual. Take, by way of example, a pay-as-you-go pension scheme in a country that is subdivided in regions. It is possible to reinsure regional pension schemes on the national level for economic and demographic shocks hitting the regions: this might do as well as a truly national pension scheme.[39] This example can be extrapolated to the supranational re-insurance of national insurance systems. The subsidiarity applied in such a two-tiered supranational scheme is first of all a matter of practical organisation, but – in the context of insurance – it might also allow participating nation-states to vary the details of the interpersonal insurance mechanism within their nation-state, according to their preferences. Subsidiarity, so conceived, does not diminish global solidarity. The idea of organising a Eurozone re-insurance for national unemployment insurance mechanisms of Eurozone countries is an example of such an approach. Whilst Andor, De Grauwe, and Ji discuss it as a functional response to a design flaw in the Eurozone, a two-tiered system of unemployment insurance can also be seen as a way to improve solidarity (with regard to the risk of short-term unemployment) by enhancing it to a supranational level; thus, it is an improvement

---

38 Note that these arguments should be distinguished from pragmatic arguments for subsidiarity on the basis of existing attitudes: such arguments accept a 'loss' in terms of ideal global justice (which is unattainable given existing attitudes) in order to settle for a second-best solution (which is attainable on the basis of existing attitudes). A pragmatic argument for subsidiarity, based on existing attitudes, is that there is insufficient 'fellow feeling' at the global level to sustain global justice.

39 For an elaboration of this example with regard to pension policy, in the context of Belgian federalism, see J. Drèze, *On the Interaction between Subsidiarity and Interpersonal Solidarity* (Re-Bel, Volume 1, 2009), available at: www.rethinkingbelgium.eu/rebel-initiative-ebooks/ebook-1-subsidiarity-interpersonal-solidarity (accessed 12 December 2016). For an application of this type of argument to the EU level, see J. Drèze. A. Durré, and J.F. Carpantier, 'Fiscal Integration and Growth Stimulation in Europe' (2014) 80 *Louvain Economic Review* 5.

in terms of justice. The design challenges touched upon briefly in the previous section can be reconsidered and reformulated in terms of responsibility-sensitive justice: Eurozone Member States would insure each other against unemployment shocks for which they do not hold – as a matter of convention or social contract – individual Member States responsible; thus, they would organise true solidarity. As explained in Section 1.2, any insurance device must address moral hazard (the fact that the insured agent might influence the liability which the insurer has to pay by deliberate behaviour, whilst the insurance contract is premised on the convention that the insured agent is not responsible for the event that creates the liability); but insurance – and solidarity – is impossible if there is an obsession with the risk of moral hazard and a desire to eliminate it completely.

The second observation (global justice requires global solidarity only if nation-states are different from each other in a relevant sense) entails a more complicated normative discussion. Suppose, for the sake of the argument, that there is a perfect correlation between the economic and demographic risks hitting a set of nation-states: an inter-state insurance against economic and demographic risks affecting their pension systems would not add any value.[40] Or, suppose for the sake of the argument, that we have a set of nation-states with identical average income levels and identical income distributions: there would be no reason to organise income redistribution across borders to implement egalitarian objectives. The argument is not purely theoretical: one might say that a European strategy of upward convergence, if it delivers, gradually creates a situation where income redistribution across Member States becomes unnecessary; in such a scenario, only income redistribution within the Member States is needed. Upward convergence, if it delivers, can be seen as a slow but politically feasible strategy to obtain at least one precondition for what the global egalitarian wants (applied to the EU), that is, that the average prosperity within Member States is equalised across Member States.

1.4.3.2 Is Upward Convergence Sufficient?

Suppose, for the sake of the argument, that we can rely on economic integration to produce upward convergence, and that this finally leads to an equalisation of average prosperity levels (I will qualify that hypothesis, which is far from evident in today's Europe, in Section 1.5). Would we then leave

---

[40] This statement is made on a high level of theoretical abstraction. De Grauwe and Ji discuss the relevance of synchronisation and non-synchronisation of business cycles in the context of a European unemployment insurance scheme on a more concrete level of analysis, and argue that a pan-European approach might be useful also in case of synchronisation.

the design of redistributive policies to national governments? Can we rely on national preferences with regard to redistribution and apply subsidiarity, without any concern, at the supranational level, for distributive justice? Two objections can be made against such a view. The first objection does not accept subsidiarity with regard to distributive preferences, or at least qualifies it. The second objection accepts subsidiarity with regard to distributive preferences, but questions the actual capacity of welfare states to implement redistributive policies in an integrated market.[41]

The first objection is, in my understanding, implicit in De Schutter's contribution in this volume, who argues that redistribution should be 'Europeanised'. Basically, De Schutter argues that the welfare of an individual (say, his income) should not depend on the level of economic prosperity of his country. Hence, he proposes that at least the funding basis of national welfare states should be subject to a pan-European redistributive scheme. Consider a scenario in which average welfare state funding is equalised via pan-European fiscal transfers, but preferences within some Member State X are such that there is hardly any redistribution of these funds towards the least advantaged in country X. I think it follows from De Schutter argument that this is incompatible with his ideal of European distributive justice: his argument that redistribution should be truly Europeanised, leaves no room, so I think, for subsidiarity-based national deviations that would contradict the objective of improving the position of the least advantaged.[42] The difficulty with that position, so it seems to me, is twofold. First, on a pragmatic level, De Schutter's description of the problem implies that we can isolate 'redistribution' as a separate function of welfare states, i.e. that we are able to make a neat distinction between the overall national architecture of welfare states (including employment policies, education, child care, etc.) and their

---

[41] These objections are not per se mutually exclusive. If the first objection is not a flat denial of subsidiarity, it is not inconsistent to justify European supranational initiatives in the domain of distributive justice on the basis of a combination of both objections.

[42] There are two reasons why this is incompatible with De Schutter's rationale. First, it seems hard to justify that an individual's position is dependent on the preferences for redistribution of his fellow citizen, but not dependent on the level of average prosperity attained in his country (which may also be a result of preferences). Second, it seems implausible that European citizens in other countries would be ready to transfer money to this Member State X, if it is not used for the stated aim, to wit, helping the least advantaged. Therefore, I understand De Schutter's position as follows: preferences for redistribution that exist at the nation-state level are not relevant from a fundamental normative point of view. Obviously, De Schutter would accept that this principled, normative point of view is conditional on its acceptance in a democratic deliberation at the EU level; and, he would accept that a country cannot be forced to be a Member State of a European Union in which distributive choices are made at the pan-European level.

redistributive outcomes. In fact, it is hard to dissociate redistribution from the overall functioning of welfare states; hence, the Europeanisation of redistribution logically entails a degree of Europeanisation of the whole welfare state edifice. Second, on a fundamental level, De Schutter's position implies that a European conception of justice (which bears on the whole welfare edifice) would trump national democratic preferences: given the historical legitimacy of the European Union and its strong emphasis on subsidiarity (not just with regard to implementation, but also with regard to social-policy objectives, notably in the realm of redistribution), such a drastic move seems highly implausible. Obviously, De Schutter might respond to this, in the sense that this 'realistic' concern carries little weight in a purely normative argument.

However, the idea that – notwithstanding subsidiarity – it is legitimate to fight for a certain conception of social justice at the EU level, with which Member States would have to comply, always had some traction in the European political debate: European countries were seen as sharing fundamental ('European') values with regard to the social model. Jointly defending and developing a 'European way of life' (as Habermas would have it, referring to an expression used by former French Prime Minister Lionel Jospin) was seen by many as a legitimate ambition per se, an ambition even at the heart of the European project.[43] Whilst the founding fathers thought that upward convergence through market integration would not contradict but facilitate the on-going development of comprehensive welfare states, driven by domestic social forces and preferences, in this view welfare state development becomes an explicit and strategic common European objective. The Open Method of Coordination (OMC) on Social Inclusion, which was launched in 2001, can be seen as an attempt to reconcile the ambition to realise a truly European social model with the traditional concern for subsidiarity, including in the domain of income distribution. OMC means that social policy objectives, including objectives with regard to minimum income protection, are formulated at the EU level, thus instantiating a European conception of justice; national diversity is accepted, both in terms of policy inputs and policy outcomes, but Member States are asked to justify their performance with regard to those principles. Thus, the OMC presupposes a commonality in objectives with regard to national distributive policies, which constitutes a conception of European justice, but without rigidly imposing these objectives. In his

---

[43] Next to arguments referring to the on-going integration of markets, seeing the upscaling of employment and social policy standards as a necessary functional corollary – arguments recapitulated in Deakin's contribution to this volume (Chapter 8).

subtle analysis of OMC, Kenneth Armstrong sees this as an exercise in social constitutionalism:

> If the function of court-led economic constitutionalism is often to prise open the nation state and require Member States to demonstrate how national policies are to be reconciled with EU economic objectives, then the function of OMC-driven social constitutionalism may equally be to put EU Member States to the test and to demand explanations of how exercises of domestic social sovereignty attain the social policy objectives and values of the Union while protecting fundamental rights. In this way, social solidarity in the name of combating poverty and social exclusion is a substantive jumping-off point to be articulated through practices of governance, but it is also an irreducible point in the sense that it cannot be avoided.[44]

Social constitutionalism via 'open coordination', so conceived, would accommodate the first objection against relegating concerns for redistribution completely to the national level, whilst accepting an important degree of subsidiarity. Admittedly, the impact of the OMC has, qua actual impact, often been perceived as weak. To make this strategy credible, it needs tangible impact.

The second objection to the idea that upward convergence might suffice as a supranational egalitarian strategy starts from the opposite vantage point. Suppose we accept, in a spirit of subsidiarity, national sovereignty with regard to national distributive preferences (contra the first objection). It may be the case that the Member States' actual capacity to achieve their redistributive objectives is diminished by the impact of economic integration.[45] In order to rescue national sovereignty – in a real sense – we may have to scale up certain aspects of redistribution to the supranational level. Corporate taxation is an example: in order to protect national governments against a race-to-the-bottom in corporate taxation, a degree of supranational regulation (for instance with regard to the tax base) is needed. Supranational regulation of

---

[44] K. Armstrong, *Governing Social Inclusion. Europeanization through Policy Coordination* (Oxford University Press, 2010), p. 262. On the relation between OMC and the idea of a common European conception of justice, see also F. Vandenbroucke, 'Sustainable Social Justice and "Open Co-ordination" in Europe', in G. Esping-Andersen (ed.), *Why We Need a New Welfare State* (Oxford University Press, 2002). For further discussion of Armstrong's view, in relation to the idea of a European approach to minimum income protection, see F. Vandenbroucke, B. Cantillon, N. Van Mechelen, T. Goedemé, and A. Van Lancker, 'The EU and Minimum Income protection: Clarifying the Policy Conundrum', in I. Marx and K. Nelson (eds), *Minimum Income Protection in Flux* (Palgrave Macmillan, 2013).

[45] These arguments are congenial to well-known arguments, revisited by Deakin in his contribution, on the need to define a pan-European floor of social rights as a corollary to the internal market.

corporate taxation is an example of *systemic support* that can be provided to
national welfare states by a European Social Union. Next to capital mobility,
labour mobility can have a negative impact on the distributive capacity of
national welfare states. Labour mobility may increase the supply of low-skilled
people in certain Member States, and put pressure, in these Member States,
on the working conditions of low-skilled people. Governments may counter
such an impact by labour-market regulation and redistributive policies. But, if
people and taxable factors of production can move freely from one Member
State to the other, this might also reduce the capacity of governments to redistribute. The low-skilled might tend to move to highly redistributive welfare
states; the high-skilled might tend to move to less redistributive welfare states;
capital will move where it is taxed least, etc.: such trends might undermine
the redistributive capacity of national welfare states. Whether or not such
trends occur in reality, is a matter of dispute (the downward pressure of capital
mobility on corporate taxation seems most evident; empirical studies learn
that cross-border mobility is mainly motivated by employment opportunities,
rather than by benefit systems). But, the point I want to make is that even in
a setting where Member States would have achieved the same average level
of prosperity, a supranational approach may be necessary to reconcile free
movement on one hand and redistribution on the other hand.

Thus, this second objection to an overly optimistic reliance on upward convergence (with a view to distributive justice on a supranational level) leads us
to what is probably the most complex discussion in the realm of European
justice: how to reconcile free movement between Member States and the
redistributive capacity of national welfare states? More fundamentally, what
is the normative rationale for free movement? Space forbids a detailed elaboration of this question. Briefly put, the thesis I would like to defend is that
free movement can be part of the legitimate opportunity structure of a just
European polity, *if* it is accommodated by principles of reciprocity. In his analysis of what he calls 'transnational solidarity in the European Union', Floris
De Witte formulates it as follows:

> if we want to reintegrate cosmopolitan dynamics within the structures of
> the nation state in the pursuit of social justice, the concept of reciprocity,
> whether understood in economic, social or political terms, might prove a
> good starting point, as it can conceptually accommodate relationships across
> borders while remaining sensitive to the preconditions for the reproduction
> of the welfare structures.[46]

---

[46] De Witte, *Justice in the EU*, n. 20 in this chapter, at p. 17.

With an explicit reference to Rosanvallon's notion of reciprocity,[47] De Witte concludes that '[R]eciprocity ... allows for the reconfiguration of justice on the national level so as to take account of the transnational relational commitments that have emerged in economic, social, or political forms'.[48]

One need not agree with De Witte's practical application of these concepts to concur with this fundamental idea. Giving mobile people who contribute to the social system of their host country (say, a Polish citizen working on a regular employment contract in Belgium) access to the social benefits of the host country (Belgium) is a matter of sound reciprocity for two different reasons, which are not always well understood. First of all, this principle reflects a generally accepted contributory principle within the existing national solidarity circles. Secondly, it justifies the fact that the Polish worker's employer pays the same social security contributions to Belgian social security as the Belgian worker's employer. In other words, non-discrimination in terms of

---

[47] Ibid., n. 20 in this chapter, at p. 48. Rosanvallon defines reciprocity as 'equality of interaction ... The equilibrium on which it depends takes two forms: equilibrium of exchange or involvement', see P. Rosanvallon, *The Society of Equals*, translated by A. Goldhammer (Harvard University Press, 2013), p. 271. He refers to Bowles's definition of reciprocity: 'a propensity to cooperate and share with others similarly disposed, even at personal cost'. A readiness to contribute to society, for those who are able to contribute, seems an essential feature of reciprocity, so conceived, see S. Bowles, in collaboration with C. Fong, H. Gintis, A. Jayadev, and U. Pagano, *Essays on the New Economics of Inequality and Redistribution* (Cambridge University Press, 2012).

[48] De Witte's account of 'transnational solidarity' is based on two arguments. First, freedom of movement, as understood in the European project, is legitimate as it enhances the freedom of European citizens to pursue their conception of the good life, beyond the borders of their nation-state. Second, solidarity between non-nationals and nationals ('transnational solidarity'), upon which access to social benefits by non-nationals is based, depends on the associative or relational interaction between non-nationals and nationals. De Witte's fundamental idea is that freedom of movement must be accommodated by principles of reciprocity: he thereby entertains a broad notion of reciprocity and solidarity: reciprocity includes contributory efforts, but also goes beyond it: living in the same country can be the basis for specific solidarities, for instance with regard to access to primary healthcare. Giving non-nationals who happen to live in one's country access to primary healthcare, simply on the basis of their residence without any further condition but 'need', is not seen as jeopardising the 'preconditions for the reproduction of the welfare structures'. In contrast, giving access to social assistance, simply based on residence without further conditions, might be seen as jeopardising the 'preconditions for the reproduction of the welfare structures'. Admittedly, this account leaves a lot to be specified: it creates a framework for deliberation but does not lead straightforwardly to conclusions, as De Witte's critical account of the European Court of Justice's case law testifies. The 'preconditions for the reproduction of the welfare structures' can be understood in an economic sense (safeguarding an equilibrium between expected revenue and expenditure), but also in a political sense (safeguarding popular support). Crucially, in this account of solidarity in the EU, *reciprocity cannot be based on nationality*: the mere fact that people are 'non-nationals' cannot be the reason why they are denied access to social policies in the Member State of residence. See De Witte, *Justice in the EU*, n. 20 in this chapter.

social rights justifies and so sustains the principle that we do not tolerate competition between the Polish and the Belgian social security system on Belgian territory. In this way, this principle contributes to safeguarding the distributive capacity of national welfare states in the EU. Therefore, the 'deal' struck by former Prime Minister Cameron with the EU leaders to avoid Brexit, which would allow the discriminating of regular Polish workers in the UK vis-à-vis British workers was fundamentally misguided.

Competition between the Polish and the Belgian social security system is exactly what happens in the context of posting of workers: a Polish worker who is 'posted' in Belgium remains integrated in Polish social security. Thus, posting is an exception to a foundational and sound principle of the European project. In order to accommodate work in other countries on short-term projects, such an exception is needed, a fortiori if one wants to develop an integrated market for services. Admittedly, the scope for this exception seems to have become too large, and there are important problems of inspection and control. The political debate on posting is analysed by Martinsen in her contribution to this volume. Feenstra also discusses posting in his discussion of the *Laval* judgment. Elsewhere I argue that the political debate badly needs an encompassing approach to the problem of posting and non-discriminatory access to social benefits for active non-nationals, in a spirit of reciprocity.[49] 'New' Member States such as Poland typically want as few limitations as possible on posting of workers (since a liberal posting regime is economically beneficial for them). Simultaneously, these Member States want as few limitations as possible on the principle of non-discrimination in social policy (since such limitations imply a social relapse for Polish citizens, who would lose social rights they now have). Thus, they apply two principles that are, in terms of rationale and justification, fundamentally at odds with each other, but that seem to serve their short-term interests best. Some of the 'old' Member States, having the most advanced welfare provision and labour-market regulation, are increasingly nervous about the impact of posting on their labour markets; similarly, they feel uneasy with the debate on access to social benefits for non-nationals, who are working on regular employment contracts. What would reciprocity mean in this context? In a European negotiation on these matters, the old Member States should address the new Member States in the following way: 'We are not in favour of discriminating against your citizens in our advanced welfare states when they come to work there on regular contracts,

49 Vandenbroucke, 'Social Benefits and Cross-border Mobility: Sticking to Principles May Yield Better Practical Results for Everybody', *Tribune*, Notre Europe Jacques Delors Institute, 17 June 2016, available at: www.delorsinstitute.eu/011-23040-Social-benefits-and-cross-border-mobility.html (accessed 12 December 2016).

hence we are in total opposition to the Cameron agenda. But, please, understand that we do not want to see our social system undermined by excesses in the application of posting.'[50] If such would be the principled approach of representatives of mature welfare states, they may strike a better deal with representatives of less developed welfare states on both issues (posting, non-discrimination), compared to a situation in which deviations from the non-discrimination principle and uncontrollable posting proliferate. If deviations from the non-discrimination principle and uncontrollable posting thrive, we will ultimately settle for an equilibrium with less social protection than in the opposite case. Everybody would lose in the end, in an archetypal example of how certain types of coordination yield Pareto-inferior solutions, compared to other types of coordination. Even for a country like the UK which seems, currently, not very worried about abuses of posting, it may ultimately be better – in terms of its national regulatory capacity – to have a controllable system of posting, rather than a free hand in the application of its in-work benefits for non-British citizens.

Although the debate about the coordination of social security and the debate on posting are now separated, Member States would be well advised to consider them from the same, principled perspective. The challenge is to find a balance between, on one hand, the need for an integrated market in services (for which posting is necessary) and the foundational principle of the EU that mobile workers should be integrated into the solidarity circle of the Member State in which they work, both in terms of wages, working conditions, and social security contributions and social policy entitlements. Thus, the principle of non-discriminatory access to social benefits for active non-nationals and the concomitant integration of non-nationals into their host country's social security schemes is fundamental, not only from the point of view of reciprocity within welfare states, but also from the point of view of reciprocity between EU welfare states.[51]

Non-discriminatory access to social benefits for non-active non-nationals is a more complex matter. The distinction drawn between non-active and

---

[50] Obviously, neither the level of child benefits nor the regulation of posting are matters for bilateral negotiations between the Dutch and the Polish government.

[51] Sangiovanni adds a principled argument against Cameron's Brexit deal on the basis of non-discrimination; in the same article, Sangiovanni also mentions arguments specific to the EU, based on 'demands of reciprocity among Member States cooperating in maintaining and reproducing the EU'. His reciprocity-argument refers to a scenario in which Britons working in other EU Member States would maintain access to social benefits in their host countries, whilst this would be denied to non-nationals (with EU citizenship) working in the UK. See A. Sangiovanni, 'Non-discrimination, In-work Benefits, and Free Movement in the EU' (2016) *European Journal of Political Theory*, Epub ahead of print.

active non-nationals in the application of the non-discrimination principle is a delicate and often controversial one. Contrary to a number of observers, I believe that distinction, as highlighted in the well-known *Dano* judgment by the Court of Justice,[52] is legitimate. That is, in a union of welfare states, it is legitimate to delineate the access to social benefits for non-active mobile citizens by specific conditions, which reflect the nature of the social relations established between the mobile citizen and his host country. Ferrera touches upon this question in his contributions to this volume.

1.4.4 *The Normative Puzzle*

In the previous subsection, I discussed two objections against the idea that upward convergence in average Member State prosperity, if successful, suffices from the point of view of European distributive justice. The first objection – in a strict variant, exemplified by De Schutter's understanding of international distributive justice in this volume – fundamentally denies subsidiarity with regard to distributive preferences. Transferring redistributive policies from the national to the European level seems hardly a realist position; however, calls to develop a true European social model, based on common principles of social justice, have been considered legitimate in the past, in so far as they have been implemented on the flexible and soft basis of the OMC, that is, with respect to diversity and substantive subsidiarity. In contrast, the second objection against the idea that upward convergence suffices, discussed in the previous subsection, fully accepts subsidiarity; the argument is that, in an integrated market with mobility of capital and people, specific aspects of national social and taxation policy have to be regulated and even centralised in order to protect the actual redistributive capacity of the Member States. A union of welfare states needs collective action with regard to principles of taxation of mobile factors (corporate taxes, wealth taxes). And it must see to it that the openness, which creates opportunities across the whole union, does not diminish the internal redistributive capacity of national welfare states. Therefore, openness must be embedded in principles of reciprocity, within and between welfare states. This can be seen as the normative rationale, underpinning Barnard's conclusion from the Brexit saga.

One should now note that this second objection, which is motivated by our concern with cohesion within national welfare states, reveals a more fundamental normative puzzle. With reference to my starting point in this section

---

[52] ECJ, judgments of 11 November 2014 in *Elisabeta Dano and Florin Dano v Jobcenter Leipzig*, C-333/13, EU:C:2014:2358.

(Van Parijs's formulation of global justice) it can be formulated as follows. Suppose we are attracted by Van Parijs's argument that the mere existence of national borders forces us to develop a conception of global justice (because national borders create an international 'basic structure' that needs a legitimation in terms of justice), and that the EU can be seen as a promising laboratory for global justice. But would we really want to give an absolute priority to global justice over domestic justice, as Van Parijs argues, and demote national welfare states to mere 'instruments' of global objectives? Let me illustrate the consequences of this instrumental position with a stylised example. Let's assume that the EU is composed of two types of Member States, rich Member States and poor Member States; within each of these types of Member States, there are two social classes, the rich class and the poor class. Hence, we have four representative social positions: one may be poor in a poor Member State; one may be rich in a poor Member State; one may be poor in a rich Member State; one may be rich in a rich Member State. The poor in the rich countries are better-off than the poor in the poor countries. I take it that we are global egalitarians, who want to make the position of the worst-off as good as possible (a maximin principle, à la Rawls). Let us suppose that we would have to choose between two scenarios: one (integration) in which the poor in rich countries see their social position deteriorate, while the poor in poor countries see their situation improve; another one (no integration) in which there is a status quo. If we think national welfare states are merely instruments for a global maximin, we would choose the 'integration' scenario without further ado.

For sure, the imaginary scenarios presented in the previous paragraph would betray the EU's founding fathers' expectations about the impact of integration: they firmly believed that upward convergence across EU Member States would go hand in hand with sustained or even improved internal cohesion within each of the EU Member States. But if these imaginary scenarios would be a true stylisation of today's reality of economic integration, they would create a tragic dilemma for anyone who thinks that both inequalities across Member States and inequalities within Member States matter. Let's call the latter view a 'dualist' view, as it entertains a dual perspective in which both relations across Member States and relations within Member States matter per se.

This dualism is 'non-reducible' in the following sense. The dual perspective cannot be reduced to a single one, as it is premised on conflicting views on the size of the solidarity circle concerned: the 'we' to which solidarity applies is differently defined. Moreover, there is no simple trade-off between the one and the other perspective, let alone an algorithm whereby national and pan-European poverty or inequality indicators may be reduced to a single indicator. One might say that such an irreducible normative dualism with regard to social justice in the EU is intrinsic to the point and purpose of the European project, and that the attractive simplicity of the instrumental view fails to do justice to the European project. Another way to formulate the dual perspective is that a European conception of justice consists of principles that apply between Member States qua collective actors (loosely put, we want to see upward convergence across Member States, which means that we want to improve the relative position of the 'worst-off Member State') and principles that apply within Member States (loosely put, we want to protect and if possible improve the relative position of the worst-off within each of the Member States). However, starting from such a dualist perspective, we may end up with ambiguity and inconsistency. By way of example, suppose we want to pursue a maximin rule (the position of the worst-off individual should be as good as is possible) both at the supranational European level and at the level of the Member States: without a clear priority for either the supranational maximin rule or the national maximin rules, we are faced with contradictory objectives. In his contribution to this volume, Ferrera suggests a less ambitious supranational objective: in addition to the redistributive efforts organised by national welfare states within their respective solidarity circles, a 'sufficientarian' standard would make sure that all EU citizens have 'enough', at least to survive. In Ferrera's view, this would instantiate a form of organised 'benevolence', a necessary complement to the stern, responsibility-sensitive application of principles of reciprocity.[53] Ferrera's organised benevolence would imply a degree of cross-border interpersonal redistribution; therefore, in order to be normatively consistent, i.e. not in contradiction with national distributive objectives, an elaboration on these objectives and on priorities is necessary.[54]

I cannot engage thoroughly with the arguments put forward by De Schutter and Ferrera in this volume. This is not my brief here. Including De Schutter and Ferrera in our project was a deliberate choice, as they exemplify two different approaches to normative theory building. Ferrera positions himself as belonging to a 'realist strand', 'combining normative and sociological reasoning';[55] in contrast, I would situate De Schutter in an 'idealist strand', in which

---

[53] Ferrera, Chapter 2 in this volume, n. 22 in this chapter. Ferrera's argument for 'benevolence' is, to some extent, congenial to my plea for compassion in Vandenbroucke, n. 30 in this chapter, which is premised on the idea that responsibility-sensitive egalitarian justice has no adequate answer to some relevant social policy questions.

[54] There is, a priori, no problem of consistency if the pan-European and the national objectives with regard to income protection in the Member States are expressed in relative terms (say, no one should have an income below 60 per cent of the median income in his Member State) and minimum income protection is not funded by cross-border transfers. For a concrete discussion of such a proposal, see Vandenbroucke et al., n. 44 in this chapter.

[55] Ferrera, Chapter 2 in this volume, n. 22 in this chapter.

normative ideals are seen as utopian dreaming in a bad sense only if human beings are truly *unable* to carry out the dream. According to Ferrera, '[i]f they aim at exerting practical effects, justificatory arguments need to be closely anchored to existing and factual states of affairs and remain highly sensitive to feasibility constraints'.[56] In contrast, proponents of the idealist strand might say that this realist approach risks polluting or even conflating moral judgments with empirical observations about how people actually think in today's societies and how institutions actually function. In other words, proponents of the idealist strand might argue that we should not conflate 'ought statements' with 'is statements'.

Whether or not we emphasise realism in contrast to idealism, my short exploration of normative arguments signals that we need a conception of justice that is based on a specific understanding of the European Union as a multi-tiered polity, with at least three sets of principles: principles to be applied between Member States as collective actors, (common) principles to be applied within Member States, and principles for regulating the mobility of citizens across Member States. In yet other words, we need an account that takes on board both the intrinsic value of global justice and the intrinsic (not purely instrumental) value of existing welfare states.

1.5 CONDITIONS FOR UPWARD CONVERGENCE AND SOCIAL INVESTMENT

In order to focus on the normative debate, my discussion in the preceding section has taken it for granted that the initial expectation of the founding fathers with regard to upward convergence would be vindicated. Formulating it more precisely, their expectation can be reconstructed as being based on two hypotheses:

(1) economic integration would lead to upward convergence in the average prosperity of Member States;
(2) that process would not diminish the capacity of the Member States to develop generous and redistributive domestic welfare states.

These hypotheses are, from an empirical point of view, not evident. In the contemporary debate on globalisation, many experts tend to accept that the first hypothesis holds on a global level (and thus also in Europe), but they question the second hypothesis (at least on the global level, but presumably also in Europe). My own view is that the empirical reality is nuanced and

---

[56] Ibid.

complex, with a lot of diversity in developments across welfare states; space forbids to pursue this here. In Section 4.3, I pointed out that mobility of labour and (most evidently) capital might exert downward pressure on the redistributive capacity of advanced welfare states, which would qualify the optimism of the second hypothesis. I should add that the first hypothesis (integration leads to upward convergence in Member States' prosperity) needs qualification too on the basis of our recent experience. First of all, in the Eurozone, we witnessed divergence rather than convergence over a number of years, due to design flaws of the monetary union. But even for the EU at large, it seems that upward convergence needs deliberate policies, which have implications for the orientation of national social models: Member States need adequate levels of investment in their human capital to sustain long-term convergence, and investment in human capital needs sufficiently egalitarian background conditions to be effective. Therefore, social investment policies can be seen as a matter of common concern in today's Europe; hence, promoting and supporting social investment should be on the agenda of a European Social Union.[57]

1.6 CONCLUSIONS

In this introductory contribution, I have argued that we need a clear-cut concept with regard to the social dimension of the EU. *Why* do we need it? The starting point is functional: two separate developments necessitate a basic consensus on the European Social Model. First, monetary integration necessitates supranational instruments for stabilisation. Stabilisation implies, in one way or other, the sharing of risks, and thus a responsibility cut (not on the basis of a metaphysical truth about individual and collective responsibility, but on the basis of a social contract, underpinning the idea of a European Social Model). Moreover, both the prevention of risks that carry externalities and the exigencies of risk-sharing put a limit on the diversity of the domestic social models that can be accommodated in a monetary union. In other words, the monetary union forces upon the participating Member States a basic consensus on the social order it has to serve. The second functional argument that triggers the idea of a Social Union is based on the need to reconcile free movement and domestic social cohesion across a heterogeneous set of Member States: this requires a common understanding of what it means to embed 'openness' in domestic cohesion.

[57] See Ferrera's reference to social investment in Chapter 2 in this volume, n. 22 in this chapter, and a discussion of convergence and social investment in Vandenbroucke and Rinaldi, n. 2 in this chapter; and A. Hemerijck (ed.), *The Uses of Social Investment* (Oxford University Press, 2017).

The EU must become a 'holding environment' that allows Member States to be flourishing welfare states. But *what* exactly is the agenda of a European Social Union? The answer to that question depends on specific normative choices. We should avoid a discourse framed in irresistible functional imperatives. As Innerarity puts it: 'Politics is conditional liberty, choices in the midst of constraints. Politics is always freedom in context, even and particularly within frameworks that are as complex as the EU.'[58] My argument is that our normative choices have to reconnect with the point and purpose of the European project, as it originally originated, but not in an uncritical way. On a foundational level, reciprocity within and between Member States is a key normative idea. On a practical level, we have to reconsider the original division of labour envisaged by the founding fathers of the project, in which economic policy would be supranational and social policy, in essence, national. But, that does not mean that we opt for a European welfare state. A holding environment would develop systemic support for national welfare states, in the form of risk-sharing (rather than cross-border redistribution), regulatory prevention of unfair tax competition, active support for social investment and upward convergence, all this based on a basic consensus on the European Social Model, and embedded in common social standards, notably with regard to key labour-market institutions and social inclusion. For the balancing act between openness and domestic social cohesion to be credible, such standards must have a tangible impact. So conceived, a European Social Union would be a laboratory not for international redistribution per se, but for developing policies that contradict the pessimistic determinism that often characterises contemporary debates on globalisation.

Since mere rhetorical references to solidarity will not suffice to clarify what is at stake, let alone convince citizens, we need, first of all, a robust understanding of the solidarities that should underpin such a Union. Therefore, I argued that we should valorise intellectual resources in academic theorising about social justice, which – surprisingly – are only rarely applied to the EU.[59]

---

58 D. Innerarity, 'After the Eurocrats' Dream, the Contingence of History', Verfblog, 22 November 2016, available at: www.verfassungsblog.de/after-the-eurocrats-dream-the-contingence-of-the-history/ (accessed 15 December 2016).

59 This is obviously not the first attempt to explore the 'justice deficit' in the European project from a normative perspective. However, whilst international distributive justice is a buoyant domain in academic normative political and social philosophy, it is rarely applied to the EU. Existing sources include the famous appeal by Habermas and the correspondence between Van Parijs and Rawls; see J. Habermas, 'Why Europe Needs a Constitution' (2001) 11 *New Left Review* 5; and his renewed insistence on the need for solidarity in Europe (yet without elaborating much on it) in J. Habermas, 'Democracy, Solidarity, and the European Crisis', lecture delivered at the University of Leuven, 26 April 2013, available at: www.kuleuven.be/euroforum/page.php?LAN=E&FILE= policy-papers (accessed 12 December 2016); P. Van Parijs and J. Rawls, 'Three Letters on the Law of Peoples and the European Union' (2013) 4 *Revue de*

I simplified my exploration of these academic resources, by assuming that market integration leads to upward convergence in average prosperity across Member States: the question then was whether upward convergence, if realised, suffices for a European conception of justice. That optimistic assumption with regard to the consequences of market integration needs qualification (and this qualification adds to the agenda of a European Social Union), but I did not develop this part of the debate. In my discussion, I highlighted the potential of the responsibility-sensitive approach to distributive justice, to frame our thinking on European Social Union; a responsibility-sensitive approach gives a particular edge to the notion of reciprocity. However, I did not argue that responsibility-sensitive egalitarian justice is in itself sufficient as a basis for social policy making.

We are in uncharted territory: there is no example of a union of welfare states in the world. Admittedly, there is one crucial precondition in this endeavour: to build a Social Union, we need a stronger sense of common purpose, in which a real sense of reciprocity fits in. The politics of reciprocity amongst democratically elected governments is inevitably complex. A union of national welfare states is a union of democracies; but even if these democracies maintain their sovereignty on the ways and means of social policy, they must agree on the common objectives of the union, on the responsibility cut, on the extent to which principles of responsibility and reciprocity have to be complemented by other normative principles, and on the extent to which in specific domains sovereignty has to be pooled. In itself, that constitutes a huge democratic challenge, which is not to be underestimated. However, it is my contention that the problem at hand is not, first and foremost, one of a 'democratic deficit' in the existing EU institutions; the problem is a 'deficit in common purpose'. Clarifying that common purpose with regard to the social dimension of the project remains an urgent intellectual and political task.

Philosophie Économique 7. Only recently has a more focused academic debate been instigated on the normative foundations of a 'Social Europe', see, for instance, P. Van Parijs, *Just Democracy. The Rawls–Machiavelli Programme* (ECPR Press, 2011); Sangiovanni, n. 25 in this chapter; see also D. Kochenov, G. de Burca, and A. Williams, *Europe's Justice Deficit* (Hart Publishing, 2015); and the contributions by, references to, and discussion of work by J. Neyer, R. Forst, J. Lacroix, K. Nicolaïdis, and other authors in the latter volume. N. Countouris and M. Freedland (eds), *Resocializing Europe in a Time of Crisis* (Cambridge University Press, 2013) critically assesses the evolution of 'social Europe' from the vantage point of 'mutualisation of risks to workers' and argues that the need for adequate employment protection and collective bargaining should be reconsidered.

2

The European Social Union: A Missing but Necessary 'Political Good'

Maurizio Ferrera

2.1 INTRODUCTION

Just like peace or the rule of law, organised solidarity is a key political good for a stable and effective functioning of both the market and democracy and for mediating their inevitable tensions. In historical perspective, the national systems of social protection can be seen as the end result of a long process of 'bounding', 'bonding', and 'binding'. During the twentieth century, the consolidation of territorial borders and of nationality filters (*bounding*) fed increasingly stronger sharing dispositions (*bonding*) among citizens, allowing for the establishment of compulsory mass social insurance (*binding*). In the absence of strong state boundaries eliciting mutual ties among insiders, the political production of organised solidarity (i.e. public welfare systems with high redistributive capacity) would have been impossible. As highlighted by the so-called state-building school on political development, the formation of the European Union is partly replicating – under drastically changed circumstanced – the process of boundary-building which, starting from the sixteenth century, led to the modern system of nation-states.[1] This time around, however, the bounding–bonding–binding nexus is considerably more complicated and its activation cannot be taken for granted. While incisively redrawing economic boundaries, the EU has indeed adopted through time a growing number of social provisions – some of them binding. But the construction of a Social Europe has been faced with a daunting mission, as it involves putting in place a new, socially friendly boundary configuration by working at the margin of the traditional and highly resilient set of state boundaries, nation-based bonds and binding redistributive schemes. This means engaging in dangerous

[1] S. Bartolini, *Restructuring Europe* (Oxford University Press, 2005); M. Ferrera, *The Boundaries of Welfare* (Oxford University Press, 2005); and P. Flora, 'Externe Grenzbildung und Interne Strukturierung. Europa und Seine Nationen' (2000) 10 *Berliner Journal für Soziologie* 151.

balancing acts between 'opening' and 'closure', with a view to cultivating pan-European sharing ties and crafting at least a minimally adequate system of inter-territorial and interpersonal redistribution, without, however, jeopardising national systems. In the absence of a modicum of collectively organised solidarity, a complex and heterogeneous institutional construction such as the EMU is unlikely to reach viable levels of political stability.

In addition to this Introduction, this chapter has six sections. Section 2.2 redefines analytically the very ambiguous notion of Social Europe and identifies its various components. Section 2.3 connects this analytical redefinition with the idea of a European Social Union (ESU), which I currently see as the most promising project for reorganising solidarity on a European scale. Section 2.4 discusses some normative principles which might underpin the most delicate dimension of the ESU project, namely encouraging cross-national bonding and binding. Section 2.5 highlights the political rationale of such principles and explains why the ESU should be considered as a key 'political good'. Section 2.6 wraps up and reflects on possible scenarios.

2.2 WHAT IS 'SOCIAL EUROPE'?

Social Europe is one of the most elusive concepts in both EU studies and political debates about the integration process. Ambiguity stems from the tension between the horizontal connotation of the concept: solidaristic goals, policies, and achievements at the national level – what the French debate calls *le social dans l'Europe* – and its vertical connotation, namely solidaristic or at least socially friendly goals, policies and achievements at the supranational level – *l'Europe dans le social*.[2] Instead of ignoring this tension and surrendering to the ensuing elusiveness, a heuristically neutral and all-encompassing definition is advisable. I thus suggest including under Social Europe the following set of constitutive components:

(1) The ensemble of social protection systems of the Member States, resting on the common, typically European tradition of a social market economy and social dialogue, but characterised by their different endowments of schemes and institutions, different logics and effectiveness in terms of market correcting and solidarity, different loads of functional and distributive problems, different degrees of stateness (administrative capacity and performance). Drawing on the state-building vocabulary, I propose to define this component the 'National Social Spaces'.

[2] Y. Chassard and P. Venturini, 'La dimension Européenne de la protection sociale' (1995) 9 *Droit Social* 63.

(2) The novel membership space – coterminous with the EU external borders – inside which all the bearers of EU citizenship or long-term residence permits enjoy a common title bestowed upon them by the Union in order to access the benefits and services of the place in which they freely choose to settle and work, according to the rules of that place. Starting from the 1970s, the EU has assembled an articulated legal framework for the coordination of social security systems of the Member States and since 2011 a directive regulates in its turn the cross-border mobility of patients. Let us define this component as the EU 'Social Citizenship Space'.

(3) The ensemble of social schemes and policies characterised by a cross-border element – a grass root development which took off in the 1990s and has gained increasing momentum. Most of such initiatives involve regions, under the legal umbrella of European Territorial Cooperation (for example euro-regions). Another interesting development on this front is the creation (mainly by the social partners) of cross-border occupational insurance schemes for pensions and health care benefits. This component may be called the 'Transnational Social Spaces'.

(4) The ensemble of those supranational policies that have an explicit social purpose, be they of a regulative or (re)distributive nature, directly funded by the EU budget (if they imply spending) and based on either hard or soft law. This component is the 'EU Social Policy' in its ordinary denotation.

(5) The set of objectives and principles of a social nature contained in the Treaties, including those that allocate responsibilities between levels of government and define decision-making procedures. Given the supremacy of EU law over national law, such objectives and rules constitute the general framework that guides and constrains the other four components. We can call this component, broadly, the 'European Social Constitution'.

As can be immediately seen, these five components are not easily kept together. More often than not, they find themselves in mutual contrast, both symbolically and practically, with negative consequences on the analytical coherence of Social Europe as a concept as well as on its mobilisation potential as a political objective. What is meant, exactly, by the demand for 'more Social Europe', often voiced in academic or public debates? The enhancement of EU Social Policy and of the EU Social Citizenship Space, that is to say the supranationalisation of welfare state functions at the EU level, as in the historical federations? The taming of the negative integration which

semi-automatically follows from free movement provisions and the EU competition regime and which tends to undermine the National Social Spaces?
The promotion by the EU of an upward convergence of national spaces,
meant however to remain the prevailing and unchallenged social sharing arenas? The creation of more margins of manoeuvre for territories and communities to re-aggregate themselves across national borders, based on interests or
identities, in order to re-channel the existing flows of solidarity? In the debate
we actually find many variants of each of these meanings.

Conceptual and political ambiguity often allows for a sympathetic dialogue
between diverse perspectives. But the dialogue remains unproductive, as
assumptions and implications are poorly compatible, if not mutually exclusive when pushed to their limits. Analytical disambiguation is always desirable
per se. In this case it would also allow – I submit – for a fruitful reframing of
some classical issues that in the last two decades have dominated debates on
the social deficit of the EU as an institutional and political construct, such
as the asymmetry between negative and positive integration, market-making
and market-correcting, EU (economic and legal) powers and national social
sovereignty. If Social Europe is a composite construct that cannot be reduced
to a single component and thus has to live with inherent tensions, there is no
single asymmetry or deficit to which weaknesses can be imputed. Likewise,
there is no single instrument or solution that can remedy such weaknesses.

The crisis has of course dramatically complicated the picture. Though
apparently more integrated and internally coherent than Social Europe, during the Great Recession EMU has proved to be itself a bundle of different
constituent elements (national economies with their governance systems and
public finances, the internal market, the euro, EMU governance institutions
and policies and so on) which can be rapidly pushed apart by international
financial markets despite a common currency and Central Bank, and made
to collide with each other by the resurgence of neo-mercantilist orientations –
especially on the side of creditor countries. The Eastern enlargements of the
2000s have in their turn given rise to a tension between old and new Member
States, which have come to be increasingly divided on free movement issues
relative to workers, persons, and services. The financial crisis and the inca-
pacity of the EU to tackle it, the explosion of core–periphery (North–South)
conflicts in the wake of the sovereign debt problems and the appearance of the
new East–West conflict line have enormously amplified the challenges faced
by Social Europe, not least in their political dimension. One perverse effect
of the crisis has been that national voters and politicians now increasingly
voice for closure, that is to say they are trying to re-establish the old boundaries around the National Social Spaces, while explicitly challenging the EU

Social Citizenship Space. The perspective of a redrawing of the boundaries of welfare on a continental scale, accompanied by occasional, but manageable bursts of contestation, and capable of gradually extending solidarity ties beyond state borders, now appears much more uncertain and problematic than in the mid-2000s.

2.3 TOWARDS A EUROPEAN SOCIAL UNION (ESU): THE SUBSTANTIVE AGENDA

Ideas on how to respond to the EU social predicament abound but lack coherence. Coined by Vandenbroucke,[3] the term European Social Union (ESU) offers a novel and convincing analytical framework. The choice of words immediately evokes a system of separate but interdependent elements, subject (as in the EMU) to common rules and principles and aimed at sustaining/promoting two types of solidarity: a pan-European solidarity between countries and between individual EU citizens, centred on supranational institutions, and the more traditional forms of national solidarity, centred on domestic institutions. The former should limit itself to pursuing redistributive goals which are functionally necessary and practically feasible. The latter's goal is 'the highest possible degree of solidarity' (although it would be appropriate to add 'taking into account the preferences expressed democratically by the voters'). Concretely, in Vandenbroucke's view, the institutional mission of ESU should be to guide and support the functioning and modernisation of national welfare states based on some common standards and shared objectives, leaving to the Member States wide margins of autonomy in the choice of ways and means.

What could be ESU's agenda in reference to the five components identified in Section 2.2? Let me briefly survey what I believe should be the major strategic priorities.

National Social Spaces. Here, as is well known, the current European landscape is characterised by marked national variations resulting from long-term policy trajectories, driven by distinct socioeconomic and cultural-political factors. To the extent that they mirror national preferences and traditions, domestic diversities in the organisation of solidarity are undoubtedly 'legitimate'.[4] Some authors argue that the EU should stay aloof from harmonisation or even any promotion of upward convergence among systems; it should rather

---

[3] F. Vandenbroucke, 'The Idea of a European Social Union: A Normative Introduction', Chapter 1 in this volume.

[4] F. Scharpf, 'The European Social Model: Coping with the Challenges of Diversity' (2002) *MPIfG Working Paper,* 02/8.

limit itself to ordering (in the German sense of *Ordnungspolitik*) institutional competition.[5] A number of factors militate, however, in favour of a more pro-active role for the Union. First, national social spaces are now confronting an increasing host of similar problems, in the wake of rapid endogenous (such as ageing) and exogenous (such as economic globalisation) transformations. A joint search for viable and effective solutions can broaden the horizons of national models and provide them with a richer and wider policy menu. Second, given the weight of policy lock-ins and path dependencies, institutional re-adaptation is a demanding task, even among good performers. The EU can help by supplying resources and incentives for overcoming organisational stickiness and political blockages to reform. Third, increased integration generates a constant flow of cross-national externalities. Very often, domestic leaders have to solve problems for their own *demos*, which are the direct and recognisable consequence of other EU *demoi* (how they behave, what they decide); in turn, the solutions that domestic leaders adopt are very likely to generate cross-border effects. The EU can provide the right incentives, the pertinent information and the appropriate arenas for identifying externalities and social risks that may require common management. Fourthly, unbridled policy competition based on the logic of (social) comparative advantages may lead to suboptimal and inefficient mutual adjustments, generating a growing dualisation between core and peripheral Member States[6] and hindering the formation of that pan-European solidarity, which is at the same time a key normative element of the integration project and a necessary political condition for its success.

The EU can and should be particularly proactive on one front: promoting a reorientation of national spaces towards social investment. As argued by a rich literature, social investments (and in particular the enhancement of human capital) are a real policy imperative if Europe as a whole wishes to reconcile economic competiveness and high prosperity/wellbeing in the context of increasing globalisation.[7] Responding to such imperative is, however, an extremely difficult exercise, precisely because of the narrow horizons, institutional constraints, and the political short-termism that characterise domestic

[5]   W. Abelhauser, 'Europa in Vielfalt einigen. Eine Denkschrift' (2014), available at: www.homes.uni-bielefeld.de/wabelsha/Denkschrift.pdf (accessed 30 March 2016).

[6]   F. Scharpf, 'The Costs of Non Disintegration', in D. Chalmers, M. Jachtenfuchs, and C. Joerges (eds), *The End of the Eurocrats' Dream* (Cambridge University Press, 2016).

[7]   A. Hemerijck, *The Uses of Social Investment* (Oxford University Press, 2017).

systems.[8] The facilitation of social investment should become a key political function of the European Social Union.

Social Citizenship Space. Here the priority should be the correct regulation and management of the free movement of persons and their access to social benefits and services in the countries of destination. The ESU could not exist as a union of welfare states if it did not rest on a common underlying space which guarantees the right to have basic social entitlements in any national system as a result of entries and exits. But, as we know, this issue has become increasingly contentious after the Eastern enlargement and lies at the basis of the East–West tension mentioned in Section 2.2. Again, without an adequate regulatory framework and normative framing, such type of tensions is likely to escalate into a fully fledged political conflict with disintegrative implications. The most emblematic and at the same time dramatic effect of anti-immigrant politics (fomented by the economic crisis) is of course the Brexit referendum. The existing Treaties are very clear: freedom of movement of workers is a core principle of the European construction. But at the constitutional level the rules are very general. In fact, the free movement of workers/persons and especially the access to social benefits are regulated by secondary legislation and Court jurisprudence.[9] It is at this level that solutions must be sought. The balance now existing between opening and closure can be recalibrated to take account of the sensitivity of certain countries' public opinion and of the demands of their governments, especially after the Brexit referendum and the risk of a dangerous domino effect.

Transnational Social Spaces. Over the last twenty years, the subnational level has significantly increased its role and importance in many areas of social protection: from health to social services, from active labour market to inclusion policies. Ever since Delors, a deliberate European strategy has been emerging (mainly supported by the Commission) to strengthen the 'third level' of government, to increase the involvement of the latter in social policy, and to encourage cross-border experimentation.[10] These novel aggregations can promote interesting forms of coordination and even fusion of social infra-structures, feed new forms of cross-border solidarity – intermediate between subnational and pan-European solidarity. A similar virtuous circle can result

[8] M. Ferrera, 'Impatient Politics and Social Investment: the EU as "policy facilitator"' (2016) *Journal of European Public Policy*, published online on 19 September 2016, available at: www.tandfonline.com/doi/full/10.1080/13501763.2016.1189451 (accessed 7 November 2016).

[9] S. Giubboni, 'Free Movement of Persons and European Solidarity: A Melancholic Eulogy', in H. Verschueren (ed.), *Where Do I Belong? EU Law and Adjudication on the Link between Individuals and Member States* (Intersentia, forthcoming).

[10] B. Wassenberg and B. Reitel, *Territorial Cooperation in Europe. A Historical Perspective* (Publication Office of the European Union, 2015).

from a second ongoing trend of social *transnationalisation*, meaning the creation of cross-border pension schemes providing supplementary benefits to employees working in different Member States.[11] Made possible by a 2003 Directive (entered into force in 2005), the establishment of such institutions works towards a de-territorialisation of solidarity by encouraging risk sharing along functional and corporate lines. The role of all these developments for the consolidation of ESU should not be underestimated also in political terms. By connecting directly the supranational level/elites and the subnational level/elites, on the one hand, and by stimulating civil society activism and social partner involvement, on the other hand, such processes open up new channels and new ways of transnational bonding and can elicit 'demoicratic' legitimacy for the EU as a whole.[12]

EU Social Policy. Here the debate is already very extensive and the agenda is crowded. An incomplete inventory should include at least the following issues and/or objectives:[13] the introduction of common standards for labour market, wage-setting, and social inclusion, in order to combat social dumping and facilitate mobility; a better use and an increase of the EU's resources for (co)financing reforms and especially social investment; significantly widening the scope of action of the European Fund for Strategic Investment from physical to social infrastructures and policies; strengthening cooperation and establishing standards in the field of education, including early childhood education and care; strengthening the European social dialogue; improving social governance arrangements within the European Semester; specifically including modernising social reforms in the list of conditions for obtaining 'flexibility' in national budgets. Within ESU, the big strategic priority of EU social policy (that is the component anchored directly to the supranational level) should be, however, the creation of a formalised instrument – equipped with adequate fiscal resources – to support solidarity between Eurozone countries in the event of asymmetric shocks. In other words, it is necessary to think of new forms of interstate insurance for cushioning the social consequences caused by dramatic and sudden economic downturns that strike with particular virulence a single country or a limited group of countries (as in the euro crisis). As highlighted by Vandenbroucke in his Introduction, it is not easy to design a similar instrument. The goals of contrasting moral hazard and

---

[11] I. Guardiancich and D. Natali, 'The Cross-border Portability of Supplementary Pensions: Lessons from the European Union' (2012) 12 *Global Social Policy* 300.

[12] K. Nicolaidis, 'European Demoicracy and its critics' (2013) 51 *Journal of Common Market Studies* 351.

[13] F. Vandenbroucke and B. Vanhercke, *A European Social Union: 10 Tough Nuts to Crack* (Friends of Europe, 2014).

reducing risks should be carefully balanced with the need to uphold the live-lihood of the least advantaged, wherever they reside. Although the technical and political obstacles are huge, this is possibly the most urgent nut to crack for triggering off an orderly and reasonable Europeanisation of solidarity.

European Social Constitution. This component is perhaps the least vis-ible to the general public but it certainly is the most important one. The Lisbon Treaty has already dug the foundation of the ESU in terms of objec-tives and, in part, of instruments.[14] Among the most important innovations we can mention the redefinition of the programmatic values and objectives of the Union, the explicit acknowledgement of the links between the inter-nal market and the achievement of full employment and social progress, the formal recognition of the Charter of Fundamental Rights, and – last but not least – the introduction of a transversal social clause. The crisis has severely weakened the transformative potential of such constitutional changes. Not only have the new rules introduced by the Six-Pack, the Two-Pack, and the Fiscal Compact strengthened the paradigm of austerity and of a 'disciplinar-ian' mode of governance but, according to some commentators, such changes are not legally in line with the general provisions of the Treaty concerning, precisely, the social sphere.[15] The agenda of the European Social Constitution must therefore restart from Lisbon, enabling the full potential of its principles and provisions. Unfortunately, the Court of Justice has been very hesitant, so far, to activate this potential.[16] The most promising springboard seems to be the social clause (Article 9 TFEU), according to which 'in defining and implementing its policies and activities, the Union shall take into account requirements linked to the promotion of a high level of employment, guar-antee of adequate social protection, the fight against social exclusion and a high level of education, training and protection of human health'. If properly operationalised, the activation of this clause might have huge effects in terms of the balance between the economic and social dimension. It could in fact serve as a barrier to undue encroachments of the market logic in domestic sol-idarity spaces. And it could act as a tool to monitor and facilitate the effective implementation of the ambitious social objectives set out in Article 3 TEU.

---

[14] N. Bruun, K. Lorcher, and I. Schonmann (eds), *The Lisbon Treaty and Social Europe* (Hart, 2012).

[15] A. Kocharov (ed.), 'Another Legal Monster? An EUI Debate on the Fiscal Compact Treaty' (2012) *EUI Working Papers*, 09.

[16] F. Costamagna, 'The Court of Justice and the Demise of the Rule of Law in the EU Economic Governance: the Case of Social Rights', *REScEU Working Paper 10/2016*, available at: www. resceu.eu/publications/working-papers/wp-10-2016-the-court-of-justice-and-the-demise-of-the-rule-of-law-in-the-eu-economic-governance-the-case-of-social-rights-2.html (accessed 9 April 2017).

Mutatis mutandis, its effect could be similar to those originated by the clause on gender mainstreaming (integration of gender equality in all EU policies) introduced in the Treaty of Amsterdam (1997).[17] What is lacking in the Lisbon Treaty is of course the explicit mention and establishment of a European Social Union as a counterpart of the Economic and Monetary Union (Article 3 TEU, paragraph 4: 'The Union shall establish an economic and monetary union whose currency is the euro'). Such step may be unnecessary and it would be certainly premature. But nothing prevents from starting a strategic reflection on the topic. The EMU was born after a long gestation period, and its formal conception occurred in 1988, when the European Council entrusted to Jacques Delors with the task of developing a concrete project. A similar initiative on the social front could serve today not only a function of analytical and technical clarification, but also a precious political legitimation function.

2.4 THE JUSTIFICATION OF A SOCIAL UNION: SOME NORMATIVE PROPOSALS

Designing and then implementing the ESU presupposes a set of coherent general ideas able to justify its functional rationale. It also requires, however, adequate normative justifications: why exactly ought we to do it? The Lisbon Treaty has already significantly expanded the axiological perimeter of the EU, but more elaboration is needed in order to enable the high symbolic and political potential of the ESU project. Any exercise of ESU justification must be placed in the context of the current predicament. The financial crisis and the ensuing Great Recession have brought to the fore burning questions of fairness and solidarity among the Member States, the peoples of Europe and their individual citizens. Fairness questions have given rise to harsh debates and conflicts in all historical federations (think of the US or Switzerland). We should not be surprised that such issues are becoming more salient today and, to some extent, we must look at this as a sign of maturation and collective reflexivity. There is, however, a tangible danger of excessive and destructive polarisation. It is thus advisable to cast justificatory arguments in a 'realist' rather than an 'idealist' perspective, combining normative and sociological reasoning. If they aim at exerting practical effects, justificatory arguments need to be closely anchored to existing and factual states of affairs and remain

---

[17] P. Vieille, 'How the Horizontal Social Clause Can Be Made to Work: The Lessons of Gender Mainstreaming', in N. Bruun, K. Lorcher, and I. Schonmann (eds), *The Lisbon Treaty and Social Europe* (Hart, 2012), p. 105.

highly sensitive to feasibility constraints. Their principles should be quickly accessible to political actors and easily applicable to the dilemmas raised by the new lines of conflict around cross-national transfers and the free movement of persons.

Solidarity practices presuppose (sociologically) a floor of trust and mutual recognition among parts. In the EU context, both have to contend with the dual nature of the parts that are relevant for determining the criteria of fairness: individual citizens and Member States. As famously argued by Habermas,[18] the continuation and deepening of a European constitutional process based on (post-Lisbon) democratic procedures can be expected to bring about new orientations of 'civic' solidarity, eventually able to justify and legitimise new forms of cross-national solidarity. Habermas's notion of civic solidarity has been the object of an articulated and at times critical debate.[19] For my purposes, this notion is limited by the fact that it tends to collapse the dimension of inter-territorial redistribution with that of interpersonal redistribution. The notion also fails to address the tension between opening and closure. Such dimensions should be kept analytically (and politically) separate.

A promising way of framing the issue of inter-territorial transfers (a pan European solidarity between peoples) is to adopt a Weberian perspective – which is the prime root of the tradition of political realism – and raise the following foundational question: what kind of community is the EU? If we adopt Weber's typology,[20] it is clear that the EU is not (yet) a fully fledged political community: it lacks the legitimate monopoly of force; its internal cohesion and the legitimacy of its authorities are not based of on affectual/identitarian orientations. It is, however, equally clear that the EU is (or has become) much more than just an economic/market association. In Weber's typology there are two other possible classificatory options. One is 'political association': a voluntary territorial *Verband* endowed with some common institutions, whose members pursue a number of shared goals essentially based on instrumental rationality. The other classificatory option is that of a 'neighbourhood community', that is to say a territorial group (typically a group of subgroups) that emerges in the wake of durable spatial proximity. Neighbours are not kin, linked by spontaneous altruism. As a matter of fact, proximity (especially if

[18] J. Habermas, *Europe: The Faltering Project* (Polity Press, 2009); J. Habermas, *The Lure of Technocracy* (Polity Press, 2015).
[19] A. Sangiovanni, 'Solidarity in the European Union', in J. Dickinson and P. Elephteriadis (eds), *in Philosophical Foundations of European Union Law* (Oxford University Press, 2012), p. 384.
[20] M. Weber, *Economy and Society*, translated by G. Roth and C. Wittich (California University Press, 1978).

unchosen) generates a wish/interest in maintaining mutual distance, in order to avoid undue interferences. Yet neighbours do tend to develop communal orientations, especially in case of need and emergencies. According to Weber, neighbourhood communities are characterised by an ethos of 'sober brotherhood': a brotherhood devoid of pathos, largely deriving from the fact of physical proximity (like the fact of kin affinity, in the case of brothers).[21] Such ethos is able to foster and sustain a minimum of solidarity, inspired by 'primitive' ethical principles. Weber cites three examples derived from the Judeo-Christian tradition: 'Do not do to others what you would not want others to do unto you', 'Siblings do not bargain on price', and 'In case of necessity you will make loans without interest' (the original connotation of *mutuum* in Roman law). In 'modern conditions', Weber adds, communal orientations among neighbours are also based on a specific 'sense of dignity', which allows for a flexible balance between self-interested distance, mutual support, and a modicum of altruistic empathy.

Sober brotherhood principles encourage exchanges which are not based on the 'shopkeeper mentality' of the *homo economicus*: they do in fact incorporate a reciprocity component, namely the disposition to give something *now* conditional upon receiving or having received something in a different temporal moment (with a relatively loose equivalence scale). In retrospect, we can say that the EU was born as a mere market association, rapidly became a political association and then evolved into a neighbourhood community – especially with the expansion of the Structural Funds aimed at supporting less prosperous regions. The euro crisis has, however, halted this development. With the new rules and programmes of financial assistance, the ethic (and politics) of brotherhood has made some backward steps, receding from soberness to stinginess. The ethos of mutual help has given way to a reaffirmation of distance – often framed in moral terms.[22]

What has gone wrong? Why has the euro crisis so rapidly dissipated significant amounts of that cross-national *Vergemeinschaftung* capital so painstakingly accumulated over the decades? In addition to the obvious answers related to institutional factors ('governing by the rules and ruling by the numbers', to quote Vivien Schmidt[23]) I submit that a key role has been played

[21] C. Burelli, 'Fraternity: a Realistic Starting Point for Solidarity, EU Visions' (2015), available at: www.euvisions.eu/fraternity-a-realistic-starting-point-for-solidarity/ (accessed 30 March 2016).

[22] K. Dyson, *States, Debt and Power* (Oxford University Press, 2014).

[23] V. Schmidt, 'The Eurozone's Crisis of Democratic Legitimacy: Can the EU Rebuild Public Trust and Support for European Economic Integration?' (2015) 15 *European Economy Discussion Papers* 1, p. 7.

by the very logic of reciprocity and, more specifically, by its 'disciplinarian' recodification through the Stability and Growth Pact.[24] As famously argued by Alvin Gouldner,[25] reciprocity is a necessary, but insufficient condition for upholding a legitimate social order and in particular its communal element. The main limitation of reciprocity is the uncertainty of the net balance of 'indebtedness' – how much is owed by whom to whom – in longstanding relationships (such as those, precisely, of each Member State with each of the others). There are epistemic limits to information about complex sequences of gives and takes: it is difficult to 'call it quits', squaring and balancing accounts. And in multimember collectivities such as the EU, reciprocity may easily lead to dyadic polarisations between the stronger creditor and the weaker debtor – a binary confrontation that neglects the larger ramifying consequences of actions and those exogenous factors, outside the control of either (or just one) part, which, however, contribute to determining the levels and scope of mutual obligations and claims. The result is the explosion of occasional bursts of mutual (or multilateral) resentment, hostility, retaliation, which may escalate into vicious spirals. The EU is experiencing today a similar syndrome. Appealing to strong reciprocity principles is not enough for sustaining and promoting more solidarity; the appeal can even be counterproductive.

Can we get out of this vicious circle? Reciprocity is a key principle of justice, but political communities (including neighbourhood communities) are capable of generating, through stable and continuous interactions, a capital of mutual leniency and indulgency (possibly underpinned – in 'modern conditions' – by the Weberian 'sense of dignity'). Some credit mechanisms – as it were – are developed, where outstanding obligations are stored and then mobilised in cases of emergencies or special need. Such mechanisms put in place a fertile ground for the activation of a second principle, different from reciprocity, which in normative jargon is called the principle of beneficence (also known as 'compassion': giving something for nothing). Partly building on Weber, Gouldner considers this principle an almost invariant component of universal religions, but he also identifies far-reaching secular roots in European culture: from Roman *clementia,* to feudal *noblesse oblige.* A long thread of solidarism does run through the history of our Continent: from ancient Judaism's brotherly love (Leviticus) to pagan republican *concordia,*

[24] K. Nicolaidis, and M. Watson, 'Sharing the Eurocrats' Dream: A Democratic Approach to EMU Governance in the Post-crisis Era', in D. Chalmers, M. Jachtenfuchs and C. Joerges (eds), *The End of the Eurocrats' Dream* (Cambridge University Press, 2016).
[25] A. Gouldner, *For Sociology. Renewal and Critique in Sociology Today* (Basic Books, 1973).

from the revolutionary *fraternité* of 1789 to the emancipatory spirit of the *Solidarnosc* movement of 1989.[26]

Beneficence plays a fundamental role in complementing the principle of reciprocity and in neutralising its inherent risk of generating vicious confrontational spirals. If appropriately cultivated, beneficent dispositions may not only serve as ignition keys for expanding reciprocity in new ambits and for pushing it beyond enlightened interest, towards brotherhood. They can also operate as a legitimating mechanism for the powerful, weakening the tendency of the lowly to view the highly as 'exploiters'. To effectively and systematically serve these purposes within a political community, beneficence cannot rest exclusively on spontaneous credit mechanisms, but must be institutionalised and formalised in a sort of moral code (gradually internalised because 'it is right') that prescribes to 'give something for nothing' in certain situations. Only if this is the case is it possible to break away from the logic of strong reciprocity in ambiguous, borderline occurrences which require urgent action. For Weber, political choices should follow an ethic of responsibility, based on consequentialist criteria complemented with some normative principles serving as 'backstops'. In handling reciprocity relations among the Member States, the EU's backstop principle ought to be: if in doubt, act benevolently.

Discussing the EU in terms of a neighbourhood community, inspired and regulated by the principle of reciprocity complemented by beneficence, has the advantage of launching a symbolic message which is easily understandable to the enlarged public and which evokes life experiences and moral intuitions widely shared and deeply rooted in European culture. Neighbours are not forced to help each other in all cases. Sober brotherhood is something much less demanding than the set of solidaristic political obligations that operate at the national level – between both citizens and regions. The prime driver of sober brotherhood remains a material interest, a strong reciprocity expectation. But it incorporates a modicum of communal empathy and loyalty capable of sustaining beneficent rules and practices over time (in normative jargon, the application of an unconditional 'sufficientarian' standard of distributive justice).

My second justificatory argument has less to do with economic solidarity via inter-territorial transfers than with finding a fair balance between opening and closure: the issue of free movement and access to benefits. The original rationale of free movement was essentially functional (market-making and thus greater economic growth). With the passing of time, a new justificatory discourse

---

[26] H. Bunkhorst, *Solidarity. From Civic Friendship to a Global Legal Community* (Massachusettes Institute of Technology Press, 2005)

started to develop, especially on the side of the ECJ and the Commission, centred on non-discrimination, equality of opportunity, transnational solidarity.[27] While pertinent and highly relevant for ideal justifications – based on ultimate and 'non-negotiable' standpoints regarding the 'good society' – these three normative principles wield very limited political purchase in the current predicament of increased contention around free movement and access to benefits. In a number of Member States, voters express a clear preference for discrimination, despite the deliberate efforts of political education on the side of their governments. As a matter of fact, insisting on non-discrimination can lead to a further destabilisation of the European polity. If the goal is that of containing conflict and preserve opening, we need to look for justifications which are perhaps less ambitious, but more realistic and sensitive to consequences.

The 'good neighbours' argument has weak traction in this case: the stake is not only whether to help from a distance, but whether to accept neighbours in one's place. Using a famous Swedish metaphor, the issue is who may enter into the *Folkhemmet*: the welfare state as the people's home – a national people. Where can we look for a normative compass on this extremely delicate front?

Europe has a long history of admitting foreigners through guest-worker regimes. As this expression implicitly suggests, the normative principle that is typically activated in case of migration flows is that of 'hospitality'. In modern political philosophy, this principle has a noble pedigree, rooted in Kantian thought. In his famous essay on perpetual peace, Kant argued that – owing to the finite size of the earth's surface – certain moral obligations arise that forbid territorial closure. The third 'definitive article of perpetual peace' defines hospitality as 'the right of a stranger not to be treated as an enemy when he arrives in the land of another … so long as he peacefully occupies his place, one may not treat him with hostility'. There are, however, two kinds of hospitality rights. The first is 'a right of temporary sojourn, which all men have'. For Kant this is an *ius cosmopoliticum* (a cosmopolitan right), which men have 'by virtue of their common possession of the surface of the earth, where, as a globe, they cannot infinitely disperse and hence must finally tolerate the presence of each other'.[28] The second kind of hospitality is more specific and demanding: 'the right to be a permanent visitor'. A special agreement is needed in order to give an outsider the right to become a fellow inhabitant. What Kant had in mind was the *ius hospitii* defined by Roman law since the early Republic: the faculty enjoyed by the citizens of Rome and of certain foreign cities or states to freely

[27] F. De Witte, *Justice in the EU: The Emergence of Transnational Solidarity* (Oxford University Press, 2015).
[28] I. Kant, 'Towards Perpetual Peace. A Philosophical Sketch', translated by J. Bennett (2010), available at: www.earlymoderntexts.com/assets/pdfs/kant1795_1.pdf (accessed 30 March 2016).

move into each other's territory and of having the same privileges except for
the *suffragium* (the right to vote).

What kind of hospitality is appropriate within the EU? If we accept the image
of a neighbourhood community of states, characterised by spatial proximity, a
common external boundary, strong interest interdependence and high flows
of transnational movements, the hospitality which Europeans ought to offer/
receive to or from each other, regardless of nationality, is surely thicker than
a mere right of temporary sojourn. The citizens of other EU nations are not,
by definition, full members of the *Folkhemmet*. But they ought to be treated
as *hospites* in the thick sense, i.e. entitled to equal treatment as regards civil
and at least some social rights. Sociologically speaking, the practice of hospitality may serve a number of important functions: it fosters mutual recognition
and respect, fights prejudices and stereotypes, ignites a process of conversion
whereby strangers are turned into fellows, friends, and even members of kin; it
promotes the internalisation and diffusion of liberal and cosmopolitan values.
As in the case of sober brotherhood, the prime drivers of hospitality dispositions are reciprocity expectations. In this case, however, the specific form and
content of expectations are more difficult to pin down. The host may expect
to become a guest of her guest at a later time (correspondence reciprocity).
But more often the expectation is addressed to returns in other ambits (such
as work, material help, financial contributions), especially if the guest is a
stranger. The important point is, however, that the reciprocity basis of hospitality exposes the latter to the potential vicious circles discussed earlier in this
section. The principle of beneficence has a very limited application in the
context of individual mobility, namely that of intra-EU migration. Apart from
extraordinary cases (refugees, asylum seekers), migrants are not necessarily in
conditions of extreme need or emergency. They are strangers who knock at the
doors of 'our' *Folkhemmet* without invitation. Some inhabitants of the latter
may be afraid to open the doors: they do not know what to expect. The stranger
seeking hospitality might be moved by predatory aims. If forced to open the
doors, the host may be tempted to respond in the same coin, for example by
overtly or covertly 'exploiting' the guest. If beneficent dispositions cannot be
mobilised or are not sufficient, what other principles and practices might contrast the potential perverse effects inherent in the logic of hospitality?

I submit that a promising candidate is a norm that could be called 'non-
dominating conditionality'. Conditionality was already envisaged by Kant
for hospitality relations and is a key principles in contemporary theories on
immigration based on 'weak' cosmopolitanism and/or 'liberal nationalism'.[29]

---

[29] D. Miller, *Strangers in our Midst* (Harvard University Press, 2016)

Conditionality allows the host to set clauses for accepting guests: for example in terms of explicit quid pro quos, in terms of the functional scope of hospitality, in terms of time and timing. Non-domination (understood here in a loose connotation) is the obligation for the host to behave fairly, to abstain from using her positional power for arbitrary and exploitative interferences in the choices of the guest, whose very status tends to generate vulnerability.

2.5 THE SOCIAL UNION AS A POLITICAL GOOD

The justificatory arguments just outlined are not aimed at defending a systematic normative view about an ideal world. They rather aim at deriving normativity from extant political facts and institutions: their point and purpose, their guiding logics. The normativity is primarily political. A well calibrated mix of reciprocity and benevolence, conditional but non-dominating hospitality rules, enshrined in the real-world institutions of the EU, is desirable – first and foremost – as a political good. Political goods are states of affairs (deliberately crafted by political actors) that are not desirable per se, but because they serve as necessary conditions for achieving other final goods. Peace, internal order, social and economic prosperity, a stable and effective institutional framework for taking decisions and arbitrating disputes: these are typically instrumental goods which facilitate social cooperation within a given political collectivity. They contain conflicts and sustain generalised compliance, thus expanding the chances of individuals and allowing them to pursue their own life projects.[30] The production of political goods must inevitably pass through institution building, ultimately responding to political 'reason'.[31] In this perspective, the *whys* of ESU are not only functional and normative, but also *political*. To the extent that ESU could bring a key contribution to the overall stability, even survival, of the EU as such, one might argue that the political rationale is located at a deeper level than the other two – it is a condition for their very pertinence and relevance.

Let me briefly discuss the institutional implications of my reasoning for the ESU project specifically, i.e. its *what*. Referring back to the analysis outlined in Sections 2.2 and 2.3 of this chapter, it can be argued that the two most crucial components are the EU Social Policy, on one hand, and the Social Citizenship Space on the other. Within the former, the challenge is

---

[30] M. Stoppino, *Potere e Teoria Politica* (Giuffre, 2002).

[31] J. Priban, 'The Evolving Idea of Political Justice in the EU: From Substantive Deficits to the Systemic Contingency of European Society', in D. Kochenov, G. De Búrca, and A. Williams (eds), *Europe's Justice Deficit?* (Hart, 2015), p. 193.

to re-organise binding reciprocity and shaping some form of organised benevolence. Within the latter, the challenge is to recalibrate free movement in
terms of organised hospitality.

The most effective tool for re-organising reciprocity is some form of risk-
pooling – the key pillar of institutionalised solidarity in the European tradition. The national welfare state, with its panoply of sharing arrangements, was
born in response to a 'social question' resulting from the spread of capitalist
markets and industrialisation. Today Europe is faced with a new, large-scale
social question, closely (and causally) linked to EMU's presence and design –
in the wider context of globalisation. Just as one century ago at the domestic
level, we need today a collective discussion about the expedience of pan-
European risk pooling. Which Member State is vulnerable to what and why is
it vulnerable? To answer this question it may be useful to distinguish between
similar and common risks. The first are the result of analogous dynamics (e.g.
demographic ageing) that have no significant link with either integration or
cross-national externalities. Here open coordination and mutual learning are
important and useful, but there is no need for joint action. Common risks are
instead directly produced by integration and/or externalities: e.g. the adverse
consequence of an asymmetric shock in the presence of EMU's constraints;
the implications of domestic trade deficits or surpluses for the overall growth
of the Eurozone, or the negative impact of sudden surges in worker mobility
or immigration from outside the EU. For such type of risks, joint action (e.g.
under the form of risk pooling or re-insurance schemes) is the appropriate
solution, on functional/normative grounds but also on political grounds, i.e.
for legitimation and loyalty-building purposes. The quantum leap that needs
to be undertaken for a tangible and credible take-off of ESU should therefore be the creation of a formalised instrument – equipped with adequate
fiscal resources – for responding to common adversities, wherever they may
hit. A first, timid step in this direction was already made in 2006, with the
establishment of the European Globalisation Adjustment Fund. Based on
what happened during the euro crisis, it is necessary to think of more ambitious forms of interstate insurance for cushioning the social consequences
caused by dramatic and sudden economic 'disasters' that strike with particular
intensity a single country or a limited group of countries (e.g. the peripheral
Member States during the sovereign debt crisis). An option which has already
been widely explored is the establishment of a EU unemployment insurance
scheme (discussed by Andor in this volume).

As to benevolence-based solidarity, the most obvious instrument would be
an EU scheme of last resort assistance. As mentioned in Section 2.4, the standard in this case should be sufficientarian: making sure that all EU citizens have

'enough', at least enough to survive. Ever since the 1992 Recommendation on sufficient resources, the Commission has been sensitive to this issue and efforts are now being made to identify 'reference budgets', that is to say indicators of absolute poverty.[32] In terms of policy action, there is a legacy which stretches back to the late 1980s, when the European food aid programme for the most deprived persons (MDP) was launched by Delors in order to redistribute agricultural surpluses. In the wake of the crisis, a new scheme has been officially created in 2014, called Fund for European Aid to the Most Deprived (FEAD), with a focus on severe material deprivation.[33] Compared to pre-existing schemes, the FEAD is more ambitious as it envisages: (1) the widening of the scope of the intervention (from food aid to the fight of material poverty and social exclusion); (2) an increase of resources (taking into account national cofinancing); (3) the shift from voluntary to compulsory participation for EU Member States. This latter element went largely unnoticed, but it is very innovative: it implies the adoption of the highly solidaristic principle: 'from each Member State according to its economic resources and possibilities, to each Member State according to its contingent needs'. A strengthening of FEAD and/or similar instruments would offer the most promising grounds for enhancing benevolence-based solidarity anchored directly to the EU. The mission of this type of solidarity should be to establish a safety net below reciprocity.

Let us now turn to the EU Social Citizenship Space. This is a foundational brick of the Social Union project and has paved the way for a gradual transnationalisation of solidarity beyond national borders. But such transnationalisation has been produced, politically speaking, in a 'parasitic' way: not through allocations, that is the creation of new social entitlements supported by dedicated resources, but only through coordinative adjustments that have forced the opening of the National Social Spaces.[34] The result has not been a pan-European system of social entitlements, offering free-standing guarantees of protection, but an area of free movement supported by the social protections offered by national welfare systems. EU law has produced new guaranteed powers to mobile persons; these powers have affected domestic constellations

[32] B. Storms, T. Goedemé, K. Van den Bosch, T. Penne, N. Schuerman, and S. Stockman, 'Pilot Project for the Development of a Common Methodology on Reference Budgets in Europe, *Review of Current State of Play on Reference Budget Practices at National, Regional, and Local Level*' (2014), available at: ec.europa.eu/social/BlobServlet?docId=12544&langId=en (accessed 12 October 2016).

[33] I. Madama, 'The Fund for European Aid to Deprived People' (2016) *REScEU Working Paper*, 09/2016, available at: www.resceu.eu/publications/working-papers.html (accessed 7 November 2016).

[34] For a similar view see De Witte, n. 27 in this chapter.

of rights and duties. From a political point of view, the social security coordination regime has given rise to a programmatically contentious juxtaposition between the (non-native) holders of the new sharing rights and the (native) bearers of the corresponding duties.

Empirical data show that the net economic balance of intra-EU migration for the receiving countries is positive.[35] But the fact of political conflicts about free movement cannot be ignored. A new balance between opening and closure is needed, based on non-dominating conditionality criteria. More concretely, what might be done is a more stringent definition of the rights of those who do not work: for example, the relatives who remain in the countries of origin residents who are not economically active, and to some extent also those who move in search of work. Partly, this can be done by applying more severely the restrictive clauses that already exist. But one can also imagine introducing legislative changes through the ordinary procedure. It is clear that the freedom of movement of workers and their entitlement to social security benefits should remain a red line not to be crossed. On other types of intra-EU migrants, however, it is reasonable to recognise that the pan-European solidarity now politically viable is more limited than that provided for by the regulatory status quo, and its general normative underpinnings based on non-discrimination principles alone. Provided that it respects the red line (the minimum level of solidarity which is necessary to speak of a EU common space), it would not be a drama to give back to the Member States a modicum of autonomy in filtering the access to social benefits on the side of non-national inactive or non-resident persons. A redirection in this sense is already detectable in recent ECJ rulings and doctrine.[36] The refugee emergency has already served as a catalyst for a thorough rethinking of conditionality clauses on who can enter and move freely across the Union. The non-domination part of this rethinking should include ways and means for assisting migrants in the exercise of their rights (however redefined) in order to avoid exploitative practices on the part of governments, citizens, bureaucratic agencies and employers.

2.6 CONCLUSION

If smartly designed and communicated, the European Social Union promises to bring about not only normatively desirable functional advantages, but also precious political goods for stabilising the EU as a collective association/community. A smart design requires the deployment of the whole array of

---

[35] Ferrera, n. 8 in this chapter.
[36] De Witte, n. 27 in this chapter.

binding and nonbinding policy instruments available to the Union: regulations, allocations, soft coordination. The journey on this road requires considerable investment on the part of EU leaders, or at least some among them. In national contexts, throughout the twentieth century the production of organised welfare largely resulted from pressure from below. The appeal to solidarity served both to cement horizontal alliances among the disadvantaged and vertical exchanges between rulers and ruled. Solidarity and political justice became irreversibly intertwined through the democratic process. But a second logic played a role as well, especially in the historical federations, where claims of social justice intersected with claims of territorial justice. In some critical historical contingencies (the New Deal in America, World War II in Switzerland), big leap forwards in terms of both social and territorial solidarity followed a top–down logic, based on *Staatsräson*, that is the wish of political authorities (local and federal) to preserve stability and consolidate the polity in the face of pressing functional challenges or dire emergencies. In today's Europe, we clearly have increasing redistributive conflicts but the organisation of voice from below encounters huge challenges. During the crisis there have been important signs of transnational mobilisation in favour of a more solidaristic EU, not only on the side of trade unions, but also civil society organisations. For example, NGOs played a key role – alongside the Commission – in the establishment of FEAD. This fund is a little drop in the sea, of course. But it is also an example of how conflict dynamics can result in the creation of new, bonding, and binding institutions. Even assuming that the ESU project might actually match the preferences and interests of social groups possibly willing to coalesce, for the time being it does not seem realistic to expect large-scale transnational mobilisations for euro-social objectives. In order to make concrete advancements, the main impulse must come from above, on the side of leaders sharing the goal of preserving the very conditions of possibility of the EU as such: political order, mutual trust, the defence of common interests, in a context of fair cooperation. The historical passage is narrow and winding. But crossing over it is not entirely impossible.

3

The Solidarity Argument for the European Union

Helder De Schutter

3.1 INTRODUCTION

Imagine you take the view that justice requires a considerable amount of socio-economic redistribution from those who are well off to those who are less advantaged. Should you then support or instead reject the project of the European Union? If the answer is to support, is the aim then to support an ambitious EU with many competences or should the EU's budget and competences be kept modest, perhaps as modest as the EU currently is in regards to its competences and its budget of 1 per cent of the GDP of the EU's Member States, or less modest than that? And should we then support further expanding the EU, keep the current 28 Member States without further enlargement, or instead seek to reduce the number of Member States (for example by encouraging Member States to step out in Brexit fashion)?

That is the question this chapter will answer; in short: should enthusiasts of redistribution support the EU, and if so, deepen and widen it? I will assume, along the way, that justice indeed requires socioeconomic redistribution, that is: I will assume you agree with what I ask you to imagine in the first sentence of this chapter. Perhaps you think redistribution is to be subjected to clear limits or to stringent conditions (such as willingness to work), and maybe you want to insist on a more precise definition of 'well off' and of 'less advantaged'. But I will take it that you do believe redistribution is important. If you disagree with this premise, then you are of course very welcome to read on, but then what follows no longer applies to you personally.

In this contribution[1] I will answer the question as follows. I argue that redistributionists like you and I have good reasons to support the existence of an ambitious European Union that is more integrated and comprises more

---

[1] The current chapter is both a translation and a significant reworking of a chapter which appeared in a book edited by Erik De Bom: H. De Schutter, 'Solidariteit als argument voor de

Member States than is currently the case. The reason for that support lies in the fact that the EU has the ability to realise social justice over and above the level of the nation-state. Redistributionists therefore have a good reason to be EU-builders.

In elaborating this answer I want to streamline and strengthen an argument that is not often mentioned and is also not sufficiently understood: a socially progressive justification of European integration and enlargement. I develop this argument in two steps. I first show why I think it is desirable that the project of distributive justice is partly decoupled from the nation. This decoupling, however, threatens the connection between redistributive state power and shared nationality. In the second step, I develop a remedy for this decoupling: a recoupling, at the level of the EU, of the connection between redistribution and nationality.

3.2 THE EUROPEAN DECOUPLING OF THE REDISTRIBUTING COMMUNITY FROM THE NATIONAL COMMUNITY

For about two centuries, the nation-state has been the anchor of political self-understanding. True to its name, the nation-state pairs the nation and the state. These two components are so frequently named together that many use them as synonyms. For example, one might speak without any difference of meaning about the French nation and the French state. Yet we can draw a crucial distinction between nation and state: the state is an amalgamate of political institutions, whereas the nation refers to a group of people sharing a common cultural identity often grounded in language, but usually also comprising other factors such as shared understandings, a shared national history, and a sense that one forms one people.

3.2.1 *The Nation-State Couples the Nation and the State*

So in the nation-state, the project of the state and the project of the nation are coupled. The nation is assumed to provide a source of unity for a state: the state is kept together by a national culture. Traditionally, a distinction is made between a German and a French way of realising the ideal of the nation-state. If the nation-state is realised as in Germany, the state follows the nation: the state is mounted on the platform of a national culture. Herder, the German father of romantic nationalism, articulated this vision in his rejection of the

Europese Unie', in E. De Bom (ed.), *Europese Gedachten. Beschouwingen over de toekomst van de Europese Unie* (Pelckmans - Klement, 2014).

multinational state: for him multinational unity could only rest on nation-external coercion (such as through dictatorial rule) and not on the natural internal cohesion that characterises a nation-state.[2] It is in part for this reason that Herder forcefully rejects European colonialism and its concomitant multinational empires.

This national culture with its distinct national language often did not yet exist, as in France, where it had to be actively created. When revolutionaries at the beginning of the French revolution researched the French proficiency of the citizens of France, they discovered that only a minority spoke French and that most citizens spoke a local *patois*. The political conclusion of the revolutionaries was to urgently 'annihilate' the *patois* and to universalise French identity and the use of French on French soil.[3] This policy was continued in the nineteenth century and was aptly described in Eugen Weber's *Peasants into Frenchmen*: the idea was to make Frenchmen out of the inhabitants.[4] When nation-state formation happens 'the French way', then the nation follows the state: we begin with a political community and we make sure it is nationally coloured.

Even though both models of nation-state formation are antipodes, they lead to the same result: a nation-state, a state with a shared national culture. Today we still live in a world dominated by this ideal of the nation-state. National unity in western states is usually no longer pursued by means of illiberal methods and goals like eradicating other languages and dialects. But states still try to provide a shared collective identity for their population by means of nation-building. The state apparatus, the educational sector, and the media raise people with a shared standard language, and shape a shared perception of reality: they are instruments of a shared national identity. This identity must provide states with sufficient stability and cohesion in order to realise common projects.

3.2.2 *State Matters Are Increasingly Detached from the Nation*

Despite its continued importance, however, the nation-state is today also undergoing significant pressures, by two evolutions. Firstly, substate nations

---

[2] J.G. Herder, *Sämtliche Werke* [1891], ed. by B. Suphan, 33 vols (Weidmann Verlag, 1994), XIII, pp. 384–5.

[3] H. Grégoire, 'Rapport sur la nécessité et les moyens d'anéantir les patois et d'universaliser l'usage de la langue française' [1794], in M. de Certeau, D. Julia, and J. Revel (eds), *Une politique de la langue. La Révolution française et les patois: l'enquête de Grégoire* (Gallimard, 2002), pp. 331–51.

[4] E. Weber, *Peasants into Frenchmen. The Modernization of Rural France. 1870–1914* (Stanford University Press, 1976).

like Flanders, Québec, Scotland, or Catalonia increasingly claim forms of recognition and political autonomy. The result is a growing acceptance of the fact that many so-called nation-states really are multinational states: states that are internally divided and host two or more national cultures. Such states often install a form of federalism, a system that enables both national autonomy and a state-wide political entity, like in Canada, Belgium, or Spain.

Secondly, more influence, state power and policy competences are transferred to echelons above and beyond the nation-states. Think of decision-making at the WTO, NATO, or the UN, or of nongovernmental actors such as the Gates Foundation. Of all decision-taking organisations above the level of the state, the European Union is the most far-reaching and integrated one.

Focusing on the EU, I am in this contribution especially interested in the second source of pressure faced by the nation-state. As a result of the increasing supranationalisation of decision-making, the 200-year old coupling between nation and state is increasingly under threat. Even though states remain crucial decision-makers, certain state matters are transferred to a higher level. Elements of the state dimension of the nation-state thereby become independent from national embedding. What are we to think of such abolishment of national ties? Is the increased decoupling of state matters from national embedding desirable?

The most intensive debate in contemporary political philosophy revolves around this question of nation-state transcending political and moral claims. Should we, in times of globalisation and appeals for global justice, continue to uphold the nation-state framework or instead seek to transcend it? Is it desirable that nations or states are privileged sites of justice, or should we strive towards extending the borders of moral concern and seek to organise global distributive justice?

3.2.3 *The Liberal Nationalist Response: Between Solidarity-Limiting and Solidarity-Creating*

Within this current debate, one school of philosophers defends the continued importance of nation-states. They are often called 'liberal nationalists' because they defend the idea of the nation in a way that is compatible with human rights and other liberal values. I will now briefly outline that liberal nationalist view, because I want to argue that there is something desirable and relevant for thinking about the EU in the reasons they see for nation-building.

Liberal nationalists attempt to show that liberalism and nationalism can be reconciled, that there is a version of nationalism that is not inherently illiberal and that liberalism does not have to be inherently anti-nationalist. The essence of the nationalism of this doctrine is the belief that the nation is and should remain the locus of political life. Normatively, liberal nationalists hold the belief that national identities matter, that the state should protect and promote them, and, that it is desirable that the boundaries of political units coincide with national (and linguistic) units.[5]

But the proposed marriage between liberalism and nationalism goes deeper than a mere reconciliation of both ideals. Liberal nationalism claims that its nationalism is not just compatible with liberalism, but in fact follows directly from it: there are liberal reasons for making nations and political units (ultimately: states) coincide. One such reason is that nationalism helps realise the left-liberal goal of social (or distributive) justice.[6] Liberal nationalism holds that there is a connection between distributive justice and sharing a national identity. Redistributive policies presuppose that people are willing to make sacrifices for 'anonymous others whom we do not know, will probably never meet, and whose ethnic descent, religion and way of life differs from our own'.[7] This kind of sacrifice requires a high level of trust – trust that sacrifices will be reciprocated. It also requires a willingness to show solidarity with anonymous others. Both trust and solidarity especially exist within national communities. The principle of nationality (which sets out to draw political boundaries around national boundaries) and policies of nation-building, according to the liberal nationalist argument, can create such a common bond between individuals that will increase their willingness to make such sacrifices.

Several liberal nationalists see this social justice argument as especially important. David Miller, for example, seems to take it as his most crucial concern: he states that a progressive policy requires a shared national identity; without such identity and its correlated willingness to share, states are no longer expected to pursue ambitious projects of distributive justice. 'Given the possibility of private insurance, we would expect states that lacked a communitarian background such as nationality provides to be little more

5 Versions of this normative recommendation to (re)draw political boundaries around national units are defended by C. Gans, *The Limits of Nationalism* (Cambridge University Press, 2003); W. Kymlicka, *Politics in the Vernacular* (Oxford University Press, 2001); D. Miller, *On Nationality* (Oxford University Press, 1995); and Y. Tamir, *Liberal Nationalism* (Princeton University Press, 1993).
6 See Miller, n. 5 in this chapter, at pp. 83–5, 98; Kymlicka n. 5 in this chapter, at pp. 225–6 and Tamir, n. 5 in this chapter, at pp. 117–21.
7 Kymlicka, n. 5 in this chapter, at p. 225.

than minimal states, providing only basic security to their members'.[8] An economic system without social corrections does not need strong national-cultural identity. But for a welfare state such shared national identity is crucial.

What, however, is there to be done when no shared national identity exists? When a national identity is missing in a polity, one solution is to abandon the project of social justice and accept living in a minimal state with minimal redistribution. But this will not satisfy people like you and me, who believe that the well-off should redistribute to the less well-off. For redistributive enthusiasts, two distinct remedies are available: to limit social justice to smaller nationally homogenous zones, or to create nations at the larger polity level. Since no such national-cultural identity exists in Europe, says Miller, we should not pursue social justice at the European level, but instead we should pursue social justice within national borders. Yet, sometimes social justice is an argument to build identity somewhere, rather than to limit justice to levels where there already is a shared identity. Social scientists and historians have in the past decades abundantly shown that nations are actively 'built'. States have actively attempted to create national cultures, by emphasising internal cohesion, by standardising the language, by designating an official language and by coercing public education to use it, or by emphasising the differences with other nations. Even though they clearly reject the illiberal nationalist methods that states have generally employed to that effect, liberal nationalists today still applaud that emergence of national identities. They emphasise the importance of the fact that solidarity, which was first limited to smaller families, clans, or villages, was able to significantly extend its scope.[9] Liberal nationalists believe that with the emergence of the nation something morally significant was created: the possibility to realise social justice and solidarity between great numbers of people.

That the nation was actively constructed where it did not exist or existed insufficiently, implies that the social justice argument can sometimes ground the creation of national identities. The social justice argument is often presented as *solidarity-limiting*: it then says that social redistribution is best limited to whoever shares the same nation. But liberal nationalism also adheres to a vision that states that nationalism can also be *solidarity-creating*; we

---

[8]   Miller, n. 5 in this chapter, at p. 72.
[9]   D. Miller, *Citizenship and National Identity* (Polity Press, 2000), pp. 81–96; and Kymlicka, n. 5 in this chapter, at pp. 221–41.

then bring solidarity to a level where no (sufficient) national feeling existed, through nation-building.

In Europe, certain redistributive and other elements of state power have been transferred to the European Union. This process has to some extent disentangled the nation-state because state power is partly decoupled from the nation. This means that in the EU the scope of the legal person has been extended: from just a group of co-nationals, to the Benelux, to the club of six states and ultimately to the current group of 28 Member States (27 after the British exit). So we can see the EU as an engine of rights extension. Comparable to the eighteenth century, when the nation-state arose, instituting a new level of rights and justice, today we see a new European level of justice surfacing. Just like liberal nationalists today understand what happened in the past two centuries as a positive increase of solidarity as a result of the creation of the nation-state which enabled for large-scale redistribution with anonymous others with a previously unseen scope, so can we now imagine that European regionalists in a few centuries will look back upon our current time as a pivotal moment in which a repositioning took place of the circle of people who form a community of shared rights and duties.

3.2.4 *European Redistribution*

I find this nationalistic lesson illustrative for the way in which progressive welfare state defenders can look at the EU. Whoever sympathises with redistribution to the least advantaged can see the EU as a way to enlarge the scope of moral concern and solidarity. This would maybe not be the case if all European Member States were comparably well off, as a result of which it would not matter a great deal if the unity of distribution and solidarity is the Member State rather than the EU. But since there are weighty inequalities between EU Member States, better-off Member States' membership of a higher redistributing unit within which also a less advantaged Member State is represented, is from the point of view of redistribution a moral gain: it spreads out opportunities and benefits the least well off. That explains my statement that whoever supports redistribution realises that sometimes we need to organise redistribution at domains where no national identity exists (yet), analogous to how contemporary liberal nationalists support the emergence of nations in the history of nationalism.

But does that argument not imply that supporters of the international pursuit of social justice have a reason to organise a shared welfare state with *all* the disadvantaged, including those not living in Europe? Yes: if you believe, as I do, that there is in principle no reason to limit the pursuit of justice or equality to co-nationals, then the scope of application of equality is global.[10] If spreading solidarity is the goal, then it is inconsistent to limit solidarity to advantaged nations and to not involve the rest of the world in the redistributive project, engaging in redistribution only among those least advantaged who are relatively speaking still very advantaged. But an expansion of domestic distributive justice to a global context of redistribution, while the only ultimately desirable situation, is currently utopian in the negative, unrealistic, sense of the word. It is politically unfeasible to bring about a world government that organises a global welfare state or at least globally equalises on a per capita basis the revenues for nation-state based projects of redistribution. We do need to actively encourage the globalisation of redistribution wherever possible: if redistributing between the well-off and the less well-off is our premise, then there is no argument for organising a circle of solidarity together with Romanians but to exclude Kenyans. But within the horizon of our time, the EU is the only supra-state project in which the realisation of such an expansion of the moral community is today not entirely incredible. The EU is the only project that allows us to start thinking about others outside of our own nation-state as 'one of us'.

This argument for an EU-wide distributive justice could be met with criticism from global distributive justice enthusiasts.[11] The objection is that a generous EU-redistributive scheme would not address the globally least advantaged: the EU would become a national system writ large, thereby reinstalling a national limitation to the social justice logic, and increasing the gap between European justice and global justice.

It will therefore not do to simply go for European justice because global justice is thought to be a chimera: we need to think about the compatibility of EU and global solidarity. It seems to me that two arguments can be brought to the defence of the compatibility view, the view that EU-builders are not engaging in global injustice by seeking to realise European solidarity.

---

[10] For a similar argument, see P. Van Parijs and Y. Vanderborght, 'Basic Income in a Globalized Economy', in R. Hasmath (eds), *Inclusive Growth, Development and Welfare Policy: A Critical Assessment* (Routledge, 2015).

[11] This tension between EU and global justice does not figure prominently in the literature. Two papers addressing this issue are E. Baycan, 'The ideal/Non-ideal Theory Distinction Applied to the Social Justice Debate beyond National Borders: European or Global?' (2016) *NCCR Working Paper Series*, 3; and S. Harb, 'Global Distributive Justice and the EU' (2016), unpublished paper.

The first argument states that the EU can be a laboratory for global justice, as defended among others by Philippe Van Parijs.[12] In the EU we are experimenting with the practical organisation of justice at levels higher than the nation-state. Such experiments can help us prepare the realisation of global justice in the future. The European experiment can give us practical, administrative, and institutional clues as to how to go about realising global justice in the future.

The second argument states that the EU can be a training ground for enlarging mentalities. Focusing on realising social justice within the EU while it is ultimately global justice that matters can be justified by the fact that the EU is a training device for identities: we learn to show solidarity towards transnational others. Once Europeans have learned to think of each other as European rather than only French, Polish, or Swedish, when it comes to redistribution, the step towards identifying with anonymous others globally seems a feasible step. The European training experience can then teach us something about how to enlarge identities.

Yet European distributionists should not let current feasibility constraints cloud the ultimate goal. While directly realising global distributive justice without a European detour is not feasible, global distributive justice is still the ultimate goal. Therefore we should, at each democratic junction along the political pathway in which a choice is presented to us that has a substantial enlargement of the moral community as one of the possible options, pick the most extended and the most global one. If a society is confronted with a practical-political choice between two paths – the path of a smaller circle and the path of a larger circle – redistributionists should choose the second path. In my view, the same argument applies domestically: faced with a choice between a Flemish and a Belgian scope of redistribution, we are to choose the Belgian one since it is larger and it includes the less well-off non-Flemish south of the country.[13] And the reasoning is also true for a domestic (say German or Dutch or Belgian) versus an EU-wide circle of redistribution. Today many such choices between different paths are presented: this is a result of the pressures faced by the nation-state, from below as a result of the growing manifestation of national minorities, as from above as a result of political globalisation processes.

None of this implies that national identities as we know them become meaningless. It is unrealistic to believe we can shed them. And it is also not

[12] Van Parijs often refers to it in teaching about the European Union (which he has done with me for years for a course called 'Political Philosophy and the European Union'). It is also implicit in Van Parijs and Vanderborght, n. 10 in this chapter.

[13] See also P. Van Parijs, 'Samenleving en Politiek' (2003) 10 *Tijdschrift voor een democratisch socialisme* 27, p. 32.

desirable: national cultures foster cultural and linguistic life-worlds, and contexts of dignity and self-respect[14], and as such deserve recognition.

But respecting national self-government is compatible with simultaneously further constructing the EU. Federalism is a political system that allows for political autonomy at both state-wide and substate levels simultaneously. If nations like Québec or Flanders can have significant political autonomy within their multinational federal states, then there is no reason why such autonomy could not also be possible within the EU. For some competences, the nation-state surely is the right level. But for redistributive solidarity, the current nation-state levels are not morally desirable, since there is no difference in the moral importance of, and our moral duties towards, co-nationals and other individuals.[15] If one believes that redistribution is desirable, one

---

[14] The notions 'life-world' and 'dignity' require explanation. A *life-world* is a set of shared assumptions and ideas about the world. In my view, language and cultural knowledge function like a key to a room: one needs to speak the language (or have access to the culture) to access what is discussed in the room. Once inside the room that the key gives access to, one is surrounded by arguments and styles of discussing that are not readily available to people who don't speak the language (or are familiar with the same culture) unless through translators who hold the key to other rooms. Each room constitutes a life-world. This idea of life-world goes back to a romantic philosophy of language, see H. De Schutter, 'The Liberal Linguistic Turn: Kymlicka's Freedom Account Revisited' (2016) 44 *Dve Domovini* 51. The idea of *dignity* is older and goes back to the defence of European vernaculars in early modern Renaissance thought. According to this view, using someone's language or affirming the status of someone's language or culture is a way of promoting that person or that group's dignity. A language is a source of collective and personal self-respect and dignity.

[15] This view has some affinity with 'the principle of subsidiarity', but differs from it in two crucial aspects. The principle of subsidiarity states 'powers or tasks should rest with the lower-level sub-units of that order unless allocating them to a higher-level central unit would ensure higher comparative efficiency or effectiveness in achieving them': A. Follesdal, 'Subsidiarity' (1998) 6 *Journal of Political Philosophy* 231. My view differs as follows. First and foremost, the principle of subsidiarity only allows for a competence to be transferred to a higher unit if this is required for 'comparative efficiency or effectiveness' in the achievement of the powers. But in my view redistributive power is to be transferred to the higher unit (the level of the EU) for a moral reason, not for the purpose of efficiency. Even if it would be more efficient to organise solidarity and redistribution at the level of the Member State, the moral reason I am articulating in this contribution justifies transferring it upwards nonetheless. Second, the principle of subsidiarity treats the Member State as the natural place for powers or competences; deviations from placing a competence there have to be argued for. As Follesdal has it, 'subsidiarity places the burden of argument on those who seek to centralise … authority', see A. Follesdal, 'Competing Conceptions of Subsidiarity', in J.E. Fleming and J. Levy, *Federalism and Subsidiarity* (New York University Press, 2014), p. 214. I see no such need for treating the Member State as the central or natural locus of power: in my view, in federal settings, we need arguments both for placing a competence at the central level and for placing it at the local level; no level has a priori competence priority. This second critique has affinities with the critique of subsidiarity 'neglecting' central solidarity in N. Walker, 'Subsidiarity and the Deracination of Political Community: The EU and Beyond', in S. Oeter, T. Repgen, and H-H Trute (eds), *Europe als Idee. Edinburgh School of Law Research paper* (2015) 15/31; *Europa Working Paper*, 15/04, pp. 12–14.

wants to support an as wide as possible pool of people among which redistri-bution is politically pursued.[16]

In this way solidarity can become an argument for the EU. In short, the solidarity argument for the EU is this: whenever extension changes of the solidarity circle appear within feasible reach, the political energy of those who believe in redistribution and the moral arbitrariness of one's place of birth must be directed towards extending the circle, and to make the redistribution more substantial. At every European juncture, be it an election, a referen-dum, a convention or a treaty change, those who support redistribution should try to extend the scope of solidarity.[17]

At this point one alternative to European redistribution should be dis-cussed. Above I noted in passing that EU-level redistribution would not be needed if all Member States were comparably well off, which they are not. But one might argue that they could become equally well off, if the right policy measures are undertaken. This is essentially the idea behind Frank Vandenbroucke's idea of a European Social Union.[18] We might set out to bring all Member States to comparably high levels (through policies such as direct foreign investment, opening up markets, educational mobility, etc.). Let me call this view the equalising Member States view (EMS) (which is part of the European Social Union), and call my alternative approach of trans-ferring the financing of redistribution in the Member States to the EU the Europeanisation of redistribution view (ER).

---

[16] I here assume both that redistribution is desirable, *and* that we have politically speaking equal moral duties towards all human beings. One might challenge this. To limit redistribution to some out of that pool (e.g. co-nationals), one would need an additional argument as to why we have more duties to co-nationals than to other human beings. Miller provides one such argument, claiming that because one shares a national identity, one morally owes more to that person than to other human beings, see D. Miller, *National Responsibility and Global Justice* (Oxford University Press, 2007).

[17] I am leaving open here the very important question of what should be the proper form of redistribution: whether it should be realised in a form that is recognisably like the one at vogue in the national welfare states, whether it should come in the form of increasing EU-wide social standards and initiatives (such as the European Social Fund) with significant redistributive components, or whether it should perhaps come in the form of a European basic income, as Van Parijs and Vanderborght, see n. 10 in this chapter. The point is that it should come in the form of EU-wide redistribution in such a way that solidarity projects are not limited to the current Member States internally but involve an EU-wide sphere of redistribution to the least advantaged.

[18] See F. Vandenbroucke and B. Vanhercke, *A European Social Union: 10 Tough Nuts to Crack* (Friends of Europe, 2014). My reasoning in this paragraph has benefited from, and depends in great part on, private communication with Frank Vandenbroucke, who pointed out this alternative to European redistribution, and who I thank for pushing me to think through the contrast between our respective normative projects.

I agree that in cases where all Member States would be roughly equally well off, justice is compatible both with a European redistribution circle (ER) and national circles to which (most of the) redistribution is limited (EMS). This means, however, that the two visions could be simultaneously pursued. From the point of view of ER, nothing would be lost if all Member States were socioeconomically more or less equally well-off, that is, if EMS had won. So we could strive towards realising both, and, from the perspective of ER defended here, if one of both scenarios comes about, justice has been reached. The political energy of a redistributive enthusiast can therefore be invested in supporting both EMS and ER at the same time. That being said, I do still see two advantages for ER over EMS.

The first is that differences in national culture seem to jeopardise EMS's project of reaching a position of rough equality between the Member States. Member States host public cultures with different histories and understandings. For example, Member State A may value economic progress whereas Member State B may be more focused on cultural opportunities. As a result, different national accents exist, and as long as there are Member States with a measure of political autonomy, as long as the EU is not a unitary political entity without Member State self-government (something which many, including myself, would regard as undesirable), these differences will persist and will have effects on welfare state results. It seems to me that the only way for EMS to cancel out significant national welfare state differences, and thereby to really neutralise the differences in the distribution of talents, is to nullify national autonomy and make sure that all Member States implement the same package of measures. EMS could then indeed proceed without needing Europe-wide redistribution, but it seems to me that it would not win much compared to ER: it would be as if a federal entity dictates what its substate provinces or regions should do, effectively erasing federalism. So there are different tracks of development, educational, and other public choices, and national cultures valuing different goods. I can see that EMS would seek to reduce those differences, but national autonomy implies the existence of differences; the differences cannot be cancelled out unless national autonomy is given up.

A second advantage of a European solidarity circle over solely having a gamut of national circles is the evidence by which solidarity could occur in times of crisis inside one Member State: in the aftermath of an acute economic or natural crisis that sets back many individuals, ER would not have to rely on outside aid: the solidarity system would immediately start benefitting the individuals in the Member State that is lagging behind.

In short, the outcomes envisioned by ER and EMS are both equally valuable, from the point of view of the solidarity argument. Yet as long as there are and are likely to continue to be significant socioeconomic differences in life opportunities between citizens depending on the Member State in which they find themselves, the project of a redistributive enthusiast, as defended here, should be about enlarging the scope of solidarity, by transferring the financing of solidarity upwards, to the level of the European Union.

3.2.5 *Difficulties*

Extending solidarity upwards, however, is complicated, because empirical dynamics are hard to assess, and difficult choices pop up along the way. Two such difficulties stand out.

The first difficulty is the trade-off between enlarging the sphere of redistribution and intensifying it, between widening and deepening EU solidarity. The argument from redistribution justifies *expanding* the EU as a means of spreading solidarity. Rather than helping the less advantaged in the Member States that have already joined and are usually richer, by including only their disadvantaged in the pool of social redistribution, it is from a perspective of global justice more desirable to include the less advantaged from non-members that may seek to join: what matters from a pure redistributive perspective is the global individual, not the national individual, and since average life conditions are lower in official candidates for membership (such as Albania and Turkey) and potential candidate-Member States (Kosovo and Bosnia and Herzegovina) than the average life conditions in the EU as whole, solidarity is gained by each enlargement.

The argument also works in the opposite direction: a non-member with a higher average life-standard than the EU-average, like Norway, has, from a redistributive position, a reason to become a member so that it can spread its wealth towards faster improving the life standard of the least advantaged. For the same reason the solidarity argument also provides a reason against exiting from the EU. This is true for both well-off and badly-off Member States: the well-off Member States have a reason to stay in in order to share their wealth with worse-off others, and the badly-off Member States have a reason to benefit their poor by staying in.[19] So the solidarity argument for the EU and for

---

[19] However, the solidarity argument does not provide a reason against exiting for Member States approaching the EU-average on socioeconomic matters for whom leaving would make no difference in terms of social justice: they have nothing to gain or lose from a solidarity perspective. But if a socioeconomically average member would decline socioeconomically after

EU solidarity provides a reason for expansion of the EU, and against exiting from the EU.

So the EU should widen. But the problem is that conflicts occur between widening and deepening. Widening can lead to a decline in cohesion and homogeneity that threatens further deepening: it is easier to deepen with six similar Member States than with 28.[20] This is especially the case given the consensus needed for new treaties to occur (or for revisions of treaties in case a Convention is called): treaties require consensus and ratification by all Member States. But the higher the number of Member States, the higher the chance of disagreement. So widening threatens deepening, for which new treaties and/or amendments are required.

Yet deepening, in the direction of further EU-wide redistribution, so that the EU, irrespective of its size, receives more political redistributive power, is demanded by the distributive argument. A lot still needs to happen before the EU citizens form a substantial socially redistributive circle of solidarity. Surely rights such as freedom of movement within the EU help foster equality, since less advantaged labourers from less advantaged areas can move to better-off Member States. And, the very existence of net contributing and net receiving Member States results in a certain level of social redistribution. But all in all, intra-EU distribution is limited, and the EU does suffer from libertarian tendencies akin to the interstate federalism preferred by Friedrich Hayek.[21]

In short, on the distributive argument, the EU needs to deepen and to widen. Deepening allows for a more significant level of EU-solidarity, and widening it leads to a further spreading of the solidarity. But widening can postpone deepening, and empirical priority conjectures must be made. It will often be wise to postpone widening until a certain 'depth' has come about. Imagine that at t₁, countries A, B, and C constitute an EU-like union called *Utopia*. Imagine, however, that they currently lack sufficient cohesion and common understanding for the emergence of significant redistribution at the level of *Utopia*: there is no redistributive 'deepening' yet. Imagine further that the citizens of C are in general less well-off than the citizens of A and B. Imagine also that there is a candidate Member State D whose citizens are similarly disadvantaged as the citizens of C (the welfare levels of the citizens of C and D are comparable). Now, A, B,

---

exiting – a reasonable expectation given its loss of access to the open market and other EU benefits – then that Member State equally has a reason not to exit. I am grateful to Geert De Baere for making me think about this latter caveat.

[20] J.A. Caporaso, *The European Union. Dilemmas of Regional Integration* (Westview Press, 2000), pp. 97–113.

[21] See M. Höpner and A. Schäfer, 'Embeddedness and Regional Integration: Waiting for Polanyi in a Hayekian Setting' (2012) 66 *International Organization* 429.

and C may want to postpone the admission D to *Utopia* with a few years until A, B, and C are further integrated. They could argue that postponing the admission of D can be better for solidarity from the well-off towards the less advantaged: (1) the less advantaged citizens of C might benefit from postponing D-membership, because the required levels of cohesion are more easily reached in a smaller and less heterogeneous union of A, B, and C, resulting in the willingness to redistribute. (2) The poor in D itself might benefit from joining later because, depending on empirical circumstances, it is well possible that *Utopia*-level redistribution may never happen if D joins now, given the daunting presence of heterogeneity.

A second difficulty faced by enthusiasts of European redistribution has to do with the fact that much of the existing deepening is not leading to more redistribution. It is not because the EU gets more power, as for example after the recent economic crisis, that the power is employed towards the pursuit of social justice. Such redistribution is also hard to realise as a result of the following problem,[22] which in fact is just the intra-EU side of the first difficulty discussed above. On the one hand, as Fritz Scharpf has explained, the EU-integration (or deepening) is dependent on the treaties that are made by the Member States, which each have veto power. On the other hand, these Member States have different traditions as far as social justice is concerned. These two factors combined result in the improbability of realising a more social market economy in Europe: the Member States can only agree on a greatest common denominator. This leads redistributionists like Fritz Scharpf to be sceptical of EU integration.[23] Some libertarians even use this argument to state that whoever is inclined to support a minimal state (and reject progressive redistribution) does well to support a federal European Union, since the government's grip will be weaker in such a setting.[24]

So surely assessing the actual impact of the EU on redistributive justice is a complicated matter, and different extra factors are relevant as well, such as the fact that the EU-limits on budget deficits can lead Member States to enforce social cuts, the fact that the EU generates fiscal competition between Member States, and the fact that the EU also liberalises energy and parts of the health industry.[25]

---

[22] See F. Scharpf, 'The Asymmetry of European Integration, or Why the EU Cannot Be a 'Social Market Economy'' (2010) 8 *Socio-Economic Review* 211.
[23] Ibid.
[24] See James Buchanan's argument in J.M. Buchanan, 'Federalism and Individual Sovereignty' (1995–96) 15 *Cato Journal* 259.
[25] See for example D.S. Martinsen and K. Vrangbæk, 'The Europeanization of Health Care Governance: Implementing the Market Imperatives of Europe' (2008) 86 *Public Adminstration* 169; and D.S. Martinsen, 'Welfare States and Social Europe', in U. Neergaard, E. Szyszczak, J.W. van den Gronden, and M. Krajewski (eds), *Social Services of General Interest in the EU* (Springer, 2013), pp. 53–71, for a critical welfare analysis of decisions by the Court of Justice.

3.2.6 *Strategic Levellism and Ideological Levellism*

But many of these discussions are not intrinsically European. If there was no EU, many issues would be raised within a nation-state context. For example, even without a EU, we would still face questions about whether we want to apply free market principles to health care, about how to bring different regions of a country with different socioeconomic challenges and traditions to agree on one national welfare standard, and whether we should avoid budget deficits by cutting social provisions. That such questions would need to be faced in any case, implies, I think, that the EU's current less-than-ideal state with respect to what redistributionists want cannot form the basis of an argument against the *existence* of the EU in itself; it can at most be the basis of an argument against current EU decisions. In fact, Euroscepticism can take two forms: the first is to be against the EU's current policies; the second is to be against the existence of the EU. EU distributionists embrace the redistributive potential of the EU, not its current policies. In fact, their position is compatible with, and generally leads to, a strong criticism of current EU policies: a Euroscepticism of the first form. Compare this situation with that of socially progressive minds in states without strong redistribution: that not enough redistribution exists in such states is not a reason for rejecting the existence of the state at stake. Rather than a rejection of the existence of the state, socially progressive opposition is a rejection of current policies. The same is true for the EU: that the current EU more closely resembles a minimal than a welfare state is not a reason for opposition against the EU but for opposition within the EU for more redistribution. The realisation of the domestic welfare state was not a sinecure either, and there is no reason to understand European shortcomings as intrinsic to the European project.

And yet this is the situation in which several left-wing parties find themselves within the Union. They are not intrinsically ideologically opposed to the existence of a supranational European Union (they are not nationalists or statists), but they are very critical of the way in which the EU is currently governed and of the lack of social policies it currently pursues. This criticism has led some of them to reject the European Union. That rejection was based on the argument that it is strategically erroneous to support the EU, because its policies are not sufficiently socioeconomically progressive. Some leftist Scandinavian parties have for example rejected EU membership because they saw the EU as a neoliberal project,[26] and the same is true for certain contemporary leftist sympathies across the continent.

---

[26] D.A. Christensen, 'The Left-Wing Opposition in Denmark, Norway and Sweden: Cases of Euro-Phobia?' (1996) 19 *West European Politics* 525.

We could call such a choice *strategic levellism*: strategic levellers opt for a policy level not in virtue of their ideology but in virtue of the chance that their ideology is going to be realised. Levellism is a view about the appropriate level for any given competence (such as immigration policy, or road maintenance). Strategic levellism is then the view that determines that level in view of the highest probability of getting one's ideology realised: strategic levellers pick that level at which the majority leans more heavily towards their ideology, or where the chances of realising it are highest. Contrast this with *ideological levellism*: ideological levellers opt for a policy level on the basis of ideology; they choose to place a certain competence at that level that their ideology requires. Left-wing European actors who are against the European Union because the EU has too many right-wing voters or right-wing policies, engage in strategic levelling. They choose the nation-state as their preferred level not because they are intrinsically ideologically nation-state based, as for example the UK Independence Party or Front National are, but because they believe that a higher probability of getting left-wing policies exists within the nation-state than within the European Union.

We can see this mechanism at work in any multilevel policy where the level for a competence can change. Take for example the Belgian federation. Strategic levellism is adhered to by certain Flemish free-market groups who are in favour of curtailing socioeconomic redistribution. They are not ideologically opposed to Belgium per se, but they realise that a Belgian context has more left-wing voters than the Flemish context, due to the higher presence of left-wing voters in Wallonia. In Flanders, socioeconomically more right-wing (and less redistribution-favouring) parties are traditionally more popular than in the south of the country. As a result, these free-market actors strategically opt for more decentralisation towards Flanders.

Such strategic choices, however, are democratically hard to justify. It is democratically tricky to counter a democratic decision you are about to lose with a threat of exit from that policy level where the issue at stake is currently being decided. But, apart from democracy, the more important problem of strategic levellism is that of social justice: just like the serious obstacles to the emergence of substantial national redistribution did not form an argument against the existence of the state in itself, so too is the difficulty of bringing about substantial European redistribution not a reason against the existence of the European Union. For those who hold that redistribution is a requirement of justice, it is important to realise redistribution on a European level. And the current opposition to such a plan is a hurdle that redistributionists have to overcome, not an intransient impossibility for such a policy. Proponents of distributive justice should not reject the EU but should critically embrace it: its Euroscepticism should attack the current EU, not its existence.

The argument I just outlined is seldom made. The EU project is more commonly normatively justified as a project of peace. EU integration, has, so the argument goes, made war between Member States nearly impossible. This long-standing peace argument is fully compatible with the solidarity argument so there is no need for solidarity defenders to reject it. It is important to remark though that the solidarity argument supports distributive deepening and further expansion of the EU. The peace argument is not typically used as an argument for further deepening and widening but it might be reformulated to do so, and it clearly has been used in the recent past to justify the EU's Eastern European enlargement.[27]

A second alternative view with respect to the justification for the EU (apart from peace) is moral indifference. This is a very popular view: it says there is no moral answer to the questions whether we should keep the EU and whether we should further integrate and enlarge. More or less Europe is then a morally neutral question without significant normative implications. *Anything goes*, is the answer, as long as it goes democratically. I think this view is wrong. Of course, we should only do what is democratically decided. But there are normative dimensions to this issue, and the solidarity argument is meant to show that redistributionists have a reason to favour the project of the EU, and to favour further integration and expansion. If democratic majorities vote against this, then we must accept this. But that should not withhold distributionists from pleading their case.

A third view, aside from peace and indifference, regarding the possible justification of the existence of the EU is the maintenance of welfare states. Habermas has argued in the past two decades that economic globalisation processes weaken the national grip on economic matters and welfare creation. This results in a positive view of Europe as a bulwark against national welfare erosion, as the European context is still big enough to be able to impact upon the economic conditions of the welfare state.[28] I think that this argument, like the one from peace, is an important argument. But it differs significantly from the solidarity argument for the EU that I am spelling out here, because the Habermasian view pleads for the EU as an instrument of maintaining domestic circles of redistribution. Instead the solidarity argument sees the EU as an instrument to realise a European circle of redistribution, and so to explicitly

---

[27] See R. Baldwin, 'The Eastern enlargement of the European Union' (1995) 39 *European Economic Review* 474.

[28] J. Habermas, 'Why Europe Needs a Constitution' (2001) 11 *New Left Review* 5.

realise a European welfare state, at least as far as the financing of solidarity is concerned.[29]

3.3 RECOUPLING THE NATIONAL AND THE REDISTRIBUTING COMMUNITY

So far I have outlined the solidarity argument for transferring components of state power to the European Union (and for enlarging the EU). Yet if we send state power to higher levels, we thereby decouple the link between state competences and national cultures, and thereby unravel the nation-state: transferred state competences then emancipate themselves from nationality. This invites the widespread liberal-nationalist criticism that social justice and other state projects ideally remain tied to a national culture and that a European Union cannot work since its citizens share no national-cultural loyalties. Above I replied to this criticism that liberal nationalism has historically often condoned moving against the coupling of nationality and state, specifically when it supports the slowly and actively constructed historical emergence of solidarity at levels where such solidarity did not yet exist, such as in France and other nation-states. So supporters of redistribution (including liberal nationalists in the past) can realise that sometimes we need to organise redistribution at levels where no national identity exists yet. This shows that the reasons for the national embedding of state matters can be sometimes overridden by other reasons: a state matter like solidarity can for instance be thought to be weightier than the general preference for the coupling of state and nationhood.

So my first reply to the objection to the EU's decoupling of state competences and national culture is that sometimes decoupling is the preferred option, even for liberal nationalists, because certain weightier issues overrule the preference for coupling state and nation. But there is a second, more fundamental reply that European redistributionists can give to the liberal-nationalist critique of the European project. This is to *re*-couple the emancipated state power to a national identity, now at a European level, through European nation-building. I will now indicate how this second reply can work.

Liberal nationalism pleads for stimulating a shared national-cultural identity within a political community. This shared identity is instrumental for state

---

[29] I am here leaving open whether the distribution of the revenues would remain a domestic matter. It is possible to plead only for a European redistribution of the revenues (the taxes), not for a Europeanisation of the organisation of the welfare state itself. In the latter option, nation-states would remain responsible for designing their own health care, poverty relief, pension systems, and other welfare dimensions.

cohesion and for social justice. Liberal nationalists argue that the extension of initially local solidarity to state-based forms of redistributive solidarity was morally desirable, and they emphasise that that solidarity was possible as a result of realising a common we-feeling that comes with national identity. What can this position imply for the European Union?

Many adherents of liberal nationalism turn out to be sceptical of European identity. For example, David Miller understands the EU as an organ without national identity that should therefore remain limited and should be governed intergovernmentally. But on the just sketched argument for nation-building, national identity is seen as instrumental for a political community, it is possible to form such an identity where it initially did not exist, and this has historically been pursued in such a way. Therefore, I see no reason why the identity that we pursue at the European level could not be similar in kind to the identity that is pursued domestically. Once we are looking at the EU today with a liberal-nationalist lens, it becomes clear that, if we want the European project to succeed and if we are interested in EU-wide redistribution, then we need to encourage a similar Europe-wide we-feeling.

For example, such an identity for the European Union could resemble the state-wide identity that is being pursued within multinational states. David Miller states that multinational states, like the United Kingdom or Belgium, require a certain overarching national identity in order to adequately function.[30] However, that state-wide nation still has to be stimulated in a way that is compatible with the substate nation-building that exists at the level of for example Wales or Flanders. But that should not be a problem, for Miller, since people can be a member of two nations at the same time: it is possible to adhere to both a Welsh national identity and a British national identity. Such 'nested identities' are in my view a helpful and progressive way of understanding identity, that grounds nationalism in a less exclusive view of identity than it is often associated with.

But if such inclusive identity is possible for many people in multinational states such as the United Kingdom and Belgium, then there is no principled reason why it cannot be theorised within a multinational European Union. It is in my view inconsistent for a liberal nationalist to be prepared to discuss nested identities in currently existing multinational states, but to not recognise such possibility for the European Union. The identity we ought to pursue at the European level should in my view not differ *in kind* from the state-wide national identities that many multinational states still provide (on top of the substate national identities they host). This nation-building would then

---

[30] Miller, n. 9 in this chapter at pp. 125–41.

occur not along the German but along the French model of nation-state unity that I discussed above: just as in France the state was made into a nation, so should we today seek to stimulate the formation of a common 'national' identity for the European Union. Surely the European nation-building we need to pursue should not imply the destruction of the domestic nations (which the French did set out to do for the *patois*): national identities don't need to disappear; instead a European identity layer can be added onto existing national identities.

What might it mean to argue for a 'national' identity at the European level? In line with my earlier definition above I mean something different by 'nation' than by 'state' (otherwise the 'nation-state' would be a pleonasm and the term 'multinational state' would be an oxymoron). Here I use the term as meaning a certain shared cultural identity. Of course such a shared European cultural identity must be appropriate for the kind of entity that the EU is, and it must be compatible with national identities. In many ways, the EU today looks like a multinational state that also needs to work out a form of national identity for the presence of state-wide allegiance. In such states, overarching nation-building can only work if it is not premised on a denial or removal of substate national identities: in a multilingual state, for example, the state-wide identity cannot be grounded in the native language of one of the present language groups. Just like federal multinational states have good reasons to seek to realise a form of state-wide (Canadian, British, Belgian) identity compatible with the existence of substate national identities, so too should the EU seek to stimulate a similar overarching identity. Apart from a principle of equal accommodation of all existing national identities, which is in itself a condition of possibility for the emergence of a European identity (similar to how the recognition of Québec is a condition of possibility for Canadian identity), we can also think at the European level of identity-stimulating matters such as the implementation of an EU-wide history curriculum that focuses on European history, creating symbolic allegiance to the European flag and the anthem, of understanding the EU's policy of multilingualism as a source of European identity (comparable with how multiculturalism became a defining feature of Canadian identity), and subsidising EU-wide public media. Several initiatives already exist, such as the European Erasmus-programme. The idea is not that a very different type of unity is to be envisaged. Instead, the same sort of identity that we have strived and are still striving, to realise domestically, be it in mono- or in multinational polities, should now be pursued for the EU: for that we do not need a distinct, less emotional or more rational basis: we can extend the old model of allegiance developed for the nation-state, with the caveat that now, in contrast to certain earlier realisations of that model, developing such allegiance must not come at the expense of the continued fostering of allegiance to substate levels.

A final example of European nation-building is stimulating, where possible, the fostering of a direct relationship between the EU and its citizens. This allows European citizens to relate to each other as individuals, and not just as citizens belonging to different states. It implies that certain 'supranational' organs within the EU such as the European Parliament can be strengthened: such institutions focus on a direct relationship between the EU and EU-citizens. They stand in contrast to intergovernmental organs such as the European Council, where the heads of state meet. Will Kymlicka, for example, defends the EU as a limited intergovernmental project: the idea is that national citizens amongst themselves decide what they think their representatives at the level of the EU should seek to realise.[31] If we follow this proposal, we get an indirect form of decision-making: collective discussions are had by citizens acting not as Europeans but as national citizens, who manage the EU as members of their Member States. Citizens debate domestically what the position of their Member State is to be at the European level. This, however, quickly leads to a 'UK-mentality' whereby Member States look at what they can get out of the EU and how the EU may benefit the national interest, and whereby an EU-wide mentality and solidarity, required for such ambitious projects as redistribution from rich to poorer EU-citizens, is slowed down.

That is why redistributionists want to enable a shift towards a second perspective, in which European citizens understand themselves as belonging to one European community, steered by European representatives. In this vision, the EU is driven by the collective will of (individual) European citizens. Perceiving others as individuals with whom one forms an overarching political entity ensures an enlargement of the moral community. It implies the readiness and the possibility to put oneself in another's shoes, whether the other is German, Czech, or Polish. So since we want to encourage European redistribution, we should ensure a perspective change from an international to an inter-individual basis of the European Union. Understood in this way we get a solidarity reason to stimulate the direct connection between the EU and its citizens: solidarity requires a 'we', and that is why we need to transform the EU-citizen from another Member State, from an anonymous other, to 'one of us', so we can understand that citizen as part of the 'we' that is needed for solidarity. We must be able to relate to fellow Europeans as members of the same *people*, even though we are also members of smaller peoples at the same

---

[31] Kymlicka, n. 5 in this chapter.

time (state and/or substate peoples such as Belgians and Flemish respectively) with competences of their own.

Such a direct, individual (as opposed to indirect and intergovernmental) relationship is sometimes argued for on democratic grounds. Democratic government, the argument goes, requires a collective European discussion that transcends Member States.[32] I am sympathetic to this argument, but the redistributive argument can ground the same goal: in order to realise an EU-wide circle of redistribution, identification with European others is required.

Importantly, this extension of the liberal-nationalist project to the European level – seamlessly possible within liberal-nationalist history and ideology, though seldom defended by contemporary liberal nationalists – allows for a remedy for the decoupling of state power from the nation. Above I discussed the pressure on the nation-state as a result of competence transfers to the European Union. The EU thereby decouples important elements of state power from the nation, assuming that power itself. Now we can see that stimulating European nation-formation constitutes a remedy for such upwards transfer of power. It allows for a new re-coupling of those competences and dimensions of now EU-power and a shared national-cultural identity.[33]

3.4 CONCLUSION

Where and when possible, we need to broaden the sphere of solidarity, for reasons of global distributive justice. In order to do so, we need to apply the following rule: whenever we are historically confronted with a policy choice between two different roads, one leading to or sustaining a smaller level of redistribution, and the other leading to or sustaining a larger level, we need to choose the larger, most cosmopolitan level. For people living in Europe today, that road is the road of the European Union. Redistributionists therefore choose for a more expanded and a socially more integrated European Union.

A larger and more redistributive EU leads to a decoupling of state power and national identity. The decoupling can be remedied by retransferring power to the nation-state but doing so is incompatible with the redistributionist demand of enlarging the sphere of solidarity. But there is a second option. The

---

[32] See for example S. Hix, *What's Wrong with the European Union and How to Fix It* (Wiley/Blackwell, 2008); and S. Rummens, 'Staging Deliberation: The Role of Representative Institutions in the Deliberative Democratic Process' (2012) 20 *Journal of Political Philosophy* 23.

[33] The word 'national', difficult in itself, refers to both the currently existing domestic spheres (Danish, Italian, and so on) and to cultural identity affairs (as in 'a nation is a cultural entity'). When I speak of 'nation'-building for the EU, I of course mean 'national' in the second sense only.

decoupling can be remedied at the European level by stimulating a process of European nation-formation. Doing so encourages a European we-feeling that brings the same cohesive ties to the EU level that once were brought to the domestic level, in a move supported by liberal nationalism. This second option does not reject an ambitious EU, nor does it seek to ground the latter on more rational foundations like non-national ties of constitutional patriotism.[34] It simply extends liberal nationalism to the platform of the European Union

While ambitious forms of EU-wide redistribution and nation-formation are far from being realised, it is still important to now make choices that later may make larger forms of solidarity possible. Normative ideals surely meet practical objections, but it is still important to have clear ideal visions in mind to strive towards. Unless the practical objections make the dream impossible in the inability understanding of impossibility (according to which the agents are not *able* to carry out the dream[35]), the normative dream itself should remain unaffected by them: whoever desires social justice should realise that the normative ideal is best served by a social EU and should attempt to build a social and redistributive Union, not to destruct or diminish that Union.

---

[34] J. Habermas, *Die postnationale Konstellation* (Verlag, 1998).

[35] See D. Estlund, 'Utopophobia' (2014) 42 *Philosophy and Public Affairs* 113. Estlund explains that it is extremely improbable that he will dance like a chicken during a lecture. But that does not mean he is unable to do so: he is perfectly *able* to dance as such during the lecture. There is an improbability and an inability understanding of impossibility: it is impossible in the probability sense that he will dance like a chicken (since probability is as good to zero), while at the same time it is not impossible, in the ability sense, for him to dance like that.

4

Social Justice in an Ever More Diverse Union

Christian Joerges

4.1 INTRODUCTION

The European Social Model, ill-defined and undertheorised as it may be in political debates, is widely perceived as the great loser in the political and institutional reconfiguration of the European integration project, which we have witnessed under the impact of the financial crisis. The state of 'Social Europe' is indeed deplorable. The turn to austerity politics has not only led to the imposition of rigid structural reforms on countries of the European South, but reflects a general retreat from the welfare state commitments that were understood in the foundational period of the EEC as a common European legacy. The search for a preservation and renewal of that legacy must not focus exclusively on topical claims and urgencies. It should instead include and depart from the decoupling of economic integration from welfare state traditions with a primacy of the former, which resulted essentially from the constitutionalisation of the economic freedoms and was deepened since 2007 by the *Laval-Viking-Rüffert* jurisprudence of the ECJ. What happened under the impact of the financial crisis continues on this avenue with ever more rigidity. The critical reconstruction in this paper argues, however, that a primacy of the economic over the social was never fully realised; the law of the internal market had to take account of a broad range of regulatory objectives and to mediate between the objectives of building the internal market and the social acquis which Member States had established in a variety of forms. These compromises are read and defended as the realisation of the 'united in diversity' vision of the Draft Constitutional Treaty of 2003. This vision is conceptualised as 'conflicts-law-constitutionalism'. It is then submitted that this reconceptualisation of the integration project has significant affinities with a 'Social Union' that does not replace the broad variety of welfare state traditions by some uniform European model but respects this variety and coordinates their further development.

4.2 STRUCTURING THE ARGUMENT

Europe's austerity politics has hit most severely the South of the Union. It has, 'because of its palpable, indeed glaring social injustice', antagonised the nations of Europe.[1] The break with European commitments is manifold. Austerity is imposed on 'zero-choice democracies'.[2] The principles of equality and mutual respect within the Union have fallen into oblivion. Both injustice within, and lack of solidarity between, Member States are interdependent. These are valid reasons militating for corrective measures. And yet, spontaneity with short-term perspectives may not provide long-term guidance. This chapter will undertake a reconstructive exercise which will reach far beyond the turning point in the outbreak of the financial crisis in 2008 and even the founding of the EEC. This reconstruction will focus on the relationship between 'the economic' (the progress of economic integration) and 'the social' (welfare regimes and social justice) in the various stages of the integration process. It will reveal ongoing tensions between these two dimensions that could never be settled by the establishment of some common transnational European social regime. The provision of welfare and social justice remained in essential respects a national agenda, albeit one that mirrored the Union's ever-growing diversity and increasing gaps in the level of welfare that the members of the Union achieved. Quests for social justice have therefore to include interstate relations. Article 3 commits the Union to promote 'solidarity among Member States'. This is a promising formula. The new Article 136 (3) TFEU as amended in 2011 reads less comfortably: financial assistance can be granted, but must be subject to 'strict conditionality'. This rigid response to the welfare gaps between the Member States did not come out of the blue. It reflects a primarily economic ordering which has been advocated in scholarship ever since it started to address the problem of justice in interstate relations back in the nineteenth century. The weight of this legacy is not so easily visible but, nevertheless, highly important.

---

[1] J. Habermas, 'Democracy in Europe: Why the Development of the EU into a Transnational Democracy Is Necessary and How It Is Possible' (2015) 21 *European Law Journal* 546, p. 550.

[2] N. Heplas, 'Supra-national Technocracy and Zero Choice Democracy: The Greek Experience', contribution to the workshop 'Technocracy and Democracy in Times of Financial Crisis', University of Darmstadt, 6–7 March 2014 (on file with author).

(1) This is why, in the first step of our reconstruction, we will recall the distinction and tension between domestic and interstate justice – of justice within and justice between distinct polities – as it has been conceptualised, famously and enormously influentially within and beyond German borders, in the nineteenth century by the most celebrated German jurist ever, Carl Friedrich von Savigny, in his treatise on private international law.[3] Savigny's message in a nutshell: the law can ensure justice only within private relations. This is conceivable also transnationally. Interstate relations, however, remain in an unruly state of nature governed by power and politics rather than law. To rephrase this in our terminology: The law is concerned exclusively with the reasonableness of private affairs. It does not try to intervene in the name of social justice into private ordering domestically let alone interfere with international affairs. Section 4.3 will elucidate this background and its continuous importance further.

(2) The two following steps deal with the tensions between the economic and the social in the process of European integration project.

- Section 4.4 will deal with the so-called foundational period. Under the Treaty of Rome, the Member States retained responsibility for social welfare and remained largely autonomous in its formation. The opening of their borders to free intra-Community trade did not interfere significantly. Political scientists have characterised this fortunate constellation as the golden age of 'embedded liberalism'.[4]

- Seemingly paradoxically, it was the success of the integration project that brought this equilibrium out of balance. Market-integration affected ever more legal fields and prompted the establishment of sophisticated regulatory machinery. These developments were, however, not accompanied or complemented by the adoption of transnational welfare regimes. The ensuing constellation has been famously characterised by Fritz W. Scharpf as a 'de-coupling' of economic integration from social integration.[5] The commitment to the 'highly competitive market economy' proclaimed in the Draft Constitutional Treaty of 2003 and by now enshrined in (Article 3(3)

---

[3] F.C. von Savigny, *System des heutigen Römischen Rechts*, vol. VIII (Veit & Company, 1849).
[4] The term was coined in J.G. Ruggie, 'International Regimes, Transactions and Change: Embedded Liberalism in the Postwar Economic Order' (1982) 36 *International Organization* 375.
[5] F.W. Scharpf, 'The European Social Model: Coping with the Challenges of Diversity' (2002) 40 *Journal of Common Market Studies* 645.

TEU) was in the view of many commentators meant to overcome this schism. Section 4.4 will submit, however, that this commitment was an undertheorised response, a political formula which failed to provide guidance in the resolution of the tensions that persisted and deepened the complex conflict constellations within a socioeconomically ever more diverse Union.

(3) The Treaty of Maastricht applied a new recipe but relied on the familiar logic. The persistence of socioeconomic diversity was acknowledged. But this was perceived as a failing that should and could be overcome through convergence. Convergence, even though it cannot be accomplished overnight, would be realised under the healthy pressure of a common currency. Accordingly, the Treaty of Maastricht promised to lead to an 'ever closer Union' with Economic and Monetary Union as its new transnational corner stone. Section 4.5 will argue that the EMU has created unresolvable conflict constellations without providing a reliable constitutional framework for their resolution.

(4) What we experienced after ratification of that treaty was, first, under the quite fortunate economic conditions that prevailed after the turn of the century, a period of muddling through, but then, after the outbreak of the financial crisis, a downfall of the economies of Southern Europe and of the Republic of Ireland, which created a state of economic and social emergency. The responses, analysed in Section 4.6, are characterised there as a move from 'integration through law' to 'crisis law', that is to say, a deep transformation of Europe's *Verfassungswirklichkeit*[6] which contrasts strikingly with Europe's once envisaged constitutional order and commitments. Does this re-ordering allow or leave political and legal space for a renewal of Europe's social commitment? We will examine the obstacles to such efforts. They stem from Europe's dedication to structural reforms that were legalised by the recent jurisprudence in the *Pringle* and *Gauweiler* judgments – once again legalisation of the primacy of the economic over the social, which will be discussed in some detail.

(5) What will happen to the European project? The Epilogue will not engage in prediction or prophecies, but will instead point to two scenarios submitted by the political economist Dani Rodrik and the political theorist Jonathan White. Both of them are not at the surface, but, in different ways, fundamentally pessimistic. We will add as a third scenario,

---

[6] 'Constitutional reality' is the best available translation; the German term captures better the tension between valid law and an extra-legal praxis. See in more detail below in Section 4.7 of this chapter.

Werner Abelshauser's defence of the variety of economic cultures as a constellation with a beneficial potential. All this should not be read as a critique of piecemeal change and pragmatism, but as a quest to reflect such activities in the framework of renewed reconstructions of the design problems of integration politics.

4.3 BACK TO AGE-OLD BEGINNINGS: THE LEGACY OF CLASSICAL PRIVATE INTERNATIONAL LAW AND EUROPE'S FOUNDATIONAL DILEMMA

Private international law (the Anglo-Saxon equivalent: conflict of laws) is an intellectual heritage with which students of European legal integration are hardly familiar. And yet, quite similar to Maitland's famous observation that 'the forms of action ... still rule us from their graves',[7] these historical roots are of topical importance. Two readily discernible aspects deserve particular attention in the present context: the first is the distinction between justice within consolidated polities on the one hand and the state of nature in the international system on the other (Section 4.3.1); the second is the relation between social justice and the institutionalisation of political democracy (Section 4.3.2).

4.3.1 Savigny's International Private Legal Ordering and the Unruliness of Interstate Relations

The distinction between domestic and international (interstate) justice originates in the categorical difference between internal and external affairs: that is, in the taming of the political and the ordering of the social by nation-states, on the one hand, and the unruliness of the state of nature in the international system, on the other. The relevant legal disciplines have conceptualised these differences quite rigidly. Beyond its recognition of the commitments undertaken in international treaties, international law was far from enthusiastic about affirming interference in the economic and social affairs of the sovereign entities that constituted it.

Private international law, however, became considerably more ambitious with Friedrich Carl von Savigny's path-breaking treatise of 1849.[8] In what has been praised as a Copernican turn, Savigny developed the vision of a truly

---

[7] See F.W. Maitland, 'The forms of action at Common Law' (1909), available at: legacy.fordham.edu/halsall/basis/maitland-formsofaction.asp (accessed 12 October 2016).

[8] Von Savigny, n. 3 in this chapter.

transnational legal order of private law relations, which depended, not on the uniformity of substantive rules, but on the readiness of courts in all spheres of jurisdiction to apply the legal order in which these private legal relationships were situated – the principle of mutual recognition as pronounced in the seminal *Cassis de Dijon* judgment[9] is the European equivalent. Private international law was not intended to strive for substantive justice, but for uniformity of decision-making. This is the distinctive character of the 'justice' that the discipline of private international law seeks to promote. Since the private law systems of all 'civilised nations' deserve to be recognised in principle, all the law needs to determine is the seat of a legal relationship (*Rechtsverhältnis*) and apply that law. Savigny's concepts were both revolutionary and realistic. They were revolutionary in the principled separation of private law from the state and its public policy. They were realistic in the delimitation of the scope of the new principles. The mutual respect of foreign legal orders, their equal treatment, and the toleration of diversity was premised upon an understanding of private law as an unpolitical order that was not permeated by public policies. This meant that the application of a foreign order would not affect the policies and interests of a particular state in any significant way.[10]

Savigny's historical premises are in many respects outdated. Private law pursues policies; the boundaries between public and private laws are often blurred. But Savigny's vision of an autonomous transnational private law ordering continues to resurface in ever new variations.[11] One such variety is 'economic constitutionalism': the core institutions of private law – party autonomy, private property, enforceability of contracts – codify and ensure the functioning of markets. This type of economic rationality legitimates the private ordering of the economy and should not be disturbed by political interventions but complemented instead by a legal protection of a system of undistorted competition. This is the creed in particular of ordoliberal scholarship, which has accompanied and influenced the development of the integration project since its inception.[12]

---

[9] ECJ, judgment of 20 February 1979 in *Cassis de Dijon*, C-120/78, EU:C:1979:42.

[10] K. Vogel, *Der räumliche Anwendungsbereich der Verwaltungsrechtsnorm* (Metzner, 1965); on the contemporary importance of this tradition, see R. Michaels, 'Globalizing Savigny? The State in Savigny's Private International Law and the Challenge of Europeanization and Globalization', in M. Stolleis and W. Streeck (eds), *Dezentralisierung. Aktuelle Fragen politischer und rechtlicher Steuerung im Kontext der Globalisierung* (Nomos, 2007); H.-P. Mansel, *Internationales Privatrecht im 20. Jahrhundert. Der Einfluss von Gerhard Kegel und Alexander Lüderitz auf das Kollisionsrecht* (Mohr Siebeck, 2014).

[11] J. Bomhoff, 'The Constitution of the Conflict of Law', in H. Muir Watt and D.P. Fernández Arroyo (eds), *Private International Law and Global Governance* (Oxford University Press, 2014).

[12] See E. Mestmäcker, 'Die Wiederkehr der bürgerlichen Gesellschaft und ihres Rechts' (1991) 10 *Rechtshistorisches Journal* 177, and more in Section 4.5 of this chapter.

4.3.2 *Social Justice through Political Democracy: The Example of Hermann Heller's 'Social Rechtsstaat'*

The order that the market generates is to be respected and protected by law – this is the message of the Savignyian tradition in Germany and equivalent conceptions that hold that free markets are not only a necessary but also suffi- cient prerequisite of a good social order. All constitutional democracies have sooner or later and in different ways departed from these premises of laissez- faire liberalism.[13] What needs to concern us in the context of our reconstruc- tion of the integration process is the dependence of these departures from a democratically legitimated order of economy and society. 'Social justice' is not a given, but an order generated through democratic processes. Suffice it here to cite the constitutional theorist Hermann Heller, who has elaborated this view after Germany's first democratic turn in the Republic of Weimar.[14] Social justice, for Heller, is not predefined by the constitution. Rather, democracy entails a mandate to define social justice and a chance of accom- plishing politically defined objectives. On this reading, Heller paved the way for a proceduralised notion of justice in constitutional democracies. Precisely the linkages that he established between democratic constitutionalism and social justice are an impasse for Social Europe. As long as the EU does not establish a comprehensive democratic order it cannot realise an equivalent to the democratic welfare states of its members. This is not to say, however, that the quest for Social Europe would pursue a false utopia. It is to understand the challenges that such quests have to be aware of. These are manifold: as constitutional democracies the Member States remain legitimated to define their social orders. As Members of the EU they not only have to respect each other but also take their concerns and interests into account. Last but not least, they have to determine what they owe to each other. To put this slightly differently: their commitments to social justice have to be complemented by commitments to interstate justice. The following sections will elaborate these suggestions step by step.

---

[13] On all this, see the magisterial overview by D.M. Kennedy, 'Three Globalizations of Legal Thought: 1850–2000', in D.M. Trubek and A. Santos (eds), *The New Law and Economic Development. A Critical Appraisal* (Cambridge University Press, 2006).

[14] See H. Heller, 'Politische Demokratie und soziale Homogenität' [1928], reprinted in: H. Heller, *Gesammelte Schriften*, ed. by M. Drath et al., in 3 vols (Sijthoff, 1971), II: 21–433. For a topi- cal comment on Heller's lasting importance see A.J. Menéndez, 'Neumark Vindicated: The Three Patterns of Europeanisation of National Tax Systems and the Future of the Social and Democratic *Rechtsstaat*', in D. Chalmers, M. Jachtenfuchs, and C. Joerges (eds), *The End of the Eurocrats' Dream: Adjusting to European Diversity* (Cambridge University Press, 2016).

4.4 THE EEC IN THE AGE OF 'EMBEDDED LIBERALISM'

In the first step of our reconstruction we return to the foundational period, which we have characterised as the 'golden age of embedded liberalism'.[15] This notion is not widely used in European legal studies. It has been coined by the Harvard political scientist John G. Ruggie, in an essay that documented the coexistence and compatibility of open borders with welfare systems within constitutional democracies.[16] The validity of this analysis is widely recognised. Its relevance in our context should be obvious: both post-war trade regimes, the GATT and the EEC, had established frameworks that left 'the participating states with very considerable freedoms to pursue their regulatory objectives and distributional policies'. This is the conclusion of Dani Rodrik, whom I cite at some length:

> The considerable manoeuvring room afforded by these trading rules allowed advanced nations to build customised versions of capitalism around distinct approaches to corporate governance, labour markets, tax regimes, business-government relations, and welfare state arrangements. What emerged in a phrase coined by the political scientists Peter Hall and David Soskice, were 'varieties of capitalism'.[17] The United States, Britain, France, Germany, or Sweden were each market-based economies, but the institutions that underpinned their markets differed substantially and bore unmistakably national characteristics.[18]

Embedded liberalism is not a legal concept, but is well compatible with both the findings of eminent historians and legal analyses. In particular, the late Tony Judt has called the post-war political commitments to social welfare 'a common legacy of European democracies'.[19] Welfare state policies and practices were, of course, controversial in many respects, but they were understood as *national* affairs. Stefano Giubboni, who has reconstructed both the mindset of the founding fathers and the political bargaining over the Treaty of Rome carefully, concludes that we have to understand this disregard of the social

---

[15] Section 4.2 of this chapter.
[16] Ruggie, n. 4 in this chapter; see also J. Steffek, *Embedded Liberalism and Its Critics: Justifying Global Governance in the American Century* (Palgrave Macmillan, 2006).
[17] P.A. Hall and D. Soskice (eds), *Varieties of Capitalism: The Institutional Foundations of Comparative Advantage* (Oxford University Press, 2005).
[18] D. Rodrik, *The Globalization Paradox* (W.W. Norton, 2011), p. 74.
[19] T. Judt, *Postwar: A History of Europe since 1945* (Penguin, 2005), p. 791 et seq.; T. Judt, *Ill Fares the Land* (Penguin, 2010), p. 127 et seq.

not as a failure but as a 'historical compromise'.[20] The lack of a stronger social imprint in the EEC Treaty seemed acceptable. Eminent left-leaning economists supported this;[21] they expected very positive effects from an opening of national *Volkswirtschaften*.[22]

It is on that background remarkable, but not necessarily deplorable that the social was treated with benign neglect in legal scholarship. This is in particular true with regard to the leading school of thought of the time. 'Integration through law' was an agenda which supported the 'constitutionalisation' of the EEC Treaty by the jurisprudence of the ECJ and advocated indeed the transformation of the unruly 'state of nature' between nation-states into a relationship now characterised by both political intergovernmentalism *and* legal supranationalism.[23]

A not so comforting agenda was pursued by Germany's ordoliberal school. Some of its core messages were fully in line with the integration through law agenda. But this agenda was redirected towards a constitutional upgrading of private law institutions and economic freedoms. As Ernst-Joachim Mestmäcker has put it famously: 'The historical importance of the EEC Treaty consists in its relating the internationality of law and political institutions to the internationality of economic relations. In this sense the EEC Treaty embodies an economic constitution. The road to peace leads via recognition of the immediate legal relations among citizens who have no public mandate to fulfil but are delegates of their own interests.'[24] This, in a nutshell, is the message and foundation of the ordoliberal reading of the EEC Treaty. To substantiate: among the core messages of ordoliberalism were the fundamental human rights dimensions of private autonomy, the economic benefits of a system of undistorted competition, the indispensability of law as a means to establish such an order and to protect its functioning, and the restriction of discretionary state interventions in society founded on private law.[25] The

---

[20] S. Giubboni, *Social Rights and Market Freedoms in the European Constitution. A Labour Law Perspective* (Cambridge University Press, 2006), p. 7; more recently, see R. Dukes, *The Labour Constitution. The Enduring Idea of Labour Law* (Oxford University Press, 2014), p. 130 et seq.

[21] See, most notably, the 'Ohlin Report': International Labour Organisation, 'Social Aspects of European Economic Co-operation. Report by a Group of Experts' (1956) 74 *International Labour Review* 99.

[22] The German term retains insights into the specifics of European economies, namely their social and political embeddedness which will be discussed in Section 4.5 of this chapter.

[23] J.H.H. Weiler, 'The Community System: The Dual Character of Supranationalism' (1981) 1 *Yearbook of European Law* 257.

[24] E. Mestmäcker, 'Power, Law and Economic Constitution' (1973) 2 *The German Economic Review* 177, pp. 190, 192.

[25] For more detailed analysis, see C. Joerges, 'What Is Left of the European Economic Constitution? A Melancholic Eulogy' (2005) 30 *European Law Review* 461.

advocates of integration through law and Germany's ordoliberals did not know much about each other. But both agreed on essential points, in particular, the reading of economic freedoms as fundamental rights – and in both of their conceptualisations, the European legal order gained a transnational validity that did not require democratic legitimacy.

What this alliance between economic constitutionalism and treaty constitutionalism also shared was its complacency with regard to social justice in Europe. In this respect, the rationales of both strands of integration theory are different in a very essential respect. The 'European economic constitution' was perceived as a shield against such extensive state activities including welfare regimes. The mainstream of European law scholarship was by no means hostile to social ambitions. They were simply not on the agenda of the foundational period.

4.5 'SOCIAL REGULATION' AND THE PROBLEMS WITH A EUROPEAN 'SOCIAL MARKET ECONOMY'

The tensions between the economic and the social, so we can summarise, were kept latent in the foundational period. They were bound to become visible with the dynamics that the integration project began to unfold from the mid-1980s. It is worth noting that these developments were shaped by integration politics but again by no means singular or specifically European. In the final sections of his famous article, John G. Ruggie discussed the advent of new challenges to the balancing of national autonomy and international economic integration that were accomplished in the era of embedded liberalism. Under the 1947 General Agreement on Tariffs and Trade (GATT) regime, he underlined, objections to free trade were essentially economic, and tariffs were a nation-state's primary means of protecting its interests. By the early 1970s, tariffs had been substantially reduced. However, what then occurred was a steady increase of so-called nontariff barriers. These barriers reflected a wide range of concerns about the protection of health, safety, and the environment. They were now dominating the bargaining over trade agreements and their implementation. Ruggie's observations on these new obstacles to free trade were anything but hostile. He acknowledged that these developments represented and fostered a new type of embeddedness of markets. However, they also created new challenges for the international trade system as a whole. Domestic regulatory objectives that are generated in a nation-state's political system and often backed by constitutional commitments were now confronted with external objections as to both their reasonableness and their protectionist implications – the quests of external actor that reached behind the borders.

Ruggie, writing in 1982, could not predict how the international trade system would adapt to this new constellation a decade later by transforming the GATT 1947 into the WTO 1994, an institutional move that created more effective means for dispute resolution and was complemented by a number of special Agreements (such as the Agreement on the Application of Sanitary and Phytosanitary Measures (SPS) and the Agreement on Technical Barriers to Trade (TBT)), with rules for balancing the economic concerns of free trade with the social concerns of regulatory objectives.

4.5.1 *Social Regulation in the EU*

Unsurprisingly, the integration project was exposed to the same challenges. The responses that Europe found and institutionalised were surprising – in a positive sense. When the European Commission, led by Jacques Delors, launched its programme on the 'Completion of the Internal Market' in the mid-1980s,[26] its proponents and critics expected both an intensified monitoring of regulations hampering competition and regulatory competition fostered by the planned obligation to recognise national legal norms mutually. Under these new competitive conditions, EC Member States would seek to defend or strengthen their economic competitiveness by loosening their regulatory policies and, hence, a 'race to the bottom' would begin. Regulation was considered a cost factor, whereas deregulation was seen as a way to gain efficiency. However, these expectations were proven wrong. What followed was no simple broad deregulation, but an intensified re-regulation, which resulted in new forms of collaboration between state and non-state actors – later termed 'new modes of governance'. The post-national constellation, which Europeanisation has generated, has eroded the regulatory powers of nation-states and their competence to assess the costs and benefits of opening national economies autonomously. Yet, Europeanisation has also established sophisticated transnational governance arrangements, which could not have been achieved by nation-states on their own.

The contents and scope of this institutional ingenuity was simply admirable: the 'new approach to technical harmonisation and standards', the rise of the committee system (comitology), the move towards agencies that were charged with the regulation of market entry and exit, or with more general informal, and policy-informing, information-gathering duties were

---

[26] COM(1985)310, *Completing the Internal Market: White Paper from the Commission to the European Council Commission White Paper to the European Council on Completion of the Internal Market* (Brussels, 14 June 1985).

promising developments. What needs to be underlined in the present con-text, however, is the growing awareness of pertinent analyses of the legit-imacy problems of these new modes of regulation.[27] Contrary to many perceptions, the famous advocate of the transformation of Europe into a 'regulatory state' shared this concern and insisted time and again on the distinction between 'social regulation' and 'social policy'.[28] Social policy with distributional implications, Giandomenico Majone argued, required the type of majoritarian legitimation that only constitutional democracies could provide.

4.5.2 *Social Justice through a 'Highly Competitive Social Market Economy'*

It is, against this background, simply amazing and deplorable how careless the problems of social justice were treated by the European politics. Gøsta Esping-Andersen's seminal study on *The Three Worlds of Welfare Capitalism* was available from 1990.[29] Everybody could hence know and should have known why a unitary European welfare state was not conceivable, that it would instead be indispensable to live with a variety of models and organise their coexistence with the option to strive for the kind of Social Union envis-aged by the Cambridge/Leuven project. This was not ruled out in principle. But the most prominent response and promise given to the advocates of a more Social Europe and critics of the neoliberal tilt of the integration project was the 'social market economy'. That occurred in some haste at a late stage of the efforts of the European Convention to produce a new legal base for the Union in the form of the Treaty Establishing a Constitution for Europe. The idea was submitted by a French–German alliance of two very prominent pol-iticians, namely Dominique de Villepin and Joschka Fischer.[30] Their motion

---

[27] See on standardisation H. Schepel, *The Constitution of Private Governance: Product Standards in the Regulation of Integrating Markets* (Hart Publishing, 2005), on comitology, C. Joerges and J. Neyer, 'From Intergovernmental Bargaining to Deliberative Political Processes: The Constitutionalisation of Comitology' (1997) 3 *European Law Journal* 273, on agencies M. Everson, 'Independent Agencies: Hierarchy Beaters?' (1995) 1 *European Law Journal* 180.

[28] G. Majone, 'The European Community between Social Policy and Social Regulation' (1993) 31 *Journal of Common Market Studies* 153.

[29] Princeton, NJ: Princeton University Press.

[30] An early draft version of 28 May 2003 used the term 'social market economy' (CONV 724/1/03 REV 1 *Draft Constitution* (Brussels, 28 May 2003)), but the text was then modified by the classification as 'highly competitive' (CONV 797/03 *revised text of part one of the European Constitutional Treaty* (Brussels, 10 June 2003)). This version made it into the Constitutional Treaty (Article I–3 (3) Constitutional Treaty), and thereafter into the Treaty of Lisbon (Article 3(3) TEU).

profited from the positive connotation of this notion.[31] We can nevertheless quite safely assume that neither of them knew much – or cared – about the original meaning of that notion. But it is worth recalling that meaning if one is to understand what actually happened.

The concept of the social market economy was submitted by Alfred Müller-Armack in 1948 programmatically as a 'third way' between a planned and a laissez-faire economy,[32] that is to say, as a synthesis, to cite Müller-Armack literally, of 'more socialism [*sic!*] with more freedom'.[33] His work gained a quasi-official status when he served as the head of the *Grundsatzabteilung* (roughly: the think tank) in Ludwig Erhard's Ministry of Economic Affairs, which was entrusted with the task of elaborating the principles upon which policy-making should be based. Müller-Armack was certainly keen to underline the compatibility of his concepts with the ordoliberal principles of the Freiburg School. But it is precisely this compatibility that is highly dubious. Müller-Armack continued to advocate 'a system of social and societal measures', which included countercyclical fiscal policies, the striving for an 'approximate full employment', redistributive policies by taxation of all income, subventions for those in need, be it welfare, pensions, subsidies for homeowners, tenants, etc.[34]

This short glance should suffice to reveal that the 'highly competitive social market economy' is an oxymoronic notion and why European Union could not become a social market economy in the original sense of this notion as spelled out by Müller-Armack.[35] To be sure, we are free – and need to be free – to redefine and reconceptualise the social market economy. But we should then be aware of the continuities and discontinuities in our operations. We should also remain sensitive for the bases of the popular appeal of this legacy. As economic historians, most notably Werner Abelshauser, have documented

---

[31] Quite successfully! To cite just one reaction: 'Les tenants d'une Europe social se félicitent de quelques avancées – la référence à 'l'économie social de marché', au plein emploi, aux service publics', *Le Monde* on 10 November 2003.

[32] A. Müller-Armack, Die 'Wirtschaftsordnungen sozial gesehen' [1948], reprinted in: A. Müller-Armack, *Wirtschaftsordnung und Wirtschaftspolitik. Studien und Konzepte zur sozialen Marktwirtschaft und zur europäischen Integration* (Verlag Rombach, 1966), pp. 171–99.

[33] A. Müller-Armack, *Genealogie der Sozialen Marktwirtschaft. Frühschriften und weiterführende Konzepte* (Haupt, 1974), p. 46.

[34] See, on all this in more detail, C. Joerges and F. Rödl, 'The "Social Market Economy" as Europe's Social Model?', in Lars Magnusson and Bo Stråth (eds), *A European Social Citizenship? Preconditions for Future Policies in Historical Light* (Lang, 2005), available at: papers.ssrn.com/sol3/papers.cfm?abstract_id=635362 (accessed 13 October 2016).

[35] See Joerges and Rödl, n. 34 in this chapter, and more recently F.W. Scharpf, 'The Asymmetry of European Integration, or Why the EU Cannot Be a '"Social Market Economy"' (2010) 8 *Socio-Economic Review* 211.

in much detail, the multifaceted praxis of the social market economy is very much in line with what the later studies on the varieties of capitalism have characterised as the 'cooperative (German) model'.[36] Equally important, in the early years of the Federal Republic, the German economy represented an exemplary case of 'social embeddedness'.[37] This finding is significant for the legal conceptualisation of the economic and the social and their interdependence to which we will return in Section 4.6.

4.5.3   *The Internal Market as 'Social Market' and the Idea of 'Conflicts-Law Constitutionalism'*

Without exploring the conceptual history of the social market economy in more detail, we can conclude that the formula of the 'highly competitive market economy' has confirmed rather than overcome the schism between the social and the economic. For a good number of years,[38] I have advocated an alternative to this dichotomy, namely, the idea that we should not democratise Europe and its law, but instead build upon and strengthen the potential of European law to compensate for the democracy-failures of the nation-state. As the essay on comitology has underlined, this compensatory function includes the compensation of governmentability impasses that stem from the eroding capability of nation-states to govern autonomously. Comitology (as we have observed it) was our example for cooperative problem-solving that could derive its legitimacy from the deliberative quality of this activity. In this vision, the legitimacy of the European project would rest upon its potential to ensure a fair and constructive management of Europe's socioeconomic and political diversity, a vision pronounced with the fortunate motto in Article I-8 of the otherwise ill-fated 2003 Draft Constitutional Treaty: 'united in diversity' should be understood as Europe's true vocation, and – this is the jurisprudential gist of the approach – its vocation can be realised through a new type of conflicts law understood as Europe's constitutional form. The social in the European market would then be realised by the mutual respect of the

---

[36]   See W. Abelshauser, *Deutsche Wirtschaftsgeschichte. Von 1945 bis zur Gegenwart* (C.H. Beck, 2nd edn, 2011), in particular, pp. 480 et seq.; 523 et seq.; W. Abelshauser, '*E pluribus unum?* Eine alternative Strategie für Europa' (2013) 11 *Zeitschrift für Staats- und Europawissenschaften* 467.

[37]   See M. Glasman, *Unnecessary Suffering. Managing Market Utopia* (Verso, 1996), p. 56 et seq.

[38]   First in the essay on comitology co-authored with J. Neyer (n. 27 in this chapter), more recently, for example, in C. Joerges, 'Unity in Diversity as Europe's Vocation and Conflicts Law as Europe's Constitutional Form', in R. Nickel and A. Greppi (eds), *The Changing Role of Law in the Age of Supra- and Transnational Governance* (Nomos, 2014). Also available at: papers.ssrn.com/sol3/papers.cfm?abstract_id=1723249 (accessed 13 October 2016).

Member States for their economic and political concerns and the cooperative search for a fair balancing between European commitments and national
concerns. This reconceptualisation of European law through a 'new type of
conflicts law' was designed as a reconstructive project which would, in essential aspects, be in line with the praxis of the integration project, in particular,
its responses to the broad range of horizontal, vertical, and diagonal tensions
generated by the variety of national *acquis sociaux*.[39] These reconstructions
delivered a nuanced and often positive assessment of the integration process.
They contrast with the characterisation of European market-building as a
neoliberal project with a Hayekian or Anglo-Saxon neoliberal imprint that
the Cologne Max-Planck Institute for the Study of Society advances.[40] In
view of the multiplicity of actors and interests and the diversity of conflict
constellations with which the Union has to cope, the ensuing heterogeneity
is anything but surprising. The defence of the social in the internal market
does not require the establishment of a supreme social market economy at
European level. It can instead be realised through the continuous realisation of fair responses to the tensions between European and national concerns.[41] These findings can be summarised in the conceptual framework of
the theory of embedded liberalism. To cite a prominent non-European voice:
'Democracies have the right to protect their social arrangements and when
this right clashes with the requirements of the global economy, it is the latter
that should give way.'[42]

The most important exception to this evaluation is the recent labour law
jurisprudence of the ECJ.[43] Simon Deakin has pointed to an irritating coincidence: this departure from embedded liberalism occurred with the advent of

---

[39] For exemplary analyses, see, for example, C. Joerges, 'The Impact of European Integration on
     Private Law: Reductionist Perceptions, True Conflicts and a New Constitutionalist Perspective'
     (1997) 3 *European Law Journal* 378.
[40] See for example, M. Höpner and A. Schäfer, *Die Politische Ökonomie der europäischen
     Integration* (Campus, 2008).
[41] See C. Joerges, n. 25 in this chapter, at p. 481 et seq. In a similar vein, for example, M. Bartl,
     'The Way We Do Europe: Subsidiarity and the *Substantive* Democratic Deficit' (2015) 21
     European Law Journal 23; D. Damjanovic, 'The EU Market Rules as Social Market Rules:
     Why the EU can be a Social Market Economy' (2013) 50 *Common Market Law Review* 1685;
     J. Mulder, 'Social Legitimacy in the Internal Market: A Dialogue of Mutual Responsiveness',
     PhD thesis EUI Florence 2016 (on file with author); in comprehensive perspectives, see C.
     Möllers, 'Denn wir wissen nicht, was wir wollen: Krisenzurechnung und legitimationsprob-
     lematik im europäischen Integrationsdiskurs' (2015) 43 *Leviathan* 339.
[42] Rodrik, n. 18 in this chapter, at p. 19 (emphasis in original).
[43] See the critique by C. Joerges and F. Rödl, 'Informal Politics, Formalised Law and the "Social
     Deficit" of European Integration: Reflections after the Judgments of the ECJ in *Viking* and
     Laval' (2009) 15 *European Law Journal* 1.

the financial crisis.[44] This is indeed the disaster to which we now have to turn. As announced in our introductory remarks, our observations will be underlining the *continuities* between what we have recently experienced and the institutionalised praxis of the integration project. The Treaty of Maastricht is the consummation of this praxis: Maastricht sought to complete the internal market by Economic and Monetary Union (EMU). It also opened new perspectives for a Social Europe through the constitutionalisation of the social dialogue.[45] It moved, to use the language of Dani Rodrik once more, towards 'deep economic integration'. The socioeconomic diversity of the Union was treated with benign neglect and an institutional framework with the potential to manage the implications of this move was not established. This prioritisation of economic integration proved to be fateful, not only for the European economy, but also for the prospects of Social Europe.

4.6 EMU AS AN IRRESOLVABLE DIAGONAL CONFLICT CONSTELLATION

What the President of the *Bundesbank* Helmut Schlesinger had argued in the Maastricht litigation[46] is, by now, common wisdom: the separation of monetary policy from fiscal and economic policy, which the Treaty of Maastricht established, is a design failure. The implications of this assessment, however, are controversial. In Schlesinger's view, EMU should have been postponed until a political union had been realised. This is a widely shared view, albeit a hypothetical one for the time being. We have to consider alternatives. One pertinent suggestion is the move towards stricter rules. On this view the financial crisis can be attributed to the all too soft framework of the EMU and the noncompliance, in particular of Germany, with the Stability Pact.[47] This is a suggestion which survived the extension of the Pact in 2005, 2011 and 2013.[48]

---

[44] S. Deakin, 'The Lisbon Treaty, the *Viking* and *Laval* Judgments, and the Financial Crisis: In Search of New Foundations for Europe's "Social Market Economy"', in N. Bruun, K. Lörcher, and I. Schömann (eds), *The Lisbon Treaty and Social Europe* (Hart Publishing, 2012).

[45] See Dukes, n. 20 in this chapter, p. 125 et seq.

[46] 2 BvR 2134/92 & 2159/92, BVerfGE 89, 155. English translation: *Manfred Brunner and Others v The European Union Treaty* (1994) 1 *Common Market Law Reports* 57.

[47] Resolution of the European Council of 17 June 1997 on the Stability and Growth Pact, [1997] OJ C 236/1; Article 126 TFEU (ex-Article 104 EC Treaty) in conjunction with Protocol No. 12.

[48] Resolution of the European Council on the Stability and Growth Pact, OJ C 236 of 2 August 1997; Article 126 TFEU (ex-Article 104 EC Treaty) in conjunction with Protocol No. 12, the Pact now consists of Council Regulation 1466/97/EC of 7 July 1997 on the strengthening of the surveillance of budgetary positions and the surveillance and coordination of economic policies, [1997] OJ L 209 (the 'preventive arm', based on Article 121 TFEU) and Council Regulation 1467/97/EC of 7 July 1997 on speeding up and clarifying the implementation of

Again we observe non-compliance and political barraging over the proper responses.[49] This suggests that the quest for stricter rules and compliance did not cure the design failures of the Pact of 1997. The account of the Maastricht compromise and its legal characterisation submitted here builds upon my reconceptualisation of European law as a new type of conflicts law, on the one hand, and on two non-legal strands of research on the other, namely analyses of the European political economy delivered by the varieties of capitalism studies[50] and the inquiries into economic cultures by the economic historian Werner Abelshauser and his school.[51] It is neither possible nor necessary to go into these foundations in any detail here. A few remarks on their core messages and their interdependences should suffice.

Let me depart from observations submitted by Simon Deakin (who is not a disciple of either of these schools): '[T]he national economies of the euro zone were on different economic growth paths. The future debtor states were mainly pursuing policies of financially driven growth that were dependent on an expansion of private credit and on increasing asset prices in the markets for commercial and residential property.'[52] This is not the language of the varieties of capitalism studies, but it is very much in line with their insights. The socioeconomic discrepancies in the Union were already substantial in 1993. To expect that these economies would converge under the pressures of a common currency was naïve, to say the least. These divergences are the result of different policy orientations, historical experiences, political struggles, successful or failed political and societal initiatives. It is important to underline

the excessive deficit procedure, [1997] OJ L 209 (the 'corrective arm', based on Article 126 TFEU); see furtherec.europa.eu/economy_finance/economic_governance/sgp/index_en.htm (accessed 13 October 2016).

[49] On 13 January 2015, the European Commission issued a communication detailing how it would apply the flexibility provisions of the Stability and Growth Pact to encourage growth-friendly fiscal consolidation, see COM(2015)12 *making the best use of the flexibility within the existing rules of the Stability and Growth Pact* (Strasbourg, 13 January 2015).

[50] Such as T. Iversen and D. Soskice, 'A Structural-Institutional Explanation of the Eurozone Crisis' (2013) available at: citeseerx.ist.psu.edu/viewdoc/download?doi=10.1.1.714.6935&rep=rep1&type=pdf (accessed 13 October 2016); P.A. Hall, 'Varieties of Capitalism and the Euro Crisis' (2014) 37 *West European Politics* 1223.

[51] W. Abelshauser, 'Europa in Vielfalt einigen. Eine Denkschrift' (2014) available at: www.homes.uni-bielefeld.de/wabelsha/Denkschrift.pdf (accessed 13 October 2016); W. Abelhauser, 'Ricardo neu gedacht: Komparative institutionelle Vorteile von Wirtschaftskulturen', in W. Abelhauser, D. Gilgen, and A. Leutzsch (eds), *Kulturen der Weltwirtschaft* (Vandenhoek & Ruprecht, 2013).

[52] S. Deakin, 'Social Policy, Economic Governance and EMU: Alternatives to Austerity', in N. Bruun, K. Lörcher, and I. Schömann (eds), *The Economic and Financial Crisis and Collective Labour Law in Europe* (Hart Publishing, 2014), p. 90.

– under the impression of the current polemics against the German obsession with rules and the blaming of Southern Europe with moral failures and economic inefficiencies – that neither the varieties school nor economic historians have ever graded the objects of their enquiries. Instead, what these schools of thought underline is that our economies build upon different institutional configurations. They submit that these configurations have proved to be surprisingly resistant against the changes that European integration policies have imposed and/or sought to accomplish. What Werner Abelshauser underlines more emphatically than, for example, Peter A. Hall is a constructive potential and option: competition between the different configurations can be beneficial, whereas the European quest for ever more uniformity with its one-size-fits-all strategies is mainly destructive.

As lawyers, we have to deliver a legal conceptualisation of the conflict constellation that Maastricht has established. One seems most obvious: the insulation of monetary policy against fiscal and economic policy was bound to generate conflicts between the two levels of European governance. This conflict is one of categorically different types of authority. The authority of the ECB in the realm of monetary policy as it is institutionalised in its independence rests upon the assumption that monetary policy is to be insulated against undisciplined political pressures, and can be understood as an essentially technocratic task that should be guided by expertise. Fiscal and economic policy, however, are exercised by politically accountable and democratically legitimated bodies. The tensions between these two types of legitimacy are, of course, well known from national systems, in particular from Germany and its *Bundesbank*. But there are two important differences. The *Bundesbank* was, in many ways, socially embedded, and its independence could be threatened by simple parliamentary majorities. Equally important, the *Bundesbank* felt responsible primarily for Germany's by and large homogeneous economy. Its independence could be understood not only as being compatible with the democratic order, but even as a stabilising element that helped to balance the political demands and long-term concerns of the national economy.[53]

The ECB is in a fundamentally different position. It cannot focus on the concerns of just one country, but must balance the interests and preferences of a variety of ever more diverse economies; it must, as Henrik Enderlein has

[53] K.-H. Ladeur, 'Die Autonomie der deutschen Bundesbank – ein Beispiel für die institutionelle Verarbeitung von Ungewißheitsbedingungen' (1992) 3 *Staatswissenschaft und Staatspraxis* 486; L.P. Feld, C. Fuest, J. Haucap, H. Schweitzer, V. Wieland, B.U. Wigger, and Stftiung Markztwirtschaftt (eds), 'Dismantling the Boundaries of the ECB's Monetary Policy Mandate' (Kronberger Kreis, 2016), available at: www.stiftung-marktwirtschaft.de/uploads/tx_ttproducts/datasheet/KK_61_OMT-Judgement_2016.pdf (accessed 13 October 2016).

put it, conduct a monetary policy for 'a country that does not exist'.[54] Europe's diversity poses two further normative challenges, which stem from an unavoidable politicisation of the ECB. The first is that, since the coordination of monetary policy with fiscal and economic policy affects different, non-converging economic and social systems, the ECB must set priorities among the members of the Eurozone; the best effort to define a proper average does not eliminate such an unequal impact. The second is even more delicate and affects our agenda more directly. It is under the common currency inconceivable to defend the prime objective of European monetary policy as long as the heterogeneity of the Eurozone persists and the economies do not converge. Christian Thimann, a former advisor to President Mario Draghi, has explained the philosophy of the ECB very lucidly in a contribution to the *Frankfurter Allgemeine Zeitung* of 2 August 2013:[55] price stability requires competitiveness, he argues, and the key to improved competitiveness are structural reforms, in particular, the lowering of wages. Under the imperatives of the common currency, internal devaluation is the only conceivable substitute to a devaluation of the currency. Structural reforms, however, concern the institutional infrastructure of the economy and its social fabric. This is why European monetary policy will impact upon a broad range of national policies. These implications have not been considered in the original design of the ECB's mandate. They are all the more problematical as they affect the *acquis sociaux* of the members of the Eurozone not only deeply but also differently.

To repeat and rephrase: the non-conferral of economic and fiscal policies to the Union level implied that the exercise of these policies by the Member States could pose fundamentally different problems to Europe's monetary policy. The resulting conflict constellations, however, were anything but uniform. They did not present the type of vertical conflict for which supremacy would provide a response. The powers needed to resolve these problems remained attributed to two distinct levels of governance. The type of conflict resolution foreseen in Article 119 TFEU is 'the adoption of an economic policy which is based on the close coordination of Member States' economic policies', as substantiated in Article 121 TFEU. As is plainly visible from the legal texts and substantiated by meticulous analyses,[56] this instrument was a *lex imperfecta*, an order devoid of meaningful sanctions. The functioning of

---

[54]   H. Enderlein, 'The Euro as a Showcase for Exploratory Governance: Why There are no Simple Answers', in Hertie School of Governance (ed.), *Governance Report 2015* (Oxford University Press, 2015), p. 29.

[55]   C. Thimann, 'Wettbewerbsfähigkeit als Leitmotiv', Frankfurter Allgemeine Zeitung, 2 August 2013, p. 12.

[56]   B. Braams, *Koordinierung als Kompetenzkategorie* (Mohr Siebeck, 2013).

the whole new regime was dependent upon good economic luck and constant political bargaining.

If the Maastricht EMU and the Stability and Growth Pact (SGP) are, legally speaking, too soft, why not fix the construct through strong rules? This question, which is so often answered in the affirmative, leads us to the true gist of the matter both in practical and in constitutional terms. The diversity of socioeconomic conditions – even within the Eurozone – continued to generate a variety of interests. The differences of institutional configurations, economic cultures, and social norms all serve to explain why European command-and-control governance cannot accomplish its objectives. The normative and constitutional implications of this conflict constellation are of fundamental importance. There is, of course, nothing unusual or inherently problematical with compromises, incoherencies, or with hybrids embodied in or generated by legal acts. What is so problematical about the European case and what distinguishes the European order from consolidated constitutional democracies is the lack of political infrastructure and the unavailability of an institutional framework in which democratic political contestation could occur and legitimate a completion or improvement of the imperfect edifice that has been established. We have to conclude, sadly, that the Maastricht arrangement was an ill-defined political compromise, rather than a sustainable accomplishment of constitutional validity and strength.

4.7 FROM 'INTEGRATION THROUGH LAW' VIA 'CRISIS LAW' TO TECHNOCRATIC RULE AND AUTHORITARIAN MANAGERIALISM

The fragility of the EMU framework soon became apparent. Germany was the most prominent, but by no means the only country to break the 'rules' of the Stability Pact.[57] And yet, for a good number of years, it seemed possible to manage the new regime, and the common currency began to look like a success story. This perception changed abruptly with the outbreak of the financial crisis in 2008 – with financial markets becoming 'nervous', rating agencies rediscovering the socioeconomic fragmentation of the euro area and adjusting their policies accordingly. The follow-up has been retold often enough in

---

[57] The often repeated narrative about this disobedience is incomplete. Germany's over-indebtedness had to do with the huge costs of German unification; the 'sick man of Europe' applied a recipe which was apparently well targeted: the structural reform imposed under the Schröder government proved to be economically successful – and damaged not only Germany's neighbours but also its social democratic advocates thoroughly; see, in great detail, P. Manow, 'Social Protection, Capitalist Production – The Bismarckian Welfare State in the German Political Economy 1880–2010' (2015) Revised habilitation thesis, Constancy, chapter 7 (on file with author).

many disciplinary perspectives. The EUI in Florence, the legendary propo-
nent of integration through law,[58] responded through the launch of a project
on 'Constitutional Change through Euro Crisis Law'.[59] 'Crisis law' is an oxymoron, as a closer look reveals. We observe enormously prolific machinery
delivering 'more Europe' than ever.[60] The 'law of "emergency Europe"'[61] may
capture the objectives and contents of this transformation more adequately.
What kind of regime did Europe establish? Is all this legal? Does it deserve
recognition? We will not embark on all these queries here.[62] Even the social
dimension of the crisis will be discussed only in a specific perspective. Our
analysis will depart from the recent judgments of the ECJ in *Pringle*[63] and
the OMT-case (*Gauweiler*).[64] These cases are important because they have
endorsed the *praxis*, in particular, the conditionality of financial aid to 'states
in difficulties' and the imposition of structural reforms as advocated in particular by the ECB.[65] The ECB has not only become an enormously influential
actor in Europe's crisis politics, it follows an agenda with clearly elaborated
conceptual contours.

The core of the controversy over the ECB's OMT programme is the decoupling of European and nation-state powers in the spheres of monetary,
economic and fiscal policies. One crucial aspect of this conundrum is the
proper understanding of the mandate of the ECB. Advocate General Cruz

---

[58] M. Cappelletti, M. Seccombe, and J.H.H. Weiler (eds), *Integration Through Law. Europe and the American Federal Experience* (Walter de Gruyter, 1985).

[59] See eurocrisislaw.eui.eu (accessed 13 October 2016).

[60] Some 800 pages of 'essential texts' have been collected by F. Losada and A.J. Menéndez for ARENA in Oslo, with the information by the European Commission being updated contin-uously, see www.sv.uio.no/arena/english/research/publications/publications-2014/menendez-losada-legal-texts-vo1-120614.pdf (accessed 13 October 2016).

[61] See J. White, 'Emergency Europe' (2015) 63 *Political Studies* 300; see, earlier, E.-W. Böckenförde, 'Kennt die europäische Not kein Gebot? Die Webfehler der EU und die Notwendigkeit einer neuen politischen Entscheidung' (Does necessity not know rules? Design flaws of the EU and the necessity of a new political decision), Neue Züricher Zeitung, 21 June 2010.

[62] But see C. Joerges, 'The European Economic Constitution and its Transformation through the Financial Crisis' (2014) 15 *German Law Journal* 985. On *Pringle* see M. Everson, 'An Exercise in Legal Honesty: Rewriting the Court of Justice and the Bundesverfassungsgericht' (2015) 21 *European Law Journal* 474; on Gauweiler and the controversy between the German Constitutional Court and the ECJ see C. Joerges, 'Pereat iustitia, fiat mundus: What Is Left of the European Economic Constitution after the OMT-litigation?' (2016) 23 *Maastricht Journal of European and Comparative Law* 99.

[63] ECJ, judgment of 27 November 2012 in *Pringle*, C-370/12, EU:C:2012:756.

[64] ECJ, judgment of 16 June 2015 in *Peter Gauweiler and Others v Deutscher Bundestag*, C-62/14, EU:C:2015:400.

[65] See Thimann, n. 55 in this chapter.

Villalòn, in his opinion of 14 January 2015, has discussed these in three steps. His first observation is that the:

> Treaties are silent ... when it comes to defining the exclusive competence of the Union in relation to monetary policy. It follows that we are left without authoritative guidance when it comes to the definition of fiscal and monetary policy and their delineation from monetary policy. The division that EU law makes between those policies is a requirement imposed by the structure of the Treaties and by the horizontal and vertical distribution of powers within the Union.[66]

Step Two: The Treaty does provide us, however, with a clear definition of the objectives of monetary policy. This was underlined by the ECJ in *Pringle*[67] and is rephrased here: '[U] under Articles 127(1) TFEU and 282(2) TFEU, the primary objective of the Union's monetary policy is to maintain price stability. The same provisions further stipulate that, without prejudice to that objective, the ESCB is to support the general economic policies in the Union, with a view to contributing to the achievement of its objectives, as laid down in Article 3 TEU.'[68] The move from a substantive definition to an orientation via objectives is literally of decisive importance because it implies that the institution that is entrusted with the implementation of the objectives of monetary policy must be in a position to determine its content. The pertinent passage of the opinion deserves to be cited at some length:

> The ECB must accordingly be afforded a broad discretion for the purpose of framing and implementing the Union's monetary policy. The Courts, when reviewing the ECB's activity, must therefore avoid the risk of supplanting the Bank, by venturing into a highly technical terrain in which it is necessary to have an expertise and experience which, according to the Treaties, devolves solely upon the ECB. Therefore, the intensity of judicial review of the ECB's activity, its mandatory nature aside, must be characterised by a considerable degree of caution.[69]

What this statement implies is a very considerable restructuring of the European economic governance and an explicit rejection of the ordoliberal project of an 'economic constitution' in which the ordering of the economy would be guided by legal rules and justiciable criteria. This disempowerment of law is complemented by a weakening of democratically legitimated politics.

---

[66] Opinion of Advocate General Cruz Villalòn in *Gauweiler*, n. 64 in this chapter, paragraph 129.
[67] ECJ, *Pringle*, n. 63 in this chapter, at paragraphs 54–5.
[68] ECJ, *Gauweiler*, n. 64 in this chapter, at paragraph 43.
[69] Ibid., paragraph 111 (references omitted).

The ordering of the economy is instead conceptualised as an epistemic task which is to be delegated to a supranational bureaucracy.

The ECJ, building upon its pronouncements in *Pringle*,[70] subscribes to the views of its Advocate General: 'It must be pointed out in this regard that the FEU Treaty contains no precise definition of monetary policy but defines both the objectives of monetary policy and the instruments which are available to the ESCB for the purpose of implementing that policy.'[71] 'This prerogative of the ECB in the assessment of the economic situation has to be recognised as long as it does not appear that it is vitiated by a manifest error of assessment.'[72] What is then left of the powers of the Member States in the sphere of economic policy? In *Pringle*, the ECJ has qualified the financial aid under the ESM-Treaty as a matter of economic policy,[73] underlining that, upon 'the basis of this case-law, purchases of government bonds may not qualify as acts of monetary policy for the sole reason that they also indirectly pursue monetary policy objectives'. In *Gauweiler*, the ECJ added that collateral effects of monetary policy measures in the realms of fiscal and economic policy cannot affect the evaluation of the measures taken by the ECB:

> [S]uch indirect effects do not mean that such a programme must be treated as equivalent to an economic policy measure, since it is apparent from Articles 119(2) TFEU, 127(1) TFEU and 282(2) TFEU that, without prejudice to the objective of price stability, the ESCB is to support the general economic policies in the Union.[74]

The links of this reasoning with the agenda of this conference become apparent when the ECJ proceeds to the conditioning of the ECB's policy:

> The point should also be made that the ESCB, in a wholly independent manner, made implementation of the programme announced in the press release conditional upon full compliance with EFSF or ESM macroeconomic adjustment programmes, thereby ensuring that its monetary policy will not give the Member States whose sovereign bonds it purchases financing opportunities which would enable them to depart from the adjustment programmes to which they have subscribed. The ESCB thus ensures that the

[70] ECJ, *Pringle*, n. 63 in this chapter, paragraph 53.
[71] ECJ, *Gauweiler*, n. 64 in this chapter, paragraph 42.
[72] ECJ, *Gauweiler*, n. 64 in this chapter, paragraph 74.
[73] In the *Pringle* case, the Court of Justice has affirmed this with regard to the European Stability Mechanism, because its aim is the stabilisation of the euro currency area as a whole. The Court of Justice has held that such an act could not be treated as equivalent to an act of monetary policy for the sole reason that it might have indirect effects on the stability of the euro, see ECJ, n. 63 in this chapter, paragraphs 56 and 97.
[74] ECJ, *Gauweiler*, n. 64 in this chapter, paragraph 59.

monetary policy measures it has adopted will not work against the effectiveness of the economic policies followed by the Member States.[75]

These somewhat extensive references should be self-explanatory: the ECB has been empowered to go ahead with its agenda. This agenda relies on the imposition of austerity measures and the control of their implementation, i.e. by the ECB itself and many other so-called structural adjustments which, in the view of the ECB, will increase the effectiveness of its policies.[76] This is what Yves Mersch, Member of the Executive Board of the ECB explained, in a speech delivered on 15 June 2015:

> Structural reforms have a direct link to inflation, inflation expectations and real interest rates through their effect on the adjustment process ... [This is] why structural reforms are relevant for monetary policy and why it is legitimate that, as a central bank, we take a view on them. In a nutshell, in the euro area, the more divergent economies become in terms of their structural conditions, the harder it ultimately becomes to achieve price stability at the euro area level.[77]

We have to take into account that the ECB is an institution with unprecedented autonomy. The understanding of its mandate, to which the ECJ gave its judicial blessing, implies that the ECB has been empowered to insist on the flexibilisation of labour markets, the reduction of entry barriers to protected sectors, the relief of entrepreneurs from administrative burdens.[78] I conclude: whatever it may take to revitalise Social Europe, it needs to be welcomed by the ECB.

4.8 EPILOGUE: 'THERE MUST BE SOME WAY OUT OF HERE'

Although all this has been legalised by the ECJ we still should ask whether it is legitimate and deserves recognition.[79]

---

[75] ECJ, *Gauweiler*, n. 64 in this chapter, paragraphs 59–60.

[76] See for a lucid analysis I. Feichtner, 'Public Law's Rationalization of the Legal Architecture of Money: What Might Legal Analysis of Money Become?' (2016) 17 No. 5 *German Law Journal* 875.

[77] Y. Mersch, 'On European Unity: Economic and Institutional Challenges Facing Europe', speech at the European Economics and Financial Centre London, 25 June 2015, available at: www.ecb.europa.eu/press/key/date/2015/html/sp150625.en.html (accessed 14 October 2016).

[78] Feichtner, n. 76 in this chapter, lists further implications of unconventional monetary policy measures such as the reduction of the revenues from investments by pension funds and (re-) distributive effects within and between the Member States.

[79] The title of this section refers to E. Achtsioglou and M. Doherty, 'There Must Be Some Way Out of Here: The Crisis, Labour Rights and Member States in the Eye of the Storm' (2014) 20 *European Law Journal* 219.

I restrict myself here to three observations:

(1) The first concerns the very idea of 'Community' and 'Union'. There are socioeconomic differences that are bound to generate a divergence of interests, and economic and political conflicts. Responses of both the Union and the Member States to such issues have to respect 'the other', shared constitutional values and human rights. Europe must not turn any Member State of the Union into a zero-choice democracy.[80] Mutual recognition and respect constitutes the Union as Union.[81]

(2) Throughout the history of the integration project, European rule has oscillated between technocratic rule and democratic constitutionalism. But the commitment to democratic legitimacy cannot be overruled. The resort to non-majoritarian institutions has to be justified and delimited. The assumption that the ESCB and ECB, as institutions that are not legitimated by a democratic vote and cannot be held accountable by Europe's citizens, can be empowered to take far-reaching distributional decisions and intervene in all policy fields, seems simply indefensible.

(3) The third query is related to the first objection and concerns the praxis of conditionality. It is irreconcilable with the foundation of the European project to transform the principles of equality, mutual respect, and cooperation into command-and-control relationships. This constitutes an inacceptable intrusion into the practice of democratic political will-formation.[82]

The long-term impact of an erosion of the legitimacy of European rule is hardly predictable. We cannot exclude that political contestation, however disorganised, will intensify, that the epistemic communities organising Europe's crisis management will be forced to reconsider their recipes, that technocratic rule cannot be shielded against the European public and politicians who are accountable to their constituencies. It may become increasingly difficult for the Member States to ensure what Max Weber has called the *Fügsamkeit* of their citizens, on which the implementation of European prescriptions depends.[83] And yet, it may be more likely that complacency will

---

[80] The term has been coined by Heplas, n. 2 in this chapter.

[81] See C. Kilpatrick, 'On the Rule of Law and Economic Emergency: The Degradation of Basic Legal Values in Europe's Bailouts' (2015) 35 *Oxford Journal of Legal Studies* 1, p. 7.

[82] See A. Albi, 'Erosion of Constitutional Rights in EU Law: A Call for "Substantive Co-operative Constitutionalism"' (2015) 9 *Vienna Journal of International Constitutional Law* 291, pp. 302–6; J. White, 'Authority after Emergency Rule' (2015) 78 *Modern Law Review* 585, p. 590 et seq.

[83] See H. Urban, 'Stabilitätsgewinn durch Demokratieverzicht? Europas Weg in den Autoritarismus' (2011) *Blätter für deutsche und internationale Politik* 77, p. 84.

win the day and the crisis management will continue to muddle through ever more difficulties, and that citizens will learn to accept and adapt, that 'normalisation' will trump 'contestation'.[84]

Political theorist Jonathan White does not believe that we will witness a return to a constitutional condition with renewed legitimate authority. He suggests it inconceivable that 'a line will be drawn under the crisis period, such that the extraordinary measures taken do not contaminate the institutional regime that ensues'. This is because the crisis may return and, after the present one, it has not been possible to establish an emergency constitution which provides for emergency responses and their termination. He predicts that 'emergency rule will tend to blend in with normal rule, to the detriment of the political order's legitimate authority'.[85]

Dani Rodrik, whom we have cited approvingly at various steps of our argument, has in his work on the globalisation of the economy submitted a 'trilemma thesis'. He asserts the impossibility of the simultaneous pursuit of economic globalisation, democratic politics, and national determination (autonomy), highlighting that only two goals can be paired: either economic globalisation and democratic politics, or democracy and national autonomy.[86] He has recently argued that the EU furnishes dramatic illustration of this trilemma.[87] The Union could transnationalise democracy through federalisation and thereby defend the advantages of the common market. Federalisation, however, would imply that it would, at the same time, be forced to establish common European politics to legitimise the necessary assumption of fiscal and social policy, with negative consequences for national sovereignty. In the absence of such a de-nationalising will, Rodrik asserts, the EU will have to

---

[84] On this dichotomy, see C. Kreuder-Sonnen, 'Global Exceptionalism and the Euro Crisis: Schmittian Challenges to Conflicts-Law Constitutionalism', in C. Joerges and C. Glinski (eds), *The European Crisis and the Transformation of Transnational Governance: Authoritarian Managerialism versus Democratic Governance* (Hart Publishing, 2014). Kreuder-Sonnen has now (July 2016) delivered his doctoral thesis at the Free University Berlin (C. Kreuder-Sonnen, 'Emergency Powers of International Organizations. Between Normalization and Containment', PhD thesis Free University Berlin 2016 (on file with author), in which he has dedicated one chapter (pp. 155–212) to the reconstruction of 'emergency politics in the euro crisis', its actor configurations, the strategies pursued, the erosion of legal prescriptions, the emergence of a new type of transnational executive rule and the so far not very promising efforts to regain constitutional grounds. As a jurist, concerned with the fate of law, I appreciate not only the illuminating disentanglement of complex processes but even more the rare readiness of a political scientist to take the law really seriously.

[85] White, n. 82 in this chapter.

[86] Rodrik, n. 18 in this chapter, at p. 85 et seq.

[87] D. Rodrik, 'The Future of European Democracy' (2014) available at: www.sss.ias.edu/files/pdfs/Rodrik/Commentary/Future-of-Democracy-in-Europe.pdf (accessed 14 October 2016).

abandon the common currency and accept the implications for economic (dis)integration.

If Rodrik were right, Europe would indeed be hopelessly entrapped – for empirical reasons because deep federalisation with all its institutional conditions is not a realistic agenda in the foreseeable future; for normative reasons because as long as we cannot even imagine how to design a democratic process through which the European citizenry could be persuaded to pursue the federal telos.[88] Under such conditions the search for alternatives is urgent. The one we have defended in this chapter is certainly complex and demanding. To substantiate our plea with respect to the social in the European project: the distinction between justice within democratically accountable polities and justice in their interstate relations disburdens the European project from false utopian ambitions. The threefold commitment of the Union, to respect the democratic autonomy of its Member States, to strive for a curtailment of external effects of their policies, and to further targeted fair cooperative problem-solving, would in all likelihood be more favourable to the generation of solidarity in the Union than the kind of we-pay-and-you-obey strategy that the European crisis management has established and legalised.

Are such visions and in particular their legal framing in the conflicts-law approach compatible with the project of a European Social Union? Important affinities are certainly discernible. The not so plainly visible is the reconceptualisation of the relationship between the social and the economic. With its understanding of the economy as a polity, the insistence on and respect of its social embeddedness, the conflicts-law approach rejects the neat separation between economic governance and social policy with the primacy of the former. With its 'united in diversity' vision, our approach not only tolerates a variety of institutional infrastructures of the economies of the union, but pleads for their recognition as a diversity of *acquis sociaux*. The understanding of the social as a dimension rather than a separate pillar of the European project

---

[88] I am of course aware of – and admire – the work of Jürgen Habermas, and I find his passionate plea for a transnational (non-federal) European democracy (see Habermas, n. 1 in this chapter) theoretically fascinating. My disappointment with Habermas's Europe is the lack of any plausible pragmatic perspective on the realisation of his visions; see, for an ardent critique W. Streeck, 'What about Capitalism? Jürgen Habermas's Project of a European Democracy', Review of Jürgen Habermas, *The Lure of Technocracy* (Polity, 2015) (on file with author). Interestingly enough, in a post-Brexit interview with the German weekly *Die Zeit* of 9 July 2016, pp. 37–8, Habermas signals agreement with a good deal of Streeck's observations on the desperate state of the EU. Transnational democracy is now a project to be pursued by a core of Member States, but open to accession by others later. Are we to assume that the members of the euro zone are willing to go ahead with such steps?

seems well compatible with these suggestions. This is even more plainly visible with respect to the rejection of any one-size-fits-all supranational welfare state model. It should, last but not least, also be true with regard to 'the core idea', namely that 'a social union would support national welfare states *on a systemic level* in *some* of their key functions'.[89]

---

[89] F. Vandenbroucke, 'The Case for a European Social Union: From Muddling Through to a Sense of Common Purpose' (2014) *University of Leuven Euroforum Paper*, 09/14 (first emphasis in original, second emphasis added).

5

The Democratic Legitimacy of EU Institutions and Support for Social Policy in Europe

Marc Hooghe and Soetkin Verhaegen

5.1 INTRODUCTION

The economic and financial crisis that hit the global economy from 2008 on has had severe destabilising consequences for the European Union. On the one hand, various political parties and organisations questioned the legitimacy of the Union, and this wave of Euroscepticism also had a strong impact on the results of the elections for the European Parliament that were held in May 2014.[1] More specifically, the cost of EU membership has been repeatedly debated in the so-called 'net contributors', and it has been a salient item in the debate leading to the Brexit referendum in June 2016. On the other hand, and in complete contrast to this Eurosceptic point of view, is the strongly emerging vision that further European integration is required to address the current economic and political crisis.[2] Various pathways have been suggested for this further integration. First, the common currency within the Eurozone requires a further integration of economic, budgetary and fiscal policies.[3] Second, it has been argued that a stronger political integration of the European Member States is only possible and legitimate if the notion of a common European identity is being strengthened.[4] Third, and finally, it has been suggested that

---

[1] O. Treib, 'The Voter Says No, but Nobody Listens: Causes and Consequences of the Eurosceptic Vote in the 2014 European Elections' (2014) 21 *Journal of European Public Policy* 1541.

[2] J. Habermas, *Zur Verfassung Europas. Ein Essay* (Suhrkamp, 2011).

[3] P. De Grauwe and Y. Ji, 'From Panic-driven Austerity to Symmetric Macroeconomic Policies in the Eurozone' (2013) 51 *Journal of Common Market Studies* 31.

[4] N. Fligstein, A. Polyakova, and W. Sandholtz, 'European Integration, Nationalism and European Identity' (2012) 50 *Journal of Common Market Studies* 106; K. Grimonprez, 'The European Dimension in Citizenship Education: Unused potential of Article 165 TFEU' (2014) 1 *European Law Review* 3; S. Verhaegen, M. Hooghe, and E. Quintelier, 'European Identity and Support for European Integration: A Matter of Perceived Economic Benefits?' (2014) 67 *Kyklos: Internationale Zeitschrift für Sozialwissenschaften* 317.

a stronger European Social Union is necessary if the goal is to address the strong discrepancies with regard to the economic and social performance of the various Member States of the Union.[5]

In this chapter, our goal is to assess the feasibility and legitimacy of proposals like the one for a European Social Union. The level of legitimacy depends on two fundamental characteristics. First, there should be support for some form of solidarity or insurance mechanisms.[6] If European citizens have the idea that current levels of development or inequality are sustainable and do not pose a moral, social or economic problem, almost self-evidently there would be no further social support for social policy at any level. Second, even if there is support within public opinion for a stronger social policy, citizens still need to identify the European Union as the adequate and most effective level to implement this policy. A preference for social policies at the national, or even at the subnational level, might even prevent the European Union from developing into a truly European Social Union, as is envisioned. This second concern finds its origin in the fact that previous studies have shown that various forms of diversity (linguistic, ethnic, or religious) might have a negative effect on the willingness to invest in solidarity mechanisms.[7] To a large extent, solidarity mechanisms imply a boundary between the 'insiders' who are allowed access and the 'outsiders' who do not received the advantages associated with the solidarity scheme. If, for most European citizens, the group of insiders is being defined as only the inhabitants of their own country, this would render it more difficult to develop a social security policy at the European level.

5.2 PREFERENCES ABOUT SOCIAL SECURITY POLICY

There is a huge variation both between individuals and between societies with regard to support for social policy, redistribution and income inequality. While some societies are inclined to accept rather high levels of inequality, this is not the case for others. At the state level, it has been claimed that existing political rules and institutions determine political support for social policies.[8] Welfare state regimes create expectations and beliefs among the

---

[5] F. Vandenbroucke, 'A European Social Union: Why We Need It, What It Means' (2013) 2 *Rivista Italiana di Politiche Pubbliche* 221; F. Vandenbroucke, 'The Idea of a European Social Union: A Normative Introduction', Chapter 1 in this volume.

[6] U. Dallinger, 'Public Support for Redistribution: What Explains Cross-national Differences?' (2010) 20 *Journal of European Social Policy* 333.

[7] M. Dahlberg, K. Edmark, and H. Lundqvist, 'Ethnic Diversity and Preferences for Redistribution' (2012) 120 *Journal of Political Economy* 41.

[8] M. Hooghe and J. Oser, 'Trade Union Density and Social Expenditure: A Longitudinal Analysis of Policy Feedback Effects in OECD Countries, 1980–2010' (2015) 23 *Journal of European Public Policy* 1.

population that will continue to shape their preferences towards future policies and their attitudes towards those that are to benefit from redistribution or
insurance efforts.[9] Building on the distinction between various welfare state
regimes that has been introduced by Esping-Andersen,[10] the reasoning in this
line of the literature is that citizens' concepts of fairness and equality are being
shaped by their institutional setting, which would also imply a large degree of
institutionally shaped path dependency, as this congruence between welfare
regimes and popular beliefs in the long run benefits a continuation of existing
policies.[11] Experiences with welfare regimes thus determine public opinion,
which by itself functions as a barrier against change in the nature of welfare
regimes and social policies.[12] Especially in countries with a long tradition in
welfare regimes, this regime hypothesis clearly explains differences in public
opinion towards social policy.[13] The finding that there are substantive differences between countries and existing welfare state regimes would imply that
it is not evident to modify the scope of welfare regimes and social policies.[14]
Countries in Europe, and therefore also public opinion in these countries,
have experienced huge differences with regard to the structure of social security.[15] Following the logic of the impact of welfare regimes on public opinion,
we should expect that there will be a level of institutional inertia that is hard
to overcome. Adding a new layer on top of these existing institutional structures will inevitably lead to the question what kind of framework has to be
implemented, as clearly countries do not agree on the specific characteristics
of welfare state regimes that should be developed.

Support for social security policies will therefore depend to a large extent
on the precise characteristics of the policy being pursued. To a large degree,
social security depends on an insurance logic: actors are willing to invest

9   M.M. Jæger, 'Welfare Regimes and Attitudes Towards Redistribution: The Regime Hypothesis
    Revisited' (2006) 22 *European Sociological Review* 157.
10 G. Esping-Andersen, *The Three Worlds of Welfare Capitalism* (Princeton University
    Press, 1990).
11 M.M. Jæger, 'United But Divided: Welfare Regimes and the Level and Variance in Public
    Support for Redistribution' (2009) 25 *European Sociological Review* 723.
12 C. Brooks and J. Manza, *Why Welfare States Persist. The Importance of Public Opinion in
    Democracies* (University of Chicago Press, 2007).
13 C.A. Larsen, 'The Institutional Logic of Welfare Attitudes: How Welfare Regimes Influence
    Public Support (2008) 41 *Comparative Political Studies* 145; T. Jakobsen, 'Welfare Attitudes
    and Social Expenditure: Do Regimes Shape Public Opinion?' (2011) 101 *Social Indicators
    Research* 323.
14 J. Kulin and S. Svallfors, 'Class, Values, and Attitudes Towards Redistribution: A European
    Comparison' (2013) 29 *European Sociological Review* 155.
15 E. Guillaud, 'Preferences for Redistribution: An Empirical Analysis over 33 Countries' (2013)
    11 *Journal of Economic Inequality* 57.

resources in a collective scheme, based on the expectation that if they are confronted with negative circumstances in their life, they will also benefit from the collective effort. If insurance is the predominant characteristic of the social security scheme, the motivation to contribute to it can to a large extent be seen as an expression of enlightened self-interest.[16] While the actor has to invest resources, s/he gains the security that in adverse conditions one can benefit from the resources that have been invested by others. Even actors who currently have high levels of economic resources, can still calculate the odds that at some moment in their life, they too will be confronted with an economic downturn, which will force them to rely on forms of insurance or social security. An insurance logic would assume that support for this kind of policy should be spread more or less equally across society, as all members of society benefit to the same extent from the insurance coverage being offered by the policy. Some gradient might still be possible, as, for example, the highly educated know that the odds that at some point they will be confronted with a loss of income is lower. The important point, however, is that they cannot have the absolute certainty that they will never be confronted with such adverse circumstances, so that for them too it remains a rational strategy to participate in the insurance scheme. However, social security can also be based first of all on a logic of redistribution, transferring resources from the wealthier segment of society to the poorer groups. If that is the case, motivations to support such a policy can shift considerably. Those who have low income levels, in this scenario can only gain from redistribution so their interest should be to support such a policy. The high-income group, on the other hand, knows that they will lose resources as their contribution to the scheme will be larger than their benefits, at least on a short-term basis. Hence, they stand to lose from such a policy. In that case, it is not self-interest that will be a motivating factor, but rather feelings of solidarity towards others with lower levels of material resources. Potentially, this feeling of solidarity might be supplemented with a more rational insight into the importance of social cohesion, and it can be assumed that this cohesion level will be higher if inequalities remain limited.[17] It remains to be investigated however, to what extent such a more abstract reasoning is indeed present within society at large.

A second important question is on what geographical level this kind of policy should be implemented. If there is an interpersonal form of insurance

[16] A. Alesina and E. La Ferrara, 'Preferences for Redistribution in the Land of Opportunities' (2005) 89 *Journal of Public Economics* 897.

[17] P. Van Parijs, 'Basic Income at the Heart of Social Europe? Reply to Fritz Scharpf', in R.J. Van der Veen and L. Groot (eds), *Basic Income on the Agenda. Policy Objectives and Political Chances* (Amsterdam University Press, 2000).

or solidarity, this would imply that resources will flow from one individual individuals to another. This poses quite a challenge for the identification of the in-group, as basically actors have to consider all the others as part of their in-group. This would imply not only that these others will be able to benefit from solidarity, but also they will be considered as more reliable with regard to keeping up their own obligations in an insurance logic. If, however, the security mechanism is situated at the country level, this kind of in-group mechanism among the population might be less necessary, as in that case the solidarity or insurance mechanism operates between states. Of course, this kind of policy decision would still need to be approved by the population at large, but the consideration of whether or not to accept others in the common pool can be expected to be mostly situated at the country level, and less at the individual level. In that case, we would be less inclined to expect that a strong common group identification would be a requirement in order to support such a scheme.

Within the literature it is suggested, however, that there is not necessarily always a strict separation between individual and country level mechanisms. An apparent vulnerability of the interpersonal solidarity mechanism is that some beneficiaries will be considered as less trustworthy as they will benefit from the collective investment, without contributing themselves to these common resources. This kind of moral hazard or free-rider behaviour might undermine social support for an interpersonal solidarity mechanism, especially if the cultural distance between the members of the group is rather large.[18] One way to circumvent this problem is to rely on the presence of a third-party enforcer that curtails the possibilities of individuals to opt for free-rider behaviour. In the case of social security, this third-party enforcer can in most cases only be the state, or some state agency that has the authority to supervise the functioning of the policy. This kind of policy shifts the trust question: it is no longer necessary that there is a form of social trust towards and attachment to other community members; it is sufficient that one trusts the institutions to adequately monitor the way the insurance or solidarity scheme is operated. Even if one assumes that some beneficiaries will show a tendency to profit in an unfair manner from the system, the knowledge that the institutions will curtail this behaviour might be sufficient to increase the willingness to invest in such a scheme. In any case: confidence in the capacity of the administering institutions, therefore, might be vital to build support for forms of social security.

---

[18]   A. Bay and A.W. Pedersen, 'The Limits of Social Solidarity: Basic Income, Immigration and the Legitimacy of the Universal Welfare State' (2006) 49 *Acta Sociologica* 419.

If we want to examine potential support among public opinion for social security policies at the EU level, it is therefore important to take into account these potential differences. It can be assumed that solidarity mechanisms require a thicker form of interpersonal trust and community feelings than insurance schemes. As was mentioned, insurance can be a matter of enlightened self-interest, and in that case there is no need for an affective bond with the beneficiary, or potential beneficiaries. As the return in a solidarity scheme might be much less palpable, this in-group trust is more important in a redistribution policy. In that case, a common in-group identification is vital for the policy. Some studies have even shown that because of this mechanism, immigration and ethnic diversity might have a detrimental effect on the willingness to support increased social security expenditure. As it is assumed that part of the immigrant population will be dependent on social security benefits, the incentives for natives to invest in social policy are expected to be reduced.[19] The willingness to support social policy among members of outgroups is in general more limited, because in that case the odds that in some way or another a form of reciprocity will occur are much more limited.[20] Historically it can indeed be observed that most current social security systems found their origin within the framework of the nation-state, and this automatically installs a boundary with regard to who can be involved in this policy scheme.[21] As Kymlicka argues:

> [T]here must be some sense of common identity and common membership uniting donor and recipient, such that sacrifices being made for anonymous others are still, in some sense, sacrifices for 'one of us'. Also, there must be a high level of trust that sacrifices will be reciprocated: i.e., that if one makes sacrifices for the needy today, that one's own needs will be taken care of later.[22]

If social security will depend mainly on a form of interpersonal solidarity, it is a straightforward assumption that support for this policy will be dependent on a shared identity as European citizens. If there is solidarity involved, this incentive will be stronger towards members of the in-group (however that

---

[19] C.A. Larsen, 'Ethnic Heterogeneity and Public Support for Welfare: Is the American Experience Replicated in Britain, Sweden and Denmark?' (2011) 34 *Scandinavian Political Studies* 332; S. Mau and C. Burkhardt, 'Migration and Welfare State Solidarity in Western Europe' (2009) 19 *Journal of European Social Policy* 213.

[20] M. Hooghe, T. Reeskens, D. Stolle, and A. Trappers, 'Ethnic Diversity and Generalized Trust in Europe: A Cross-National Multilevel Study' (2009) 42 *Comparative Political Studies* 198.

[21] K. Banting and W. Kymlicka (eds), *Multiculturalism and the Welfare State. Recognition and Redistribution in Contemporary Democracies* (Oxford University Press, 2006).

[22] W. Kymlicka, *Politics in the Vernacular: Nationalism, Multiculturalism, and Citizenship* (Oxford University Press, 2001), p. 226.

group might be defined), than towards members of the outgroup. To put it differently: if a European social security depends on solidarity, we would expect that it will be supported mainly by those individuals who have developed a strong sense of European identity. If this common identity is not developed, it is much less likely to have feelings of solidarity directed towards other citizens of the European Union. We use the concept of European identity here in the sense that, for example, Risse and Herrmann and Brewer use the term, that is, as a strong and affective bond between the individual and the larger group of all European citizens. For an insurance system, on the other hand, this kind of affective bond is less vital, as this kind of self-interested exchange can in principle be conducted with a large variety of others.[23]

There seems to be only one functional equivalent for this in-group requirement, and this is the reliance on political institutions. These institutions will be necessary, either because the social security scheme is conceived as a mechanism operating at the level of the political system, and not on the level of the individual citizen, or because the institutions function as a third-party enforcer, making sure that the moral hazard of the social security system remains limited and viable. It is therefore not necessary to expect that the specific individual that now receives a benefit will also compensate this by contributing personally at a fixed time in the future. The principle of 'generalised reciprocity' means that there is a reasonable expectation that, somewhere in the future, one will be able to rely on reciprocity, no matter who is expected to contribute for that at a given moment. This expectation of generalised reciprocity therefore does not depend on an assessment of the trustworthiness of individual others within the exchange network. Governing institutional norms, or the impact of state institutions that can function as a third-party enforcer, might be equally effective in this regard.[24] While in the past national social security systems mainly played this role, it remains to be investigated whether institutions at different policy levels might be equally effective in this regard. An alternative reading to these findings is that moral norms do play an important role in the willingness to invest in social policy.[25] In that case,

[23] T. Risse, *A Community of Europeans? Transnational Identities and Public Spheres* (Cornell University Press, 2010); and R.K. Herrmann and M.B. Brewer, 'Identities and Institutions: Becoming European in the EU', in R.K. Herrmann, T. Risse, and M.B. Brewer (eds), *Transnational Identities: Becoming European in the EU* (Rowman & Littlefield Publishers, 2004).

[24] Z. Barta, J. McNamara, D. Huszár, and M. Taborsky, 'Cooperation among Non-relatives Evolves by State-dependent Generalized Reciprocity' (2011) 278 *Proceedings of the Royal Society B* 843.

[25] S. Bowles and H. Gintis, 'Reciprocity, Self-Interest, and the Welfare State' (2000) 26 *Nordic Journal of Political Economy* 33.

too, however, previous research indicates that the set of norms individuals use might vary considerably between countries, partly as a result of past experiences with currently existing social security schemes.

Also the regime hypothesis implies that institutions play an important role in this regard. Citizens show a tendency to internalise and support the norms that are being applied by the institutions that are responsible for implementing social policy. Hetherington has shown that support for redistributive policies in the United States does not just depend on levels of interpersonal solidarity and connectedness, but also on trust in the political institutions that have to implement social security policies.[26] Even citizens who do support solidarity as an abstract principle, will be less inclined to spend scarce resource on social security when they have the feeling that the institutions that have to implement these policies will not do this in a responsive and effective manner. Trust in both national and European institutions should thus help us to explain a preference to transfer redistributive policies from the national to the European level. Support for social security can find its origins both in interpersonal solidarity, as in belief in the legitimacy of the institutions that will implement this redistribution. Given the current Eurosceptic climate in a number of Member States, this might pose a challenge for the project of a European Social Union.

Theorising about public support for a European Social Union, or more broadly about a social policy at the European level, therefore leads to a number of conflicting expectations. On the one hand, it can be assumed that national welfare regimes will continue to have an effect on public opinion in the various Member States, and these persistent cross-national differences will render it more difficult to achieve a European consensus on the way such a European social policy could be implemented. On the other hand, a shared feeling of community among EU citizens and political trust in EU institutions could challenge this national perspective. Identifying with fellow-Europeans could increase feelings of solidarity on the EU level. However, we know from previous research that European identity is only weakly developed in most European Member States.[27] The institutional perspective rather leads to the expectation that if citizens perceive the EU institutions as trustworthy, they will be more inclined to support social policies developed at that level.

[26] M. Hetherington, *Why Trust Matters: Declining Political Trust and the Demise of American Liberalism* (Princeton University Press, 2005).

[27] S. Verhaegen, M. Hooghe, and C. Meeusen, 'Opportunities to Learn about Europe at School. A Comparative Analysis among Adolescents in 21 European Member States' (2013) 45 *Journal of Curriculum Studies* 838.

We thus expect a positive relationship between European political trust and support for social policy on the EU level. Also, a negative relationship is expected between national political trust and support for social policies on the EU level as respondents with low trust in their national political institutions are expected to compensate for this by diverting their expectations for social redistribution to a different level, for instance the EU level. Respondents with high trust in national political institutions are not expected to divert to the EU level. Additionally, we expect a positive relationship between having a (stronger) European identity and support for social policies at the EU level. Finally, in line with the insurance logic, we expect that citizens who are more likely to benefit, are more likely to support solidarity on the EU level.

5.3 DATA

The data used in this study are derived from a recent survey wave of Eurobarometer: Eurobarometer 79.3. This specific dataset is selected as it includes the necessary information to test the factors expected to drive support for social security on the EU level. Eurobarometer 79.3 contains data on all 27 EU Member States the EU consisted of in 2013. About a thousand respondents were interviewed in May 2013 in each Member State. A total of 26,605 respondents are included in the dataset. Respondents were selected using a multi-stage random probability sample and were face-to-face interviewed. By using multilevel regression analyses, we take the structure of the data into account (individuals are nested in Member States) and we can control for country level indicators which could explain differences in preferences for or against social policies at the EU level, as expected by the regime hypothesis.

5.4 OPERATIONALISATION

In this section the used variables are presented. We explain why they are included in the analysis and how they are measured. Descriptive statistics for all variables can be found in Table 5.2 in the appendix to this chapter.

5.4.1 *Support for Social Security on the EU Level*

We operationalise 'support for social security on the EU level' as expecting the EU to provide measures of social security. Respondents were asked in an open-ended question what their expectations are about the EU. Some respondents answered they expected 'social security' from the EU. For our analyses, respondents that mentioned this topic receive code 1, others receive code o. As this is a binary dependent variable, logistic multilevel regression analyses will be used.

5.4.2 Self-Interest, In-Group Solidarity, Institutional Trust

To test the relationship between self-interest and support for social security, we include the perceived financial situation of the respondent. According to the insurance logic, citizens base their preferences for social security on an assessment of their own financial situation. The more positive they perceive their own financial situation, the less in favour they are expected to be of social security. Respondents were asked: 'How would you judge the current situation in each of the following? The financial situation of your household'. Responses range on a 4-point Likert scale from 'very bad' (code o) to 'very good' (code 3). A measure for perceived financial situation of the household is used as previous research has shown that perceptions of one's financial situation are a better explanation for the attitudes of citizens about the EU than measures of the actual financial situation of an individual.[28] Additionally, this is a good measure as we should take into account that citizens are not always willing to report on their actual family income in a comprehensive or reliable manner.

The theory of self-interest, however, also leaves room for solidarity, as explained in the theoretical Section (2). Yet, an important restriction to this solidarity is the expectation that it is limited to the in-group. It is thus expected that citizens who have a stronger feeling of a 'European in-group' will be more in favour of social redistribution on the EU level. In other words, citizens with a stronger European identity are expected to be more supportive of European social policy. Strength of European identity is in Eurobarometer 79.3 measured with the following survey item: 'For each of the following statements, please tell me to what extent it corresponds or not to your own opinion. You feel you are a citizen of the EU'. The response options to this question ranged on a 4-point Likert scale ranging from 'no, definitely not' (code o) to 'yes, definitely' (code 3).

In contrast to the hypothesis that support for social security depends on whether it is organised for the in-group identified with, is the idea that citizens' trust in the institutions that organise this policy is crucial. Accordingly, a measurement is included for both national and European political trust as

---

[28] L. Hooghe and G. Marks, 'Calculation, Community and Cues Public Opinion on European Integration' (2005) 6 *European Union Politics* 419; M. Loveless and R. Rohrschneider, 'Public Perceptions of the EU as a System of Governance' (2011) 6 *Living Reviews in European Governance* 5.

citizens are expected to more easily accept social security when they trust the institutions that organise this policy. A sum scale is constructed for national political trust including whether respondents trust their national parliament and government. For European political trust, a sum scale was constructed of trust in the European Parliament, in the European Commission, in the Council and in the EU in general. Both sum scales are recoded to range between 0 and 1.

5.4.3 *Control Variables*

We included control variables on both the individual level and on the country level. On the individual level controls are included for a number of sociodemographic variables (citizenship status, age, gender, and educational level). On the country level the analysis contains a control for being part of the 'GIIPS'-group and the Eurozone.

We control for citizenship status as this is expected to be related with European identity, so with the feeling to be part of the in-group.[29] The data allow us to distinguish between natives and non-natives, based on the nationality respondents have. Educational level was measured by asking respondents when they ended their full-time education. Based on this information, categories were constructed indicating whether the respondent ended his/her full-time education before the age of 15, between the age of 16 and 19 years old, after the age of 20, whether the respondent is still a student or whether the respondent never had full-time education. As the most common category is to study until 16–19 years old (44 per cent of the respondents studied until this age), this category is selected as the reference category.

As we expect that having experience with a particular social welfare regime has an effect on citizens' social policy preferences, we also expect that experience with further EU integration influences citizens' preferences about social policy on the EU level. While social welfare is still mainly a national competence, members of the Eurozone are already more strongly economically and financially integrated. We therefore expect that there will be broader public support for social security – a form of financial integration – in these Member States. Given the fact that citizens of the Eurozone already have a wide experience in public authorities being exercised at a supranational level, a path dependency explanation might be that for these citizens, it will be relative

---

[29] O. Agirdag, P. Huyst, and M. Van Houtte, 'Determinants of the Formation of a European Identity among Children: Individual- and School-Level Influences' (2012) 50 *Journal of Common Market Studies* 198.

easily to transfer also other competences to such a level. For citizens from a country that holds on to its financial sovereignty, on the other hand, transferring social security authority to a new entity might be a rather difficult step to take. A dummy distinguishing between Eurozone and non-Eurozone members is thus included in the analysis. Finally, as the survey took place during the euro crisis, we included a dummy variable on the country level that distinguishes between the Member States that were most severely struck by this crisis (also known as the GIIPS-countries). Greece, Ireland, Italy, Portugal, and Spain were therefore attributed code 1, the other Member States were attributed code 0. We expect that citizens in countries facing economic problems will be more in favour of social security measures on the EU level because this would most likely mean that they would benefit from these measures. Supporting EU level security would thus be favoured because of self-interest at the national level.

5.5 ANALYSES

5.5.1 *Levels of Support for Social Security on the EU Level*

Before we investigate support for social security on the EU level, it is useful to have a look at the absolute figures. Respondents were asked what they expect from the EU. They could respond whatever they liked to this open-ended question so the options were numerous. Only 5.07 per cent of the respondents expect social security from the EU.

Figure 5.1 shows that significant country differences exist in support for social redistribution on the EU level. The strongest expectations about social security on the EU level can be found in Latvia, Estonia, and Austria; expectations are the weakest in, for example, Portugal, Cyprus, and Finland. Hence, not only the clustered sampling of the respondents, but the accordingly clustered levels of support for European social security show that it is important to take the multilevel structure of the data into account.

5.5.2 *Explaining Support for Social Security on the EU Level*

Following this presentation of the varying levels of support for European social security in each Member State, multivariate multilevel analyses are carried out in order to test which factors can explain whether a citizen supports social security on the EU level.

As can be observed in the null model (ICC in Table 5.1), 9.97 per cent of the total variance between Member States in support for social security is

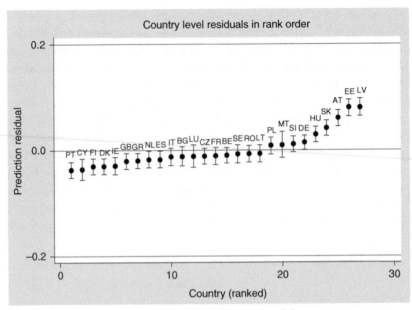

FIGURE 5.1: Support for social security on the EU level, by country.
Source: Eurobarometer 79.3.

accounted for by the clustering in Member States. This indicates that 9.97 per cent of the difference in support for European social security can be attributed to country-specific factors. A likelihood-ratio test shows that taking into account the clustered structure of the data significantly improves the model. Hence, we can distinguish substantive and significantly different levels of support for European social security between Member States (Figure 5.1). This is indicated by both the variance and the intra-class correlation.

In Model II, the relationship between the explanatory variables and support for European social security is presented. First, we find support for the idea that preferences about social security are driven by self-interest: respondents that have a more positive perception of the financial situation of their household are significantly less supportive of European social security (B= −0.341, p<0.001). All else being equal, scoring one unit higher on perceived financial situation of the household makes a respondent 29 per cent less likely to expect the EU to take care of social security issues. This confirms previous findings that especially those who stand to gain from social policy schemes will be in favour of their implementation, while the reverse holds for actors that are less likely to ever benefit themselves from these schemes. Second, we do not find a significant relationship between

TABLE 5.1: *Modelling support for social security at the EU level*

	Model I Null model	Model II Expectation social security EU	Model III Model with controls
		B	B
Individual mechanisms of solidarity and insurance			
Perceived financial situation household		−0.341[a]	−0.334[a]
European identity		0.009	0.071
National political trust		−0.192[c]	−0.266[b]
EU political trust		0.309[a]	0.305[a]
Welfare regime hypothesis			
Eurozone member		0.112	0.393[c]
Individual level control variables			
Citizenship status (ref: native)			
Non-native			−0.214
Age			0.019[a]
Gender (ref.: male)			0.376[a]
Education (ref. is studied until 16–19 years old)			
Until 15 years old			0.157[c]
Over 20 years old			−0.218[b]
Still in education			−0.468
No full-time education			−0.795
Country level control variables			
GIIPS country			−1.304
Intercept	−2.983[a]	−2.648[a]	−3.385[a]
Log likelihood	1986.8307	2028.3895	2140.802
Variance (country level)	0.393	0.434	0.275
Intra-class correlation (ICC)	9.97%	11.67%	7.71%

Footnotes: [a] $p<0.001$, [b] $p<0.01$, [c] $p<0.05$. Bivariate correlation tests and VIF statistics indicated that there are no problems of multicollinearity.

Notes: Regression coefficients of logistic multilevel regression analyses using GLLAMM are presented. N(individual level)=18,584 after list wise deletion of cases with missing on the used variables.[30] N(country level)=27. While log odds are presented in this table, the text speaks in terms of odds ratios, which are calculated as exp(B).

Source: Eurobarometer 79.3.

[30]   J.J. Hox, *Multilevel Analysis. Techniques and Applications* (Routledge, 2010).

strength of European identity and expecting the EU to take care of social security. The hypothesis that citizens are more easily willing to accept social security within the in-group is thus not confirmed. These findings (which remain stable when the control variables are included in Model III) hint at the conclusion that support for a European Social Union should not particularly be based on interpersonal solidarity and identity, as it does not seem to matter.

Third, we find a significantly negative relationship between trust in national political institutions and support for European social security. When a respondent trusts the national political institutions, they are 23 per cent less likely (in Model III) to be supportive of European social security. The observation that this relationship is significant, while there is no significant relationship between European identity and support for social security on the EU level is in line with the expectation that citizens rather look at political institutions for the organisation of social security, than at fellow citizens. Put differently, citizens who do not trust their national institutions much tend to divert their expectations to the European level. This can also be seen in the relationship between trust in European political institutions and support for social security on the EU level. This relationship is significantly positive (B= 0.305, p<0.001), which confirms the expectation that respondents who trust the EU institutions to function in a trustworthy manner are also more likely to invest in this level and are willing to pass new competences to it. When a respondent trusts the EU institutions, this increases their likelihood to support European social security by 36 per cent, all else being equal.

Fourth, the significantly positive relationship in Model III (B=0.393, p<0.05) between being a member of the Eurozone and supporting social security on the EU level hints at the path dependency hypothesis to be useful when studying the European integration project. Eurozone members are more strongly integrated in the EU in a financial way. As taking social security measures is an even stronger way of cooperation, we expected that citizens in Eurozone Member States would be more supportive of social security within the EU. This is shown in the results as respondents who live in a Eurozone country are 48 per cent more likely to support European social security (all else being equal). It thus makes a difference whether the respondent lives inside or outside the Eurozone. Citizens of a country that holds on to its financial sovereignty, are thus also more likely to reject the transfer of social policies to the European level.

Finally, for the control variables, we find that female respondents are more supportive of social security on the EU level than men and that older respondents are more likely as well to support social security on the EU level. For education we find that, compared to respondents that went to school until 16–19 years old, respondents who studied shorter have a significantly higher probability to expect the EU to take social security measures, while respondents that studied longer (over 20 years old) have a lower probability to expect this. No significant correlation is found for living in a GIIPS country. Respondents that live in one of the EU Member States that are most severely hit by the euro crisis are not more (nor less) likely to be in favour of European social security.

5.6 DISCUSSION

The goal of the current study was to investigate the determinants of support for social security policies at the EU level. In this regard, we mainly followed an institutional logic, leading to the assumption that the way in which these social policies are organised, also has a strong impact on public opinion.

In this study, we do not wish to argue about the incentives actors receive to invest resources in social security across Europe. Indeed, Vandenbroucke and Vanhercke claim that an important incentive might be that a stronger European Social Union is a prerequisite to ensure the long-term stability of the entire Eurozone, which will have a positive effect on the economic development levels of all citizens of the Eurozone.[31] It has to be observed, however, that this reciprocity mechanism does not operate at the individual level, but on the country level. For the inhabitant of one of the richer EU Member States the incentive to invest is not the hypothetical possibility that, one day, an inhabitant of the poorer EU countries will pay for her/his pension or social security scheme. The odds that such an event will occur in the foreseeable future are indeed very limited, given the strong economic divergences between the Member States. Rather, the insight has to be that the state of the economy of the richer EU Member States too will be affected by an economic downturn in one of the poorer EU states. In that case, a European social union is not founded on interpersonal solidarity or reciprocity, but rather on a realisation of the high level of interdependency between European economies.

At first sight, such a state level reciprocity mechanism might seem an unlikely foundation for a programme for more social security within Europe. Such a foundation might seem rather abstract, for citizens who are not familiar with economic policies, European rules and basic knowledge about economic cycles. But on the other hand, the entire literature on regime effects

---

[31] F. Vandenbroucke and B. Vanhercke, *A European Social Union: 10 Tough Nuts to Crack* (Friends of Europe, 2014), p. 51.

on support for social security is equally abstract. This literature suggests that willingness to invest in social security schemes on a national level, is not dependent on an assessment of the morality of individual recipients of social security efforts. From an institutionalist perspective, it can be argued that this support is based on an expectation about how the institutions will behave in the future, and what benefits the actor will receive from these institutions and the policies they embody.[32] In a similar manner, on a EU level too, these institutions might have a similar effect. If European citizens are convinced that the European political, monetary and social framework has tangible benefits for their own level of well-being, gradually support might develop to add a stronger social dimension to the European institutional framework. An advantage of such a scheme is also that it does not respond to a zero-sum logic. Placing the emphasis on social exchange between the richer and the poorer EU Member States inevitably means that every euro that is transferred from rich to poor, is lost for those rich countries, while the odds are rather small that the transfer will be reversed in the near future. Developing a European social architecture, however, implies that this jumping scale has beneficiary effects on all European economies, and this leads to the development of a win–win situation. Framed this way, inhabitants of the rich EU Member States no longer should have the feeling that they are asked to make a 'sacrifice' for the poorer EU countries.

Vandenbroucke and Vanhercke note that a stronger social dimension of the European Union can be based both on solidarity and mutual insurance, and most likely 'a mixture of both'.[33] The solidarity mechanism 'implies a propensity to cooperate and share with others similarly disposed, even at personal cost'.[34] The current analysis suggests that this interpersonal solidarity mechanism currently is only weakly developed within Europe. Not only is the sense of a European identity not all that widespread, but we have even seen that identifying as a European might not have any impact on the willingness to support redistribution at the European level. To put it differently: it would be wrong to expect that if Europeans gradually identify to a larger extent as European, this will automatically lead to the establishment of interpersonal ties of solidarity across the European continent. The common bonds between European citizens, for the time being, remain too weak to support the development of a strong social policy that is based on interpersonal solidarity. The fact

---

[32] Brooks and Manza, n. 12 in this chapter.
[33] Vandenbroucke and Vanhercke, n. 31 in this chapter, at p. 61.
[34] H. Gintis, *Game Theory Evolving: A Problem-centered Introduction to Modeling Strategic Behavior* (Princeton University Press, 2000) p. 288.

that we can observe such a strong and significant effect of one's own income position suggest that among the wealthier segments of European society, there is less willingness to invest resources into this kind of social security.

This does not imply, however, that the proposal for a European Social Union as such should be dismissed. It does imply that the insurance element of the proposal, especially at the aggregate level, will need to be emphasised in order to strengthen the public legitimacy of this proposal. From a functionalist perspective, this is a likely development. The European monetary union is a well-established fact, and its functioning and stability could and should have an effect on public opinion that is more than eager to preserve the economic benefits of this governance scheme. The fact that support for a European social security is higher in countries that are a member of the Eurozone, supports this path dependency hypothesis. For Europeans that have become used to have a joint currency and a joint financial policy, apparently it is also easier to imagine a common social security policy. In a way, this reverses the policy logic.

This institutional logic does not only apply to Eurozone members; also citizens' attitudes about EU institutions influence their support for EU level social policy. If citizens have the conviction that the EU institutions function in an effective and trustworthy manner, this does increase their willingness to transfer new policy domains to these European institutions. From an institutionalist perspective, we can argue that what matters most is trust in the institutions, and to a lesser extent, trust in each and every one of one's fellow citizens. This logic implies that a European Social Union should not just be seen as an individual mechanism of insurance or solidarity. If we focus on individuals, the insurance element is rendered very unlikely. Social security would imply that resources will be transferred from the archetypical Swedish dentist to the retired Greek worker. The likelihood that this individual solidarity will ever be reversed is almost zero, given the huge differences with regard to economic development levels within the EU. The focus therefore has to be at the country level. A more prosperous and cohesive European Union has important economic benefits, also for the Swedish dentist. Defined in this manner, a European Social Union can be conceptualised as a common good, with benefits flowing to all members, whether or not they as an individual receive resources from the system. As such, we can relate to a long line of studies on the sustainability of common goods.[35] Governing the commons does not require a high level of trust in each and every individual that might benefit from joining these common pools of resources. This form of trust in

---

[35] E. Ostrom, *Understanding Institutional Diversity* (Princeton University Press, 2005).

the political institutions does remain necessary in two different scenarios. On the one hand, it could be possible to organise the social security scheme on the country level, but that would still imply that these countries receive a sufficiently high level of legitimacy from their population in order to embark on such an ambitious policy scheme. On the other hand, even if one would envision an interpersonal social security scheme, the political institutions might still function as a third-party enforcer, and in that case too, it seems vital that citizens trust the institutions that will implement the social policy. In both cases, public support ultimately seems to be dependent on trust in the institutions that will have to implement the new policy.

But it does require a high level of trust in the effectiveness of the institutions that will govern these commons and this is most likely the main challenge for the European institutions as they currently function. The European institutions have been faced with an enormous challenge in their struggle to uphold the levels of prosperity of European citizens. These efforts have not always been successful, and the outcome of the European elections of May 2014 and the Brexit referendum of June 2016 suggest that this has further eroded the legitimacy of the European Union. But simultaneously the EU needs higher levels of legitimacy, if it wants to play its role and protect the European social model. The long-term answer to the prevailing climate of Euroscepticism is not less Europe, but more and more effective, and therefore also a more legitimate Europe.

5.7 APPENDIX

TABLE 5.2: *Descriptive statistics of the used variables*

Variable	Mean	Minimum	Maximum
Perceived financial situation household	1.605	0	3
National political trust	0.297	0	1
EU political trust	0.459	0	1
European identity	1.729	0	3
Age	48.66	15	94

	Proportion
Gender	
Male	48.43%
Female	51.57%
Citizenship status	
Native	98.09%
Non-native	1.91%
Education	
Until 15 years old	16.20%
Until 16–19 years old	44.25%
Over 20 years old	32.02%
Still in education	6.94%
No full-time education	0.59%
Eurozone member	65.89% is member
GIIPS country	20.06% is member

Notes: N= 18,584 after list-wise deletion of cases with missings on the used variables.
Source: Eurobarometer 79.3 (2013).

PART II

Topics in European Governance

6

The Impact of Eurozone Governance on
Welfare State Stability

László Andor

6.1 INTRODUCTION

The European Union, also in its Treaty, is committed to economic, social, and territorial cohesion, balanced growth and upward convergence. After years of financial, economic, and social crises, the gap between these ideals and the reality has to be noted, and taken seriously. However, the gap is not only a product of the recent crisis, but is a product of a longer period of transformation. In the last 25 years, Europe was transformed by two main projects. The first project is the establishment of a Single Market and a single currency. The second one is the Eastward enlargement (2004, 2007, and 2013). The impact of these two projects on cohesion and convergence is a critical question for academic studies and public policy at the same time. In the following sections, we analyse the nature of asymmetry, divergence and imbalances in the Eurozone, and outline the relevant policy responses that have been developed or considered to address these imbalances. Furthermore, we elaborate on what is still missing, if our aim is to stress welfare state resilience in particular.

6.2 EURO AREA IMBALANCES AND DIVERGENCE

The dual transformation of Europe has resulted in a deeply imbalanced union. South–North imbalances can be interpreted as a core–periphery relation, which gave rise to dangerous divergences at the time of the recent crisis, with severe implications for the national welfare systems on the Eurozone periphery. In this section we analyse the origin of divergence and its manifestation within the social dimension.

6.2.1 Core and Periphery in the EU and the Eurozone

Core and periphery used to be a conceptual framework to describe the world (economic) system. Western Europe, a geographical area of former colonial powers, formed part of the core of the world system. Countries of East Central Europe have formed part of a semi-periphery, with various historical cycles of attempted 'catching-up' with the West, and often finding itself in a dependent relation with it. In recent years, core and periphery have been increasingly used to describe relations within Europe, within the EU, and within the Eurozone.[1] Various components of dependency theory and the original core–periphery analysis have inspired the study of intra-European political economy: the international division of labour, the functioning of transnational corporations, international capital flows, as well as currency regimes and exchange rate policy. The interventions and policies of international financial institutions in the 1980s and 1990s created a bridge between the global South and the European East. However, while both East and South in Europe are often referred to as periphery, the nature of core–periphery relations differs if we look at the East and South of Europe, and their connection with specific layers of European integration. The Eastern European periphery has been mainly connected with and an issue for the imbalances within the Single Market (Eastern Member States are either outside the Eurozone or just recently joined.) On the other hand, the South–North polarisation became an issue of the monetary union.

The political dividing lines have been eliminated between East and West, but the economic gaps, in particular productivity and income gaps, have continued to exist.[2] For sure, in spite of the recent economic crisis, and the marked vulnerability of some Eastern Member States, the wide income gap between old and new Member States continued to diminish in the years of EU membership. However, these existing gaps have created tensions in the social dimension of the Single Market, which highlights the importance of social legislation, employment policy coordination, and cohesion policy.[3]

---

[1] L. Bruszt and B. Greskovits, 'Transnationalization, Social Integration, and Capitalist Diversity in the East and the South' (2009) 44 *Studies in Comparative International Development* 411; and W. Dymarski, M. Frangakis, and J. Leaman (eds), *The Deepening Crisis of the European Union: The Case for Radical Change* (Poznan University Press, 2014).
[2] B. Galgóczi, J. Leschke, and A. Watt, *EU Labour Migration since Enlargement: Trends, Impacts and Policies* (Ashgate, 2013).
[3] E. Vaccarino and Z. Darvas, ' "Social dumping" and posted workers: a new clash within the EU', Bruegel, 7 March 2016, available at: bruegel.org/2016/03/social-dumping-and-posted-workers-a-new-clash-within-the-eu/ (accessed 31 October 2016).

While there are various structural differences across countries that constitute the Eurozone, their internal imbalances tend to be linked to the issue of handling economic cycles, and require the establishment and proper functioning of financial and monetary instruments. The EMU has been built around the assumption of convergence and specific convergence criteria (ex ante but also after joining). However, in the absence of a capacity to deal with cyclicality and asymmetry within the EMU, this convergence becomes either temporary or illusory. The discrepancy between nominal and real convergence is therefore the key to understanding these imbalances specific to the Eurozone.

East and West, North and South are often used as synonyms for core and periphery in the EU. In reality, South and North only vaguely cover the groups of countries in asymmetric situations in the EMU. The actual 'financial' South, meaning the Eurozone periphery, also includes Ireland, the three Baltic states, together with Slovenia and Slovakia, which were pioneers among Eastern Member States to adopt the euro as their national currencies, but without jumping to the developmental level of the continental core.

The Maastricht model lead to a situation in which EMU membership for peripheral countries entails greater confidence and consequently favourable pricing of finance – for private as well as public actors – in times of growth. In contrast, during times of recession, financial fragmentation increases the costs of borrowing and also the risk of insolvency for these Member States. Capital flight usually aggravates this situation, also in connection with the lack of full confidence in the future of the Eurozone, or in its composition.

Since 2007, Eurozone peripheries experienced deep and long recessions, and subsequently painful periods of fiscal adjustment. The recent financial crisis has practically undone much of the previous convergence between Eurozone periphery and core. The available adjustment mechanism, which is based on internal devaluation, focused on cost competitiveness, but at the same time it weakened the human capital base of peripheral Member States while public debt to GDP ratios continued to rise. In contrast, debt ratios either stagnated or increased only moderately in the core countries, leading to polarisation within the Eurozone. At the same time, Member States diverged in terms of welfare state capacity and industrial relations, which is not less important. Arguably, divergences between the core and the periphery of the Eurozone are a greater danger to the sustainability of the EMU and the stability of the EU than imbalances within the Single Market, which are mainly related to East–West relations. Therefore, the social dimension of this asymmetry requires specific attention.

6.2.2 *The Social Impact of the Crisis and the Crisis Response*

The sovereign debt crisis of 2010 and the subsequent fiscal consolidation strategies have substantially weakened the welfare state in peripheral Eurozone countries.[4] In particular, they have weakened the effectiveness of so called automatic fiscal stabilisers at the national level. In other words, the ability of states to immediately act in a countercyclical way as tax revenues drop and social expenditure increases, was adversely affected.

Unemployment increased to 11 per cent in the EU and 12 per cent in the euro area in 2013, but it became twice as high in the Eurozone periphery. Unemployment amounted to a quarter of the workforce in both Spain and Greece in 2013, and youth unemployment rates peaked above 50 per cent in both. In these two countries, income inequality (as measured by the GINI index) was already higher than the EU average before the crisis, and it continued to grow further in the crisis years. In other adjusting countries, where economic growth was negative and unemployment was on the rise in 2011–13, poverty has also risen significantly. Demand for the services of food banks has grown and many young people lacking opportunities choose to emigrate, often to other continents, which by definition results in a loss of human capital for Europe as a whole. These developments resulted in the adoption of a Communication on Strengthening the Social Dimension of the EMU by the European Commission (October 2013). In this document a scoreboard of key employment and social indicators was proposed. The scoreboard demonstrated that overall unemployment and youth unemployment and inactivity, along with income inequality and poverty, showed significant and dangerous divergence during the crisis, especially inside the Eurozone.[5]

Why did Europe become so divided in terms of economic and social outcomes? A key factor has been the design of the EMU, with monetary policy being centralised at the ECB, but fiscal and structural policies being predominantly under the responsibility of national governments, without there being any Eurozone budget in place. This means that instruments that were

[4] D. Vaughan-Whitehead (ed.), *The European Social Model in Crisis: Is Europe Losing Its Soul?* (Edward Elgar, 2015); and J.E. Dolvik, and A. Martin (eds), *European Social Models from Crisis to Crisis. Employment and Inequality in the Era of Monetary Integration* (Oxford University Press, 2015).

[5] European Commission, *Employment and Social Developments in Europe 2014* (Publications Office of the European Union, 2015).

historically used to limit the social impact of crises were not available any more, while there was nothing to replace them.

Europe's jobs crisis is linked to its weak macroeconomic performance, and notably to less effective fiscal and monetary responses than in the US and Japan.[6] European labour markets are being adversely affected by a persistent gap in most Member States between effective aggregate demand and potential output, in a context of high unemployment, the large overhang of private debt, low inflation and nominal interest rates that are close to their lower limit. Due to the imperfect nature of the EMU, adjustment to economic shocks tends to occur not through expansionary fiscal or monetary policies that would temporarily drive up inflation and reduce unemployment, but through internal devaluations in deficit countries, which lead to low inflation – or outright deflation – and are accompanied by high levels of unemployment. Yet wage-inflationary pressures are much less likely nowadays than in the 1970s or 1980s because of the changes undergone by weakened trade unions – collective bargaining has become more decentralised and is easier to opt out of. In many EU countries, such as Spain and Germany, nominal unit labour costs have not kept up with increases in overall prices due to deliberate wage constraint or inefficient product markets. The result has been a further compression of aggregate demand and an even more pronounced impact on unemployment.

In 2010, the EU adopted a long-term strategy, Europe 2020, which, among other goals, aimed at increasing employment to 75 per cent (within the 20–64 years age group) and reduce the number of people living at risk of poverty or social exclusion by at least 20 million. However, the functioning of the single currency (especially at a time of crisis) makes the Europe 2020 targets de facto unattainable, even with a big delay. A stronger social dimension, which is crucial for the legitimacy of the European project, requires a fresh look at the original design of the single currency.

6.3 THE ORIGIN OF DIVERGENCE

The EMU was established with an unprecedented divorce between the main monetary and fiscal authorities,[7] with the idea of moving progressively towards common economic governance. The incompleteness of the EMU, however, was fatally exposed once the financial crisis hit, and has often been pointed out

---

[6] L. Andor, 'Is High Unemployment Here to Stay?' Europe's World, 26 March 2015, available at: europesworld.org/2015/03/26/high-unemployment-stay/#.WBdP_SRimfk (accessed 31 October 2016).

[7] C. Goodhart, 'The Two Concepts of Money: Implications for the Analysis of Optimal Currency Areas' (1998) 14 *European Journal of Political Economy* 407.

as key determinant of the long recession.[8] The removal of the exchange rate risk fostered capital flows,[9] which acted as a system of transfers – intermediated by financial markets[10] – instead of a common fiscal capacity.[11] At the same time, the lack of exchange rate precluded the use of an important adjustment mechanism, without creating a new one. The financial imbalances accumulated during the pre-crisis period were paving the way for an asymmetric effect of the shock caused by the financial crisis.[12] The post-Lehman financial sudden stop and the Great Recession affected countries differently: deficit countries were forced to adjust and, in the process, were further harmed; surplus countries could choose not to adjust, and effectively made that choice.

In the absence of self-correcting mechanisms, the first decade of the EMU made some countries more vulnerable through accumulating financial imbalances in the private sector. Some have noted that the whole EMU existence has been characterised by symmetric divergences in the current account balances and unemployment rates of the participating countries;[13] up to the crisis, unemployment rates were converging while the external balances were diverging. Once the sudden stop occurred and the external imbalances had to be adjusted, however, unemployment rates started to diverge dramatically. The problem of divergence seems intrinsically entrenched with the Maastricht model of the EMU architecture.[14] Nicholas Kaldor's fear[15] that a monetary union, imposed under inappropriate conditions, could backfire and generate political pressures against integration, is being proved right. In the EU, monetary integration takes place among countries that belong to different models of capitalism.[16] However, monetary integration would need a much wider toolkit to handle this variety than is currently available. The lack of a robust toolkit, either in governance or redistribution, has resulted in a high

---

[8] M. Obstfeld, 'Finance at Center Stage: Some Lessons of the Euro Crisis' (2013) *Economic Papers*, 493.

[9] P.R. Lane, 'Capital Flows in the Euro Area' (2013) *European Economy – Economic Papers*, 497.

[10] Obstfeld, n. 8 in this chapter.

[11] P. Pasimeni, 'An Optimum Currency Crisis' (2014) 11 *European Journal of Comparative Economics* 173.

[12] A. Regan, 'The Imbalance of Capitalisms in the Eurozone: Can the North and South of Europe Converge?' (March 2015) *Comparative European Politics*.

[13] P. Pasimeni, 'The Economic Rationale of an EMU Fiscal Capacity', contribution to the workshop 'Towards a Genuine Economic and Monetary Union', Oesterreichische Nationalbank, 10 September 2015.

[14] L. Andor, 'Can We Go Beyond the Maastricht Ortodoxy?', VoxEU.org, 13 December, 2013, available at: www.voxeu.org/article/can-we-move-beyond-maastricht-orthodoxy (accessed 31 October 2016).

[15] N. Kaldor, 'The Dynamic Effects of the Common Market', *New Statesman*, 12 March 1971.

[16] Regan, n. 12 in this chapter.

degree of divergence but also in instability, which in turn, is the source of low investment and growth and an erosion of national welfare systems.

At the time of the crisis, the euro re-divided Europe in terms of economic and social polarisation between 'South and North', risking the future of EU integration in.[17] Symmetric shocks may be as serious a problem as asymmetric ones are,[18] but in a monetary union of such diverse members even simultaneous shocks can be sources of polarisation. In the absence of well-functioning financial markets (perfect factor mobility), the Eurozone became a club of creditors and debtors, which significantly enhanced the dominance of core countries, and especially those with an AAA rate, over the deficit countries.

The gravity of the Eurozone crisis is shown by the high number of comprehensive EU initiatives that have been put forward to address and overcome this crisis. Most importantly, in 2012, the Presidents of the European Council, the Commission, the ECB, and the Eurogroup came forward with a long-term plan for the reconstruction of the EMU.[19] Monetary reform became a key component of the EU recovery strategy, and in 2015 the 2012 Report was followed up by another one signed by five presidents. The 2015 five presidents' report diagnosed the Eurozone with severe divergences and summed up key arguments for revamping the EU's economic and monetary architecture.[20] The divergences developed within the euro area represent the main threat to the existence of the single currency, and to the stability of the EU as a whole. Hence the need to reform the EMU architecture, and in particular to strengthen its real economic performance and its social dimension. This ambition should go beyond securing the short-term survival of the single currency.

6.4 POLICY RESPONSE TO EURO AREA IMBALANCES: EMU REFORM

Since the deepening of the financial and monetary crisis in Europe, reforms have been promoted at the national as well as the European level. In this section we argue that such reforms continue to be ineffective if they remain

---

[17] J. Stiglitz, *The Euro: How a Common Currency Threatens the Future of Europe* (WW. Norton and Company, 2016).

[18] P. De Grauwe and Y. Ji, 'Booms and Busts and the Governance of the Eurozone', Chapter 7 in this volume.

[19] H. Van Rompuy, 'Towards a Genuine Economic and Monetary Union, report in close collaboration with J.M. Barroso, J.C. Juncker, and M. Draghi ("The Four Presidents Report")' (2012), available at: ec.europa.eu/priorities/sites/beta-political/files/5-presidents-report_en.pdf (accessed 20 October 2016).

[20] J.C. Juncker, 'The Five Presidents' Report: Completing Europe's Economic and Monetary Union, report in close cooperation D. Tusk, J. Dijsselbloem, M. Draghi and M. Schulz' (2015), available at: ec.europa.eu/priorities/sites/beta-political/files/5-presidents-report_en.pdf (accessed 30 March 2016).

contained at the national level or at the level of the Eurozone without the creation of a fiscal capacity to deal with asymmetries and cyclicality. We explore the arguments pointing towards fiscal shock absorption, and the possibility of EMU unemployment insurance.

6.4.1 *The Pursuit of Better Governance*

The EU crisis response since 2009 has been dominated by a cautious cycle of financial sector regulation, fiscal consolidation, and structural reforms. Since 2012, the reform of the monetary union has also been on the agenda, while policy documents also called for boosting the demand side of the labour market as well as social investment.[21] However, the EU's efforts to develop the demand side of labour-market policy have been constrained.[22] These efforts by the Commission can be seen in the area of macroeconomic policymaking: the disinflationary bias in monetary policy, and its bias towards internal devaluation.

During the crisis, EU economic governance went through a major transformation in the pursuit of reforms that can boost productivity and the long-term growth potential of the economy.[23] After the launch of the European Semester (2011), the share of the 'economic' and 'social' components have changed by making the process – including the country-specific recommendations (CSRs) – more social,[24] and thus more balanced.

However, structural reforms, even if defined in a constructive way, cannot be the main answer to cyclical developments. Fiscal instruments are needed not just to replace but also to supplement other adjustment mechanisms, like structural reforms, and labour mobility. Structural reforms play an important role to respond to crises but they primarily provide a boost to long-term growth potential, without a short-term capacity to stimulate the economy. In the history of emerging economy financial crises, they always functioned in combination with currency devaluation. Labour mobility in principle (in textbooks) offers a solution to imbalances, but in reality it only plays a minor role,

---

[21] See the Employment Package, communicated in COM (2012) 0173, *Towards a Job-rich Recovery* (Brussels, 18 April 2012); but also related initiatives, available at: ec.europa.eu/social/main.jsp?catId=1039 (accessed 31 October 2016).

[22] L. Andor, 'Europe's Quest for Growth', *Prime Economics*, 23 March 2015, available at: www.primeeconomics.org/articles/europes-quest-for-growth (accessed 31 October 2016).

[23] M.J. Rodrigues, and E. Yiarchogiannopoulou (eds), *The Eurozone Crisis and the Transformation of EU Governance: Internal and External Implications* (Ashgate, 2014).

[24] See P. Vanheuverzwijn, 'Promoting the Agenda for a Social Economic and Monetary Union: Attention, Credibility and Coalition-building' (2014) *Bruges Political Research Paper*, no. 37.

especially in such a fragmented labour market as the EU. The Eurozone crisis has triggered new migration of workforce, but often towards other continents, causing a long-term human capital loss to the EU.

Two important conclusions have to be drawn. First, social crises in the context of EMU instability cannot be considered as a matter of subsidiarity. Secondly, social policy alone, even if national welfare systems are reformed, cannot offset the social consequences of the Eurozone crisis.[25] Given the constraints which membership in a (minimalist) monetary union implies, it is fundamental to recreate possibilities of macroeconomic adjustment inside the Eurozone whereby aggregate demand and economic growth can be maintained. This is only possible if the Eurozone can optimise economic growth for the Eurozone as whole, instead of focusing on fiscal goals and structural reforms within specific Member States. The weak recovery potential derives from the lack of such optimisation capacity. And, in a deflationary environment, a protracted period of low or negative growth will cause the decline of both human and fixed capital, which in turn will undermine the EU's growth potential. Unemployment caused by a cyclical downturn will become structural if the downturn is not tackled in time.

Given the very limited chances of overcoming such imbalances through increased labour mobility in the EU, a rule-based stabiliser mechanism becomes a very desirable solution. If short-term shocks and private sector deleveraging cannot be mitigated by autonomous monetary policy, they have to be absorbed by fiscal policy. Creating a procedure to deal with macroeconomic imbalances (MIP) was intellectually well-founded, but in practice it did not succeed in enforcing symmetrical adjustment in the Eurozone. The minimalist Monetary Union turned diversity into divergence. This means that without adequate macroeconomic intervention capacity, only limited temporary results will be achieved. Better governance and a stronger coordination of structural policies is always possible, but insufficient to restore the potential of convergence without broader monetary reform, which is a transition towards an EMU 2.0.

6.4.2 Launched: Banking Union and Investment Plan

As a first step in EMU reform, a banking union is in the process of being implemented, which has the potential to relieve pressure on government that

---

had to bail out major commercial banks. The banking union is built around common financial sector regulation, the application of the bail-in principle and a Single Resolution Mechanism at the European level, together with a strengthened common rulebook. To the extent that the banking union can be trusted to perform equally for all its Member States and their banks during financial crises, it would reduce financial fragmentation in the Single Market and boost EMU resilience already today. However, the establishment of the full banking union itself takes a long time, and the EU had to rely on other means for stabilisation and recovery. ECB intervention since 2012, therefore, has been critical in restoring the chance of recovery on the periphery and reducing the risk of deflation. However, in order to consolidate the ECB in this stabilising function, it needs to be explicitly empowered to act as a true European institution and consider employment as much among its goals as price stability.

In July 2014, following the European Parliament elections, the policy reform continued with the announcement of an investment plan.[26] Boosting investment was declared a priority by the newly elected Commission President Jean-Claude Juncker. He identified one of the Vice-Presidents as the investment chief of the EU, and presented his investment plan to the European Parliament as early as November 2014. According to the Juncker Plan, the EU provides €16 billion from its own budget, supplemented by an additional €5 billion from the European Investment Bank. With this seed capital, the European Fund for Strategic Investment hopes to attract almost €300 billion in private sector investment. Member States are also encouraged to contribute, and indeed in early 2015 there are initial signs that this will happen. Moreover, President Juncker has announced in his 2016 State of the EU that the Commission will upgrade the programme.

In 2014, it had to be recognised that while the banking union is a vital reform, it either does not happen with the necessary speed, or it does not lead to the right kind of financing to promote economic recovery. There is a need to go beyond the minimalist banking union but, at least at this current stage, there is no political momentum to put plans for a fiscal union on the agenda. The investment plan is in between. It is an effort to overcome the depression through more intensive political coordination of investment activities in the absence of a demand side stimulus.

With these features, the investment plan, even in an upgraded version, falls short of an economic policy instrument that would be able to deal with cyclicality and asymmetry. These features were excluded from the original design,

---

[26] Andor, n. 6 in this chapter.

and require the extension of the EMU reform process to the area of fiscal capacity.

6.4.3 Outstanding: Fiscal Capacity and Shock Absorption

The relevance of a common fiscal capacity in monetary unions was first pointed out by Kenen,[27] and the specific case of the EMU was also widely discussed in literature before the adoption of the euro.[28] Indeed, rebalancing the Eurozone is a key issue today, which points to the need of establishing a fiscal capacity. This, however, may not necessarily entail a fiscal union and 'federal' redistribution. A Eurozone finance minister, for example, would in principle be a fiscal official with the capacity to enforce symmetrical adjustment under the MIP, and could help to overcome cyclical downturns and the deflationary bias of the EMU in general. Creating a Treasury for the Eurozone is another frequently discussed direction that seems obvious for a community of democratic states sharing a single currency. Various models of rule-based – though limited – mechanism of solidarity to strengthen people's and markets' confidence in the euro – and thus to create a better institutional foundation for the recovery of demand and investment – have also been explored.

Hostility around bailout programmes and their conditionality have not created a constructive atmosphere in which more solidarity could be easily promoted, especially if solidarity would involve forms of fiscal transfers. However, there is virtually no serious assessment of the functioning of the euro that predicts longevity of the currency without a fiscal capacity and risk sharing,[29] ideally in some form of automatic stabilisers that can limit the damage from cyclical downturns. From a macroeconomic point of view, stabilisation means dealing with asymmetries and cyclicality.[30] Since a perfect ex ante solution (through policy coordination) cannot be attained, it is necessary to have ex post possibilities, which means we need to have a fiscal capacity for shock absorption. This also means introducing elements of a fiscal union, or in other words, transfers. An automatic stabiliser at the EMU level is needed for several reasons. It would help uphold aggregate demand at the right time in crises,

[27] P. Kenen, 'The Theory of Optimum Currency Areas: An Eclectic View', in R. Mundell and A. Swoboda (eds), *Monetary Problems of the International Economy* (University of Chicago Press, 1969).

[28] For example, R. Mundell, 'Uncommon Arguments for Common Currencies', in H.G. Johnson and A. Swoboda (eds), *The Economics of Common Currencies* (Allen & Unwin, 1973).

[29] P. De Grauwe, 'Design Failures in the Eurozone: Can They Be Fixed?' *LSE 'Europe in Question' Discussion Paper Series*, 57/13.

[30] L. Andor, 'Basic European Unemployment Insurance – The Best Way Forward in Strengthening the EMU's Resilience and Europe's Recovery' (2014) 49 *Intereconomics*.

and it would help prevent short-term crises from unleashing longer-lasting divergence.[31] It would reduce – or in an ideal case eliminate – the macroeconomic bias against full employment in the EU. The political complexity of implementing these solutions should not be underestimated. However, the EU is in a race against time if it is to make the single currency sustainable and legitimate.

6.5 EURO AREA UNEMPLOYMENT INSURANCE UNDER CONSIDERATION

In democratic countries, unemployment insurance developed not just as an instrument of social policy, but it has also been identified as a crucial fiscal stabiliser. Stabilisation instruments do not necessarily have to be tied to the unemployment rate, but those which are, can perform a double (or triple, see Section 6.5.2 below) stabilisation function. While political hurdles should not be underestimated, the added value in terms of economic and social outcomes has been proven in a variety of independent studies.[32]

6.5.1 *Options for Fiscal Stabilisation Instruments*

In discussions on Eurozone fiscal capacity, experts speak about three possible models of automatic stabilisers. These models have different implications in terms of the frequency of cross-country transfers, the definition of final beneficiaries, the need for harmonisation and governance, as well as the sourcing of the model. Some experts have explored the possibility of automatic income support for situations of major economic downturns, defined on the basis of the 'output gap'.[33] Most likely, such a solution would be in line with the current Treaty, but it also has disadvantages. The output gap is a concept too abstract for many people, and when it is calculated, it is often corrected ex post, which may lead to perverse outcomes. In addition, it entirely lacks a

[31] L. Andor (2016) 'Towards Shared Unemployment Insurance in the Euro Area' (2016) 5 *IZA Journal of European Labor Studies* 1.

[32] For example, M. Dolls, C. Fuest, D. Neumann, and A. Peichl, 'An Unemployment Insurance Scheme for the Euro Area? A Comparison of Different Alternatives Using Micro Data' (2014) ZEW-*Centre for European Economic Research Discussion Paper*, 095/14; A. Brandolini, F. Carta, and F. D'Amuri, 'A Feasible Unemployment-Based Shock Absorber for the Euro Area', *Questioni di Economia e Finanza Occasional Papers*, 254; and M. Beblavý, D. Gros, and I. Maselli, 'Reinsurance of National Unemployment Benefit Schemes' (2015) *Centre for European Policy Studies research paper*, 401.

[33] H. Enderlein, L. Guttenberg, and J. Spiess 'Making One Size Fit All: Designing a Cyclical Adjustment Insurance Fund for the Eurozone' (2013) *Notre Europe Institute Policy Paper*, 61.

social focus (meaning that it is not certain at all that the beneficiaries of such transfers would be the most vulnerable victims of economic crises).

With regard to automatic stabilisers that are directly and explicitly linked to unemployment, the discussion so far has revolved around two competing models: basic common unemployment insurance, which would be created by a partial pooling of national systems,[34] and a so called re-insurance mechanism, also known as a rainy day model.[35] 'Partial pooling' of national systems means receiving unemployment benefit from a common fund for a limited period (for example 6 months), and sharing the costs of that among the Member States. Individual workers become part of a risk community. The scheme would be based on a few basic parameters agreed in advance, and its functioning would be entirely predictable and calculable on the basis of these clear rules. The European scheme would not completely replace national ones, being an additional, complementary tool.[36] The levels of the contribution and of the benefit should represent a relatively low common denominator between the rules of national schemes, to ensure a fairly basic standard of support during short-term unemployment. Each Member State should be free to levy an additional contribution and pay out a higher or longer unemployment benefit on top of this European unemployment insurance. The jobseekers would continue to interact with national authorities (public employment services). However, every month these national authorities would send to the European fund the basic contribution from all their employed workers. Likewise, every month the European fund would pay to the national authorities an amount corresponding to the sum of all the basic European unemployment benefit payments to be made that month in the country. Member States can still top up payments from the common pool and also extend coverage from their own resources. But the common pool represents EU solidarity for countries experiencing temporary hardships due to the limitations of their macroeconomic toolbox inside the monetary union.

Designing re-insurance seems easier than partial pooling. The national fiscal capacity for dealing with cyclical unemployment would be supported, but transfers would only be triggered by major crises. Such a scheme would make a more visible impact at times of crisis, while lacking a role during more modest fluctuations. Since countries (instead of individuals) form the risk

---

[34] S. Dullien, *A European Unemployment Benefit Scheme. How to Provide for More Stability in the Euro Zone* (Brookings, 2014).

[35] Beblavý et al., n. 32 in this chapter.

[36] Trésor Economics, 'An Unemployment Insurance Scheme for the Euro Area' (2014) available at: www.tresor.economie.gouv.fr/File/403124 (accessed 31 October 2016).

community, the political acceptance is probably 'easier' than in the previous case.[37] The risk of this model lies in setting the trigger too high (in terms of how fast unemployment would need to rise above 'standard' levels), and thus making the mechanism less effective than it could otherwise be.

6.5.2 The Added Value of Eurozone Unemployment Insurance

An automatic fiscal stabiliser in the form of a basic European unemployment insurance would have a meaningful macroeconomic effect in counteracting a cyclical downturn.[38] This means helping EMU countries to share part of the financial risk associated with cyclical unemployment caused by a drop in aggregate demand, but not compensating for structural differences caused by skills mismatches, less efficient labour-market institutions and the like.

Both models (partial pooling and re-insurance) can deliver three types of stabilisation. First, they could contribute to economic stabilisation by shifting demand and purchasing power to countries and regions which otherwise would need to implement fiscal 'adjustment' and internal devaluation. Second, social stabilisation could be enacted as well, by directing the flow of funds towards more vulnerable groups, and helping to tame the rise of poverty among the working age population (which has been a major trend in recent years in Europe). The third type is institutional stabilisation. EMU is based on rules but the application of these rules has been the subject of academic as well as political debates. Member States agreed on tightening those rules but pragmatic considerations often point towards more flexibility (the 2016 cases of Spain and Portugal being a typical controversy). While some experts simply recommend ignoring the rules and giving up on them entirely.[39] it is more likely that a modus vivendi could be found through the creation of stabilisation tools that would allow the reconciliation of uniform fiscal rules with the need to maintain national welfare safety nets and social investment capacities.

Had either of these insurance mechanisms existed in EMU from the start of the single currency, all Member States would have been beneficiaries at some point in time. Countries experiencing a severe recession would have received fiscal transfers, helping them towards a faster recovery and avoiding

[37] M. Hooghe and S. Verhaegen, 'The Democratic Legitimacy of EU Institutions and Support for Social Policy in Europe', Chapter 5 in this volume; and L. Andor and R. Hess, 'Automatic Fiscal Stabiliser: Make It Happen!' *EPC discussion paper.*
[38] Brandolini et al., and Dolls et al., n. 32 in this chapter.
[39] See for example, P. Legrain, *European Spring. Why Our Economies and Politics Are in a Mess and How to Put Them Right* (CB Books, 2014).

a perception that for the arbitrary EU fiscal targets are more important than democracy and social cohesion. Through such a scheme, it should be possible to create a European safety net for the welfare safety nets of individual Member States, strengthening the ability of national governments to support an economic recovery. Citizens would directly benefit from EU solidarity at times of hardship, and Member States would be required to upgrade their employment services and labour-market institutions to the best EU standards.

The issue of convergence in unemployment insurance regulation is an important one, and should be addressed in the design phase of the scheme. If the Member States agree to pool more financial, budget, and economic sovereignty, this inevitably calls for a clear framework for social coordination and convergence. Otherwise, it will only lead to more fierce competition between the Member States, lowering of social standards and jeopardising of the social model.

6.5.3 *Institutional Requirements and Political Feasibility*

While delivering clear benefits, either of the two models would also come with some new requirements. To start with a pivotal one, both would require the acceptance of limited transfers in the Eurozone – even if neither of these models entail permanent transfers in the long run. The Single Market already leads to a modest level of redistribution under the heading of cohesion policy, and a similar-sized stabilisation fund would be just as obvious for the Monetary Union as well. A European unemployment insurance offers this in a transparent, orderly and rule-based fashion.

The second key requirement is a limited amount of harmonisation of labour markets. Both models, but especially partial pooling, would come with defining some common minimum standards across countries (such as a minimum replacement ratio and a minimum benefit duration). As Padoan has recently argued,[40] such a scheme would provide incentives to increase convergence in labour-market regulation, enhancing the capacity for labour-market adjustments at the aggregate Eurozone level. Harmonisation in a diverse EU is always hard, in every sector from fishery to banking. However, in this particular case, what would make things easier is that only cyclical unemployment would need to be linked to EMU fiscal capacity. Longer-term unemployment

---

[40] P.C. Padoan, 'Couldn't Brussels Bail Out the Jobless?', *The Guardian*, 10 June 2015, available at: www.theguardian.com/commentisfree/2015/jun/10/russels-bail-out-jobless-european-union-unemployment (accessed 31 October 2016).

– which is largely due to national factors rather than EU driven fiscal adjustments – would remain an issue for national and local actors. Thus, a large-scale harmonisation is unnecessary.

Transparent governance has to be mentioned as a third requirement. Design, but also supervision, would need to strike the right balance between national responsibility and European solidarity. Related issues are often discussed under the umbrella of moral hazard, with the assumption that a cross-country unemployment insurance fund, just like any other fiscal instrument, needs to have safeguards against gaming the system.[41] Inviting representatives of employers as well as employees to a supervisory board, and using experience rating and clawbacks (of contributions/pay-outs), could help to minimise the chance of abuse.

The funding of an EMU unemployment insurance is a further question. Neither model is tied to a specific form of funding. There are many ways of combining sources, but one thing surely has to be decided at the start: whether the fund would be allowed to borrow or not. Allowing it to borrow would help maximise the economic stabilisation impact (adding an intertemporal dimension to the interregional one). This capacity would still exist if borrowing is not allowed, but in that case the greater emphasis would be on the social stabilisation effect as opposed to the economic one.

6.6 CONCLUSIONS

Asymmetries, imbalances, and divergence raise the questions of sustainability and legitimacy in the European Union. All EU countries are supposed to be welfare states with the capacity to control unemployment, poverty, and inequality, while this capacity has significantly weakened during the Eurozone crisis. In the Eurozone, convergence cannot be restored without overcoming the deep and dangerous polarisation that has developed in the crisis years. For that, the reform of the EMU has to continue beyond better governance, ideally with developing a fiscal capacity that can help dealing with cyclicality and asymmetries.

The social dimension of the EMU is crucial for the legitimacy of the European project but also – given the deepening economic governance – for the legitimacy of Member States policies. But, it cannot be pursued in the same way as the social dimension of the Single Market. The latter is mainly a

---

[41] F. Vandenbroucke and C. Luigjes (2016) 'Institutional Moral Hazard in the Multi-tiered Regulation of Unemployment and Social Assistance Benefits', *Centre for European Policy Studies research paper*, 137.

question of legislation, while strengthening the social dimension of the EMU is fundamentally a question of fiscal and monetary instruments. Hence, the reconciliation of the monetary union with national welfare systems necessitates a broader and more substantial reconstruction of the EMU, and automatic stabilisers in particular.

7

Booms, Busts and the Governance of the Eurozone

Paul De Grauwe and Yuemei Ji

7.1 INTRODUCTION

Since the eruption of the sovereign debt crisis in the Eurozone, substantial efforts have been made to create a new form of governance for the Eurozone that will make the Monetary Union more robust in absorbing future economic and financial shocks. Much of the drive to adapt the governance of the Eurozone has been influenced by the traditional theory of optimal currency areas (OCA), which stresses the need for flexibility in product and labour markets. As a result, the Eurozone countries have been pushed towards structural reforms that aim to reduce the structural rigidities in product and labour markets, in the hope that this would lead to a more resilient monetary union capable of withstanding future asymmetric shocks.

Figure 7.1, which presents the OECD product market legislation index, shows that the Eurozone countries have introduced structural reforms at a faster pace than the rest of the OECD countries. Figure 7.2, which presents the OECD index of employment protection, shows how the Eurozone has significantly reduced its tight employment protection, especially since the sovereign debt crisis in 2010. It is interesting to note that since the early 1990s the non-Eurozone OECD countries have followed a reverse trend of increasing employment protection. In this chapter, we ask whether this movement towards structural reform as part of the push for new governance is going in the right direction. We will argue that this is not the case. The main reason is that the nature of the shocks that have hit the Eurozone does not correspond to the pattern of asymmetric shocks that has been identified by the OCA theory to require more flexibility. We will argue that what is needed in the Eurozone

We gratefully acknowledge the comments and suggestions from Daniel Gros, André Sapir, Frank Vandenbroucke.

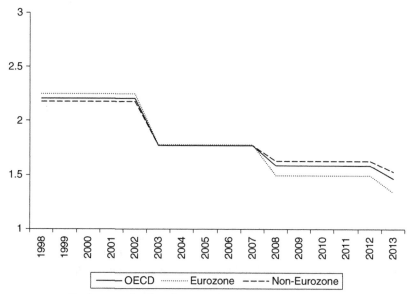

FIGURE 7.1: Product market legislation index.
Source: OECD.

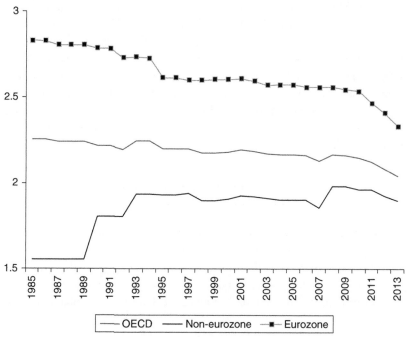

FIGURE 7.2: Employment protection legislation index.
Source: OECD.

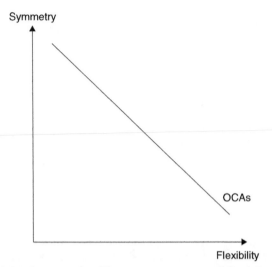

FIGURE 7.3: OCA theory trade-off between symmetry and flexibility.

is not more structural reforms but a better mechanism capable of dealing with the classical boom and bust dynamics that are inherent to capitalism.

Hyman Minsky's classic analysis of booms and busts in capitalist systems stresses the need to stabilise using government mechanisms.[1] We will ask whether the Eurozone, which has moved towards more flexibility, provides for this stabilising mechanism.In Sections 7.2 and 7.3, we analyse what the OCA theory has to say about the need for flexibility and stabilisation in the face of asymmetric shocks. In Sections 7.4 and 7.5 we analyse empirically the nature of these shocks in the Eurozone and in Sections 7.6 and 7.7 we study what this evidence might means for the governance of the Eurozone. We conclude in Section 7.8.

7.2 STANDARD OCA THEORY AND THE GOVERNANCE OF THE EUROZONE

The theory of OCA has created a set of ideas that has a significant influence on the governance of the Eurozone and on views about how this governance should be strengthened in the future. The best way to make this clear is to present the core of the OCA theory, using a well-known graphical representation of this theory.[2] This is done in Figure 7.3. On the horizontal axis we set

---

[1] H. Minsky, *Stabilizing an Unstable Economy* (Yale University Press, 1986).
[2] See P. De Grauwe, *Economics of Monetary Union* (Oxford University Press, 11th edn, 2016).

out the degree of flexibility in the labour and goods markets. This measures the degree to which wages and prices adjust freely to shocks and the degree to which workers are mobile. We assume that these different dimensions of flexibility can be represented by one index. On the vertical axis we set out the degree of symmetry between countries, that is the degree of co-movement (correlation) of macroeconomic variables such as output and employment. Thus, when there are a lot of asymmetric shocks we move downwards along the vertical axis. By contrast, when shocks become less asymmetric we move upwards along the vertical axis. The downward sloping OCA line represents the trade-off between symmetry and flexibility. Hence, when the degree of symmetry declines (there are more asymmetric shocks) countries in a monetary union need more flexibility to deal with these shocks. The OCA-line separates the space into two zones. The OCA-zone above the OCA-line contains the collection of points at which symmetry and flexibility are high enough to guarantee that the benefits of the monetary union exceed the costs. The points below the OCA-line are the points at which symmetry and flexibility are too low, meaning that countries located in that zone will find that the costs of the monetary union exceed the benefits. The OCA-line that separates the two zones can therefore also be defined as the collection of points for which the benefits and the costs of the monetary union are equal.

This theory has been very influential for the governance of the Eurozone and continues to be so. It is at the core of the policy prescriptions that call for structural reforms so as to make the labour and goods markets more flexible. In fact, since the start of the sovereign debt crisis in 2010 member countries have been pressured by the European Commission to introduce a whole set of structural reforms. The member countries that turned to the Eurozone for financial support (Greece, Ireland, and Portugal) were given this support conditional on introducing a series of structural reforms that would make labour and goods markets more flexible. The underlying rationale was the OCA theory that stresses the need for flexibility to deal with asymmetric shocks in a monetary union.

One of the underlying assumptions of this theory and its prescription for flexibility is that the asymmetric shocks are permanent. When shocks are permanent, such as a change in preferences that leads consumers in one country to buy more of the foreign than of the domestic good, or a productivity increase in one but not in another country, then there is really no other way in a monetary union to deal with such a shock other than changing relative prices (wages or product prices) or by a movement of labour and capital. Things are very different, however, when shocks are temporary. In that case, it can be argued that flexibility is not necessary. In fact it can even be harmful. Take the case of business-cycle movements. When these are asymmetric, in other

words when they are not synchronised, it makes little sense to adjust by relative price changes and/or by movements of labour and capital. Flexibility may
in fact exacerbate the business-cycle movements and its asymmetry. For example, if country A experiences a recession and country B a boom the movement
of labour from A to B is likely to exacerbate the recession in country A and
the boom in country B. Or take flexibility of wages. If during the recession
country A is forced to reduce wages, the immediate effect of the wage cuts will
be a decline in aggregate demand, which will make the recession in country
A more severe. From the preceding analysis it follows that temporary shocks,
such as business-cycle movements, should be dealt with differently: by stabilisation efforts that smooth consumption over time.

However, the OCA theory that focuses on the trade-off between flexibility
and symmetry was developed on the assumption that asymmetric shocks are
permanent. These shocks are also typically exogenous, like meteor impacts.
There is nothing one can do about these. One is forced to adjust by making
the system more flexible. Business-cycle shocks, by contrast, can be said to
be endogenous. They are the result of endogenous movements in optimism
and pessimism that lead to booms and busts. These movements have been
endemic in capitalism and will continue to do their work also in a monetary
union. They have been described by Minsky and Kindleberger.[3] To the extent
that these movements are not synchronised, they do not call for more flexibility; rather they call for insurance mechanisms that allow countries experiencing a downturn to be compensated by countries that experience a boom,
in such a way that when the fortunes of countries are reversed the transfers
are reversed. It has long been recognised that such an insurance mechanism
requires some form of budgetary union. Thus, endogenous and asymmetric
business-cycle movements call for very different institutions in the union from
the permanent and exogenous shocks that have been at the core of the OCA
analysis.

7.3 GOVERNANCE OF A MONETARY UNION IN THE FACE OF TEMPORARY SHOCKS

In this section we consider what the nature of the institutions of a monetary
union should be when the shocks are endogenous, temporary, and asymmetric. We will focus on business-cycle movements that are driven by 'animal spirits', that is to say, movements of optimism and pessimism that lead to booms

---

[3] Minsky, n. 1 in this chapter; C. Kindleberger, *Manias, Panics and Crashes. A History of
   Financial Crises* (John Wiley & Sons, 4th edition, 2001).

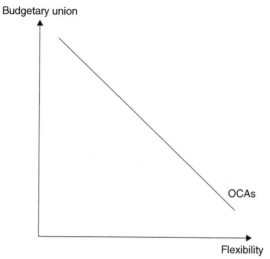

FIGURE 7.4: Trade-off between budgetary union and flexibility.

during periods of optimism and recessions during periods of pessimism. In this section we focus on the theory. In the next section we analyse the empirical question of the nature of the asymmetric shocks in the Eurozone. We start from a similar trade-off to the one in Figure 7.3, but now we concentrate on the trade-off between flexibility and budgetary union. We define a budgetary union as a (partial) transfer of the national power to tax and to spend to European institutions. A budgetary union has the effect of creating an insurance mechanism that allows countries experiencing bad economic times to be compensated by countries that fare well. The way this trade-off is constructed is as follows (Figure 7.4). On the vertical axis we set out the degree of budgetary union. The higher the degree of budgetary union the more we move upwards along the vertical line. On the horizontal axis we set out the same measure of flexibility as that used in Figure 7.3. The OCAs line now measures the minimum combinations of budgetary union and flexibility needed to make a monetary union economically attractive (higher benefits than costs). It is negatively sloped for the following reason. When budgetary union increases, insurance against asymmetric shocks increases, making monetary union less costly. As a result, there is less need for flexibility. We move upward along the negatively sloped OCAs line.[4]

---

[4] We call this trade-off the OCAs line because the idea of such a trade-off comes from André Sapir, see A. Sapir, 'Architecture Reform for an Heterogeneous EMU: National vs. European

This is an important insight. Flexibility may sound great for many economists and central bankers, but it is costly for those people who are forced to
be flexible. Flexibility means that these people may have to accept a wage cut
or be forced to emigrate. We learn from Figure 7.4 that a movement towards
budgetary union alleviates the (painful) need to be flexible. It may also make
a monetary union more acceptable to large segments of the population. At
the same time, however, it may make those who are asked to transfer revenue
unhappy, resisting such a 'Transfer Union'.

We can use the insights of Figure 7.4 to analyse the importance of the nature
of the asymmetric shocks. We have made the distinction between asymmetric
shocks that are exogenous and permanent, and asymmetric shocks that are
temporary and endogenous. We have argued that when a permanent (exogenous) shock occurs, flexibility is the only option to adjust to this shock. By
contrast, when business-cycle movements are synchronised it is not optimal to
use flexibility. In that case an insurance mechanism is the appropriate way to
govern the monetary union. A budgetary union provides this.

It can now be shown that the nature of the shocks influences the slope of
the trade-off.[5] When the shocks are mainly of the permanent type, we obtain
a steep trade-off. We show this in Figure 7.5. We have also put the Eurozone
of 19 members below the OCA_S-line, suggesting that the present Eurozone
is not an OCA. The steep trade-off implies that a small increase in flexibility
leads us more quickly into the OCA zone than a budgetary union. In the
most extreme case – when all shocks are of a permanent nature – the trade-off
becomes vertical. In that case no amount of budgetary union will bring us into
the OCA-zone. There is then no other way but to increase flexibility.

Things are very different when the shocks are temporary, driven by business-
cycle movements. In that case the trade-off is flat (Figure 7.6). As a result,
much flexibility is needed to move the Eurozone into the OCA area compared to budgetary union. A relatively small increase in budgetary union will
bring us into the OCA-zone. In the most extreme case – when all shocks are
of a temporary nature – the trade-off is horizontal. In that case no amount of
flexibility will succeed in bringing the Eurozone into the OCA-zone. The
only way to achieve optimality will be through a budgetary union.

One complication that arises here has to do with hysteresis. Sometimes
temporary shocks can lead to hysteresis effects. For example, a recession typically leads to plant closures and dismissal of workers. To the extent that these

Institutions', contribution to the conference 'Adjustment in European Economies in the
Wake of the Economic Crisis', Bank of Portugal, 9 May 2015.
5   We are grateful to Frank Vandenbroucke for suggesting that the nature of the shocks affects the
slope of the trade-off.

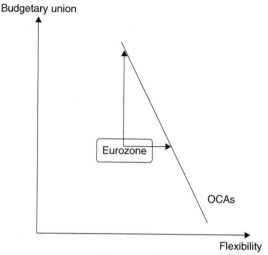

FIGURE 7.5: How to move the Eurozone towards the OCA$_s$-area when permanent shocks dominate?

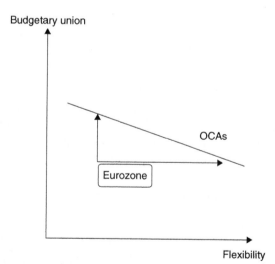

FIGURE 7.6: How to move the Eurozone towards the OCA$_s$-area when business-cycle movements dominate?

workers have developed firm specific skills that are lost when the firm disappears, the workers lose part of their human capital making it difficult to find another (comparable) job. Unemployment can then become protracted. Another example relates to the nature of the boom. If, as was the case in

Ireland and Spain, the boom is concentrated in the housing market, many workers are attracted to this sector during the boom. After the crash they are dismissed. They may find it difficult to use their skills acquired in the housing market in other sectors of the economy. There is a large literature on sources of hysteresis.[6]

The existence of hysteresis has implications for our discussion. It implies that if a business-cycle shock occurs it matters a great deal to try to use stabilisation so as to avoid hysteresis effects. If temporary business-cycle shocks have permanent effects the need to set up schemes that will mitigate the impact of these shocks becomes even more important. Figures 7.5 and 7.6 lead to another interesting insight. Flexibility in labour markets is something national governments can do. There is no need for further integration to increase flexibility. Budgetary union, however, is of a different nature. It requires political integration. In other words, while flexibility is in the realm of national governments, budgetary union is a European affair.[7] When shocks are permanent they have to be dealt with at the national level while when shocks are temporary the response should be at the level of the Eurozone.

7.4 THE NATURE OF SHOCKS IN THE EUROZONE: EMPIRICAL EVIDENCE

It is not always easy to separate permanent from temporary shocks in economic time series. Here we use a Hodrick-Prescott filter (HP) that allows us to estimate the long-term trend component in GDP. The cyclical component is obtained by subtracting the trend component from the observed GDP (for more detail, see the appendix to this chapter (Section 7.9), where we also analyse the robustness of the results for changes in the smoothness parameter lambda in the HP filter).[8] The results of this exercise are shown in Figure 7.7. We present, for each Eurozone country, trend growth and the

---

[6]   See O.J. Blanchard and H.L. Summers, 'Hysteresis and the European Unemployment Problem' (1986) 1 *NBER Macroeconomics Annual* 15; L.M. Ball, 'Hysteresis in Unemployment: Old and New Evidence' (2009), *US National Bureau of Economic Research (NBER) Working Paper*, 14818; A. Fatas and L. Summers, 'The Permanent Effects of Fiscal Consolidations' (2015) available at: voxeu.org/sites/default/files/file/DP10902.pdf (accessed 19 October 2016).

[7]   Sapir, n. 4 in this chapter.

[8]   There is a literature based on Blanchard and Quah (O. Blanchard and D. Quah, 'The Dynamic Effect of Demand and Supply Disturbances' (1989) 79 *American Economic Review* 655), which is based on estimating a VAR and, after imposing identifying restrictions, is able to estimate the temporary and the permanent component in output shocks. We discuss this literature in P. De Grauwe and Y. Ji, 'Crisis Management and Economic Growth in the Eurozone', in F. Caselli, M. Centeno, and J. Tavares (eds), *After the Crisis: Reform, Recovery and Growth in Europe* (Oxford University Press, 2016).

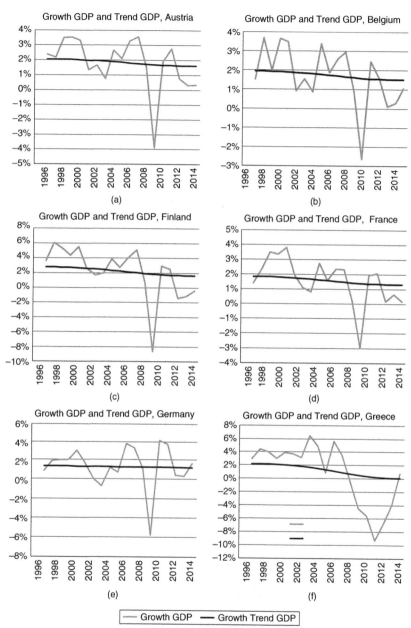

FIGURE 7.7: Cyclical and trend components in GDP growth (1999–2014): (a) Austria; (b) Belgium; (c) Finland; (d) France; (e) Germany; (f) Greece; (g) Ireland; (h) Italy; (i) Netherlands; (j) Portugal; (k) Spain.

Sources: Eurostat and own calculations.

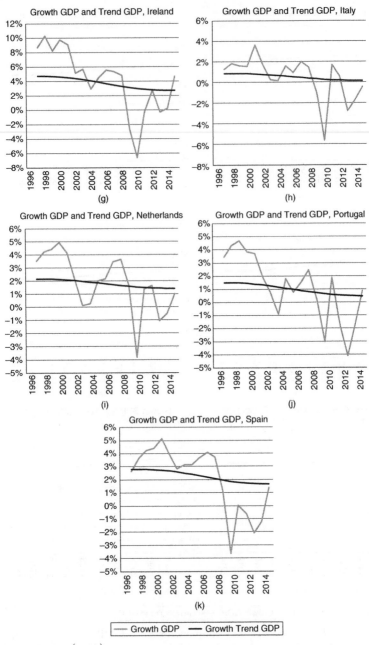

FIGURE 7.7: (*cont.*)

TABLE 7.1: *Mean (absolute) trend growth and mean (absolute) business-cycle change in GDP (as a percentage) during 1999–2014*

	Mean cycle	Mean trend	Ratio
Austria	1.79%	1.77%	1.01
Belgium	1.72%	1.67%	1.03
Germany	1.55%	1.23%	1.26
France	2.15%	1.49%	1.44
Netherlands	2.66%	1.66%	1.60
Finland	4.35%	2.02%	2.15
Spain	4.58%	2.07%	2.21
Ireland	8.01%	3.35%	2.39
Portugal	3.67%	0.81%	4.53
Italy	2.86%	0.41%	7.05
Greece	9.09%	0.90%	10.11

Notes: (as a percentage) during 1999–2014.
Source: Computations based on data from Eurostat.

observed growth rates (the cyclical component is obtained by subtracting the observed from the trend growth).[9] Two results stand out. First, we observe for all Eurozone countries (except for Germany) a decline in the long-term growth rate of GDP. This decline is particularly significant in Greece, Ireland, Finland, Spain, Portugal, and Italy. Second, there is great variability in the business-cycle (temporary) component of GDP growth. In order to gauge the relative importance of cyclical and trend components in GDP growth we compare the mean (absolute) cyclical growth of GDP with the (absolute) mean trend growth of GDP for each country.[10] We show the results in Table 7.1. We observe that for the core countries (Austria, Belgium, Germany, and the Netherlands) the cyclical growth and trend growth components are of similar magnitudes, although the cyclical component is systematically larger than the trend component. In the countries of the periphery (Spain, Portugal, Ireland, Italy, and Greece) this is very different. We observe that for these countries the cyclical growth component is much larger than the trend growth component (the most extreme case being observed for Greece). Thus, in the peripheral

---

[9] We only include the original Eurozone countries. The new Eurozone countries entered too late to provide a sufficiently long time series.

[10] As the cyclical component alternates between positive and negative numbers we have to take the absolute values.

TABLE 7.2: *Correlation coefficients of cyclical components of GDP growth*

	Aus.	Bel.	Fin.	Fra.	Ger.	Gre.	Ire.	Ita.	Net.	Por.
Austria										
Belgium	0.9									
Finland	0.9	0.9								
France	0.9	0.9	0.9							
Germany	0.6	0.5	0.5	0.5						
Greece	0.7	0.8	0.8	0.7	0.0					
Ireland	0.8	0.8	0.9	0.9	0.4	0.8				
Italy	0.9	0.9	0.9	0.9	0.5	0.8	0.9			
Netherlands	0.9	0.9	0.9	0.9	0.6	0.7	0.8	0.9		
Portugal	0.9	0.8	0.8	0.8	0.3	0.8	0.8	0.9	0.9	
Spain	0.8	0.9	0.94	0.8	0.2	0.9	0.9	0.9	0.8	0.9

Source: Own calculations based on Eurostat.

countries the GDP growth rates have been dominated by cyclical movements in economic activity of the boom–bust type.

What are the implications of these results? First, since the start of the Eurozone, cyclical (temporary) movements have been the dominant factor behind growth variations in GDP. This is especially the case in those peripheral countries where cyclical movements in economic growth are many times higher than the long-term growth rates. Thus, as mentioned earlier, booms and bust in economic activity seem to be the overwhelming characteristic of movements in GDP in the countries of the periphery.

Second, it appears that the cyclical movements of GDP are highly correlated in the Eurozone. This is made clear by Table 7.2, which shows the correlations in the cyclical components of GDP growth across the Eurozone. We observe high correlation coefficients of bilateral cyclical components of GDP growth, typically 0.8 or more.[11] It is interesting to note that the country with the lowest correlation coefficients is Germany (although the German correlation coefficients are all positive). Thus, one can conclude that the business cycles of the Eurozone countries were highly correlated. Germany stands out as the country with the lowest (positive) correlations of its business cycle with the rest of the Eurozone.

---

[11]   We study a behavioural macroeconomic model and show that in such a model 'animal spirits' can easily get correlated internationally, producing high correlations of business cycles. This study can be found in P. De Grauwe and Y. Ji, 'The International Synchronisation of Business Cycles: The Role of Animal Spirits' (2017) 28 *Open Economies Review* 1.

Thus, the asymmetry between the Eurozone countries is to be found not so much in a lack of correlation in business-cycle movements but in the *intensity* of the boom–bust dynamics of growth rates. Put differently, Eurozone countries' business cycles seem to have been relatively well correlated. The difference between these countries was that some (mainly in the periphery) experienced much higher variance in business-cycle fluctuations than others (in the core). As a result, the asymmetry between member countries is to be found in the variance of the business cycles. This feature is striking in Figure 7.8, which shows the movements of the business-cycle components in the different Eurozone countries. These appear to move together but are of

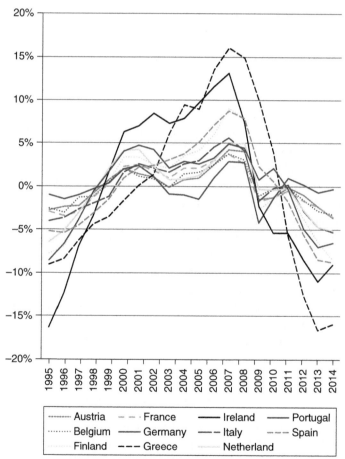

FIGURE 7.8: Business-cycle component of GDP growth.
Source: Own calculation based on Eurostat.

TABLE 7.3: *Slope of regression domestic cycle on euro-cycle*

	Slop
Germany	0.21
Belgium	0.48
Austria	0.49
France	0.55
Italy	0.77
Netherlands	0.80
Portugal	1.02
Finland	1.21
Spain	1.22
Ireland	2.07
Greece	2.18

Source: Own calculations.

very different amplitude. Some countries like Ireland and Spain experience a very strong boom and later bust, while countries like Belgium, Austria, and Germany experience similar cycles but of much less amplitude.

In order to obtain a more precise estimate of the asymmetry in the amplitudes of the business cycles, we regressed each country's domestic cyclical component on the Eurozone common cyclical component. The estimated slope coefficients reveal the extent to which the domestic cycles are smaller or lower in amplitude than the common cycle. The estimated slope coefficients are presented in Table 7.3. It is striking to find how different these slope coefficients are. Germany, Belgium, Austria, and France have slope coefficients that are significantly lower than 1, suggesting cycles of significantly lower amplitude than the euro-cycle. Conversely, Finland, Spain, and especially Ireland and Greece, have slope coefficients significantly higher than 1. This suggests that these countries experienced much higher amplitudes in their business cycles than the common euro-cycle.

7.5 WHAT KIND OF FLEXIBILITY

In the previous sections we lumped together labour-market and product market flexibility. This may make sense when discussing the trade-off between stabilisation and flexibility but not when analysing the long-term growth potential of countries. Labour-market and product market flexibility may have different implications for long-term growth. In order to analyse this issue, in a previous study we performed an econometric analysis of the separate effects of labour-market and product market rigidities in the OECD countries during the period 1980–2014.[12] We used standard econometric growth analysis of panel data. The measures of labour-market rigidity were the OECD employment protection index and for product market rigidity the OECD product market legislation index. The most striking aspect of the results is the finding that these measures of the labour and product market rigidities do not seem to have any influence on the growth rate of GDP per capita in OECD countries. Similar results were obtained by IMF.[13]

The conclusion is that employment protection is of no visible importance for economic growth may seem surprising. The 'Brussels–Frankfurt consensus' has stressed that employment protection has a negative effect on hiring and in so doing reduces prospects for growth. This may be true but there is another phenomenon that may more than compensate the positive effect of flexibility. In economies where employment protection is weak the incentives for firms to invest in its labour force is weak. When turnover is high firms are unlikely to invest in personnel that are likely to quit early. In addition, employees that can be fired quickly have equally weak incentives to invest in firm-specific skills. As a result, labour productivity is negatively affected. More generally, the quality of human capital will be low.

The same conclusion holds for product market regulations. Product market regulations do not seem to matter in the process of economic growth. Again this goes against current mainstream thinking, which has been much influenced by, among others, Aghion et al., which stresses that the model of perfect competition with free entry and price flexibility boosts innovation among firms that are close to the technological frontier.[14] There is an older literature, however, going back to Joseph Schumpeter stressing that innovation, investment and growth are better promoted in an environment of market imperfections and market power. The empirical evidence suggests that both opposing views may be at work, thereby offsetting each other.

[12] De Grauwe and Ji, n. 8 in this chapter.
[13] International Monetary Fund, *World Economic Outlook: Uneven Growth – Short- and Long-term Factors* (International Monetary Fund, 2015), pp. 104–7 (chapter 3, Box 3.5 on 'The Effects of Structural Reforms on Total Factor Productivity').
[14] P. Aghion, C. Harris, P. Howitt, and J. Vickers, 'Competition, Imitation and Growth with Step-by-Step Innovation' (2001) 68 *Review of Economic Studies* 467.

7.6 IMPLICATIONS FOR THE GOVERNANCE OF THE EUROZONE

The findings reported in the previous sections put the need for stabilisation in the Eurozone in a new light. We analyse two implications that involve steps towards budgetary integration. First, the finding of the overwhelming importance of the cyclical and temporary component of output growth should lead to the conclusion that efforts to stabilise the business cycle should be strengthened relative to the efforts that have been made to impose structural reforms. In terms of our theoretical analysis this means that Figure 7.6 is probably the relevant one. Again, this does not mean that flexibility can be disposed of.

7.6.1 *Common Unemployment Insurance*

A second implication of our empirical results relates to the many proposals made to create a fiscal space at the Eurozone level in the form of a common unemployment insurance system.[15] The proposals for such an insurance system have very much been influenced by the standard assumption made in the OCA-theory that shocks are asymmetric, in other words, that when one country experiences a recession, and thus increasing unemployment, the other country experiences a boom, and declining unemployment. This facilitates the workings of the common unemployment insurance system. The booming country transfers resources to the country in a recession and thereby smooths the business cycles in the two countries. Technically and politically such a system encounters relatively few problems.

Problems may arise when, as we have found, business cycles are relatively well synchronised but of very different amplitudes in the different member countries. In that case most countries will tend to experience a recession at about the same time; in some countries the recession will be mild but in others very intense. This creates both an economic and a political problem. First, countries with a mild recession are asked to transfer resources to countries experiencing a stronger recession. This tends to reduce the intensity of the

---

[15] See, for example, H. Van Rompuy, 'Towards a Genuine Economic and Monetary Union, Report in Close Collaboration with J.M. Barroso, J.C. Juncker, and M. Draghi ("The Four Presidents Report")' (2012), available at: ec.europa.eu/priorities/sites/beta-political/files/5-presidents-report_en.pdf (accessed 20 October 2016); Tommaso Padoa-Schioppa Group, 'Completing the Euro: A Road Map towards Fiscal Union in Europe' (2012), available at: www.notre-europe.eu/media/completingtheeuroreportpadoa-schioppagroupnejune2012.pdf?pdf=ok (accessed 20 October 2016); M. Beblavy, G. Marconi, and I. Maselli, 'European Unemployment Benefits Scheme: The Rationale and the Challenges Ahead' (2015), available at: www.ceps.eu/system/files/CEPS%20SR%20No%20119%20EUBS_0.pdf (accessed 20 October 2016).

recession in the latter country at the expense of making it more intense in the former country. It is not clear that this improves welfare. Second, it is likely to create important political problems in the former country that is asked to transfer resources when the economy is not doing well. Another way to formulate the previous insights is the following. The traditional proposals for a Eurozone unemployment insurance mechanism are predicated on the view that there is a need to smooth differences in unemployment changes across countries. That is, it is assumed that some countries experience increases, others declines in unemployment. The insurance mechanism then smooths these intercountry differences. We have noted, however, that this is not a typical Eurozone asymmetry. What we found is that most countries are likely to experience a boom and a recession at about the same time, with different intensities and amplitudes. There is therefore relatively little need for intercountry smoothing of business-cycle movements. The more pressing need is to smooth volatilities over time.

The previous analysis suggests that common unemployment insurance schemes should put emphasis on smoothing over time and not so much on intercountry smoothing. This can be achieved by allowing the common unemployment insurance scheme to accumulate deficits and surpluses over time. The fiscal rule that could be imposed is that the insurance scheme balances over the business cycle. Beblavy and Maselli have performed interesting simulations of several schemes that impose such a fiscal rule.[16] In general it appears from these simulations that such an insurance mechanism can be implemented. Such a rule would make it possible to automatically balance the need for intercountry and intertemporal smoothing.

The previous analysis makes clear, however, that given the importance of common business-cycle movements, a common unemployment insurance mechanism will need a capacity to issue bonds during recessions when the payments made by the insurance scheme will exceed the contributions by the Member States. During these periods the deficits of the scheme will have to be financed by the issue of common bonds, which one may want to call Eurobonds. Put differently, the common unemployment insurance mechanism will have to work like a common fund that is capable of issuing debt during recessions. If this is not allowed, a common unemployment insurance system cannot contribute much to common stabilisation efforts. Thus,

---

[16] M. Beblavy and I. Maselli, 'An Unemployment Insurance Scheme for the Euro Area: A Simulation Exercise of Two Options' (2014), available at: www.ceps.eu/system/files/CEPS%20Special%20Report%20An%20EU%20Unemployment%20Insurance%20Scheme%20Beblavy%20and%20Masselli.pdf (accessed 20 October 2016).

a workable common unemployment benefit scheme will necessarily imply some form of budgetary union.

Such a budgetary union can be kept relatively mild by imposing the fiscal rule mentioned earlier: that during common booms, the bonds issues during the recession are retired, thereby insuring that there is no long-term accumulation of common bonds. Today, this is probably as far as one can go in the direction of a budgetary union.

7.6.2 *National Stabilisation?*

In principle, intertemporal smoothing could be done at the national level, by allowing the national budgets to do the job. However, the large differences in the amplitude of business-cycle movements make such a purely national approach problematic, as it leads to large differences in the budget deficits and debt accumulation between countries. These differences quickly spill over into financial markets when countries that are hit very hard by a downward movement in output are subjected to sudden stops and liquidity crises.[17] This is likely to force them to switch off the automatic stabilisers in their national budgets.[18] As we argued, this can push countries into a bad equilibrium. Put differently, in the absence of a budgetary union, large differences in the amplitude of the business cycles are likely to hit the countries experiencing the more severe recession by 'sudden stops', that is to say, by large liquidity outflows that force them to abandon any ambition to stabilise the business-cycle shocks. In addition, these liquidity outflows are inflows in some other countries in the monetary union, typically those that are least hit by the recession.[19] Their economic conditions improve at the expense of the others. The stabilisation of common business shocks with different amplitudes at the national level makes the system unstable.

In this respect, the research of Alcidi and Thirion is relevant.[20] These authors find that while the core Eurozone countries have been able to stabilise part

---

[17]   See P. De Grauwe, 'The Governance of a Fragile Eurozone' (2011) *CEPS Working Documents*, No. 346.

[18]   P. De Grauwe and Y. Ji, 'Self-fulfilling Crises in the Eurozone: An Empirical Test' (2012) 34 *Journal of International Money and Finance* 15.

[19]   This is confirmed by the empirical work of Furceri and Zdzienicka (D. Furceri and M.A. Zdzienicka, 'The Euro Area Crisis: Need for a Supranational Fiscal Risk Sharing Mechanism?' (2013) *IMF Staff Discussion Note*, No. 13–198) and Hoffmann and Nitschka (M. Hoffmann and T. Nitschka, 'Securitization of Mortgage Debt, Domestic Lending, and International Risk Sharing' (2012) 45 *Canadian Journal of Economics* 493) who find that during recessions risk sharing through financial markets declines dramatically.

[20]   C. Alcidi and G. Thirion, *Feasibility and Added Value of a European Unemployment Benefit Scheme: Interim report* (CEPS, 2015).

(about 50 per cent) of the business-cycle shocks at the national level since the eruption of the debt crisis in 2010, the peripheral countries have been unable to do so, and also unable to profit from insurance mechanisms at the level of the Eurozone. As a result, most (90 per cent) of the business-cycle shocks had to be absorbed by drops in consumption (and therefore in employment). National stabilisation efforts do not work but introduce an element of instability into a monetary union, mainly because they leave the countries most hit by the business-cycle shocks unable to stabilise. Thus, when business-cycle shocks dominate (as we have shown in the previous section) it will be necessary to follow a common approach to the stabilisation of the business cycles. The common unemployment insurance mechanisms discussed in the previous section move us in this direction. Whether these schemes are important enough to perform a significant stabilising role remains to be seen. The common insurance mechanisms now being proposed have a relatively small intertemporal smoothing component, amounting to no more than 0.1 to 0.2 per cent of GDP over the business cycle, certainly insufficient to produce a significant intertemporal smoothing at the EU-level.[21]

Thus, in the long run further steps towards a budgetary union will be necessary. By centralising part of the national budgets into a common budget managed by a common political authority, the different increases in budget deficits following from a (common) recession translate into a budget deficit at the union level. As a result, the destabilising flows of liquidity between countries disappear, and the common budgetary authority can allow the automatic stabilisers in the budget to do their role in smoothing the business cycle. In fact, because a common budget also generates implicit intercountry transfers the countries with the deepest recession will profit from the automatic stabilising features of the common budget most. As a result, a common budget provided the most effective way to stabilise the business cycle. It is clear, however, that a budgetary union in which a significant part of national taxation and spending is transferred to a European government and parliament is far off. For the time being less ambitious efforts, such as the common unemployment insurance systems, are all that is feasible. They are important though in that they make clear the direction the Eurozone institutions will have to take in the future.[22]

---

[21]   Beblavy and Maselli, n. 16 in this chapter.
[22]   See also, on this, F. Vandenbroucke, 'The Case for a European Social Union. From Muddling Through to a Sense of Common Purpose', in B. Marin (ed.), *The Future of Welfare in a Global Europe* (Aldershot, 2015).

7.7 COMPLETING THE MONETARY UNION WITH POLITICAL UNION

The present institutional setup of the Eurozone is characterised by the fact that a number of bureaucratic institutions have acquired significant responsibilities without political accountability. Thus, there has been a transfer of sovereignty without a concomitant democratic legitimacy. Here we concentrate on the European Commission. Elsewhere, we discussed the European Central Bank.[23]

7.7.1 *The European Commission and Political Union*

The European Commission has seen its responsibilities increase since the eruption of the sovereign debt crisis in the Eurozone. This has been motivated by the desire of the creditor nations to impose budgetary and macroeconomic discipline on the debtor nations. As a result, the Stability and Growth Pact has been strengthened, and the European Commission has been entrusted with the responsibility of monitoring macroeconomic imbalances and to force debtor nations to change their macroeconomic policies.[24] The idea that macroeconomic imbalances should be monitored and controlled is a good one. The emergence of such imbalances was at the origin of the euro-crisis. Yet the way this idea has been implemented is unsustainable in the long run. The new responsibilities of the European Commission create a problem of democratic legitimacy. The European Commission can now force countries to raise taxes and reduce spending without, however, having to bear the political cost of these decisions. These costs are borne by national governments. This is a model that cannot work. Governments that face the political costs of spending and taxation will not continue to accept the decisions of unelected officials who do not face the cost of the decisions they try to impose on these governments. Sooner or later governments will go on strike, like the German and French governments did in 2003–04. Only the small countries (Portugal, Belgium, Ireland, etc.) will have to live with this governance. Large countries will not.

7.7.2 *Bureaucratic versus Political Integration*

Increasingly, European integration has taken the form of bureaucratic integration as a substitute for political integration. This process has started as soon as the European political elite became aware that further political integration

[23] De Grauwe, n. 2 in this chapter.
[24] In principle, the macroeconomic imbalance procedure should work symmetrically. It is, however, very unlikely to work that way. In fact, we see already today that the European Commission exerts more pressure on deficit countries than on surplus countries.

would be very difficult. This process has become even stronger since the start of the sovereign debt crisis in the Eurozone. The outcome of this crisis has been that the European Commission and the European Central Bank have seen their powers increase significantly, without any increase in their account-ability. More and more these two institutions impose decisions that affect mil-lions of people's welfare, but the people who are affected by these decisions do not have the democratic means to express their disagreements. Political scientists make a distinction between output and input legitimacy. Output legitimacy means that a particular decision is seen to be legitimate if it leads to an increase in general welfare. In this view, a government that is technocratic can still be legitimate if it is perceived to improve welfare. This view is very much influenced by the Platonic view of the perfect State. This is a State that is run by benevolent philosophers who know better than the population what is good for them and act to increase the country's welfare. Input legitimacy means that political decisions, whatever their outcome, must be based on a process that involves the population, through elections that allow people to sack those who have made bad decisions.

Much of the integration process in Europe has been based on the idea of output legitimacy. The weak part of that kind of legitimacy becomes visible when the population is not convinced that what the philosophers at the top have decided, has improved welfare. That is the situation today in Europe. In many countries there is a perception that the decisions taken in Brussels and Frankfurt have harmed their welfare.

7.8 CONCLUSION

Since the sovereign debt crisis in the Eurozone, member countries have been pushed towards introducing more flexibility into labour and product mar-kets. This drive towards structural reforms was very much influenced by the traditional theory of OCA. This theory stresses that in the face of asymmet-ric shocks member countries should have a sufficient degree of labour and product market flexibility to adjust to these shocks. Without such flexibility adjustment will be impossible, thereby undermining the sustainability of the monetary union. The underlying assumption of the OCA prescription for structural reform is that asymmetric shocks are permanent (such as perma-nent changes in preferences or productivity shocks). When the shocks are temporary it does not follow that more flexibility is the answer. More specifi-cally, when the shocks are the result of unsynchronised business-cycle move-ments, the way to deal with them is by stabilisation efforts. In this chapter we have provided empirical evidence to suggest that the most significant shocks in the Eurozone have been the result of boom and bust, driven by waves of optimism and pessimism. These business-cycle movements have been relatively well-synchronised. What was not synchronised was the amplitude of these business-cycle movements, where some countries experienced much greater amplitude in business cycles than others. In principle, these business-cycle movements could be stabilised at the national level without the need for budgetary union. However, as the amplitude of these movements is so different, countries experiencing the deepest recession are likely to be hit by 'sudden stops', meaning liquidity outflows triggered by fear and panic, which forces them to switch off the automatic stabilisers in the budget, preventing them from conducting any stabilisation. We argued that the best possible way to deal with the business-cycle movements whose amplitude is unsynchronised is by introducing a budgetary union. By centralising part of the national budgets into a common budget managed by a common political authority, the various increases in budget deficits following from a (common) recession translate into a budget deficit at the union level. As a result, the destabilising flows of liquidity between countries during the recession disappear, and the common budgetary authority can allow the automatic stabiliser in the common budget to perform its role in smoothing the business cycle. It is highly unlikely that the governance of the Eurozone will move in the direction of creating institutions capable of providing the necessary stabilisation of booms and busts that national governments are no longer able to provide. The willingness to move in this direction is minimal. This has much to do with the absence of a 'deep variable' in the monetary union. This deep variable is the sense of belonging to the same (European) nation and that creates the political basis for organising transfers between countries. The absence of this deep variable makes it inevitable that one looks for schemes that introduce some stabilisation at the Eurozone level without going all the way towards budgetary union.

We discussed common unemployment insurance schemes that are now being proposed and stressed that these have to put more emphasis on intertemporal insurance and less on intercountry insurance. This also implies that they should have the capacity to issue bonds during recessions, and to do the opposite during an economic boom, making sure that over the business cycle there would be no net issue of common bonds.

The unwillingness to create a political union has also led to a continuing temptation to resort to technical solutions to the problem. Thus, there has been a proliferation of technical schemes to introduce Eurobonds.[25] We have

---

[25] See J. Delpla and J. Von Weizsäcker, 'The Blue Bond Proposal' (2010) 2010 Bruegel Policy Brief 1; P. De Grauwe and W. Moesen, 'Gains for All: A Proposal for a Common Euro

discussed a common unemployment insurance mechanism in this chapter. They are necessary to indicate the direction in which the Eurozone will have to move. There is a danger, however, that they create a fiction that technical solutions (and therefore also bureaucratic integration) can be a substitute for political unification. As a result, they comfort policy-makers in their decision to set aside all further attempts towards a political union.

7.9 APPENDIX

As suggested in the main text, the choice of the smoothing parameter (lamda) in the Hodrick-Prescott (HP) filter has a significant influence on the estimate of the cyclical and permanent components of GDP-growth. In this appendix we illustrate this by comparing estimates, using a high and a low lamda. The high lamda is the same as the one used in the text and was set equal to 1200; the low lamda was set equal to 100. We compare the results in Figure 7.9. It is immediately evident that in the low lamda estimates the long-term growth line follows the observed output growth line more closely. As a result, the cyclical component is on average smaller than in the high lamda case. This is made clear in Table 7.4, which shows the mean absolute changes in the trend and cyclical components. Even in the case of a low lamda we find that the peripheral countries have been subjected to larger cyclical than permanent movements in output.

Table 7.5 presents the correlation coefficients of the cyclical components of GDP growth for low lamda. It should be compared with Table 7.2 in the text. We observe that in the low lamda estimates the correlation coefficients are of a similar order of magnitude as in the high lamda case. Thus, one of our main conclusions, that business cycles have been highly correlated, is maintained. This is also made clear in Figures 7.10 and 7.11 that show the evolution of the business-cycle component in the two estimates. Obviously, in the low lamda estimate the business-cycle components are generally lower than in the high lamda estimate. In both cases, though, we observe similarly correlated booms and busts in the Eurozone. And, as Figure 7.12 indicates, the divergence in the amplitude of the business cycles across countries tends to increase during the boom years prior to the crisis. This

Bond' (2009) 44 *Intereconomics* 132; J. Von Hagen and G.W. Hammond 'Regional Insurance against Asymmetric Shocks: An Empirical Study for the European Community' (1998) 66 *The Manchester School* 331; J. Drèze, A. Durré, and J. Carpantier, 'Fiscal Integration and Growth Stimulation in Europe' (2012) 80 *Recherches économiques de Louvain* 5; H. Enderlein, L. Guttenberg, and J. Spiess, *Blueprint for a Cyclical Shock Insurance in the Euro Area, Studies & Reports No. 100* (Jacques Delors Institute, 2013).

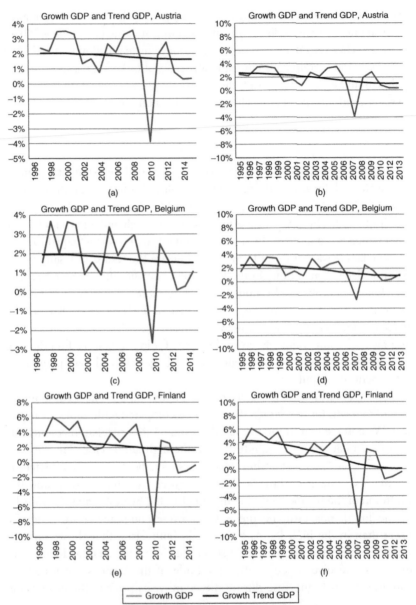

FIGURE 7.9: Cyclical and trend components in GDP growth (1999–2014), side-by-side comparison high lamda (HL) (Figure 7.7) and low lamda (LL): (a) Austria (HL); (b) Austria (LL); (c) Belgium (HL); (d) Belgium (LL); (e) Finland (HL); (f) Finland (LL); (g) France (HL); (h) France (LL); (i) Germany (HL); (j) Germany (LL); (k) Greece (HL); (l) Greece (LL); (m) Ireland (HL); (n) Ireland (LL); (o) Italy (HL); (p) Italy (LL); (q) Netherlands (HL); (r) Netherlands (LL); (s) Portugal (HL); (t) Portugal (LL); (u) Spain (HL); (v) Spain (LL).

Sources: Eurostat and own calculations.

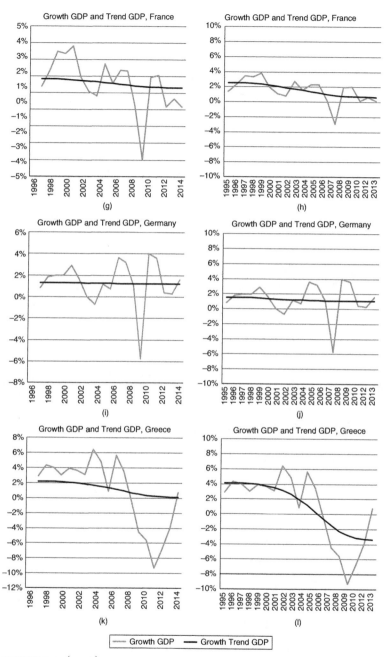

FIGURE 7.9: *(cont.)*

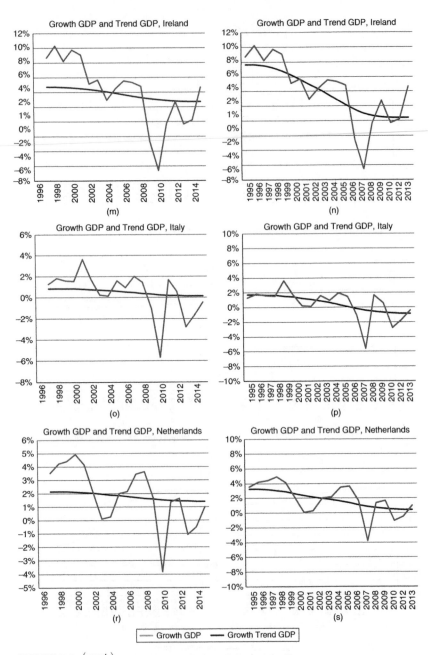

FIGURE 7.9: (cont.)

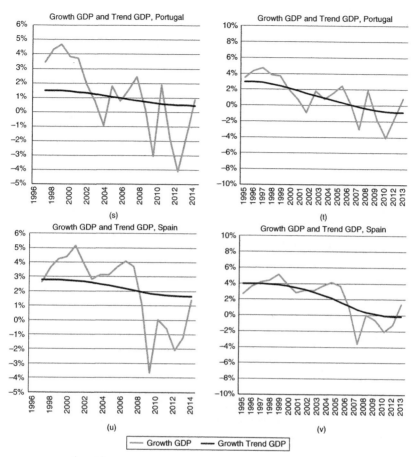

FIGURE 7.9: (*cont.*)

TABLE 7.4: *Mean (absolute) trend growth and mean (absolute) business-cycle change in GDP (as a percentage) during 1999–2014, side-by-side comparison low lamda and high lamda (Table 7.1)*

	Low lamda				High lamda		
	Mean cycle	Mean trend	Ratio		Mean cycle	Mean trend	Ratio
Belgium	0.97	1.47	0.66	Austria	1.79%	1.77%	1.01
Austria	1.18%	1.58	0.75	Belgium	1.72%	1.67%	1.03
Spain	1.69	2.22	0.76	Germany	1.55%	1.23%	1.26
France	1.04	1.27	0.82	France	2.15%	1.49%	1.44
Portugal	1.63	1.40	1.16	Netherlands	2.66%	1.66%	1.60
Netherlands	1.61	1.33	1.21	Finland	4.35%	2.02%	2.15
Germany	1.49	1.18	1.27	Spain	4.58%	2.07%	2.21
Ireland	3.26	2.48	1.31	Ireland	8.01%	3.35%	2.39
Finland	2.08	1.53	1.36	Portugal	3.67%	0.81%	4.53
Italy	1.37	0.96	1.42	Italy	2.86%	0.41%	7.05
Greece	4.50	2.85	1.58	Greece	9.09%	0.90%	10.11

Notes: see Table 7.1.
Source: Computations based on data from Eurostat.

is also what we found using estimates with a high lamda. Thus, one of our major empirical conclusions still stands, even when one uses a low lamda. This is that the asymmetry in the business cycles of the Eurozone countries is to be found in the divergence in the amplitude of the business cycle. The business cycles themselves tended to be highly correlated. There is reason to believe that the low lamda estimates bias the business-cycle components downwards and thus the long-term growth component upwards (in absolute value). This is made clear from Tables 7.6, which compares the estimates of long-term growth in 1995 and 2014 in the two lamda scenarios. We find that in the low lamda estimates the decline in long-term growth in a number of periphery countries is implausibly high. In the cases of Ireland and Greece long-term growth declines by more than 7 percentage points. (The corresponding declines in the high lamda case is 2 per cent.)

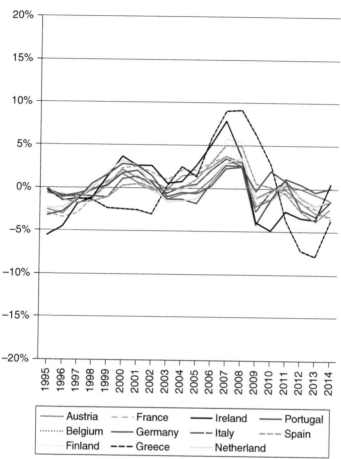

FIGURE 7.10: Business-cycle component of GDP growth, low lamda.
Source: Own calculation based on Eurostat.

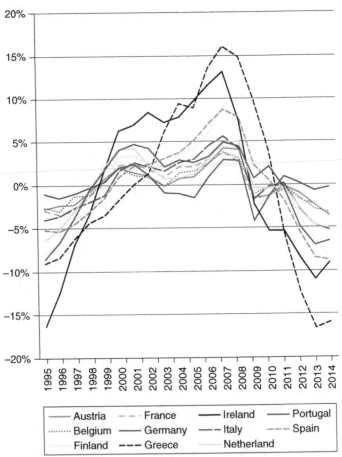

FIGURE 7.11: Business-cycle component of GDP growth, high lamda.
Source: Own calculation based on Eurostat (Figure 7.8).

TABLE 7.5: *Correlation coefficients of cyclical components of GDP growth, low lamda*

	Aus	Bel	Fin	Fra	Ger	Gre	Ire	Ita	Net	Por
Austria										
Belgium	0.9									
Finland	0.9	0.9								
France	0.9	0.9	0.9							
Germany	0.8	0.7	0.7	0.8						
Greece	0.3	0.4	0.5	0.2	−0.0					
Ireland	0.7	0.7	0.7	0.8	0.5	0.4				
Italy	0.8	0.8	0.9	0.9	0.7	0.5	0.7			
Netherlands	0.8	0.8	0.8	0.7	0.7	0.3	0.6	0.7		
Portugal	0.9	0.7	0.6	0.5	0.5	0.4	0.5	0.6	0.8	
Spain	0.6	0.7	0.7	0.6	0.3	0.9	0.7	0.8	0.6	0.6

Source: Own calculations based on Eurostat.

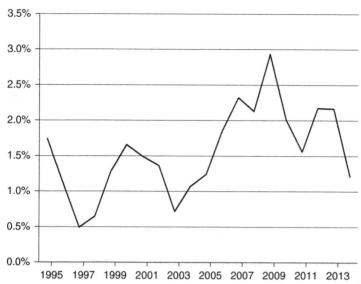

FIGURE 7.12: Standard deviation cyclical component, low lamda.

TABLE 7.6: *Estimates of long-term growth in 1995 and 2014*

Low lamda				High lamda			
	Tre	Tre	Cha		Tre	Treo14	Cha
Austria	2.58	1.02	−1.56	Austria	2.0	1.6	−0.
Belgium	2.49	0.90	−1.59	Belgium	1.9	1.5	−0.
Finland	4.20	0.09	−4.11	Finland	2.7	1.6	−1.
France	2.53	0.69	−1.84	France	1.8	1.3	−0.
Germany	1.55	1.11	−0.43	Germany	1.3	1.2	−0.
Greece	4.12	−3.37	−7.49	Greece	2.1	0.1	−2.
Ireland	7.66	0.41	−7.26	Ireland	4.7	2.7	−2.
Italy	1.71	−0.86	−2.57	Italy	0.8	0.1	−0.
Netherlands	3.27	0.45	−2.83	Netherlands	2.1	1.4	−0.
Portugal	2.98	−0.87	−3.85	Portugal	1.5	0.4	−1.
Spain	3.99	−0.14	−4.13	Spain	2.8	1.6	−1.

Source: *De Grauwe and Ji, n9 above.*

8

What Follows Austerity? From Social Pillar to New Deal

Simon Deakin

8.1 INTRODUCTION

In the autumn of 2016 the future of the European Union was more in doubt than at any point in the preceeding five decades. Politics appeared to be taking a post-liberal turn in Britain, following the Brexit referendum of 23 June, and in the United States, following the presidential election of 8 November. A common thread linking these developments was scepticism towards policies of austerity. Post-Brexit, Britain's Conservative government abandoned fiscal targets put in place by the Coalition government and maintained after the General Election of 2015,[1] but the autumn statement delivered in November 2016 did not mark a major change in the substance of macroeconomic policy.[2] At the same time, one of its principal measures was the introduction of tax cuts for middle-income and higher earners,[3] hardly a break with recent practice.

---

[1] The Conservative–Liberal Democrat Coalition government which held office between May 2010 and May 2015 had a target of achieving a fiscal surplus by 2020, and this was reaffirmed by the Conservative government which took office in May 2015. The target, which was embodied in the Charter of Budget Responsibility agreed by Parliament in October 2015, was modified in the Autumn Statement of November 2016, and now consists of a mandate to reduce public sector net borrowing (the 'structural deficit') to below 2 per cent by 2020–21. It is currently 4 per cent. The revised mandate also involves reducing public sector debt as a percentage of GDP in 2020–21; previously the target was to reduce the debt–GDP ratio in every year up to and including 2020–21. Public sector debt is currently over 80 per cent of GDP. See Office of Budget Responsibility, *Economic and Fiscal Outlook November 2016* (HMSO, 2016), pp. 197–9.

[2] 'Confronted by a near-term economic slowdown and a structural deterioration in the public finances, the Government has opted neither for a large near-term fiscal stimulus nor for more austerity over the medium term. Instead, the Chancellor has proposed a much looser "fiscal mandate" that gives him scope for almost 2.5 per cent of GDP (£56 billion) more structural borrowing in 2020–21 than his predecessor was aiming for in March [2016].' Office of Budget Responsibility, n. 1 in this chapter, at p. 5.

[3] The changes made to personal allowances, raising the threshold at which income tax is paid and at which the higher rate of income tax applies, disproportionately benefit average and higher earners, see HMRC and HM Treasury, 'Autumn Statement 2016: tax updates

The Trump administration which took office in the USA in January 2017 made tax cuts for middle income earners and cuts in corporation tax its fiscal policy priorities,[4] with no substantive plan for infrastructure spending along the lines set out during the election campaign. An end to austerity was advocated by movements of the social democratic left[5] before it was taken up by conservative politicians, and the unexpected result of the British General Election of June 2017 appears to have further discredited austerity policies in the United Kingdom.

The situation is very different in the European Union and in particular in the Eurozone. There, the policy of austerity has been reinforced to the point of being embedded in intergovernmental agreements, most notably the Treaty on Stability, Coordination, and Governance of March 2012,[6] which commits its signatories to enact constitutional or equivalent legal measures ruling out the use of fiscal deficits to counter the effects of economic recession. In 2014 the intervention of the European Central Bank effectively prevented the adoption of an anti-austerity policy by the Syriza-led administration in Greece; had the government proceeded as it intended, and as it was mandated to do by a referendum, the ECB would have withdrawn its support for Greece's commercial banks, and the domestic economy would most likely have collapsed.[7] Thus it seems that whether by legal-constitutional means, or via the power to control national economic policy which the ECB is capable of exercising during a fiscal crisis, ending austerity is not an option for Eurozone states or, in practice, for the vast majority of other EU Member States, for which Eurozone membership continues to be a long-term goal.

and technical changes' (2016) available at:www.gov.uk/government/uploads/system/uploads/ attachment_data/file/571251/AS_UTC_-211116_.pdf (accessed 5 December 2016).

[4] BBC, 'Mnuchin Promises to Boost US Growth as Treasury Boss', BBC News, 30 November 2016, available at:www.bbc.co.uk/news/business-38157228 (accessed 5 December 2016).

[5] BBC, 'Labour Leadership: Corbyn on Austerity and Poverty', BBC News, 12 September 2015, available at:www.bbc.co.uk/news/uk-politics-34232479 (accessed 5 December 2016); B. Sanders, 'The Pro-worker, Pro-growth Experiment in Greece Is Under Threat', *The Guardian*, 17 February 2015, available at: (www.theguardian.com/commentisfree/2015/feb/17/ the-pro-worker-pro-growth-experiment-in-greece-is-under-threat (accessed 5 December 2016).

[6] Treaty on Stability, Coordination, and Governance in the EMU of 2 March 2012. For analysis of this Treaty, see S. Deakin, 'Social Policy, Economic Governance and EMU: Alternatives to Austerity', and L. Obendorfer, 'A New Economic Governance through Secondary Legislation? Analysis and Constitutional Assessment: from New Constitutionalism, via Authoritarian Constitutionalism to Progressive Constitutionalism', both in N. Bruun, K. Lörcher, and I. Schömann (eds), *The Economic and Financial Crisis and Collective Labour Law in Europe* (Hart, 2014).

[7] See J. Stiglitz, *The Euro and its Threat to the Future of Europe* (Allen Lane, 2016), pp. 156–7; P. Mason, *Postcapitalism: A Guide to Our Future* (Penguin, 2016), p. xi.

Simon Deakin

We might, nevertheless, question whether the Eurozone's approach can be indefinitely maintained. Much may depend on whether governments in Britain and America make a clean break with austerity and can be seen to make alternatives work. But leaving the examples of these other systems to one side, the effects of austerity policies, in terms of increasing inequalities and depressing growth, will surely at some point require a rethink for the euro area. This point will arrive sooner rather than later to the extent that the current crisis comes to be understood as nothing less than an existential one for the Eurozone and even for the wider Union.

At this moment of unique danger or opportunity, or both, for the European project, the Commission's proposal for a European Pillar of Social Rights[8] might appear, at first sight, somewhat underwhelming. As a restatement of the goals of European social policy, the Pillar lacks the ambition and sense of purpose of earlier instruments to which it bears some resemblance, such as the Community Charter of the Fundamental Social Rights of Workers of 1989,[9] which, with the benefit of hindsight, appear radical by comparison. It is tempting then to see the Pillar as offering nothing more than the 'mirage' or 'illusion' of the kind of social policy which Europe needs at this time of crisis. On the other hand, a Commission initiative on social policy which does not simply call for yet further deregulation in the name of market integration is a rare event. In both tone and substance, the documentation on Social Pillar is very different from the labour-market pronouncements of the Barroso Commission.[10] So it merits a closer look.

[8] COM(2016)127 *Launching a Consultation on a European Pillar of Social Rights* (Strasbourg, 8 March 2016). In addition to the 2016 Communication, there was an Annex setting out an Outline of the Pillar itself consisting of a series of 'principles' (this is the term used in the Explanatory Note to the Outline). Then in April 2017 the Commission published a Recommendation (C(2017)2600) and a Proposal for an Interinstitutional Proclamation (COM(2017)251) setting out what was intended to be the final text of the Pillar, in anticipation of its adoption at the Gothenburg Summit planned for November 2017. A number of supporting documents were published at the same time. The Social Pillar was first prefigured in documents prepared by the Presidency of the European Council in 2013, in response to a call from the December 2012 Council to develop a 'social dimension of the EMU', see Cabinet of the President of the European Council, 'Towards a Genuine Economic and Monetary Union: State of Play of the Consultations with Member States and Institutional Actors – Summary Note' (2013), available at: www.consilium.europa.eu/uedocs/cms_data/docs/pressdata/en/ec/137665.pdf (accessed 5 December 2016).

[9] The Community Charter was adopted by the heads of state or government of the then 11 Member States meeting at Strasbourg on 9 December 1989. The text is reproduced in 1 *Social Europe* 1990, pp. 46–50, available at: www.eesc.europa.eu/resources/docs/community-charter–en.pdf (accessed 5 December 2016).

[10] In particular the Green Paper, COM(2006)708 *Modernising Labour Law to Meet the Challenges of the 21st Century* (Brussels, 22 November 2006).

With this aim in mind, the present chapter unfolds as follows. Section 8.2 briefly does some scene setting by explaining how we came to be where we are now: why there is no pan-European labour code, why social policy remains fragmented at the level of EU law and practice, and how it came to be subordinated to economic and monetary policy in the process of constituting the internal market and currency union. Section 8.3 reviews the proposals set out by the Commission in the documents it published on the Social Pillar in March 2016, in so far as they relate to labour and social security law, and to labour-market regulation more generally. Section 8.4 sets out the case for thinking of the Social Pillar as a step on the road leading away from austerity and towards an integrated economic, monetary and social policy response to the problems besetting European economies – in other words, towards a European New Deal.

8.2 HOW WE GOT HERE: EUROPEAN SOCIAL POLICY IN RETROSPECT

In 1897, Sidney and Beatrice Webb wrote of the incomplete and fragmented nature of labour-market regulation in Britain in these terms:

> [the] policy of prescribing minimum conditions, below which no employer is allowed to drive even his most necessitous operatives, has yet been only imperfectly carried out. Factory legislation applies, usually, only to sanitary conditions and, as regards particular classes, to the hours of labour. Even within this limited sphere it is everywhere unsystematic and lop-sided. When any European statesman makes up his mind to grapple seriously with the problem of the 'sweated trades' he will have to expand the Factory Acts of his country into a systematic and comprehensive Labour Code, prescribing the minimum conditions under which the community can afford to allow industry to be carried on; and including not merely definite precautions of sanitation and safety, and maximum hours of toil, but also a minimum of weekly earnings.[11]

In the course of the twentieth century, most European nations implemented a version of the plan set out by the Webbs, but to this day there is no pan-European labour code, and the fragmentation they described as characteristic of British labour law at an early stage in its development very well describes the European Union labour law of today. In so far as there is a 'floor of rights' in European labour law setting minimum standards with which Member States must comply, it is partial and incomplete.[12] In discrimination law and in

---

[11] S. Webb and B. Webb, *Industrial Democracy* (Longman, Green and Co., 1897), p. 767.
[12] See C. Barnard and S. Deakin, 'Social Policy and Labour Market Regulation', in E. Jones, A. Menon, and S. Weatherill (eds), *The Oxford Handbook of the European Union* (Oxford University Press, 2012).

relation to health and safety there is something approaching comprehensive regulation through a combination of Treaty provisions and Directives,[13] but there is no systematic standard-setting in the area of employment termination.[14] Certain areas, most notably freedom of association and the law governing industrial action, are more or less untouched by social policy directives.[15] There is no European-level legal floor to wages, and no basic standard-setting in relation to forms and levels of collective bargaining.

The failure to embed transnational labour standards in the process of constructing the European Union can be traced to decisions taken at the time of the drafting of the Treaty of Rome in the 1950s.[16] The founding Member States rejected arguments for the harmonisation of social policy on the grounds that, in a common market, wages and conditions would tend to level up under the influence of the forces of convergence.[17] Social policy would remain a matter for individual states within a legal framework designed to encourage cooperation between them but falling short of mandating acceptance of common standards.[18] Differences in wages and living standards *across* the Member States largely reflected differences in productivity and any comparative advantages enjoyed by low-cost states would be cancelled out by movements in exchange rates.[19] Only where this was not the case because of cross-sectoral differences *within* Member States was there a case for centralised regulation. This rather technical justification for transnational harmonisation provided the original basis for the inclusion in Article 119 of the Treaty of Rome of

[13] See C. Barnard, *EU Employment Law* (Oxford, 4th edn, 2012), Parts III and IV respectively.
[14] There is no single measure for the harmonisation of dismissal laws. Such directives as exist relate to the laws governing collective redundancies, business transfers and insolvencies (Barnard, n. 13 in this chapter, Part V). Employment termination is an issue requiring unanimity in the Council if a directive is to be adopted: TFEU, Article 153(2).
[15] Pay, freedom of association, the right to strike and the right to lock out are excluded from the competence of the Union to adopt directives in the social policy field under Article 153 (see Article 153(5)).
[16] See S. Deakin, 'Labour Law and Market Regulation: The Economic Foundations of European Social Policy', in P. Davies, A. Lyon-Caen, S. Sciarra, and M. Weiss (eds), *European Community Labour Law Principles and Perspectives: Liber Amicorum* Lord Wedderburn (Oxford University Press, 1996).
[17] '[W]age and interest rates tend to level up in a common market ... This is a consequence rather than a condition of the common market's operation.' Comité Intergouvernemental Créé par la 1Conférence de Messine, *Rapport des Chefs de Délégation aux Ministres des Affaires Etrangères* (Comité Intergouvernemental Créé par la Conférence de Messine, 1956), English translation in (1956) 405 *Political and Economic Planning* 233. This view was eventually embedded in Article 117 of the Treaty of Rome: Deakin, n. 16 in this chapter, at pp. 69–70.
[18] This was the logic underlying Article 118 of the Treaty of Rome (now Article 156 TFEU).
[19] This view was set out in the 'Ohlin Report' commissioned by the six founding Member States from the ILO. International Labour Organisation, 'Social Aspects of European Economic Co-operation. Report by a Group of Experts' (1956) 74 *International Labour Review* 99.

the principle of equal pay between women and men.[20] A further and some-what more pragmatic justification for not harmonising labour laws in general was that the original six Member States were all committed by one means or another, in some cases through constitutional texts, to maintaining social rights and strong welfare states.[21]

Whatever the merits of the original decision to downplay the importance of transnational social policy, it should have been revisited at the point when the building blocks of the Economic and Monetary Union (EMU) were being put in place in the late 1980s and early 1990s. The deepening of the internal market following the Single Act of 1986 implied a step change in levels of labour and capital mobility, particularly the latter, which would test the theory that convergence would naturally lead to levelling up. If standards in product and capital markets were to be harmonised, leaving labour standards up to national legislatures would invite a 'race to the bottom' in social policy. Monetary union, by removing exchange rate flexibility and locking in a uniform interest rate, would leave states with few ways to respond to fiscal shocks except by depressing wages and living standards.

The need for a pan-European floor of rights to respond to these risks was recognised at the time,[22] but the harmonisation of labour laws stopped short of what was needed. The Single Act paved the way for uniform rules on health and safety[23] and the Maastricht Treaty expanded the social policy competences of the Union as well as widening the scope for qualified majority voting on labour law matters, although wage regulation and most aspects of collective labour law remained beyond the reach of even these new powers.[24] The failure to make more systematic progress in the period between the adoption of the Community Charter of Social Rights in the 1989 and the Social Chapter of the Maastricht Treaty in 1991 can be attributed to a number of political factors including the opposition of the United Kingdom to an extension of social policy. The UK took the position it has consistently maintained in relation to efforts to deepen European integration: diluting the content of harmonising measures, on the one hand, and then securing opt-outs from these weakened provisions, on the other. By the time the UK signed up to the Social

---

[20] Now contained in Article 157 TFEU. See Ohlin Report, n. 19 in this chapter, at p. 107.

[21] Ohlin Report, n. 19 in this chapter, at p. 112.

[22] U. Mückenberger and S. Deakin, 'From Deregulation to a European Floor of Rights: Labour Law, Flexibilisation and the European Single Market' (1989) 3 *Zeitschrift für ausländisches und internationales Arbeits- und Sozialrecht* 157.

[23] The Single Act led to the insertion of Article 118b into the EC Treaty. See now Article 153(1)(a)–(b) TFEU.

[24] See now Article 153 TFEU.

Chapter in the late 1990s the opportunity for further labour law harmonisation had been lost, as the focus of policy-making turned to the use of alternative, 'soft-law' mechanisms of regulation, and open coordination methods came to be preferred to legally binding standards. The prospect of a floor of rights in social policy further receded in the 2000s as the UK was joined in resisting any expansion of social policy by accession states from central and eastern Europe, which accepted the incomplete 'social acquis' as a condition of membership, but otherwise viewed labour law in unfavourable terms as a legacy of socialist dirigisme.[25]

Towards the end of the first decade of the millennium EU policy towards social policy shifted from one of 'legislative deadlock'[26] to outright conflict between the goals of labour protection and market integration. This shift was not inevitable and it remains reversible, but it was, nonetheless, an entirely predictable result of the failure to embed social policy more deeply in the institutional framework of the EMU. The Court's rulings in *Viking*[27] and *Laval*[28] marked the first step in this process as they elevated to the level of legal dogma the argument that cross-national differences in labour standards distorted the operation of the internal market.[29] It is worth recalling that this very argument was rejected in the preparatory documents of the Treaty of Rome: a common market did not require uniformity of wages and living costs.[30] It is hard to discern any argument of economic principle in *Viking* and *Laval* other than the subjection of labour law to the logic of atomistic competition, which is common to neoclassical and ordoliberal conceptions of the market. At the core of this vision of the 'European economic order' is a 'social contract' according to which 'workers throughout Europe must accept the recurring negative consequences that are inherent to the common market's creation of increasing prosperity, in exchange for which society must commit itself to the general improvement of their living and working conditions, and to the provision of economic support to those workers who, as a consequence of market forces,

[25] On the evolution of EU social policy during the 1990s and 2000s see Barnard, ch. 1, n. 13 in this chapter.
[26] Barnard and Deakin, n. 12 in this chapter.
[27] ECJ, judgment of 11 December 2007 in *International Transport Workers' Federation and Finnish Seamen's Union* ('Viking'), C-438/05, EU:C:2007:772.
[28] ECJ, judgment of 18 December 2007 in *Laval un Partneri*, C-341/05, EU:C:2007:809.
[29] For discussion, see S. Deakin, 'Regulatory Competition after *Laval*' (2008) 10 *Cambridge Yearbook of European Legal Studies* 581.
[30] '[C]ompetition does not necessarily require a complete harmonisation of the different elements in costs; indeed, it is only on the basis of certain differences – such as wage differences due to differences in productivity – that trade and competition can develop'. Spaak Report, n. 17 in this chapter, at p. 233.

come into difficulties'.[31] It is not difficult to see in this comment the source of much contemporary disenchantment with the European project.[32]

The second phase in the conflict between market integration and protective labour regulation occurred with the response of the Union's institutions (notably the Commission and the ECB, acting in conjunction with the International Monetary Fund to form the 'Troika') to the sovereign debt crisis which emerged in the Eurozone from 2009.[33] As a condition of extending financial support to the debtor states, the Troika insisted on 'structural reforms' to national-level labour and social security laws, the object of which was to restore fiscal balances by depressing wages and social security benefits.[34] As social policy was (and remains) largely a matter for the Member States, which the Union possessing only limited powers to legislate directly on matters of wage determination and social security provision, the Troika's interventions operated at the intergovernmental level, sidelining Union law while undermining, in practical terms, the autonomy supposedly enjoyed by Member States under the Treaties.[35] Attempts to engage the Court in arguments over the incompatibility of the Memoranda of Understanding with social rights set

[31] Opinion Advocate General Poiares Maduro in *International Transport Workers' Federation and Finnish Seamen's Union* ('*Viking*'), C-438/05, EU:C:2007:772, at p. 59.

[32] On links between the logic of the *Viking* and *Laval* cases, labour trafficking and the Brexit referendum vote, see S. Deakin, 'Brexit, Labour Rights and Migration: Why Wisbech Matters to Brussels' (2016) 17 *German Law Journal* (Brexit Supplement) 14.

[33] See Deakin, n. 6 in this chapter; S. Deakin and A. Koukiadaki, 'The Sovereign Debt Crisis and the Evolution of Labour Law in Europe', in N. Countouris and M. Freedland (eds), *Resocialising Europe in a Time of Crisis* (Cambridge University Press, 2013); Z. Adams and S. Deakin, 'Structural Adjustment, Social Policy and Social Policy in a Regional Context: The Case of the Eurozone Crisis', in A. Blackett and A. Trebilcock (eds), *Research Handbook on Transnational Labour Law* (Edward Elgar, 2015).

[34] See A. Koukiadaki and L. Kretsos, 'Opening Pandora's Box: The Sovereign Debt Crisis and Labour Market Regulation in Greece' (2012) 41 *Industrial Law Journal* 276; V. Monastiriotis, N. Hardiman, A. Regan, C. Coretti, L. Landi, J.-I. Conde-Ruiz, and R. Cabral, 'Austerity Measures in Crisis Countries – Results and Impact on Mid-term Development' (2013) 48 *Intereconomics* 4; K. Busch, C. Hermann, K. Hinrichs, and T. Schulten, 'Euro Crisis, Austerity Policy and the European Social Model: How Crisis Policies Threaten Europe's Social Dimension' (2013), available at: library.fes.de/pdf-files/id/ipa/09656.pdf (accessed 5 December 2016).

[35] The issues of wages and collective bargaining are excluded from the scope of Article 153 TFEU and social protection is a matter requiring unanimity. These provisions go back to the Social Chapter of the Maastricht Treaty: see Barnard, ch. 1, n. 13 in this chapter. On the argument that the MoUs are contrary to the exclusion of wage determination and collective labour law issues from Article 153 TFEU, implying that these are areas over which the Member States have exclusive competence, see M. Schmitt, 'Evaluation of European Union Responses to the Crisis Having Regard to Primary Legislation (European Union Treaties and Charter of Fundamental Rights)', in N. Bruun, K. Lörcher, and I. Schömann (eds), *The Economic and Financial Crisis and Collective Labour Law in Europe* (Hart, 2014).

out in the Union Treaties and in the Charter of Fundamental Rights of the European Union proved to be futile.[36] It is difficult to see in this process anything other than the further subordination of social policy to an ultra-liberal conception of market integration.[37]

8.3 THE EUROPEAN PILLAR OF SOCIAL RIGHTS: POTENTIAL AND LIMITS

It was into this unpromising environment that the initiative for the Pillar of Social Rights was launched. Ostensibly, the Pillar is designed to deepen the process of the EMU.[38] Can this really be done while simultaneously strengthening social protection? To explore this question, the analysis in this section will focus on the rationale of the Pillar; its relationship to the wider EMU process; the proposed scope of the Pillar, in terms of the rights, principles, and areas of worker protection so far identified as possibly forming part of it; and the mechanisms through which the Pillar may take effect.

8.3.1 *The Rationale of the Pillar*

According to the Commission Communication of April 2016, the Pillar draws on the concept of a 'competitive social market economy'. Underlying this idea are a number of claims about the relationship between social policy and the economic goals of the Union:

(1) Social policy is a 'productive factor' which can contribute to growth and competitiveness.
(2) Social policy achieves this end by reducing inequality, maximising job creation, and enhancing the formation of human capital.

---

[36] Schmitt, n. 35 in this chapter.

[37] A. Supiot, *La gouvernance par les nombres* (Fayard, 2015).

[38] Outline, Explanatory Note: the principles set out in the draft Pillar 'address concerns for a deeper and fairer Economic and Monetary Union, such as the need to boot competitiveness, to increase participation in the labour market, develop adequate social protection floors, make full use of people's potential, ensure the sustainability of public finances and increase the adjustment capacity and resilience of adjustment structures'. The Pillar is intended to apply only to states in the auro area 'but would also be open for other Member States to join on a voluntary basis'.

(3) There is empirical evidence for this view: the Member States with the most advanced social systems are also those with the most advanced and successful economies.

(4) It is particularly important that social policy plays this role in supporting the EMU at a time when the European economies are recovering from the crisis.

(5) Social policy has a specific role in 'deepening' EMU and thereby contributing to integration.[39]

The emphasis on social policy as a productive factor is welcome, although it is not new. The idea of a competitive social market economy, or close variants of it, goes back at least to early 2000s in the debate over the Constitutional Treaty. The essence of the idea is to be found in a number of current Treaty provisions, including Article 3 TEU.[40]

However, the emphasis given to social policy as an input into sustainable economic growth, and not just an outcome of growth, can be seen positively. It implies that mechanisms of worker and social protection should be embedded in the process of economic integration, not as a side effect of EMU nor, for example, to reverse growing inequality if that were to result from EMU (a 'market reversing' function). Rather, social policy is there to help ensure that a more long-lasting, stable, and ultimately successful EMU can be achieved (a 'market constituting' function). The idea that social policy is an input into growth and integration, and not just a result of it or response to it, chimes with many recent developments in the social science literature on labour markets and growth,[41] and this wider literature can be called on to defend the idea against claims that social policy is a fetter on growth or distorts markets.

---

[39] COM(2016)127, n. 8 in this chapter: 'social policy ... should be conceived as a productive factor, which reduces inequality, maximises job creation and allows Europe's human capital to thrive. This conviction is confirmed by evidence on social and economic performance. The best performing Member States in economic terms have developed more ambitious and efficient social policies, not just as a result of economic development, but as a central part of their growth model.'

[40] 'The Union shall establish an internal market. It shall work for the sustainable development of Europe based on balanced economic growth and price stability, a highly competitive social market economy, aiming at full employment and social progress, and a high level of protection and improvement of the quality of the environment. It shall promote scientific and technological advance.'

[41] See S. Deakin, 'The Contribution of Labour Law to Economic Development and Growth' (2016) 92 *Bulletin for Comparative Labour Relations* 19.

8.3.2 *The Role of the Social Pillar within the Wider Framework of EMU*

According to the Commission Communication, a number of specific roles for the Pillar are envisaged within the wider EMU process:

(1) Social policy mechanisms can address inequalities which inhibit human capital formation, limit opportunities, and thereby hamper growth.[42]

(2) Social policy mechanisms have a role to play in addressing imbalances within the Eurozone which threaten its stability. These imbalances have become worse since the onset of the current crisis.[43]

(3) Strong welfare states help buffer the effects of economic 'shocks' of the kind recently experienced in many parts of the Eurozone.[44]

This aspect of the Pillar should also be welcomed. However, the Commission Communication does not sufficiently clearly spell out how social policy can help address the issues of imbalances and shocks. This lack of clarity not only risks diluting the message that social policy should be central to EMU, but it also opens the door to a deregulatory interpretation of the role of social policy. This can be seen in the reappearance, in the Communication, of the much criticised and (it might have been thought) largely discredited idea of 'flexicurity'.[45]

The imbalances and shocks referred to in the Commission Communication reflect a larger problem with EMU as currently constituted, namely that its institutional architecture is 'asymmetrical'. In particular, the relationship between social/economic policy, on the one hand, and monetary policy, on the other, is unbalanced.[46] Monetary policy is unified under a single, Union-level competence, the administration of which is largely in the hands of the ECB. Economic policy and social policy are shared competences: that is, they are partitioned between the Member States and the Union institutions,

---

[42] COM(2016)127, n. 8 in this chapter, at paragraph 2.2.

[43] Ibid., paragraph 2.3: building well-functioning welfare systems 'is not just a political or social imperative, it is also an economic necessity'.

[44] Ibid., paragraph 2.3: 'it is clear that the future success of the euro area depends, in no small measure, on the effectiveness of national labour markets and welfare systems and on the capacity of the economy to absorb shocks'. In the version of the Pillar published in April 2017, the Preamble, paragraph 12, states: 'A stronger focus on employment and social performance is particularly important to increase resilience and deepen the Economic and Monetary Union', see COM(2017)251, n. 8 in this chapter.

[45] Ibid., paragraph 2.2. The flexicurity concept was at the core of the 2006 Green Paper on the 'modernisation' of labour law. Para 2.2 of the Communication, referring obliquely to this, states that 'the concept of flexicurity is not new but in the aftermath of the crisis, and in light of a changing world of work, it is time to redefine how it can best be applied in practice'.

[46] See Deakin, n. 6 in this chapter.

with the balance of competences very much in favour of the Member States.[47]

Putting in place a single monetary policy without counterbalancing institutions for economic and social coordination at central level is now widely understood to have been a major cause of the crisis in the Eurozone which began in 2008–9. That crisis was triggered by divergences between the national economies of the Eurozone. During the 2000s, certain countries (the future debtor states) were experiencing relatively high growth based on credit expansion and wage inflation. This was achieved at the cost of decreasing productivity and competitiveness. Others, the future creditor states, were experiencing slower growth with limited expansion of domestic credit and restraints on wages. This mix of conditions led to higher productivity and steadily improving competitiveness in the future creditor states.[48]

The superior economic performance of the future creditor states was reflected in trade surpluses not just with third countries beyond the Eurozone, but with the future debtor states within it. To offset these surpluses, capital flows from the creditor to debtor states increased. This led to further speculative lending and credit bubbles in the future debtor states. The ECB's single interest rate policy exacerbated these imbalances as it was not able to take account of the different macroeconomic conditions prevailing in the different states. The rigidity of monetary policy was thus a further factor in triggering the crisis.[49]

The problem of imbalances remains an unresolved issue for the Eurozone. It has not been addressed in any systematic way by the responses to the crisis of the Troika since 2008–9. Imposing austerity on the debtor states addresses the wrong problem (because 'welfare profligacy' was not the cause of their economic vulnerability) and is making matters worse in several respects.[50] Austerity policy does have the side effect of helping to maintain the solvency of banks in the creditor states which had lent incautiously to the debtor states – but that is a different story.

To address the issue of imbalance and shocks means addressing the institutional asymmetry that is inherent in the design of the Eurozone. From the point of view of social policy, it means putting in place a coordinated approach to wage determination and social protection within the Eurozone. This should be seen as an essential part of making EMU sustainable.

---

[47] On the distinction (for this purpose) between the Union's unique competence in monetary policy, and the shared competencies in economic and social policy, see ECJ, judgment of 27 November 2012 in *Pringle*, C-370/12, EU:C:2012:756.
[48] See generally, Deakin, n. 6 in this chapter.
[49] See generally Stiglitz, ch. 6, n. 7 in this chapter.
[50] Stiglitz, chs 7 and 8, n. 7 in this chapter.

Social policy could help address the issue of imbalances in a number of ways but the following two are among the potentially most important.

8.3.2.1 Wage Determination

Centralisation of collective bargaining at sector and national level, together with national level of coordination of wages policies through dialogue between governments and the social partners, was features of the labour-market regimes of virtually all the creditor states prior to the crisis, and continues to be so. Centralised collective bargaining together with national coordination enables wage increases to be linked to productivity growth across the whole economy. It is a solidaristic means of maintaining competiveness since it allows the benefits of a strong economic performance to be widely shared across different industries and between the private sector (which is the main driver of competitiveness) and the public sector. By contrast, in the future debtor states, the level of sectoral and national-level coordination of wages during the 2000s was weak (or weaker than in the creditor states). This was a factor which contributed to wage inflation and the loss of competitiveness in those states and hence to the imbalances which precipitated the crisis.[51] Against this background there is a case to be made for instituting a common approach to wage determination across the Eurozone, based on the desirability of maintaining and strengthening institutions of collective bargaining at sector and national level.

8.3.2.2 Employment Protection Laws (EPL)

EPLs that are relatively strong in terms of their control over the dismissal decision and also avoid segmenting the labour market (by, for example, excluding fixed-term and agency work from protection) have a role to play in encouraging industrial upgrading by firms and helping to create the conditions for innovation. Most of the creditor states have relatively strong EPL laws with wide coverage and limit the permissible degree of differential treatment of fixed-term and agency workers. Many of the debtor states, on the other hand, have EPL regimes characterised by a high level of protection for a small core of workers, offset by a lower degree of protection for workers in so called non-standard jobs. There is evidence that this mix of policies fails to support economy-wide upgrading (as firms come to rely on insecure and low-cost labour in the secondary labour market in order to survive) and also has regressive effects (as workers in non-standard employment experience greater insecurity of work and incomes).[52] This is another area in

---

[51]   This discussion is further elaborated in Deakin, n. 6 in this chapter.

[52]   For a summary of the evidence on the effects of EPL on labour market segmentation, see Z. Adams and S. Deakin, 'Institutional Solutions to Inequality and Precariousness in Labour Markets' (2014) 52 *British Journal of Industrial Relations* 779.

which the failure to arrive at a common approach to labour-market regulation within the Eurozone led to economic divergences prior to the crisis and exacerbated its effects once it struck. Countering it requires consideration to be given to developing a more unified approach to EPL across the Eurozone.

It may be noted that polices of centralising collective bargaining and strengthening EPLs while reducing segmentation run exactly counter to those implemented by the 'Troika' in the debtor states since 2009,[53] but this reinforces the point that the response of the European institutions has so far been not just misguided but actively counterproductive in terms of addressing the institutional shortcomings of the Eurozone.

8.3.3 *The Scope of the Social Pillar*

The contents of the Pillar were initially set out in the Outline contained in the Annex to the Commission Communication of April 2016 and subsequently in the Commission Recommendation and Proposal for an Interinstitutional Proclamation of April 2017.[54] The areas of labour law addressed in chapter II of the draft Pillar include:

(1) Minimum wages[55]
(2) The right to a written contract of employment[56]
(3) Length of probation or qualifying periods[57]
(4) The right to a certain period of notice prior to dismissal[58]
(5) Procedural fairness in dismissal[59]
(6) Health and safety[60]
(7) Social dialogue.[61]

---

[53] Stiglitz, ch. 7, n. 7 in this chapter.
[54] For the appendix to COM(2016)127, n. 8 in this chapter, see eur-lex.europa.eu/legal-content/en/TXT/?uri=CELEX:52016DC0127 (accessed 5 December 2016), and for the 2017 version of the Pillar, see COM(2017)2600 and C(2017)251, n. 8 in this chapter. In addition to a chapter on 'Fair Working Conditions' (chapter II, which is the focus of the discussion here), there are chapters on 'Equal Opportunities and Access to the Labour Market' (I) and 'Social Protection and Inclusion' (III). These lie outside the scope of the present chapter.
[55] COM(2017)251, n. 8 in this chapter, Article 6.
[56] Ibid., Article 5d, this provision also states: 'Employment relationships that lead to precarious working conditions shall be prevented, including by prohibiting abuse of atypical contracts'.
[57] Ibid., Article 7b (which indicates that the information should be provided to the worker 'at the start of employment').
[58] Ibid.
[59] Dismissal not be 'unjustified' as well as being preceded by reasonable notice: ibid., Article 7c.
[60] Ibid., Article 10. See also Article 10 on work-life balance issues.
[61] Ibid., Article 8.

The first problem with this list is what is omitted. It is not straightforward to infer from the Pillar a role for common standards on collective bargaining. The Outline refers to minimum wages, which are one form of centralised wage determination. However, no reference is made to sector-level or nationally coordinated wage bargaining above the basic wage floor. The section on social dialogue does not address the issue of levels of collective bargaining.

A second problem relates to the level of social protection, which the Pillar appears to regard as adequate. Thus the Article on dismissal provides that the termination decision must not be 'unjustified', that there must be a reasonable period of notice, and some compensation provided. No reference is made to the possibility of reinstatement other than a general reference to a right to 'redress' for an unjustified dismissal. This is an extremely weak dismissal standard by reference both to international (ILO and ESC) norms, and also by reference to current Member State practice.[62] Thus, if it were to form a benchmark for future practice, it would imply levelling down of many existing laws.

The issue of 'secure and adaptable employment' is addressed in Article 5 of the Pillar.[63] In the April 2016 Communication, segmentation of the labour market is seen to be a problem, but the Communication does not suggest effective ways of addressing it. Rather than eliminating differences between the separate categories of work relationships,[64] the Communication argues that there should continue to be a lower level of protection for non-standard jobs, which are described as providing a 'gateway' to the labour market. This is a problematic response to the role played by dualism in creating in-work poverty and insecurity.

8.3.4 Mechanisms for Delivering the Social Pillar

The Communication of April 2016 notes that social policy regimes across the EU currently differ considerably in the level of regulation and protection they provide and in their impact on outcomes.[65] It refers to a number of initiatives

---

[62] On this, see K. Lörcher and I. Schömann, 'The European Pillar of Social Rights: Critical Legal Analysis and Proposals' (2016) *ETUI report*, 139.

[63] COM(2016)251, n. 8 in this chapter, referring to various policy goals including the fostering of transitions to 'open-ended forms of employment', ensuring the necessary flexibility for employers to adapt swiftly to changes in the economic context', and fostering 'innovative forms of work', entrepreneurship and self-employment, while preventing 'precarious working conditions' and 'prohibiting abuse of atypical contracts'.

[64] On the importance of this approach for avoiding discrimination between workers in different forms of work, see Adams and Deakin, n. 52 in this chapter.

[65] COM(2016)127, n. 8 in this chapter, paragraph 2.4: 'situations differ widely across Member States'.

and developments which could lead in future to a higher degree of coordination of social policy, including the emergence of 'social indicators' as part of the European Semester process.[66] It also makes reference to the 'Better Regulation' concept.[67] The Communication states in a number of places that the Pillar is designed to 'build on' and 'complement' the social acquis,[68] but also indicates in another part of the text that it would be appropriate to 'revisit' the acquis.[69]

The Communication's account of regime diversity is accurate as far as it goes, but is just restating the problem of the Eurozone's asymmetrical design and the resulting divergences of social law and practice across the Eurozone. The Communication does not suggest bringing forward proposals for the harmonisation of national labour laws using Treaty powers. This is not surprising given the likely political difficulty of getting agreement on such initiatives, and given the focus of the Pillar on the institutional regime of the Eurozone by contrast to that of the wider Union.

How far the emergence of social indicators as part of the European Semester process enhances the role of social policy in the deepening of EMU remains to be seen. There is a danger that indicators could be designed in a way which heightens deregulatory pressures. This could be the case if social indicators were constructed in a way that described worker-protective labour laws as 'distortions' of the market or 'burdens' on business. As the debate over indicators unfolds it will be necessary to counter this way of thinking by pointing to the potentially beneficial impact of, for example, minimum wage laws, EPLs, and centralised collective bargaining.

The reference in the Communication to the Better Regulation agenda, and the suggestion that the existing social acquis be revisited, open the door to a deregulatory logic. If this was pursued, it would be the opposite of the approach needed to ensure that social policy plays an active role in the deepening of EMU. Deregulation of labour laws would undermine the capacity of social policy mechanisms to counter the effects of imbalance and provide a 'buffer' against shocks. It would also make it more difficult to deliver on the objective of inclusive growth. For these reasons, any suggestion that the Pillar

---

[66] Among the mechanisms through which the Pillar could be implemented, it is suggested, are 'greater attention to social considerations in the European Semester of economic policy coordination, the use of social indicators in the so called macroeconomic imbalances procedure, [and] the promotion of "social benchmarking"': ibid., paragraph 2.4.

[67] '[T]he logic of better regulation ... is not less regulation, but an approach to regulation that takes full account of the economic, social and environmental impact on the ground, to make sure that each initiative reaches its goal in the best manner', ibid., paragraph 2.4.

[68] Ibid., paragraph 3.

[69] Ibid., paragraph 3.2.

could be used to roll back national-level protections should be resisted as contrary to the goal of deepening the EMU.

8.3.5 *Assessment*

Elements of the Social Pillar should be welcomed. These include the rationales suggested for the Pillar: the general rationale of making social policy an input into competitiveness and growth; and the specific rationale of using social policy to address imbalances and shocks in the operation of the Eurozone. Where the Pillar is less successful is in the relationship between means and ends. Put simply, the Pillar does not suggest appropriate means for achieving its supposed ends. In terms of its scope, the Pillar is weak and partial in its response to the problems it identifies. In terms of mechanisms, it fails to identity means by which more effective coordination of social policy regimes could be achieved and the asymmetries in the Eurozone addressed.

The Social Pillar could have contained a much clearer commitment to policies which could help build inclusive and sustainable growth inside the Eurozone, in particular legal support for centralised (sector-level and national) wage determination, and non-discriminatory employment protection laws. It could also have suggested more concrete ways in which common standards around policies of this kind could be achieved. What is at stake is not simply the issue of a just and equitable EMU, but whether EMU is sustainable. In its current form, it isn't, in large part because of the weakness of social policy.

8.4 TOWARDS A EUROPEAN NEW DEAL?

The Social Pillar, despite its shortcomings, envisages a more central role for social policy in the process of EMU, in contrast to the peripheral one it has had until now. Such a development, while welcome, would be insufficient to revive EMU. Austerity is producing a toxic combination: the Eurozone is suffering not just rising inequality and insecurity, but also economic stagnation.[70] This mix is driving disenchantment with the European project and the rise of illiberal political movements in several countries. If this trend continues, the fragmentation and eventual breakup of the Union become more than just a possibility.

The response of the European institutions to the sovereign debt crisis was to use the instruments of Eurozone governance to inflict structural adjustment programmes on the debtor states of exactly the kind which had repeatedly failed when implemented by the IMF in other parts of the world. Can the same instruments be used to organise a very different kind of response to

[70] Stiglitz, n. 7 in this chapter.

the crisis, one which aims to promote social cohesion, wage-based growth, and ecologically sustainable development – in short a European New Deal?[71] There are straws in the wind to this effect which include the discussion (adverted to in the April 2016 Communication[72]) of embedding social metrics in the European Semester process, and the use of social dialogue mechanisms to promote a floor in transnational collective bargaining.

A more fundamental step would be to accept the need for fiscal mechanisms to play a greater role in economic policy. Quantitative easing (QE), as practised by all the major central banks including the ECB, has not only failed to generate sustainable growth, but has added to wealth inequalities by artificially inflating the value of assets.[73] The increasingly evident failure of QE is behind the growing calls for fiscal expansion as a route out of stagnation in the USA and UK. Within the Eurozone, fiscal loosening is apparently ruled out by the Treaty on Stability, Coordination, and Governance, but, fortunately if somewhat contingently,[74] this measure does not form part of Union law and so may prove to be less of an obstacle than it might seem. If not easily unwound in the short term, it can be still treated as the dead letter it will mostly likely become, without harming the operation of Union law. Secondary legislation along the lines of the regulations constituting the 'Six-Pack' and 'Two-Pack' would have to be revoked or amended but this would not require a change to the Union Treaties. Nor would a coordinated expansionary approach to economic policy, in itself, involve any conflict with the Union's exclusive competence in the area of monetary policy, nor with the legal independence of the ECB.[75]

If flexibility in fiscal policy provides one part of the measures needed to restore growth in the Eurozone, another would be policies designed to place a floor under wages and to enhance the purchasing power of lower income groups, thereby aiding consumption and underpinning demand for goods and services, at the same time as helping to reverse the trend towards inequalities

---

[71] T. Piketty, 'A New Deal for Europe', *New York Review of Books*, 25 February 2016, available at: www.nybooks.com/articles/2016/02/25/a-new-deal-for-europe/ (accessed 5 December 2016).

[72] COM(2016)127, n. 8 in this chapter, paragraph 2.4.

[73] For relevant discussion of the perverse effects of QE, see W. Streeck, 'How Will Capitalism End?' (2014) 87 *New Left Review* 35, pp. 38–40.

[74] The embedding of the 'fiscal compact' in Union law was vetoed by the United Kingdom. See Deakin, n. 6 in this chapter.

[75] The flexibility available to the Union is one of the more beneficial side effects of the *Pringle* judgment. For discussion, see Deakin n. 6 in this chapter. Those recently calling for a greater role for fiscal policy in macroeconomic management include the Governor of the Bank of England ('we must grow our economy by rebalancing the mix of monetary policy, fiscal policy and structural reforms', see M. Carney, 'The Spectre of Monetarism', Roscoe Lecture, Liverpool John Moores University, 5 December 2016, available at: www.bankofengland.co.uk/publications/Documents/speeches/2016/speech946.pdf (accessed 9 December 2016).

of wealth and earnings. Here a critical role could be played by sector-level collective bargaining, the decline of which since the 1990s, and even more so since the start of the crisis in 2008, is responsible for much of the rise in earnings inequality across the EU Member States.[76] The development of cross-national benchmarks for sectoral collective bargaining can be addressed through the European Semester process, in effect bypassing the exclusion of issues of pay determination from the scope of the Union's competences to adopt directives in the social policy field.[77] If this path is taken, the adoption of social and employment indicators that explicitly take as their goal the improvement of bargaining outcomes for the lowest paid and the narrowing of the pay gap across the earnings distribution should be actively pursued.[78]

8.5 CONCLUSION

This chapter has offered an analysis and critique of the consultation on a European Pillar of Social Rights launched by the Commission in March 2016. Particularly when viewed in the long-run of the evolution of European social policy, the Pillar is an initiative which can be given a cautious welcome. As a restatement of social rights it leaves much to be desired, but this is not its main purpose. It should be understood as a much overdue attempt to reintegrate social policy into the evolving process of EMU. Its emphasis on social policy as an input into sustainable economic development, and not simply the result of market integration, is the right approach to take at this critical moment, and if rolled out at the level of concrete change to Eurozone governance would have far-reaching repercussions. If the Social Pillar can be used to hasten the end of austerity in Europe, it would prove genuinely useful. Such is the scale of the crisis facing the Union that this shift in economic policy, once inconceivable, may soon be understood as unavoidable. When that moment arrives, social policy must again be at the core of the debate.

---

[76] J. Visser, S. Hayter, and R. Gammarano, 'Trends in Collective Bargaining Coverage: Stability, Erosion or Decline?' (2015) *Inclusive Labour Markets, Labour Relations and Working Conditions Branch Issue Brief*, 1.

[77] Article 153(5) TFEU. See n. 15, in this chapter.

[78] This process has already begun, with the change in real growth of household disposable income and inequality in the distribution of income among the indicators used in the 'scoreboards' contained in the Joint Employment Report and Macroeconomic Imbalances Procedure within the European Semester process. See Directorate General for Internal Policies, 'Mainstreaming Employment and Social Indicators into Macroeconomic Surveillance' (2016) Study for the EMPL Committee, available at: www.europarl.europa.eu/RegData/etudes/ STUD/2016/569985/IPOL_STU(2016)569985_EN.pdf (accessed 9 December 2016). In this context, consideration could be given, for example, to including collective bargaining coverage and union membership as additional indicators.

9

Social Dialogue: Why It Matters – European Employers' Perspective

Philippe de Buck and Maxime Cerutti

9.1 INTRODUCTION

Social dialogue is not inherent to employee relations throughout the world. But it is a longstanding feature of national industrial relations systems in Europe. And it has developed into an important vehicle of social policy-making in the context of EU integration in particular throughout the last three decades. This chapter draws an employers' picture of social dialogue development in Europe, focusing on the European social dialogue (ESD). The fact that the current European Commission decided to make the re-launch of the ESD one of its top priorities makes such a consideration timely. But beyond this, thinking about the role of social dialogue is perhaps more essential today than ever before, because the world order is currently being reshaped. New power relations between the regions of the world are being tested. And the dynamics of European integration are endangered from within by political demagogy and a growing anti-EU rhetoric. In such turbulent times, social partners can be a vector of stability because they are key players of market economies and political democracies.

To have a bright future, Europe needs to build on its strengths. Our culture of social dialogue can definitely be an asset for Europe in the changing world. This means avoiding the pitfalls of a dialogue of insiders protecting the status quo. This means engaging in a renewed conception of social dialogue as a tool for responsible change and fair share of the benefits of growth. To succeed, Europe needs to be an attractive location for investments. And the human potential of the European workforce needs to be fully seized in innovative enterprises. Moreover, the rapid adaptation of Europe's enterprises and workers to economic and social change will be essential. One of the main challenges for employers in the future will be to find the people with the right skills in sufficient numbers.

At the present juncture of history, the challenge is to move away from a tradition whereby the purpose of social dialogue is primarily seen as an instrument to achieve social peace by adding to existing social rights. In the future, a key factor to encourage enterprises and their organisations to invest in social dialogue is to ensure that it positively contributes in terms of competitiveness. Essential in this respect is that companies have enough flexibility to adapt their workforce to changing economic circumstances, notably in terms of working time, wages, and contracts. Social problems in Europe are not due to a deficit of social policy but to a lack of global competitiveness. Further social progress will not be decided by laws; it can only be achieved through the competitiveness and successes of private enterprises. Once economic success is achieved, an important challenge for policy-makers is to translate it into jobs and more equal opportunities. Employers consider social progress as an important objective for policy, in particular social policy, and they share the ultimate goal of social well-being and equity. But the truth is that the only sustainable way to achieve this is economic growth.

Many policies have an impact on the competitiveness of enterprises and job creation, not least macroeconomic, energy and climate, and trade policies. Employment and social policy frameworks also play an important role for companies to have access to a sufficient and sufficiently skilled workforce and to ensure a good match between labour demand and supply. In this context, social partnership can play a major role. Because economic and social challenges are often interlinked, enterprises and workers are well placed to identify the solutions they need to achieve better economic and social outcomes. This requires the social partners on both sides accepting the fundamentals of a social market economy. They can also provide useful information and advice to public authorities when taking their own actions to improve the capacity of our economies to grow and achieve fair, dynamic, mobile, and inclusive labour markets.

Member States and national social partners are the key players in the field of employment and social affairs. This means that European social partners' added value is about putting in place frameworks and tools that can help national social partners converge towards shared diagnoses of the challenges they face, and towards possible solutions to overcome them. In this light, the ESD should be about building a shared understanding of challenges that are common to European countries with a view to supporting more ownership for the necessary actions and decisions at national level. The ESD should also underpin mutual learning and the sharing of experiences between social partners across Europe, rather than aiming to solve problems across the board at European level. To bring its full contribution, the ESD should draw on the various means of action that exist such as joint analyses, advice, and recommendations; and/or tripartite activities. For example, the joint labour-market analyses agreed by the European social partners in 2007 and 2015 could be better used at national level to achieve more progress in the design and delivery of reforms.

A key challenge ahead for the social partners and policy-makers is to better understand the links between the way in which collective bargaining frameworks are designed and competitiveness outcomes, to ensure that social dialogue is increasingly recognised as a vector of competitiveness. It is positive that in 2015 the European social partners were able to conclude successfully two important negotiations on an in-depth employment analysis[1] and on a social dialogue work programme for 2015–17, and in March 2017 an autonomous framework agreement on active ageing and an intergenerational approach.[2] But more progress is needed to ensure a more meaningful ESD.

Finally, if social dialogue is sometimes rooted in more than a century of relations between employers and workers and their representatives, there are also some countries in Europe where the framework conditions for an autonomous social dialogue are still missing. Member States where social dialogue structures are comparatively weak need to support the development of strong and autonomous social partner organisations and, where appropriate and based on the request of national social partners, help to organise an autonomous social dialogue.

9.2 HISTORY OF THE EU SOCIAL DIALOGUE

The launch of bipartite social dialogue at European level has been promoted since the mid-1980s by former Commission President Jacques Delors. Social dialogue at community level evolved from then on into a genuine European forum for negotiation. A key milestone was the social partners' agreement of 31 October 1991, which was subsequently incorporated in the Treaty of Maastricht's Social Protocol. With this agreement, the social partners affirmed their willingness to take an active part in EU social policy-making. Whereas the Single Market programme was under way, its social dimension included the transfer of important competences from the national to the EU level on issues such as working

---

[1] European Social Partners, 'In-Depth Employment Analysis' (2015) available at: erc-online.eu/wp-content/uploads/2015/11/Joint-IDEA-report-July-2015-final.pdf (accessed 18 October 2016).

[2] European Social Partners, 'European Social Partners' Autonomous Framework Agreement on Active Ageing and an Inter-Generational Approach (2017), available at: www.businesseurope.eu/publications/european-social-partners-autonomous-framework-agreement-active-ageing-and-inter (accessed 7 June 2017).

conditions, in particular health and safety at work, and information and consultation of workers. Employers had an interest in taking a direct role in the shaping of this emerging social dimension through negotiations with the European Trade Union Confederation (ETUC) to make sure that EU social policies and regulations were adapted to new and changing economic and social realities.

Since 1992, the role of social partners has been officially recognised by EU primary law (currently Articles 154 and 155 TFEU). Before proposing a directive in the social field, the Commission is obliged to consult social partners at two stages. The first consultation concerns the question of the need to act on a given issue at the EU level. The second consultation relates to the content of envisaged legislation. At any of these two stages, the social partners can decide to start negotiations. If they do, the right of initiative granted to the Commission by the Treaty is frozen. The social partners have nine months to come to an agreement. If the negotiations are successful, the European social partners have the choice between implementing their agreement either:

- by the national members of the signatory parties in accordance with their national industrial relations practices, which leaves the choice to national social partners in terms of their preferred implementation method, or;
- by asking the Commission to transmit the agreement to the Council so that it transforms it into a directive that Member States are responsible to implement, in some cases leaving the responsibility to implement to national social partners.

If the negotiations fail, the Commission can reactivate its right of initiative and the normal legislative procedure is launched: proposal of the Commission, discussions in Council and European Parliament.

The procedure introduced by the Maastricht Treaty was a genuinely new model that took into account the differences between pre-existing national systems. It was invented by the European social partners, namely BusinessEurope (former name UNICE), European Centre of Employers and Enterprises providing Public Services (CEEP) and ETUC. This consultation approach has had some influence on the way in which some national governments consult with national social partners. For example, in France, the law of 31 January 2007 on social dialogue modernisation created a new consultation phase, similar to European level consultations, before the French government tables any legislative proposals in the field of employment and social affairs.[3]

---

[3]   Law of 31 January 2007 *de modernisation du dialogue social*, consolidated version of 18 October 2016, NOR: SOCX0600184L.

To date, the European social partners at cross-industry level have started nine negotiations of framework agreements, including one revision of an existing agreement. All but one led to a positive conclusion. The only failure to reach an agreement was in the early 2000s on temporary agency work. It took the Council and Parliament until 2008 to agree on a directive on this issue. Another interesting case is the Recast Directive 2009/38/EC on European works councils (EWCs).[4] Employers offered negotiations, which were rejected by the trade unions. However, the European social partners agreed on a joint advice after the Commission made its proposal in 2008, which was well reflected in the Recast Directive that was adopted by the Council and the European Parliament in 2009. Of the agreements reached, three were implemented by way of a directive – parental leave (1995, revised in 2009); part-time work (1997) and fixed-term work (1999).[5] Four were implemented in accordance with national industrial relations practices – telework (2002); stress at work (2004); harassment and violence at the work place (2007) and inclusive labour markets (2010). The inclusive labour-markets agreement was the first 'purely autonomous agreement' in the sense that it was negotiated and agreed as a result of a social dialogue work programme, without being triggered by a Commission consultation.

9.2.1 Lessons Learned

Over the last three decades, the ESD has been linked closely to the European integration process:

- 1980s: accompanying the Single Market programme;
- 1990s: accompanying the European Monetary Union;
- 2000s: accompanying the EU growth and jobs strategy;

What employers have learned over this period is that in order to be effective, the ESD should not attempt to address issues that can only be negotiated at

4   Directive 2009/38/EC of the European Parliament and of the Council of 6 May 2009 on the establishment of a European Works Council or a procedure in Community-scale undertakings and Community-scale groups of undertakings for the purposes of informing and consulting employees, [2009] OJ L 122/28.
5   Council Directive 96/34/EC of 3 June 1996 on the framework agreement on parental leave concluded by UNICE, CEEP and the ETUC, [1996] OJ L 145/5; Council Directive 2010/18/EU of 8 March 2010 implementing the revised Framework Agreement on parental leave concluded by BUSINESSEUROPE, UEAPME, CEEP and ETUC and repealing Directive 96/34/EC, [2010] OJ L 68/13; Council Directive 97/81/EC of 15 December 1997 concerning the Framework Agreement on part-time work concluded by UNICE, CEEP and the ETUC, [1997] OJ L 14/9; Council Directive 1999/70/EC of 28 June 1999 concerning the framework agreement on fixed-term work concluded by ETUC, UNICE and CEEP, [1999] OJ L 175/43.

national level or by companies themselves. The role of the EU is not to regulate very different labour markets in the way that national social partners do. Its added value is to steer national employment and social policies in order to modernise social systems in a way that responds effectively to the structural challenges European countries are all confronted with as part of the global economy. European level policy discussions should focus on issues that have a genuine European dimension. This encompasses issues that have a cross-border dimension. But also those which require an adequate degree of coordination to ensure that actions by the relevant actors converge towards commonly agreed goals.

Going forward, the first priority for the EU social policy is to build consensus on how to renew the 2007 flexicurity principles[6] and develop as part of this a number of European benchmarks.[7] To be helpful, such benchmarks should provide a point of reference for assessing progress towards reform goals and comparison between Member States. This should contribute to improving implementation of the European Semester process.

9.3   EU SOCIAL PARTNERSHIP AND DIALOGUE IN THE TWENTY-FIRST CENTURY

9.3.1   *Work Programmes*

Over the years, the EU social dialogue has become more autonomous. This means that the social partners increasingly take the lead in choosing the issues that they discuss and negotiate on, rather than being prompted by the Commission. In return, the social partners expect to implement their agreements without interference from the Commission.

At the turn of the new millennium, the European social partners took on new responsibilities for acting upon the most relevant issues that need to be addressed at EU level to improve the functioning of labour markets. Since then, they adopted multi-annual autonomous work programmes. An autonomous work programme is the result of a bipartite negotiation between EU employers and workers' representatives, during which they discuss the priority

---

[6]   Council of the European Union, 'Draft Conclusions: Towards Common Principles of Flexicurity' of 22 November 2007, available at: register.consilium.europa.eu/doc/srv?l=EN&f=ST%2015497%202007%20INIT (accessed 18 October 2016).

[7]   For more information, please see BusinessEurope, 'European Pillar of Social Rights – BusinessEurope contribution to the debate' (2016) available at: www.businesseurope.eu/publications/european-pillar-social-rights-businesseurope-contribution-debate (accessed 18 October 2016).

issues to address as well as the most appropriate instruments to deal with them (negotiation, seminar, project, etc.). This approach was used for the five autonomous work programmes that have been negotiated to date.[8] The key challenge is to identify issues and actions that add value to the European policy agenda, while ensuring that the agreed actions are useful for national social partners in 28 Member States facing diverse realities. Progressively, a similar approach based on autonomous work programmes has been followed by some EU sectoral social partners, for example in the commerce and construction sectors.

The first work programme of the European cross-sectoral social partners for the period 2003–05 encompassed practical activities, such as seminars, mixed with negotiations for example on the issue of stress at work. It made provision for completion of 19 joint initiatives focused on employment and enlargement of the EU. At this time, it was crucial for the EU social partners to give support to the Lisbon Strategy, which was launched in 2000 and aimed at turning Europe into the most competitive knowledge-based economy in the world, capable of sustainable economic growth, with more and better jobs and greater social cohesion.

Providing assistance to social partners of the new Member States joining the EU social dialogue was also at the core of the autonomous initiatives included in this first work programme. Since the 1990s, the reunification of Europe has been high on the EU social partners' agenda. Their activities focused on deepening the understanding of the realities of the new Member States and candidate countries, looking at the effects of EU accession in those countries, identifying the key economic and social issues for each country as seen through the eyes of the local social partners, and gaining direct experience of how local social partners approach and debate those issues. The underlying assumption was that social partners in the new Member States faced common challenges. These countries had to perfect the functioning of either relatively small and insular or young market economies. At the same time, they had to carry out the necessary adjustments linked to joining the European Union and implementing its legal acquis. The institutional context is important when looking at the outcomes of the first work programme. With the Lisbon strategy, a new phase started for EU economic and social policies, whereby the coordination of actions between EU and national actors grew in importance. Recognising the role of autonomous work programmes, the Commission has been increasingly relying on social partners to shape the EU social policy,

[8] The list of autonomous work programmes is available at: erc-online.eu/european-social-dialogue/social-partners-autonomous-workprogramme/ (accessed 18 October 2016).

including on how best to balance economic and social considerations. The first work programme therefore successfully contributed to strengthening the EU social dialogue, and adapting it to the changing realities of an enlarged European Union.

The second work programme for the period 2006–08 reflected a desire to maintain the momentum of the previous one, while taking into account the new context of an enlarged EU of 25 Member States, and later 27. The work on integration of social partners of the new Member States in the ESD was continued. Likewise, the contribution of the EU social partners to the Commission's Growth and Jobs strategy remained an important focus, with increased efforts to coordinate with national social partners an EU social partner yearly assessment of the progress made in implementing the strategy. The EU social partners urged the national governments to involve their social partners to improve results. Importantly, for the first time, the EU social partners decided to work on a joint labour-market analysis identifying the main challenges and priorities for action for public authorities and the social partners. An autonomous agreement was negotiated to tackle the issue of harassment and violence at the work place.[9] And the capacity-building approach initially focused on the 10 New Member States was extended to the EU-15, with a study on how social partners were dealing with restructuring and economic and social change. The context of this second programme was a Europe in political crisis. This period followed the rejection in 2005 of the Constitutional Treaty in France and the Netherlands, and there were great difficulties to agree on EU budget guidelines for 2007–13. This clearly showed that Europe needed to modernise its system of governance.

The third work programme for the period 2009–2010 (extended to 2011) was negotiated in the context of the aftermath of the financial crisis and of great economic uncertainty. The work programmes 2003–05 and 2006–08 were based on a three-year cycle. By contrast, the third work programme covered a two-year period so as to be synchronised with the Growth and Jobs strategy. It was extended in 2011 to conclude a number of initiatives and negotiate the following work programme with the new ETUC leadership elected in 2011. This work programme focused on contributing to the post-2010 Lisbon agenda, taking into account the context of the crisis. Social partners also agreed to jointly monitor the common principles on flexicurity, and a new focus was put on addressing the employment aspects and consequences of climate change.

9   European Social Partners, 'Framework Agreement on Harassment and Violence at Work' (2007) available at: erc-online.eu/wp-content/uploads/2016/03/Framework_Agreement_Harassment_and_Violence_at_Work.pdf (accessed 18 October 2016).

A new autonomous agreement on inclusive labour markets was negotiated as part of this work programme.[10]

The fourth work programme for the period 2012–14 was negotiated with the goal of ensuring an ambitious and realistic work programme, focusing on a limited number of well-targeted priorities. The overarching challenge identified for this period was employment. The European social partners recognised that Europe could only succeed in creating enough jobs to reach the 2020 75 per cent employment rate target if sound macroeconomic policies were put in place. At the height of the crisis, a clear sense of urgency was stressed by the social partners to focus on putting forward solutions to EU labour markets problems. The EU social partners agreed on the need to set up a useful framework for national discussions on the policies and reforms needed. As the focus was on employment, the social partners started with the negotiations of a new framework of actions on youth employment.[11] This was followed by the negotiation of a second analysis of the functioning of labour markets.[12] Social partners also agreed on a declaration setting out their role as part of the renewed EU economic governance.[13]

Additionally, the social partners fostered a renewed focus on capacity building, by renewing their approach to their capacity building activities across Europe. This is linked to the fact that social dialogue is only possible with sufficiently strong and independent employers' organisations and trade unions, in other words, with a certain level of knowledge and expertise in social and labour-market issues, an understanding of and willingness to discuss common themes and an acknowledgement of the responsibilities in delivering on the outcomes of the social dialogue. This then translates in the EU social dialogue, since for an organisation to become a recognised EU level social partner, it must be organised at the EU level and capable of taking part in consultations and negotiating agreements. The European Social Partners also revisited the 2005 framework of actions on gender equality[14] with the creation

---

[10] European Social Partners, 'Framework Agreement on Inclusive Labour Markets' (2010) available at: erc-online.eu/wp-content/uploads/2014/04/Framework-Agreement-on-Inclusive-Labour-Markets-25032010-2010-00836-E.pdf (accessed 18 October 2016).

[11] European Social Partners, 'Framework of Actions on Youth Employment' (2013) available at: erc-online.eu/wp-content/uploads/2014/05/2013-00635-E.pdf (accessed 18 October 2016).

[12] See European Social Partners, n. 1 in this chapter.

[13] European Social Partners, 'Social Partner Involvement in the European Economic Governance: Declaration by the European Social Partners' (2013) available at: erc-online.eu/wp-content/uploads/2014/05/Declaration-on-Social-Partners%E2%80%99-involvement-in-European-Economic-Governance-24102013-2013-01319-E.pdf (accessed 18 October 2016).

[14] European Social Partners, 'Framework of Actions on Gender Equality' (2005) available at: erc-online.eu/wp-content/uploads/2014/04/2005-00680-EN.pdf (accessed 18 October 2016).

of a practical toolkit[15] aiming at informing and supporting the work of social partners at national, sectoral, and company levels by promoting examples of social partner actions from across Europe.

The fifth and current work programme for the period 2015–17 was negotiated in the context of the restarting of the EU social dialogue initiated by the new European Commission led by President Jean-Claude Juncker, who stated: 'I would like to be a President of social dialogue'.[16] In this context, employers, and notably BusinessEurope, call for a reform partnership, building upon a common understanding around priority areas for reforms. Implementation of the fifth work programme begins in 2016 with the negotiation of an autonomous framework agreement on 'fostering active ageing and an intergenerational approach'. Social partners also agreed to develop joint conclusions on promoting better reconciliation of work, private and family life and gender equality to reduce the gender pay gap. Other issues that will be addressed are: EU mobility and legal migration, investments, apprenticeships, skills needs in digital economies and active labour-market policies. Equally important, the current work programme includes a number of actions to improve the implementation of EU social dialogue instruments at national level.

These work programmes demonstrate the efforts invested by European and national social partners in playing a proactive role in shaping the EU social policy. An important challenge for the future, however, is to improve the synergies between the ESD work programmes and the Commission's work programmes, while respecting their respective responsibilities and autonomy. Respecting social partners' autonomy means that the Commission should refrain from interfering with social partners' autonomous activities. For example, the European social partners agreed autonomously to address the issue of work-life balance in their 2015–17 work programme. Their autonomy was undermined by the Commission in 2015–17 when it launched social partner consultations on work-life balance, which have challenged their previously agreed actions in this field[17] and published in April 2017 a legislative proposal repealing the parental leave Directive 2010/18/EC that derived from a social partner agreement of 1995, as revised already once in 2009.

[15] The Toolkit for Gender Equality in Practice is available at: erc-online.eu/gendertoolkit/#/ (accessed 18 October 2016).

[16] J.C. Juncker, 'A New Start for Europe: My Agenda for Jobs, Growth Fairness and Democratic Change' (2014) available at: ec.europa.eu/priorities/docs/pg_en.pdf (accessed 18 October 2016).

[17] Commission's website on work-life balance: ec.europa.eu/social/main.jsp?catId=1311&langId =en (accessed 7 June 2017); and BusinessEurope, 'European Pillar of Social Rights – right aims, wrong approach', press release of 25 April 2017, available at: www.businesseurope.eu/ publications/european-pillar-social-rights-right-aims-wrong-approach (accessed 7 June 2017).

9.3.2 *Labour-Market Analyses*

Employers consider the publication of joint labour-market analyses – in 2007[18] and 2015[19] – as major achievements of the ESD. On both occasions, the publications started with a factual description and analysis of relevant data, from which key challenges were identified and policy recommendations to the EU, Member States, and social partners were made. The analyses need to be seen in the context of the periods in which they were undertaken, with one being conducted prior to the onset of the financial crisis and the other shortly after its peak. While the labour-market and wider macroeconomic environment have gone through important changes between these periods, there is a degree of continuity evident in the policy recommendations. This demonstrates the need for consistency in EU policy-making and provides the foundations for an ESD built on a partnership for labour-market reforms.

The first analysis was carried out in 2006–07 at a time when Europe's economy was experiencing a relatively prolonged period of economic growth and employment. Real growth in Gross Domestic Product (GDP) averaged 2.4 per cent over the ten years between 1996 and 2006 and the EU's average employment rate stood at 64.4 per cent in 2006, up from 62.2 per cent in 2000. Hopes were high that the Lisbon strategy would further enhance competitiveness in the recently enlarged EU and that it would lead to increased productivity and employment. However, these generally positive trends could not mask the fact that nearly 16 million people were unemployed, highlighting that a sound policy mix was required if the Lisbon target of 70 per cent employment was to be achieved. Chief among these was tapping into the potential of so-called flexicurity policies – measures that address both the flexibility and security aspects of employment for workers and employers alike. The European social partners considered that this concerns 'labour law and contractual arrangements, effective and high quality active labour-market policies, lifelong learning policies, efficient and sustainable social protection systems and social dialogue'.[20] Of particular importance for BusinessEurope was the possibility for employers to be able to use different forms of contractual arrangements to allow them to adapt to their needs, noting that at the time, 85 per cent of contracts were of indefinite duration.[21] This is also important to help workers

[18] European Social Partners, 'Key challenges facing European labour markets: a joint analysis of European Social Partners' (2007) available at: www.businesseurope.eu/sites/buseur/files/media/imported/2007-01436-E.pdf (accessed 18 October 2016).
[19] European Social Partners, n. 1 in this chapter.
[20] European Social Partners, n. 17 in this chapter.
[21] Ibid., p. 19.

combine work and family life and to combat labour-market segmentation. In addition, it was highlighted that flexicurity policies need to be underpinned by sound macroeconomic policies and tax and benefit systems that encourage employment participation.

The second analysis was undertaken in 2013–15 to assess the short-term challenges arising from the financial crisis and longer-term structural issues, and to identify appropriate policy responses. This analysis, which in comparison to the first one covers a wider set of issues having a direct or indirect impact on employment, is embedded in a different economic and social context. In contrast to the pre-crisis situation, average GDP for the period 2008–13 decreased by 0.2 per cent, and as a consequence the average EU employment rate decreased from a peak of 65.7 per cent in 2008 to 64.1 per cent in 2013. A substantial increase in unemployment was also apparent, reaching a high of 26.4 million people in early 2013, compared with around 16 million in 2006. The Europe 2020 strategy followed in the footsteps of Lisbon with the aim of fostering competitiveness and achieving 75 per cent employment rate in the EU. However, the evidence continues to suggest that this headline target is likely to be unreachable and the recommendations in the latest analysis continue to focus on the need to foster growth, investment and job creation. In this context, employers welcomed the fact that this second analysis comprises a stronger focus on competitiveness and an agreement between the EU social partners on the main elements of the competitiveness concept.[22]

As regards labour-market policies, this includes returning to the flexicurity principles, with the European social partners noting that while 'contracts of indefinite duration are and should remain the most widespread form of employment contract in Europe, diverse contractual arrangements can be useful to match employers' and workers' needs'. It is also observed that 'social partners have a key role to play in assessing, designing and agreeing on internal and certain forms of external flexibility, including for SMEs, especially to overcome short-term rises in the number of orders or to fill in for absent employees due to sickness or family duties'. This reflects the enduring emphasis that employers place on having an appropriate number of different forms of contractual arrangements at their disposal.

---

[22] Social partners agreed that 'as part of the concept of competitiveness an enabling environment for enterprises is key. It encompasses a wide number of factors that ultimately influence a country's growth and jobs performance favourably such as: macroeconomic fundamentals, labour market policies, innovation and investment in R&D, business environment including infrastructure, skills, education and training, labour cost and high performing public services', see European Social Partners, n. 1 in this chapter, at p. 26.

Another important issue that came to the fore in the second analysis is increasing levels of youth unemployment (15–24 year olds). The data demonstrate that this is a structural challenge and a longer-term trend with EU youth unemployment rate being twice as high as the overall unemployment rate in many countries well before the crisis started in 2008. The challenge has been exacerbated by the crisis with youth unemployment rising from 15.2 per cent in 2008 to 23.8 per cent in 2013, with a slight improvement to 21 per cent in 2016. At the same time, there are around 2 million job vacancies in the EU. BusinessEurope believes that well-functioning labour markets are characterised by smooth transitions from education to employment. To facilitate these transitions, there needs to be a good match between skills supply and demand on the one hand, and labour-market conditions that encourage employers to hire people on the other. However, these figures point towards a mismatch between the skills that people have when they enter the labour market and those required by employers. Therefore, this analysis highlights the need to ensure that people's expectations and the needs of labour markets are 'reflected in education and training schemes so that enterprises can grow and people find jobs in line with their skills, expectations and competences'.

The 2015 In-Depth Employment Analysis provides a good starting point for addressing the actions in the European social partners' work programme 2015–17. Agreeing on a shared diagnosis of the state-of-play of labour markets is indeed an important prerequisite to identify which actions would add value – at which level of policy-making and by whom – and to pave the way for a sufficient engagement and ownership of the measures needed. This is not about new rights, but about trying to reach an agreement on economic developments with a view to adjust the systems in place accordingly. One important objective is to provide jointly agreed European cross-country evidence and analysis to the national social partners across Europe, thereby nurturing their debates on the way forward for their country.

9.3.3 *EU Economic Governance Process, European Semester*

The European Semester is one of the most important and influential policy coordination and agenda-setting programmes in the EU. Within this process the Commission proposes, on the basis of the Annual Growth Survey and country reports, a selected number of Country Specific Recommendations (CSRs) to be adopted by the Council. The monitoring of the implementation of the CSRs is expected to improve the impact of the recommendations at national level as well as to decide whether progress was made in a given area. The process aims at converging European economies towards shared objectives. This greater convergence is needed and welcome as long as it is fully coherent with the goal of increasing Europe's competitiveness while respecting subsidiarity as defined in the Treaty.[23] What is required to be meaningful is to make sure that the European Semester process really has an impact, through effective implementation of country recommendations and respect of fiscal rules.

As part of the European Semester and the CSRs, many issues are related to the daily work of the social partners, from labour-market reforms to employment or reconciliation policies. Given the importance of the reform process and the issues covered, the European and national social partners are consistently asking to be closely involved and consulted ever since the launch of the Lisbon Strategy. More recently, they have clarified the way they wish to be involved in the renewed EU economic governance in a declaration in 2013.[24] A consultation of the EU social partners on employment and social aspects is organised in September each year ahead of the publication of the Annual Growth Survey. This allows for exchanges of views to inform the European Commission of the employers' and trade unions' priorities. The consultation is not only oral but also in written form, since the social partners send their contribution to the Commission and it is subsequently officially published.

Today, to contribute to a more cohesive and competitive European Union, the ESD needs to evolve to contribute to shaping and implementing necessary EU and national reforms, which in turn reflect the needs of more diverse economic and social situations in the enlarged European Union. BusinessEurope member federations point out in BusinessEurope's 2016 Reform Barometer[25] only 20 per cent of CSRs have been satisfactorily implemented despite the Commission identifying the key issues for reform in Member States. This is also the case for employment and social objectives, where member federations generally view their national situation as not satisfactory or even poor. Countries faced with greater difficulties as a result of the crisis have pushed forward reforms more forcefully than others in recent years, and several Member States improved their reform implementation. However, in some countries that are traditionally very competitive, with strong growth and employment performance, BusinessEurope member federations report that reform implementation has slowed.

---

[23] Articles 3(3) and 5(3) TEU.
[24] European Social Partners, n. 13 in this chapter.
[25] BusinessEurope, 'Reform Barometer: Reform to Perform, Spring 2016' (2016) available at: www.businesseurope.eu/sites/buseur/files/media/reports_and_studies/reform_barometer_2016/reform_barometer_spring_2016.pdf (accessed 18 October 2016).

More progress is needed to address the implementation gap. As part of this, the recent agreement by Council[26] – which is still to be put in place – to set up productivity boards made up of independent experts within the euro area, could be helpful in encouraging greater awareness of both the need for reforms and their potential impact on competitiveness. As recognised by the Council decision, these boards should analyse competitiveness performance in a broad sense and 'neither interfere with the wage-setting process and the role of social partners, nor harmonise wage setting systems'.

It is also important for the Commission to understand the social partners' assessment of reforms. And there is a lot to gain from mutual learning among national social partners as part of the EU level social dialogue. The EU social partners now advocate a closer cooperation at all levels. Whilst the EU part of the process seems to function well, the consultation of social partners at national level is not of the same quality. The existence of European Semester officers[27] in the great majority of Member States does not mean that social partners are systematically and consistently consulted on the country reports, prior to the adoption of the CSRs or in the monitoring process. In addition, it is still the case that in some countries social partners would be invited along with representatives of civil society, NGOs or non-profit organisations, whereas an approach recognising the specific role of social partners on the labour markets is needed.

Some country examples show that social dialogue can bring a meaningful contribution to the solutions needed, such as the Finnish competitiveness pact of September 2016 and the 2014 reform of the pensions system by the Finnish social partners. To enhance the positive contribution that social dialogue can bring throughout Europe, the European social partners have an important role to organise a process of mutual learning between their respective members. This can contribute to more ownership of the reforms needed by the social partners, and therefore contribute to reducing the implementation gap of the European Semester process.

9.4 EU SECTORAL SOCIAL DIALOGUE

Of course, it is impossible to discuss the EU social dialogue without mentioning the sectoral level. EU sectoral social dialogue was formalised by

[26] Council of the European Union, 'Outcome of the Council meeting' 3475th Economic and Financial Affairs Council Meeting of 17 June 2016, p. 13, available at: www.consilium.europa.eu/en/meetings/ecofin/2016/06/st10324_en16_pdf/ (accessed 18 October 2016).

[27] European Semester Officers are now placed in the European Commission representation office in each EU Member State capital city.

the Commission Decision of 20 May 1998 on the establishment of Sectoral Dialogue Committees promoting the dialogue between the social partners at European level.[28] The decision to set up a sectoral social dialogue committee has to be based on a joint request from the social partners in the sector. It is also required that the employers' and workers' organisations making the request relate to specific sectors or categories and are organised at European level; consist of organisations that are themselves an integral and recognised part of Member States' social partner structures; have the capacity to negotiate agreements; are representative of several Member States; and have adequate structures to ensure their effective participation in the committees' work. Initially, 21 sectoral social dialogue committees were created in 1999, in industries formerly covered by joint committees and working parties. Since then the sectoral social dialogue has been developing rapidly and there are now 43 sectoral social dialogue committees.[29] The organisations involved represent a range of different sectors, some broader (for example metalworking/engineering) – others more specific (for example aviation handling). There is a wide range of sectors for which organisations are recognised as social partners at the European level. This diversity is steadily increasing. Although this is not a problem per se, to ensure the legitimacy of their actions at the European level and the legitimacy of the EU social dialogue overall, it is critical that the representativeness of EU sectoral social partners is thoroughly checked and assured. In this respect, some criticisms have been made recently of laxity in the application of the provisions on representativeness as set out in EU primary law and the Commission Decision from 1998[30] setting up EU sectoral social dialogue structures. It is important to ensure a consistent and full application of these provisions.

It goes without saying that respect for the autonomy of social partners, and for the outcomes of their dialogue, as enshrined in EU primary law, must apply to the sectoral social partners as to the cross-industry social partners. This means that, as with the cross-sectoral social dialogue, the European Commission is formally obliged[31] to consult with the employers' and workers' organisations involved in the sectoral social dialogue committees on social and employment policy issues. The sectoral social partners also have the same possibilities at

---

[28] European Commission Decision 98/500/EC of 20 May 1998 on the establishment of Sectoral Dialogue Committees promoting the Dialogue between the social partners at European level, [1998] OJ L 225/27.

[29] For an overview see the website of the Commission at: ec.europa.eu/social/main.jsp?-catId=480&langId=en (accessed 18 October 2016).

[30] European Commission Decision 98/500/EC, n. 27 in this chapter.

[31] Articles 154 and 155 TFEU.

their disposal to negotiate EU level agreements, which may be implemented autonomously by their members – or where it is jointly requested by the signatory parties, as binding EU legislation. In practice this latter option entails that the social partners that sign the agreement, can ask the Commission to turn it into a legislative proposal which the Commission then has to assess with a view to making a proposal for adoption by the Member States in the Council.

The obligations of the Commission to facilitate and promote social dialogue also apply to the sectoral social dialogue. Some concerns have been raised by EU sectoral social partners regarding, for example, the practical arrangements for their social dialogue. Although this may appear to be a marginal issue, in fact, it is crucial in supporting the work of the social partners. It is important not only to look at the obligations of the Commission in terms of sectoral social dialogue, but also at what are the boundaries of its action, as enshrined in EU primary law. The Commission should not go beyond its role of facilitator of sectoral social dialogue. In other words, it must not interfere in the dynamics of the dialogue. This includes not favouring certain types of outcomes. In this context, one of the criticisms made is that there is, on occasion, an implicit preference of the Commission for binding agreements as opposed to non-binding or other types of initiatives. This does not adequately respect the autonomy of the social partners to decide what type of instrument(s) they wish to develop. Similarly, there should not be an implicit preference for certain topics – the social partners are best placed to decide on the most relevant areas for their joint action.

Tangible results have been achieved in the sectoral social dialogue through a wide range of outcomes, including sectoral agreements implemented through EU legislation, framework agreements implemented by the social partners, guidelines, codes of conduct, handbooks, presentations of good practices, and others. Sectoral agreements implemented by EU legislation have been prevalent in the transport sector, in particular to deal with the needs of certain sectors regarding working time. This includes the 1998 agreement on seafarers' working time,[32] transposed into national legislation by 2002 and the 2000 agreement on working time of mobile civil aviation staff,[33] transposed in 2003. These examples are an illustration of how the EU social dialogue can allow for a tailor-made approach for different sectors, by respecting the overall existing

---

[32] Council Directive 1999/63/EC of 21 June 1999 concerning the Agreement on the organisation of working time of seafarers concluded by the European Community Shipowners' Association (ECSA) and the Federation of Transport Workers' Unions in the European Union, [1999] OJ L 167/33.

[33] Council Directive 2000/79/EC of 27 November 2000 concerning the European Agreement on the Organisation of Working Time of Mobile Workers in Civil Aviation, [2000] OJ L 302/57.

EU legislative framework (in this case EU legislation on working time), whilst making specific adaptations to the rules to suit the sector concerned.

Another agreement which the signatory partners asked to be implemented by EU legislation is the hairdressing sector agreement.[34] However, the nature of this agreement is very different to those mentioned above. Firstly, it is broader, dealing with a wide range of health and safety matters. Secondly, it lays down principles and obligations of importance for the sector, but crucially, if the agreement becomes EU law and retains this broad scope, some of these obligations could apply to employers from other sectors. The agreement has caused much debate and as yet the Commission has not met the request of the signatory parties, to turn the agreement into a proposal for EU legislation for adoption by the Council. In fact, the sectoral social partners were asked by the Commission to rework the agreement taking into account the concerns raised by the Commission. This agreement has now been revised by the social partners in the sector and the final version was signed on 23 June 2016. It is positive that a solution could be found respecting at the same time the role of social partners and the nature of EU social legislation. The sectoral social partners are now waiting for the Commission to formally launch the process to turn the agreement into a proposal for EU legislation. Clearly, as recognised by EU sectoral social partners, the autonomy of the hairdressing sector to conclude an agreement and request implementation by EU legislation must be respected. At the same time, it is crucial that the agreement, if it is to be implemented as EU law, fulfils certain principles, as is obligatory for any EU legislative proposal. This means that the Commission's assessment of the representativeness of the signatory parties, as well as the assessment whether the proposal adheres to the subsidiarity and proportionality principles[35] and whether it is in line with existing EU health and safety legislation, is equally necessary in the case of agreements that stem from the autonomous initiative of social partners.

Although important, sectoral social partner agreements implemented by EU legislation are only the tip of the iceberg and in reality, the majority of actions by the social partners in the different sectors do not fall into this category. In this respect, it is important to recognise the value of the different types of tools/actions developed. For example, in 2011 social partners in the chemicals sector agreed on a framework agreement to be implemented by their respective members, which lays down minimum core competences

---

[34] Coiffure EU and UNI Europa, 'European Framework Agreement of 23 June 2016 on protection of occupational health and safety in the hairdressing sector' (2016) available at: ec.europa. eu/social/main.jsp?catId=521&langId=en&agreementId=5460 (accessed 18 October 2016).

[35] Article 5(3) and (4) TEU.

for process operators and first-line supervisors in the sector across Europe.[36] Furthermore, guidelines have been agreed by social partners in many sectors, including agriculture, electricity, telecommunications, and commerce. Although less common than guidelines, codes of conduct are another tool developed by sectoral social partners, for example in the hospitals, private security, sugar industry, woodworking, hairdressing, footwear, leather/tanning, commerce, and textiles sectors. In general, they deal with employment standards, but also increasingly corporate social responsibility.

These examples highlight the richness of the outcomes of the EU sectoral social dialogue, whereas this is in fact only a snapshot. There is also a broadening of the role of sectoral social partners, as the Commission increasingly involves them in areas which were not previously considered as part of EU social dialogue. This includes many parallel processes to sectoral social dialogue, as well as initiatives led by Commission departments other than DG Employment. This is a positive development, and can help cement the role of sectoral social partners more broadly in EU policy, under the condition that the principles of autonomy and representativeness are adhered to, and the areas are of relevance for the sectors concerned.

In conclusion, ESD should stem from recognised industrial relations actors at national level across Member States. Where industrial relations do not exist across different Member States for a specific sector, the artificial creation of EU social dialogue structures should be avoided. Secondly, representativeness should be based on a clear and sustainable mandate, as provided by national members, also to negotiate agreements. Finally, European social partners should have a certain structure, resources, expertise, and experience in social policy related questions to be in a position to make a worthwhile contribution to ESD.

9.5 SOCIAL DIALOGUE AT COMPANY LEVEL – EUROPEAN WORKS COUNCILS

In addition to the development of EU social dialogue at cross-industry and sectoral levels, since 1994 EU legislation provides for employee information and consultation in large companies on a European scale in the form of EWCs. EWCs are bodies through which European employees are informed and consulted by the management on important developments in the company and

---

[36] ECEG and EMCEF 'European Framework Agreement, 15 April 2011 European Framework Agreement on Competence Profiles for Process Operators and First Line Supervisors in the Chemical Industry' (2011) available at: ec.europa.eu/social/main.jsp?catId=521&langId=en&agreementId=5193 (accessed 18 October 2016).

on significant decisions that affect employment or working conditions and have transnational dimension. The right to establish EWCs exists in companies or groups of companies with at least 1000 employees in the EU and the European Economic Area, when there are at least 150 employees in each of two Member States. The initial EU Directive on EWCs was amended by the Recast Directive, which took effect on 6 June 2011.[37]

In 2004, BusinessEurope together with the ETUC, conducted a series of seminars and case studies on the EWCs, and drew conclusions on their functioning.[38] Employers acknowledge that a EWC can bring benefits for a company. It can help develop corporate culture and improve information flows between employees and management. It can also facilitate large change management processes, in particular as discussions in the EWC can lead to a better understanding among employees of the rationale behind changes and to smoother implementation processes. Another clear finding is that the climate of mutual trust between management and workers in the EWC is important for a good functioning of this body. The quality of communication in the EWC can be affected by employees' ability to understand complex issues discussed in this body. In this context, investing in training of employee representatives can be useful. The project also concluded that ensuring ownership of the EWC by the entire workforce is important for a good functioning of this body, but often can be a challenge. Another challenge lay in organising quality information and consultation without creating undue delays and uncertainties since managing multiple layers of information and consultation can pose difficulties. Finally, it was apparent that good functioning of EWCs is an adaptive and an evolving process. Creating a good working atmosphere and added value of the EWC requires time, openness and efforts from both sides.

In line with the outcomes of this project, during the negotiations of the Recast Directive, the following issues were important to BusinessEurope:

- The Directive should continue to give priority to company level solutions negotiated by social partners at the company level. In other words, management and workers' representatives should be given the opportunity to agree on the composition and modalities of operation of EWCs, so that it can be adapted to the situation of a specific company. The subsidiary

---

[37] Council Directive 94/45/EC of 22 September 1994 on the establishment of a European Works Council or a procedure in Community-scale undertakings and Community-scale groups of undertakings for the purposes of informing and consulting employees, [1994] OJ L 254/64; and Council Directive 2009/38/EC, n. 4 in this chapter.

[38] European Social Partners, 'Lessons Learned on European Works Councils' (2005) available at: erc-online.eu/wp-content/uploads/2014/04/2005-00684-EN.pdf (accessed 18 October 2016).

requirements set in the Directive should apply only in the absence of this agreement.

- Existing EWC agreements which were in force should continue in operation, in particular the EWCs set up in accordance with article 13 of the original 1994 Directive.[39]
- EWC should deal only with truly transnational issues, affecting at least two countries.
- Information and consultation processes should be timely and effective but the EU rules should not unduly delay decision making in companies. This has become an important competitiveness factor in fast changing markets and business environments.
- There should be a confidentiality clause, making it possible for management not to disclose certain information on confidentiality grounds as well as requiring Special Negotiating Body and EWC members not to reveal any information which has expressly been provided to them in confidence.

More recently, BusinessEurope has supported a research project by the University of Leuven to gather information on recent management perspectives in relation with the functioning of their EWC.[40] EWCs have become an important vehicle of regular information exchange, cooperation and dialogue between social partners in larger companies. This research provides evidence of a 'learning curve' for improvements to the functioning of EWCs, which mainly derives from the trust-based cooperation of management and labour in companies.

The European Commission is currently reviewing the Recast Directive and will present its evaluation report. It is clear that only four years after the end of the transposition phase, the impact of the Recast Directive on the operation of EWCs is not yet fully seen. However, some early observations can be made. The number of EWCs has been steadily increasing. According to the European Trade Union Institute (ETUI – the research branch of the ETUC) database,[41] there has been an increase from 939 EWCs in 2008 to 1071 in 2015.

---

[39] Council Directive 94/45/EC, n. 36 in this chapter, according to article 13, EWC agreements concluded voluntarily before the deadline for transposition of Directive 94/45 (22 September 1996) remain valid also after this date. Also, already concluded 'article 13 agreements' can be renegotiated/prolonged on the basis of article 13 even after 22 September 1996.

[40] For all materials on the Perspective of Management on European Works Councils project, see: soc.kuleuven.be/ceso/wo/erlm/research/permewc-2013-the-perspective-of-management-on-european-works-councils (accessed 18 October 2016).

[41] The ETUI European Works Councils Database is available at: www.etui.org/Services/European-Works-Councils-Database-EWCDB (accessed 18 October 2016).

It is worth noting that the establishment of a EWC is a right for employees, not an obligation. The fact that not all companies within the scope of the Recast Directive have established a EWC is not a problem nor a sign of failure of the Recast Directive. Many large companies already have EWCs. Sometimes – especially in relatively smaller companies – there is simply no need for such a structure of information and consultation, and other communication channels are used. The new rules introduced by the Recast Directive appear to be sufficiently clear, and companies gradually learn to work on the basis of these rules. There have not been many disputes regarding the new rules. Provisions that leave scope for interpretation (such as the notion of 'means required' for EWC members to apply the rights arising from the Directive; the definition of 'transnational', or the modalities of expert assistance) can be further clarified by the contracting partners in their EWC agreements. The Recast Directive has created new requirements for companies, increasing compliance costs (such as providing expert assistance to a Special Negotiating Body or providing training to members of EWC). However, the nature of the Directive has by and large been preserved as it continues to give priority to company level solutions negotiated by social partners at the company level. Ensuring that this remains the case in the future is a key concern for BusinessEurope. In this light, employers believe that there is no need to change the legislation on the EWCs. Companies are still in the phase of adaptation to the Recast Directive, and try to ensure discussions in EWC bring increased added value for management and workers.

9.6 A DIVERSE AND EVER-EVOLVING NATIONAL SOCIAL DIALOGUE AND THE LINK TO THE EU SOCIAL DIALOGUE

Whilst often embedded in long-established cultures and traditions, national industrial relations systems are not static. National frameworks on collective bargaining continually need to adapt in order to create and maintain an appropriate space for social partners' negotiations, which is to the mutual benefit of enterprises and workers. Mutual trust, representativeness and willingness on both sides, as well as acceptance of the fundamentals of the global economy remain key factors for successful social dialogue at national level.

At the same time, industrial relations systems as well as characteristics of social partners' organisations differ greatly between EU countries. EU-level policy makers should – in BusinessEurope's view – take into account and respect this diversity. Diversity of industrial relations systems takes many forms. For example, the levels at which collective bargaining predominantly takes place differ. In the United Kingdom, Ireland or Poland collective bargaining mainly takes place at the company level. In some other countries (such as Germany, Italy, Belgium, the Netherlands or France) employers and workers delegate the negotiation of employment conditions to collective bargaining specialists, but the level at which collective bargaining usually takes place varies: regional sectoral level in Germany or national sectoral level generally combined with national cross-sectoral negotiations in countries like Belgium, Italy or France. At the same time, in the recent years, a trend can be observed of collective bargaining shifting to more decentralised levels. According to the European Commission,[42] in 2000 'the prevalent bargaining level in the EU remained the sectoral or industry level, by 2013 the balance had shifted towards company and intermediate bargaining (alternating between sector and company level)'. BusinessEurope believes that whatever the level at which working conditions are negotiated, it is important to ensure that wage agreements leave enough flexibility to the company level to take maximum account of productivity developments. For example, German social partners increasingly use 'opening clauses' in sectoral collective agreements, which provide flexibility for companies to adapt national rules to their particular situation. Other examples include the possibility to agree on a variable starting date of the agreed wage increase, lump sum payments, variable elements of the wage; and working time accounts.

There is also a wide diversity of situations in terms of thresholds for collective bargaining that need to be observed by social partner organisations, which usually vary for national, sectoral, and company negotiations. Depending on countries, this may be based on union membership, a licence system, or a minimum threshold of votes cast in works council elections. More generally, collective bargaining coverage varies a lot across the European Union, with coverage rates ranging from less than 30 per cent in some Central and Eastern European countries such as Lithuania, Latvia, Estonia, Hungary, and Slovakia to nearly full coverage in Sweden, Finland, Belgium, France, and Austria.

Another area of diversity is the room left for collective bargaining by the legislator. In Denmark, for example, trade unions and employers concluded an agreement of mutual recognition more than a 100 years ago. Employment conditions in the private sector are almost exclusively defined by collective agreements and there is practically no legislation applicable to firms in the private sector. Labour law is reserved for the public sector. By contrast, in France for example, state intervention in labour-market regulation is a deeply

---

[42] European Commission, *Industrial Relations in Europe 2014* (Publications Office of the European Union, 2015).

rooted tradition, even though the recent trend has been for State authorities to leave more space to social dialogue negotiated solutions.

The nature of the agreements negotiated by the social partners and their relationship with legislation also differ. In the United Kingdom, for example, collective agreements have no legal value. They are 'gentlemen's agreements', but those who sign them respect the commitments made. In Denmark, agreements are only applicable to the workers and enterprises affiliated to the organisations signing them. In some other countries, for example Belgium, France, and Italy, agreements concluded between employers and trade unions can be made universally applicable through legislation or an executive decree. There is therefore a certain link between negotiations and legislation. To encourage more dynamic collective bargaining and outcomes more in tune with rapid economic and social change, some countries such as Portugal have introduced recently some new rules aiming to reduce the expiry period of collective agreements and the period of their continuation upon expiry.

Furthermore, the degrees of autonomy of social partners also differ. There are countries where social partners have a total autonomy of negotiation. In such cases there is no state intervention, and when negotiations encounter difficulties or fail, conflict resolution mechanisms are purely voluntary and rely above all on the power relations between the two sides. This is the case in Denmark. Other countries, such as Belgium, France, Spain, or Italy, have semi-autonomous systems. Even though the state is not a party in the negotiations of national agreements, it can have an influence on the outcome, because a failure in negotiations can lead either to the legislator taking over or compulsory arbitration.

The ways in which the right to strike is defined also differs a lot between EU countries. In many European countries, the right to strike is a collective right and not an individual one. Consequently, during the whole validity period of a collective agreement and as long as the commitments made are respected, a strike is illegal. An important exception is France, where the right to strike is an individual right guaranteed by the constitution, which cannot be suspended.

Another source of diversity is the concept of representativeness of social partners. There are countries where representativeness is mainly dependent upon mutual recognition (such as Denmark and the UK) and others where representativeness is based upon fulfilling requirements set out in legal regulation (such as France and Germany). As a recent Eurofound report concludes: 'Given this core duality and the complexity of intervening arrangements, it is today as difficult (or impossible) a task as it was in 1993 to propose any single all-embracing European definition of representativeness'.[43]

The diversity of industrial relations systems across the EU has implications for EU-level social dialogue and for EU social policy-making. It explains the different ways in which EU-level social partners' agreements are implemented at national level (such as national cross-industry agreements, sectoral agreements, guidance documents and changes to legislation). Moreover, it also has implications for the scope of EU social policy-making. For example, according to Article 153(5) TFEU 'pay, the right of association, the right to strike or the right to impose lock-outs' are excluded from EU competences. In the employers' view, it is important for the EU-level actors to respect and to build on the diversity of national industrial relations systems across Europe. Any attempts from EU-level actors to impose harmonisation of industrial relations systems would be counterproductive. At the same time, the commitment of national social partners to engage in the ESD shows their belief that it can add value to their national social dialogues: by raising awareness of effective employment and social policies, by providing a framework for mutual learning, by reinforcing the capacity of social partners, or by promoting new issues on the national agenda. A key objective for European employers in the next years is to achieve better coordination between EU and national social agendas, notably by setting up a framework for national discussions on the content of policies and reforms needed.

9.7 CONCLUSION

There is recognition across Europe that social dialogue can be a tool to promote both competitiveness and fairness, contributing to harmonious economic and social development. This is also the belief of BusinessEurope. Fostering social dialogue is recognised as an element of the European social model, and after more than thirty years of existence, the ESD has demonstrated its positive role as part of EU policy-making. Much has been achieved, and the development towards more autonomy in the EU social dialogue is testament to its success and its growing maturity. This success continues to rely on a climate of trust, confidence, and cooperation between employers, trade unions, and policy-makers. In this respect, it is positive to see that Eurofound company surveys regularly give evidence of a good climate of trust between

---

[43] Eurofound, 'The concept of representativeness at national level and at European Level' (forthcoming) some information is already available at: www.eurofound.europa.eu/observatories/eurwork/representativeness-studies (accessed 18 October 2016).

social partners. The last of these surveys published in 2015[44] indicated that 83 per cent of employee representatives surveyed agreed with the statement that the management can be trusted; 80 per cent of the representatives agreed that management was making sincere efforts to involve the employee representation in solving joint problems; and 52 per cent of the employees reported having had at least some influence on the most important decision taken in the establishment in recent years.

As part of the re-launch of the ESD, consideration is being given to the best means of reinvigorating the role of social dialogue. On 27 June 2016, the European social partners, the Commission, and the Dutch Presidency of the Council adopted a tripartite statement on 'a new start for social dialogue'.[45] This is the outcome of more than one year of technical work following the high-level conference organised on 5 March 2015 in the presence of the Commission President Mr Jean-Claude Juncker. The statement includes actions by the signatories aiming to support a more substantial involvement of the social partners in the European Semester, a stronger emphasis on capacity building of national social partners, a strengthened involvement of social partners in EU policy and law-making, and a clearer relation between social partners' agreements and the better regulation agenda. This is the first time that such a shared roadmap on social dialogue is agreed between Commission, Council, and the European social partners. It is now important to transcribe this into real actions, in particular in countries where social partners need support. Achieving results together will depend on our capacity to act with ambition but also on a sense of realism of what can be achieved.

The employers' view is that this discussion should not focus excessively on further institutionalising the dialogue, either in bipartite or tripartite settings, as the currently available structures and methods are overall satisfactory. With already at least 70 social directives providing adequate minimum standards and well-developed social systems at national level, the priority is to support where needed a more even implementation of the existing rules. Conversely, further social minimum standards which place an additional burden on companies should not be introduced.

[44] Eurofound, *Third European Company Survey – Overview report: Workplace Practices – Patterns, Performance and Well-being* (Publications Office of the European Union, 2015), p. 106.
[45] The Council of the European Union, the European Commission and European Social Partners, 'A New Start for Social Dialogue' (2016) available at: www.businesseurope.eu/sites/buseur/files/media/position_papers/social/2016-06-27_quadri-partite_statement_signed_on_a_new_start_for_social_dialogue.pdf (accessed 18 October 2016).

What will be essential in the future, is that the EU social partners converge more on how to foster economic growth and social prosperity in Europe. And in this respect, employers stress that one of the key challenges for Europe in the years to come remains creating more jobs and reduce unemployment. To win the battle for employment, employers call for a renewed EU strategy based on flexicurity principles. And in terms of emerging challenges for labour-market policies, public authorities, and social partners in Europe will have a lot to do in the next years to support labour-market adaptation to the digitisation and greening of our economies.

The European Social Dialogue: What Is the Role of Employers and What Are the Hopes for the Future?

Philippe Pochet and Christophe Degryse

10.1 INTRODUCTION

In 2015, the European social dialogue (ESD) officially celebrated its 30th anniversary. The European Commission organised a major conference on 6 March 2015 to 'revive' the dynamics of the ESD, which, according to most observers, have broken down since the 2000s. The ESD no longer produces new social rights (except the extension of parental leave by one month in 2009) and shows little sign of ambition.[1] Yet it remains one of the fundamental pillars of social Europe, and is one of the elements of the European integration process that distinguishes it from other systems of regional integration. In this sense, the social dialogue is intrinsic to European identity itself.

In this chapter, we first recall the milestones of the European social dialogue. We then examine the dynamics of the parties; in particular the employers, because it is they who generally decide on the de facto 'acceptable' level of ambition for the ESD. The novelty of this chapter is to highlight and question the strategy of the employers' organisations and European multinationals in the ESD. The chapter will also examine the possible revival of the ESD following the crises of European integration and threats to the internal market.

10.2 THE MAJOR MILESTONES OF THE ESD

During the first 30 years of European integration – roughly, the period from 1957 to 1985 – 'social Europe' was developed primarily through the adoption

[1] S. Clauwaert, 'Main Developments in European Cross-industry Social Dialogue in 2009: Bargaining in Many Shadows', in C. Degryse (ed.), *Social Developments in the European Union 2009* (European Trade Union Institute, 2010); C. Degryse (ed.), 'European Social Dialogue: State of Play and Prospects' (2011), available at www.etuc.org/IMG/pdf/Dialogue_social_2010_Rapport_OSE_CES_EN.pdf (accessed 25 October 2016).

of legislative measures, namely directives and regulations on, for example, the coordination of social security schemes, equal pay, and workplace restructuring. However, as a response to the political deadlock that had frustrated the development of these social rights (which was significantly related to the coming to power of Margaret Thatcher in the UK), from the mid-1980s a new social engine was promoted by the European Commission: the ESD between social partners. This dialogue brought together trade unions via the European Trade Union Confederation (ETUC), employers in the private sector via BusinessEurope (then called UNICE) – later joined by the European Association of Craft, Small and Medium-sized Enterprises (UEAPME), which represented SMEs – and public sector employers via the European Centre of Employers and Enterprises providing Public Services (CEEP). There were three important stages to the development of the ESD. The first, 1985–1991 (from Val Duchesse to the Treaty of Maastricht), was one of experimentation and the establishment of collective bargaining actors. This was the period of the first 'joint opinions', through which employers and workers got to know each other and started negotiating fairly general and non-binding joint texts.[2]

The second stage, 1992–99, involved the negotiation of agreements made legally binding *erga omnes* by their incorporation into Council Directives, using the procedure newly introduced by the Treaty of Maastricht. This period is still seen today as 'the golden age' of the ESD, as it exemplifies the use of social dialogue as an instrument of social regulation.

The third period, beginning in the early 2000s, was one of difficult experimentation with European autonomous agreements, implemented at national level by national partners under the terms of the Treaty. Due to pressure from the employers, but with the agreement of the unions, there was an increasing demand for an autonomous European social dialogue, with greater independence from the European Commission. First, from 2003 autonomous multiannual work programmes began to be developed by the social partners, detailing various joint actions to be carried out over a period of time that would go beyond the mere negotiation of the framework agreements. Second, the negotiated agreements were no longer implemented by means of directives; the favoured approach was now an autonomous one based on implementation by the national social partners.[3]

---

[2] C. Didry and A. Mias, *Le Moment Delors. Les syndicats au cœur de l'Europe sociale* (P.I.E-Peter Lang, 2005); J. Lapeyre, *Le dialogue social européen – Histoire d'une innovation sociale* (ETUI, forthcoming).

[3] A. Branch, 'The Evolution of the European Social Dialogue towards Greater Autonomy: Challenges and Potential Benefits' (2005) 21 *International Journal of Comparative Labour Law and Industrial Relations* 321. See Article 155(2) TFEU.

These autonomous agreements immediately raised questions about their implementation in the Member States in accordance with national traditions. However, the word 'traditions' does not always have a very clear or coherent meaning in a world of changing national industrial relations, which in general are going through a process of decentralisation and not always in an orderly fashion. Furthermore, such traditions simply do not exist in the countries of Central and Eastern Europe since the collapse of the Soviet Union in late 1991. In 1992, at the signing of the Maastricht Treaty that formalised the terms of the European social dialogue, it was not anticipated that an increasing number of (future) EU member countries would have no national institutions through which to extend to all – employers and workers – the results of a European collective bargaining. This partly explains why even today, autonomous agreements that are expected to be transposed at national level 'in accordance with the procedures and practices specific to management and labour and the Member States'[4] only cover a limited number of workers in these Central and Eastern European countries (not only there, however, but in all countries where there is no tradition of extension of agreements, such as the UK).

The third period is therefore perceived by the trade unions as a period of gradual yet significant weakening of the social dialogue under the pressure of employers (see Section 10.3 below) and its transformation into an experience-sharing forum and a place to exchange good practice.[5] This period also coincided with the Barroso Commissions I and II (2004–14) and the Juncker Commission (from 2014), whose major projects included the reduction of administrative 'burdens'.[6] Legislation – and in particular social legislation – was increasingly represented as an administrative burden for businesses and not as a way to resolve a problem together or to create a level playing field for enterprises across the whole of Europe.

Finally, the crisis since 2008 has not, as might have been expected, revived the social dialogue at European, sectoral or cross-industry level, despite neither industry nor workers being responsible for its development. It has instead helped to radicalise the employers' positions on social dialogue issues.[7] As of 2010, the crisis has been used by the troika, the Commission and many

4   Article 155(2), TFEU.
5   C. Degryse (ed.), *European Social Dialogue: State of Play and Prospects* (European Social Observatory, 2011)
6   E. Vanden Abeele 'The EU's REFIT Strategy: A New Bureaucracy in the Service of Competitiveness?' (2014) *ETUI, Working Paper*, 05.
7   I. Schömann and S. Clauwaert, 'The Crisis and National Labour Law Reforms: A Mapping Exercise' (2012) *ETUI Working Paper*, 2012.04.

Member States to weaken or remove the institutions of collective bargaining at both sectoral and cross-industry level in a majority of countries.[8]

Since 2015, however, there has been a desire promoted by the new Juncker Commission to revive the social dialogue at European level and to revive the social side of the European integration.

10.3 THE STRATEGIES OF THE ACTORS

While the different stages of this evolution are quite clear, there is little explanation for the transitions from one stage to another, particularly from stages two to three: from the 'golden age' to the age of trade union disenchantment. Very often the weakness of the ESD is explained by the withdrawal of the Commission and its increasingly diminished role and/or the inability of unions to create a transnational balance of power. Little has been said, however, about the attitude of employers, who are clearly key players.

We can start from the premise that the level of ambition for the social dialogue is by definition higher among trade unions (representing as they do the demands of workers for social progress and improvements). However, the unions have a limited capacity to use levers of power at the transnational level. European strikes are not possible in the current context mainly because of significant differences between national rules on the right to strike; for example, in many Member States solidarity strikes are forbidden or strikes are forbidden during the time of collective agreement, but it is also true that in some cases strikes, particularly in case of restructuring, did not take place because of a lack of solidarity). In the absence of a genuine balance of power, it is the employers' organisations who define what an acceptable level of ambition is for themselves and their members, thereby dictating the terms for the quality of the ESD and its results.

Our central argument is that the position and role of the employers' organisations in Europe is twofold. On the one hand, they form an important institution in the European integration process (now perhaps in the process of disintegration) and, on the other hand, they are ideological actors with their own predominant interests. In 1992, UNICE adopted a comprehensive strategy that it put into action as soon as the opportunity arose. An internal note dated 30 April 1992 gives us an insight into the level of ambition of this key actor.[9] In it, the employers' organisation states:

---

[8] C. Degryse, M. Jepsen, and P. Pochet, 'The Euro Crisis and Its Impact on National and European Social Policies' (2013) *ETUI Working Paper*, 2013.05.

[9] We thank Jean Lapeyre for sharing it with us.

UNICE could focus its strategy on two main approaches:

(1) ensuring that Article 3b (subsidiarity) [now Article 5 TEU] is actually applied to social policy and accompanied by appropriate instruments, such as a *'fiche'* annexed to all legislative proposals, explaining why the proposed action should be carried out at Community level;
(2) making effective use of our statutory right to consultation and (potential) negotiation to prevent, delay, or modify excessive centralisation of social policy or legislation that is too prescriptive and detrimental to the competitiveness of enterprises [own translation original in French].

The decision to negotiate depends on several factors:

• the nature of the legislation (for example, the employers' organisation does not want to negotiate on health and safety);
• the content (the more damaging it is in terms of carrying risks, the more it will be open to negotiation);
• the chances of adoption (no negotiation if the chances are low).[10]

These are fundamental issues for the employers' organisation, and they raise the question: what led UNICE/ BusinessEurope to nevertheless sign several agreements? In the study of UNICE by Branch and Greenwood[11] the authors conclude:

Although institutional forces, socialisation and learning have been important, the attitudes of these organisations towards social partnership and social dialogue are nevertheless instrumental. The shift in UNICE's position [following the Treaty of Maastricht] did not, then, reflect a conversion to a new philosophy. Instead, its attitude was one of 'realpolitik', namely a change in strategy in response to changing political realities.

A confluence of very particular circumstances produced the most dynamic period of social dialogue. In the 1980s, large enterprises in Europe were often presented as 'national champions'; they were relatively little Europeanised, and still less internationalised. The completion of the internal market in 1993, the desegmentation of national markets, European liberalisation policies, and the development of a set of common technical standards all contributed to the gradual emergence of a more Europeanised capitalism. It is in this context that the Delors Commission and the European Parliament argued with some success for the single market to be given a social dimension (Charter of Social

---

[10] Unice, internal note, 1992.
[11] H. Compston and H. Greenwood (eds), *Social Partnership in the European Union* (Palgrave Macmillan, 2001), p. 43.

Rights of Workers and the 1989 Action Programme). Amidst the opening up of markets and liberalisation policies at that time, there was therefore also a space for the negotiation of collective agreements to create trans-European social rights for workers. In particular, this included the development of common standards for so-called 'atypical' workers: fixed-term, part-time, etc.

As Markus Beyrer, Secretary General of BusinessEurope, emphasised: 'When the European social dialogue was founded, the big project for Europe was to create a single market. The European social dialogue then contributed to shape the social dimension of this emerging single market and to define European standards for working conditions which had become an EU competence.'[12]

In the 1990s, large multinational companies rapidly expanded and advanced from European to global level.[13] With the opening up of international trade, these companies began to expand their field of operation into Asia and the United States. Europe was now competing with other increasingly dynamic spaces.

The internal market continued to establish itself, its priority status in Europe less and less disputed following the fall of the Berlin Wall. But as the new century dawned, the Commission's focus increasingly moved away from actual social regulation of the internal market towards 'coordinated strategies' (for employment, social inclusion, pensions, etc.). From facilitator and arbitrator of the social dialogue, its role became increasingly administrative, as a mere witness to the power relations between the social partners. The terms of possible trade-off negotiation thus underwent a profound transformation from what they had been in the 1990s. In this new climate much more favourable to its own interests, UNICE was able to impose its strategy.

During this transition to the third phase of the European social dialogue, employers' organisations began to turn their backs on the process ever more overtly, while the Commission, hiding behind the 'the autonomy of the social partners', relinquished its role as a mediator (remember our original premise of 'imbalance').

In this new configuration, the unions found themselves at a disadvantage; they continued to call for a social dialogue that produced standards, but now

[12] BusinessEurope, 'High level Conference "A New Start for Social Dialogue", Opening Session "Building a Common Approach to a New Start for Social Dialogue"' (2015) available at: www.businesseurope.eu/sites/buseur/files/media/imported/2015-00186-E.pdf (accessed 25 October 2016).

[13] See B. Van Apeldoorn, 'Transnational Class Agency and European Governance: The Case of the European Round Table of Industrialists' (2000) 5 *New Political Economy* 157, on the changes in agenda and composition of the European Round Table of Industrialists (ERT), the powerful lobby of European multinationals.

without the necessary means of influence or any institutional allies. The nego-tiation of autonomous agreements therefore seemed to be in some respects a last chance for social dialogue. For union leaders of the time, the idea was that if these autonomous agreements did not produce satisfactory results, there would be a strong case for forcing the Commission to act.[14]

This new approach was thus launched in 2002, with the signing of the first of the autonomous agreements on the issue of telework. Other such agree-ments followed: on stress at work in 2004 and on harassment and violence at work in 2007. The themes addressed in this new form of negotiation mainly concerned the new challenges of the world of work, both in Europe and in the rest of the world, and were often discussed in the context of corporate social responsibility.

In reality, however, we see that the desire for autonomy expressed in the employers' discourse actually led to a great disparity in the quality of imple-mentation of the texts that had been negotiated at European level. In 25 per cent of EU countries, autonomous agreements were simply not transcribed at national level; in the eyes of the ETUC, this was clearly a failure.[15] Ramos and Visser found no less than seven ways to implement the autonomous agreements at national level: (1) common guidelines, recommendations, and model agreements; (2) autonomous national agreements; (3) separate guide-lines and model agreements by the social partners; (4) collective agreements in sectors, companies or institutions; (5) national agreements transformed into legislation; (6) legislation following consultations; (7) legislation without con-sultation of the social partners.[16]

This third phase of social dialogue was then carried to its extreme. Companies invested heavily in future growth areas; Europe, with its ageing population and saturated markets, no longer offered attractive growth pros-pects. The debate was now focused on the transfer of key areas of activity such as research and development to other centres of growth, particularly China (where the Chinese government used all of its assets to promote these stra-tegic transfers).Large multinational companies did express their willingness to engage in social dialogue, but only provided it turned into a 'partnership for structural reforms'. At the conference on social dialogue in March 2015, Emma Marcegaglia, President of BusinessEurope, declared: 'We need a joint vision with our social partners on the challenges ahead, especially on

---

[14] Lapreye, n. 2 in this chapter.
[15] Degryse, 'European Social Dialogue', n. 1 in this chapter.
[16] J. Visser and N. Ramos Martín, 'A More "Autonomous" European Social Dialogue: The Implementation of the Framework Agreement On Telework' (2008) 24 *International Journal of Comparative Labour Law and Industrial Relations* 511.

the labour markets. The European social dialogue should be a facilitator for necessary reforms. Trade unions should acknowledge that European companies face severe global competition, and improved competitiveness alone will allow us to keep Europe's social model functioning'.[17]

The most recent failure in negotiations on the issue of working time gives a clear indication that the employers are only interested in reforms that promote greater flexibility in labour markets rather than greater safety for workers. In the ETUC view, it is rather surprising that BusinessEurope could contemplate having the support of the trade unions on this issue.[18] In 2015 the Commission tried to revive the social dialogue and called for the social partners to reach an overall agreement. Surprisingly, the social partners managed to do just that, not only between themselves but also with specific requests for the Commission and the Member States. It was the Commission, having requested to be involved in the development of the text and having followed the negotiation process, which now wavered at the prospect of being subjected to obligations imposed by the social partners. Finally, however, a quadripartite document was signed in conjunction with both the Commission and the Council in June 2016. The social partners also managed to agree on a statement in support of the integration of refugees and another on the challenges of digitalisation, which they presented at the Social Summit.

10.4 A NEW DYNAMIC IN DESPERATE TIMES

Do these recent developments, still very cautious, foreshadow a significant change in the overall dynamic? We believe that the 'polycrisis' that afflicts Europe, and that only continues to deepen, could in fact offer a window of opportunity for the European social dialogue to advance to the next stage of its evolution. The great fear in 2015–16 has been that the successive financial and euro crises have triggered an existential crisis in the European Union. This can already be seen in, firstly, the Schengen crisis and the issue of asylum seekers and, secondly, the crisis in the domestic market, exacerbated by Brexit and a renewed surge of populist criticism. This new twofold crisis may yet sound the death knell for the European Union in its current form. Euroscepticism is reflected in the rise of populist political parties (in Austria, Germany, Finland,

---

[17] BusinessEurope, 'Social Dialogue Should Develop in the Direction of a Reform Partnership', press release of 5 March 2015, available at: www.businesseurope.eu/sites/buseur/files/media/imported/2015-00187-E.pdf (accessed 16 November 2016).

[18] See www.worker-participation.eu/EU-Social-Dialogue/Latest-developments/Failure-of-the-revision-of-the-working-time-Directive-negotiations (accessed 14 December 2016).

Netherlands, Hungary, Poland, etc.), while the UK's Brexit referendum has revealed the potential fragility of the adhesion to the European project.

Of course, even in the case of the Brexit vote, we can identify that a significant part of the European population continues to support the European idea, and in some parts that support is increasing.[19] But paradoxically, an increasing number of national governments want to deconstruct certain fixtures of the integration project, for motives ranging from electoral to nationalist to opportunist. This 'deconstruction' affects the internal market and the Schengen area, thereby threatening what business and companies see as the most valuable asset of the EU. The single market and free movement seemed established facts; we now know that they are mortal. Yet the economic cost of reintroducing borders has been calculated at between 470 and 1400 billion euros over a ten-year period.[20] The very idea of dismantling the European internal market brings industrialists, entrepreneurs, and exporters across the EU out in a cold sweat. The ERT knows this very well, as can be seen from its sudden reaffirmation of everything that is good about the European Union.[21]

Might this threat of deconstruction feed a kind of desperate energy to save what is left of the European project? The question is whether the employers' organisations can make the necessary link between the rise of Euroscepticism, nationalism and Europhobia on the one hand, and the deterioration of living and working conditions and increasing insecurity of whole sections of the population on the other. History has shown that European integration is supported by the people of Europe only when it succeeds in balancing the benefits it provides to the world of business with the social progress it brings to citizens; one does not automatically result in the other, as we know. Europe's great failure over the past ten or fifteen years, for which we are undoubtedly paying today, is to have forgotten this form of social compact. The European system has favoured the accumulation of profits by reducing everything that is presented as a 'burden' (regulatory, tax, administrative, and social), leaving the average citizen even less protected in the face of economic insecurity, unemployment, the crisis, and austerity. The relevance of the European social

---

[19] According to a survey organised in six Member States (Belgium, France, Germany, Italy, Poland, Spain) by IFOP on behalf of the 'Fondation Jean-Jaurès' and the 'Fondation européenne d'études progressistes', 15 July 2016, available at: www.ifop.fr/media/poll/3442-1-study_file.pdf/ (accessed 14 December 2016).

[20] N. Barkin, 'Schengen Collapse Could Cost EU up to 1.4 Trillion Euros over Decade', Reuters, 22 February 2016, available at: www.reuters.com/article/us-europe-economy-schengen-idUSKCN0VVoQG (accessed 16 November 2016).

[21] European Round Table of Industrialists, 'Why Europe Matters' (2016) available at: www.ert.eu/sites/ert/files/generated/files/document/why_europe_matters_-_en.pdf (accessed 25 October 2016).

dialogue is therefore self-evident. It is the principal means by which to create a new social pact that can produce a new balance between capital and labour, and by which Europe can concretely demonstrate what it has to offer to its citizens and workers in terms of improving their living and working conditions. In this sense, it is has an important role to play in showing the 240 million European workers that the EU is also designed for them and can bring them social progress. European employers can easily recognise that for them the cost of a results-oriented European social dialogue is lower than that of a populist dismantling of Schengen and the single market. For their part, the governments would do well to remember that any attempt to build Europe without the support of Europe's citizens and workers is doomed to failure.

Such a revival of the social dialogue requires the emergence of a visionary leadership by the employer organisations; the strategy to keep alive a stagnating process risks a complete breakdown. As for political responsibilities, they are also central to this issue. The President of the European Commission, Jean-Claude Juncker, rightly felt that his Commission provided the 'last chance' to regain the support of citizens. History has shown how its role could be decisive in the dynamics of social dialogue. Today, the Commission must regain its position as a stimulating force for the social partners, and for this 'last chance' it needs the best possible allies.

10.5 WHAT CHALLENGES LIE AHEAD?

Assuming a willingness to negotiate on the part of the employers, we identify two possible major themes: firstly, the issues and effects of digitalisation (on which subject a joint text has already been signed;[22] and secondly, the challenges related to climate change and the consequent restructuring of production and consumption. Over the short, medium, and long term, both these phenomena will bring about crucial and potentially disruptive transformations in our systems of production.

The digital transformation, alongside climate change, will have a potentially enormous impact on the labour market, not only in terms of the destruction of jobs that have become 'obsolete' and the creation of new ones, but also in the emergence of new qualifications, new forms of work organisation, and new production processes. What some people call the Fourth Industrial Revolution – the internet of things, 3D printers, digital platforms, etc. – could

---

[22] Tripartite Social Summit, 'Statement of the European Social Partners on Digitalisation' (2016) available at: www.businesseurope.eu/sites/buseur/files/media/position_papers/social/2016-03-16_tss_-_statement_on_digitalisation.pdf (accessed 16 November 2016).

lead to a fundamental shift in the way that we produce goods and provide services. Any job could be affected: from the manual worker, the service technician, the farmer, the taxi driver, the hotelier, and the translator, to the executive, the human resources manager, the tax specialist, the journalist, the legal advisor, and the personal assistant.[23] The disruptive potential of this phenomenon merits a central focus in the European social dialogue. Here we discuss some of the challenges that mark this transition into the digital economy.

We can identify four types of impact on the labour markets: the changing number of jobs (between those destroyed and those created), the nature of these jobs, their displacement via globalised subcontracting, and the new forms of management and monitoring of workers.

Concerning the loss of jobs, certain studies predict that almost half of all current jobs in the United States risk being destroyed in the next 15–20 years. In Europe, this figure stands at more than 50 per cent, while in the United Kingdom more than a third of jobs are seriously threatened. Other studies,[24] however, are less alarmist and predict that 'only' 9 per cent of jobs are at high risk of disappearing. There is therefore little consensus between these statistics and, as Valenduc and Vendramin are right to point out, it is the organisation of work around the automation of tasks that is a central issue here.[25] A robot replaces one (or several) task(s), but a job does not only consist of the accomplishment of one task. It is therefore dangerous to try to predict how many jobs robots will replace. This is why it would be helpful to have a more detailed picture of the impact of robotisation on the number of jobs in individual sectors; here the social partners could play a central role.

The development of digital labour raises many questions. What is the status of a worker on a digital platform? Are they a 'freelancer' or an 'independent contractor'? What is the nature of the employment relationship? Is the employee in a subordinate position to the employer? Who is the employer and what are their responsibilities? What control do they have over the worker? We also need to take into account the increase in multiple forms of atypical work, which include freelance workers, 'nomads', occasional service providers, and so forth. Workers may be seeking transition jobs or just some extra income, but is there a risk of them becoming stuck in a cycle of precarious work? Furthermore, are regulations on health and safety, workplace accidents, and

[23] C. Degryse, 'Digitalisation of the Economy and Its Impact on Labour Markets' (2016) *ETUI Working Paper*, 2016.02.

[24] OECD, 'Automation and Independent Work in a Digital Economy' (2016) May *OECD Policy Brief on the Future of Work*, 16.

[25] G. Valenduc and P. Vendramin, 'Work in the Digital Economy: Sorting the Old from the New' (2016) *ETUI Working Paper*, 2016.03.

working time respected? And what about professional insurance, social insurance, and taxation? The social partners could look into these issues and find common ground, as they did in the case of teleworking.

The digital economy does not recognise any borders. More and more companies, whether SMEs or transnational corporations, use the internet to subcontract tasks that can be done by crowd-workers anywhere in the world, who are available around the clock. This subcontracting is made possible (and significantly easier) by digital platforms. Is there a risk of 'normal' jobs being split up into small tasks that can be handed over to crowd-workers through these platforms? What kind of job is most endangered by this new form of digital Taylorism? But also, how can the crowd-workers organise themselves to avoid being drawn into a downward spiral of competition over prices? Considering what rules and regulations should be in place along the chain of production is a priority for the future.

Other new social risks are also emerging. For example, one of the challenges facing 'traditional' employees in offices or factories is their new relationship with corporate computer systems. The software for managing each step of the production process down to the smallest detail is being increasingly perfected. Workers can only play a subordinate role to these ultra-sophisticated IT systems, which diminishes their autonomy and increases their stress levels. The new means of 'digital management' represent yet another challenge, and the debate over how to define a 'reasoned and reasonable' limit to employee monitoring in the digital economy is a good subject for the social dialogue. The issues of digitalisation have already been tackled by both BusinessEurope[26] and the ETUC,[27] as well as in a document that was jointly adopted[28] by these two European social partners in 2016. In view of the profound digital and environmental transformations that are upon us, and all the uncertainties they entail with regards to the question of transition, we believe that the challenges identified above will come to define a renewed and ambitious social dialogue.

10.6 CONCLUSION

To conclude, the European social dialogue has undergone different stages of development throughout its history: experimentation, progressive building of trust, dynamisation, then slowdown, or even almost total failure. Because of

---

[26] BusinessEurope, n. 12 in this chapter.
[27] ETUC, 'Resolution on Digitalisation: 'Towards Fair Digital Work' (2016) available at: www.etuc.org/documents/etuc-resolution-digitalisation-towards-fair-digital-work#.WCxapCRimfk (accessed 16 November 2016).
[28] Ibid.

its institutional role, the European Commission has always influenced these developments, helping to strengthen or weaken them. After many years of neglect, the Juncker Commission is now trying to relaunch this social dialogue, an ambition shared by the European Trade Union Confederation. But that is the subject of a significant difference of interpretation with BusinessEurope. Employers now see European Social Dialogue as an instrument for structural reforms on the labour market, reforms often seen as a threat by the trade union as mainly aimed at flexibilising labour markets (working time, wages, etc.) and even neutralising collective bargaining. On the contrary, the relaunch of the social dialogue is seen by the ETUC as having to promote the negotiation of binding agreements containing new social rights for workers. This is the meaning of a resolution adopted by the executive committee of the trade union organisation: the ETUC must now stop 'wasting time' on subjects of minor importance, joint analysis, and reports, and concentrating on few but strategic issues, in order to obtain a clear commitment from the employers' organisations on their willingness to negotiate and reach ambitious agreements – without which the ETUC will change its strategy. A resolution adopted, rare occurrence, by acclamation by the executive committee of 15 December 2016.

11

The European Semester Process: Adaptability and Latitude in Support of the European Social Model

Sonja Bekker

11.1 INTRODUCTION

The establishment of the European Semester and its stricter economic governance has sparked off many debates, also addressing the impact on the European Social Model (ESM). Research has focused mainly on mapping out the new EU regulatory framework, or on assessing national-level structural reforms. Much less attention has been given to the exchange between the EU Institutions and the Member States, within the so-called 'throughput' phase of policy-making. This chapter gives more insight into this interaction by answering the question of to what degree the European Semester adapts its goals to new challenges and what leeway Member States have to implement alternative policies. The degree of adaptability and latitude indicate the perspective of social goals within the European Semester. The chapter scrutinises EU socioeconomic governance between 2009 and 2015. It looks at the changes in EU-level goals and the responses of France, Germany, Poland, and Spain in three key dossiers: unemployment, wage-setting, and pension schemes. The conclusion is that the European Semester adapts its goals. It tailors recommendations to specific national challenges and changes its focus from time to time. This goes to show that the European Semester is not a static but an evolving governance structure. Moreover, Member States have latitude to deal with EU demands in different ways. All four Member States question some of the Commission's evaluations and recommendations. They propose alternative views on sound socioeconomic policies and may even implement policies that go against the EU recommendations. They do so based on a range of arguments, including that of safeguarding social policies. Both the adaptability of the European Semester and the leeway of Member States are important ingredients of the governance process. It offers scope for learning and evolution and thereby provides opportunities for strengthening the ESM.

11.2 THE EUROPEAN SEMESTER AND ITS SOFT-LAW ROOTS

The European Semester has been introduced after the start of the crisis. One of its purposes was to make Member States comply better with fiscal rules and to avoid macroeconomic imbalances that could spill over to other countries. The Semester integrates a range of socioeconomic coordination mechanisms, including the Europe 2020 Strategy, the Macroeconomic Imbalances Procedure (MIP) and the Stability and Growth Pact (SGP). The Six-Pack (2011) and the Fiscal Compact (2013) strengthened the already existing SGP and introduced the MIP for the early detection of national macroeconomic imbalances. Both these fiscal and economic coordination cycles have a preventative but also corrective arm that may result in financial penalties for euro area countries. The Europe 2020 Strategy has remained a soft coordination cycle and mostly addresses employment and social policies, including the integrated guidelines for economic and employment policies. Europe 2020 hosts ambitious goals such as reducing the number of people who experience poverty, thereby supporting the ESM. However, during the first years of the economic crisis the EU's focus was on reducing national public expenditure. There was much less consideration for social goals. The fiscal focus coincided with numerous accounts of austerity measures and structural reforms at the national level, which often harmed social policy initiatives.[1] However, in spite of this correlation between stricter EU fiscal rules and national reforms, questions remain on the nature and magnitude of a causal link between the EU rules and the national outcomes. These questions are inspired by the pre-crisis literature on soft governance of employment and social policies via the Open Method of Coordination (OMC) and the limited competences the EU has to mingle into national social domains.[2] Such questions are furthered by more recent literature pointing at the importance of the throughput phase of policy-making.[3] This throughput phase ties the input of a decision-making (for instance the rules) process to its output (for instance domestic policy changes).

---

[1]   E. Achtsioglou and M. Doherty, 'There Must Be Some Way Out of Here ... The Crisis, Labour Rights and Member States in the Eye of the Storm' (2014) 20 *European Law Journal* 219; C. Degryse, M. Jepsen, and P. Pochet, 'The Euro Crisis and Its Impact on National and European Social Policies' (2013) *European Trade Union Institute (ETUI) Working Paper*, 05; and J. López and S. Canalda Criado, 'Breaking the Equilibrium between Flexibility and Security: Flexiprecarity as the Spanish Version of the Model' (2014) 5 *European Labour Law Journal* 22.

[2]   J. Zeitlin, P. Pochet, and L. Magnussen (eds), *The Open Method of Coordination in Action: The European Employment and Social Inclusions Strategies* (P.I.E.-Peter Lang, 2005).

[3]   V. Schmidt, 'Democracy and Legitimacy in the European Union Revisited: Input, Output and "throughput"' (2013) 61 *Political Studies* 2.

From a legal perspective, Member States have much autonomy to develop social policies according to their own needs. Soft coordination gives the EU a means to set common goals, yet also acknowledges that Member States have different ways to reach these goals. This soft coordination is still the basis of the Europe 2020 Strategy. The pre-crisis literature argues that a choice for soft coordination is not necessarily 'second-best' in absence of 'hard' competences. Benefits of soft coordination over top–down and uniform rules have been documented well. Leaving policy design and implementation to the national level makes it easier to take a complex set of factors and institutions into account when developing policies.[4] Soft coordination also offers higher degrees of flexibility, the participation of actors in various stages of policy or law formation, and moreover makes it possible to adapt targets to new challenges.[5] The OMC also initiates an iterative process of mutual learning, stimulating actors to meet and reflect on policies and its purposes.[6] Within the setting of the EU, this would imply that an exchange between the EU-level institutions and the Member States takes place. The European Semester increasingly offers such moments to exchange views. Its 2015 version includes for instance bilateral meetings between the EU and the Member States. During such meetings, the whole range of socioeconomic realities, targets and priorities might be discussed and weighed against each other. This could offer opportunities to argue for a social agenda. Such exchanges happen in the throughput stage of policy-making, and co-determine policy-making outcomes.[7] The throughput stage is however relatively unexplored, especially in the context of the European Semester. This chapter offers a first exploration by assessing the adaptability of the European Semester and the latitude of Member States to discard EU demands or to bring alternative ideas into the process. If the European Semester can adapt its goals, this might give space for social goals to anchor deeper into the process. Likewise, if Member States have leeway to develop alternative policies, then a stronger social dimension may be built into national socioeconomic policies.

---

[4] J. Lenoble, 'Open Method of Coordination and Theory of Reflexive Governance', in O. De Schutter and S. Deakin (eds), *Social Rights and Market Forces: Is the Open Coordination of Employment and Social Policies the Future of Social Europe?* (Bruylant, 2005); J. Scott and D.M. Trubek, 'Mind the Gap: Law and New Approaches to New Governance in the European Union' (2002) 8 *European Law Journal* 1.

[5] B. Eberlein and D. Kerwer, 'New Governance in the European Union: A Theoretical Perspective' (2004) 42 *Journal of Common Market Studies* 121; and J.S. Mosher and D.M. Trubek, 'Alternative Approaches to Governance in the EU: EU Social Policy and the European Employment Strategy' (2003) 41 *Journal of Common Market Studies* 63.

[6] Eberlein and Kerwer, n. 5 in this chapter.

[7] Schmidt, n. 3 in this chapter.

11.3 THE EUROPEAN SEMESTER AS A HYBRID GOVERNANCE STRUCTURE

The introduction of stricter economic governance to improve Member State compliance with EU fiscal targets suggests a limited space for Member States to develop socioeconomic policies. It is challenging to typify coordination within the European Semester, as it yokes together different instruments and coordination mechanisms within one time-frame, using structures that resemble intergovernmentalism as well as the Community Method.[8] Several characteristics would justify seeing the Semester as a hybrid governance process. Hybrid governance structures contain both hard and soft processes within the same domain and these affect the same actors.[9] A first indication of its hybrid character is the Semester's combination of the coercive SGP and MIP surveillance with the soft Europe 2020 Strategy coordination. A second indication is the hybrid character of two of the Semester's coordination mechanisms: the SGP and the MIP. They both have a rather soft, preventative arm and a hard, corrective arm. The Excessive Deficit Procedure (EDP) is the corrective arm of the SGP and the Excessive Imbalance Procedure (EIP) is the MIP's corrective arm.

In operation, the hybrid character of the Semester gains complexity. Firstly, only euro area countries that perpetually fail to meet fiscal rules (SGP), or keep having severe macroeconomic imbalances (MIP), may eventually get a sanction. It means that for some countries surveillance is much stricter than for others. Still, it is hard to determine when exactly a penalty is given. Practice shows that deadline postponements for meeting fiscal rules occur frequently. A recent Communication explains which flexibility the SGP rules have.[10] During the 2016 European Semester, speculations were made on stepping up the EDP for Spain and Portugal. The Commission argued, however, that it was economically and politically not the right moment to do so. It decided to give the two countries an additional year to bring deficits down, while demanding strong and rapid reform efforts.[11] Thus, being in the corrective stage of the SGP might not necessarily lead to punitive actions rapidly.

---

[8] K.A. Armstrong, 'The New Governance of EU Fiscal Discipline' (2013) 38 *European Law Review* 601; and M. Dawson, 'The Legal and Political Accountability Structure of "Post-Crisis" EU Economic Governance' (2015) 53 *Journal of Common Market Studies* 976.

[9] D.M. Trubek, P. Cottrell, and M. Nance '"Soft Law," "Hard Law," and European Integration: Towards a Theory of Hybridity' (2005) *University of Wisconsin Legal Studies Research Paper*, 1002.

[10] COM(2015)012 *Making the Best Use of the Flexibility within the Existing Rules of the Stability and Growth Pact* (Brussels, 14 January 2015).

[11] P. Moscovici, *Live Read-out of the College Meeting of 18/05/2016* (Ref: I-121291, 18 May 2016).

Actually, the toughest surveillance is placed upon Member States that fall outside the scope of the European Semester: the bailout or programme countries. These countries have received financial assistance packages on the condition of, among others, drastic cuts in social expenditure and major structural reforms. This has harmed the social state of these countries considerably, leaving them little room to invest in citizens and society.[12] In 2016, only Greece was in such a macroeconomic adjustment programme, while in 2015 both Greece and Cyprus were in an adjustment programme. The largest group of countries thus falls within the scope of ordinary surveillance via the European Semester. Secondly, in its everyday operation the three distinct coordination mechanisms of the European Semester influence each other.[13] Thus, in spite of the fact that the coordination mechanisms have their own legal basis, mutual influence occurs. It is caused by the separate coordination mechanisms evaluating the same policies.[14] For example, the pension system is interesting to evaluate from a social policy perspective, yet also co-determines the government's fiscal situation. It has therefore been an element in the SGP, the MIP as well as Europe 2020.[15] Especially the Country Specific Recommendations (CSRs) demonstrate the coordination mechanisms' interest in similar policies. CSRs are the outcome of the European Semester and advise each Member State which policies to implement. From 2011 onwards, the CSRs of the three coordination mechanisms have been placed together into one list of recommendations. Especially the MIP frequently assesses items that also belong to soft employment and social policy coordination domains, including topics such as unemployment, minimum wages, and the labour-market integration of vulnerable groups. This mutual influence could result in a stronger coordination of social policies.[16] Indeed, new EU economic coordination may inhibit quite fundamental choices for roads to political integration.[17] At the same time it has important limitations such as weak accountability for central prescription and control of economic and fiscal policies and a significant differentiation of

[12] Achtsioglou and Doherty, n. 1 in this chapter; F. Costamagna, 'Saving Europe "Under Strict Conditionality": A Threat for EU Social Dimension?' (2012) *LPF Working Paper*, 7; and C. Kilpatrick and B. De Witte, 'A Comparative Framing of Fundamental Rights Challenges to Social Crisis Measures in the Eurozone' (2014) 7 *SIEPS European Policy Analysis* 1.

[13] Armstrong, n. 8 in this chapter.

[14] S. Bekker, 'EU Coordination of Welfare States after the Crisis: Further Interconnecting Soft and Hard Law' (2014) 19 *International Review of Public Administration* 296.

[15] S. Bekker, 'European Socioeconomic Governance in Action: Coordinating Social Policies in the Third European Semester' (2015) *OSE Research Paper Series*, 19.

[16] Bekker, n. 14 in this chapter.

[17] A. Hinarejos, 'Fiscal Federalism in the European Union: Evolution and Future Choices for EMU' (2013) 50 *Common Market Law Review* 1621.

obligations between states.[18] These fundamental choices for roads to political integration, as well as the system's limitations, intensify if budgetary coordination starts dealing with social policies. At the same time, there is little insight into the causal mechanisms, linking the setup of the Semester to implications for national reforms. Moreover, the fact that the MIP and SGP address social policies does not reveal whether their recommendations support or harm the obtainment of social goals. Both the SGP and the MIP are capable of supporting social goals.[19]

11.3.1 *Analytical Framework*

One opportunity to strengthen the ESM emerges when the European Semester is able to adapt its goals to new social challenges. Another opportunity is national latitude to develop socioeconomic policies. This section proposes the following analytical framework to measure the degree of adaptability and leeway. Features of adaptability at the EU level include:

- general EU-level targets change from year to year;
- changes in the 'strictness' of coordination, exploring whether countries move from preventative to corrective stages, or from corrective to preventative stages;
- emergence or disappearance of new topics in CSRs.

The analysis combines these indicators with assessing whether the Semester gives tailor-made advice to countries, adjusted to national challenges. Another important indicator is whether or not the Commission's recommendations are precise or vague. Vagueness allows for further specification at national level, thus providing scope for giving reforms a national flavour. Getting imprecise CSRs is especially relevant once countries proceed into the corrective arm of surveillance, where pressure to comply is expected to be higher. The following indicators suggest latitude of Member States to hold conflicting opinions or to develop alternative policies:

- presenting alternative policies to meet the challenges addressed by a CSR, or to meet the EU's overall socioeconomic goals;
- implementing policies that go against a CSR;
- perpetual noncompliance with CSRs, thus discarding EU policy advice.

---

[18] Dawson, n. 8 in this chapter.
[19] Bekker, n. 15 in this chapter; J. Zeitlin and B. Vanhercke, *Socializing the European Semester? Economic Governance and Social Policy Coordination in Europe* 2020 (SIEPS, 2014).

- disagreeing with EU calculation methods to measure policy outcomes or the socioeconomic state of a country;
- presenting alternative ideas or philosophies about sound socioeconomic policies.

These indicators are quite relevant to assess the space for bottom-up initiatives and ideas to emerge into the coordination process.

The analysis takes a longitudinal approach, covering the years 2009 to 2015. It captures trends in the Semester's goals and priorities, as well as including the national reforms and subsequent EU-level reaction. The time period covers the last coordination cycle of the Lisbon Strategy and the five subsequent European Semester policy cycles. The analysis includes the EU on the one hand, and the reactions of France, Germany, Poland, and Spain on the other hand, and specifically looks at the topics of pensions, wages, and unemployment. The assumption is that the four countries experience different degrees of pressure to comply with EU target, while also experiencing different degrees of freedom to develop alternative policies. Germany and Poland are likely to feel the lowest pressure to comply. Germany has mostly been in preventative coordination stages, having left the EDP in 2012. Poland has been in the EDP until 2015, however, does not belong to the euro area and therefore cannot get fines. Still, as Poland has the ambition to join the Euro, it could feel the need to meet fiscal targets nevertheless. The assumption is also that Spain and France perceive the highest pressure to comply with EU demands. Both countries have been in EDP in all years scrutinised. Spain moreover signed for a loan to support its financial sector, likely resulting in additional pressure to comply.[20] Furthermore, as of 2012 Spain and France have been part of an In-Depth Review (IDR), the second stage of the MIP. Germany was subject to an IDR only as of 2014, while Poland has never been suspected of having macroeconomic imbalances. Data sources include all European Semester documents that are relevant for the four countries in the years scrutinised: National Reform Programmes (NRPs) and Stability or Convergence Programmes of national governments and the CSRs and Country Reports (formerly divided into separate staff working papers and IDRs) of the EU. In total over 43 national-level and more than 44 EU-level documents have been explored, using a qualitative content analysis technique.[21]

---

[20] Kilpatrick and De Witte, n. 12 in this chapter.
[21] A full overview of the findings, including an extensive reference list is available in S. Bekker, 'Is There Flexibility in the European Semester Process? Exploring Interactions between the EU and Member States within Post-crisis Socio-economic Governance' (2016) 1 *SIEPS report* 1.

11.4 THE EUROPEAN SEMESTER: ADAPTING ITS GOALS TO NEW PRIORITIES AND COUNTRY-SPECIFIC CHALLENGES

Before introducing stricter economic governance, the European Commission's initial crisis response was to stimulate the economy by asking Member States to increase public expenditure. This policy was codified in the European Economic Recovery Plan in 2009. Only after 2009, meeting debt and deficit rules were prioritised. Thus, the initial response of increasing public expenditure was changed into active policies to reduce public expenditure. However, as time progressed, the concern for social policies emerged, largely resulting from worries about (youth) unemployment rates, growing poverty, and rising inequality.[22] After 2012, such concerns became part of the Annual Growth Survey, which started addressing unemployment and the social consequences of the crisis, and later on also investments. The Commission moreover launched an Employment Package (2012), a Social Investment Package (2013) and a Youth Guarantee (2013). Furthermore, as of 2014 the Joint Employment Report has incorporated a scoreboard of key employment and social indicators. This demonstrates that the EU is able adapts its primary goals to new challenges. It has offered social goals a chance to integrate better within the overall set of EU socioeconomic goals. The CSRs show a likewise adaptability. They vary from year to year. This change does not necessarily relate to national compliance and policy implementation, as the following sections will demonstrate. One major change relates to the instalment of the Juncker Commission that wanted to focus the CSRs on priorities. It led to a large reduction in the number of CSRs in 2015, and moreover made CSRs less precise. Current CSRs include less often very specific policies that should be amended before a given deadline.[23] The European Semester also demonstrates adaptability in the changing strictness of coordination. Sometimes, countries have moved from corrective into preventative coordination stages. For instance, the French pension system has been explored often from the SGP, yet this ceased to be the case in 2015. Moreover, as was the case before the crisis, CSRs are still tailored to the challenges of a specific country. They thus do not necessarily have a uniform approach to all countries. Still, social policies are more frequently explored from economic coordination mechanisms. In particular the MIP evaluates an increasing amount of social policy areas. Both in 2013 and 2015 about half of the CSRs addressed at least one social policy item. However, whereas in 2013 about

---

[22] COM(2013)083 *towards Social Investment for Growth and Cohesion – Including Implementing the European Social Fund 2014–2020* (Brussels, 20 February 2013).

[23] See also Bekker, n. 14 in this chapter.

50 per cent of the social policy CSRs were attached to the MIP and/or SGP in 2015 this has risen to around 70 per cent.

Thus, while EU socioeconomic coordination might be judged as stricter governance, there are also signs of adaptability and quite loose enforcement, including frequent postponement of deadlines for meeting fiscal rules. Although the SGP and MIP evaluate social policies as well, it is too early to judge whether this means tighter coordination of social policies. Recent ideas presented by the Five Presidents' Report and the subsequent Communication on completing the Economic and Monetary Union,[24] do not give conclusive answers. On the one hand, the Commission wants to toughen surveillance further. For example, the national budgetary policies should be consistent with the SGP recommendations and, where appropriate, with the MIP recommendation. Also the European Social Funds (ESF) are tied to implementing the CSRs. National ESF-programmes should have objectives, financial allocations, and investment priorities that contribute to Europe 2020 goals, the challenges in the NRP, and the CSRs. Failure may result in fines and/or suspension of up to five European Funds. On the other hand, the Commission says to value the diversity among Member States and mentions that Member States should not necessarily follow the same policies. Only the outcome matters. The Commission also wants more focus on employment and social performance: a Social Triple A. These different thoughts on future governance do not articulate how distinct coordination mechanisms should relate to each other or how much room Member States should have to develop sound social policies. The next sections zoom in on the three selected policy areas and further explores the adaptability of the European Semester.

11.4.1 Unemployment

The topic 'unemployment' demonstrates the different focus per country and per year, as well as the Semester's ability to show a social face. In the Commission's evaluation of France, unemployment has not been a very pressing issue. In 2009, unemployment is only mentioned in a CSR addressing the support of labour-market entry and transitions, especially of young people. Two years later, the Council concluded that France's economic stabilisers, although being costly, had lowered the impact of the economic crisis considerably. In 2013, unemployment was still not seen as the most urgent matter for France, but related recommendations were expanded nevertheless. Such

---

[24] COM(2015)0600 *Steps Towards Completing Economic and Monetary Union* (Brussels, 21 November 2015).

expansion was in line with the growing precision of CSRs in those years. It moreover correlated with new regulations requiring the Commission to draft more specific recommendations if a country progresses into corrective surveillance. In 2013 and 2014, France's unemployment recommendations were tied to the IDR. In 2015, after refocusing all CSRs to priorities only, unemployment was no longer specifically addressed, in spite of remaining challenges. The Country report 2015 on France even saw an increase in unemployment, particularly among young people, older workers, and the low-qualified.

Also for Germany, unemployment has not been a key issue in EU socioeconomic coordination. Aspects of the quality of employment have been addressed frequently, however. It underlines the Semester's ability support social goals. The Commission pointed continuously at the low quality of German mini-jobs, including their low pension entitlements and low transition prospects into stable jobs.[25] The Commission's background documents perpetually addressed the inequality related to mini-jobs, but did not translate it into CSRs every year. For instance, despite remaining challenges, it was absent in the 2014 CSR. It reappeared in the 2015 CSRs calling Germany to revise the fiscal treatment of mini-jobs in order to facilitate the transition into other jobs. Similarly, for Poland unemployment was not really an issue, yet the quality of jobs was. After 2012 the high youth unemployment became a concern, including the effects of labour-market segmentation. The Commission analysed that temporary contracts insufficiently act as a stepping-stone into regular employment, include a large wage penalty, and have a negative impact on human capital and productivity in Poland. This issue was taken up more vigorously in 2012 and 2013; however, the Commission did not really observe progress in the subsequent years. It included the issue of the excessive use of temporary contracts again in the 2015 CSRs. In the analyses of the Spanish labour-market unemployment has been highly relevant. In 2011, the Commission worried because Spain was severely hit by the crisis, yet also expected unemployment to decrease after 2012. This expectation was not met and by 2013 the word 'critical' was used to describe the Spanish labour market. In 2014 youth unemployment remained high and long-term unemployment grew to almost 50 per cent. Accordingly, between 2009 and 2015 the CSRs addressed unemployment, including references to reducing labour-market segmentation, tackling youth unemployment, modernising public employment services, and improving training and job-matching. On the one hand such concerns easily match with social issues. On the other hand, the large labour-market reforms that Spain implemented in the past years have

[25] S. Bekker and S. Klosse, 'EU Governance of Economic and Social Policies: Chances and Challenges for Social Europe' (2013) 2 *European Journal of Social Law* 103.

been judged as undermining social fairness.[26] Reforms included sensitive dossiers such as employment protection legislation and the collective bargaining system. Overall, the Commission was positive about the Spanish reforms, even though it kept underlining that the magnitude of the necessary corrections require continuous and strong policy measures. In 2016 this was followed by the speculations mentioned in Section 11.3, about sanctions and increased pressure to continue reforming.

11.4.2 Wages

Also regarding wages, the European Semester shows adaptability as well as the tailored policy-advice to countries. For France wages were not addressed in 2009, yet, after 2011 it gradually turned into a main issue. The Commission related wages to the competitiveness of France and tied it to the IDR after 2012. The attention for wages culminated in long and rather precise CSRs in 2013 and 2014. Even the 2015 CSRs paid much attention to reducing labour costs, reforming the wage-setting process to align wages with productivity, and minimum wages. The Commission thus kept addressing a range of wage-related issues, especially from an economic perspective. The 2015 CSR remained quite precise, in spite of the Commission's aim to focus on priorities. The Commission observed noncompliance with CSRs on wages, and even a reform going against a CSR. In 2012, France increased the minimum wage slightly, regardless of requests to view the minimum wage in line with job creation and competitiveness. France thus saw space to develop alternative policies, even though the CSR on minimum wages was tied to the IDR of the MIP. In 2014, the Commission's evaluation was somewhat milder. This evaluation sustained in 2015, seeing significant progress in dossiers such as the tax credit for competitiveness and employment, which reduce labour costs. Conversely, the Commission judged that only limited progress was made in reducing the cost of labour at the lower end of the wage scale. Also in the surveillance of Germany, wages have been addressed frequently. As of 2011, the high tax wedges have been a relevant issue. In 2012 this was related to the unemployment of low-wage earners, and further defined into reducing high taxes and social security contributions for this group in 2013 and 2014. The purpose of the reform was giving low-wage earners better job prospects. From 2012 onwards the Commission started suggesting to increase wages by letting these grow in line with productivity and to support domestic demand.[27] All

---

[26] López and Canalda Criado, n. 1 in this chapter.
[27] See also Bekker and Klosse, n. 25 in this chapter.

these issues have been addressed via soft coordination. In 2014 a third topic was added, and this issue was attached to the IDR: the minimum wage. It resulted from Germany's announcement to introduce a national minimum wage. The CSR requested Germany to monitor the impact of the minimum wage on employment, so as to avoid job destruction. In the surveillance of Poland, wages have not been a great concern. CSRs at times referred to in-work-poverty, suggesting that wage levels are too low rather than too high. Thus, also poverty reduction may be part of European Semester coordination, thus supporting social goals. In 2012, in-work-poverty was linked to youth unemployment and the segmented labour market. It addressed the partial abuse of self-employment and civil law contracts that fall beyond the scope of Labour Law. For temporary workers in Poland, in-work poverty is twice as high as for workers on permanent contracts, also due to wage penalties related to flex work. Moreover, due to a low statutory minimum wage, low net transfers to low-income earners and stringent eligibility rules, people tend to be trapped in poorly paid jobs. In 2013, continuing worries on this issue were translated into a CSR again; however, the 2014 CSRs no longer addressed in-work-poverty. It kept being part of the concerns expressed in the Commission's Country reports. Only labour-market segmentation remained part of the CSRs in 2014 and 2015.

In the surveillance of Spain, wages have continuously been addressed in the background documents, yet did not always result in a CSR. In 2009, the Commission observed that Spanish wage developments should be aligned better with productivity developments, in order to improve competitiveness. No CSR was issued then. In 2011 this changed. The CSRs called to proceed with the implementation of a comprehensive reform of the collective bargaining process and the wage indexation system. Perhaps due to the reform efforts along the line of the CSRs, the 2012 and 2013 CSRs no longer mentioned wages. However, it became part of the 2014 CSRs again, albeit in a completely different manner. The suggestion was to lower employer's social security contributions, in particular for low-wage jobs, and to promote real wage developments that support job creation. The part on social security contribution was even attached to both the SGP and the IDR, whereas the issue of real wage development was tied to the IDR. In the 2015 CSRs, the wage issue changed again into addressing the alignment of wages and productivity. This Spanish monitoring cycle indicates that the Commission may stop giving CSRs on a certain topic if reforms have been implemented. This does not mean that topics disappear from the monitoring cycle completely, however. Issues may recur when new challenges arise. This demonstrates a certain degree of adaptability of the coordination process.

11.4.3 Pension System

Also regarding pensions, coordination adapted itself to the country and its challenges. France received a CSR on pensions in all years. Between 2011 and 2014 this was tied to the SGP and in addition linked to the IDR between 2013 and 2015. The pension CSRs to France also became much more detailed after 2013, including a very precise description of how to reform pensions. At first, the Council[28] seemed satisfied with the French pension reform of 2010, which increased the pension age to 67, set a higher minimum pension age (from 60 to 62) and phased out early retirement schemes. However, in the same year the Council predicted that more measures would be needed, especially due to high public debt. In 2012, a similar CSR was given, adding the need to review the adequacy of the pension system in addition to its sustainability. The language of the 2013 CSR was much firmer, stating that France should take new measures to bring the pension system into balance by 2020, and giving a precise list of examples of how France could do this. This firm language related to the partial rollback of the 2010 pension reforms, which explicitly went against the 2012 CSR. This rollback was installed by a newly elected French government. This again shows that France found opportunities to implement reforms that countered CSRs. In December 2013 France implemented another pension reform, and the Commission valued this reform to some extent. It was followed by a somewhat milder CSR which was no longer tied to the SGP in 2015. For Germany, the topic of pensions was only converted into a CSR in 2014. However, it was addressed in the Commission's background analyses for longer. Worries concerned the low employment rate of older workers and the low attainment of pension rights for people in a mini-job. It moreover saw lower pension contributions as a partial answer to decrease wage-related taxes. This minor interest in the German pension system changed in 2014, when the topic was suddenly explored from both the SGP and the IDR. This had to do with the German pension reform that aimed at improving early retirement conditions as well as increasing pension levels for certain groups, for instance for people who raised children born before 1992. The Council found that the reform was at odds with the cost-effectiveness of public spending and the development of disposable income, worrying also about the potentially negative effects on the take-up of the second and third pillar pensions. The 2015 CSRs no longer addressed pensions, signalling that it no longer belonged to

---

[28] Council Recommendation (2011/C 213/03) of 12 July 2011 on the National Reform Programme 2011 of France and delivering a Council opinion on the updated Stability Programme of France, 2011–14, [2011] OJ C 213/8.

the Commission's priorities. In the surveillance of Poland, the pension system was an item in all years, especially the KRUS pension provisions for farmers. The Commission observed only minor changes in the Polish system. In the assessments of Spain, pensions were hardly at the core of evaluations.

11.5 NATIONAL RESPONSES TO EU-LEVEL SOCIOECONOMIC TARGETS

The annual national reports give insight into the reasoning of Member States in coordination processes and the reform choices they make. In spite of the fact that all four countries underline their commitment to reaching the EU-level goals, the national documents reveal disagreement as well. There are conflicting views on what sound socioeconomic policy entail, different insights in calculation methods of deficits and reform effects, and some issues concerning legitimacy. Moreover, Member States find that they cannot influence all aspects of globalised economies. Indeed, their policy instruments are more limited than the European Semester's surveillance logic supposes. Whereas all of these arguments are to some extent interconnected, the following subsections present them separately.

11.5.1 *Ideas on the Nature of Sound Socioeconomic Policies*

The 2012 NRP reveals France's reform philosophy: to combine fiscal consolidation with high growth potential in order to revive economic growth and support the labour market. This also means limiting the negative social consequences of the crisis and promoting social cohesion. In support of its reform philosophy, it referred to the Commission's social goals, such as the Compact for Growth and Jobs (2013) and the European Youth Employment Initiative. Germany communicated a similar philosophy in many NRPs. It is a social market economy, giving equal importance to economy and competition as to equal opportunities and social inclusion. At times, such philosophies explain reform choices of the two countries. For example, whereas the 2014 CSRs worried about the German pension reforms from a budgetary viewpoint, Germany explained these reforms as a means to reach the EU target on social inclusion and poverty reduction. Germany wanted to prevent old-age poverty and therefore improved the pensions of people with a reduced earning capacity.

The consecutive Polish NRPs show increasing awareness of the effects of cuts in public expenditure as well as the difficulties to predict the effects of reforms for public budgets. Around 2009, the Polish government expressed readiness to reduce the fiscal imbalance, and even found that its imbalances were a result of past neglect to restructure. It prepared a reform package, whilst searching for some balance between investing in growth and consolidating public finances. The NRP 2009 further explained this as an aim to create a basis for long-lasting socioeconomic development which should also result in better living standards. Such aims remained an item in subsequent Polish national reports. In 2011, Poland defended some form of public expenditure by explaining that investments in social infrastructure (for example education, health care, culture) are a way to unleash regional potential and contribute to social inclusion. In 2013 and 2014 the country highlighted again the importance of a growth-friendly fiscal consolidation. It no longer saw further cuts in public expenditure as the sole remedy for economic misery. Poland clarified that bringing deficits below 3 per cent was difficult, despite restructuring efforts. Although the Commission gave a positive evaluation of Poland's reform plans, these efforts did not generate the expected budgetary goals. Even reform plans that were predicted to exceed the deficit reduction target, did not generate the expected results. In 2014 Poland explained this by pointing at the negative impact of fiscal consolidation on economic growth. It challenged the EU recommendations, arguing that a further reduction of the deficit would be strongly pro-cyclical and consequently affect economic growth prospects. This would reduce tax revenues, and subsequently increase the government deficit. Despite this plea for investing in growth, Poland presented further measures to limit deficit growth.

11.5.2 Conflicting Views on Calculation Methods and Reform Effects

The Polish example in Section 11.5.1 shows how different ideas on sound socioeconomic policies are tied to disputes on how to forecast future deficits. If cutting public expenditure does not have the desired effect, then investing in growth perhaps would. In their national reports all four Member States disagreed with the Commission's calculations from time to time. Whereas such disputes may address minor details, these details become quite important if resulting in negative evaluations.

Germany's account surplus was a topic of analysis. On the causes of this account surplus, Germany both agreed and disagreed with the Commission. It underlined the Commission's analysis that price competition plays a minor role in the expansion of the trade balance. The federal government also shared the view that the increase in consumer spending was below the Eurozone average, and that this partly resulted from the moderate wage development of the past 14 years. However, the country disputed that it should implement policies to increase wages. It referred to a study of the Commission which concluded that wage moderation only marginally affects account surpluses.

Moreover, Germany found past wage moderation necessary, in light of the high unemployment rates, the weak economy and the poor profitability conditions of businesses. Furthermore, Germany gave an alternative reason for the low consumer spending: the high savings related to the ageing society and the pension system. The country thus found that the Commission did not take all relevant elements into account when calculating and explaining the account surplus. Still it made further plans to stimulate internal growth. This included the introduction of a legal minimum wage and investments in childcare facilities which should support female labour-market integration. The Commission was not overly enthusiastic about this minimum wage and feared negative effects on employment, however. Germany believed that further government intervention was not necessary, as the good economy would automatically result in more jobs and higher wages. This would then raise household income and subsequently increase consumption.

Alternative explanations for growing public expenditure are visible in several national documents. Poland explained the high deficit in 2011 by its peak in public investment supporting growth, which was at that time in line with the 2009 European Economic Recovery Plan. Moreover, it pointed at expenses related to the absorption of EU funds, which are mostly cofinanced, and spending on infrastructure and the organisation of the 2012 European Football Championship. Complaints also related to the use of outdated information. For instance, Poland reacted to the Commission's forecast of an above-target deficit in 2015 by arguing that these projections did not take into account recently announced consolidation measures. In 2014 also France complained that the Commission's deficit predictions did not take into account its newly announced savings. In fact, 2015 forecasts were based on a no policy change assumption. It did not incorporate a new reduction of central government expenditure, the lowering of the national healthcare expenditure growth target, the delay in the increase of social benefits, and the impact of the Responsibility and Solidarity Pact. France concluded that differences in calculation methods could have great consequences for judgments about meeting EU targets. Moreover, France pointed out that the Commission's predictions sometimes change rather quickly, turning endorsed draft budgets into new worries about deficits. This is a similar issue raised by Poland in the Subsection 11.5.1. France recalled that the Commission endorsed a draft budget in November 2013, but, as soon as the winter 2014 forecast showed a deviation from the targets, the Commission changed their opinion and wanted France to take extra measures. Such deviations in forecasts and actual spending paces also have major consequences for the assessment of effective action in accordance with the Commission's methodology.

11.5.3 *Legitimacy and Democracy*

The disputes on what sound socioeconomic policies entail and how to measure and predict reform effects show that the effectiveness of prescribed reforms is challenged frequently. The word 'legitimacy' as such is not often mentioned, however. The four countries often write down that they agree with the EU-level aims and instruments. Only a few times legitimacy and democracy is raised. For example, in its stability programme 2014 France argued that the Commission's opinions following the budgetary surveillance of the Two-Pack of are not legally binding, even though France acknowledged that a failure to comply could lead to an acceleration of the EDP. In its 2014 NRP Germany called to improve democratic legitimacy by involving citizens and national parliaments into decision-making. A more pronounced viewpoint is included in the opinion of the French stakeholders, which was annexed to the 2015 NRP. It pleaded to give full meaning to the notion of solidarity so as to re-legitimise the European project in the eyes of citizens. The stakeholders noticed that citizens feel that their society changes and combines the market economy less and less with social protection. Therefore, the social dimension should become a guiding principle of all European policies. Correlations between aspects of democracy and alternative policy implementation may be viewed in Germany and France, however. For instance, the rollback of the French pension reforms coincided with the instalment of a newly elected government. Also the German pension reform, improving the pensions of people with a reduced earning capacity, was introduced by a newly installed government. Reforms going against a CSR or diverting from main EU-level goals, could thus stem from the demands of the electorate.

11.5.4 *National Governments Cannot Influence Everything*

All four countries partly explain their inability to reach fiscal goal via reforms, by referring to the overall EU economic slowdown. If all EU countries face economic difficulties, taking austerity measures only will not lead to economic growth. The four countries also argued that they cannot influence the economic state of other countries. In 2014 France, for instance, argued that its reform effects were limited due to the general economic slack in the EU. Spain argued that an important economic burden was the international financial crisis as well as the adjustment in its housing sector, the increasing unemployment rate and deteriorating public finances. Some of these dossiers fall outside government control. In addition, the increased interest rate was problematic, causing Spain to consolidate more speedily. Also Poland gave two pronounced reasons for its economic slowdown, some years after the start of the crisis: the economic downturn in Poland's main export markets and a rather restrictive macroeconomic policy resulting from EU recommendations. Germany even referred to the weather to explain the lower-than-expected growth in the winter of 2012/13.

Of the four countries in this study, Spain's views seem to conflict least with the Commission's analyses. It implemented major reforms which were largely along the lines of the Commission's proposals.[29] However, Spain's confidence to generate fast results decreased over time. The 2011 national reports were still fairly optimistic. Spain was committed to present a programme to exit from the crisis, including fiscal consolidation as well as structural reforms. The country called its fiscal efforts 'very ambitious', and the Commission agreed with this viewpoint. In 2011, Spain based fiscal consolidation measures mainly on nonfinancial expenditure adjustments, while prioritising sustainable growth as much as possible, improving the efficiency of expenditure and restructuring of the public sector. In spite of these efforts the imbalances remained significant. After 2011, the economic and financial situation worsened. A new strategy included a major transformation in 2012, encompassing among others labour-market reforms and reforms in collective bargaining.[30] Spain tried to build confidence based on past performance: its proven ability to overcome difficult situations by committing to economic stability and structural reforms. However, Spain was also aware that financial imbalances could not be corrected overnight. Instead, the adjustment pathway would be gradual and steady. Spain assured that it would strive for the largest adjustment of budgetary imbalance in the shortest period of time, but also asked for time and trust.

11.6 CONCLUSION

The analysis supports that the European Semester is not a static but an evolving governance system. It adapts its goals to new challenges. The evolving nature of the Semester is relevant to support the ESM. It allows new goals to be included, for instance responding to youth unemployment challenges. Moreover, as was the case in pre-crisis EU social governance, the Semester gives tailor-made

---

[29] M.L. Rodriguez, 'Labour Rights in Crisis in the Eurozone: the Spanish Case' (2014) 1 *European Journal of Social Law* 128.

[30] A range of scholars agrees with this classification of reforms being radical, C. Barnard, 'EU Employment Law and the European Social Model: The Past, the Present and the Future' (2014) 67 *Current Legal Problems* 1; López and Canalda Criado, n. 1 in this chapter; Rodriguez, n. 29 in this chapter; and B. Suarez Corujo, 'Crisis and Labour Market in Spain' (2014) 5 *European Labour Law Journal* 43.

policy advices to countries. It means that the Semester does not have a uniform effect on all Member States, also not in social policy domains. The recommendations are contextualised to a large degree and at times give support
for prioritising social goals. The analysis also shows that Member States have
room to develop alternative socioeconomic policies, even if these go against
the EU's recommendations. This is especially the case for countries that are
in preventative stages of coordination. However, examples demonstrate that
even in corrective arms of coordination, countries may discard EU-level policy
advices. Also EU recommendations that support social goals have not always
been implemented. It is also important that, within the European Semester,
countries bring alternative views into the debate, communicating reform philosophies or questioning the Commission's calculation methods and forecasts.
Such arguments can be highly supportive of a social agenda. Member States
for instance call to combine consolidation with investment, to spend money
on poverty reduction, or to take long-term goals into account. Member States
can base these arguments on 'evidence': their experiences with reform effects
or their citizens' preferences.

The chapter thus indicates that the throughput stage of the European
Semester is relevant in order to understand how new EU socioeconomic
coordination offers support to social goals. At least some of the characteristics
of the Open Method of Coordination still apply to the European Semester.
There is discussion and debate, meaning also that the basic ingredients for
mutual learning are still present. However, these characteristics are neither
really explicated, nor openly valued for their contribution to effective policy-
making. Recent EU policy documents continue to be rather vague on these
aspects. They seem to attempt to unite better compliance with valuing diversity among Member States. This means that the Semester remains quite
complex, making verdicts about Member States that seem rather surprising
given the rules and regulations. It continues to give the throughput phase an
important role in determining the outcome the decision-making process, yet
does nothing to make this throughput stage more transparent. More insight
is needed in how the different economic and social coordination mechanisms relate to each other and how the value of social and economic goals are
weighed against each other. Also, more insight is needed in which stakeholders make decisions at what moments in time. Such insights would give other
relevant stakeholders, such as the social partners or national parliaments, a
better view on when to move into the debate to support social goals.[31] Also,

---

[31] M. Ferrera, 'Social Europe and its Components in the Midst of the Crisis: A Conclusion'
(2014) 37 *West European Politics* 825.

better information about how social and economic goals are prioritised might give national-level actors more arguments to defend national choices that support social goals.

The replies of Member States in their national reports show that they already give some reasons for a stronger social perspective. At times they use the Commission's own social goals to support national choices. Such active communication from the national to the EU level may prove to be a valuable input to advance the entire socioeconomic coordination process. In other words, national arguments might trigger learning effects within EU institutions as well. The Commission is already aware of the complex reality of socioeconomic policies and demonstrates this in its Country reports. These explore social and economic policies in a broad and integrated manner. Such rich evaluations could serve as a more justified basis to make a final verdict about a country. The latitude of Member States, bringing in new arguments, but also prioritising alternative policies, can likewise be viewed as a strength of the European Semester. It not only gives Member States space to follow their own reform logic, but also to search for better solutions based on social, economic, and political considerations. If exchanges between the EU and the Member States prove to become positive learning moments for all, then the openness and adaptability of the European Semester becomes an asset.

12

Balancing Economic Objectives and Social Considerations in the new EU Investment Agreements: Commitments versus Realities

Rumiana Yotova

12.1 INTRODUCTION

This chapter assesses whether and in what ways the new EU Investment Agreements (IAs) balance economic objectives with social considerations. The European Union acquired exclusive competence in the area of foreign direct investment (FDI) following the entry into force of the Lisbon Treaty,[1] which entails at least two important consequences for the new EU IAs. First, the EU, in particular the Commission, lead the negotiation with third states.[2] This limits the ability of Member States to introduce tailored provisions, particularly in the areas of shared competences such as social policy. The Council of the EU has a role limited to the very beginning and end of the process – it authorises the opening of the negotiations, the negotiation directives and the signing of the IAs.[3] Second, these agreements have to comply with the EU's own Founding Treaties, including the obligation to act in accordance with the principles and objectives of the Union's external action.[4] These principles include the respect for human rights and human dignity, as well as the principles of equality and solidarity.[5] Notably, through its external action, the EU undertakes to '*foster the sustainable economic, social and environmental development of developing countries*',[6] as well as to promote solidarity in its relations with the wider

---

The author wishes to express special thanks to the organisers of the European Social Union Conference, Prof. Catherine Barnard, Prof. Geert De Baere, and Prof. Frank Vandenbroucke, as well as to all of the participants in the conference for the stimulating discussion.

[1] Article 207 TFEU.
[2] Article 207(3) and (4) TFEU.
[3] Article 218 (2), (5), and (6) TFEU.
[4] Article 207(1) TFEU.
[5] Article 21(1) TEU.
[6] Article 21(2)(d) TEU.

world.[7] Accordingly, it is important to assess the extent to which social considerations match these high aspirations by being reflected in the new EU investment policy and in the actual IAs negotiated with third states. The assessment will be done by reference to the EU's own Founding Treaties and the internal acts of its institutions setting out the new European International Investment Policy, as well as to the existing international framework of IAs.

At present, investment law is set out in over 3,300 IAs, 90 per cent of which are bilateral investment treaties (BITs), while the rest are treaties containing investment chapters, most commonly free trade agreements (FTAs).[8] While the older generations of IAs were exclusively focused on the economic objectives of promoting and protecting FDI, a new, reformed generation of IAs is emerging,[9] characterised by the integration of non-economic public interest considerations (including social policy).[10] The question of 'balancing' economic and social considerations in the new EU IAs is part of the broader debate about this new generation of Ias,[11] which started in North America with the 2004 US Model BIT. The shift is commonly associated with the US experience of having its public interest regulatory measures challenged in investment arbitrations instituted under the North American Free Trade Agreement (NAFTA).[12] The US experience is not isolated, as the approaches of investment tribunals towards balancing public interest considerations with economic protection are inconsistent, with some taking the view that the public interest can serve as a complete justification for good-faith non-discriminatory regulation, even where it affects the investment negatively.[13] Other tribunals, however, have held that the public interest motivation of the regulation is irrelevant, and that only the economic effect of the measure determines

---

[7] Article 3(5) TEU.

[8] UNCTAD, *World Investment Report* (United Nations, 2016), p. 101.

[9] Ibid.

[10] K. Gordon, J. Pohl, and M. Bouchard, 'Investment Treaty Law, Sustainable Development and Responsible Business Conduct: A Fact Finding Survey' (2014) *OECD Working Papers on International Investment*, 2014/01.

[11] S. Spears, 'The Quest for Policy Space in a New Generation of International Investment Agreements' (2010) 13 *Journal of International Economic Law* 1037; J. Alvarez and K. Sauvant, *The Evolving International Investment Regime: Expectations, Realities, Options* (Oxford University Press, 2011); and C. Henckels, 'Protecting Regulatory Autonomy through Greater Precision in Investment Treaties: The TPP, CETA and TTIP' (2016) 19 *Journal of International Economic Law* 27.

[12] J. Alvarez, 'The Return of the State' (2011) 20 *Minnesota Journal of International Law* 223, pp. 234 et seq.

[13] See for example, *Methanex Corp.* v *USA*, Final Award, 3 August 2005, paragraph 410; *S.D. Myers Inc.* v *Canada*, Partial Award, 13 November 2000, paragraph 281; *Tecmed SA* v *United Mexican States*, Award, 29 May 2003, ICSID Case No. ARB (AF)/00/2, paragraph 119.

whether compensation has to be paid.[14] States are responding to this regulatory challenge by modifying their IAs to strike a better balance between their economic and non-economic public interests.

Given that investment treaties are a function of the global economic process,[15] other factors catalysing change include the increasing reciprocity of FDI flows between developing and developed states,[16] as well as the global economic and financial crisis, specifically the responses of developed states and the correlated need of increasing their regulatory space to protect their public interest.[17]

International law and the UN with its specialised agencies too provide an impetus for reform. For example, according to the UN Addis Ababa Action Agenda, IAs should be crafted 'with appropriate safeguards so as not to constrain domestic policies and regulation in the public interest'.[18] The United Nations Conference on Trade and Development (UNCTAD) warns that the standards of protection in IAs can have a stabilising effect on regulatory freedom to protect the public interest, stressing 'the need to strengthen the development dimension of IIAs [International Investment Agreements] … preserving the right to regulate for sustainable development policies'.[19] In a similar vein, the International Labour Organisation (ILO) cautioned that while FDI can make an important contribution to the promotion of social welfare, it may also lead 'to conflicts with national policy objectives and with the interest of workers'.[20] According to the ILO, the way to balance economic objectives with the social considerations in an investment context is by respecting the sovereign rights of states to regulate in the public interest with due consideration to international

---

[14] See for example, *Southern Pacific Properties Limited* v *Arab Republic of Egypt*, Award on the Merits, 20 May 1992, ICSID Case No. ARB/84/3, paragraphs 158–9; *Metalclad Corp* v *Mexico*, Award, 30 August 2000, ICSID Case No. ARB(AF) 97/1, paragraphs 103, 111; and *Compañía del Dessarrolo de Santa Elena SA* v *Costa Rica*, Final Award, 17 February 2000, ICSID Case No. ARB/96/1, paragraphs 71–2.

[15] M. Reisman, 'Negotiating Investment Treaties: Mechanisms for Anticipating and Controlling Textual Drift' (2016) *Yale Law and Economics Paper*, 546, p. 19.

[16] B. Boie, 'Labour Related Provisions in International Investment Agreements' (2012) *ILO Employment Working Paper*, 126, p. 8.

[17] S. Franck, 'Considering Recalibration of International Investment Agreements: Empirical Insights', in J. Alvarez and K. Sauvant (eds), *The Evolving International Investment Regime* (Oxford University Press, 2011), pp. 73–5.

[18] United Nations, 'Addis Ababa Action Agenda of the Third International Conference on Financing for Development' (2015) GA Res 69/313, paragraph 91.

[19] UNCTAD, *Investment Policy Framework for Sustainable Development* (United Nations, 2015), p. 69.

[20] International Labour Organization, *Tripartite Declaration of Principles Concerning Multinational Enterprises and Social Policy* (International Labour Office, 4th edn, 2006), paragraph 1.

standards.[21] The express incorporation of the right to regulate in EU IAs is probably their most important innovation and mechanism for balancing economic objectives with non-economic public interest considerations.

According to quantitative studies, the developed capital-exporting states are the primary drivers of change in the investment regime, often motivated by the experience of other states in the growing number of arbitration proceedings (around 40 per cent of the totality of 444 known investment cases have been brought against developed states)[22] and by their own experience as respondents in investment cases.[23] The position of developed states as the main drivers of change in investment law is also linked to their administrative and legal capacity to draft international treaties, as well as by the relative strength and diplomatic power of their bargaining position.[24] Accordingly, given its membership and leading economic role, the EU is in a very strong position to influence, if not lead, the ongoing reform of the investment treaty regime.

Given these legal developments, the integration of the public interest in investment law and arbitration is attracting considerable scholarly attention,[25] mostly focusing on the environmental[26] and human rights aspects.[27] Social considerations, in contrast, have so far attracted very little attention and when they have, the emphasis has been on labour rights.[28] This is perhaps because

[21] Ibid., paragraph 8.
[22] UNCTAD, n. 8 in this chapter, at pp. 105–7.
[23] M. Manger and C. Peinhardt, 'Learning and Diffusion in International Investment Agreements' (2014) available at: www.uni-heidelberg.de/md/awi/peio/manger__peinhardt_26.08.2013.pdf (accessed 11 August 2016); see also K. Gordon and J. Pohl, 'Investment Treaties Over Time – Treaty Practice and Interpretation in a Changing World' (2015) OECD *Working Papers on International Investment*, 02.
[24] Manger and Peinhardt, n. 23 in this chapter, at pp. 9–10.
[25] T. Treves, F. Seatzu, and S. Trevisanut (eds), *Foreign Investment, International Law and Common Concerns* (Routledge, 2014); and L. Mouyal, *International Investment Law and the Right to Regulate: A Human Rights Perspective* (Routledge, 2016).
[26] Gordon and Pohl, n. 23 in this chapter; S.W. Schill, C. Tams, and R. Hofmann (eds), *International Investment Law and Development: Bridging the Gap* (Edward Elgar Publishing, 2015).
[27] B. Simma, 'Foreign Investment Arbitration: A Place for Human Rights?' (2011) 60 *International and Comparative Law Quarterly* 573; and C. Reiner and C. Schreuer, 'Human Rights and International Investment Arbitration', in P.M. Dupuy, F. Francioni, and E.U. Petersmann (eds), *Human Rights in International Investment Law and Arbitration* (Oxford University Press, 2009).
[28] Boie, n. 16 in this chapter; S. Brungatelli, 'International Investment Law and International Protection of Workers' Rights', in T. Treves, F. Seatzu, and S. Trevisanut (eds), *Foreign Investment, International Law and Common Concerns* (Routledge, 2014); and V. Prislan and R. Zandvliet, 'Mainstreaming Sustainable Development into International Investment Agreements: What Role for Labor Provisions?', in S.W. Schill, C. Tams and R. Hofmann (eds), *International Investment Law and Development: Bridging the Gap* (Edward Elgar Publishing, 2015).

social policy has not yet been directly challenged in investment arbitration, even though aspects of the labour regulations of host states have been brought before arbitral tribunals.[29] Furthermore, according to empirical studies, labour standards are the least frequently referred to non-economic public interest considerations in investment arbitration, compared to environmental standards and human rights.[30] Finally, while there are studies on how the EU uses its trade policy to promote human rights[31] and social issues,[32] the effect of the European social model on the new EU IAs remains unstudied. As does the potential of using EU IAs to promote social considerations, given the leading role of the EU as both an exporter and a destination of FDI. The EU is in a very strong position both to draft and negotiate new generation IAs accommodating, if not promoting, its social model. This chapter will assess whether the EU IAs concluded so far have managed to strike a good balance between economic objectives and social considerations not only from the perspective of the constitutional law of the EU with its social values, but also in the context of the global trends in investment law.

12.2 BALANCING FDI AND SOCIAL CONSIDERATIONS UNDER THE FOUNDING TREATIES OF THE EU

The EU is a sui generis international organisation under international law whose Member States have 'limited their sovereign rights' and transferred their sovereign powers to the organisation in certain fields.[33] Accordingly, the EU has a high degree of integration with strong if not primary economic focus.[34] And indeed, the new EU competence in FDI is part of the Common Commercial Policy (CCP) which represents the economic dimension of the Union's External Action,[35] having as main objective the progressive abolition

---

[29] See for example, *Centerra Gold Inc and Kumtor Gold Company* v *Kyrgyz Republic*, Termination Order, 29 June 2009, PCA Case No. AA278; and *Sergei Paushok, CJSC Golden East Company and CJSC Vostokneftegaz Company* v *Mongolia*, Award on Jurisdiction and Liability, 18 April 2011.

[30] Gordon, Pohl and Bouchard, n. 10 in this chapter, at p. 23.

[31] M. Hirsch, 'Identity Matters: The Enforcement of Global Human Rights Treaties by European Union's Trade Instruments' (2016) *Hebrew University of Jerusalem International Law Forum Working Series*, 04–16.

[32] L. Bartels, 'Social Issues: Labour, Environment and Human Rights', in S. Lester and B. Mercurio (eds), *Bilateral and Regional Trade Agreements: Commentary, Analysis and Case Studies* (Cambridge University Press, 2nd edn, 2015).

[33] ECJ, judgment of 15 July 1964 in *Flaminio Costa* v *E.N.E.L*, C-6/64, EU:C:1964:66, pp. 1158–9.

[34] See in general R. Baldwin and C. Wyplosz, *The Economics of European Integration* (McGraw-Hill, 3rd edn, 2009).

[35] Part V, Title II, TFEU.

of restrictions to international trade and investment.[36] Given the historic
development of the EU and its economic objectives, it is no surprise that the
EU has the exclusive competence to act with respect to the CCP.[37] The economic focus of the Founding Treaties in general and the EU CCP policy in
particular plays an important role in the definition and in the interpretation
of how economic objectives are to be weighed and balanced with other considerations in the new EU IAs.

The regulation of EU Social Policy is more nuanced. While certain aspects
of it form part of the objectives of the EU and the principles governing its external action,[38] including the CCP and FDI, it is an area of shared competence
between the EU and its Member States.[39] Thus, the EU primarily supports
and complements the social policies of the Member States[40] and they can
adopt more stringent social policy measures than those harmonised at the EU
level.[41] However, the EU may still legislate and adopt binding acts in the area
of social policy[42] and take initiatives to ensure coordination of the Member
States' employment and social policies.[43] According to the Declaration on
European Identity, social justice 'is the ultimate goal of economic progress'
and a 'fundamental element of the European identity'.[44] The TFEU formulates social protection as an overarching objective that ought to be taken into
account and integrated in all EU actions, setting out that: 'In defining and
implementing its policies and activities, the Union shall take into account
requirements linked to the promotion of a high level of employment, the
guarantee of adequate social protection, the fight against social exclusion, and
a high level of education, training and protection of human health.'[45]

The TFEU defines the EU social policy broadly, including the protection
of the fundamental social rights, the promotion of employment, improved
living and working conditions, proper social protection, dialogue between
management and labour, the development of human resources with a view
to lasting high employment and the combating of exclusion.[46] Furthermore,

[36] Paragraph 6, Preamble, TFEU.
[37] Article 3(1)(e) TFEU.
[38] See n. 3 in this chapter.
[39] Article 4(2)(b) TFEU.
[40] Article 153(1) TFEU.
[41] See Article 153(4) TFEU.
[42] Articles 2(2) and 4(2)(b) TFEU.
[43] Articles 2(3) and 5(2)–(3) TFEU.
[44] Heads of State or Government of the nine Member States of the enlarged European
   Community, 'Declaration on European Identity, Copenhagen, 14 December 1973' (1973) 12
   Bulletin of the European Communities 118.
[45] Article 9 TFEU.
[46] Article 151 TFEU.

Member States are obliged to conduct and coordinate their economic policies in such a way as to strengthen economic and social cohesion.[47] Notably, the attainment of high standards of social protection is also included in the EU Charter of Fundamental Rights, which in its chapter IV on Solidarity sets out a number of social rights, such as the right to fair and just working conditions,[48] the prohibition of child labour and the protection of young people at work,[49] the right of protection in the event of unjustified dismissal,[50] as well as the right to social security and health care.[51]

Based on the regulation of Social Policy in the Founding Treaties, it can be concluded that the broad EU social objectives are to be upheld and integrated, if not actively promoted, in the exercise of the new competence in FDI and in the conclusion of the new IAs with third states. This conclusion, while straightforward in theory, is delicate to achieve in practice, raising the question of how to balance the primary economic objectives of the EU and its IAs with the social considerations at hand. It is useful to try tentatively to define the meaning of 'balancing', as the term evokes a connotation of conflict and asymmetric weight. The ordinary meaning of 'balance' according to the Oxford English Dictionary is somewhat ambivalent, being 'a situation in which different elements are equal or in the correct proportions'.[52] This ambivalence is relevant to the considerations at hand, being often overlooked due to the common assumption that balance necessarily implies symmetry or equal weight. However, given the constitutional characteristics of the economic and social objectives of the EU as defined in the Founding Treaties, it is more likely that the balancing between the two, including in the conclusion of IAs, is a question of identifying the appropriate proportions rather than of striving for a perfect equilibrium. The question of this balancing act is pertinent and unsettled in investment law too, as will be discussed later (Section 3).

It should be noted that the Founding Treaties of the EU themselves purport to strike a certain balance between the economic and the social objectives of the organisation. On the one side, the TEU refers to 'upholding and promoting' the EU's values in the relations with the wider world, including solidarity and the eradication of poverty,[53] as well as to 'fostering' sustainable economic

---

[47] Article 174 and 175 TFEU.
[48] Article 31 Charter of Fundamental Rights of the European Union (EU Charter).
[49] Article 32 EU Charter.
[50] Article 30 EU Charter.
[51] Article 34 and 35 EU Charter.
[52] Oxford English Dictionary, online edition, available at: www.oxforddictionaries.com/ (accessed 19 January 2016).
[53] Article 3(5) TEU.

and social development in the context of EU external action.[54] The use of these terms seems to indicate a requirement for pro-activeness from the EU. With respect to weighing between the economic and the social, however, the TFEU takes a much more conservative approach requiring that the EU 'takes into account' social considerations in defining and implementing its economic policies,[55] and the TEU in similar vein refers to promoting economic progress while '*taking into account* the principle of sustainable development', which carries a more passive connotation of not jeopardising social considerations while striving to achieve economic objectives.[56] Notably, the Lisbon European Council in 2000 stressed the importance of ensuring a mutually reinforcing interaction between the EU's economic, social, and employment policies as part of the Lisbon Strategy.[57] These formulae suggest a dual requirement of not jeopardising social objectives and actively working to attain them. The question is whether and how this is reflected in current EU IA practice.

12.3 SOCIAL CONSIDERATIONS AND THE NEW EUROPEAN INTERNATIONAL INVESTMENT POLICY

In addition to the Founding Treaties, the acts of the Commission, the European Parliament, and the Council are also relevant in shaping the new EU International Investment Policy. Notably, the three EU institutions had very different visions about the appropriate balance to be struck between social considerations and the underlying economic objectives in the area of FDI. These visions of the Commission, the European Parliament, and the Council will be used as one of the reference points in assessing the IAs concluded so far.

While acknowledging the complexity of the relationship between FDI, economic growth and welfare, the Commission's Communication on a comprehensive European International Investment Policy underlined that FDI has a positive impact on growth and employment.[58] The Communication focused on the economic objectives of FDI but also noted the need of balancing them

[54] Article 21(2)(d) TEU.
[55] Article 9 TFEU.
[56] Paragraph 9, Preamble, TEU (emphasis added).
[57] The European Council, 'Part I Employment, Economic Reform and Social Cohesion', in 'Lisbon European Council Presidency Conclusions', Lisbon European Council meeting of 23–24 March 2000, available at: www.europarl.europa.eu/summits/lis1_en.htm (accessed 13 October 2016); see also COM(2001)0313 *Council Conclusions on Employment and Social Policies: A Framework for investing in Quality* (Brussels, 20 June 2001).
[58] COM(2010)343 *Communication from the Commission towards a Comprehensive European International Investment Policy* (Brussels, 7 July 2010), p. 3.

with social considerations. This balance had some passive aspects focused on maintaining the status quo, including the view that the economic objectives *'should be consistent with* the other policies of the Union and its Member States, including policies on … decent work, health and safety at work, consumer protection'[59] and is *'to be guided by* the principles and objectives of the Union's external action, including human rights and sustainable development'.[60] Notably, the Commission identified and highlighted some positive aspects too, including the need of 'a clear formulation of the balance between the different interests at stake', in particular the protection against unlawful expropriation on the one side and the need to ensure 'the right of each Party to regulate in the public interest', including for social protection, on the other.[61] Another proactive aspect in the Communication is that EU IAs ought to *'promote'* sustainable development, recalling the OECD Guidelines for Multinational Enterprises as an instrument 'to help balance the rights and responsibilities of investors' in this respect.[62]

Overall, the Commission Communication seems to adopt the middle ground approach on how to integrate social and other non-economic considerations in the new EU investment policy, focusing mainly on maintaining the status quo by not jeopardising social policy by concluding IAs. However, it identifies the need of balancing the interests at stake in treaty-making and formulates a two-fold understanding of the needed balance. On the one side, there is a balance to be struck between protecting economic rights and ensuring the rights of the Parties to regulate in the public (including the social) interest. On the other, there is the need to balance between the rights and duties of investors. Notably, according to the Commission this is to be done not by the EU IAs themselves, but rather by reference to the extraneous and voluntary OECD Guidelines.

The European Parliament adopts the most ambitious and progressive position in its balancing views, requiring a proactive approach in the drafting of EU IAs. The Parliament notes that the 'EU investment policy … necessitates striking a *delicate balance* between protecting investor's rights and the right of public authorities to regulate'.[63] Accordingly, it calls on the Commission 'to include in all future agreements specific clauses laying down

[59] Ibid., p. 9 (emphasis added).
[60] Ibid., p. 2 (emphasis added).
[61] Ibid., p. 9.
[62] Ibid., p. 2 (emphasis added).
[63] European Parliament, 'International Trade Committee report of 17 March 2011' (2011) (emphasis added), available at: www.europarl.europa.eu/pdfs/news/expert/infopress/20110314IPR15476/20110314IPR15476_en.pdf (accessed 21 October 2016).

the right of parties to the agreement to regulate, inter alia, in the areas of protection of … workers' and consumers' rights'.[64] The Parliament stresses that the new European International Investment Policy and related agreements must include corporate social responsibility clauses, as well as 'effective social clauses'[65] and clauses preventing the watering-down of social legislation in order to attract investment.[66]

The European Parliament calls for concrete balancing steps to be taken in the drafting and negotiation of EU IAs to uphold, but also to actively promote social protection. It formulates the necessary balance as one between the protection of the economic rights of the investor on the one side, with the right of the public authorities to regulate, inter alia, to protect social standards, on the other.

Not surprisingly, the Council of the EU adopted the most conservative approach with respect to the need of balancing, emphasising the economic and social benefits of FDI for fostering growth, job creation, consumer benefits, competitiveness, and productivity[67] and highlighting as the main objective of the new investment policy 'the objective of the Union remaining the world's leading destination and source of investment'.[68] While recognising 'the importance of the social and environmental dimension of foreign direct investment, as well as the rights and the obligations of investors', the Council made no commitments in this respect, drawing attention instead to the valuable contribution of organisations like the OECD, UNCTAD, and the ILO, as well as to corporate social responsibility,[69] falling short of acknowledging the role of the EU and its IAs. The only commitment that the Council made was that the 'new European International Investment Policy should be *guided* by the principles and objectives of the Union's external action', including sustainable development,[70] and that it should *take into account* 'the other policies of the Union and its Member States'.[71]

Accordingly, it is fair to observe that the Council was primarily concerned with the economic objectives of the new IAs and much less so with balancing

---

[64] European Parliament Resolution 2010/2203(INI) of 6 April 2011 on the future European International Investment Policy, [2012] OJ L 296/34.
[65] Ibid., paragraph 28.
[66] Ibid., paragraph 28.
[67] European Council, 'Conclusions on a comprehensive European international investment policy', 3041st Foreign Affairs Council Meeting of 25 October 2010, paragraph 1, available at: www.consilium.europa.eu/uedocs/cms_data/docs/pressdata/EN/foraff/117328.pdf (accessed 14 October 2016).
[68] Ibid., paragraph 6.
[69] Ibid., paragraph 16.
[70] Ibid., paragraph 17.
[71] Ibid.

them with other considerations, which it saw as fitting better in the remit of other international organisations. The Council's vision of the new EU International Investment Policy was to act in accordance with the Founding Treaties and not to compromise social objectives – maintaining the status quo. The Council conclusions seem to take for granted the fact that an increase in FDI will automatically lead to social benefits, without necessitating much further EU action. This assumption fits in the somewhat dated 'neoliberal' economic theory minimising the role of the regulator as one of protecting property rights and leaving the market to self-regulate.[72] This approach can be traced in the history of the EU regulation of human rights. These were not originally included in the Founding Treaties of the European Economic Community (EEC), which had an economic focus and were left to be protected by the Member States.[73] Similarly, Article 117 of the EEC Treaty on social policy whereby the Member States confirmed the need to promote the improvement of labour conditions assumed that 'such a development will result ... from the functioning of the Common Market which will favour the harmonisation of social systems'.[74]

Notably, the Commission revised and strengthened its commitments on the balancing between the economic and the social considerations in FDI in its new Trade and Investment Strategy of 2015. This shift is particularly important, because the Commission leads the negotiations of IAs on behalf of the EU. The Commission stated that it 'must pursue a policy that benefits society as a whole and promotes ... values alongside core economic interests' and that it ought to safeguard the European social model, benefiting companies, consumers and workers alike.[75] In order to achieve the proposed balance, the Commission undertakes to carry out sustainability impact assessments including in-depth analysis of the potential social and other impacts of IAs and free trade agreements (FTAs).[76] Furthermore, the Commission adopted a much more proactive approach, emphasising that 'the EU is best placed and has a special responsibility to lead the reform of the global investment regime',[77] including by putting stronger emphasis on the right to regulate,[78]

---

[72] Spears, n. 11 in this chapter, at pp. 1041–2.
[73] G. De Burca, 'The Evolution of EU Human Rights Law', in P. Craig and G. De Burca (eds), *The Evolution of EU Law* (Oxford University Press, 2nd edn, 2011), p. 475; and Hirsch, n. 31 in this chapter, at pp. 14–15.
[74] For further discussion, see G. De Baere and K. Gutman, 'The basis in EU constitutional law for further social integration', Chapter 14 in this volume.
[75] European Commission, *Trade for All: Towards a More Responsible Trade and Investment Policy* (Publications Office of the European Union, 2015), pp. 1, 7 and 18.
[76] Ibid.
[77] Ibid., p. 21.
[78] Ibid.

ensuring that economic growth goes hand in hand with high social justice and high labour standards[79] and using the CCP to promote the social pillar of sustainable development.[80] The Commission formulated these commitments more concretely with respect to treaty making, by undertaking to 'promote an ambitious and innovative sustainable development chapter in all trade and Investment Agreements'[81] to include 'far-reaching commitments on all core labour rights in line with the fundamental conventions of the ILO, as well as on ensuring high levels of occupational health and safety and decent working conditions in accordance with the ILO Decent Work Agenda'[82] and to 'prioritise work to implement effectively the core labour standards, as well as health and safety at work'.[83]

Despite the differences in the visions of the EU institutions, there are two key identifiable similarities too. First, all three institutions agreed that the new EU IAs should preserve the ability of the parties to regulate in the public interest, including for social protection.[84] Despite this general agreement, however, the institutions fell short of indicating where this balance should lie more precisely, leaving room for negotiation and concrete formulation in the EU IAs. Second, the institutions agreed that the new IAs should draw on 'the best practices of the Member States BITs'.[85] This is curious, given the prevailing economic focus of the EU Member States' BIT's and the fact that they belong to the older generations of BITs characterised by a distinct lack of reference to, let alone balance with, non-economic considerations, including social standards. Notably, at the time when the European International Investment Policy was developed in 2010, the overwhelming majority of Model BITs of the Member States contained no references to non-economic considerations.[86]

---

[79] Ibid., p. 22.
[80] Ibid., p. 23.
[81] Ibid., p. 24.
[82] Ibid.
[83] Ibid.
[84] COM(2010)343, n. 58 in this chapter, at p. 9; European Parliament Resolution, n. 64 in this chapter; European Council, n. 67 in this chapter.
[85] COM(2010)343, n. 58 in this chapter, at p. 6; European Parliament, n. 64 in this chapter, at paragraph 9; European Council, n. 67 in this chapter, at paragraph 70.
[86] See for example, Denmark Model BIT 2000, Preamble, Articles 2, 3, and 5; Greece Model BIT 2001, Preamble, Articles 3, 4, and 5; Sweden Model BIT 2002, Preamble, Articles 2, 3, and 4; Austria Model BIT 2002, Article 5; Belgo-Luxembourg Economic Union Model BIT, Preamble, Articles 3, 4, and 5; UK Model BIT 2005, Preamble, Articles 2 and 5; France Model BIT 2006, Preamble, Articles 2, 3, and 5; Germany Model BIT 2008, Preamble, Articles 2, 3, and 4.

There are, however, a few exceptions to this trend, including the Netherlands, Finland, and Austria Model BITs.[87]

Despite some isolated examples of good practices of balancing the economic with the non-economic considerations, overall, the European Member States lagged behind the trend of modernising BITs by balancing economic and social considerations, including the promotion of internationally recognised labour rights, identifiable in North America: in the US Model BITs of 2004[88] and 2012,[89] as well in the Canada Model BIT.[90] NAFTA is also relevant in this context. Its investment chapter preserves the ability of the states' parties to adopt social security and welfare measures, provided they are not inconsistent with the chapter.[91] and affirms that it is inappropriate to encourage investment by relaxing domestic health and safety measures.[92]

The questions that remain to be answered are whether and to what extent has this new trend and promise of not only protecting, but also promoting social considerations in EU IAs materialised, and how it fits not only in its regional and historical European context but also globally, in light of the most recent trends in IAs?

12.4 THE SOCIAL CONSIDERATIONS IN THE NEW EU INVESTMENT AGREEMENTS

Having looked at the question of balance between the social and the economic considerations in FDI from the perspectives of the Founding Treaties, the European International Investment Policy and in the IAs of the Member States before Lisbon, this section turns to the most critical question in this chapter, namely, how the balance is struck in the new EU IAs and whether it lives up to the commitments and expectations discussed above.

Since the entry into force of the Lisbon Treaty in 2009, the EU has exercised its new exclusive competence in FDI by including investment chapters

---

[87] Austria Model BIT 2002, Preamble, paragraph 3 referring to 'internationally recognised labour standards'. See also Netherlands Model BIT 2004, Preamble, paragraph 4; and Finland Model BIT 2001, Preamble, paragraph 6. These preambular references, however, did not find expression in any of the substantive clauses of the Model BITs.

[88] US Model BIT 2004, Preamble paragraph 5, Article 8(3)(c)(i) exception to Performance Requirements, Article 13 Investment and Labour, Annex B Expropriation.

[89] US Model BIT 2012, Preamble, paragraph 5, Annex B on Expropriation, Article 8(3)(c)(i) exception to Performance Requirements, Article 13 Investment and Labour.

[90] Canada Model BIT 2004, Preamble, paragraph 1 reference to promoting sustainable development, Article 7(2) Performance Requirements, Article 10 General Exceptions, Article 11 Health, Safety and Environmental Measures, Annex B.13(1) on Indirect Expropriation.

[91] Article 1101(4) NAFTA.

[92] Ibid., Article 1114(2).

in FTAs with third states.[93] FTAs are different from BITs, being a more modern instrument with broader economic objectives, including the regulation of international trade, investment and issues shared between the two such as intellectual property rights and trade in services.[94] Furthermore, FTAs commonly include separate chapters regulating non-economic interests, such as the protection of the environment, labour, and sustainable development.[95] Accordingly, FTAs have innovative potential for the integration of non-economic values.[96] This is well-illustrated in FTA practice: according to statistical surveys, while only 10 per cent of BITs contain language balancing non-economic considerations with their economic objectives, 96 per cent of the FTAs and Economic Partnership Agreements provide for such balance.[97] Empirical studies also show that references to labour issues are far less common in the treaty practice of emerging economies and developing states, compared to the practice of developed economies, arguably due to the perceived risk of losing a competitive advantage in attracting FDI based on lower costs.[98] These statistics are valuable in evaluating the EU IAs approach vis-à-vis different treaty partners in the context of the global investment treaty-making trends. The EU is currently negotiating a few stand-alone IAs too, with Myanmar and China, yet no EU BITs have yet been concluded or made public. The existing investment chapters in FTAs will be assessed chronologically with reference to the types of social protection provisions they contain.

Four extraneous considerations should be borne in mind when interpreting the EU IAs as possible factors affecting treaty-making. First, the context and chronology of the global economic and financial crisis of 2007–08 and its negative effects on the EU as a leading capital exporter and importer of FDI.[99] The economic crisis formed part of the context of the negotiations of IAs and FTAs, possibly motivating the weight given to economic objectives. Notably, in 2012 the EU gave up its leading position as a source and destination of FDI due to its capital inflows and outflows dropping by over 50 per cent.[100] The EU has been recovering since. According to UNCTAD's 2016

---

[93] See for example CETA; 2015 EU–Singapore FTA; and the latest EU–Vietnam FTA of 2 December 2015.

[94] Boie, n. 16 in this chapter, at pp. 19–20.

[95] See for example, 2009 US-Oman FTA, chapters 16 Labour and 17 Environment.

[96] Boie, n. 16 in this chapter, at p. 19.

[97] Gordon, Pohl, and Bouchard, n. 10 in this chapter, at p. 14.

[98] Boie, n. 16 in this chapter, at p. 26.

[99] European Commission, 'Economic Crisis in Europe: Causes, Consequences and Responses' (2009) 7 *European Economy* 1.

[100] Eurostat, FDI statistics available at: ec.europa.eu/eurostat/statistics-explained/index.php/Foreign_direct_investment_statistics (accessed 15 February 2015).

World Investment Report, in 2015 global FDI flows rose by 40 per cent.[101] The major driver behind this surge was the re-emergence of European multinational companies whose investments rose by 85 per cent compared to previous years.[102] Accordingly, it is not surprising that the EU is redoubling its efforts in concluding IAs to protect European investors abroad.

The second consideration is the identity of the third state with whom the EU negotiated and concluded the agreement. It is arguable that the EU would have had a stronger negotiating position and correspondingly, more ability to influence outcomes when in dialogue with developing, capital-importing states. In contrast, two of the agreements are with developed states, namely Canada and the US, who are in a similar bargaining position as the EU, not only due to their relative economic strength, but also to their interests as traditional capital-exporting states with increasing stakes in capital imports. Furthermore, Canada and the US already have established good practices of integrating social considerations in their Model BITs, much stronger than the practices of the EU Member States in this respect.

Thirdly, it should be recalled that the opening of the negotiations of a trade and investment agreement with the US caused significant public debate within the EU, which motivated a public consultation in 2014.[103] In response to the 150,000 replies received, the EU decided to reform its investment approach to better accommodate the public concerns, including the balancing of economic and non-economic values and objectives.[104]

Finally, it should be borne in mind that the EU does not have any direct experience of being a respondent in investment treaty arbitration, despite the interventions of the Commission as *amicus curiae* in a few investment arbitrations between EU Member States on questions of the compatibility of IAs with EU law, such as in the *Micula* v *Romania* case on the question of state aid under EU law.[105] Accordingly, the EU's experience of the practical consequences of investment treaty making is only derivative from that of the Member States under their older generation IAs, which is to be expected given how recent the EU FTAs with investment chapters are. For example, Germany is currently facing a challenge by Swedish investors under the

---

[101] UNCTAD, n. 8 in this chapter, at p. 10.

[102] Ibid., p. 6.

[103] Online public consultation on investment protection and investor-State dispute settlement in TTIP, available at: trade.ec.europa.eu/consultations/index.cfm?consul_id=179 (accessed 14 February 2016).

[104] European Commission, n. 75 in this chapter.

[105] *Ioan Micula, Viorel Micula, S.C. European Food S.A, S.C. Starmill S.R.L. and S.C. Multipack S.R.L.* v *Romania*, ARB/05/20, *amicus curiae* briefs not publicly available (on file with author).

Energy Charter Treaty (ECT) against its public-interest-based decision to phase out nuclear power generation in *Vattenfall* v *Germany*.[106] Even though the EU too is a party to the ECT, it is not directly engaged in responding to the challenge and tailoring the defence, let alone facing the consequences of the arbitration. This lack of direct experience, however, is somewhat mitigated by the increased transparency of investor-state arbitration and the public availability of most arbitral awards.[107]

12.4.1 *EU–South Korea FTA*

Notably, the EU–South Korea FTA, which was one of the first of the new generation FTAs, initiated in 2009 and finalised in 2010, did not include an investment chapter, nor did it affect the rights and obligations under existing BITs between the Member States and Korea.[108] The FTA did contain a few general provisions aimed at liberalising investment, including listing as objective the promotion of 'foreign direct investment without lowering or reducing labour or occupational health and safety standards … in the application and enforcement of … labour laws of the Parties'.[109]

The inclusion of this provision indicates the parties' intention to maintain the social model status quo by not lowering their existing standards. While this is an example of one of the weakest social commitments in investment treaty practice, it nonetheless constitutes an improvement on the existing framework of IAs between EU Member States and Korea, as they do not contain any substantive social standards provisions at all.[110] Furthermore, chapter 13 on Trade and Sustainable Development affirms the right of the parties to regulate and establish their own levels of labour protection, as well as their obligations deriving from ILO membership.[111] Even though this FTA does not directly regulate investment, it can still be taken into account by investment tribunals by way of systemic integration given that it contains relevant rules applicable between the parties.[112]

---

[106] *Vattenfall AB and Others* v *Federal Republic of Germany*, registered 31 May 2012 (pending), ICSID Case No. ARB/12/12.

[107] See for example www.italaw.com (accessed 14 October 2016).

[108] 2010 EU–Korea FTA, Preamble, paragraph 5.

[109] Ibid., Article 1(2)(h).

[110] See for example, 1964 Germany-Korea BIT; 1976 UK-Korea BIT; 1979 France-Korea BIT; 1988 Denmark-Korea BIT; 1991 Austria-Korea BIT; 1993 Finland-Korea BIT; 2005 Netherlands-Korea BIT.

[111] 2010 EU–Korea FTA, Articles 13.3 and 13.4.

[112] Article 31(3)(c) VCLTIO.

Notably, labour featured prominently in the discussions during the fourth meeting of the Committee on Trade and Sustainable Development established under the FTA, demonstrating the effectiveness of the diplomatic mechanism and the potential of IAs to promote social considerations.[113] In particular, the 'Parties updated each other on work towards ratification and effective implementation of ILO fundamental, priority and other up-to-date conventions',[114] including the progress made by individual EU Member States and the developments concerning EU labour-market policies. Furthermore, the EU called on Korea to speed up the ratification of the fundamental ILO Conventions.[115] While not legally binding, the joint statement indicates the value of diplomatic pressure in the context of economic cooperation for promoting social and labour standards, as well as the ability of the EU to influence not only the protection, but also the promotion of social rights through its economic agreements.

12.4.2 *EU–Canada Comprehensive Economic and Trade Agreement*

The first new generation FTA containing an investment chapter is the Canada–EU Comprehensive Economic and Trade Agreement (CETA) of 2014, revised in February 2016. According to the European Commission, CETA is 'the best and most progressive' EU FTA containing, inter alia, 'strong rules on the protection of labour rights'.[116] Commentators opine in a similar vein that CETA is one of the three landmark agreements that will shape international investment in the twenty-first century, along with the TPP and TTIP,[117] describing it as the groundwork for a pan-European investment approach.[118] It is probably fair to say that CETA is the most important example of the new EU IA approach to date, especially following its revision in 2016 that aligned it with the 2015 Draft TTIP.

---

[113] CTSD, 'Joint Statement of the 4th EU–Korea Trade and Sustainable Development Committee', '4th meeting the Committee on Trade and Sustainable Development of 9 September 2015', available at: trade.ec.europa.eu/doclib/docs/2015/september/tradoc_153802. pdf (accessed 14 October 2016).

[114] Ibid., p. 2.

[115] Ibid.

[116] European Commission, 'European Commission proposes signature and conclusion of EU–Canada trade deal', press release of 5 July 2016, available at: europa.eu/rapid/press-release_IP-16-2371_en.htm (accessed 14 October 2016).

[117] A. Bjorklund, J.P. Gaffney, F. Gelinas, and H. Woss, 'TDM CETA Special-Introduction' (2016) 13 *Transnational Dispute Management* 1.

[118] Y. Fortier, 'Preface – Canada' (2016) 13 *Transnational Dispute Management* 1.

Interestingly, comprehensive investment regulation was not provided for in the first negotiating directives of the Commission issued in 2009,[119] which noted generally that sustainable development was an overarching objective for the Parties and that the agreement ought to discourage the lowering down of labour and occupational health and safety standards in order to encourage investment.[120] The directives also foresaw the undertaking of an independent Sustainability Impact Assessment to tailor the negotiation process.[121] However, it was only in the second round of negotiating directives of 2011 that the Commission recommended that the Council modifies the negotiating mandate to include investment.[122] These specified that attaining the highest possible level of investment protection was to be without prejudice to the right of Member States and the EU to adopt and enforce measures necessary to protect public policy objectives, including social goals.[123]

The 2014 CETA contained a few express references to social considerations. The Preamble affirmed the commitment of the parties to promote sustainable development, including its social dimensions,[124] to implement the agreement 'in a manner consistent with the enhancement of the levels of … labour protection and the enforcement of … labour policies, building on their international commitments on labour',[125] as well as to preserve the right to regulate and the flexibility in achieving legitimate public policy objectives.[126] While the reference to the right to regulate is progressive and welcome in the context of global treaty making trends, the preambular language referring to internationally recognised labour rights is not that innovative and can be traced back to US BITs from the 1990s. It has been characterised as the 'softest form of introducing labour standards in BITs'.[127] Yet, compared with the BIT practice of most Member States, this is a step forward. For instance, the

---

[119] European Commission, 'Recommendation from the Commission to the Council in order to authorise the Commission to open negotiations for an Economic Integration Agreement with Canada, 24 April 2009' (2009), available at: data.consilium.europa.eu/doc/document/ST-9036-2009-EXT-2/en/pdf (accessed 21 October 2016). See in particular Title 1 Objectives.

[120] Ibid., paragraph 7.

[121] Ibid.

[122] European Commission, 'Recommendations from the Commission to the Council on the modification of the negotiating directives for an Economic Integration Agreement with Canada in order to authorise the Commission to negotiate, on behalf of the Union, on investment, 14 July 2011' (2011), available at: data.consilium.europa.eu/doc/document/ST-12838-2011-EXT-2/en/pdf (accessed 31 October 2016).

[123] Ibid., paragraph 26a.

[124] CETA, Preamble, paragraph 4.

[125] CETA, Preamble, paragraph 5.

[126] CETA, Preamble, paragraph 10.

[127] Boie, n. 16 in this chapter, at pp. 11–12.

2002 Belgian Model BIT affirmed that it will 'increase prosperity and welfare', without specifying how or referring to any specific social considerations. The 2008 Austrian Model BIT, however, was more progressive than the CETA preambular language, affirming the commitment of the parties to promote internationally recognised labour standards, to create labour opportunities and improve living standards. Austria implemented this Model with its 2012 BITs with Tajikistan, in 2013 with Nigeria and in a somewhat watered-down form in 2012 with Kazakhstan.

Following the numerous ambitious references to social considerations in the preamble, however, the substantive clauses of CETA 2014 fell short of meeting the established high expectations. Only three of the provisions were relevant to social considerations: one of them concerned performance requirements and preserved the ability of the Parties to condition the receipt of an advantage in connection with an investment on compliance with a requirement to employ domestic workers.[128] Performance requirements are a controversial policy tool used by some developing states to channel FDI towards contributing to their development, by requiring that investors employ a certain per cent of local workforce.[129] A relatively small number of BITs, mostly originating from the US, Japan, and Canada,[130] contain clauses prohibiting performance requirements and potentially creating tension with domestic social policy. However, the CETA performance requirement provision seemed to strike a delicate balance by exempting the employment of domestic workers from the prohibited performance requirements.

The second substantive provision balancing public interest and economic considerations is more significant in practice, as it sets out the definition of indirect expropriation striking a balance between investment protection and the right to regulate for public welfare weighing heavily in favour of the latter:

> For greater certainty, except in the rare circumstance where the impact of the measure or series of measures is so severe in light of its purpose that it appears manifestly excessive, non-discriminatory measures of a Party that are designed and applied to protect legitimate public welfare objectives, such as health, safety and the environment, do not constitute indirect expropriations.[131]

This definition establishes a high threshold of 'severe impact' to be assessed in light of the purpose of a non-discriminatory measure that ought to amount to 'manifest excessiveness' in order for a public welfare measure to constitute

---

[128] Article X.5 (3)(a) CETA.
[129] Boie, n. 16 in this chapter, at p. 10.
[130] Ibid., p. 18.
[131] CETA, Annex X.11(3) Expropriation.

expropriation. Accordingly, the so-defined balance lies heavily on the side of public interest regulation and seems to require a high standard of proof by the investor to show otherwise. This implies that in assessing this standard, a tribunal ought to show a high level of deference to the regulatory measures and arguably, to adopt a less invasive standard of review subject to the meeting of the high threshold. However, the definition does not give guidance as to the balance to be struck between the social and the economic considerations once the threshold is passed. For instance, the definition does not require that social measures meet a necessity and proportionality requirement.[132] Nor does it grant them a blank exemption from ever being indirect expropriation. In the absence of a general exception for public welfare regulation[133] or more clear guidance as to the weight to be ascribed to the economic and public interest considerations, the final act of balancing under this provision is left to the discretion of the arbitrators.

It should be noted that there is some disagreement among scholars as to whether or not the list of public welfare objectives is exhaustive or indicative, with some arguing that social considerations are implicitly included[134] and others opining that they are not.[135] Given the drafting of the provision and the qualification 'such as' preceding the list of objectives, the first view is preferable. Last but not least, the definition of indirect expropriation is not rooted in EU practice, as it does not appear in the BITs of the Member States. It is almost identical to the wording of Annex B.13(1) of the 2004 Canada Model BIT and very likely to have been influenced, if not motivated by it. The Canada Model BIT provision was in turn influenced by the 2004 US Model BIT, which codified the holding of the US Supreme Court in *Penn Central Station* v *New York City*.[136] Accordingly, the introduction of this provision in CETA is an example of the EU treaty practice being influenced by the investment (and public law) experience of other states.

Thirdly, chapter 28 setting out the general exceptions to CETA provides a broad exception to the establishment and the non-discriminatory treatment of investments for the protection of public order, defined as situations where 'a genuine and sufficiently serious threat is posed to one of the fundamental

[132] Some scholars, however, read such a requirement as implicit, see U. Kriebaum, 'FET and Expropriation in CETA' (2016) 13 *Transnational Dispute Management* 1, p. 11; and Henckels, n. 11 in this chapter, at p. 43.
[133] See the India Model BIT 2016, Article 5.4; ASEAN Comprehensive Investment Agreement 2009, Annex 2(4); and 2007 COMSEA Common Investment Area Agreement, Article 20(8).
[134] Prislan and Zandvliet, n 28 in this chapter.
[135] Mouyal, n. 25 in this chapter, at p. 170.
[136] United States Supreme Court, 438 US 104 (*Penn Central Station* v *New York City*), 26 June 1978.

interests of society'.[137] It is arguable that social measures might fall under this exception.

It is somewhat surprising that the 2014 CETA did not contain more social provisions, such as preserving expressly the right of the Parties to regulate in order to protect the social model or even imposing the minimum obligation not to lower the existing labour standards. This approach was inconsistent with the commitments of the institutions with respect to the Founding Treaties and the new European Investment Policy, as well as with CETA itself, which contains a whole chapter on Trade and Sustainable Development, endorsing progressive social provisions,[138] guaranteed by an international diplomatic process rather than by international dispute settlement. Notably, CETA also contains a Trade and Labour chapter expressly preserving the parties' right to regulate and provide high levels of labour protection, as well as to promote their international obligations under multilateral labour agreements, but none of these provisions contain an express reference to investment and as such, their relevance could be open to doubt.[139] The only provision in the chapter that specifically applies to investment is the minimal requirement that the parties should not lower or derogate from their domestic labour law standards.[140] Similarly to the Sustainable Development chapter, the Labour chapter does not fall under the jurisdiction of an investment tribunal and can only be taken into account in the interpretation of the investment provisions as forming part of the context of the treaty in accordance with Article 31(2) of the Vienna Convention on the Law of Treaties between states and International Organisations (VCLTIO), which is not yet into force but codifies the customary rules of treaty interpretation.[141] According to this general rule, the context of the treaty for the purposes of its interpretation comprises,

---

[137] Article 28.3(2) CETA.

[138] Chapter XX, Article 1 and 3, CETA.

[139] Chapter 23 Trade and Labour, Article 2 and 3, CETA. See also the North American Agreement on Labour Cooperation 1993 adopted under the framework of NAFTA, available at: www.labour.gc.ca/eng/relations/international/agreements/naalc.shtml#naalc (accessed 31 October 2016).

[140] CETA, n. 139 in this chapter, Article 4.

[141] Article 31 VCLTIO is identical to Article 31 VCLT, whose customary status has been confirmed, inter alia, in ICJ, judgment of 3 February 1994 in *Territorial Dispute (Libyan Arab Jamahiriya / Chad)*, ICJ Reports 1994, p. 21, paragraph 41; ICJ, judgment of 12 December 1996 in *Oil Platforms (Islamic Republic of Iran v United States of America)*, Preliminary Objections, ICJ Reports 1996 (II), p. 8 12, paragraph 23; ICJ, judgment of 13 December 1999 in *Kasikili/Sedudu Island (Botswana/Namibia)*, I.C.J. Reports 1999, p. 1045, paragraph 18; and by the ECJ, the most recent example being ECJ, judgement of 17 February 2016 in *Air Baltic Corporation AS v Lietuvos Respublikos specialiuju tyrimu tarnyba*, C-429/14, EU:C:2016:88, paragraph 24.

inter alia, the text of the treaty, including its preamble and annexes. Indeed, in the case of *Al Tamimi* v *Oman*, the arbitral tribunal took into account the environmental chapter in the US-Oman FTA as relevant context in interpreting the substantive investment standards, despite it not falling directly under its jurisdiction.[142] Finally, in contrast to some other FTAs, CETA does not provide that the Trade and Labour chapter is to prevail over the Investment chapter in case of an inconsistency.[143]

The substantive social provisions in the 2014 CETA stand in contrast with the ambitious Canada Model BIT. In particular, the Model BIT provides that the adoption and enforcement of domestic laws and regulations, including those relating to social protection, constitutes a general exception to the investment obligations under the treaty, subject to the requirement that they do not constitute arbitrary, discriminatory or a disguised restriction on investment.[144] Furthermore, the Canada Model BIT contains a special clause on health, safety and environmental measures, providing for the non-watering down of health and safety in order to promote investment.[145]

Overall, when assessed from the perspective of the 'best practices' of EU Member States and their Model BITs, the 2014 CETA was definitely a welcome step forward in establishing a better balance between economic objectives and social considerations, be it only in the context of indirect expropriation. Seen in a global context, however, it fell rather short of meeting the good practices of social clauses in IAs.[146] Accordingly, it was not too big a surprise that the EU initiated a renegotiation of CETA to align it with its new investment approach set out in the 2015 EU Proposal on TTIP. The new CETA was finalised and published on 26 February 2016 and is now aligned with the EU–Vietnam FTA and the 2015 Draft TTIP, striking a much better balance between the economic and the social considerations at hand, as will be discussed below. Most notably, the revised CETA contains a special provision in the investment chapter reaffirming the right of the Parties to regulate to achieve legitimate public policy objectives, expressly including social and consumer protection.[147] This is arguably the most important innovation in CETA and in the EU approach towards IAs in general. It codifies the 'police

---

[142] *Adel A Hamadi Al Tamimi* v *Sultanate of Oman*, Award, 3 November 2015, ICSID Case No. ARB/11/33, paragraphs 388–90.
[143] See the US FTAs, such as 2005 US-CAFTA DR FTA, Article 10.2.
[144] Canada Model BIT 2004, Article 10(1).
[145] Ibid., Article 11.
[146] See the Trans Pacific Partnership 2015.
[147] Article 8.9 (1) CETA.

powers doctrine' from customary international law,[148] confirming the sovereign authority of the state to regulate,[149] which has been subject to inconsistent treatment in investment arbitration where some tribunals have ordered states to pay compensation for passing general public interest legislation adversely affecting foreign investments.[150] Furthermore, due to its systematic position in the investment chapter, the right to regulate applies to and qualifies all standards of investment protection, including not only expropriation, being the most extreme form of interference with economic rights, but also the FET standard, which has been found to be violated by public interest measures in the past.[151] The express reference to social protection strongly suggests that social considerations are also implicit in the list of public welfare objectives in the definition of indirect expropriation.

Finally, it should be noted that there is some ambiguity as to whether EU IAs should be signed solely on behalf of the EU or rather as mixed agreements, on behalf of the EU and the Member States. The Commission referred the question of exclusive and shared competences in the signing of EU FTAs to the Court of Justice of the EU and the CJEU found that the Member States ought to sign and ratify IAs due to their competence in the areas of portfolio investments and with respect to international dispute settlement.[152] Notably, however, the Commission has recently recommended that CETA be signed as a mixed agreement in light of the ambiguities and in the interest of time.[153] This is a welcome development, as it confirms that the right of the 'Parties' to regulate for social matters applies not only to the EU, but also to the Member States. This approach might also benefit the protection of the public interest under EU IAs more generally, given that a number of its aspects, including the protection of the environment, are shared competences where both the EU and the Member States can regulate.

---

[148] See *Philip Morris Brands Sàrl, Philip Morris Products S.A. and Abal Hermanos S.A. v Oriental Republic of Uruguay*, Award, 8 July 2016, ICSID Case No. ARB/10/7, paragraphs 292–301.

[149] For detailed analyses, see J. Vinuales, 'Sovereignty in Foreign Investment Law', in Z. Douglas, J. Pauwelyn, and J. Vinuales (eds), *The Foundations of International Investment Law: Bringing Theory into Practice* (Oxford University Press, 2014), pp. 6–12.

[150] See *Saluka Investments BV v The Czech Republic*, Partial Award, 17 March 2016, paragraphs 255–62 and *Compañía del Desarrollo de Santa Elena S.A. v Republic of Costa Rica*, n. 14 in this chapter, paragraphs 71–2.

[151] For example *Saluka Investments BV v The Czech Republic*, n. 150 in this chapter, at paragraphs 407 et seq.

[152] ECJ, opinion 2/15 of 15 May 2017 *pursuant to Article 218(11) TFEU*, EU:C:2017:376.

[153] COM(2016)444 *Proposal for a Council Decision on the Signing on Behalf of the EU of CETA between Canada of the One Part, and the EU and its Member States, of the Other Part* (Brussels, 5 July 2016).

12.4.3 *EU–Vietnam FTA*

The EU–Vietnam FTA of 2 December 2015 sets out social considerations in two preambular paragraphs, one affirming the determination of the parties to promote investment 'in a manner mindful of high levels of … labour protection and relevant internationally recognised standards and agreements',[154] as well as to strengthen investment relations in accordance with the objective of sustainable development, including its social dimensions.[155] Second, the parties stress their desire to raise living standards and create new employment opportunities.[156] The substantive provisions of the EU–Vietnam FTA are more ambitious in balancing the social considerations than earlier EU IAs. In particular, the very first of the general provisions of the FTA setting out its objectives affirms the right of the parties to regulate and to enforce measures pursuing legitimate public policy objectives, including explicitly 'the protection of society'.[157] This is reinforced in a special provision on Investment and Regulatory Measures, identical to the one in CETA 2016 discussed above, reaffirming the right to regulate including for social protection, providing that the standards of investment protection ought not to be interpreted as a commitment that the parties will not change their legal frameworks in a manner that might negatively affect investments and the investor's profit expectations.[158] Thirdly, the definition of indirect expropriation exempts non-discriminatory measures adopted for legitimate public policy objectives with a wording identical to that of CETA.[159]

The EU–Vietnam FTA along with CETA 2016 represent the best available EU practice so far of an IA balancing economic objectives with social considerations defined broadly as protection of society.

Still, it could be argued that the FTA could have gone even further in actively promoting internationally recognised labour standards drawing inspiration from the 2002 Belgian Model BIT, whereby each party 'shall strive to ensure that its labour legislation provides for labour standards consistent with international labour standards', reaffirming their obligations as members of the ILO.[160] It could have also followed the innovative Model International

---

[154] Free Trade Agreement between the European Union and the Socialist Republic of Vietnam, 2 December 2015, Preamble, paragraph 4.
[155] Ibid.
[156] Ibid., paragraph 5.
[157] Ibid., Article 1 (2) Objectives, coverage, and definitions.
[158] Ibid., Article 13bis(2).
[159] Ibid., Annex Expropriation, paragraph 3.
[160] Belgium Model BIT 2002, Article 6 Labour, paragraphs 1 and 3. This model was not consistently implemented by Belgium in its BIT practice but could be found in Article 12 of the 2009 BeLux-Barbados BIT, Article 6 of the 2006 BeLux-Botswana BIT, neither of which are yet into

Agreement on Investment for Sustainable Development and introduced a requirement that investments are managed and operated in accordance with the ILO core labour standards and with domestic labour laws.[161] Furthermore, it could have required that the parties provide high levels of labour protections in their domestic laws and that these are consistent with the 1998 ILO Declaration on Fundamental Principles and Rights of Word.[162] As it stands, the EU–Vietnam FTA strikes a good balance for the protection of social considerations but falls short of actively promoting them.

12.4.4 *Transatlantic Trade and Investment Partnership*

The past negotiations of the much-debated Transatlantic Trade and Investment Partnership (TTIP) are also relevant in assessing the balance between economic and social considerations in EU IAs. It is fair to say that TTIP was the most controversial IA negotiated to date,[163] arguably because of the unprecedented level of publicity in its negotiations, drawing the attention of the general public for the first time to the existence and content of IAs, even though they have been proliferating since 1959. The new system of investor-state dispute settlement (ISDS) established in the first Draft TTIP was the biggest innovation of the draft agreement and its most controversial aspect, institutionalising the settlement of investment disputes through the creation of a two-tier investment court system.[164] This development may have had some bearing on the balancing of economic and non-economic considerations in light of the criticisms expressed by some that ad hoc arbitration modelled after private dispute settlement is not the optimal mechanism for assessing the public interest regulation of states, that it lacks transparency, consistency, as well as the perception that it has a pro-investor bias.[165] The new ISDS system proposed in TTIP and implemented in the 2016 CETA has generated

force. In contrast, the 2005 BIT with China contains no references to labour and the 2009 BIT with Colombia contains no reference to international labour standards in its Article 8 on Labour.

[161] IISD 'Model International Agreement on Investment for Sustainable Development', Article 14 Post-establishment obligations, available at: www.iisd.org/pdf/2005/investment_model_int_agreement.pdf (accessed 14 October 2016).

[162] Ibid., Article 21 Minimum standards for environmental, labour and human rights protection.

[163] For general criticisms from NGOs, pressure groups and trade unions, see stop-ttip.org, see also Corporate Europe Observatory at www.corporateeurope.org and Seattle to Brussels Network at www.s2bnetwork.org (accessed 12 August 2016).

[164] Chapter 2, Section 3, Draft TTIP 2015.

[165] Spears, n. 11 in this chapter; and S. Schill, 'The European Commission's Proposal of an Investment Court System for TTIP' (2016) 20 *ASIL Insights* 1. But also see J. Alvarez, 'Is Investor-State Arbitration "Public"?' (2016) *Global Administrative Law Series Working Paper*, 6.

very polarised opinions among scholars with some arguing that it does not go far enough[166] and others that it goes too far in reforming the existing ISDS regime.[167] However, it remains to be tested in practice whether the new EU model of ISDS would in any way affect the balance struck between the economic and non-economic considerations in the interpretation of IAs.

On the positive side, TTIP has been described as 'the biggest bilateral trade [and investment] deal in history' given that the EU–US economic relationship 'is the largest in the world', making up nearly half of the global GDP.[168] Indeed, the president of the European Council described TTIP as exemplifying 'Europe and America's role as the world's standard-setters'.[169] Notably, following much public debate and criticism, the negotiating mandates of the EU and the US, as well as the 2013 and 2015 drafts have now been made public. These documents are instructive as to the evolving position of the Parties on the balancing between the economic protections and social considerations. The negotiation mandates are also relevant for interpreting TTIP in accordance with Article 32 VCLTIO, codifying the principle that the preparatory works of the treaty and the circumstances of its conclusion can be used as a supplementary means of interpretation in case of ambiguity of the treaty text.

The EU Directives for negotiation of 2013 stress that TTIP should be an 'ambitious, comprehensive, [and] *balanced*'[170] agreement based on common values and principles, including the commitment to sustainable development, 'full and productive employment and decent work for all', the right to regulate for the protection of labour and the aims of ensuring

---

[166] Schill, n. 165 in this chapter; P. Hainbach, 'The EU's Approach to Investor-State Arbitration in CETA' (2016) 13 *Transnational Dispute Management* 1; B. Cappiello, 'ISDS in European International Agreements: Alternative Justice or Alternative to Justice?' (2016) 13 *Transnational Dispute Management* 1, p. 25; and European Parliament 'ISDS Provisions in EU IIAs' (2014) 2 *Studies* 1.

[167] J. Weiler, 'European Hypocrisy: TTIP and ISDS', EJIL:Talk!, 21 January 2015, available at: www.ejiltalk.org/european-hypocrisy-ttip-and-isds/ (accessed 14 October 2016); Fortier, n. 118 in this chapter; S. Schwebel, 'CETA: Keynote Remarks' (2016) 13 *Transnational Dispute Management* 1; and M. Lalonde, 'The Public Interest and Recent Treaties' (forthcoming) *ASIL Proceedings* 2016.

[168] The White House, 'Remarks by President Obama, UK Prime Minister Cameron, European Commission President Barroso, and the European Council President Van Rompuy on TTIP', press release of 17 June 2013, available at: www.whitehouse.gov/the-press-office/2013/06/17/remarks-president-obama-uk-prime-minister-cameron-european-commission-pr (accessed 15 February 2016).

[169] Ibid.

[170] Council of the European Union, 'Directives for the negotiation of the Transatlantic Trade and Investment Partnership between the European Union and the United States of America', 17 June 2013, paragraph 2 (emphasis added), available at: data.consilium.europa.eu/doc/document/ST-11103-2013-DCL-1/en/pdf (accessed 14 October 2016).

respect for international labour agreements and standards, as well as promoting high levels of labour protection.[171] The directives on the investment chapter itself, however, were more modest, weighing heavily towards the objective to provide the highest possible standard of legal protection and certainty for European investors in the US and mentioning only briefly that this should be without prejudice to the right of Member States to regulate in a non-discriminatory manner, including for social protection.[172] The US negotiation objectives seemed far less focused on the balancing between economic and non-economic considerations. For instance, the 2013 Obama Administration letter to the US Congress on the opening of negotiations refers to an 'ambitious, comprehensive, and high standard TTIP',[173] omitting any reference to the need of balance the non-economic considerations. The underlying assumption that permeates the directives is that investment will 'be an even stronger driver for job creation' and that the agreement will automatically and by itself benefit workers, fully in line with neoliberal traditions and past EU experiences discussed above.[174] The only mention of social considerations is in the context of the US intending to obtain commitments by the EU with respect to internationally recognised labour rights and the effective enforcement of domestic labour laws.[175] It is only the detailed goals of the Administration that mention 'the objective of ensuring that governments maintain the discretion to regulate in the public interest'.[176]

Based on these negotiation positions, it could be inferred that the EU had more ambitious goals and greater focus on ensuring that TTIP was a balanced economic agreement integrating social considerations, whereas the US seemed to favour a laissez-faire neoliberal approach, assuming that job creation and improvement of workers' conditions will follow naturally from the increase in FDI. With respect to the social considerations, the US emphasised only the internationally recognised labour rights, whereas the EU defined social considerations more broadly.

---

[171] Ibid., paragraphs 1, 6 and 8.

[172] Ibid., paragraphs 22–3.

[173] Executive Office of the President, 'Letter to Congress of 20 March 2013', paragraph 4, available at: ustr.gov/sites/default/files/03202013%20TTIP%20Notification%20Letter.PDF (accessed 22 January 2016).

[174] Ibid., 1–2.

[175] Ibid., 4.

[176] Available at: ustr.gov/trade-agreements/free-trade-agreements/transatlantic-trade-and-investment-partnership-t-tip/t-tip-5 (accessed 22 January 2016).

Turning to the evolution of TTIP, the first 2013 draft was leaked in the public domain in 2014.[177] Somewhat disappointingly, the Investment Chapter contained a single provision relevant to social protection in the definition of indirect expropriation providing that:

> non-discriminatory measures of general application taken by a Party that are designed to protect legitimate public policy objectives do not constitute indirect expropriation, if they are *necessary and proportionate* in light of the above mentioned factors and are applied in such a way that they *genuinely meet* the public policy objectives for which they are designed.[178]

The wording of this exception is significant because it subjects the balance between economic rights and the right to regulate to a proportionality analysis, which on the one side imposes a greater burden on the State or the EU to justify the legality of its social measures, compared to the high-threshold exceptions in CETA and the other EU FTAs. In contrast, this balance weighs more heavily towards protecting the economic rights than the regulatory space of the state, by allowing for a more intrusive standard of review. On the other side, however, this formula gives clearer guidance to arbitrators as to how to weigh the competing considerations, limiting their discretion in striking the appropriate balance.

The 2013 draft TTIP also contained a general provision affirming that each party retains the right to adopt, maintain and enforce measures necessary to protect society.[179]

The 2015 EU Proposal on Draft TTIP made public by the Commission indicates a few important developments with respect to striking a better and broader balance between the economic and the social considerations at hand.[180] In particular, the draft of the Investment chapter included an express provision affirming the right of the parties to regulate to achieve legitimate public policy objectives, including social protection, identical to the one in CETA and the EU–Vietnam FTA discussed above.[181] Notably, the definition of indirect expropriation was changed and aligned with the definitions in CETA and the other EU FTAs, no longer requiring a proportionality analysis but instead the manifest excessiveness of the impact of the measure in light of

[177] Released by the German weekly Die Zeit, see P. Pinzler 'Freihandelsabkommen: Endlich wird öffentlich gestritten', *Die Zeit*, 28 February 2014, available at: eu-secretdeals.info/ttip/ (accessed 22 January 2016).
[178] Ibid., 13, Annex Expropriation (emphasis added).
[179] Ibid., Article 1(1) Objective, coverage and definition.
[180] Draft TTIP 2015, available at: trade.ec.europa.eu/doclib/docs/2015/november/tradoc_153955.pdf (accessed 22 January 2016).
[181] Ibid., Article 2 Investment and Regulatory Measures/Objectives.

its purpose.[182] Overall, the social consideration provisions of TTIP were largely similar to those of the EU–Vietnam FTA and the 2016 CETA. This, interpreted together with the negotiation directives of both parties, could be indicative of an EU initiative lying behind the stronger social protection provisions. Given that the 2013 Draft TTIP was the first published document containing the new EU approach to IAs balancing investment protection with public interest considerations, it can be speculated that it served as a model for the later negotiations. This new EU model was clearly informed by the Founding Treaties and the EU International Investment Policy, but also by the sudden public outcry against TTIP and the public consultation that followed. This latter aspect indicates a democratisation of the process of investment treaty negotiations, which is a welcome development in the time of a legitimacy crisis of the investment arbitration regime.[183]

The 2015 Draft TTIP also contained a chapter on sustainable development with references to social considerations in the context of investment regulation, including: the recognition that the benefit of considering investment-related labour issues is part of a global approach towards sustainable development;[184] the commitment to promote investment in a way contributing to, inter alia, the realisation of the ILO Decent Work Agenda;[185] the right to regulate to promote and realise multilateral labour standards and agreements;[186] a commitment to implement effectively global standards and agreements on labour matters in domestic laws, including all ILO Conventions they have ratified;[187] a commitment to make sustained efforts to ratify the fundamental ILO Conventions and their Protocols;[188] and an obligation to effectively enforce domestic labour laws.[189] Notably, the chapter set out specific labour commitments with respects to a number of internationally recognised rights, including the freedom of association and the right to collective bargaining, the elimination of forced or compulsory labour, the effective abolition

---

[182] Ibid., Annex I Expropriation, paragraph 3. Footnote 1 defines labour as including employment promotion, social protection and dialogue, fundamental principles and rights at work, as well as non-discrimination, referring to the ILO Decent Work Agenda and the 2008 Declaration on Social Justice for a Fair Globalisation.

[183] S. Franck, 'The Legitimacy Crisis in Investment Treaty Arbitration: Privatizing Public International Law through Inconsistent Decisions' (2005) 73 *Fordham Law Review* 1521; and M. Waibel (ed.), *The Backlash against Investment Arbitration* (Kluwer, 2010).

[184] Draft TTIP, n. 180 in this chapter, Part III, chapter on Trade and Sustainable Development, Article 1(3) Context.

[185] Ibid., Article 1(1).

[186] Ibid., Article 3.

[187] Ibid., Article 4(4).

[188] Ibid., Article 4(2)(b).

[189] Ibid., Article 4(6).

of child labour, as well as the equality and non-discrimination in respect of employment and occupation.[190]

Overall, the 2015 TTIP represented a significant step towards striking a better and broader balance between the economic objectives and the social considerations underlying IAs, establishing a new EU global approach. The draft TTIP set a new level of good practice not only from the perspective of the IAs of the Member States, but also in comparison with North America, that is, in light of the 2012 US Model BIT. Article 13 of the US Model BIT on Investment and Labour provides for a much narrower regulatory space of the state for labour matters,[191] merely encourages the maintaining of the domestic status quo of labour protection by not lowering labour standards,[192] and does not promote the implementation or commitment to international labour agreements, but merely notes the existing ILO commitments in this respect.[193] TTIP, in contrast, encouraged a proactive approach of contributing to sustainable development, introducing higher levels of social protection, effectively implementing MLAs and enforcing labour obligations. It is regrettable that the TTIP negotiations are unlikely to be finalised in the current political circumstances.

12.4.5 *Procedural Aspects of the Balance between Economic and Social Considerations*

Even though the concept of balancing economic objectives and social considerations has primarily a substantive connotation, there are certain procedural aspects that can contribute to the better attainment of the balancing act in the course of investor-state arbitration. It has long been recognised that transparency is one such aspect.[194] All of the EU FTAs surveyed above contain important transparency guarantees which are fully in line with the best practices and international trends in this respect. These include the application of the UNCITRAL Transparency Rules,[195] the ability of the tribunal and the parties to appoint experts on factual issues, arguably including social and labour ones,[196] as well as the power of the tribunals to accept *amicus curiae*

---

[190] Ibid., Article 5–8.
[191] US Model BIT 2012, Article 13(3) and (5).
[192] Ibid., Article 13(2).
[193] Ibid., Article 13(1).
[194] J. Maupin, 'Transparency in International Investment Law: The Good, the Bad and the Murky', in A. Bianchi and A. Peters (eds), *Transparency in International Law* (Cambridge University Press, Cambridge, 2013); see in general D. Euler, M. Gehring, and M. Scherer (eds), *Transparency in International Investment Arbitration* (Cambridge University Press, 2015).
[195] See for example, 2016 EU–Vietnam FTA, Article 20 Transparency of Proceedings.
[196] Ibid., Article 26 Expert Reports.

submissions in disputes touching on the public interest.[197] These procedural requirements help incorporate social matters in the course of investor–state arbitration[198] and help inform the public interest groups about the social implications of investment law.

12.4.6 APPRAISAL

So far, scholarly opinions on the evaluation of the new EU IAs have been polarised. On the one side of the spectrum, there are the optimists who see the EU IAs as 'the dawning of a new era … of EU's better practices'.[199] On the other side, there are the sceptics who observe that the recent EU investment practice 'is less interesting and innovative than one might have expected'.[200] It is arguable that these opposing views could be reconciled by changing the point of reference. While Titi's optimistic views apply fully to the new EU IAs when compared with the best practices of the Member States before Lisbon, Paparinskis' observations held true when observing the global trends in investment treaty practice until 2015 when the EU introduced its new investment approach.

The development trajectory of the EU IAs discussed above indicates certain distinct trends. Chronologically, since 2010, there is an identifiable trend of strengthening the social provisions in investment chapters, starting with the single provision of not watering labour standards to encourage investment in the 2010 EU–Korea FTA[201] and culminating in the numerous and much stronger social and labour provisions in the 2015 EU–Vietnam FTA, the revised CETA and the draft TTIP. This evolutionary trend is undoubtedly the result of larger and complex processes at play, including the recovery from the economic crisis, the strong public concern about TTIP and the EU response, as well as the accretion of the investment treaty practice of the EU itself.

Second, all EU IAs so far contain express references to social considerations in their preambles. While not legally binding, preambles form part of the context of the treaty for the purposes of interpretation and could set out the object and purpose of the agreement. Accordingly, preambular paragraphs

---

[197] Draft TTIP 2015, n. 180 in this chapter, Article 23 Intervention by third parties.

[198] See Maupin, n. 194 in this chapter.

[199] C. Titi, 'International Investment Law and the European Union: Towards a New Generation of International Investment Agreements' (2015) 26 *European Journal of International Law* 639.

[200] M. Paparinskis, 'International Investment Law and the European Union: A Reply to Catharine Titi' (2015) 26 *European Journal of International Law* 663.

[201] For analysis of similar provisions in the US Model BIT 2012, see L. Caplan and J. Sharpe, 'US Model BIT', in C. Brown (ed.), *Commentaries on Selected Model Investment Treaties* (Oxford University Press, 2013), pp. 805–6.

have a special interpretative role with respect to the substantive provisions of IAs, which ought to be interpreted by taking into account the context of the treaty.[202] Notably, preambular references to non-economic considerations have led tribunals to adopt a balanced interpretative approach of the substantive protections in IAs.[203]

Thirdly, the EU FTAs containing investment chapters also have separate chapters on sustainable development. The latter usually set out more ambitious and specific labour commitments, including not only maintaining the social status quo in domestic law, but also promoting the strengthening of labour standards and the better implementation of MLAs. Notably, the first EU FTAs concluded after Lisbon limited the relevance of these chapters to trade. However, there is a shift since 2015 towards broadening the applicability of some of their provisions to cover investment, evidenced in the EU–Vietnam FTA, as well as in the 2015 Draft TTIP. This shift is welcome as it broadens the scope of the balancing between investment and social considerations. While the sustainable development chapters have their own dispute settlement mechanisms, which are distinctly inter-state and as such fall outside of the scope of jurisdiction of investment tribunals, they still have interpretative relevance similar to, if not stronger than, that of preambles by forming part of the text and context of the treaty.[204] This approach of balancing economic and social considerations was described by the then Deputy-Head of the Cabinet of the EU Trade Commissioner in his academic writings as 'intelligent integration' of social standards supported unanimously by all Member States, in light of the controversy surrounding the inclusion of an explicit reference to the right to regulate for the purposes of 'counteracting' the broad investment standards.[205] Indeed, it has been suggested that EU investors did not welcome the inclusion of social and sustainable development considerations in the new EU IAs, advocating that they do not form part of the best practices of the Member States and their existing BITs.[206] For example, representatives of the services industry advocated before the Commission that social and other public interest considerations should not be included in the IA with China as they would have the effect of reducing the existing standards of investment

---

[202] H. Ciurtin, 'Beyond the Norm: Hermeneutic Function of Treaty Preambles in Investment Arbitration and International Law' (2015) 36 *Revista Romana de Arbitraj* 64.

[203] *Saluka Investments BV v The Czech Republic*, n. 150 in this chapter, paragraphs 300, 305 and *S.D. Myers Inc. v Canada*, n. 13 in this chapter, paragraphs 196–204 and 220–1.

[204] *Adel A Hamadi Al Tamimi v Sultanate of Oman*, n. 142 in this chapter, paragraphs 388–9.

[205] F. Hoffmeister and G. Unuvar, 'From BITs and Pieces towards European Investment Agreements' (2013) 7 *Studies in International Investment Law* 57, p. 72.

[206] W. Shan and S. Zhang, 'The Potential EU–China BIT: Issues and Implications' (2013) 7 *Studies in International Investment Law* 87, p. 109.

protection and prolonging negotiations.[207] Accordingly, the balance struck between investment protection and the social considerations is motivated not only by the negotiation positions of the parties to the treaty, but also by the relative strength of the industry lobby within them. As observed by Lowe, the relevant balance in BITs 'is not between the interests of the signatories, the two states parties. Rather, it is between the host State and the investors'.[208]

Finally and most importantly, there is a detectable trend towards strengthening and broadening the balance between economic objectives and social considerations in the substantive provisions of the EU IAs. It started with the important first step of acknowledging the need of striking such balance in the 2010 EU–Korea FTA. The trend developed further in 2014 CETA, where the balance was struck between the right of the state to regulate for social protection and the right of the investor not to be subject to indirect expropriation. This balance was pitched at a high threshold to be satisfied by the investor,[209] requiring manifest excessiveness of the impact of the measure in light of its purpose, rather than the lower threshold proportionality analysis employed by some arbitral tribunals.[210] Notably, the definition of indirect expropriation in effect establishes a presumption that non-discriminatory social measures do not constitute indirect expropriation, except in rare circumstances. This formulation of the balance also shifts the traditional focus on the economic impact of the challenged regulatory measure towards a focus on its public interest objective.

The trend of balancing culminated in 2015 with the EU–Vietnam FTA and the 2015 draft TTIP, both of which influenced the revised CETA. In addition to the balancing built in the definition of indirect expropriation, these agreements expressly acknowledge the right of the states and the EU to regulate for social protection in a general manner in the Investment chapter. Accordingly, this sovereign right ought to be taken into account and balanced against all economic standards in the IAs, including FET and full protection and security. Moreover, the balancing has a prospective element to it, previewing the possibility of future strengthening of the social regulations of the

[207] European Services Forum, 'Letter Sent to Commissioner De Gucht Outlining the European Services Industry's Views on EU Investment Policy towards China, 3 October 2011' (2011) available at: www.esf.be/new/wp-content/uploads/2011/10/ESF2011-07-Karel-De-Gucht-EU-China-Investment-Agreement-Final.pdf (accessed 15 November 2016).
[208] V. Lowe, 'Regulation or Expropriation' (2002) 55 *Current Legal Problems* 447, p. 450.
[209] For commentary of a similar provision in the US Model BIT 2012, see Caplan and Sharpe, n. 201 in this chapter, at pp. 791–2.
[210] *Tecmed SA v United Mexican States*, n. 12, in this chapter, paragraph 122 and footnote 140 in *Tecmed SA v United Mexican States* award, quoting the case law of the ECHR. ARB/04/4, paragraphs 398–405.

state and allowing for it to prevail over the investor's expectations for profit. These provisions are an ambitious and innovative explicit guarantee of the right of the state to regulate for social protection and constitute an important development of the balancing on the international plane. For instance, the contemporaneous Trans Pacific Partnership has a narrower and more conservative provision on investment and non-economic objectives, falling short of acknowledging the right to regulate in general but merely affirming the right of the party to adopt and enforce measures in order to ensure that investment is undertaken in a manner sensitive to 'environmental, health and other regulatory objectives'.[211] The new balancing approach in EU IAs affirming the right to regulate reinforces the views of scholars like Lowe and Vinuales, who argue that the regulatory powers of the State are 'an essential element of the permanent sovereignty of each State over its economy' rather than 'the accidental result of the failure of investment treaties to eliminate them'.[212] Accordingly, these provisions are probably the most important mechanism for balancing economic and public interest considerations in the new EU IAs.

The evolution of the EU IAs treaty language on balancing economic objectives with social considerations will no doubt have significant implications for the case law. At present, the case law on the consequences of challenges to public interest regulation is split.[213] The divergent approaches have been criticised for creating the danger of a 'regulatory chill'[214] and strongly motivated the introduction of balancing in the latest generations of IAs so as to better accommodate the public interest.

The precise interpretation and application of the new social consideration clauses in EU IAs remains to be tested and established in future investment awards. It is likely, however, that these provisions will have important systemic implications, not only because of their strong and broad formulation, but also because of the EU push towards institutionalising the system of investment arbitration by the creation of investment courts and appeal tribunals discussed above. It is possible that the case law of such semi-permanent institutions will

---

[211] Article 9.15 Investment and Environmental, Health and Other Regulatory Objectives TPP.
[212] Lowe, n. 208 in this chapter, at p. 450. See also Vinuales, n. 149 in this chapter, at p. 317.
[213] T. Waelde and A. Kolo, 'Environmental Regulation: Investment Protection and "Regulatory Taking" in International Law' (2001) 50 *International and Comparative Law Quarterly* 811; A. Titi, *The Right to Regulate in International Investment Law* (Hart, 2014) and Mouyal, n. 25 in this chapter.
[214] Special Representative of the Secretary General on the Issue of Human Rights, Transnational Corporations and Other Business Enterprises, 'Business and Human Rights: Towards Operationalising the 'Protect, Respect and Remedy' Framework, report to the UN General Assembly', A/HRC/11/13' (2009) available at: www2.ohchr.org/english/bodies/hrcouncil/docs/11session/A.HRC.11.13.pdf (accessed 15 November 2016), paragraph 30.

be more sensitive towards the systemic role of balancing the economic rights on the one side and the right to regulate for social protection on the other.

12.5 CONCLUSIONS

In conclusion, the new EU IAs have evolved significantly in the first five years of their infancy from falling short of meeting the commitments expressed in the new EU International Investment Policy and the Founding Treaties in the early agreements, to striking a clearer and more explicit balance to protect the right of the states and the EU to regulate for social protection. Given the recent example of the reshaping of CETA to align it with the new and better EU investment approach, it can be hoped that the EU–Korea FTA will also be revised in similar vein so as to guarantee balancing the economic and the social considerations at hand. However, while the new EU IAs introduce a number of guarantees for the protection of social considerations in an investment context, they still fall short of actively promoting them, which is regrettable given the particularly strong position of the EU to do so.

Nonetheless, the new EU investment model established since 2015 is a significant improvement compared to the BIT practice of the Member States, aligning it with the latest trends in North American IAs. Moreover, the EU model introduces innovations of its own, most notably in the form of acknowledging the right of the states and the EU to regulate to protect the public interest even where this negatively affects investment, as well as the introduction of institutionalised ISDS. Nonetheless, the interpretation and application of this new balancing model under the EU IAs remains to be tested and affirmed in the practice of investment courts and arbitral tribunals.

PART III

Legal and Institutional Challenges

13

How Can the Viking/Laval Conundrum Be Resolved? Balancing the Economic and the Social: One Bed for Two Dreams?

Sjoerd Feenstra

13.1 INTRODUCTION

On the eve of the 60th anniversary of the Treaties of Rome, Europe is facing a number of unprecedented existential, constitutional and (democratic and social) legitimacy challenges.[1] The financial crisis became an economic crisis morphing into one in the Eurozone.[2] Grexit and the refugee crisis to which now Brexit can be added. Europe and the European integration process are at a crossroad. The 'European Union is at a defining moment and therefore it is not the time for business as usual.'[3] The alleged lack of sufficient social dimension of the EU as well as the numerous challenges the European Social Model is faced with are at the core of the discussions concerning the necessary reforms of the EU.

I am extremely grateful for the comments and remarks of the participants of the Cambridge-Leuven Euroforum Conference 'Social Policy and the EU: Ways Forward' (September 2015) to whom I presented orally in a round table the main thrust of this contribution. Special thanks to C. Barnard for our regular thought-provoking, lively discussions over the years. Her, Geert De Baere's and Frank Vandenbroucke's comments and suggestions on the first (revised) draft were also very useful. The usual disclaimer applies. All views and opinions expressed are purely personal.

[1] J.H.H. Weiler, 'Europe in Crisis – on "Political Messianism", "Legitimacy" and "The Rule of Law"' (2012) *Singapore Journal of Legal Studies* 248. See also: J. Habermas, *The Crisis of the European Union – A Response* (Polity, 2012); and for an impressive analysis A.J. Menéndez, 'The Existential Crisis of the European Union' (2013) 14 *German Law Journal* 453.
[2] See for an extensive overview: K. Tuori and K. Tuori, *The Eurozone Crisis – A Constitutional Analysis* (Cambridge University Press, 2014); A. Hinarejos, *The Euro Area Crisis in Constitutional Perspective* (Oxford University Press, 2015); and J. Pisani-Ferry, *The Euro Crisis and Its Aftermath* (Oxford University Press, 2014). See also: C. Barnard, 'The Financial Crisis and the Euro Plus Pact: A Labour Lawyer's Perspective' (2012) 41 *Industrial Law Journal* 98.
[3] J.C. Juncker, 'State of the Union Address 2015', speech delivered before the European Parliament, available at: ec.europa.eu/priorities/soteu/docs/state_of_the_union_2015_en.pdf (accessed 20 October 2016).

However, even before the crisis, the different – though inseparable – twins *Viking*[4] and *Laval*[5] (very quickly joined by their progeny *Rüffert*[6] and *Commission v Luxembourg*,[7] becoming the infamous 'Laval quartet') highlighted the potential tension between the economic and social dimension of the EU and became the subject of polemic controversy.

The rulings of the Court were subject to intense academic and public debate, lengthy discussions, unfortunately often dogmatic, as well as wide-ranging criticism.[8] This in itself should not be surprising bearing in mind the politically very sensitive issues at stake, fundamentally of constitutional importance, linked to the legitimacy of the European Union itself.

Therefore, revisiting those 'hot files' of the 'past'[9] may provide very useful insights and background information when addressing the legal and constitutional challenges of embedding the social dimension in the European Union after the Crisis.

In this respect this chapter will only focus on the most important parts of 'the elephant lurking in the European social model',[10] meaning the *Laval*'s regulatory conundrum[11] concerning the implications of the Court's ruling for collective standard-setting with respect to posted workers in the framework of the provision of services (Section 13.3), as well as the *Viking* conundrum which concerns the balancing of economic freedoms and fundamental social rights in the EU (Section 13.4).

Before considering in more detail the distinct, though linked *Laval* and *Viking* conundrum (respectively Sections 13.3 and 13.4), some preliminary remarks will be made with respect to the relationship between the economic and social dimension of the EU (Section 13.2). Having been described as 'a

---

4   ECJ, judgment of 11 December 2007 in *International Transport Workers' Federation and Finnish Seamen's Union* ('*Viking*'), C-438/05, EU:C:2007:772.
5   ECJ, judgment of 18 December 2007 in *Laval un Partneri*, C-341/05, EU:C:2007:809.
6   ECJ, judgment of 3 April 2008 in *Rüffert*, C-346/06,:EU:C:2008:189.
7   ECJ, judgment of 19 June 2008 in *Commission v Luxembourg*, C-319/06, EU:C:2008:350.
8   References to the main contributions can be found in the articles cited. For a more complete list: www.etui.org/Topics/Social-dialogue-collective-bargaining/Social-legislation/The-interpreta-tion-by-the-European-Court-of-Justice/Reaction-to-the-judgements (accessed 20 October 2016). For an overview of the main issues at stake see: C. Barnard, 'Viking and Laval: An Introduction', 10 *Cambridge Yearbook of European Legal Studies* 463.
9   M. Freedland and J. Prassl (eds), *Viking, Laval and Beyond* (Hart, 2014); C. Barnard, 'The Calm after the Storm: Time to Reflect on EU (labour) law scholarship following the decisions in *Viking* and *Laval*' (2015) *Legal Studies Research Paper Series*, 55/15.
10 B. Bercusson, 'The Trade Union Movement and the European Union: Judgment Day' (2007) 13 *European Law Review* 279, p. 305.
11 C. Kilpatrick, 'Laval's Regulatory Conundrum: Collective Standard-setting and the Court's New Approach to Posted Workers' (2009) *European Law Review* 844.

legacy of unresolved tensions,'[12] this might explain the controversy these rulings provoked rather than their substantive influence in the various Member States, apart from Sweden (and Denmark to a far lesser degree) and the United Kingdom (for different reasons though).[13] Section 13.5 will look at the future, drawing some tentative conclusions and indicate possible ways forward to resolve the conundrum (if any).

13.2 THE RELATIONSHIP BETWEEN THE SOCIAL AND ECONOMIC DIMENSION OF ECONOMIC INTEGRATION IN THE EU: LEGACY OF (UNRESOLVED) TENSIONS?

Discussions about the relationship between the economic and social dimension date back to the 1956 Spaak report,[14] when the EEC was launched primarily as a European economic project. Its social component was largely 'neglected', with the exception of the principle of equal pay for equal work for men and women explicitly enshrined in the Treaty and a provision concerning the coordination of social security schemes necessary to provide freedom of movement for workers. This 'initial thinness of social policy provisions within the EU integration project was premised on a consensus that the creation of a common market would not require harmonisation of labour standards or national systems of labour law'.[15] Equalisation of social and labour standards would be the result of, rather than the condition precedent to the market integration project. The near absence of specific social provisions in the original EEC Treaty clearly reflected an ordoliberal vision of the primarily economic rationality of the European project in which social policies were considered a categorically distinct subject left to Member States, and the competences between the Community and its Member States in that respect fundamentally different. While at the supranational level the former would implement the economic objectives of the law-based order guaranteeing economic freedoms and a system of undistorted competition, social matters remained in

---

[12] C. Joerges and F. Rödl, 'Informal Politics, Formalised Law and the "Social Deficit" of European Integration: Reflections after the Judgments of the ECJ in Viking and Laval' (2009) 15 *European Law Journal* 1 (emphasis added).

[13] See Freedland and Prassl, n. 9 in this chapter.

[14] Comité Intergouvernemental Créé par la Conférence de Messine, *Rapport des Chefs de Délégation aux Ministres des Affaires Etrangères* (Comité Intergouvernemental Créé par la Conférence de Messine, 1956), pp. 60–6.

[15] D. Ashiagbor, 'Unravelling the Embedded Liberal Bargain: Labour and Social Welfare Law in the Context of EU Market integration' (2013) 19 *European Law Journal* 303, p. 307. See also P. Syrpis, 'Should the EU Be Attempting to Harmonise National Systems of Labour Law?' (2010) *European Business Law Review* 143.

principle at the national level and redistributive (social) policies exclusively in the remit of the latter. Thus, economic integration could (and should) be decoupled from the welfare state and its redistributive (social) policies.[16]

What happened subsequently is well known.[17] While the process of economic integration continued through law and politics, the attempts to promote economic integration systematically challenged the different varieties of national capitalism.[18]

The increasing economic integration led to numerous actions and legislative initiatives at EU level, including in the area of employment and social policy, thus helping to develop and promote social matters at EU level. Subsequent Treaty changes extended the EU's competences concerning social policy matters[19] and increased the importance of social objectives considerably (they have even been formally recognised as being as important as economic objectives[20]).

However, due to one of the best-known dichotomies of European integration, the distinction between negative and positive integration, increased economic integration has not been (at least not totally) compensated for by the development of social policies at EU level. As such this is not surprising: it

---

[16] Ordoliberalism was developed by (political) economists and legal scholars in Germany between 1930 and 1950. It had a major influence on the development of the social market economy model in post-war West Germany. As a doctrine, its concept and vision equally played an important role in the theoretical discussions on the economic integration process in Europe and in the context of the development of the economic and monetary union pre-Maastricht Treaty as well as the European Constitution subsequently, particularly with respect to the legitimization and orientation of Europe's integration process. See for its role, importance and influence also: C. Joerges, 'The Market without the State? The "Economic Constitution" of the European Community and the Rebirth of Regulatory Politics' (1997) *European Integration Online Papers*, 19; C. Joerges and F. Rödl, ' "Social Market Economy" as Europe's Social Model?' (2004) *EUI Working Paper Law*, 8/04; C. Joerges, 'What is Left of the European Economic Constitution?' (2004) *EUI Working Paper Law*, 13/04; Joerges and Rödl, n. 12 in this chapter; K. Tuori, 'The European Financial Crisis – Constitutional Aspects and Implications' (2012) *EUI Working Paper Law* 28/12; G. Dale and N. El-Enany, 'The Limits of Social Europe: EU Law and the Ordoliberal Agenda' (2013) 14 *German Law Journal* 613.

[17] Ashiagbor, n. 15 in this chapter.

[18] J. Snell, 'Varieties of Capitalism and the Limits of European Economic Integration' (2011) 13 *Cambridge Yearbook of European Legal Studies* 415.

[19] However, despite the fact that competences of the EU in social policy matters may have been addressed more systematically in the Treaties over time, by becoming more and more precise and/or including specific provisions for certain matters, subsequent Treaty changes may have put limitations on their effective exercise in practice.

[20] Conclusions Paris summit meeting of the Heads of State and Government of the Member States April 1972; ECJ, judgment of 8 April 1976 in *Defrenne*, 43/75, EU:C:1976:56, paragraph 10; see ECJ, *Viking*, n. 4 in this chapter, paragraph 79; and ECJ, *Laval un Partneri*, n. 5 in this chapter, paragraph 105; both referring to the fact that the Union has 'not only an economic but also a social purpose'.

is easier to promote integration by reducing state legislation interfering with economic activities (negative integration) than by creating common standards and regulatory frameworks for economic agents (positive integration).[21]

More importantly, over the years more and more national social standards and welfare systems were challenged due to the broad scope and functional interpretation given to market integration rules. The judicial 'activism' of the Court of Justice.[22] also generated spill over effects[23] in terms of adding legal constraints limiting the scope for possible regulatory action at national level, resulting in deregulatory pressures. The Court became more and more perceived as being part of the social legitimacy problem of the European integration process itself and not only as part of the solution.[24]

These developments had a 'negative' impact on the further construction of the social dimension of the European integration project, resulting in what is referred to as the fundamental 'constitutional asymmetry' of EU integration between policies promoting market efficiencies and those promoting social protection and equality[25] or the European 'social deficit'.[26]

Despite efforts to strengthen the social dimension of the internal market, the impossibility of counterbalancing the (from a national regulatory point of view not always positively perceived) effects of negative integration with positive integration measures at the same speed became more than clear. In addition, the increasing infiltration of the social domain by economic rules and values[27] resulted in 'competitive deregulation'[28] or (defensive) 'regulatory

---

[21] M. Poiares Maduro, 'Striking the Elusive Balance between Economic Freedom and Social Rights in the EU', in P. Alston, M. Bustelo, and J. Heenan (eds), *The EU and Human Rights* (Oxford University Press, 1999), p. 464. See also F. Scharpf, 'Balancing Positive and Negative Integration: The Regulatory Options for Europe' (1997) *MPIfG Working Paper*, 97/8.

[22] See for an overview M. Poiares Maduro, *We The Court – the European Court of Justice and the European Economic Constitution* (Bloomsbury, 1998); and N. Shuibhne, *The Coherence of EU Free Movement Law – Constitutional Responsibility and the Court of Justice* (Oxford University Press, 2014).

[23] However, principles of collective labour law did also "spill over" into EC law, see B. Bercusson, 'Trade Union Rights in the EU Member States' (1997) *Social Affairs Series*, 12.

[24] J.H.H. Weiler, 'The Political and Legal Culture of European Integration: An Exploratory Essay' (2011) 9 *International Journal of Constitutional Law* 678, p. 688.

[25] F. Scharpf, 'The Asymmetry of European Integration, or Why the EU Cannot Be a 'Social Market Economy' (2010) 8 *Socio-Economic Review* 211; as well as F. Scharpf, 'The European Social Model: Coping with the Challenges of Diversity' (2002) 40 *Journal of Common Market Studies* 645.

[26] Ibid.; F. de Witte, 'EU Law, Politics, and the Social Question' (2013) 14 *German Law Journal* 581, p. 588.

[27] S. Klosse, 'Balancing Europe's economic and social objectives: fighting a losing battle' (2012) July-August, *European Journal of Social Law*, 176.

[28] Scharpf, n. 25 in this chapter.

competition',[29] meaning a 'race to the bottom', between national social systems.

Therefore, despite their interdependence, the relation between the economic and social dimension of the European integration process constitutes more a legacy of unresolved tensions than a happy marriage.

While the internal market integration may have also promoted the development of European social policies and social rights, the advances made with respect to the social dimension have been more limited than in the case of the economic freedoms. Moreover, the further development of social policies and rights often appears to be 'prisoner' of the objectives of the economic integration process. As a result, European economic integration generated deregulatory pressures and challenged social standards. Therefore, 'the social rights deficit vis-à-vis economic freedoms in European integration is more a story of what has not been than what has been'.[30]

Bearing in mind that the relationship between the internal market and social policy has not been an easy one.[31] it is understandable that the landmark decisions in *Viking* and *Laval* (to which I will turn in a moment) came to symbolise the insoluble antagonism between social and labour rights and the internal market.[32]

As the Monti report[33] puts it, these decisions 'revived an old split that never had been healed: the divide between advocates of greater market integration and those who feel that the call for economic freedoms and for breaking up regulatory barriers is an alibi for dismantling social rights protected at national

[29] S. Deakin, 'Regulatory Competition after Laval' (2008) 10 *Cambridge Yearbook of European Legal Studies* 518; S. Giubboni, 'Social Rights and Market Freedom in the European Constitution: A Re-appraisal' (2010) *European Labour Law Journal* 161. See also S. Deakin, 'Legal Diversity and Regulatory Competition: Which Model for Europe?' (2008) 12 *European Law Review* 440; C. Barnard and S. Deakin, 'Market Access and Regulatory Competition' (2001) *Jean Monnet Working paper*, 9/01; and A. Saydé, 'One Law, Two Competitions: An Enquiry into the Contradictions of Free Movement Law' (2011) 13 *Cambridge Yearbook of European Legal Studies* 365, stressing equally that negative integration without 'positive integration' – *even if intended to promote regulatory neutrality* (that is, creating a level playing field among private parties) – inevitably leads to more intense forms of regulatory competition within the internal market, p. 377 (emphasis added).

[30] Poiares Maduro, n. 21 in this chapter, at p. 464.

[31] M. de Vos (ed.), *European Union Internal Market and Labour Law: Friends or Foes?* (Intersentia, 2009).

[32] DG for Internal Policies, 'EU Social and Labour Rights and EU Internal Market: study for the EMPL Committee' (2015), p. 94, available at: www.europarl.europa.eu/RegData/etudes/STUD/2015/563457/IPOL_STU(2015)563457_EN.pdf (accessed 21 October 2016).

[33] M. Monti, 'A New Strategy for the Single Market: At the Service of Europe's Economy and Society – Report to the President of the European Commission' (2010), pp. 68–9, available at: ec.europa.eu/internal_market/strategy/docs/monti_report_final_10_05_2010_en.pdf (accessed 21 October 2016).

level'. It also stressed that the Court's cases have exposed the 'fault lines' that run between the single market and the social dimension at national level in two ways, bringing to the surface:

- the strains to which the regulatory framework for posting of workers is subject in a context of divergent social and employment conditions and perceived risks of social dumping and unfair competition;
- the extended reach of EU law to collective labour disputes, bringing social partners and collective action straight into the heart of the economic constitution of the single market.

It is on those two points that the remainder of this chapter will focus.

13.3 LAVAL'S REGULATORY CONUNDRUM: COLLECTIVE STANDARD-SETTING IMPLICATIONS FOR POSTED WORKERS' BY HOST STATES – REGULATORY COMPETITION IN EUROPE?

13.3.1 *Scene Setter: The Regulatory Framework of the Posting of Workers Directive*

Posting of workers in the framework of the provision of services[34,35] is for many a 'nightmare file'; highly contested (even before its adoption), technically complex, politically very sensitive, and surrounded by myths and negative connotations, such as 'social dumping' or a 'race towards the bottom' as far as working conditions are concerned.

This may be explained by the fact that labour mobility, not taking place in the context of the free movement of workers but in the form of posting of workers in the framework of the freedom to provide services in another Member State temporarily,[36] raises different, legally complex questions relating to

---

[34] Directive 96/71/EC of 16 December 1996 concerning the posting of workers in the framework of the provision of services, [1997] OJ L 18/1.

[35] P. Davies, 'Posted Workers: Single Market or Protection of National Labour Law Systems?' (1997) 34 *Common Market Law Review* 571. See for a more extensive overview: PhD thesis M.S. Houwerzijl, 'De Detacheringsrichtlijn – Over de achtergrond, inhoud en implementatie van Richtlijn 96/71/EC' (2005) *Europese Monografieën* (Kluwer, 2005); S. Feenstra, 'Detachering van werknemers in het kader van het verrichten van diensten – Het arbeidsrechtelijke kader – Richtlijn 96/71/EC', in Y. Jorens (ed.), *Handboek Europese detachering en vrij verkeer van diensten* (Die Keure, 2009).

[36] See for the objectively different situation of the two and its legal implications also recitals 1 to 3 of Directive 2014/67/EU of 15 May 2014 on the enforcement of Directive 96/71/EC concerning the posting of workers in the framework of the provision of services and amending Regulation (EU) No 1024/2012 on administrative cooperation through the Internal Market Information System, [2014] L 159/11.

politically and socially highly sensitive matters: Trojan horses threatening to undermine the territorial application of labour and social security law,[37] provoking dilemmas of protection or protectionism,[38] or (worse) protection proclaimed but protectionism clearly aimed at?[39]

From a regulatory perspective, the starting (or turning)[40] point is the *obiter dictum* in the *Rush Portuguesa* case,[41] which acquired nearly mythical status:

> [I]n response to the concern expressed in this connection by the French Government, that Community law does not preclude Member States from extending their legislation, or collective labour agreements entered into by both sides of industry, to any person who is employed, even temporarily, within their territory, no matter in which country the employer is established; nor does Community law prohibit Member States from enforcing those rules by appropriate means.[42]

Thus, broadening considerably a similar statement referring only to minimum wages in a previous judgment.[43]

Subsequent (re-)regulatory initiatives at national level in several Member States[44] which, in turn, risked provoking an unacceptable degree of regulatory

---

[37] H. Verschueren, 'Cross-border Workers in the European Internal Market: Trojan Horses for Member States' Labour and Social Security Law?' (2008) *International Journal Comparative Labour Law and Industrial Relations* 167.

[38] N. Countouris and S. Engblom, 'Protection or Protectionism – A Legal Deconstruction of the Emerging False Dilemma in European Integration' (2015) *LRI Working Paper*, 1/15; See M. Biagi, 'The "Posted Workers" EU Directive: From Social Dumping to Social Protectionism' (1998) *Bulletin of Comparative Labour Relations* 173.

[39] See R. Giesen, 'Posting: Social Protection of Workers vs. Fundamental Freedoms?' (2003) 40 *Common Market Law Review* 143, for an interesting overview of the case law prior to *Laval* which would show that social protection of workers and the fundamental freedoms are basically not contradictory and that the judges are seriously concerned with ensuring social protection, without overlooking the fact that this argument was partly used only as an excuse to protect local markets.

[40] See COM(75)653 *Amended Proposal for a Regulation of the Council on the Provisions of Conflict of Laws on Employment Relationships within the Community* (Brussels, 28 April 1976), which, although never adopted, interestingly dealt with the respective subject matter explicitly referring to the free movement of workers (instead of the freedom to provide services subsequently used to regulate this specific form of labour mobility further).

[41] Concerning the legality of an administrative fine imposed for not having the necessary work permits in France for the Portuguese workers of a Portuguese company carrying out works on several TGV sites in France.

[42] ECJ, judgment of 27 March 1990 in *Rush Portuguesa*, C-113/89, EU:C:1990:142, paragraph 18.

[43] ECJ, judgment of 3 February 1982 in *Seco v EVI*, C-62/81 and C-63/81, EU:C:1982:34, point 15.

[44] See for an interesting overview of the respective developments: W. Eichhorst, 'European Social Policy between National and Supranational Regulation: Posted Workers in the Framework of Liberalized Services Provision' (1998) *MPIfG Discussion Paper*, 98/6; G. Menz, *Varieties of Capitalism and Europeanization – National Response Strategies to the Single European Market* (Oxford University Press, 2005); Houwerzijl, n. 35 in this chapter, at pp. 75–6; and

competition and uncertainty, provided the necessary political grounds for the adoption of Directive 96/71/EC. The Directive 'enacted in order to prevent wage-cost competition':[45]

> [A]ims to reconcile the exercise of the freedom to provide cross border services enshrined in the Treaty, on the one hand, with the appropriate protection of the rights of workers temporarily posted abroad to provide them, on the other. In order to do that it identifies the mandatory rules of general interest at Community level that must be applied to posted workers in the host country.[46]

Thus, the Directive establishes a hard core of 'clearly defined terms and conditions of work and employment for minimum protection of workers that must be complied with by the service provider in the host country'.[47]

Providing a significant level of protection for posted workers, 'the Directive also plays a key role in promoting the necessary climate of fair competition between all service providers (including those from other Member States) by guaranteeing a *level playing field*, as well as legal certainty for service providers, service recipients, and workers posted within the context of the provision of services'.[48]

Where those terms and conditions of employment are laid down by law, regulation or administrative provisions, Member States must apply them to workers temporarily posted to their territory in the context of the provision of services. Member States must equally apply them to posted workers *if* they are laid down by collective agreements or arbitration awards that have been declared universally applicable within the meaning of Article 3(8), *insofar as* they concern the activities referred to in the Annex to the Directive (building work). With regard to other activities, Member States are left the choice of imposing terms and conditions of employment laid down by such collective agreements or arbitration awards (Article 3(10),

---

S. Evju, 'Safeguarding National Interests – Norwegian Responses to Free Movement of Services, Posting of Workers and the Services Directive', in S. Evju (ed.), *Cross-Border Services, Posting of Workers, and Multilevel Governance* (University of Oslo, 2013). See further: S. Evju 'Regulating Transnational Labour in Europe: The Quandries of Multilevel Governance', in S. Evju (ed.), *Cross-Border Services, Posting of Workers, and Multilevel Governance* (University of Oslo, 2013).

[45] Joerges and Rödl, n. 12 in this chapter, at p. 17.
[46] Which include the most important terms and conditions of employment, such as working time, minimum rates of pay, minimum paid annual holidays.
[47] See COM(2012)131 *Explanatory Memorandum of the Proposal for an Enforcement Directive 96/71/EC Concerning the Posting of Workers in the Framework of the Provision of Services* (Brussels, 21 March 2012), p. 2.
[48] Ibid. (emphasis added).

second indent). They may also, in compliance with the Treaty, impose terms and conditions of employment in matters other than those referred to in the Directive in the case of public policy provisions (Article 3(10), first indent).[49]

The Directive's double objective (promoting freedom to provide services while also protecting workers) may already have constituted a 'mission impossible'.

Before turning to the *Laval* case itself, it is important to underline that Directive 96/71/EC itself contains different regulatory layers. It does impose a mandatory level of protection for construction sector activities with respect to terms and conditions as laid down in universally applicable collective agreements *but* at the same time leaves considerable regulatory margin to the Member States on, for example:

- the material content of the mandatory rules (that is, terms and conditions of employment) to be respected;
- the definition of a worker (left to the host Member State);
- the concept and constituent elements of the important notion of 'minimum rates of pay' (to be defined by national law and/or practice);
- the setting or introduction of minimum wages;
- specific derogations[50] with respect to certain terms and conditions (that is, paid annual holidays and/or minimum rates of pay), which are provided for and may be used;
- equal treatment of temporary agency workers and 'local' workers, which may be provided;[51]
- the mandatory level of protection resulting from the relevant universally applicable collective agreements, which may be extended to other sectors/activities than the building/construction;[52]
- matters concerning public policy provisions.[53]

---

[49] Ibid., p. 3 (emphasis added). Idem COM(2007)304 *Posting of Workers in the Framework of the Provision of Services – Maximising Its Benefits and Potential while Guaranteeing the Protection of Workers* (Brussels, 30 August 2008), p. 2.

[50] See Directive 96/71/EC, n. 34 in this chapter, Article 3 paragraph 2 (concerning initial assembly and/or first installation of goods not exceeding 8 days), paragraph 3 and 4 (if length of posting not exceeding one month) as well as paragraph 5 (if amount of work to be done is not significant).

[51] Ibid., Article 3 paragraph 9.

[52] Ibid., Article 3 paragraph 10, 2nd indent.

[53] Ibid, Article 3 paragraph 10, 1st indent.

In addition, ensuring the correct application and monitoring of compliance with, as well as enforcement of, the applicable rules[54] is in principal also left to the Member States.

13.3.2 *Laval: Collective Standard-setting in EU Perspective*

At the origin of the case is the very specific and particular situation in Sweden where most terms and conditions of employment referred to in Directive 96/71/EC are laid down in national legislation, with the exception of the minimum rates of pay which are not laid down by law but left to the social partners to regulate via negotiation on a case by case basis (and may be enforced by means of collective action, including the right to strike[55]). It is this fundamental feature of the Swedish model, and in particular its compatibility with prevailing EU law in cross-border situations, which employers decided to litigate on and which ended up before the Court of Justice. A further complicating factor resulted from the fact that the Swedish building sector collective agreement to which the Latvian service provider was requested to sign up to, contained other matters not specifically referred to in the nucleus of mandatory rules of the Directive,[56] such as pecuniary contributions for the pay review,[57] and a 'special building supplement' and a number of insurance premiums.[58]

In its ruling, the Court focussed extensively on the specificities and complexity of the Swedish regulatory framework. However, this could not prohibit the rather devastating conclusion that: the Treaty and Article 3 of the Posting Directive precluded trade unions:

> [I]n a Member State in which the terms and conditions of employment covering the matters referred to in Article 3(1), first subparagraph, (a) to (g) of that directive are contained in legislative provisions, save for minimum rates of pay, from attempting, by means of collective action in the form of a blockade ('blockad') of sites such as that at issue in the main proceedings, to force a provider of services established in another Member State to enter into negotiations with it on the rates of pay for posted workers and to sign a collective agreement the terms of which lay down, as regards some of those matters, more favourable

---

[54] See for an interesting in-depth overview of the different practices and traditions in Germany, the Netherlands and Sweden: M. Kullmann, 'Enforcement of Labour Law in Cross-Border Situations' (2015) 14 *Series Law of Business and Finance*.

[55] Collective actions being at the core of the *Viking* dispute (see Section 13.4) will not be the focus here as far as the respective part of the judgment in the *Laval* case is concerned.

[56] Directive 96/71/EC, n. 34 in this chapter, Article 3 (1) 1st subparagraph (a) to (g).

[57] See with respect to similar wage monitoring contributions: ECtHR, judgment of 13 February 2007 in *Evaldsson and Others v Sweden*, 75252/01.

[58] ECJ, *Laval un Partneri*, n. 5 in this chapter, paragraph 83.

conditions than those resulting from the relevant legislative provisions, while other terms relate to matters not referred to in Article 3 of the directive.[59]

Possible explanations for this rather harsh judgment can be found in the fact that the 'national context was characterised by a lack of provisions, of any kind, which are sufficiently precise and accessible that they do not render it impossible or excessively difficult in practice'[60] to determine the obligations which the service provider is required to comply with. Social policy goals being used as a pretext for protectionism,[61] and the potentially cloaked protectionist nature of the measures involved, has also been offered as a possible explanation.[62]

Nevertheless, the first reactions[63] gave a flavour of the harsh criticism that followed: the Court's 'new' approach to posted workers[64] exhaustively and restrictively interpreting the Posting Directive would have turned the minimum floor of rights under the Posting Directive into a ceiling[65] with devastating

[59] Ibid., paragraph 121 under 1
[60] Ibid., paragraph 110 as well as 71 which refers to the necessity to negotiate on a case-by-case basis.
[61] C. Semmelmann, 'The European Union's Economic Constitution under the Lisbon Treaty: Soul-searching among Lawyers Shifts to Focus to Procedure' (2010) 35 *European Law Review* 516, p. 536. See for another interesting example of alleged protectionism: ECJ, judgment of 18 September 2014 in *Bundesdruckerei*, C-549/13, EU:C:2014:2235, requiring tenderers and their subcontractors to respect national legislation imposing minimum hourly wage even if activities are performed in another Member State.
[62] K. Lenaerts and J.A. Gutiérrez-Fons, 'The Constitutional Allocation of Powers and General Principles of Law' (2010) *Common Market Law Review* 1629, p. 1666. According to their analysis, in *Viking* and *Laval* trade unions sought protectionist measures by struggling to keep jobs at home and shield their local labour markets. For the same reasons, the ECJ may have felt that granting a margin of appreciation to trade unions in such a broad way as if they were Member States authorities, was inappropriate. See for an alternative explanation of the latter: L. Azoulai, 'The Court of Justice and the Social Market Economy: The Emergence of an Ideal and the Conditions for its Realization' (2008) 45 *Common Market Law Review* 1335, p. 1351. The clear anxiety on the part of the Court over protectionism is also referred to by Ashiagbor, n. 15 in this chapter, p. 316.
[63] See Deakin, n. 29 in this chapter, *Regulatory Competition after Laval*; A. Davies, 'One Step Forward, Two Steps Back? The Viking and Laval Cases in the ECJ' (2008) 37 *Industrial Law Journal* 126; P. Syrpis and T. Novitz, 'Economic and Social Rights in Conflict: Political and Judicial Approaches to Their Reconciliation' (2008) 33 *European Law Review* 411; J. Malmberg and T. Sigeman, 'Industrial Actions and EU Economic Freedoms: The Autonomous Collective Bargaining Model Curtailed by the European Court of Justice' (2008) 45 *Common Market Law Review* 1115.
[64] Kilpatrick, n. 11 in this chapter; C. Kilpatrick, 'British Jobs for British Workers? UK Industrial Action and Free Movement of Services in EU Law' (2009) *LSE Working Paper*, 16/09, pp. 11–14. See also: C. Kilpatrick, 'Internal Market Architecture and the Accommodation of Labour Rights. As Good as It Gets?' (2012) March *European Journal of Social Law* 4, p. 17.
[65] C. Kilpatrick, n.11 in this chapter, at p. 848; Semmelmann, n. 61 in this chapter, at p. 536; slightly more cautious ('could be read') S. Deakin, 'Regulatory Competition in Europe after Laval' (2008) *Centre for Business Research Working paper*, 364; and Syrpis and Novitz, n. 63 in this chapter, p. 416 acknowledging that it may be 'overstating to suggest that Laval turns the floor into a ceiling'.

effects on the role and function of (collective) standard setting mechanisms, collective bargaining and (labour) law in cross-border situations.[66] From saviour of the integration process the Court became its worst enemy overnight, alienating important segments of public opinion from the European project.

Before turning to possible ways to resolve the regulatory conundrum, some criticised elements of the Court's interpretation need to be addressed. First, the allegedly limited interpretation by the Court of Article 3(7) of the Posting Directive (allowing for the application of more favourable conditions),[67] which would not allow host Member States to go beyond the nucleus of mandatory rules, may have come as a shock but is completely in line with the '*travaux préparatoires*' and predicted by some.[68] However, a different interpretation would de facto and de iure have rendered Article 3(10),[69] as well as the possibility of applying equal treatment with respect to temporary agency workers (Article 3(9)), redundant: why would there be a need for these specific derogations if paragraph 7 would already have provided a 'blank cheque'?

Secondly, the Court did *not* give a substantive interpretation of the derogation under Article 3(10) in the *Laval* judgment itself.[70] The potentially devastating (negative) aspects resulted far more from subsequent rulings than *Laval* itself.[71] Indeed in the case *Commission v Luxembourg*[72] the Court gave a restrictive interpretation of the public policy derogation addressed to

---

[66] T. van Peijpe, 'Collective Labour Law after Viking, Laval, Rüffert and Commission v Luxembourg' (2009) 25 *International Journal of Comparative Law* 81.

[67] Directive 96/71/EC, n. 34 in this chapter, paragraphs 79–80.

[68] Davies, n. 35 in this chapter; S. Evju, 'Posting Past and Present – The Posting of Workers Directive – Genesis and Current Contrasts' (2009) *Formula Working Paper*, 8, p. 31; Evju, *Safeguarding National Interests*, n. 44 in this chapter, pp. 242, 257; as well as S. Evju, 'Revisiting the Posted Workers Directive: Conflict of Laws and Laws of Contrast' (2010) 12 *Cambridge Yearbook of European Legal Studies* 151.

[69] M. Franzen and C. Richter, 'Case C-346/06, Rechtsanwalt Dr. Dirk Rüffert, in his capacity as liquidator of *Objekt und Bauregie GmbH & Co. KG v Land Niedersachsen*, [2008] ECR I-1989' (2010) 47 *Common Market Law Review* 537, pp. 549–50.

[70] ECJ, *Laval un Partneri*, n. 5 in this chapter, paragraph 82–4 referring explicitly to the fact that the Swedish national authorities had decided not to have recourse to Article 3(10) (paragraph 84 1st sentence). See in this respect also the COM(2003)458 *on the implementation of Directive 96/71 in the Member States* (Brussels, 25 July 2003), underlining that 'the group of experts which prepared the transposal of the Directive considered that the concept of 'public policy provisions' referred to in Article 3(10) covers provisions concerning fundamental rights and freedoms as laid down by the law of the Member State concerned and/or by international law, such as freedom of association and collective bargaining', p. 14.

[71] S. Evju and T. Novitz, 'The Evolving Regulation: Dynamics and Consequences', in S. Evju (ed.), *Regulating Transnational Labour in Europe: The quanderies of multilevel governance* (University of Oslo, 2014), p. 63

[72] ECJ, *Commission v Luxembourg*, n. 7 in this chapter.

Member States (Article 3(10)). Furthermore, in the *Rüffert case*[73] the Court decided that obligations concerning the rate of pay to be respected, which were laid down in a collective agreement not being declared universally applicable and referred to in legislation applying solely to public procurement contracts and *not* private contracts, could not be imposed pursuant to the Posting of Workers Directive, interpreted in light of Article 56 TFEU.[74] Many saw the alleged 'rigid' interpretation in *Laval* confirmed. In particular, the (artificial) distinction between public and private sector contracting, used as reason to reject the worker protection justification, was heavily criticised.[75] This distinction indeed appears to ignore that sectorial differentiation *as such* is *not* incompatible but totally in line with the (technically complex) regulatory framework of the Posting of Workers Directive itself. The latter only prescribes a mandatory level with respect to construction sector activities, leaving considerable regulatory margin with respect to other sectors to the Member States. Therefore, the clarification of this aspect of the *Rüffert* case provided for by the Court in the *RegioPost* case[76] with respect to a minimum wage laid down in public procurement specific legislation should be more than welcomed.

13.3.3 *The Existential Question: Is There a Laval's Regulatory Conundrum with Respect to Collective Bargaining in Host Member States and If So, How Can It Be Resolved?*

Different elements in *Laval*, as well as subsequent developments, provide an answer to the question whether there is a regulatory conundrum, and if so, how it can be resolved.

At the *national level*, contrary to the criticisms and alarm expressed, *Laval* did not lead to the modification of existing legislation,[77] with the exception of Sweden (and Denmark[78] to a far lesser degree). The Swedish legislation

---

[73] ECJ, *Rüffert*, n. 6 in this chapter.

[74] Ibid., paragraphs 29, 39; ECJ, *Bundesdruckerei*, n. 61 in this chapter. See however also ECJ, judgment of 17 November 2015 in *RegioPost*, C-115/14, EU:C:2015:760, paragraphs 62–5 and 71–7.

[75] Kilpatrick, 'Internal Market Architecture', n. 64 in this chapter, at pp. 18–21.

[76] ECJ, *RegioPost*, n. 74 in this chapter, in particular paragraph 62–5 and 71–7.

[77] See for an overview of the different national responses: A. Bücker and W. Warneck, 'Viking – Laval – Rüffert: Consequences and Policy Perspectives' (2010) *ETUI Report* 111; S. Evju (ed.), *Cross-Border Services, Posting of Workers, and Multilevel Governance* (University of Oslo, 2013); and Freedland and Prassl, n. 9 in this chapter, Part II at pp. 113–276.

[78] See for further information, M. Gräs Lind, 'Danish Law on the Posting of Workers', in S. Evju (ed.), *Cross-Border Services, Posting of Workers, and Multilevel Governance* (University of Oslo, 2013), in particular pp. 97–101 and 131–4.

was modified, but this did not stop the trade unions from continuing their Europeanisation efforts, of what fundamentally should have remained a national issue. They also challenged the compatibility of the modifications to the 'Lex Laval' with international obligations both at International Labour Organisation (ILO) level[79] and in Strasbourg before the European Committee of Social Rights.[80]

The predicted potentially unlimited exposure of trade unions to litigation and threats of significant claims for damages[81] proved largely unfounded, apart from the BALPA case in the UK (where British Airways effectively alleged a breach of Article 49 TFEU if the BA pilots had gone on strike),[82] which, together with the challenges the rulings would provoke with respect to the territorial approach to labour law in the UK[83] and the possibility of subjecting industrial actions to a substantive proportionality test on top of existing statutory procedural requirements in the UK, thus potentially limiting even further the exercise of the right to strike, explains the important role *Laval* and *Viking* subsequently played in the public debate in the United Kingdom.

---

[79] Resulting nearly in a deadlock situation in 2012 with respect to ILO Convention 87 and 98; C. La Hovary, 'Showdown at the ILO? A Historical Perspective on the Employers' Group's 2012 Challenge to the Right to Strike' (2013) 42 *Industrial Law Journal* 1.

[80] ECSR, decision of 3 July 2013 in *LO and TCO v Sweden*, 85/2012; M. Rocca, 'A Clash of Kings – The European Committee of Social Rights on the "Lex Laval" ... and on the EU Framework for the Posting of Workers' (2013) 3 *European Journal of Social Law* 217. See for an overview also: S. Evju, 'The Right to Collective Action under the European Social Charter' (2011) 2 *European Labour Law Journal* 196.

[81] See further L. Hayes, T. Novitz, and H. Reed, 'Applying the Laval Quartet in a UK Context: Chilling, Ripple and Disruptive Effects on Industrial Relations', in A. Bücker and W. Warneck (eds), '*Reconciling Fundamental Social Rights and Economic Freedoms after Viking, Laval and Rüffert*' (Nomos, 2011), pp. 195–244; and K. Apps, 'Damages Claims against Trade Unions after Viking and Laval' (2009) 34 *European Law Review* 141; See also S. Guadagno, 'The Right to Strike in Europe in the Aftermath of Viking and Laval' (2012) *European Journal of Social Law* 241.

[82] See further K. Ewing, *Fighting Back: Resisting 'Union Busting' and 'Strike Breaking' in the BA Dispute* (IER, 2011); K.D. Ewing and J. Hendy QC, 'The Dramatic Implications of Demir and Baykara' (2010) 39 *Industrial Law Journal* 2, pp. 44–7; and Barnard, n. 9 in this chapter, at p. 12. See also: Kilpatrick, n. 64 in this chapter; C. Barnard, ' "British Jobs for British Workers": The Lindsey Oil Refinery Dispute and the Future of Local Labour Clauses in an Integrated EU Market' (2009) 38 *Industrial Law Journal* 245; and C. Kilpatrick, 'Has Polycentric Strike Law Arrived in the UK? After Laval, After Viking, After Demir?' (2014) 30 *International Journal of Comparative Labour Law and Industrial Relations* 293. For a critical review of the court decisions in the UK: N. Countouris and M. Friedland, 'Injunctions, Cyanamid, and the Corrosion of the Right to Strike in the UK' (2010) 1 *European Labour Law Journal* 489.

[83] Applying all national labour laws to all those working in its territory (that is, including posted workers). See C. Barnard, "The UK and the Posted Workers: The Effect of Commission v Luxembourg on the Territorial Application of British Labour Law' (2009) 38 *Industrial Law Journal* 122.

In Norway, the *Laval* (and *Viking*) ruling had no immediate impact, but the Laval quartet as such did fuel discussions on the Norwegian membership of the European Economic Area (EEA).[84] In addition, the question whether various provisions on rates of pay and specific allowances laid down in a nationwide collective agreement in Norway was compatible with the Posting of Workers Directive and the EEA Agreement (Article 36) ended up in the EFTA Court[85] but the effect of the EFTA Court's ruling was considerably 'watered down' subsequently in the Norwegian Supreme Court's controversial final decision.[86]

At the *European level*, there has been only one further case, *Fonnship*,[87] which facts predated *Laval*. More importantly, after tense and lengthy negotiations within and between the Council and the European Parliament, an enforcement Directive of the Posting of Workers Directive was adopted.[88] It contains a comprehensive and delicately balanced package of measures to improve considerably the protection of posted workers and prevent circumvention and abuse of the rules applicable (including for situations which do not qualify as genuine posting in the context of the temporary provision of services). It also provides a more transparent and predictable legal framework for service providers helping to ensure a level playing field contributing to fairer competition and facilitating (further) cross-border provision of services.[89] In particular, with respect to collective standard setting, the important role of social partners is reiterated,[90] including the possibility of determining the different levels of the applicable minimum rates of pay, alternatively or simultaneously.

The Directive gives a clear signal: Europe does not accept fraud and abuse of the applicable rules at the expense of (posted) workers and circumvention of applicable rules should be tackled. To achieve this, it provides for a number of tools to fight social dumping effectively, which should improve and reinforce implementation, application and enforcement in practice of the Posting of Workers Directive. Thus it further diminishes possible regulatory

---

[84] S. Evju, 'The "Norwegian Model" in Broad Outline', in M. Freedland and J. Prassl (eds), *Viking, Laval and Beyond* (Hart, 2014).

[85] EFTA Court, judgment of 23 January 2012 in *STX Norway and Others*, E-2/11.

[86] C. Barnard, 'Posting Matters' (2014) 11 *Arbeitsrett* 1.

[87] ECJ, judgment of 8 July 2014 in *Fonnship A/S*, C-83/13, EU:C:2014:2053.

[88] Directive 2014/67/EU, n. 36 in this chapter. See also for the original proposal COM(2012)131, n. 47 in this chapter.

[89] See for an overview: A. Defossez, 'La directive 2014/67/UE relative à l'exécution de la directive 96/71/CE concernant le détachement de travailleurs: un premier pas dans une bonne direction' (2014) 4 *Revue Trimistielle de Droit Européen* 833.

[90] See Directive 2014/67/EU, n. 36 in this chapter, Article 5 (4) and recital 15.

competition between Member States while ensuring a level playing field capable of dealing with the new socioeconomic diversity, following the 2004 and 2007 enlargements.

Moreover, and even more importantly for those who so harshly criticised the Court, the Court of Justice itself in *Sähköalojen ammattiliitto*[91] clarified that a number of elements of pay, such as a calculation of minimum wage for hourly work and/or piecework according to pay groups, holiday pay, a daily allowance and compensation for daily travelling time, which were laid down in a universally applicable collective agreement, could be applied to posted workers.

With respect to special contract performance conditions requiring specific minimum hourly wages to be respected in the context of public procurement, the Court in *RegioPost*[92] 'deviated' from its previous position in *Rüffert*. It stated that such a requirement was justified by the objective of workers' protection and that the mere fact that it only applied in the context of public contracts did not call this conclusion into question.[93]

13.3.4 Interim Conclusion

In summary, looking back, the *Laval* regulatory conundrum is far smaller than some have argued, if it exists at all.

Opponents of *Laval* focused in particular on the alleged negative impacts for the protection of workers.[94] Most ignored the very specific and particular national context and/or the technically complex regulatory framework of Directive 96/71 with its different layers, thus exaggerating considerably the potential consequences of the Court's ruling. More importantly, their criticism often appeared to have been prejudiced by a more fundamental contestation of the very phenomenon of posting of workers in the framework of the temporary provision of services.

The relationship between the Posting of Workers Directive and Article 56 TFEU may not have been that clear for all and/or still provide considerable food for thought and/or further discussion.[95] However, using the Court's ruling in *Laval* in this dogmatic politicised discussion fundamentally contesting

---

[91] ECJ, judgment of 12 February 2015 in *Sähköalojen ammattiliitto*, C-396/13, EU:C:2015:86.
[92] ECJ, *RegioPost*, n. 74 in this chapter.
[93] See ibid., in particular paragraphs 62–5 and 71–7.
[94] See for a fundamentally different approach and opposite criticism: N. Reich, 'Free Movement v. Social Rights in an Enlarged Union – the Laval and Viking Cases before the ECJ' (2008) 9 *German Law Journal* 125; and D. Kukovec, 'Whose Social Europe? The Viking and Laval Judgments and the Prosperity Gap' *IGLP Working paper Series*, 3/11.
[95] See further Barnard, n. 86 in this chapter.

the phenomenon of posting in the framework of the provision of cross-border services as such, or considering that such posted workers should benefit from equal treatment in comparison to national workers (instead of 'only' the nucleus of mandatory rules of protection provided for by the Directive), would be incorrect. It is an example of shooting the messenger, not the message.

There is, however, one matter that gives pause for concern. Considering the combined effect of the *Viking* and *Laval* cases, trade unions do appear to get the worst of both worlds: Articles 49 and 56 TFEU are directly applicable to them but, unlike Member States, they cannot avail themselves of the public policy derogation for Member States in Article 3(10) of Directive 96/71/EC.[96] This may be due to the rather strict and literal interpretation by the Court of that provision addressed explicitly to Member States, thus limiting it to national public authorities. Or, as others have argued, it could be explained by the alleged protectionist tenor of the measures and social policy objectives pursued by trade unions which sought to shield their local labour markets, keep their members' jobs at home and insufficiently took into consideration the interests of other workers. This would have led the Court to the conclusion that granting a margin of appreciation to trade unions in such a broad way as if they were Member States' authorities, would be inappropriate.[97] Whatever the view taken,[98] the approach of the Court imposing on trade unions the same limits the Court imposes on Member States authorities while refusing to entrust trade unions with the task of determining the nature of the public social order[99] and leave them a certain margin of appreciation when pursuing (public) social policy objectives appears at odds with the different regulatory instruments (including the implementation of Directives by social partners) used in Member States to attain public policy objectives.[100] In addition, the combined effect remains all the more striking, bearing in mind that in other cases concerning labour and anti-discrimination law the Court has acknowledged that the right to collective standard-setting does require a certain margin of appreciation ('broad discretion') in defining social objectives and

[96] ECJ, *Laval un Partneri*, n. 5 in this chapter, paragraphs 84, 98; and *Viking*, n. 4 in this chapter, paragraphs 56–66.
[97] K. Lenaerts and J.A. Gutiérrez-Fons, n. 62 in this chapter, p. 1666.
[98] See for a more nuanced approach Syrpis and Novitz, n. 63 in this chapter, arguing that it may be appropriate to apply the free movement provisions only to private parties, including trade unions, when they are exercising regulatory tasks which would otherwise be exercised by public authorities but not if that's not the case.
[99] Azoulai, n. 62 in this chapter, at p. 1351.
[100] S.A. de Vries, 'The Protection of Fundamental Rights within Europe's Internal Market after Lisbon – An Endeavour for More Harmony', in S.A. de Vries, U. Bernitz, and S. Weatherill (eds), *The Protection of Fundamental Rights in the EU after Lisbon* (Hart, 2013), pp. 91–2.

balancing different interests and may not be subject to full judicial review.[101] Having dealt with the *Laval* regulatory conundrum, it's now time to turn the *Viking* case.

13.4 RECONCILING ECONOMIC FREEDOMS AND FUNDAMENTAL SOCIAL RIGHTS, THE VIKING CONUNDRUM

13.4.1 *Introduction and Scene Setter*

The way in which fundamental rights are balanced with internal market freedoms raises complex questions of law and principle.[102] Some consider the need to engage in such a delicate, complex balancing exercise as a logical consequence of the 'constitutional coming-of-age' of fundamental rights protection within the EU.[103] Others wonder whether this is not fighting a losing battle, though stressing the crucial need for appropriate legal and political responses to rebalance the Union's social and economic dimension.[104]

Therefore, it should be no surprise that, while many critics of the judgment(s) welcomed the recognition of the right to take collective action, including the right to strike, 'as a fundamental right which forms an integral part of the general principles of Community law the observance of which the Court ensures',[105] they were more than concerned about the balance struck between the economic freedoms and fundamental social rights, as well as the method applied by ECJ, in particular in *Viking* (where the exercise of the right to strike was more strictly scrutinised than in *Laval*). The mere necessity to reconcile the exercise of the right to strike with economic freedoms was equally questioned.

---

[101] See further: C. Schubert, 'Collective Agreements within the Limits of Europe – Collective Autonomy as Part of the European Economic System' (2013) 4 *European Labour Law Journal* 146, in particular the examples concerning anti-discrimination law (the ban on age discrimination) indicated on pp. 166–7. See for the Court's control of the exercise of the right to collective bargaining also: M. Schmitt, 'Evaluation of EU Responses to the Crisis with Reference to Primary Legislation (European Union Treaties and Charter of Fundamental Rights)', in N. Bruun, K. Lörcher, and I. Schönmann (eds), *The Economic Crisis and Collective Labour Law in Europe* (Bloomsbury, 2014).

[102] J. Morijn, 'Balancing Fundamental Rights and Common Market Freedoms in Union Law: Schmidberger and Omega in the Light of the European Constitution' (2006) 12 *European Law Journal* 15.

[103] S.A. de Vries, 'Balancing Fundamental Rights with Economic Freedoms According to the European Court of Justice' (2013) 9 *Utrecht Law Review* 169.

[104] Klosse, n. 27 in this chapter.

[105] ECJ, *Viking*, n. 4 in this chapter, paragraph 44; and *Laval un Partneri*, n. 5 in this chapter, paragraph 91.

Some argued that the recognition of the right to take collective action, including the right to strike, as a fundamental right was of 'little more than rhetorical value'.[106] Others considered that the true essence of balancing would require a symmetrical reconciliation and pragmatic compromise which was allegedly denied by the Court by the absolute primacy reserved to economic freedoms vis-à-vis the right to take collective action. Therefore, 'the explicit acknowledgement of the right to strike as a fundamental social right revealed instrumental to its radical compression and effective sterilisation in the 'balancing exercise' with the conflicting economic freedoms', thus 'largely and effectively 'anaesthetised' on the basis of a fictitious and only 'rhetorical' balancing act'.[107]

The wide-ranging criticism and controversy accordingly focussed on the following arguments/points of the ruling:

- the fact that the exercise of the right to take collective action, including the right to strike, did not as such fall outside the scope of EU law;[108]
- the direct effect of primary law in 'conflicts' between private parties, through the horizontal application of Article 49 TFEU with respect to collective actions of 'private bodies/associations', meaning trade unions;[109]
- the denial of the (alleged) primacy of social rights over economic freedoms;
- the mere need to strike a balance in case of conflicts;[110]
- the lack of recognition of a (wide/broader) margin of appreciation for the Member States and/or social partners in view of the objectives pursued;

---

[106] C. Barnard, 'Employment Rights, Free Movement under the EC Treaty and the Services Directive' (2008) *Mitchell Working Papers*, 2/08, p.14. See for a more positive appreciation stressing the possibility that the recognition as such could well develop its own dynamics: S. Prechal and S.A. de Vries,'Viking/Laval en de grondslagen van het internetmarktrecht' (2008) 11 SEW *Tijdschrift voor Europees en Economisch Recht* 425, p. 433. In that respect, they refer to the developments in the area of gender equality and non-discrimination on grounds of nationality where the principle of equal treatment and non-discrimination has been transformed into a human rights standard. See S. Prechal, 'Equality of Treatment, Non-discrimination and Social Policy: Achievements in Three Themes' (2004) 41 *Common Market Law Review* 533.

[107] S. Giubboni, 'Social Europe after the Lisbon Treaty. Some Sceptical Remarks' (2011) *European Journal of Social Law* 244, pp. 248–9.

[108] ECJ, *Viking*, n. 4 in this chapter, paragraphs 33–55; and *Laval un Partneri*, n. 5 in this chapter, paragraphs 86–90.

[109] ECJ, *Viking*, n. 4 in this chapter, paragraphs 57–66; and *Laval un Partneri*, n. 5 in this chapter, paragraphs 97–8.

[110] ECJ, *Viking*, n. 4 in this chapter, paragraph 79; and *Laval un Partneri*, n. 5 in this chapter, paragraph 105.

- the (unnecessarily) strict application of the principle of proportionality accepting the objective of protecting workers' rights as a justification ground but giving it a very strict interpretation, while at the same time limiting the use of the right to strike to situations when no other means are available, that is only as an ultimate resort.[111]

Bearing in mind first, the highly sensitive and political nature of the controversy; second, their 'poisoning' effect and possible negative impact on future policy initiatives; third, concerns that clarification should not be left to future occasional litigation before the ECJ or national courts; and fourth, amending the Treaty (to clarify the alleged primacy of social rights over economic freedoms or exclude them in general from its scope) and/or regulating the right to strike (Article 153(5) TFEU) not being politically or legally[112] feasible, further action was required.

13.4.2 *Possible Ways Envisaged to Resolve the Viking Conundrum*

The idea of a further clarification was put forward by the Commission (as proposal 30) in its Communication initiating the public debate on the relaunch of the single market[113] and subsequently as legislative clarification in key action 2.10 in the *Single Market Act I*.[114] The underlying reason was that the single market was not an end in itself but a tool for implementing other policies, including social policy. The relaunch was thus used as a vehicle for potentially delivering the necessary clarification.

There were multiple difficulties: without reversing the case law of the Court, a clear political signal was required, while taking due account of the inherent limitations in the Treaty (that is, Article 153(5) TFEU), as well as the fundamentally different factual situation in the *Spanish strawberries*[115] and

---

[111] ECJ, *Viking*, n. 4 in this chapter, paragraphs 85–90; and *Laval un Partneri*, n. 5 in this chapter, paragraphs 106–11. According to K. Lenaerts and J.A. Gutiérrez-Fons analysis, 'The Constitutional Allocation of Powers and General Principles of Law' (2010) *Common Market Law Review* 1629, p. 1666, this might be explained by the protectionist nature of the measures concerned which sought to keep jobs at home and shield their local labour markets.

[112] See points 69–70 of the opinion of Advocate General Sharpston of 19 December 2012 in *Epitropos tou Elegktikou Synedriou*, C-363/11, EU:C:2012:584.

[113] COM(2010)608 *Towards a Single Market Act, For a Highly Competitive Social Market Economy 50 Proposals for Improving Our Work, Business and Exchanges with One Another* (Brussels, 27 October 2010).

[114] COM(2011)206 *Single Market Act, Twelve Levers to Boost Growth and Strengthen Confidence 'Working Together to Create New Growth'* (Brussels, 13 April 2011).

[115] ECJ, judgment of 9 December 1997 in *Commission v France*, C-265/95, EU:C:1997:595.

the *Viking* case.[116] The envisaged solution was put forward in a proposal, the so-called (draft) Monti II Regulation,[117] which despite its remarkable shortness (only five articles long) did a quite astonishing job in antagonising many.[118] However, obtaining the necessary political support turned out to be a mission impossible. The need to reconcile social and economic rights was contested, others wanted social rights to have primacy over economic freedoms, some favoured no legislative action at all, and many were revealed to be too 'afraid' of the proportionality principle.[119] Thus, the proposal died a sudden death after having been the first 'casualty' of the so-called yellow card procedure.[120] However, the real 'kiss of death' had already been given: the ferocious opposition to a leaked unofficial draft version (which nobody pretended to have seen

[116] While the first one concerned the total lack of French public authorities to intervene and take all necessary and proportionate measures in order to prevent the free movement of fruit and vegetables ('*Spanish strawberries*') from being frequently obstructed by recurrent actions by private French individuals, the latter merely concerned a threat of collective action by trade unions in order to deter Viking-Line from reflagging one of its vessels from the Finnish flag to that of another Member State. While in the French situation only State intervention could remedy the situation and guarantee the proper functioning of the internal market, such intervention would have amounted to unjustified or unnecessary obstacles to the effective exercise of the right to strike in *Viking*.

[117] COM(2012)130 *On the Exercise of the Right to Take Collective Action within the Context of the Freedom of Establishment and the Freedom to Provide Services* (Brussels, 21 March 2012).

[118] G. Barrett, 'Monti II: The Subsidiarity Review Process Comes to Age ... Or Then Again Maybe It Doesn't' (2012) 4 *Maastricht Journal of European and Comparative Law* 595.

[119] See N. Bruun, A. Bücker, and F. Dorssemont, 'Balancing Fundamental Social Rights and Economic Freedoms: Can the Monti II Initiative Solve the EU Dilemma' (2012) 28 *International Journal of Comparative Labour Law and Industrial Relations* 279; F. Dorssemont, 'De ontwerp-Verordening Monti II, oude wijn (azijn) in nieuwe zakken?' (2012) 11 *Arbeidsrechtelijke Annotaties* 3; M. Rocca, 'The Proposal for a (So-called) 'Monti II' Regulation on the Exercise of the Right to Take Collective Action within the Context of the Freedom of Establishment and the Freedom to Provide Services – Changing without Reversing, Regulating without Affecting' (2012) 13 *European Labour Law Journal* 19; Guadagno, n. 81 in this chapter, in particular pp. 261–77. See also for more positive assessment: S.A. de Vries, 'Het ex-Monti II-voorstel: "Paard van Troje" of zege voor sociale grondrechten?' (2013) 4 *Nederlands tijdschrift voor Europees recht* 123, p. 133, qualifying Monti II as a serious and underestimated effort to embed social interests and social rights stronger in the legal analysis of conflicting in case of collision of rights and freedoms.

[120] F. Fabbrini and K Granat, '"Yellow Card, But No Foul": The Role of the National Parliaments under the Subsidiarity Protocol and the Commission Proposal for an EU Regulation on the Right to Strike' (2013) 50 *Common Market Law Review* 115; M. Goldoni, 'The Early Warning System and the Monti II Regulation: The Case for a Political Interpretation' (2014) 10 *European Constitutional Law Review* 90; I. Cooper, 'A Yellow Card for the Striker: How National Parliaments Defeated EU Strikes Regulation' (2015) *Journal of European Public Policy* 1406–25.

but intensely discussed and largely commented on by different stakeholders)[121] proved lethal.

This is not the place to dwell on the birth, life, and death of Monti II which, according to some, was 'short, brutal and nasty',[122] nor on its contents. However, two points should be made. While the Monti II proposal may have been 'the wrong idea, in the wrong place, at the wrong time', action at EU level could have counterbalanced the Court's perceived cold rationality of the common market and anchored fundamental social rights more strongly in the legal balancing exercise.[123] Furthermore, as far as EU law is concerned, what remains is a hard truth. It is still easier to prevent the adoption of new EU rules even if it comes at the cost of being stuck with worse case law.[124] Regrettably, as a result no fundamental substantive discussion or open, interactive exchange of views has taken place since the demise of Monti II on a matter of such utter importance.

13.4.3 Possible Alternatives

Unlike some have argued,[125] putting 'our' faith in the European Court of Human Rights (ECtHR) to come up with a more satisfactory solution will not get us any further. First of all, accession of the EU to the European Convention on Human Rights might not be that imminent, Opinion 2/13 of the Court[126] having identified a considerable number of issues with regard to the compatibility of the draft accession agreement with EU law. Second, the relevance of the decisions in *Demir and Baykara* and *Enerji Yapi-Yol*[127] in the present context can be questioned because the cases concerned a sectoral

---

[121] See K.D. Ewing, 'The Draft Monti II Regulation: An Inadequate Response to Viking and Laval' (March 2012) *Institute of Employment Rights Briefing* 1; G. Orlandini, 'La proposta di regolamento Monti II ed il diritto di sciopero nell'Europa post-Lisbona' (2012) available at: www.europeanrights.eu/public/commenti/Monti_II_final.pdf (accessed 25 October 2016); N. Bruun and A. Bücker, 'Critical Assessment of the Proposed Monti II Regulation – More Courage and Strength Needed to Remedy the Social Imbalances' (2012) *ETUI Policy Brief*, 4/12.

[122] See The Adoptive Parents, 'The Life of a Death Foretold: The Proposal for a Monti II Regulation', in M. Freedland and J. Prassl (eds), *Viking, Laval and Beyond* (Hart, 2014), p. 108.

[123] de Vries, n. 119 in this chapter, at p. 133.

[124] C. Unseld, 'POMFR: Viking, Laval and the Question If Anybody Cares', European Law Blog, 22 September 2015, available at: europeanlawblog.eu/?p=2896 (accessed 25 October 2016).

[125] Ewing and Hendy, n. 82 in this chapter; F. Dorssemont, 'How the European Court of Human Rights Gave Us Enerji to Cope with Laval and Viking', in M-A. Moreau (ed.), *Before and After the Economic Crisis: What Implications for the 'European Social Model'* (Edward Elgar, 2011).

[126] ECJ, Opinion 2/13 of 18 December 2014 *pursuant to Article 218(11) TFEU*, EU:C:2014:2454.

[127] Respectively ECtHR, judgment of 12 November 2008 in *Demir and Baykara*, 34503/79; and ECtHR, judgment of 21 April 2009 in *Enerji Yapi-Yol Sen*, 68959/01.

prohibition on having recourse to collective action. Thus, they relate to fundamentally different factual situations to those at stake in the *Laval* and *Viking* cases. Third, it can be questioned whether the approaches followed by the two Courts in general are really that different: the ECJ may favour using a proportionality test, but it bears close resemblance to the 'margin of appreciation test' used by the ECtHR[128] and lead to similar results in practice. Fourth, having qualified the freedom of association as an essential element of the freedom of collective bargaining (*Demir*) and considering the right to strike as an important tool to use the collective bargaining freedom effectively and thus to protect workers' interest (*Enerji Yapi-Yol*), the ECtHR, notwithstanding its transformed approach to collective bargaining in Article 11 of the European Convention on Human Rights,[129] more recently considered the complete ban on secondary action in the UK to remain within the wide margin of appreciation accorded to States.[130]

Others have pointed to changes made by the Treaty of Lisbon, such as the increased commitment to the protection of fundamental rights and the inclusion of the respect of human rights as foundational value of the EU (Article 2 TEU) as well as the obligation to respect the national identities of Member States, inherent in their fundamental structures, political and constitutional (Article 4(2) TEU), which would constitute important elements to influence (and preferably change) the Court's approach and future jurisprudence. However, the Lisbon Treaty does not make any qualitative change to the structure and scope of the provisions governing free movement. Notwithstanding the increased references to fundamental rights, their economic focus is thus not 'softened'; no silver bullet has been provided for.[131]

I also disagree with those who have argued that the horizontal clause ('cross-cutting 'social protection mainstreaming' clause) inserted in Article 9 TFEU by the Lisbon Treaty might help. The 'fundamental' innovation of Article 9 TFEU may have been highlighted by Europe 2020, but for the time being its introduction has been more of symbolic importance than of operational effectiveness, not least due to its different, less binding wording than other

---

[128] de Vries, n. 103 in this chapter, at pp. 188–9.

[129] Kilpartick, n. 82 in this chapter.

[130] ECtHR, judgment of 8 April 2014 in *RMT*, 31045/10; A. Bogg and K. Ewing, 'The Implications of the RMT Case' (2014) 43 *Industrial Law Journal* 221.

[131] S. Weatherill, 'From Economic Rights to Fundamental Rights', in S.A. de Vries, U. Bernitz, and S. Weatherill (eds), *The Protection of Fundamental Rights in the EU after Lisbon* (Hart, 2013), pp. 29–36.

horizontal clauses in the Treaty.[132] Further, even if a mainstreaming method could be used as a tool for avoiding the risk of social asymmetries and combining economic competitiveness with social justice, this in itself will not suffice to reduce such asymmetries.[133]

The mere fact that the EU has the vocation of being a (highly competitive) social market economy (as prescribed in Article 3(3) TEU) will not do the trick either. Even if Article 3(3) TEU is to be considered as the expression of a constitutional principle, its potential for rebalancing (if not inverting) the relationship between the economic and social dimensions of Europe or helping to overcome Europe's social deficit in practice is highly questionable.[134] Its impact is largely symbolic.[135] Therefore, its effect may be limited to interpreting EU market rules as social market rules,[136] and have no concrete implications for the relationship or balance to be struck between economic freedoms and fundamental rights as such.[137]

What about the Court's own case law? With a few exceptions, this does not – yet – give much hope either. One of the exceptions can be found in the opinion of Advocate General Cruz Villalón in *Santos Palhota*[138] concerning the compatibility with EU law of an obligation to send a prior declaration of posting and not start the works before having received the notification with a registration number. Having stressed the significance of the changes introduced by the Treaty of Lisbon, he argued that this meant that overriding

---

[132] See V. Papa, 'The Dark Side of Fundamental Rights Adjudication? The Court, the Charter and the Asymmetric Interpretation of Fundamental Rights in the AMS Case and Beyond' (2015) 6 *European Labour Law Journal* 190, p. 213.

[133] M.D. Ferrera, 'The Horizontal Social Clause and Social and Economic Mainstreaming: A New Approach for Social Integration?' (2013) *European Journal of Social Law* 288, p. 296. See for a more positive view: P. Vielle, 'How the Horizontal Social Clause Can Be Made to Work: The Lessons of Gender Mainstreaming', in N. Bruun, K. Lörcher, and I. Schöman (eds), *The Lisbon Treaty and Social Europe* (Bloomsbury, 2012); and P. Vielle, 'How the Horizontal Social Clause Can Be Made to Work: The Lessons of Gender Mainstreaming' (2010) *ETUI Policy Brief* 6/10.

[134] Scharpf, n. 25 in this chapter; Joerges and Rödl, n. 16 in this chapter.

[135] J. Snell, 'Varieties of Capitalism and the Limits of European Economic Integration' (2011) 13 *Cambridge Yearbook of European Legal Studies* 415, p. 428.

[136] S. Deakin, 'The Lisbon Treaty, the Viking and Laval Judgments and the Financial Crisis: In Search of New Foundations for Europe's "Social Market Economy"', in N. Bruun, K. Lörcher, and I. Schöman (eds), *The Lisbon Treaty and Social Europe* (Bloomsbury, 2012); D. Damjanovic, 'The EU Market Rules as Social Market Rules: Why the EU Can Be a Social Market Economy' (2013) 50 *Common Market Law Review* 1685. See also: Azoulai, n. 62 in this chapter; L. Andor, 'Building a Social Market Economy in the European Union', speech at the Manchester Business School, 20 October 2011.

[137] Semmelmann, n. 61 in this chapter, at p. 522.

[138] Opinion of Advocate General Cruz Villalón of 7 October 2010 in *Santos Palhota and Others*, C-515/08, EU:C:2010:245, paragraph 52–4.

reasons relating to public interest (such as safeguarding a certain level of social protection) justifying a restriction of an economic freedom should no longer be considered something exceptional and should not be interpreted strictly.[139] In his view, this would be expressed in practical terms by applying the proportionality test. However, in that respect he 'only' refers to the appropriateness and necessity test though,[140] which the Court in its ruling subsequently in line with previous case law applied without paying any attention to the Lisbon changes.

The approach defended by Advocate General Trstenjak with respect to the principle of proportionality in a case concerning the possibility of partial conversion of earnings entitlement into occupational pension rights on the basis of collective agreements in the public sector (*Entgeltumwandlung*) in Germany could reveal more promising.[141] Having stressed the equal status between fundamental rights and fundamental freedoms, in her opinion 'that general equality in status implies, first, that, in the interests of fundamental rights, fundamental freedoms may be restricted. However, second, it implies also that the exercise of fundamental freedoms may justify a restriction on fundamental rights'.[142] In addition, 'for the purposes of drawing an exact boundary between fundamental freedoms and fundamental rights, the principle of proportionality is of particular importance. In that context, for the purposes of evaluating proportionality, in particular, a three-stage scheme of analysis must be deployed where (1) the appropriateness, (2) the necessity and (3) the reasonableness of the measure in question must be reviewed'.[143] Therefore, 'a fair balance between fundamental rights and fundamental freedoms is ensured in the case of a conflict only when the restriction by a fundamental right on a fundamental freedom is not permitted to go beyond what is appropriate, necessary and reasonable to realise that fundamental right. Conversely, however, nor may the restriction on a fundamental right by a fundamental freedom go beyond what is appropriate, necessary and reasonable to realise the fundamental freedom'.[144] Such a double, symmetrical proportionality test via a three-pronged scheme (appropriateness, necessity, and reasonableness) is

---

[139] See in this respect also opinion of Advocate General Trstenjak of 14 April 2010 in *Commission v Germany*, C-271/08, EU:C:2010:183.

[140] Opinion of Advocate General Cruz Villalón, *Santos Palhota*, n. 138 in this chapter, paragraphs 53 and 54.

[141] Opinion of Advocate General Trstenjak, *Commission v Germany*, n. 139 in this chapter, in particular paragraphs 75–84, 186–99 and 202–4.

[142] Ibid., point 81 (see also points 84 and 204).

[143] Ibid., point 189.

[144] Ibid., point 190.

no doubt rich in promise,[145] certainly when the exercise of fundamental rights as such is accepted as a legitimate interest and a self-standing justification ground instead of being dealt with in the context of an unwritten justification of 'overriding reasons of public interest'.[146]

In view of Advocate General Trstenjak's opinion, the ruling of the Court in this case[147] may, at first sight, be thought disappointing. However, upon closer examination, its reasoning and the test applied differs significantly from the one applied in *Viking*. With respect to the need to reconcile and strike a fair balance, the Court does not only refer 'by analogy'[148] to its judgment in the *Schmidberger* case,[149] a case often referred to by those criticising the Court's approach in *Viking*, but also the subsequent application of the principle of proportionality[150] differs considerably from the rather straight forward, one-sided approach in *Viking* resulting in the conclusion that 'compliance with the directives … does not prove irreconcilable with attainment of the social objective pursued … in the exercise of their right to bargain collectively'.[151] In comparison to *Viking*, the fundamental differences in approach and final result are more than striking. The lessons from this for litigants should be clear: do not focus only on providing justifications for restrictions on economic freedoms by social objectives/fundamental rights (like the German

---

[145] V. Trstenjak and E Beysen, 'The Growing Overlap of Fundamental Freedoms and Fundamental Rights in the Case Law of the CJEU' (2013) 38 *European Law Review* 293.

[146] de Vries, n. 103 in this chapter, at p. 188; Morijn, n. 102 in this chapter. See also: T. Novitz, 'A Human Rights Analysis of the Viking and Laval Judgments' (2007) 10 *Cambridge Yearbook of European Legal Studies*, p. 357; and Malmberg and Sigeman, n. 63 in this chapter, at p. 1130.

[147] ECJ, judgment of 15 July 2010 in *Commission v Germany*, C-271/08, EU:C:2010:426.

[148] Ibid., paragraph 52 (a similar reference is not contained in *Viking*).

[149] ECJ, judgment of 12 June 2003 in *Schmidberger*, C-112/00, EU:C:2003:333. In this case, concerning a 30-hour complete blockade of the Brenner motorway in order to allow an environmental group to organise a demonstration, the Court considered the restrictions to the free movement of goods arising through the exercise of fundamental rights to be justified. Having first of all stressed the wide margin of discretion of the competent authorities when striking a fair balance between different interests (paragraph 81/82), it subsequently not only examined in detail whether the obstacles to the free movement of goods through the exercise of the fundamental right to freedom of expression and freedom of assemble were proportionate to the protection of those rights (paragraph 82 et seq.), but equally whether strict enforcement of the free movement of goods would have resulted in excessive interference in the exercise of fundamental rights (paragraph 89 et seq.). It thus reflected the idea of an equal ranking of fundamental rights and economic freedoms, which, ultimately, were brought into balance by an examination of the proportionality of the restrictions of both the exercise of the economic freedom and the exercise of the fundamental right in question. In addition, the protection of fundamental rights appeared to be used as a self-standing unwritten category of justification grounds.

[150] Ibid., paragraph 53–65.

[151] Ibid., paragraph 66.

Government did),[152] but equally (if not only) on the restricting effects of the economic freedoms for the effective exercise and protection of social objectives/rights.[153]

Interesting in this respect is also the final decision of the Swedish Labour Court in the *Fonnship* case.[154] It applied the double proportionality test via a three-pronged scheme referring explicitly to the proposal for the Monti II Regulation.[155] Moreover, Judge Pinto de Albuquerque considered 'the more balanced approach' of the ECJ in its judgement in case C-271/08 as 'coming closer to the imperative direction set by the Court in *Demir and Baykara*'.[156]

13.4.4 Interim Conclusion

In summary, unlike *Laval*'s regulatory conundrum, the question how to balance economic freedoms and fundamental social rights (the *Viking* conundrum) appears far from resolved.

The judicial methodology used by the Court in *Viking* (and *Laval*) may have been in line and consistent with its classical internal market case law and economically inspired framework of analysis.[157] However, the way in which the delicate balancing exercise was performed and in particular the principle of proportionality was applied, appears far from satisfactory or consistent in comparison to other rulings.

Because of the existing constitutional pluralism with respect to the right to take collective action and the different regulatory national traditions and practices with respect to wage-setting, many had expected that the Court would at least have given a margin of discretion to protect the fundamental rights at stake and/or a less strict application of the principle of proportionality. The assumed protectionist nature of the objectives pursued by the collective actions in *Viking* (and *Laval*) in combination with not sufficiently taking into considerations the interests of other groups of workers, may well explain

---

[152] A point also stressed by in Opinion of Advocate General Trstenjak, *Commission v Germany*, n. 139 in this chapter, paragraph 203.

[153] Phil Syrpis in his comments on this case, *Industrial Law Journal* 2011 pp. 222–9.

[154] Arbetsdomstolen, judgment of 25 November 2015, A-14/02, A-39/02, A-53/03 and A-137/03, 70/15, p. 48.

[155] COM(2012)130, n. 117 in this chapter.

[156] ECtHR, judgment of 27 November 2011 in *Hrvatski Lijecnicki Sindicat v Croatia*, 36701/09, see footnote 21 of his Concurring Opinion.

[157] Prechal and de Vries, n. 106 in this chapter; and S. Reynolds, 'Explaining the Constitutional Drivers behind a Perceived Judicial Preference for Free Movement over Fundamental Rights' (2016) 53 *Common Market Law Review* 643.

the hesitations of the Court but does not make the final result of its rulings less 'devastating' from a fundamental social rights point of view, in particular because the use of the right to strike in *Viking* seemed to be limited to situations where no other means are available.

Some argued that the differences in outcome in other rulings may give the impression that the Court would be more inclined to give preference to those fundamental rights which are based on moral or ethical considerations or essential elements of the democratic system than to rights which (as in *Viking* and *Laval*) are based on economic and social interests.[158] Others summarise the Court's emerging approach as: 'the more sensitive and the more remote from commercial considerations the matters advanced in the context of justification of trade barriers are, the more generous the Court is to the available scope for justification and also to the breadth of the margin of appreciation enjoyed by the regulator'.[159]

On the positive side, the recognition of the right to take collective action, including the right to strike, as a fundamental right should certainly be welcomed and might as such well develop its own dynamic.[160] In addition, the more recent case law referred to in the previous paragraph demonstrate that the judicial adjudication methodology of the Court in the context of the balancing exercise when trying to reconcile economic freedoms and fundamental social rights may well have different outcomes, thus providing interesting indications on possible future avenues.

Therefore, the 'clash of titans by analogy'[161] is far from over. All the more reason to look forward and elaborate on possible ways to (re)balance the economic and social, for which the current particularly historic momentum for the future of the Union[162] (particularly in the light of Brexit and its aftermath) might provide an excellent opportunity.

---

[158] J. Malmberg and T. Sigeman, n. 63 in this chapter.

[159] Weatherill, n. 131 in this chapter, at p. 25.

[160] See Prechal and de Vries, n. 106 in this chapter, at p. 433, referring in that respect to developments in the area of gender equality and non-discrimination on grounds of nationality where the principle of equal treatment and non-discrimination has been transformed into a human rights standard (see for further details: Prechal, n. 106 in this chapter).

[161] de Vries, 'The Protection of Fundamental Rights within Europe's Internal Market after Lisbon – An Endeavour for More Harmony', in S.A. de Vries, X. Groussot, and G. Thor Petursson (eds), *Balancing Fundamental Rights with the EU Treaty Freedoms: The European Court of Justice as 'Tightrope' Walker* (Eleven International Publications, 2012), p. 9.

[162] D. Tusk, 'Letter from President Donald Tusk before the Bratislava Summit' (2016) available at: www.consilium.europa.eu/en/press/press-releases/2016/09/13-tusk-invitation-letter-bratislava/ (accessed 26 October 2016).

13.5 SOCIAL EUROPE MATTERS – GIVING TEETH TO
THE EU'S SOCIAL DIMENSION

Crisis-ridden, battered and bruised,[163] Europe is at a cross-road facing major existential, constitutional, institutional,[164] and legitimacy challenges. It is at a crucial,
defining moment.At this particularly historic momentum, defining the Union's
social objective is even more a necessity rather than a luxury.[165] Against this background,[166] Social Europe is faced with many challenges but also a number of
opportunities.

The social rights deficit vis-à-vis economic freedoms in European integration may have been 'more a story of what has not been than what has been',
a picture further aggravated by the economic crisis and the numerous measures taken in the context of the EU's economic governance since,[167] and
their repercussions for democratic legitimacy and social rights.[168] The number of country-specific recommendations concerning social and employment policy matters as well as the presence of social and employment
oriented issues within the macroeconomic imbalance procedure may have
increased since the beginning of the euro crisis but that does not necessarily imply that their content and the economic governance process as such
have become more social. Reforms undertaken in the framework of the
crisis, in particular those related to labour law, labour-market regulation[169]

---

[163] D. Phinnemore, 'Crisis-ridden, Battered and Bruised: Time to Give Up on the EU' (2015) 53
Journal of Common Market Studies 61.

[164] B. de Witte, 'Euro Crisis Responses and the EU Legal Order: Increased Institutional Variation
or Constitutional Mutation?' (2015) 11 *European Constitutional Law Review* 434.

[165] F. Vandenbroucke, 'Europe: The Social Challenge: Defining the Union's Social Objective Is
a Necessity Rather Than a Luxury' (2012) *Opinion paper OSE*, 11/12

[166] P. Tsoukala, 'Narratives of the European Crisis and the Future of (Social) Europe' (2013) 58
Texas International Law Journal 241.

[167] S. Bekker and S. Klosse, 'EU Governance of Economic and Social Policies: Changes
and Challenges for Social Europe' (2013) *European Journal of Social Law* 103. See
also: S. Clauwaert, 'The Country-specific Recommendations (CSRs) in the Social Field – An
Overview and Comparison' (2015) *ETUI Background Analysis*, 03/15.

[168] See for an extensive overview: K. Tuori and K. Tuori, *The Eurozone Crisis – A Constitutional
Analysis* (Cambridge University Press, 2014); A. Hinarejos, *The Euro Area Crisis in Constitutional
Perspective* (Oxford University Press, 2015); and J. Pisani-Ferry, *The Euro Crisis and Its
Aftermath* (Oxford University Press, 2014). See also: N. Bruun, K. Lörcher, and I. Schönmann
(eds), *The Economic Crisis and Collective Labour Law in Europe* (Bloomsbury, 2014).

[169] See for an overview: I. Schömann, 'Labour Law Reforms in Europe: Adjusting Employment
Protection Legislation for the Worse?' (2014) *ETUI Working Paper* 02/14. See A. Koukiadaki,
I. Tavora, and M. Martinez Lucio (eds), *Joint Regulation and Labour Market Policy in Europe
during the Crisis* (ETUI, 2016).

and social protection, had a considerable impact on national and European social policies.[170]

Therefore, (re)socialising Europe in a time of crisis is a must,[171] not least to avoid further alienation of important segments of public opinion from the European project, in particular its social and democratic legitimacy. In addition, with the deepening of the asymmetry, the social deficit of European integration is at risk of converting into a crisis for the Union's social and democratic legitimacy.[172] Moreover, not reforming the structure and legal framework of the Eurozone and the policies imposed on the member countries risks creating a considerable political threat to the future of Europe.[173] Therefore, a credible response to the social deficit would be a pre-condition and political necessity for the legitimacy of any intensified integration project.[174]

At the same time, taking into consideration the unprecedented challenges Europe is currently facing, this may not be the time for utopian visions or revolutionary thinking, but instead realistic pragmatism is required, focusing on practical but ambitious solutions.[175] Further development of the social dimension within the framework of the current treaties may be difficult, but – within limitations – possible.[176]

Despite the fact that there is no hierarchical relationship between fundamental freedoms and fundamental rights as far as EU law is concerned,[177]

---

[170] C. Degryse, M. Jepsen, and P. Pochet, 'The Euro Crisis and Its Impact on national and European social policies' (2013) *ETUI Working paper* 05/13.

[171] See also: F. Vandenbroucke, 'Sociaal beleid in een muntunie: puzzels, paradoxen en perspectiven', inaugural lecture at the University of Amsterdam, 1 June 2016, available at: www.frankvandenbroucke.uva.nl/wp-content/uploads/2016/07/Oratie-2016-Vandenbroucke_preprint_v5_12.7.2016.pdf (accessed 25 October 2016).

[172] S. Giubboni, 'European Citizenship and Social Rights in Times of Crisis' (2014) 15 *German Law Journal* 935, p. 952.

[173] J.E. Stiglitz, *The Euro and Its Threat to the Future of Europe* (Penguin, 2016).

[174] Joerges and Rödl, n. 12 in this chapter, at p. 2.

[175] D. Tusk, 'Speech President Tusk at the Bruegel Annual Dinner', speech at the Bruegel Annual Dinner, 7 September 2015, available at: bruegel.org/2015/09/speech-by-president-donald-tusk-at-the-bruegel-annual-dinner/ (accessed 25 October 2016).

[176] A. Schellinger, 'Giving Teeth to the EU's Social Dimension – Dismal Failure and Promising Potential' (2015) *Friedrich Ebert Stiftung*, 09/15.

[177] V. Skouris 2005, 'Fundamental Rights and Fundamental Freedoms: The Challenge of Striking a Delicate Balance' (2006) 17 *European Business Law Review* 225, p. 239; Schubert, n. 101 in this chapter, at pp. 163–4; D. Leczykiewicz, 'Conceptualising Conflict between the Economic and the Social in EU Law after Viking and Laval', in M. Freedland and J. Prassl (eds), *Viking, Laval and Beyond* (Hart, 2014). Idem: opinion Advocate General Poiares Maduro in *International Transport Workers' Federation and Finnish Seamen's Union* ('*Viking*'), C-438/05, EU:C:2007:772, point 23; opinion of Advocate General Mengozzi of 23 May 2007 in *Laval un Partneri*, C-341/05, EU:C:2007:291, point 84; and opinion of Advocate General Trstenjak, *Commission v Germany*, n. 139 in this chapter, points 81 and 186. For a slightly different view:

in a situation characterised by multilevel governance and legal pluralism, it appears highly unlikely that the economic and social dimension will genuinely be placed on an equal footing.[178] Therefore, the idea of a 'Social Progress Protocol',[179] proposed in order to solve the problems of balancing economic freedoms and social rights (and which according to the main defenders should establish a primacy of the social over the economic),[180] should not be presented as merely a 'technical solution'.[181] It would at least require Treaty amendment,[182] which has no chance whatsoever politically, at least in the near future, and thus is 'nothing else but alibi politics',[183] if desirable at all.

Instead, all the existing possibilities, including the potential of the Lisbon Treaty, should be used to its full extent. However, bearing in mind the so-called structural social deficit of the EU and the fundamental asymmetry between the economic and social dimensions of the European (economic) integration process, a mere (re)balancing may not be that easy or sufficient to achieve the desired outcome. Multiple paths and different combinations may have to be envisaged, in particular in the medium and long term, for which numerous proposals, including the ideas put forward in the five Presidents report for the completion of the EMU,[184] might provide the necessary sources of inspiration.

In any case, as far as the balancing between the economic and the social is concerned, it will be necessary to have a more human developmental and fundamental rights approach, using every possibility to reflect, improve, and

de Vries, n. 161 in this chapter, at p. 32, who considers that it may be very difficult and not really desirable to establish an a priori hierarchy between the two.

[178] Ashiagbor, n. 15 in this chapter, at p. 324.

[179] ETUC, 'Paris Manifesto – Stand Up in Solidarity for Quality Jobs, Workers' Rights and a Fair Society in Europe 2015' (2015) available at: www.etuc.org/documents/paris-manifesto-stand-solidarity-quality-jobs-workers%E2%80%99-rights-and-fair-society-europe#.WA9HqiTz-fk (accessed 25 October 2016). See also: J. Dutheil de la Rochère, 'Challenges for the Protection of Fundamental Rights in the EU at the Same of the Entry into Force of the Lisbon Treaty' (2010) 33 *Fordham International Law Journal* 1787, stressing that fundamental rights do not prevail over fundamental freedoms, at least not under the Treaty.

[180] See for instance: A. Bücker, 'A Comprehensive Social Progress Protocol Is Needed More than Ever' (2013) 4 *European Labour Law Journal* 4.

[181] N. Bruun, 'Economic Governance of the EU Crisis and its Social Policy Implications', in N. Bruun, K. Lörcher, and I. Schöman (eds), *The Lisbon Treaty and Social Europe* (Bloomsbury, 2012).

[182] R. Blanpain, 'The Treaty Needs to be Amended' (2013) 4 *European Labour Law Journal* 28.

[183] M. Weiss, 'The Potential of the Treaty Has to be Used to Its Full Extent' (2013) 4 *European Labour Law Journal* 24.

[184] J.C. Juncker, 'The Five Presidents' Report: Completing Europe's Economic and Monetary Union, report in close cooperation D. Tusk, J. Dijsselbloem, M. Draghi, and M. Schulz' (2015), available at: ec.europa.eu/priorities/sites/beta-political/files/5-presidents-report_en.pdf (accessed 30 March 2016); see also the documents referred to in n. 200 in this chapter.

correct the current system in order to link economic and social policy in a more systematic way.[185] A first step required in this respect concerns the theoretical foundations of the balancing mechanism and judicial methodology applied by the Court.[186] This will have to be refined by a recalibration of the proportionality principle, giving it the necessary teeth in situations where the exercise of fundamental rights has to be reconciled with economic freedoms. The proportionality principle[187] is not something to be afraid of. It may have many faces and no clear-cut 'legal arithmetic', but it constitutes a general principle of law and an important standard for judicial review, the intensity of which depends on whether the restriction of an (individual) right or a complex balancing between different policy fields is at stake.[188] It is, in principle, equally an appropriate tool to balance between the economic and social rights of the EU, provided the Court follows a different, alternative approach than the very strict application of proportionality in *Viking*.

The double, symmetrical proportionality test via a three-pronged scheme (appropriateness, necessity, and reasonableness) suggested by Advocate General Trstenjak,[189] is rich in promise,[190] certainly when the exercise of fundamental rights as such is accepted as a legitimate interest and a self-standing justification ground instead of being dealt with in the context of an unwritten justification of 'overriding reasons of public interest'.[191] Focussing not only on providing justifications for restrictions on economic freedoms by social

---

[185] Deakin, n. 136 in this chapter; de Vries, n. 103 in this chapter, at pp. 187–91.

[186] X. Groussot and G.T. Petursson, 'Balancing as a Judicial Methodology of EU Constitutional Adjuducation', in S.A. de Vries, X. Groussot, and G. Thor Petursson (eds), *Balancing Fundamental Rights with the EU Treaty Freedoms: The European Court of Justice as 'Tightrope' Walker* (Eleven International Publiation, 2012). See also: J.H. Gerards, 'Belangenafweging bij rechterlijke toetsing aan fundamentele rechten', inaugural lecture at the University of Leiden, 4 April 2006, available at: media.leidenuniv.nl/legacy/Schriftelijke%20versie%20oratie.pdf (accessed 25 October 2016).

[187] See further: C. Barnard, 'A Proportionate Response to Proportionality in the Field of Collective Action' (2012) 37 *European Law Review* 117; T.-I. Harbo, 'The Function of the Proportionality Principle in EU Law' (2010) 16 *European Law Journal* 158-; N. Reich, 'How Proportionate is the Proportionality Principle?', Paper Oslo Conference 'The Reach of Free Movement', May 2011, www.jus.uio.no/ifp/forskning/prosjekter/markedsstaten/arrangementer/2011/free-movement-oslo/speakers-papers/norbert-reich.pdf (accessed 25 October 2016); N. Hös, 'The Principle of Proportionality in Viking and Laval: An Appropriate Standard of Judicial Review?' (2010) 1 *European Labour Law Journal* 236.

[188] Semmelmann, n. 61 in this chapter, at p. 538 including the references in footnote 151.

[189] Opinion of Advocate General Trstenjak, *Commission v Germany*, n. 139, in particular paragraphs 75–84, 190–2 and 202–4).

[190] Trstenjak and Beysen, n. 145 in this chapter.

[191] Morijn, n. 102 in this chapter, at p. 39; opinion of Advocate General Trstenjak, *Commission v Germany*, n. 139 in this chapter, paragraphs 183–5. See also: Novitz, n. 146 in this chapter, at p. 357; and Malmberg and Sigeman, n. 63 in this chapter.

objectives/fundamental rights, but also (if not only) on the restricting effects of the economic freedoms for the effective exercise and protection of social objectives/fundamental rights, will certainly merit further attention in this respect. Equally useful is the idea that not the weight or intrinsic value of a fundamental right or interest would be decisive, but the seriousness of the infringement and the importance of the right in realising the general interest and/or social objective.[192]

In addition, Europe's crisis, in combination with deepening and completing EMU, may also provide pathways to Europe's future,[193] its architecture and institutional framework in which the social dimension should play a prominent role.[194] The Eurozone crisis and policy measures taken in that context had a huge impact on national and European social policies[195] but, together with Brexit, also prompted one of the most intense debates about the Union's future and the challenges it is faced with. These ongoing discussions are not only crucial for the legitimacy of the EU's integration process as such but also for the future of social policy matters at EU level.[196] They should provide a window of opportunity to increase its social side and face. Building a more social Europe will no doubt require several steps and one step at a time.

In this respect, possible topics (some of which are dealt with in more detail in other chapters of this book) and future opportunities relate to reinforcing the social and employment dimension of the economic governance in the

---

[192] R. Alexy, *A Theory of Constitutional Rights* (Oxford University Press, 2010), p. 102, referred to in de Vries, n. 161 in this chapter, at p. 33.

[193] K. Dervis and J. Mistral (eds), *Europe's Crisis, Europe's Future* (Brookings Institute, 2014); see also G. Majone, *Rethinking the Union of Europe Post-Crisis – Has Integration Gone Too Far?* (Cambridge University Press, 2014) and G. Majone 'Rethinking European Integration after the Debt Crisis' (2012) *UCL Working Paper*, 3/12.

[194] See further: F. Vandenbroucke and B. Vanhercke, *A European Social Union: 10 Tough Nuts to Crack* (Friends of Europe, 2014); F. Vandenbroucke, 'The Case for a European Social Union – From Muddling Through to a Sense of Common Purpose', in B. Marin (ed.), *The Future of Welfare in a Global Europe* (Ashgate, 2015), pp. 489–520; see also the *New Pact for Europe Project* publications: New Pact for Europe, *Strategic Options for Europe's Future* (King Baudouin Foundation, the Bertelsmann Stiftung and the European Policy Centre, 2013); and New Pact for Europe, *Towards a New Pact for Europe* (King Baudouin Foundation, the Bertelsmann Stiftung and the European Policy Centre, 2014).

[195] C. Degryse, M. Jepsen, and P. Pochet, n. 170 in this chapter; D. Vaughan-Whitehead, 'The European Social Model in Times of Crisis: An Overview', in D. Vaughan-Whitehead (ed.), *The European Social Model in Crisis – Is Europe Losing Its Soul?* (Edward Elgar, 2015), in particular Table IA.I containing an overview of the diversity and different magnitudes of the changes made.

[196] C. Barnard, 'EU Employment Law and the European Social Model: The Past, the Present and the Future' (2014) *Legal Studies Research Paper Series*, 43/14. See also: S. Sciarra, 'Social Law in the Wake of the Crisis', *Working Paper Centre for the Study of European Labour Law 'Massimo d'Antona'*, 108/14.

EU;[197] (further) socialising the European Semester;[198] fostering upwards social convergence (including agreeing on set of common high-level benchmarks, specific standards and indicators); as well as more generally enhancing and strengthening the coherence and consistency of provisions that implement both economic and social goals.

The suggestion of introducing a (new) social policy conditionality (to be built into EU economic policy at the earliest Treaty amendment) is also an interesting idea,[199] while the European Pillar of Social Rights[200] and the Reflection Paper on the Deepening of the Economic and Monetary Union (adopted on 31 May 2017) contain important indications to further concretise the political top priorities in this respect.

Creating an 'ever closer union' among the peoples of Europe can only move forward through daring initiatives and closer integration of social objectives and social policies. Whether this will lead to a profound constitutional mutation of the EU legal order or increased institutional variation,[201] differentiated integration or enhanced cooperation, unity in diversity or diversity in unity remains to be seen. However, that by far exceeds the topic of this contribution: how to resolve the *Viking* and *Laval* conundrum.

[197] J. Delors, 'Economic Governance in the European Union: Past, Present and Future' (2013) 51 *Journal of Common Market Studies* 169.

[198] See for a number of policy recommendations: B. Vanhercke, J. Zeitlin, and A. Zwinkels, 'Further Socializing the European Semester: Moving Forward for the "Social Triple A"?' (2015) available at: www.ose.be/files/publication/2015/vanhercke_zeitlin_2015_EuropeanSemester_report_dec15.pdf (accessed 25 October 2016).

[199] Bruun, n. 181 in this chapter.

[200] Officially adopted on 26 April 2017 following a public consultation launched on 8 March 2016; see for further information and the relevant documents (including a first preliminary outline): ec.europa.eu/priorities/deeper-and-fairer-economic-and-monetary-union/towards-european-pillar-social-rights_en (accessed 25 October 2016). See for a flavour of possible topics also M. Joao Rodrigues, 'Report on the European Pillar of Social Rights' (2016) available at: www.europarl.europa.eu/sides/getDoc.do?pubRef=-//EP//TEXT+REPORT+A8-2016-0391+0+DOC+XML+V0//EN (accessed 25 October 2016).

[201] de Witte, n. 164 in this chapter.

14

The Basis in EU Constitutional Law for Further Social Integration

Geert De Baere and Kathleen Gutman

14.1 INTRODUCTION

Now is the moment for a major rethink of the relationship between European economic and social integration, if not the European project generally, and for an evaluation of what can be done through law to promote the European Social Model. At the heart of any discussion about the future lies the matter of competence, apparently a dry legal issue but one of utmost consequence. Indeed, the perennial issues (and tensions) underlying the EU's competence in the field of social policy make this subject not only of great practical importance in terms of the crisis, but also valuable from an EU constitutional law perspective.

The objective of this contribution is therefore to analyse the extent of the EU's competences in the field of social policy to further social integration under the Treaties. In essence, this contribution aims to set out the possibilities under EU law to put into action what is decided at EU level. This analysis will be done in four main sections. Section 14.2 sets out the EU constitutional framework in social policy, involving consideration of the fundamental principles governing EU competence, the potential breadth of EU 'social' competences, and the relevant changes brought about by the entry into force of the Lisbon Treaty. Section 14.3 delves into the development of the traditional route of EU social policy legislation so far and some proposals going forward. Section 14.4 explores certain alternative routes: enhanced cooperation, international agreements, and amendment of the Treaties, while Section 14.5 examines the so-called 'horizontal social clause' of Article 9 TFEU.

In undertaking this analysis, there are several challenges that must be recognised at the outset. These include, first, the diversity of the Member States'

Many thanks to Catherine Barnard and Frank Vandenbroucke for their helpful comments and suggestions. The usual disclaimer applies. The views and opinions expressed in this chapter are personal.

social systems that generally precludes a one-size-fits-all approach; secondly, the apparent lack of political will of the Member States and the social partners;[1] thirdly, the perceived frailty or weakness of the EU's competences in social policy,[2] which prompted calls for amending the Treaties in this regard;[3] and fourthly, the assessment in devising proposals for EU-level action, of what is really needed, at what level, and for whom, amid a vast array of regulatory methods situated at various levels and involving various actors as encapsulated in the Treaties. Therefore, it may be useful before embarking on our exploration to establish a semantic framework for our discussion and make clear what we will focus on. In the first place, we draw a distinction between EU social policy *sensu lato* and *sensu stricto*. This is because EU social policy *sensu lato* (as well as terms such as EU social law) can potentially cover and is entangled with many policy areas (for example, free movement, equal treatment, citizenship, services of general economic interest, transport, employment policy, education, vocational training and youth, internal market, public health, economic, social, territorial cohesion, and trade) in addition to EU social policy *sensu stricto* as covered by Title X of the TFEU (in which there are references to some of these areas), all of which cannot be discussed in depth. In the second place, the expression 'further social integration' embodies different dimensions; in this contribution, it is meant to denote (upward) social convergence. The question then becomes: what legal instruments are at the disposal of the EU (or subsets of the Member States) to promote upward convergence in social standards?

Without discounting the importance of matters of substance in devising EU rules on a particular topic of social policy (in terms of the complex and delicate choices to be made in light of the diverse approaches of the Member States) and the wide variety of means available (for example, money via the European Social Fund and other funding vehicles or coordination of national policies via the Open Method of Coordination (OMC)),[4] this

---

[1] See for example C. Barnard, 'EU Employment Law and the European Social Model: The Past, the Present and the Future' (2014) 67 *Current Legal Problems* 199, 213–14.

[2] The steady stream of metaphors and phrases in the literature is indicative of this. See for example R. Blanpain, *European Labour Law* (Kluwer, 13th rev. edn, 2012) ('The EU boat, in relation to social policy, is a small vessel with very short paddles'), p. 146; K. Tuori and K. Tuori, *The Eurozone Crisis: A Constitutional Analysis* 233 (Cambridge University Press, 2014) ('constitutional underdog'); A. Somek, 'Concordantia Catholica: Exploring the Context of European Antidiscrimination Law and Policy' (2005) 14 *Transnational Law and Contemporary Problems* 949, 976 ('social and nowhere to go: competences').

[3] See for example R. Blanpain, 'The Treaty Needs to be Amended' (2013) 4 *European Labour Law Journal* 28; K. Lörcher, 'Social Competences', in N Bruun, K Lörcher and I Schömann (eds.), *The Lisbon Treaty and Social Europe* (Hart, 2012), pp. 191–4.

[4] For general discussion of the OMC in social policy, see for example K.A. Armstrong, *Governing Social Inclusion: Europeanization through Policy Coordination* (Oxford University

contribution focuses on the scope of the EU's constitutional competence to achieve its social objectives on the basis of the existing Treaty framework. Exploring the extent of the EU's competence in social policy establishes a template for the assessment of possible proposals for EU legislation and alternatives to such legislation contemplated in this setting going forward.

14.2 THE EU CONSTITUTIONAL FRAMEWORK GOVERNING FURTHER SOCIAL INTEGRATION

14.2.1 *The Place of Social Policy in European Integration*

The drafters of the 1957 Treaty of Rome were convinced that European economic integration was to be organised at the level of the European Economic Community: it would boost economic growth and create upward convergence, thereby contributing to the development of prosperous national welfare states, whilst leaving social policy concerns essentially at the national level.[5] That much is clear from Article 117 TEEC, which will be examined below.

Under the current Treaties, social policy *sensu lato* can fall under several different categories of competences, which in turn has an impact on what type of further integration, if any, is possible. For example, social policy is a shared competence 'for the aspects defined in the TFEU'.[6] At the same time, social policy is listed under Article 5(3) TFEU as a possible coordination competence, i.e. the 'Union may take initiatives to ensure coordination of Member States' social policies', and employment policy is likewise a 'coordination competence'.[7] However, before delving into the analysis of the social competences and legal bases in the Treaties on social matters, it is important to recall the principles that govern the conferral of competences on the Union.

Press, 2010); B. Cantillon, H. Verschueren, and P. Ploscar (eds), *Social Inclusion and Social Protection in the EU: Interactions between Law and Policy* (Intersentia, 2012); M. Dawson, *New Governance and the Transformation of European Law: Coordinating EU Social Law and Policy* (Cambridge University Press, 2011); E. Marlier and D. Natali (eds), *Europe 2020: Towards a More Social EU?* (Peter Lang, 2010).

[5] See F. Vandenbroucke, 'The Idea of a European Social Union: A Normative Introduction', Chapter 1 in this volume.

[6] Articles 2(2) and 4(2)(b) TFEU.

[7] Articles 2(3) and 5(2) TFEU.

14.2.2 *Specific and General Legal Bases*

14.2.2.1 Specific Legal Bases

The Union acts ordinarily on the basis of 'specific powers',[8] which are not necessarily the express consequence of specific provisions of the Treaties but may also be implied from them.[9] The original Treaty of Rome contained no specific legal basis for 'social' matters. Its limited Title on social policy only contained provisions relating to equal pay[10] and paid holiday schemes,[11] and even these provisions contained no express powers for the EU to act in these fields. The main substantive provision relating to workers was not found in the social Title but in the Title on free movement.[12]

The key to understanding the Treaty drafters' limited ambitions in the social field lay in Article 117 TEEC.[13] The provision provided that the Member States agreed upon the need to promote improved working conditions and an improved standard of living for workers, so as to make possible their harmonisation while the improvement is being maintained. The Member States then affirmed their belief that such a development would ensue not only from the functioning of the common market, which would favour the harmonisation of social systems, but also from the procedures provided for in the EEC Treaty and from the approximation of provisions laid down by law, regulation or administrative action.[14]

Article 117 TEEC therefore encapsulated two ideas. First, harmonisation in social matters would follow spontaneously from economic integration. Secondly, only the latter ought to be pursued at the level of the (then) Community. The Member States would be in charge of any social policies they thought would need to be adopted.[15] This could be regarded as an example of the application of the subsidiarity principle in its pre-constitutional version, that is, as implicitly underpinning the Treaties as a political principle that does not govern the exercise of competences that have been conferred on

---

[8] The terms 'competences' and 'powers' will be used interchangeably in the present chapter.

[9] Opinion 2/94 of 28 March 1996, EU:C:1996:140, paragraph 25.

[10] Article 119 TEEC (now Article 157 TFEU).

[11] Article 120 TEEC (now Article 158 TFEU).

[12] Articles 45 and 46 TFEU. Compare the equivalent enabling provisions for freedom of establishment and free movement of services: Articles 53(1) and 62 TFEU.

[13] Now amended Article 151 TFEU. See C. Barnard, *EU Employment Law* (Oxford University Press, 4th edn, 2012), pp. 4–8.

[14] See further F. Vandenbroucke and B. Vanhercke, *A European Social Union: 10 Tough Nuts to Crack* (Friends of Europe, 2014), p. 24.

[15] Ibid., p. 64.

the Union (as the subsidiarity principle in Article 5(3) TEU does), but oversees the actual conferral of powers.[16] The reflection on the appropriate level of government at which to pursue social policy found explicit expression in the attribution of competence in Article 117 TEEC. The upshot is that the EU was never initially conceived as a 'social union'.

That view began to change in the 1970s, in part for economic reasons: countries with higher social standards feared that they were at a competitive disadvantage. Eventually, this led to the introduction of a specific legal basis for social policy matters by the Single European Act, namely Article 118a TEEC in the field of health and safety, which allowed for qualified majority voting (QMV) in the Council.[17]

The content of Article 118a TEEC can currently be found in Article 153 TFEU, which envisages a significantly increased range of competence for the EU in the social field. The subsidiarity principle that was present in its pre-constitutional sense already in Article 117 TEEC remains of great importance in the current EU competences on social matters, and as is clear from the text of Article 153 TFEU, has a dual dimension in the current Treaty provisions on social policy:[18] on the one hand, those provisions reflect the subsidiary nature of Union action in relation to that of the Member States;[19] on the other hand, they give a role to management and labour in the formulation or implementation of measures at Union level.[20]

Furthermore, Article 153(2)(a) TFEU provides for the European Parliament and the Council to 'adopt measures designed to encourage cooperation between Member States through initiatives aimed at improving knowledge, developing exchanges of information and best practices, promoting innovative approaches and evaluating experiences, excluding any harmonisation of the laws and regulations of the Member States'. This reflects the increasing use of the OMC.[21]

The directives adopted pursuant to Article 153(2)(b) TFEU are intended to lay down minimum requirements. That much is also clear from Article

---

[16]   On that aspect of the subsidiarity principle: K. Lenaerts and P. Van Nuffel (eds), *European Union Law* (Sweet & Maxwell, 2nd edn, 2011), pp. 132–4, paragraph 7–027; G. De Baere, '"Единство в многообразието": balancing unity and diversity in EU competences through subsidiarity, proportionality and flexibility' (2015) XII *Evropeiski praven pregled* 36.

[17]   See Barnard, n. 13 in this chapter, at pp. 8–12 and 50–3.

[18]   Lenaerts and Van Nuffel, n. 16 in this chapter, at pp. 132–4, paragraph 7–027 and the citations therein. See also Vandenbroucke, n. 5 in this chapter, and C. Barnard, '(B)Remains of the Day: Brexit and EU Social Policy', Chapter 19 in this volume.

[19]   Article 153(1), (2) and (4) TFEU.

[20]   Articles 153(3) and 154 TFEU.

[21]   Barnard, n. 13 in this chapter, at pp. 54–5.

153(4) TFEU, which provides that the provisions adopted pursuant to Article 153 TFEU are not to 'prevent any Member State from maintaining or introducing more stringent protective measures compatible with the Treaties'. As the Court of Justice[22] held in the *Working Time Directive* case, that provision 'does not limit [Union] action to the lowest common denominator, or even to the lowest level of protection established by the various Member States, but means that Member States are free to provide a level of protection more stringent than that resulting from [Union] law, high as it may be'.[23] Furthermore, Article 153(4), first indent, TFEU adds that EU action in social policy areas on the basis of Article 153 TFEU must not 'affect the right of Member States to define the fundamental principles of their social security systems and must not significantly affect the financial equilibrium thereof'.

In addition, Article 153(5) TFEU expressly excludes four areas of high sensitivity (pay, the right of association, the right to strike and the right to impose lock-outs) from EU competence under Article 153 TFEU.[24] Another relevant example is that Union action in the area of industry on the basis of Article 173 TFEU cannot 'provide a basis for the introduction by the Union of any measure which could lead to a distortion of competition or contains tax provisions or provisions relating to the rights and interests of employed persons'.[25] Furthermore, Union measures in the field of employment exclude harmonisation of the laws and regulations of the Member States.[26] The same counts for the adoption by the Union of social policy measures 'designed to encourage cooperation between Member States through initiatives aimed at improving knowledge, developing exchanges of information and best practices, promoting innovative approaches and evaluating experiences'[27] and action in the field of industry.[28]

However, even in areas excluded from EU competence, the ECJ has made clear that the Member States and social partners still have to exercise their competence consistently with EU law, including the principle of

---

[22] Under Article 19(1), first subparagraph TEU, the institution of the Court of Justice of the EU encompasses the Court of Justice ('ECJ'), the General Court ('EGC') and specialised courts. The only court falling in the latter category, the Civil Service Tribunal ('EU Civil Service Tribunal' or 'ECST'), established in 2004, ceased to operate on 1 September 2016 after its jurisdiction was transferred to the EGC in the context of the reform of the EU's judicial structure.

[23] ECJ, judgment of 12 November 1996 in *United Kingdom v Council* ('*Working Time Directive*'), C-84/94, EU:C:1996:431, paragraph 56. See Barnard, n. 13 in this chapter, at pp. 55–6.

[24] But see further, Section 14.3.2.1 in this chapter.

[25] Article 173(3), second subparagraph TFEU.

[26] Article 149, second paragraph TFEU.

[27] Article 153(2), first subparagraph (a) TFEU.

[28] Article 173(3), second subparagraph TFEU.

non-discrimination[29] and the four freedoms. This can be seen in the controversial but highly significant decisions of *Viking* and *Laval*.[30] There, the Court applied the freedom of establishment and to provide services to an area expressly excluded from EU competence (strikes), thereby creating a legislative vacuum. While as a consequence of the judgments national rules potentially had to be amended or even removed from the books entirely, the EU itself could not remedy the vacuum, given the absence of competence to act. This is one aspect of the so-called social deficit in the EU. In fact, an attempt was made, in the Monti II proposal, to address the problem. As will be seen below, this proposal was introduced using one of the general legal bases, Article 352 TFEU, but the proposal prompted such fierce criticism from all sides that it was rapidly withdrawn.[31]

In addition to Article 153 TFEU, equipping the EU with specific competence to take action in the field of social policy[32] and Article 155 TFEU, providing a legal basis for the conversion into EU measures of collective (or framework) agreements negotiated by the social partners in matters covered by Article 153 TFEU,[33] Article 157(3) TFEU constitutes a legal basis for measures to ensure the application of the principle of equal opportunities and equal treatment in matters of employment and occupation, including the principle of equal pay for equal work or work of equal value.[34]

Mention should also be made of specific legal bases outside social policy *sensu stricto* but arguably within social policy *sensu lato*. First, Article 19 TFEU,

[29] ECJ, judgment of 10 June 2010 in *Bruno and Pettini*, C-395/08 and C-396/08, EU:C:2010:329, paragraph 39.

[30] ECJ, judgments of 11 December 2007 in *The International Transport Workers' Federation and The Finnish Seamen's Union* ('*Viking*'), C-438/05, EU:C:2007:772; and of 18 December 2007 in *Laval un Partneri*, C-341/05, EU:C:2007:809. See S. Feenstra, 'How Can the Viking/ Laval Conundrum Be Resolved: One Bed for Two Dreams?', Chapter 13 in this volume; and Barnard, n. 1 in this chapter, at pp. 205–7.

[31] See Section 14.3.2.1 in this chapter.

[32] See ECJ, judgment of 14 January 2010 in *Commission v Czech Republic*, C-343/08, EU:C:2010:14, paragraph 67.

[33] See Article 155(2) TFEU. For general discussion of these agreements and other texts issued by the social partners, see for example C. Barnard and G. De Baere, *Towards a European Social Union: Achievements and Possibilities under the Current EU Constitutional Framework* (University of Leuven Euroforum, 2014); P. Craig, *EU Administrative Law* (Oxford University Press, 2nd rev. edn, 2012), pp. 219–41.

[34] See for example COM(2012)614 *Proposal for a Directive of the European Parliament and of the Council on Improving the Gender Balance among Non-executive Directors of Companies Listed on Stock Exchanges and Related Measures* (Brussels, 14 November 2012). At the time of writing, it has not yet been adopted. See also the Opinion of the Committee on Legal Affairs on the Legal Basis, annexed to the European Parliament's Report of 25 October 2013 on this proposal, which mentions other measures adopted under what is now Article 157(3) TFEU and discusses this legal basis in further detail.

which is to be found in Part Two Non-Discrimination and Citizenship of the Union, provides for the Council acting unanimously in accordance with a special legislative procedure and after obtaining the consent of the European Parliament, to 'take appropriate action to combat discrimination based on sex, racial or ethnic origin, religion or belief, disability, age or sexual orientation', without prejudice to the other provisions of the Treaties and within the limits of the powers conferred by them upon the Union. As a legal basis, that provision has a clear potential to be of significant value to social policy issues, as can be seen from the fact that it (or more accurately its predecessor Article 13 EC) was used to adopt two crucial measures to combat discrimination.[35]

Secondly, as mentioned above, employment is an entirely different type of Union competence from social policy *sensu stricto*. EU action with respect to employment is based on a new approach referred to as OMC, which is based on target setting, peer review, and guidelines. Pursuant to Article 145 TFEU, Member States and the Union are to 'work towards developing a co-ordinated strategy for employment and particularly for promoting a skilled, trained and adaptable workforce and labour markets responsive to economic change'. Article 147 TFEU requires the Union to contribute to a high level of employment by encouraging cooperation between Member States and by supporting and, if necessary, complementing their action, all the while respecting, the competences of the Member States. Article 148 TFEU further provides that the Council is to adopt certain labour-market policies, albeit in the form of soft law, drawing up guidelines on employment. These guidelines have been revised a number of times but they generally contain a mix of active labour-market policy (education, training) with exhortations to Member States to deregulate to make the labour market more flexible. The change of approach signalled by the Employment Title suggested that the old 'Community method or 'ordinary Union method'[36] was running out of steam.

---

[35] Council Directive 2000/43/EC of 29 June 2000 implementing the principle of equal treatment between persons irrespective of racial or ethnic origin, [2000] OJ L 180/22; and Council Directive 2000/78/EC of 27 November 2000 establishing a general framework for equal treatment in employment and occupation, [2000] OJ L 303/16.

[36] See G. De Baere, 'European Integration and the Rule of Law in Foreign Policy', in J. Dickson and P. Eleftheriadis (eds), *Philosophical Foundations of European Union Law* (Oxford University Press, 2012), pp. 361–6, outlining the characteristics of the ordinary Union method, and arguing that while it is often regarded as the cornerstone of European integration, it is in fact a method aimed at subjecting Member State action to the rule of law.

14.2.2.2 General Legal Bases

As we have seen, the original Treaty of Rome contained no express competence for the EU to legislate in the field of social policy, which was seen as a matter for domestic law. However, the idea that economic policy should be designed at EU level while social policy-making remains in neatly separated national or regional arenas was, at best, naive. As the premise for EU social policy, it was a recipe for a dwindling capacity of the Member States to direct their own social policies (since they were ever increasingly constrained by their commitments about expenditure at EU level), without greater steering capacity on the part of the EU.[37]

The unsustainability of the original setup was recognised by the early 1970s, when the Heads of State agreed that the attainment of a social dimension was, to them, as important as economic union. This precipitated a flurry of legislative activity in three policy domains: gender equality, protection of employees in the restructuring of their business, and health and safety. In the absence of any specific legal bases, all of these measures were adopted under general legal bases contained in the Treaties.

These include in particular what are now Articles 114 and 115 TFEU, and the so-called 'flexibility clause' in Article 352 TFEU. The general legal bases are intended to serve a residual function, applying only in the absence of a specific basis. They may not be used as a legal basis in order to circumvent an express exclusion of harmonisation laid down in specific articles of the Treaties.[38]

Article 114 TFEU can serve as a legal basis where there are differences between the laws, regulations, or administrative provisions of the Member States which are such as to obstruct the fundamental freedoms and where the measures proposed have as their object to contribute to the functioning of the internal market.[39] To justify recourse to Article 114 TFEU, what matters is that the measure adopted on that basis must actually be intended to improve the conditions for the establishment and functioning of the internal market.[40] While a reasonably broad scope of measures could

---

[37] F. Vandenbroucke, 'Europe: The Social Challenge. Defining the Union's Social Objective Is a Necessity Rather than a Luxury' *Observatoire social Européen Opinion Paper*, 11/12, p. 24.

[38] ECJ, judgment of 5 October 2000 in *Germany v Parliament and Council ('Tobacco Advertising I')*, C-376/98, EU:C:2000:544, paragraph 79.

[39] ECJ, judgment of 4 May 2016 in *Philip Morris Brands and Others*, C-547/14, EU:C:2016:325, paragraph 58 and the case law cited there. See also judgments of 4 May 2016 in *Poland v Parliament and Council*, C-358/14, EU:C:2016:323; and *Pillbox 38*, C-477/14, EU:C:2016:324.

[40] ECJ, judgment of 12 December 2006 in *Germany v Parliament and Council ('Tobacco Advertising II')*, C-380/03, EU:C:2006:772, paragraph 80. For a detailed discussion of the scope of Article 114 TFEU, see K. Gutman, *The Constitutional Foundations of European Contract Law: A Comparative Analysis* (Oxford University Press, 2014), pp. 325–58 and citations therein.

be pursued on that basis, it appears safe to assume that measures in the broader realm of social policy regarding, for example, the fundamentals of pensions, the redistribution of wealth through a reform of the tax system or the size of the expenditure on health are beyond the limits of that competence.[41] The usefulness of Article 114 TFEU as a legal basis for social policy measures is also limited by the fact that it cannot apply to 'fiscal provisions, to those relating to the free movement of persons nor to those relating to the rights and interests of employed persons'.[42] Article 115 TFEU contains no such exclusion, but measures on that legal basis are adopted in accordance with a stricter decision-making procedure, requiring unanimity in the Council.

In the absence of a specific legal basis for Union action in the Treaties, recourse may be had to Article 352 TFEU. That provision enables the Union to adopt the appropriate measures if action by the Union should prove necessary, within the framework of the policies defined in the Treaties, to attain one of the objectives set out in the Treaties, and the Treaties have not provided the necessary powers.[43] The competence under Article 352 TFEU 'does not create an obligation, but confers on the Council an option, failure to exercise which cannot affect the validity of proceedings'.[44] Put differently, it is not true that if something can be done under Article 352 TFEU, it has to be done instead of under Member State competences. The Council has a large discretion to determine whether action is necessary.[45] Nevertheless, this discretion is limited. First, recourse to Article 352 TFEU is justified only where no other provision of the Treaties either expressly or impliedly gives the Union institutions the necessary power to adopt the measure in question.[46] Secondly, any recourse to Article 352 TFEU should, in accordance with the principle of conferral, stay within the scope of the Treaties. This was borne out by the Court's reasoning on Article 308 TEC (Article 352 TFEU's predecessor) as a possible legal basis

---

[41] A. Hinarejos, 'The Euro Area Crisis and Constitutional Limits to Fiscal Integration' (2011–12) 14 *Cambridge Yearbook of European Legal studies* 261.

[42] Article 114(2) TFEU.

[43] Article 352(1) TFEU.

[44] ECJ, judgment of 31 March 1971 in *Commission v Council* ('ERTA'), C-22/70, EU:C:1971:32, paragraph 95.

[45] For example ECJ, judgment of 12 July 1973 in *Hauptzollamt Bremerhaven v Massey Ferguson*, C-8/73, EU:C:1973:90, paragraphs 3–6.

[46] ECJ, judgment of 11 June 1991 in *United Kingdom, France and Germany v Council*, C-51/89, C-90/89, and C-94/89, EU:C:1991:241, paragraph 6; Opinion 2/92 of 24 March 1995, EU:C:1995:83, paragraph 36.

for accession of the then Community to the European Convention on Human Rights[47] in Opinion 2/94.[48]

Should the Union wish to act on the basis of Article 352 TFEU, the Council must act unanimously on a proposal from the Commission and after obtaining the consent of the European Parliament.[49] Also since Lisbon, the Commission has the obligation to draw national parliaments' attention to proposals based on Article 352.[50]

If necessary, the Union can combine Article 352 TFEU with other Treaty provisions if they in themselves do not constitute a sufficient legal basis.[51] There are indications in the case law that where recourse is made to Article 352 TFEU in combination with other legal bases, the relevant procedural requirements are to be combined. The Court thus allows for the unanimity requirement of Article 352 TFEU to be combined with other procedures, such as, notably, the ordinary legislative procedure, which would otherwise provide for QMV.[52] However, crucially, measures based on Article 352 TFEU may not entail harmonisation of Member States' laws or regulations in cases where the Treaties exclude such harmonisation.[53]

[47] Convention for the Protection of Human Rights and Fundamental Freedoms of 4 November 1950, 213 UNTS 221.
[48] For example Opinion 2/94 of 28 March 1996, EU:C:1996:140. Article 6(2) TEU now provides for the Union to accede to the ECHR. However, the ECJ held that the agreement on the accession of the EU to the ECHR was 'not compatible with Article 6(2) TEU or with Protocol (No 8)' relating to Article 6(2) TEU on the accession of the Union to the ECHR: Opinion 2/13 of 18 December 2014, EU:C:2014:2454. See for example P. Eeckhout, 'Opinion 2/13 on EU Accession to the ECHR and Judicial Dialogue: Autonomy or Autarky' (2015) 38 *Fordham International Law Journal* 955–92; J. Odermatt, 'A Giant Step Backwards? Opinion 2/13 on the EU's Accession to the European Convention on Human Rights' (2015) 47 *New York University Journal of International Law and Politics* 783–797.
[49] Article 352(1) TFEU.
[50] Article 352(2) TFEU, though not of proposals based on Article 114 TFEU. See S. Weatherill, 'Better Competence Monitoring' (2005) 30 *European Law Review* 36, arguing that this difference is accidental and deploring this.
[51] See for example ECJ, judgment of 3 September 2008 in *Kadi and Al Barakaat International Foundation*, C-402/05 P and C-415/05 P, EU:C:2008:461, paragraphs 211–14.
[52] ECJ, judgment of 3 September 2009 in *Parliament v Council* ('*International Fund for Ireland*'), C-166/07, EU:C:2009:499, paragraph 69. This should be contrasted with the Court's approach in the judgment of 11 June 1991 in *Commission v Council* ('*Titanium Dioxide*'), C-300/89, EU:C:1991:244. See for example T. Corthaut, Case note (2011) *Common Market Law Review* 1271; G. De Baere, 'From 'Don't Mention the *Titanium Dioxide* Judgment' to 'I Mentioned it Once, But I Think I Got Away with it All Right' — Reflections on the Choice of Legal Basis in EU External Relations after the *Legal Basis for Restrictive Measures* Judgment' (2012–14) 15 *Cambridge Yearbook of European Legal Studies* 537; Gutman, n. 40 in this chapter, at pp. 287–91. See, for example, Ministero dell'Economia e delle Finanze, *A European Unemployment Benefit Scheme: Nine Clarifications* (Ministero dell'Economia e delle Finanze, September 2016), p. 5, contemplating the establishment of a European Fund for unemployment benefits on the basis of Article 175(3) TFEU, and possibly Article 136 TFEU and/or Article 352 TFEU.
[53] Article 352(3) TFEU.

Article 352(1) TFEU stipulates that action on that legal basis must be 'necessary to attain one of the objectives set out in the Treaties'. These objectives notably include the establishment of an internal market and in that connection (since Lisbon) working 'for the sustainable development of Europe based on balanced economic growth and price stability, a highly competitive social market economy, aiming at full employment and social progress, and a high level of protection and improvement of the quality of the environment'.[54] Nevertheless, the fact that the Union is to pursue its objectives by appropriate means commensurate with the competences conferred upon it in the Treaties, combined with the impossibility since Lisbon of using Article 352 TFEU to circumvent the lack of a harmonisation competence[55] together imply that the usefulness of that provision directly to pursue the social objectives in the Treaty is limited.[56] This was demonstrated by the Monti II saga, examined further below.[57]

Any assessment of the potential use of Article 352 TFEU must also take into account the national constitutional orders of Member States.[58] An example of a national constitutional court's impact on the debate is the *Bundesverfassungsgericht's* view in its *Lisbon Urteil* that Article 352 TFEU can be construed in such a way that the integration programme envisaged there can still be predicted and determined by the German legislative bodies.[59] However, the *Bundesverfassungsgericht* warned that the provision meets with constitutional objections:

> with regard to the ban on transferring blanket empowerments or on transferring *Kompetenz-Kompetenz*, because the newly worded provision makes it possible substantially to amend treaty foundations of the European Union without the constitutive participation of legislative bodies in addition to the Member States' executive powers.[60]

The duty to inform national parliaments pursuant to Article 352(2) TFEU does not alter that assessment because the Commission is only required to draw the national parliaments' attention to the relevant proposal. The

---

[54] Article 3(3) TEU.
[55] Article 352(3) TFEU.
[56] Armstrong, n. 4 in this chapter, at pp. 244–5. See in general De Baere, n. 16 in this chapter, at pp. 29–36.
[57] See Feenstra, n. 30 in this chapter.
[58] See G. van der Schyff, 'EU Social Competences and Member State Constitutional Controls: A Comparative Perspective of National Approaches', Chapter 15 in this volume.
[59] German Federal Constitutional Court, BVerfGE 123, 267 (*Lisbon*) of 30 June 2009, at [322].
[60] Ibid., at [328].

Bundesverfassungsgericht therefore imposes an important procedural limit on the use of Article 352 TFEU:

> Because of the indefinite nature of future application of the flexibility clause, its use constitutionally requires ratification by the German Bundestag and the Bundesrat on the basis of Article 23.1 second and third sentence of the Basic Law. The German representative in the Council may not express formal approval on behalf of the Federal Republic of Germany of a corresponding lawmaking proposal of the Commission as long as these constitutionally required preconditions are not met.[61]

Such requirements pose a clear limitation on the potential for the use of the flexibility clause in social policy as in other areas.

14.3 THE TRADITIONAL ROUTE OF EU SOCIAL POLICY LEGISLATION

14.3.1 *Arrested Development of EU Social Policy Legislation*

Several key measures that may be considered to comprise an important part, if not the core, of EU social policy legislation are based on the EU's competence under what is now Article 153 TFEU (and by cross-reference what is now Article 155 TFEU).[62] These measures illustrate three salient points concerning the state of EU social policy legislation and the EU's competence in this field.

First, it is apparent that the majority of measures were adopted in the heyday of the 1970s, '80s, and '90s,[63] and many of the more recent measures are merely codifications (or consolidation in the case of the Collective Redundancies Directive[64]) of these earlier measures,[65] meaning that the original act and its

---

[61] Ibid., at [328] and [417].

[62] For an overview, see for example Commission Staff Working Document, The EU social acquis, SWD (2016)50 final, accompanying the Communication launching a consultation on a European Pillar of Social Rights (COM(2016)127 *Communication on Launching a Consultation on a European Pillar of Social Rights* (Strasbourg, 8 March 2016)). For related documents and activities, see the Commission website, ec.europa.eu/priorities/deeper-and-fairer-economic-and-monetary-union/towards-european-pillar-social-rights_en (accessed 15 December 2016).

[63] For background, see for example C. Barnard, 'EU 'Social' Policy: From Employment Law to Labour Market Reform', in P. Craig and G. De Búrca (eds), *The Evolution of EU Law* (Oxford University Press, 2nd edn, 2011), pp. 641–62; J. Piris, *The Lisbon Treaty: A Legal and Political Analysis* (Cambridge University Press, 2010), pp. 309–13.

[64] Council Directive 75/129/EEC of 17 February 1975 on the approximation of the laws of the Member States relating to collective redundancies, [1975] OJ L 48/29, now consolidated as Council Directive 98/59/EC of 20 July 1998 on the approximation of the laws of the Member States relating to collective redundancies, [1998] OJ 1998 L 225/16 (Collective Redundancies Directive).

[65] See for example Council Directive 77/187/EEC of 14 February 1977 on the approximation of the laws of the Member States relating to the safeguarding of employees' rights in the event

subsequent amendments are presented in a single text without any substantive amendments (for example, changes to the legal basis) allowed.[66] This is not to say that there has been no legislative activity on the basis of Article 153 TFEU in recent years, but it has been limited.[67]

Secondly, it is unlikely that certain measures adopted under the EU's internal market competence of what was then Article 100 TEEC (later Article 94 EC, now Article 115 TFEU) would have been adopted under that legal basis today. This is so, with particular regard to Directive 75/129 on collective redundancies[68] and Directive 77/187 on transfers of undertakings,[69] taking into account their aim and content. The Employer Insolvency Directive,[70] while originally adopted under Article 100 TEEC, was subsequently amended by way of Directive 2002/74,[71] which was based on former Article 137(2) EC now Article 153(2) TFEU],[72] with the result that the codified version, Directive 2008/94,[73] is also based on this provision. In the proposal for Directive 2002/

---

of transfers of undertakings, businesses or parts of businesses, [1977] OJ L 61/26, now codified as Council Directive 2001/23/EC of 12 March 2001 on the approximation of the laws of the Member States relating to the safeguarding of employees' rights in the event of transfers of undertakings, businesses or parts of undertakings or businesses, [2001] OJ L 82/16 (Transfer of Undertakings Directive); Council Directive 80/987/EEC of 20 October 1980 on the approximation of the laws of the Member States relating to the protection of employees in the event of the insolvency of their employer, [1980] OJ L 283/23, now codified as Directive 2008/94/EC of the European Parliament and of the Council of 22 October 2008 on the protection of employees in the event of the insolvency of their employer, [2008] OJ L 283/36 (Employer Insolvency Directive); Council Directive 93/104/EC of 23 November 1993 concerning certain aspects of the organization of working time, [1993] OJ L 307/18, now codified as Directive 2003/88/EC of the European Parliament and of the Council of 4 November 2003 concerning certain aspects of the organization of working time, [2003] OJ L 299/9 (Working Time Directive).

[66] See the Commission's website, ec.europa.eu/dgs/legal_service/ (accessed 15 December 2016). In contrast to codification and consolidation, recasting involves new substantive changes, for example Directive 2009/38/EC of the European Parliament and of the Council of 6 May 2009 on the establishment of a European Works Council or a procedure in Community-scale undertakings and Community-scale groups of undertakings for the purposes of informing and consulting employees (Recast), [2009] OJ 2009 L 122/28 (European Works Council Directive).

[67] See for example Lörcher, n. 3 in this chapter, at p. 191.

[68] See n. 64 in this chapter.

[69] See n. 65 in this chapter.

[70] Ibid.

[71] Directive 2002/74/EC of the European Parliament and of the Council of 23 September 2002 amending Council Directive 80/987/EEC on the approximation of the laws of the Member States relating to the protection of employees in the event of the insolvency of their employer, [2002] OJ L 270/10.

[72] See further COM(2000)832 *Proposal for a Directive of the European Parliament and of the Council Amending Council Directive 80/987/EEC on the Approximation of the Laws of the Member States Relating to the Protection of Employees in the Event of the Insolvency of Their Employer* (Brussels, 23 May 2016).

[73] See n. 65 in this chapter.

74, the Commission explained that in the absence of a specific legal basis for measures to improve working conditions, it was necessary to refer to the general legal basis for the approximation of legislation; however, in light of the amendments introduced by the Amsterdam Treaty, then Article 137(2) EC constituted the specific and appropriate legal basis for legal instruments aimed at improving working conditions, such that this Directive should take that Article as its legal basis.[74]

Consequently, the fact that certain older directives were based on the EU's internal market competences does not necessarily predicate the recourse to such competences when it comes to the assessment of the legal bases of future measures. This does not rule them out either. Depending on the aim and content of the measure, this may implicate the use of Article 153 TFEU by itself or in combination with other legal bases, including Article 115 TFEU and possibly Article 114 TFEU to the extent that the measure does not fall within the excluded areas listed in Article 114(2) TFEU.[75]

Thirdly, a striking feature of these measures is that they generally do not indicate what field(s) enumerated in Article 153(1) TFEU ((a) through (i) in the case of directives pursuant to Article 153(2)(b) TFEU) is/are being relied on. This is understandable in respect of the earlier measures based on former Article 118a TEEC (adopted before the entry into force of the Maastricht Treaty), since that Article did not provide much of a choice, setting forth the EU's competence to adopt directives in order to achieve the objective of 'encouraging improvements, especially in the working environment, as regards the health and safety of workers'. Yet, with subsequent Treaty amendments starting with the Maastricht Treaty's Social Policy Protocol and Agreement, the list of fields was developed, then placed inside the Treaty framework into two groups (distinguished by decision-making procedures) under the Amsterdam Treaty and eventually consolidated by the Nice Treaty under ex Article 137(1) EC, which was taken over by the Lisbon Treaty in what is now Article 153(1) TFEU. Thus, depending on the measure concerned, one has to examine its content and the preparatory documents, often the Commission's proposal, in order to determine the relevant field(s) that constitute(s) the grounding for such measure.

---

[74] COM(2000)832, n. 72 in this chapter, point 6.
[75] Regarding the relationship between Articles 114 and 115 TFEU, see for example Gutman, n. 40 in this chapter, at pp. 313–24 and citations therein. Regarding consideration of 'social' objectives in EU internal market legislation, see for example B. De Witte, 'A Competence to Protect: The Pursuit of Non-market Aims through Internal Market Legislation', in P. Syrpsis (ed.), *The Judiciary, the Legislature and the EU Internal Market* (Cambridge University Press, 2012), p. 25; G. Davies, 'Democracy and Legitimacy in the Shadow of Purposive Competence' (2015) 21 *European Law Journal* 2.

Looking closely at some of the measures, several fields of Article 153(1) TFEU have been used by the EU legislator to varying degrees. Among those that stand out are: (a) improvement in particular of the working environment to protect workers' health and safety as illustrated by the Framework Directive on health and safety[76] and the Working Time Directive;[77] (b) working conditions as illustrated by the Employer Insolvency Directive,[78] the Directive on part-time work,[79] the Directive on fixed-term work,[80] and the Directive on temporary agency work;[81] (e) the information and consultation of workers as illustrated by the Information and Consultation Directive[82] and the European Works Council Directive;[83] and (i) equality between men and women with regard to labour-market opportunities and treatment at work as illustrated by the original and revised Directives on parental leave.[84]

[76] Council Directive 89/391/EEC of 12 June 1989 on the Introduction of Measures to Encourage Improvements in the Safety and Health of Workers at Work, [1989] OJ L 183/1 (Framework Directive on Health and Safety), first recital.

[77] See Working Time Directive, n. 65 in this chapter, first recital.

[78] See COM(2000)832, n. 72 in this chapter, point 6, at third paragraph.

[79] Regarding Council Directive 97/81/EC of 15 December 1997 concerning the Framework Agreement on Part-time Work concluded by UNICE, CEEP, and the ETUC, [1998] OJ L 14/9, see COM(1997)398, point 40.

[80] Regarding Council Directive 1999/70/EC of 28 June 1999 concerning the framework agreement on fixed-term work concluded by ETUC, UNICE, and CEEP, [1999] OJ L 175/43, see COM(1999)203, point 44.

[81] Regarding Directive 2008/104/EC of the European Parliament and of the Council of 19 November 2008 on temporary agency work, [2008] OJ L 327/9, see COM(2002)149 *Proposal for a Directive of the European Parliament and the Council on Working Conditions for Temporary Workers* (Brussels, 21 March 2002), point 4.

[82] Although the title and content of the Directive 2002/14/EC of the European Parliament and of the Council of 11 March 2002 establishing a general framework for informing and consulting employees in the European Community, [2002] OJ L 80/29 indicate this, point (e) (or the preceding third indent of Article 2(1) of the Social Policy Agreement annexed to the Social Policy Protocol) is not cited expressly in the Directive itself or the Commission's proposals, which merely reiterate the language of this point. See COM(1998)612 *Proposal for a Council Directive Establishing a General Framework for Informing and Consulting Employees in the European Community* (Brussels, 17 November 1998), part V; COM(2001)296 *Amended Proposal for a Directive of the European Parliament and of the Council Establishing a General Framework for Improving Information and Consultation Rights of Employees in the European Community* (Brussels, 23 May 2001), points 1–2.

[83] European Works Council Directive, n. 66 in this chapter, ninth recital; and COM (2008)419 *Proposal for a European Parliament and Council Directive on the Establishment of a European Works Council or a Procedure in Community-scale Undertakings and Community-scale Groups of Undertakings for the Purposes of Informing and Consulting Employees* (Brussels, 2 July 2008), point 23.

[84] Regarding Council Directive 96/34/EC of 3 June 1996 on the framework agreement on parental leave concluded by UNICE, CEEP, and the ETUC, [1996] OJ L 145/4, see Proposal, COM(96)26, point 31. Regarding Council Directive 2010/18/EU of 8 March 2010 implementing the revised Framework Agreement on Parental Leave concluded by BUSINESSEUROPE,

At the same time, these measures help to illuminate that other fields of Article 153(1) TFEU have been resorted to rarely, if at all, in respect of directives adopted pursuant to Article 153(2)(b) TFEU (or via Article 155(2) TFEU),[85] as compared to the adoption of 'soft' measures pursuant to Article 153(2)(a) TFEU in the sense of 'measures designed to encourage cooperation between Member States' excluding the harmonisation of national laws. To take some recent examples, while the Council Recommendation on a Quality Framework for Traineeships,[86] based on Articles 153, 166, and 292 TFEU, does not say so explicitly, the Commission cited paragraphs (b) working conditions, (c) social security and social protection of workers, (h) integration of persons excluded from the labour market, and (j) the combating of social exclusion, as part of the justification for recourse to Article 153 TFEU in the proposal.[87] Similarly, regarding the Decision on establishing a European Platform to enhance cooperation in the prevention and deterrence of undeclared work,[88] based on Article 153(2)(a) TFEU, the Commission declared that the EU has the competence to act in the field of undeclared work based on the social policy provisions of the TFEU, pointing to paragraphs (b) working conditions, (h) integration of persons excluded from the labour market, and (j) the

---

UEAPME, CEEP, and ETUC and repealing Directive 96/34/EC, [2010] OJ L 68/13, see first recital; and Proposal, COM(2009)410, point 3.1. Regarding the relationship between Articles 153(1)(i) and 157(3) TFEU, see Opinion of the Committee on Legal Affairs on Legal Basis, annexed to the second European Parliament Report of 5 March 2010, on the proposal for a Directive on Maternity Leave, COM(2008)637 *Proposal for a Directive of the European Parliament and of the Council Amending Council Directive 92/85/EEC on the Introduction of Measures to Encourage Improvements in the Safety and Health at Work of Pregnant Workers and Workers Who Have Recently Given Birth or Are Breastfeeding* (Brussels, 3 October 2008), proposing the use of Articles 153(2) and 157(3) TFEU: see point 3. However, the proposal was withdrawn in 2015.

[85] For example, the EU legislator has not yet utilised point (c) in this regard: see H. Verschueren, 'Union Law and the Fight Against Poverty: Which Legal Instruments?', in B. Cantillon, H. Verschueren, and P. Ploscar (eds), *Social Inclusion and Social Protection in the EU: Interactions between Law and Policy* (Intersentia, 2012), pp. 205, 211. See also Staff Working Document, n. 62 in this chapter, points 3.1.9, 3.2.

[86] Council Recommendation of 10 March 2014 on a Quality Framework for Traineeships, [2014] OJ C 88/1. Article 166 TFEU (regarding vocational training) is added as a legal basis to cover traineeships that are not remunerated, and Article 292 TFEU provides for the adoption of Council recommendations on the basis of a Commission proposal in areas of Union competence.

[87] COM(2013)857 *Proposal for a Council Recommendation on a Quality Framework for Traineeships* (Brussels, 4 December 2013), point 3.

[88] Decision (EU) 2016/344 of the European Parliament and of the Council of 9 March 2016 on establishing a European Platform to enhance cooperation in tackling undeclared work, [2016] OJ L 65/12.

combating of social exclusion.[89] Moreover, paragraph (h) the integration of persons excluded from the labour market is cited, perhaps not surprisingly given the title, in Commission Recommendation 2008/867 on the active inclusion of people excluded from the labour market.[90]

With the current approach, it is easy to lose sight of the fact that Article 153(1) TFEU provides in principle an extensive list of fields that may be the subject of EU legislation, more than any other provision establishing a sectoral competence for the EU in the Treaties.[91] In other words, this Treaty provision essentially lays out an 11-point 'laundry list' of fields within the scope of EU competence, nine of which may be the subject of EU (minimum[92]) harmonisation by way of directives, though at least half have remained dormant in much of the EU legislative activity to date. Taking stock of key pieces of EU social policy legislation therefore highlights, along the lines of the European Parliament's Resolution 'Towards a genuine Economic and Monetary Union',[93] that there is arguably untapped potential for EU legislative action under Article 153 TFEU, particularly in relation to paragraph (h) as well as other paragraphs, such as (c) social security and social protection for workers and (d) protection of workers where their employment contract is

---

[89] COM(2014)221 *Proposal for a Decision of the European Parliament and of the Council on Establishing a European Platform to Enhance Cooperation in the Prevention and Deterrence of Undeclared Work* (Brussels, 9 April 2014), point 3.1.

[90] Commission Recommendation 2008/867/EC of 3 October 2008 on the active inclusion of people excluded from the labour market, [2008] OJ L 307/11, first recital; see also COM(2008)629 Commission Communication on this Recommendation (Brussels, 15 October 2008), point 1, first paragraph; and Council of the European Union, 'Conclusions on Common Active Inclusion Principles to Combat Poverty More Effectively' 2916th Employment, Social Policy, Health and Consumer Affairs Council Meeting of 17 December 2008, point 5, available at: www.consilium.europa.eu/ueDocs/cms_Data/docs/pressData/en/lsa/104818.pdf (accessed 15 December 2016). This Recommendation is based on ex Article 211 EC, which was repealed and replaced, in substance, by Article 17(1) TEU. It builds on Council Recommendation 92/441/EEC of 24 June 1992 on common criteria concerning sufficient resources and social assistance in social protection systems, [1992] OJ L 245/46, based on ex Article 235 TEEC [now Article 352 TFEU], and related institutional documents pertaining to the establishment of adequate minimum income schemes in the Member States. See further Section 14.3.2 in this chapter.

[91] For example Article 81(2) TFEU, concerning the EU's competence in judicial cooperation in civil matters, lists eight matters on which measures may be adopted in that field. See further for example Gutman, n. 40 in this chapter, at pp. 423–36 and citations therein.

[92] See Article 153(4), second indent, TFEU.

[93] European Parliament Resolution of 20 November 2012 with recommendations to the Commission on the report of the Presidents of the European Council, the European Commission, the European Central Bank and the Eurogroup 'Towards a Genuine Economic and Monetary Union', available at: www.europarl.europa.eu/sides/getDoc.do?pubRef=-//EP//NONSGML+TA+P7-TA-2012-0430+0+DOC+PDF+V0//EN (accessed 15 December 2016), recital AP.

terminated, which would appear to be highly relevant in the present discussion of EU-level action to further social integration in the wake of the crisis.[94] In fact, some of these paragraphs have already filtered into the consideration of proposals for EU legislation, which leads to the next subsection.

14.3.2 *Proposals for EU Social Policy Legislation*

Generally speaking, there is a vast and growing array of proposals put forward by scholars and policy-makers for EU legislation and other types of EU-level action on many subjects relating to the field of social policy,[95] not to mention broader calls for a more systematic approach to social policy in the EU,[96] taking into account the national and subnational levels, all of which cannot be discussed here in detail.

One of the most concrete and longstanding proposals for EU social policy legislation that has recently gathered steam in the literature and policy documents concerns the adoption of a directive establishing minimum standards on an adequate minimum income,[97] which builds on certain Recommendations issued by the Council and Commission on the subject.[98] For example, the European Anti-Poverty Network[99] has repeatedly advocated the adoption of a directive on adequate minimum income,[100] based on Article

---

[94] For example in connection with the EU Pillar of Social Rights, see Communication, n. 62 in this chapter, point 3.2, second paragraph.

[95] For a brief selection, see Barnard, n. 1 in this chapter, at pp. 231–6; Barnard and De Baere, n. 33 in this chapter, at pp. 26–35; B. Cantillon and N. Van Mechelen, 'Between Dream and Reality … On Anti-Poverty Policy, Minimum Income Protection and the European Social Model', in B. Cantillon, H. Verschueren, and P. Ploscar (eds), *Social Inclusion and Social Protection in the EU: Interactions between Law and Policy* (Intersentia, 2012), pp. 173, 174–5.

[96] See for example European Parliament Resolution, n. 93 in this chapter, Annex, Recommendation 3.2 on a social pact for Europe; Barnard, n. 1 in this chapter, at pp. 224–31 (concerning the creation of a European Social Compact); F. Vandenbroucke, *The Case for a European Social Union: From Muddling Through to a Common Sense of Purpose* (University of Leuven Euroforum, 2014).

[97] For background, see for example Cantillon and Van Mechelen, n. 95 in this chapter; A. Van Lancker, *Toward Adequate and Accessible Minimum Income Schemes in Europe: Analysis of Minimum Income Schemes and Roadmaps in 30 Countries Participating in the EMIN Project Synthesis Report* (European Minimum Income Network, 2015), available at: emin-eu.net (accessed 15 December 2016] (2015 EMIN Synthesis Report), point 5.3 (indicating emerging consensus at European level involving Union institutions and other constituents).

[98] See n. 90 in this chapter.

[99] For other organisations calling for such an initiative: see Opinion of the European Economic and Social Committee on European Minimum Income and Poverty Indicators, [2014] OJ C 170/23, point 1.3 fn 2.

[100] See A. Van Lancker, *Working Document on a Framework Directive on Minimum Income* (European Anti-Poverty Network, 2010), available at: www.eapn.eu/en/ (accessed 15 December 2016).

153(1)(h) TFEU.[101] This legal basis – as with the need for an EU legislative initiative on the subject[102] – finds some support in institutional documents.[103] Some commentators are sceptical, doubting whether Article 153 TFEU provides a proper legal basis for such a measure.[104] Although the feasibility of this proposal remains uncertain,[105] it is instructive for fleshing out several issues relating to the scope of the EU's competence under Article 153 TFEU, namely, the exceptions set forth in Article 153(5) TFEU and the viability of, and relationship between, certain fields listed in Article 153(1) TFEU, which are highly relevant to initiatives that may be considered in the future.

14.3.2.1 Article 153(5) TFEU

First, this proposal concerns the adequacy of minimum income schemes, which are intended to ensure a minimum standard of living for individuals and their dependents when they have no other means of financial support.[106] It does not appear to regulate minimum wages,[107] a topic which has also garnered its fair share of attention in the wake of the crisis.[108] This is important in view of Article 153(5) TFEU, which states: 'The provisions of this Article shall not apply to pay, the right of association, the right to strike or the right to impose lock-outs.' Indeed, on the basis of this provision, the Commission has underlined that the EU has no competence to establish minimum requirements

---

[101] Ibid., pp. 6–8. See also 'An EU Directive on Adequate Minimum Income: A Legal Assessment', available at: www.eapn.eu/en (accessed 15 December 2016) (EAPN Legal Assessment). This proposal has filtered into later documents of the European Minimum Income Network (EMIN), a two-year project (2013–14) sponsored by the European Parliament, funded by the Commission, and promoted by the EAPN: see for example 2015 EMIN Synthesis Report, n. 97 in this chapter, pp. 33–4.

[102] See for example European Parliament Resolution of 15 November 2011 on the European Platform against poverty and social exclusion, [2013] OJ C 153E/57, paragraph 95; Opinion of the Committee of the Regions on 'The European Platform against Poverty and Social Exclusion', [2011] OJ C 166/18, point 7.

[103] See for example Opinion of the European Economic and Social Committee, n. 99 in this chapter, point 2.4. See also n. 90 in this chapter.

[104] See for example Verschueren, n. 85 in this chapter, at pp. 211–13.

[105] See F. Vandenbroucke, B. Cantillon, N. Van Mechelen, T. Goedemé, and A. Van Lancker, 'The EU and Minimum Income Protection: Clarifying the Policy Conundrum', in I. Marx and K. Nelson (eds), *Minimum Income Protection in Flux* (Palgrave Macmillan, 2013), p. 271.

[106] 2015 EMIN Synthesis Report, n. 97 in this chapter, at p. 3. See also for example EAPN Explainer #2, *Adequacy of Minimum Income in the EU* (EAPN, 2010). More general definitions are provided in the Council and Commission Recommendations, n. 90 in this chapter.

[107] See for example Opinion of the European Economic and Social Committee, n. 99 in this chapter, point 2.1.

[108] See for example Eurofound, *Pay in Europe in the 21st Century* (Publications Office of the European Union, 2014).

on pay and that it is the responsibility of the national governments and/or the social partners to decide whether or not a minimum wage is established, and, if so, at what level and under what modalities.[109] Yet, what about the potential impact on minimum wages?[110] In a growing body of case law, the ECJ has made clear that while Article 153(5) TFEU rules out direct interference with pay, as would be the case with minimum wages, it does not preclude the adoption of EU rules that touch on or have an indirect impact on pay.

In *Del Cerro Alonso*,[111] involving the interpretation of Directive 1999/70 on fixed-term work,[112] the Court held that since Article 153(5) TFEU derogates from paragraphs 1 to 4 of that Article, the matters reserved by that paragraph must be interpreted strictly so as not to unduly affect the scope of paragraphs 1 to 4, nor to call into question the aims pursued by Article 151 TFEU.[113] It observed that the exception relating to 'pay' set out in Article 153(5) TFEU is explained by the fact that fixing the level of wages falls within the contractual freedom of the social partners at the national level and within the relevant competence of the Member States, and thus, in the present state of Union law, it was considered appropriate to exclude determination of the level of wages from harmonisation under Article 151 TFEU et seq.[114] The 'pay' exception 'cannot, however, be extended to any question involving any sort of link with pay; otherwise some of the areas referred to in Article [153(1) TFEU] would be deprived of much of their substance'.[115]

Thereafter, in *Impact*,[116] also involving the interpretation of the Directive on fixed-term work,[117] the Court recalled its ruling in *Del Cerro Alonso*[118] and underlined that the 'pay' exception under Article 153(5) TFEU 'must therefore be interpreted as covering measures – such as the equivalence of all or some of the constituent parts of pay and/or the level of pay in the Member States, or *the setting of a minimum guaranteed [Union] wage* – which amount to direct interference by [Union] law in the determination of pay within the [Union]'.[119] The

[109] Answer given by Mr. Andor on Behalf of the Commission to Question E-002257/14 by P. Le Hyaric, 'European Minimum Wage (or Income)', [2014] OJ C 365/271; see also for example Answer Given by Mr. Andor on Behalf of the Commission to Question E-011735/13 by M. Tarabella, 'European Minimum Wage', [2014] OJ C 218/234.
[110] See for example Cantillon and Van Mechelen, n. 95 in this chapter, at p. 200.
[111] ECJ, judgment of 13 September 2007 in *Del Cerro Alonso*, C-307/05, EU:C:2007:509.
[112] See n. 80 in this chapter.
[113] ECJ judgment, *Del Cerro Alonso*, n. 111 in this chapter, at paragraph 39.
[114] Ibid., paragraph 40.
[115] Ibid., paragraph 41.
[116] ECJ, judgment of 15 April 2008 in *Impact*, C-268/06, EU:C:2008:223.
[117] See n. 80 in this chapter.
[118] See ECJ judgment, *Impact*, n. 116 in this chapter, at paragraphs 122–30.
[119] Ibid., paragraph 124 (emphasis added). See also Opinion of Advocate General Kokott of 9 January 2008 in *Impact*, C-268/06, EU:C:2008:2, points 165–81.

Court has reiterated these points in subsequent judgments,[120] such as *Bruno*,[121] involving the interpretation of the Directive on part-time work, and *Specht*,[122] which dealt with the interpretation of Directive 2000/78 establishing a general framework for equal treatment in employment and occupation.[123]

Of note, one issue that has not yet been fully addressed in the Court's case law concerns the extent to which the exceptions set out in Article 153(5) TFEU may be the subject of regulation, including harmonisation measures, under other provisions of the Treaties. To recall, the wording of Article 153(5) TFEU stipulates that, 'The provisions of this Article shall not apply' to the four topics listed therein (pay, the right of association, the right to strike, and the right to impose lock-outs). Accordingly, commentators take different positions on the effect of Article 153(5) TFEU on other Union competences, such as Article 352 TFEU.[124] Although the Court has not yet pronounced on the relationship between Articles 153(5) and 352 TFEU, certain Opinions of Advocates General suggest that despite the delimitation of Article 153(5) TFEU to measures adopted under Article 153 TFEU, the EU legislator may not resort to other legal bases in order to circumvent Article 153(5) TFEU.[125]

---

[120] See also for example Opinion of Advocate General Sharpston of 20 September 2012 in *Epitropos tou Elegktikou Synedriou*, C-363/11, EU:C:2012:584, points 67–71 in relation to the Directive on fixed-term work, n. 80 in this chapter (the Court did not have the opportunity to rule on the matter, as it held the case inadmissible: judgment of 19 December 2012 in *Epitropos tou Elegktikou Synedriou*, C-363/11, EU:C:2012:825); Opinion of Advocate General Trstenjak of 16 June 2011 in *Williams and Others*, C-155/10, EU:C:2011:403, points 61–2 in relation to the Working Time Directive, n. 65 in this chapter, and Council Directive 2000/79/EC of 27 November 2000 concerning the European Agreement on the Organisation of Working Time of Mobile Workers in Civil Aviation concluded by the AEA, ETF, ECA, ERA and IACA, [2000] OJ L 302/57, adopted pursuant to Article 155(2) TFEU (the Court did not pronounce on the issue: judgment of 15 September 2011 in *Williams and Others*, C-155/10, EU:C:2011:588).

[121] ECJ judgment, *Bruno and Pettini*, n. 29 in this chapter, at paragraphs 35–7.

[122] ECJ, judgment of 19 June 2014 in *Specht and Others*, C-501/12 to C-506/12, C-540/12 and C-541/12, EU:C:2014:2005, paragraphs 33–7. See also Opinion of Advocate General Bot of 28 November 2013 in *Specht and Others*, EU:C:2013:779, points 42–50.

[123] Directive 2000/78/EC, n. 35 in this chapter, based on what is now Article 19(1) TFEU [ex Article 13(1) EC]. Its legal basis is exceptional in the sense that it states: 'Without prejudice to the other provisions of the Treaties and within the limits of the powers conferred by them upon the Union', which prompted the referring court's question on the relationship between a certain provision of this Directive and Article 153(5) TFEU: see *Specht and Others*, n. 122 in this chapter, at paragraph 32.

[124] See for example F. Rödl, 'The Labour Constitution', in A. von Bogdandy and J. Bast (eds), *Principles of European Constitutional Law* (Hart and Verlag CH Beck, 2010), pp. 636–7 and citations therein. With particular regard to Article 352 TFEU; see also for example Lörcher, n. 3 in this chapter, at pp. 179–80 and p. 183.

[125] See Opinion of Advocate General Mengozzi of 23 May 2007 in *Laval un Partneri*, C-341/05, EU:C:2007:291, points 52–7 (the ECJ's judgment did not deal with this issue in *Laval*, n. 30 in this chapter); Opinion of Advocate General Jääskinen of 20 November 2014 in *United*

This issue came to the fore in the context of the proposal for the so-called Monti II Regulation.[126] Following the Court's judgments in *Laval*[127] and *Viking*[128] (as well as related case law together referred to as the '*Laval* quartet'[129]), the Commission put forward this proposal in order 'to clarify the general principles and applicable rules at EU level with respect to the exercise of the fundamental right to take collective action within the context of the freedom to provide services and the freedom of establishment, including the need to reconcile them in practice in cross-border situations'.[130] Its proposed legal basis was Article 352 TFEU.[131] In the Commission's view, 'the fact that Article 153 does not apply to the right to strike does not as such exclude collective action from the scope of EU law'.[132] The Commission's assertions did not go unchallenged. As is well-known, this proposal constituted the first time that the national parliaments invoked the 'yellow card' procedure introduced by the Lisbon Treaty to ensure compliance with the principle of subsidiarity.[133] Several national parliaments disputed the use of Article 352 TFEU as the legal basis and contended that the Commission relied on this legal basis to circumvent Article 153(5) TFEU.[134] The Commission ultimately withdrew the proposal on other grounds (lack of political support in the European Parliament

Kingdom v Parliament and Council, C-507/13, EU:C:2014:2394, points 111–14 (the case did not proceed to judgment: Order of 9 December 2014 in *United Kingdom v Parliament and Council*, C-507/13, EU:C:2014:2481).

126 COM(2012)130 *Proposal for a Council Regulation on the Exercise of the Right to Take Collective Action within the Context of the Freedom of Establishment and the Freedom to Provide Services* (Brussels, 21 March 2012) (Monti II proposal) and particularly points 2.1 and 3.4.1.

127 *Laval*, n. 30 in this chapter.

128 *Viking*, n. 30 in this chapter.

129 See COM(2012)130 (Monti II proposal), n. 126 in this chapter and points 1 and 2.1. With the continuation of cases (for example ECJ, judgment of 12 February 2015 in *Sähköalojen ammattiliitto*, C-396/13, EU:C:2015:86, the 'sequel' to *Viking*: Opinion of Advocate General Wahl of 18 September 2014 in *Sähköalojen ammattiliitto*, C-396/13, EU:C:2014:2236, point 26), this so called 'quartet' may soon become an 'orchestra': A. Bücker, F. Dorssemont, and W. Warneck, 'The Search for a Balance: Analysis and Perspectives', in A. Bücker and W. Warneck (eds), *Reconciling Fundamental Social Rights and Economic Freedoms after Viking, Laval and Rüffert* (Nomos, 2011), p. 331 fn 45.

130 COM(2012)130 (Monti II proposal), n. 126 in this chapter and points 3.1 and 3.3.

131 Ibid., point 3.2. As noted therein (ibid., point 2.1), in 2008, the European Trade Union Confederation put forward a Proposal for a Social Progress Protocol, available at: www.etuc.org/proposal-social-progress-protocol (accessed 15 December 2016), which includes a provision explicitly allowing for the use of Article 352 TFEU in this context. For further discussion of this Protocol, see for example (2013) 4 *European Labour Law Journal* 2.

132 COM(2012)130 (Monti II proposal), n. 126 in this chapter, point 3.3.

133 Article 7(2) Protocol (No 2) on the application of the principles of subsidiarity and proportionality OJ 2016 C202/206.

134 See www.ipex.eu/IPEXL-WEB/dossier/dossier.do?code=APP&year=2012&number=0064&applng=EN (accessed 15 December 2016); COM (2013)566 *Report from the Commission Annual Report 2012 on Subsidiarity and Proportionality* (Brussels, 30 July 2013), point 3.

and Council).[135] It ignited much debate in the literature on the workings of this procedure, which in turn implicates the competence issues raised by the proposal.[136]

Arguably, the proposal may not have been a strong 'test case' to flesh out the relationship between Articles 153(5) and 352 TFEU, since it did not seek to harmonise the laws of the Member States in one of the areas, *in casu* the right to strike, listed in Article 153(5) TFEU. In fact, it purported to do very much the opposite.[137] While further case law on the matter would be welcome, the Court's judgments so far evidence a strict reading of Article 153(5) TFEU so as to ensure that it does not undercut the possible range of measures that may be adopted under Article 153 TFEU.

14.3.2.2 Fields Listed in Article 153(1) TFEU

Another issue highlighted by the proposal on adequate minimum income relates to the identification of the applicable fields set forth in Article 153(1) TFEU. The main contender appears to be point (h) the integration of persons excluded from the labour market on the grounds that it corresponds to the main objective to ensure an adequate minimum income for persons who are unable to carry out remunerated work and have no other means of support. This is also because a directive may be adopted in this field pursuant to Article 153(2)(b) TFEU.

By comparison, other fields listed in Article 153(1) TFEU have been deemed less suitable. In particular, point (j) the combating of social exclusion would appear to be relevant in light of the proposed directive's aim, and its wording has filtered into the previous Recommendations issued by the Council and Commission.[138] Yet, this

---

[135] See Annual Report, n. 134 in this chapter, point 3; Withdrawal of obsolete Commission proposals, [2013] OJ C 109/7.

[136] See for example F. Fabbrini and K. Granat, "'Yellow Card But No Foul': The Role of the National Parliaments under the Subsidiarity Protocol and the Commission Proposal for an EU Regulation on the Right to Strike' (2013) 50 *Common Market Law Review* 115, pp. 133–5; M. Goldoni, 'Reconstructing the Early Warning System on Subsidiarity: The Case for Political Judgment' (2014) 39 *European Law Review* 647, 659–60; D. Jančić, 'The Game of Cards: National Parliaments in the EU and the Future of the Early Warning Mechanism and the Political Dialogue' (2015) 52 *Common Market Law Review* 939, p. 953.

[137] See COM(2012)130 (Monti II proposal), n. 126 in this chapter, point 3.4, particularly point 3.4.3. See further for example G. Barrett, 'Monti II: The Subsidiarity Review Process Comes of Age ... Or Then Again Maybe It Doesn't' (2012) 19 *Maastricht Journal of European and Comparative Law* 595; G. Orlandini, 'The Monti II Proposal for the Regulation and the Right to Strike in Post-Lisbon Europe' (2012) *European Journal of Social Law* 224.

[138] See for example Council Recommendation 92/441, n. 90 in this chapter, Article A; Commission Recommendation 2008/867, n. 90 in this chapter, Article 4(a), first paragraph.

field[139] is not included among those allowing for the use of directives under Article 153(2)(b) TFEU. On account of this limitation, it does not appear likely that points (h) and (j) may be combined. This also raises questions concerning the relationship between the points set out in Article 153 TFEU that provide for the adoption of directives pursuant to Article 153(2)(b) TFEU and those that merely allow for the adoption of 'soft' measures pursuant to Article 153(2)(a) TFEU. Here, while an argument may be made that proceeding by way of point (h) undercuts the restricted scope of measures in the field covered by point (j), arguably, some overlap is to be expected in view of the interrelationship between the various fields listed in Article 153(1) TFEU and this by itself does not preclude recourse to point (h).

In addition, point (c) social security and social protection of workers has been considered inappropriate because even assuming a broad interpretation of 'social security' or 'social protection' that could be linked to the aim and content of the proposed directive,[140] it pertains to 'workers'.[141] It requires a special legislative procedure (unanimous voting in the Council and consultation of the European Parliament) and is the only field (as compared to points (d), (f), and (g)) that is not subject to the 'passerelle' clause enshrined in Article 153(2) TFEU) to render the ordinary legislative procedure applicable.[142] Moreover, under the first indent of Article 153(4) TFEU, measures adopted under Article 153 TFEU 'shall not affect the right of Member States to define the fundamental principles of their social security systems and must not significantly affect the financial equilibrium thereof'.[143] This provision is a potential roadblock for proposals based on point (c), though so far as can be discerned, the proposal does not appear to be geared at regulating aspects of the national social security systems that would implicate this provision.

Hypothetically, it may be wondered whether point (c) could be combined with point (h) with a view to ensuring that, however their status may be defined, persons needing this kind of social assistance would not be excluded from the scope of application of the proposed directive. At face

---

[139] As well as point (k) the modernisation of social protection systems without prejudice to point (c).

[140] See for example Council Recommendation 92/441, n. 90 in this chapter, tenth recital; Articles A, D; Commission Recommendation 2008/867, n. 90 in this chapter, Article 4(a)(i).

[141] See for example Verschueren, n. 85 in this chapter, at p. 211; EAPN Legal Assessment, n. 101 in this chapter, at p. 9. See also in this regard EGC, judgment of 19 April 2016 in *Constantini v Commission*, T-44/14, EU:T:2016:223, paragraphs 38–9.

[142] See Article 153(2), fourth to fifth paragraphs TFEU. But see Article 48(7) TEU.

[143] At present, there is limited case law on this provision. See for example ECJ judgment, *Commission v Czech Republic*, n. 32 in this chapter.

value, the decision-making procedures for these two points are incompatible – point (h) prescribes the ordinary legislative procedure (which may be part of the reason enticing the European Parliament to its use), whereas, as just mentioned, point (c) requires in ironclad terms the special legislative procedure – thus entailing a choice between one or the other depending on the objectives to be achieved by the measure concerned. While in principle there are instances allowing for a combination of seemingly incompatible legal bases following largely from the Court's judgment in *International Fund for Ireland*,[144] it is not yet clear whether this judgment may be extrapolated beyond Article 352 TFEU.[145] Awaiting further case law on the matter, such a combination here would appear to be precluded. In this way, the proposal brings to light various questions relating to the scope of the EU's competence under Article 153 TFEU, as well as limitations associated with the use of this provision for the adoption of EU social policy legislation, which prompts inquiry into other possible routes for further social integration.

14.4 ALTERNATIVE ROUTES FOR FURTHER SOCIAL INTEGRATION

While the previous sections have set out the possibilities for adopting measures aiming for further social integration (as defined above) on the basis of the existing Treaty framework and on the assumption that the applicable decision-making procedures would be followed, implying the participating of all Member States as represented in the Council, the present section sketches out three routes towards further social integration that could be explored if the ordinary routes were not available. In particular, this section explores, first, enhanced cooperation, which is intended to allow for measures to be adopted within the EU legal framework despite the lack of political will of some of the Member States. Second, the use of international agreements is explored as a means of achieving further social integration despite the fact that some or all of the Member States do not wish to see such integration taking shape within the framework of the current Treaties. Third, this section briefly examines the situation in which it would be considered necessary to amend the Treaties in order to allow for the necessary further integration.

---

[144] ECJ judgment, *International Fund for Ireland*, n. 52 in this chapter.
[145] See for example Opinion of Advocate General Mengozzi of 29 January 2015 in *Commission v Council*, C-28/12, EU:C:2015:43, point 80 fn 53; Opinion of Advocate General Wahl in Opinion 3/15, EU:C:2016:657, point 116 fn 68.

14.4.1 *Enhanced Cooperation*

14.4.1.1 Overview

As Advocate General (AG) Bot recalls in his Opinion in the *Unitary Patent* case, the establishment of an enhanced cooperation mechanism was:

> inspired by the growing heterogeneity of the Member States and their respective interests or specific needs. That mechanism aims to enable and encourage a group of Member States to cooperate inside rather than outside the Union, where it is established that the objectives pursued by that cooperation cannot be achieved by the Union as a whole.[146]

Arguably, that heterogeneity is certainly present with respect to the Member States' social systems and preferences with respect to further social integration.[147]

14.4.1.2 Legal Framework for Enhanced Cooperation

The legal framework for enhanced cooperation between Member States is enshrined in Title IV of the TEU (Article 20 TEU) and Title III of Part Six of the TFEU (Articles 326 to 334 TFEU). Member States can establish enhanced cooperation between themselves within the framework of the Union's non-exclusive competences.[148]

Enhanced cooperation must be aimed at furthering the objectives of the Union, at protecting its interests and at reinforcing its integration process,[149] and must comply with the Treaties and Union law.[150] Those conditions help prevent enhanced cooperation being used to turn back the integration process.[151] In addition, it must not undermine the internal market or economic, social, and territorial cohesion, must not constitute a barrier to, or discrimination in, trade between Member States, and must not distort competition between them.[152]

---

[146] Opinion of Advocate General Bot of 11 December 2012 in *Spain and Italy* v *Council* ('*Unitary Patent*'), C-274/11 and C-295/11, EU:C:2012:782, point 82.

[147] See Barnard and De Baere, n. 33 in this chapter, at pp. 37–43.

[148] Article 20(1) TEU.

[149] Article 20(1), second subparagraph TEU.

[150] Article 326, first paragraph TFEU.

[151] See E. Pistoia, 'Joined Cases C-274 & 295/11, *Kingdom of Spain and Italian Republic* v *Council of the European Union*, Judgment of the Court of Justice (Grand Chamber) of 16 April 2013, nyr.' (2014) 51 *Common Market Law Review* 256.

[152] Article 326, second paragraph TFEU.

Acts adopted in the framework of enhanced cooperation also do not form part of the acquis that has to be accepted by candidate States for accession to the Union.[153] At the same time, enhanced cooperation must respect the competences, rights, and obligations of those Member States that do not participate in it. Those Member States, in turn, must not impede its implementation by the participating Member States.[154] In the *Unitary Patent* judgment, the ECJ clarified that while it is

> essential for enhanced cooperation not to lead to the adoption of measures that might prevent the non-participating Member States from exercising their competences and rights or shouldering their obligations, it is, in contrast, permissible for those taking part in this cooperation to prescribe rules with which those non-participating States would not agree if they did take part in it.[155]

If, for example, an agreement could be reached between the required number of Member States to establish enhanced cooperation for a measure based on Article 153(1)(h) TFEU on minimum standards for any type of income support for people excluded from the labour market, the fact that some non-participating Member States would dislike the resulting measures would be no obstacle to their adoption.

Enhanced cooperation must involve at least nine Member States, and the Council must give its authorisation as a last resort only, when it has established that the objectives of such cooperation cannot be attained within a reasonable period by the Union as a whole.[156] The ECJ held in the *Unitary Patent* judgment that the impossibility referred to in Article 20(2) TEU 'may be due to various causes, for example, lack of interest on the part of one or more Member States or the inability of the Member States, who have all shown themselves interested in the adoption of an arrangement at Union level, to reach agreement on the content of that arrangement'.[157]

Nevertheless, the ECJ held the 'last resort' condition to be particularly important, concluding that the expression 'as a last resort' highlights 'the fact that only those situations in which it is impossible to adopt such legislation in the foreseeable future may give rise to the adoption of a decision authorising enhanced cooperation'.[158] AG Bot noted that for this condition to be fulfilled,

---

[153] Article 20(4) TEU.
[154] Article 327 TFEU.
[155] ECJ, judgment of 16 April 2013 in *Spain and Italy v Council ('Unitary Patent')*, C-274/11 and C-295/11, EU:C:2013:240, paragraph 82.
[156] Article 20(2) TEU.
[157] ECJ judgment, *Unitary Patent*, n. 155 in this chapter, at paragraph 36.
[158] Ibid., paragraphs 48–50.

it is not necessary for a legislative proposal to have been rejected by a vote, but rather the presence of a genuine deadlock at some stage of the legislative process, which demonstrates that reaching a compromise is impossible,[159] and the Court agreed.[160]

Crucially, when enhanced cooperation is being established, it is to be open to all Member States.[161] The Commission and the Member States participating in enhanced cooperation are to ensure that they promote participation by as many Member States as possible.[162]

The provisions on enhanced cooperation allow Member States to make use of the Union's institutions and exercise its competences by applying the relevant provisions of the Treaties.[163] This means that the procedure to be followed is that prescribed in the Treaty provision constituting the substantive legal basis. While all members of the Council may take part in the relevant deliberations, only those representing participating Member States are to take part in the vote.[164]

Of importance if enhanced cooperation were to be contemplated with respect to proposals based on, for example, Article 352 TFEU, is that the ECJ clarified in the *Unitary Patent* judgment that nothing forbids the Member States from establishing enhanced cooperation within the ambit of those competences for which the Council must decide unanimously. In that case, provided that the Council has not decided to act by QMV, it is the votes of only those Member States taking part that constitute unanimity.[165] Indeed, not being able to resort to enhanced cooperation in areas in which unanimity applies would defeat the purpose of the mechanism to a significant extent, as the type of deadlock enhanced cooperation is intended to overcome is particularly likely in matters that require unanimity in the Council.[166] That opens up the possibility of using enhanced cooperation to adopt a number of measures in the area of social policy *sensu lato* for which the Council needs to act unanimously. That is notably the case with respect to the following examples:

(1) directives adopted on the basis of Article 153(1)(c), (d), (f), and (g) TFEU in the fields of social security and social protection of workers; protection of workers where their employment contract is terminated;

---

[159] Opinion in *Unitary Patent*, n. 146 in this chapter, points 111–16.
[160] ECJ judgment, *Unitary Patent*, n. 155 in this chapter, at paragraphs 53–4.
[161] Article 20(1), second paragraph TEU and Article 328(1), first subparagraph TFEU.
[162] Article 328(1), second subparagraph TFEU.
[163] Article 20(1), first subparagraph TEU.
[164] Article 20(3) TEU and Article 330, first paragraph TFEU.
[165] ECJ judgment, *Unitary Patent*, n. 155 in this chapter, at paragraph 35.
[166] See Opinion in *Unitary Patent*, n. 146 in this chapter, point 85.

representation and collective defence of the interests of workers and employers, including co-determination, subject to the condition that they should not apply to pay, the right of association, the right to strike or the right to impose lock-outs; conditions of employment for third-country nationals legally residing in Union territory, respectively;

(2) measures adopted on the basis of Article 115 TFEU; and

(3) measures adopted on the basis of Article 352 TFEU.

Enhanced cooperation has not been directly used to combat the euro area crisis, but is explicitly contemplated in the Treaty on Stability, Coordination, and Governance in the Economic and Monetary Union (TSCG),[167] which will briefly be examined in the next section. At any rate, enhanced cooperation is only possible with respect to competences that have actually been conferred on the Union. As the ECJ held in *Pringle*, it is clear from Article 20(1) TEU that 'enhanced cooperation may be established only where the Union itself is competent to act in the area concerned by that cooperation'.[168] In other words, enhanced cooperation is not intended as a means to circumvent the principle of conferral, but to remedy the lack of political will of some of the Member States to exercise specific EU competences.[169] Nevertheless, the question remains whether what the ECJ said *a contrario* in *Pringle* means that where the Union does have the relevant competences, the Member States ought to have recourse to enhanced cooperation rather than mechanisms set-up outside the EU legal order, such as the European Stability Mechanism (ESM).[170] It could be argued on the basis of the principle of sincere cooperation in Article 4(3) TEU that the Member States in such circumstances must at least make an honest attempt to take the enhanced cooperation route before heading off on their own extra-Union affair.[171]

A significant advantage of relying on enhanced cooperation for further social integration as compared with ESM-like constructions is that it takes place entirely within the EU legal order and the EU institutional and constitutional framework, including its guarantees of democratic representation through the

---

[167] Article 10 Treaty on Stability, Coordination, and Governance in the Economic and Monetary Union.

[168] ECJ, judgment of 27 November 2012 in *Pringle*, C-370/12, EU:C:2012:756, paragraph 167.

[169] Hinarejos, n. 41 in this chapter, at p. 260. Compare Gutman, n. 40 in this chapter, at pp. 457–8.

[170] Editorial Comments, 'What Do We Want? "Flexibility! Sort-of …" When do we want it? "Now! Maybe …"' (2013) 50 *Common Market Law Review* 673.

[171] See in that sense also R. Repasi, *Legal Options for an Additional EMU Fiscal Capacity* (European Parliament, Directorate General for Internal Policies Policy Department C: Citizens' Rights and Constitutional Affairs, Constitutional Affairs, 2013), p. 12; and compare P. Craig, 'Two-speed, Multi-speed and Europe's Future: A Review of Jean-Claude Piris on the Future of Europe' (2012) 37 *European Law Review* 809.

European Parliament and judicial protection through the Union courts. The ECJ exercises judicial review as regards the Council authorisation to engage in enhanced cooperation, decisions to allow a Member State to participate in enhanced cooperation after it has been established, and the implementation of enhanced cooperation.[172] Furthermore and crucially, regardless of whether the Charter applies to action by the EU institutions or the Member States within the ESM or similar structures regarding social policy *sensu lato*,[173] setting such mechanisms up through enhanced cooperation would make the applicability of the Charter unassailable.[174] Enhanced cooperation also provides those Member States unwilling to participate with the assurance that their interests will be protected through the specific guarantees in the Treaties referred to above and the participation of the EU institutions within the EU legal order.[175]

Finally, of course, the benefits of enhanced cooperation must be weighed against the fact that, as the Court acknowledged in *Spain* v *Parliament and Council*, 'the implementation of enhanced cooperation inevitably leads to a certain fragmentation of the rules applicable to the Member States in the area concerned'.[176]

14.4.2 *International Agreements*

Could steps towards further social integration be taken by means of international agreements between the Member States or with third states? The question raises many issues of constitutional import to the Union and its Member States, all of which cannot be covered within the scope of this paper. Nevertheless, a number of points can be made. As is well-known, the Member States have in the recent past taken a number of crucial steps towards further economic integration in order to combat the euro area crisis. For various reasons, they have to a significant extent done so through international

---

[172] See ECJ, judgment of 30 April 2014 in *United Kingdom* v *Council* ('Financial Transactions Tax'), C-209/13, EU:C:2014:283, paragraphs 33–4.

[173] See ECJ, judgment of 20 September 2016 in *Ledra Advertising and Others* v *Commission and ECB*, C-8/15 P to C-10/15 P, EU:C:2016:701, paragraph 67; Opinion of Advocate General Bot in *Florescu and Others*, C-258/14, EU:C:2016:995, and Opinion of Advocate General Saugmandsgaard Øe in *Associação Sindical dos Juízes Portugueses*, C-64/16, EU:C:2017:395. See further Chapter 17 by Lenaerts and Gutiérrez-Fons, as well as Chapter 16 by Kornezov, in this volume.

[174] See in that sense M. Schwarz, 'A Memorandum of Misunderstanding – The Doomed Road of the European Stability Mechanism and a Possible Way Out: Enhanced Cooperation' (2014) 51 *Common Market Law Review* 417.

[175] However, various institutional questions remain open. See e.g. J. Piris, *The Future of Europe: Towards a Two-Speed EU?* (Cambridge University Press, 2012), pp. 56–7 and 117–20; Editorial Comments, n. 170 in this chapter.

[176] See ECJ, judgment of 8 September 2015 in *Spain* v *Parliament and Council*, C-44/14, EU:C:2015:554, paragraph 55.

agreements that fall outside the four corners of the EU legal framework, notably the ESM and the TSCG. Could that model be followed for social integration? This section briefly looks at two examples, namely the possibility of establishing a common minimum wage through an international agreement between the Member States, and the possibility of initiating social integration through so-called contractual arrangements with Member States.

First, the exclusion of Union competence to harmonise minimum pay would allow Member States to establish a common minimum wage[177] on the basis of their own competences, which they have retained in accordance with Articles 4(1) and 5(2) TEU. The Member States could arguably do so jointly through an international agreement. However, they would do well to frame the (presumably) higher common standard contained in the international agreement as being in turn a minimum standard,[178] in order to avoid a potential infringement of exclusive external Union competence on the basis of Article 3(2) TFEU, which grants the Union exclusive competence 'for the conclusion of an international agreement ... in so far as its conclusion may affect common rules or alter their scope'.[179] That said, given that the Union lacks the competence directly to legislate on pay, the risk of existing Union rules being affected by an agreement between the Member States on minimum pay is less marked than it would be if the Union did have legislative competence in that area.

Secondly, Vandenbroucke and Vanhercke suggest that well-conceived contractual arrangements between the EU and the Member States may be a way forward if they are based on the genuine reciprocity that is objectively needed in the EU today.[180] Could such contractual arrangements take the

[177] Compare in that sense Piris, n. 175 in this chapter, at p. 112.
[178] See ECJ, Opinion 2/91 of 19 March 1993, EU:C:1993:106, paragraph 18; Opinion 1/03 of 7 February 2006, EU:C:2006:81, paragraph 123 and 127; and (*a contrario*) the judgment of 4 September 2014 in *Commission v Council*, C-114/12, EU:C:2014:2151, paragraph 91, and Opinion 3/15 (Marrakesh Treaty on access to published works) of 14 February 2017, EU:C:2017:114, paragraphs 120–21. See further G. De Baere, 'EU External Action', in C. Barnard and S. Peers (eds), *European Union Law* (2nd edn, Oxford University Press, 2017).
[179] That phrase originates from ECJ judgment, *ERTA*, n. 44 in this chapter, at paragraph 22. See ECJ, judgment, *Commission v Council*, n. 178 in this chapter, at paragraph 66; judgment of 26 November 2014, *Green Network*, C-66/13, EU:C:2014:2399, paragraph 27; Opinion 1/13 of 14 October 2014, EU:C:2014:2303, paragraphs 69–74; and Opinion 2/15 of 16 May 2017, EU:C:2017:376, paragraphs 170–72. The Court has also confirmed that Article 3(2) TFEU applies to agreements between Member States in the ECJ judgment, *Pringle*, n. 168 in this chapter, at paragraphs 100–1. Contra: Opinion of Advocate General Kokott in *Pringle*, C-370/12, EU:C:2012:675, point 98.
[180] Vandenbroucke and Vanhercke, n. 14 in this chapter, at p. 92. See for example the proposals in the Commission Communication, COM(2013)165 *towards a Deep and Genuine Economic and Monetary Union. The Introduction of a Convergence and Competitiveness Instrument* (Brussels, 20 March 2013); and European Council 19–20 December 2013 Conclusions (EUCO 217/13), p. 19, paragraph 36.

form of international agreements? The Union itself has legal personality[181] and in each of the Member States, it is to enjoy the most extensive legal capacity accorded to legal persons under their respective laws.[182] However, of the institutions listed in Article 13(1) TEU, only the ECB has legal personality.[183] The European Investment Bank (EIB), though not an institution within the meaning of Article 13(1) TEU, also has legal personality.[184] In other words, only the ECB and the EIB could conclude binding agreements with other legal persons in their own name, while all other institutions listed in Article 13(1) TEU can only enter into obligations on behalf of the Union. However, while the Union indisputably has the competence to conclude agreements with third states and international organisations in the circumstances listed in Article 216(1) TFEU, the same cannot be said for international agreements with its own Member States.[185]

The contractual arrangements could perhaps be established through an agreement not with the Union or the ECB or EIB, but between the Member States of the Union. As the Court made clear in *Pringle*, such agreements would have to be framed so as not to conflict with Article 3(2) TFEU.[186] Specifically with respect to Belgium, the Netherlands, and Luxembourg, such arrangements could perhaps even be contemplated within the framework of the Benelux, for which Article 350 TFEU explicitly makes provision, on condition that such arrangements comply with the applicable requirements set by the ECJ.[187]

Thirdly, what if Member States would wish to 'repatriate' such an international agreement in the EU legal order? Could they, for example, do so by way of enhanced cooperation? That eventuality is in fact explicitly contemplated in Article 10 TSCG.[188]

The Member States of course did not need the TSCG to tell them they could make use of the enhanced cooperation mechanism.[189] However, to

---

[181] Article 47 TEU.
[182] Article 335 TFEU.
[183] Article 282(3) TFEU.
[184] Article 308 TFEU.
[185] Repasi, n. 171 in this chapter, at p. 20.
[186] ECJ judgment *Pringle*, n. 168 in this chapter, at paragraphs 100–1.
[187] See ECJ, judgment of 14 July 2016 in *Brite Strike Technologies*, C-230/15, EU:C:2016:560, paragraph 57 and the case law cited there, where the ECJ held that that provision enables Belgium, Luxembourg, and the Netherlands 'to leave in force, by way of derogation from the EU rules, the rules which apply within their regional union, in so far as that regional union is further advanced than the internal market', while specifying that in order to be justified, 'that derogation must also be indispensable for the proper functioning of the Benelux regime'.
[188] Note that the TCSG's integration in the EU legal order is provided for in its Article 16.
[189] Hinarejos, n. 41 in this chapter, at p. 256. The Member States probably did not need the TSCG at all, as most of what it did could have been done under existing EU competences: P. Craig,

recall, enhanced cooperation can only be used to remedy a lack of political will on the part of some of the Member States, and not to remedy a lack of competence on the part of the Union: it is limited to activities for which there exists a proper legal basis. In other words, only an agreement the content of which could have been adopted under EU competences, but was not for political reasons, could be brought inside the EU legal order through enhanced cooperation. That would not be the case, for example, with respect to an agreement between the Member States establishing a common minimum wage. Such an agreement could only be integrated in the EU legal order by amending the Treaties or through a Protocol if certain Member States do not wish to participate, as was done with the Schengen acquis.[190]

Alternatively, could Article 352 TFEU be used? In *Pringle*, the ECJ studiously avoided committing itself to whether the ESM could have been set up on the basis of Article 352 TFEU.[191] In its blueprint for a deep and genuine EMU, published on the day after *Pringle* was rendered, the Commission argued that while it would not be excluded to integrate the ESM into the EU framework under the current Treaties via a decision pursuant to Article 352 TFEU and an amendment to the EU's own resources decision,

> it appears that, given the political and financial importance of such a step and the legal adaptations required, that avenue would not necessarily be less cumbersome than operating an integration of the ESM through a change to the EU Treaties. The latter would also allow the establishment of tailor-made decision-making procedures.[192]

That appears to be a sensible assessment, which leads to the final subsection.

'The Stability, Coordination and Governance Treaty: Principle, Politics and Pragmatism' (2012) 37 *European Law Review* 233; A. Dashwood, 'The United Kingdom in a Re-formed European Union' (2013) 38 *European Law Review* 743.

[190] Protocol (No 19) on the Schengen acquis integrated into the Framework of the European Union, [2016] OJ C 202/290. See further S. Peers, *EU Justice and Home Affairs Law, Volume I: EU Immigration and Asylum Law* (Oxford University Press, 4th edn, 2016), pp. 13–17 and 29–32.

[191] ECJ judgment, *Pringle*, n. 168 in this chapter, at paragraph 67, referring to *ERTA*, n. 44 in this chapter, at paragraph 95. See Schwarz, n. 174 in this chapter, taking the view that Article 143(2) TFEU combined with Article 121 TFEU makes a strong case for a possible future implementation via Article 352 TFEU to include granting loans by the Union to euro area members if compatible with Article 125 TFEU as interpreted by the ECJ in *Pringle*.

[192] COM(2013)165, n. 180 in this chapter, at p. 34. Compare European Parliament Resolution, n. 93 in this chapter, at p. 7, recital CT, taking the view that the ESM could be integrated into the Union legal framework through Article 352 TFEU in combination with Article 136 TFEU; and B. de Witte and T. Beukers, 'The Court of Justice approves the creation of the European Stability Mechanism outside the EU legal order: *Pringle*' (2013) *Common Market Law Review* 834, arguing that the incorporation of the ESM into the Union legal order could be achieved either through the ordinary Treaty amendment procedure or by using Article 352 TFEU.

14.4.3 Amending the Treaties

It seems clear that redistributive social policy *sensu lato* has remained within the competence and,[193] as Armstrong put it, the 'normative embrace' of domestic institutions of social solidarity.[194] In consequence, both Habermas and Lenaerts have argued that if the adoption of socioeconomic redistributive rules were to be the solution to avoid future crises, an amendment of the Treaties would be necessary, which would have to go hand in hand with a substantial increase in the democratic legitimacy of the Union level.[195]

The Commission in substance appears to agree with that assessment. In its blueprint for a deep and genuine EMU, it argued that a proper fiscal capacity with a stabilisation function would require Treaty amendments.[196] The European Parliament likewise has taken the view that the completion of a genuine EMU within the Union will require in the medium-term a Treaty amendment, and that a substantial improvement of the democratic legitimacy and accountability at Union level, in its view through an increased role for itself, is an absolute necessity.[197]

The EU is in that respect faced with a constitutional conundrum. While the enhancement of the social identity of the Union is intended to galvanise its capacity to attract legitimacy, there may well be an unwillingness to view the Union as a defender of social values, without stronger democratic institutions at EU level or stronger national bonds of collective affinity. Even if the Member States are losing or have lost their capacity adequately to defend social values, it does not necessarily follow that the EU can generate the popular legitimacy necessary to defend such values. The relationship between giving the Union a stronger social identity and legitimacy, on the one hand, and granting it greater competences in social matters, on the other, may therefore be a classic instance of a 'chicken and egg' problem.[198]

---

[193] Hinarejos, n. 41 in this chapter, at p. 244.

[194] Armstrong, n. 4 in this chapter, at p. 232.

[195] J. Habermas, *Democracy, Solidarity, and the European Crisis* (University of Leuven Euroforum, 2013); and K. Lenaerts, *Economic Integration, Solidarity and Legitimacy. The EU in a Time of Crisis* (University of Leuven Euroforum, 2013), p. 32. See also K. Lenaerts and J.A. Gutiérrez-Fons, 'The European Court of Justice as the Guardian of the Rule of EU Social Law', Chapter 17 in this volume; and Hinarejos, n. 41 in this chapter, at pp. 264–5.

[196] COM(2013)165, n. 180 in this chapter, p. 33. Compare European Parliament Resolution, n. 93 in this chapter, at p. 7, recital CG. Compare COM(2013)690 *Strengthening the Social Dimension of the Economic and Monetary Union* (Brussels, 2 October 2013), p. 11.

[197] European Parliament Resolution, n. 93 in this chapter, recital AJ and at paragraph 9.

[198] Armstrong, n. 4 in this chapter, at p. 234.

Finally, even if the Member States were to agree to confer new competences on the Union with respect to social policy, they would do well to take heed of national constitutional limitations as imposed by their constitutional courts.[199] For example, it seems safe to assume that an amendment to the Treaties that would grant the Union the competence to build a substantive fiscal or social policy would skirt the shores of these limits as imposed by the *Bundesverfassungsgericht*, and risk running aground the German involvement in such an enterprise.[200]

However, the European Parliament notes in its Resolution 'Towards a genuine Economic and Monetary Union' that 'the Commission should list current legislative initiatives that must not be delayed by the long-term institutional developments', and 'future Treaty changes should not be an obstacle to the swift implementation of what can already be achieved under the existing Treaties'.[201]

14.5 THE 'HORIZONTAL SOCIAL CLAUSE' OF ARTICLE 9 TFEU

This section examines a provision in the current Treaties that could help further social integration not because any positive measures could be based on it, but because it may lead to upward social convergence through the incorporation of social policy objectives in other policies, such as notably the areas of the internal market, competition, and state aid.[202] Its contribution is therefore intended to be preventative or reactive with a view to avoiding harm to upward social convergence.

The idea of including a statement of fundamental principles of social protection in the Treaties originated in the observation made by Vandenbroucke in the margins of the Convention for the Future of Europe that the ECJ in its case law tried to weigh up the social objectives of the national systems when

---

[199] Such as notably the *Bundesverfassungsgericht* in its *Lisbon Urteil*, n. 59 in this chapter, at [251]–[252] (emphasis added). See further also German Federal Constitutional Court, BVerfG, 2 BvR 987/10 (European Financial Stability Facility (EFSF)) of 7 September 2011. German Federal Constitutional Court, BVerfG, 2 BvR 1390/12 (European Stability Mechanism) of 18 March 2014, at [164] [166]. See more broadly S. Rummens and S. Sottiaux, 'Democratic Legitimacy in the Bund or "Federation of States": the Cases of Belgium and the EU' (2014) 20 *European Law Journal* 576.

[200] See, with respect to fiscal policy, Hinarejos, n. 41 in this chapter, at pp. 266–7. As a further illustration of the close watch the *Bundesverfassungsgericht* is keeping on all economic and monetary measures taken at EU level, see its first ever reference for a preliminary ruling, which led to the ECJ judgment of 16 June 2015 in *Peter Gauweiler and Others v Deutscher Bundestag*, C-62/14, EU:C:2015:400.

[201] European Parliament Resolution, n. 93 in this chapter, recitals AI and AO.

[202] Vandenbroucke and Vanhercke, n. 14 in this chapter, at p. 59.

deciding upon the applicability of market rules, but did not have the possibility of taking into account all the possible consequences of its decisions without clearer guidance from the Treaty.[203] That idea found its way into what is now Article 9 TFEU,[204] which provides:

> In defining and implementing its policies and activities, the Union shall take into account requirements linked to the promotion of a high level of employment, the guarantee of adequate social protection, the fight against social exclusion, and a high level of education, training and protection of human health.

Opinions differ widely on whether it has made or can make any actual difference in the Union's policies.[205] Notably, the European Parliament in its Resolution 'Towards a genuine Economic and Monetary Union' mentioned Article 9 TFEU among the provisions of the current Treaties regarding employment and social policies the full potential of which has up to now been untapped.[206] In that regard, it is important to be clear, first, on what Article 9 TFEU is and is not and, second, on what it was designed to achieve.

First, while Article 9 TFEU obliges the Union to take 'social issues' into account in all its policies and activities, it does not constitute a new conferral of competences and can therefore not as such be used as a legal basis for initiatives leading to further social integration, or indeed for any EU act. It is also a textbook example of a programmatic provision that will be difficult to use independently as a basis for claims in individual cases.[207]

Secondly, what purpose then does Article 9 TFEU serve? The ECJ referred to Article 9 TFEU in *Deutsches Weintor*, holding that 'the protection of public health constitutes, as follows also from Article 9 TFEU, an objective of general interest justifying, where appropriate, a restriction of a fundamental freedom'.[208] That suggests that not only the protection of human health, but also the other goals in Article 9 TFEU, notably the promotion of a high level of employment, the guarantee of adequate social protection, the fight against social exclusion, and a high level of education and training could constitute

---

[203] F. Vandenbroucke, 'The EU and Social Protection: What Should the European Convention Propose?' (2002) *MPIfG Working Paper*, 02/6, section 3.2.

[204] The corresponding provision in the Treaty establishing a Constitution for Europe ([2004] OJ C 310/1) was Article III-117.

[205] Barnard and De Baere, n. 33 in this chapter, at pp. 36–7.

[206] European Parliament Resolution, n. 93 in this chapter, recital AP.

[207] For example ECST, judgment of 3 December 2014 in *DG v ENISA*, F-109/13, EU:F:2014:259, paragraph 60.

[208] ECJ, judgment of 6 September 2012 in *Deutsches Weintor*, C-544/10, EU:C:2012:526, paragraph 49.

an objective of general interest justifying, where appropriate, a restriction of a fundamental freedom. That interpretation would seem to accord with the original intention for a horizontal social clause to offer the ECJ a ground in the Treaties to take into account more readily the social objectives of the Union and its Member States.[209] AG Cruz Villalón put it in starker terms in his Opinion in *Dos Santos Palhota*:

> To the extent that the new primary law framework provides for a mandatory high level of social protection, it authorises the Member States, for the purpose of safeguarding a certain level of social protection, to restrict a freedom, and to do so without European Union law's regarding it as something exceptional and, therefore, as warranting a strict interpretation.[210]

Furthermore, recent ECJ case law indicates that Article 9 TFEU, where relevant in combination with other provisions of the Charter of Fundamental Rights of the EU ('Charter') and the Treaties, can also be used as part of a balancing exercise between different fundamental rights and freedoms to assess the legality of an EU act.[211]

Article 9 TFEU's function as a horizontal clause chimes with the idea of not adding a parallel social pillar to the EMU, but to mainstream the social dimension into all EMU initiatives.[212] The main relevance of Article 9 TFEU is therefore its potential to require EU measures not to affect in a disproportionate manner the social objectives listed in it.[213] As AG Wahl put it in his Opinion in *AGET Iraklis*, 'from the point of view of the EU legislature, it follows from Article 9 TFEU that a high level of employment and adequate social protection are considerations which the European Union must take account of when defining and implementing its policies and activities'.[214] A key tool for systematically ensuring that the EU's common social objectives are mainstreamed in all relevant EU policy areas is the social

---

[209] Vandenbroucke, n. 202 in this chapter.

[210] Opinion of Advocate General Cruz Villalón of 5 May 2010 in *Dos Santos Palhota and Others*, C-515/08, EU:C:2010:245, point 53.

[211] See, specifically regarding the promotion of a high level of employment and the guarantee of adequate social protection: ECJ, judgment of 21 December 2016 in *AGET Iraklis*, C-201/15, EU:C:2016:972, paragraph 78; regarding the protection of public health: ECJ, *Deutsches Weintor*, n. 207 in this chapter; judgment of 17 December 2015 in *Neptune Distribution*, C-157/14, EU:C:2015:823; *Pillbox 38*, n. 39 in this chapter; *Philip Morris Brands*, n. 39 in this chapter.

[212] Vandenbroucke and Vanhercke, n. 14 in this chapter, at p. 62.

[213] See with respect to social exclusion: P. Schoukens, *From Soft Monitoring to Enforceable Action: A Quest for New Legal Approaches in the EU Fight Against Social Exclusion* (University of Leuven Euroforum, 2013), p. 22.

[214] Opinion of Advocate General Wahl of 9 June 2016 in *AGET Iraklis*, C-201/15, EU:C:2016:429, point 56.

impact assessment within the Commission's general Impact Assessment System (IAS).[215]

The ECJ could in turn play its role by scrutinising the arguments on the basis of which the Union thought it necessary to introduce certain measures by directly looking at the justification put forward in the Impact Assessment. AG Sharpston adopted such an approach in *Spain v Council* with respect to the principle of proportionality, which likewise forms part of Impact Assessments, taking the view that the Union legislator had infringed that principle, inter alia, because no Impact Assessment had been carried out.[216] The Court could arguably use Impact Assessment reports in combination with the duty to give reasons as laid down in Article 296, second paragraph, TFEU to review the justification of a particular proposed measure on the basis of the social objectives listed in Article 9 TFEU.[217] That way, the ECJ could at least make sure that the EU legislature had in fact duly considered the social impact of any particular measure it wishes to introduce.

In light of the case law so far, there is a good case to be made that this provision may help to ensure the recognition of EU social policy aims in the EU legislative process regarding measures in all EU policy areas, as well as the Court's interpretation of such measures, possibly in conjunction with Articles 2 and 3 TEU on the Union's values and objectives, respectively, and the relevant provisions of the Charter. At the same time, the wording of Article 9 TFEU appears to be not as strong as Article 11 TFEU, which contains the horizontal clause concerning environmental protection, and is phrased rather more snappily.[218] There may also be a risk of 'watering down', given the number of horizontal clauses listed in Title II and other parts of the TFEU. In other words, while it remains doubtful whether Article 9 TFEU can achieve much in a 'positive'

---

[215] See European Commission, 'Impact Assessment Guidelines (SEC(2009)92)' (2009) available at: ec.europa.eu/smart-regulation/impact/commission_guidelines/docs/iag_2009_en.pdf (accessed 16 December 2016). See further Opinion of the European Economic and Social Committee on 'Strengthening EU Cohesion and EU Social Policy Coordination through the New Horizontal Social Clause in Article 9 TFEU' (own-initiative opinion), [2012] OJ C 24/29, paragraph 1.4.

[216] Opinion of Advocate General Sharpston of 16 March 2006 in *Spain v Council*, C-310/04, EU:C:2006:179, points 82–96.

[217] See in that sense regarding subsidiarity: P. Craig, 'The ECJ and *Ultra Vires* Action: a Conceptual An alysis' (2011) 48 *Common Market Law Review* 427.

[218] Note, however, that in holding 'that the objective of sustainable development henceforth forms an integral part of the common commercial policy', the Court relied inter alia on Articles 9 and 11 TFEU read together: Opinion 2/15 of 16 May 2017, EU:C:2017:376, paragraphs 146–47. Specifically with respect to Article 9 TFEU, that would seem to imply that the objective of guaranteeing 'adequate social protection' now indisputably forms an integral part of every trade agreement concluded by the EU.

sense by way of further social integration on its own, its importance, especially in relation to both the process of drafting EU austerity measures and their judicial review by the ECJ and the EGC, must not be discounted.

14.6 CONCLUSION

This chapter demonstrates that the current Treaties provide a number of possibilities for taking important, if incremental, steps towards further social integration. Specifically, this includes, first, unlocking the potential of Article 153 TFEU through adoption of EU social policy legislation especially in light of underused paragraphs of Article 153 TFEU: second, considering enhanced cooperation as a workable alternative to international agreements and Treaty amendment, which both have significant drawbacks; and third, making use more readily of Article 9 TFEU, which may not be sufficient by itself but arguably constitutes a viable tool in combination with other provisions and principles of EU law.

The Union should make full use of that potential while actively considering the long-term options. Nevertheless, in contemplating the conferral of additional competences on the Union in this setting, heed should be taken of a paradox: the more competences the EU has been given, the harder it has been to adopt EU legislation, including using the ordinary legislative procedure. [219] Indeed, an expanded and increasingly heterogeneous EU means that it is ever more difficult to regulate on any topic. This problem is aggravated by the subject area: social policy is seen as sensitive in many national systems, as is illustrated by the fact that of the three instances at which national parliaments have used the yellow card procedure, it was twice in respect of a proposal for a piece of social legislation, namely the Monti II proposal, intended to address some of the consequences of *Viking* and *Laval*,[220] and the revised Posted Workers Directive.[221]

Furthermore, it appears fairly clear that expedients outside the EU legal order such as the TSCG could not be used to effect the institutional changes that a genuine EMU would entail.[222] Enhanced cooperation appears to be

---

[219] Barnard, n. 1 in this chapter, at pp. 213–14.

[220] Ibid., p. 214.

[221] COM(2016)128 *Proposal for a Directive of the European Parliament and of the Council Amending Directive 96/71/EC of The European Parliament and of the Council of 16 December 1996 Concerning the Posting of Workers in the Framework of the Provision of Services* (Brussels, 8 March 2016). See D. Sindbjerg Martinsen, 'The European Social Union and EU Legislative Politics', Chapter 18 in this volume.

[222] Dashwood, n. 189 in this chapter, at p. 754.

at least in part a workable alternative to get quite a few incremental things done, and the Union should not fear it. Differentiation 'in the sense that not all Member States are subject to the same rules or accept the same commitments, is and always has been a central organising principle of the Union's constitutional order'.[223] Indeed, the euro area is currently a form of differentiation structurally ingrained in the EU legal order.

At any rate, the Union has no choice about whether or not to address the social issues facing its citizens:

> The functional requirements for a sustainable monetary union and the principled assertion that, at its core, the European project is a social model point in the same direction: the search for a strong consensus on the content of the European Social Model is no longer a superfluous luxury, but a necessity.[224]

Put differently, social integration is an integral part of the Union's project.[225] This paper has established that EU constitutional law provides a basis not just to preserve the current social acquis, but also to build on it, and to foster further social integration. In other words: the question is not if, but when and how.

---

[223] Ibid., p. 740.
[224] Vandenbroucke, n. 37 in this chapter, at p. 24.
[225] Barnard, n. 1 in this chapter, at p. 201.

15

EU Social Competences and Member State Constitutional Controls: A Comparative Perspective of National Approaches

Gerhard van der Schyff

15.1 CREATING A EUROPEAN SOCIAL UNION

At the heart of the European Economic Community in 1957 lay the creation of a common internal market, with free movement of goods, services, and people. According to the theory of neofunctionalist spillover, integration in one field would trigger the need for integration in other fields.[1] Economic regulation, for instance, would also lead to social, political, and constitutional integration, as economic decisions could not be taken independent of such contexts. The theory certainly goes some way in explaining the integration process to date, as ever-increasing economic integration has not left many fields of traditional state competence intact.

The spillover effect, though, has not always resulted in complete integration. The case of EU social competences is a good example in this regard. While notable strides have been made in this field since the initial Member States committed themselves to constantly improve 'the living and working conditions of their peoples' in the preamble to the Treaty of Rome, social policy can, at best, still be described as resembling a work in progress. Neofunctionalist spillover in social matters has been far from complete in the EU, to the extent that some argue that while at supranational level the EU is committed to 'economic rationality and undistorted competition', 'redistributive (social) policies' are left to the various national participants.[2] While this distinction might be too stark, it does sketch a rough idea of the division of labour.

---

[1] P. Craig, 'Integration, Democracy and Legitimacy', in P. Craig and G. de Búrca (eds), *The Evolution of EU Law* (Oxford University Press, 2nd edn, 2011), p. 14.

[2] C. Joerges and F. Rödl, 'Informal Politics, Formalised Law and the "Social Deficit" of European Integration: Reflections after the Judgments of the ECJ in Viking and Laval' (2009) 15 *European Law Journal* 1, pp. 3–4.

This division can obviously be explained in part by reference to economic integration as the core with which to spur the European project. Prioritising economic integration over social integration has been the political choice made since the early days of the European project. Although the logic of spill-over might point in the direction of further integration in the social field, the process is not self-executing or otherwise inevitable. So long as political hesitancy prevails, integration will necessarily lag behind what may be deemed desired or necessary in establishing a balance between the levels of economic and social integration.

A further factor has emerged which has influenced the creation and strengthening of a European social union, namely the limits to integration presented by the constitutional orders of the Member States of the EU. Viewed from this angle, the process of integration is not simply a question of whether national political actors choose to meet the demands created by the logic of spillover, but whether and how national constitutional orders allow states to respond to the perceived need for further social integration. Increased social integration is therefore not only dependent on mustering enough political will, but importantly also on respecting national constitutional constraints.

It is precisely this constitutional question that will be studied in this contribution. I wish to focus on the reaction of national constitutional orders to social integration in the EU. As the competence of the EU has increased in range and in depth, national constitutional responses have become increasingly important in restricting what Member States can agree to at EU level. This is because national constitutional orders have only been qualified by European integration, thereby enlarging the field of possible contact between national orders and the EU. Admittedly national constitutional reaction has not been focused on the social field in any great measure. However, the principles underlying general or specific national reactions to enhanced integration can be applied to the social field. In studying such national responses, two lines of enquiry will be pursued. The first concerns the possible impact of a national constitutional order on the *transfer* of social competence to the EU; this will be referred to as 'a priori constitutional control' (Section 15.3). It will be shown that constitutional orders increasingly raise the bar for consenting to the transfer of national competences to the EU.

The second line will focus on possible constitutional reaction to the *exercise* of such a competence by the EU; this will be referred to as 'ex post constitutional control' (Section 15.4). In addition to explaining national participation in EU decision-making processes, this section will analyse some Member States' refusal to accept the unqualified primacy of EU law. It will become clear that both a priori and ex post controls in the social field are often aimed at protecting fundamental constitutional principles, sometimes also referred to as 'constitutional identity'. In this regard, 'reshaping' a constitutional order, understood as ordinary change, is not necessarily as problematic as 'reshaping' such an order in the sense of fundamental change, to make use of Walter F. Murphy's distinction in describing different shades of constitutional change.[3]

In studying these questions, I will endeavour to sketch the range of possible actions corresponding to the two lines of enquiry and will refer to pertinent examples in the social field where they exist. The focus will fall on the EU's foundational treaties, namely the TEU and the TFEU, which will be referred to as the 'Treaties', as opposed to the term 'treaties' that refers to all international treaties including the TEU and the TFEU. Treaties entered into by the EU fall outside the scope of this study, given that they cannot be understood as essentially national responses to European integration.

15.2 'SOCIAL FIELD' DELINEATED

As the term 'social field' is quite vague, the concept needs to be delineated a bit more for present purposes. Neither EU primary law nor the various national constitutional laws provide a precise definition of what the social field encompasses. As the enquiry rests on understanding national constitutional responses to social integration at the European level, the focus will fall on the increase and exercise of the EU's social competence as provided for in the Treaties. This allows for a common platform from which to proceed, but also raises the question as to what such competence entails.

In this regard a distinction can be made between the core of EU social policy and matters related to that core. At the heart of these issues is Title X of the TFEU on 'Social Policy'. Title X regulates the primary spillover effects of economic integration borne of the inherent tension and the need for societal compromise between capital and labour, thereby capturing what in German literature has been called the 'labour constitution'.[4] Article 153(1) TFEU provides an overview of some of the topics covered by this Title, including working conditions, social security and social protection of workers, the termination of employment contracts and the representation and collective defence of the interests of workers and employers. Linked

[3] W.F. Murphy, 'Slaughter-house, Civil Rights, and Limits on Constitutional Change' (1987) 32 *American Journal of Jurisprudence* 1, p. 17.
[4] See further F. Rödl, 'The Labour Constitution', in A. von Bogdandy and J. Bast (eds), *Principles of European Constitutional Law* 2nd ed. (Oxford/München: Hart/CH Beck/Nomos, 2011), pp. 623–58, 625–7.

to such core topics are a variety of conceivable policy areas, ranging from discrimination law to economic, social, and territorial cohesion, that can influence the tension at the base of the labour constitution.[5] Is it worth noting that the list in article 153(1) TFEU does not cover housing and education, while these topics are often construed as social policy issues by the Member States.

The complexity of the social field is exacerbated further by the fact that while article 4(2)(b) TFEU identifies social policy as a shared competence 'for the aspects defined in this Treaty', articles 5(2) and 5(3) TFEU list employment policies and social policies as topics on which the EU may only coordinate Member State action. Focussing on article 153(1) TFEU, the EU can act to support and complement Member States with regards to the various topics listed in the provision.[6] In this regard, article 153(2)(b) TFEU allows for minimum standards directives to be adopted for nine of the 11 topics mentioned in article 153(1) TFEU.[7] In respect of the other two topics, the combatting of social exclusion and the modernisation of systems of social protection listed in article 153(1)(j) and (k) TFEU, the EU may adopt measures designed to encourage cooperation between Member States. According to article 153(2)(a) TFEU this may not result in the harmonisation of the laws and regulations of the Member States. It is also important to note that any provisions adopted pursuant to article 153(1) may not affect the right of Member States to define the fundamental principles of their social security systems and also prevents the EU from affecting the financial equilibrium of such systems in a fundamental way.[8]

Although the range of topics entrusted to the EU is apparently quite broad under article 153(1), it becomes clear that the EU's powers to act in the social field are not as far-reaching as in some other fields or on a par with Member States' competences. As a result, the social rights guaranteed in the Charter on Fundamental Rights of the EU are more generous than the range of competences to which they apply, a situation characterised by Florian Rödl as the 'missing congruence' in the labour constitution.[9]

[5] For example Articles 2, 3(3) TEU; Article 10, Title XVIII TFEU.
[6] See A. Rosas and L. Armati, *EU Constitutional Law: An Introduction* (Hart, 2nd edn, 2012), p. 211.
[7] More particularly Article 153(1)(a)–(i) TFEU. When acting on four of these topics, the Council shall act unanimously, in accordance with a special legislative procedure, this concerns the topics in Article 153(1)(c), (d), (f), and (g) TFEU.
[8] Article 153(4) TFEU.
[9] See Rödl, n. 4 in this chapter, at pp. 637–9.

15.3 A PRIORI CONSTITUTIONAL CONTROL

In general, Member States have become more protective of their constitutional orders than probably ever before in the history of the European project. This is particularly evident when it comes to transferring national competences to the EU. Article 5(1) TEU establishes the principle of conferral, which means that the EU does not possess any inherent powers of its own, but that it relies on the transfer of competences from the Member States by means of the Treaties. As explained in article 5(2) TEU, competences not conferred upon the EU remain with the Member States, and therefore are part of their constitutional orders, broadly conceived. A priori constitutional control relates to national rules on the transfer of such competences to the EU. EU law has little if any role in this regard, as it is essentially for the Member States to decide these issues.

The bedrock of Member States' rules in this regard is political in nature, to which rules of a judicial nature may be added. When transferring national competences to the EU, a minority of states including Belgium and the Netherlands emphasise the importance of the political approach, allowing treaties to be approved by a simple majority in parliament without adding extra hurdles as a matter of course.[10] This means that the competences governing the national labour constitution of these states can be Europeanised without much difficulty, provided that sufficient political will has been mustered and the correct approval procedure followed. Were the government so to decide and parliament did not object, treaties in the Netherlands could even be approved tacitly without requiring an act of parliament.[11] While the Dutch approach can be described as relatively straightforward and simple, this changes when a treaty contradicts the Constitution. Article 91(3) of the Constitution requires that such a contentious treaty be adopted by a two-thirds majority in parliament. This provision has so far not proved to be a real hurdle to social integration, as the Treaties have never been found to gainsay the Constitution.[12]

---

[10] Article 91(1)–(2) of the Constitution of the Netherlands; Articles 33, 53, and 167 of the Constitution of Belgium.

[11] See Article 4–5 of the Kingdom Act on the Approval and Publication of Treaties of 1994; L. Dragstra, N.S. Efthymiou, A.W. Hins, and R. de Lange, *Beginselen van het Nederlandse staatsrecht* (Kluwer, 18th edn, 2015), pp. 196–7.

[12] The Constitution of Portugal knows a similar procedure in Article 279(4), with the difference that a finding of unconstitutionality by the Constitutional Court forces such a vote, in which instance two-thirds of the members of the Assembly of the Republic must vote in favour of ratifying the unconstitutional treaty.

Other states, though, insist on qualified legislative majorities as a matter of course whenever constitutional issues arise in approving a treaty and not only when the Constitution is contradicted. For instance, article 85(1) to (2) of the Bulgarian Constitution requires that a treaty always be approved by two-thirds of the National Assembly in the event of the country participating in international organisations and treaties concerning political matters or fundamental rights. The required majority increases to a demanding five-sixths in the Danish Parliament in the event that executive, legislative or judicial powers were to be transferred according to article 20(1) to (2) of the country's Constitution. The effect is to raise the bar quite high in transferring social competences to the EU. Indirect democratic approval can also be augmented by direct democratic approval. For instance, the draft Constitutional Treaty was put to the vote by the governments in France and the Netherlands in 2005 and subsequently rejected by the voters, which meant that the Treaty was cast aside although the votes were not binding.[13]

Apart from relying on the executive to take the lead in calling a referendum, legislators can also take the initiative in some states including Slovenia, Spain, and Poland in the event any treaty necessitates constitutional amendments.[14] Even though the Constitution is not amended, a majority of parliamentarians in Poland can call a referendum to ratify a treaty that transfers constitutional competences to an international organisation, thereby supplanting parliamentary ratification by means of a two-thirds legislative majority.[15] In the case of Ireland, the Treaties have always been adopted after approval in a binding referendum, as they were viewed as amending the Constitution, thereby forcing a vote.[16]

A number of examples can be identified of Member States that consider the adoption of additional measures in order to protect their constitutional orders. For instance, although the constitutional order of the Netherlands has been quite open to further European integration, an amendment to the Constitution has been tabled that will require any amendment to the Treaties

---

[13] See P. Hainsworth, 'France Says No: The 29 May 2005 Referendum on the European Constitution' (2006) 59 *Parliamentary Affairs* 98–117; A. Nijeboer, 'The Dutch Referendum' (2005) 1 *European Constitutional Law Review* 393.

[14] Article 170 of the Constitution of Slovenia allows a referendum to be called at the request of 30 parliamentarians; Article 167(3) of the Constitution of Spain at the request of at least 10 per cent of the member of either legislative chamber; Article 235(1) of the Constitution of Poland at the behest of the Senate or 20 per cent of the members of the lower chamber.

[15] Article 90(3)–(4) of the Constitution of Poland, see also Article 235(6).

[16] See Article 47(1) of the Constitution of Ireland and L.F.M. Besselink, M. Claes, Š. Imamović, and J.H. Reestman, *National Constitutional Avenues for Further EU Integration* (European Parliament, 2014), pp. 32, 136, 140. The study is available at: www.europarl.europa.eu/studies (accessed 5 January 2016).

to be adopted by a two-thirds parliamentary majority in the event powers are transferred to the EU, and not only in the event of the Constitution being contradicted in the sense of article 91(3).[17] As the Treaties have always been adopted by at least a two-thirds majority in parliament the proposed amendment might seem superfluous, but given the increase in Eurosceptic politics this might not be certain in the future.[18] Were this amendment to be successful it will provide another potential barrier to further European integration.

Another instrument to consider in the Netherlands is the Advisory Referendum Act of 2014, which requires a nonbinding referendum to be held on a variety of issues including the ratification of treaties upon 300,000 voters having signed a petition.[19] This threshold has not proved a deterrent: soon after the Act came into force in 2015, nearly 428,000 voters supported a referendum on the proposed Association Agreement between the EU and Ukraine.[20] In the event, 61 per cent of voters rejected the Association Agreement in a referendum held on 6 April 2016, leaving the government to consider how it will respond. The transfer of any social competences to the EU in future could be met with the same reception.

The trend to erect more political barriers to European integration was also evidenced by the adoption of the European Union Act (EUA) 2011 in the United Kingdom.[21] Although the United Kingdom is on the verge of leaving the EU after its referendum of 23 June 2016, the country's approach deserves attention given the example it might set for other states considering parliamentary hurdles with which to check further European social integration. In this regard, section 2 EUA requires that, in addition to approval by an act of parliament, a referendum must be held in some cases were the Treaties to be amended or replaced according to the ordinary revision procedure in article 48(2)–(5) TEU. The referendum requirement can also be triggered by the simplified revision procedure in article 48(6) TEU. This means that the respective Treaty can only be ratified or an article 48(6) TEU decision agreed to by the United Kingdom, once a majority of voters has supported the move. This effectively placed a 'lock' on the transfer of more national competences to the EU. All such referendums are valid irrespective of the turnout, which

---

[17] Parliamentary Papers I, 2015–16, 30 874 (R1818), no. A; Parliamentary Papers II, 2006–07, 30 874 (R 1818), nos. 2, 6.
[18] See also Besselink et al., n. 16 in this chapter, at p. 159.
[19] See Articles 2–3 of the Act.
[20] See the announcement by the Electoral Council, available at: www.kiesraad.nl/nieuws/bekendmaking-uitslag-definitieve-fase-referendumverzoek-associatieverdrag-eu-oekra%C3%AFne (accessed 5 January 2016).
[21] See further M. Gordon and M. Dougan, 'The United Kingdom's European Union Act 2011: "who won the bloody war anyway?"' (2012) 37 *European Law Review* 3.

meant a minority of the overall electorate could effectively block any revision on a low turnout. This stands in contrast with advisory referendums in the Netherlands that require a minimum turnout of 30 per cent of the electorate to be valid, according to article 3 of the Advisory Referendum Act.[22]

A referendum is required, according to the European Union Act, when the content of the Treaty revision or the article 48(6) TEU decision falls into one of the categories listed in section 4 EUA. According to section 4(3) EUA, a matter falling within one of these categories will not trigger a referendum where it concerns the codification of an existing practice, does not apply to the United Kingdom, or concerns the accession of a new Member State. When studying the various categories in section 4 EUA, it becomes clear that in fact very little was excluded from the referendum requirement. The requirement would, for instance, be activated by among others an extension of the objectives of the EU as set out in article 3 TEU, such as the organisation's commitment to develop a social market economy aimed at full employment, as well as the creation of new, or the extension of existing, EU competences. In particular, article 4(1)(f)(i) of the Act explicitly covers the extension of the competence of the EU in relation to the coordination of economic and employment policies. Noteworthy is also section 4(1)(m) read with section 4(3)(a) of the Act, which require a referendum in the event of 'any amendment' of article 48 TFEU 'that removes or amends the provision enabling a member of the Council, in relation to a draft legislative act, to ensure the suspension of the ordinary legislative procedure'. According to article 48 TFEU, a Member State can request such suspension where a draft legislative act in support of the freedom of movement of workers would affect important aspects of that state's social security system. The European Council can then choose not to suspend the procedure, or refer the matter back to the European Commission or take no action, both of which will result in the proposal not being adopted.

In addition to insisting on stronger political barriers in preventing the substance of a national competence from being integrated into the EU too easily, attention should also be turned to the role of national courts in this matter. Jurisdictions such as the United Kingdom and the Netherlands largely limit or exclude the courts from deciding procedural or substantive constitutional issues. The UK's European Union Act may again serve as an example. Section 5 provides that the relevant minister must lay a statement before parliament on whether a Treaty amendment or article 48(6) TEU requires the holding of a referendum. While it seems that a British court could be approached to

---

[22] The turnout in the Dutch referendum on the EU–Ukraine Association Agreement of 6 April 2016 was 32 per cent.

compel a minister to make such a statement where one is not forthcoming, the traditional view on the sovereignty of parliament would mean that a court may not refuse to apply an act of parliament that disregards the referendum requirement in section 2 of the Act altogether.[23]

In other jurisdictions, courts do play a leading and at times decisive role in deciding whether treaty changes will affect the country's constitutional order and which rules to apply in approving such treaties. In this regard, the Supreme Court of Estonia may declare treaties unconstitutional, a power which applies to unratified and even to ratified treaties.[24] As to the standard of review, reference can be made to article 1 of the Constitution of the Republic of Estonia Amendment Act of 2003 that allows the country to belong to the EU in accordance with the *fundamental* principles of the Constitution. These principles have not been enumerated in the Constitution and the Supreme Court has never reviewed the constitutionality of a treaty to date. Academic opinion, though, has identified a variety of such principles including the social state.[25]

Estonia is not alone in this regard. Its approach mirrors the situation in states such as the Czech Republic, Poland, and especially Germany, where the social state has been identified as a fundamental principle that may not be infringed by European integration. In France, references to the social state, or the 'social republic' in the preamble to the Constitution, can equally be understood as including normative expressions regarding the labour constitution that capture the need for values such as solidarity and justice to be factored in when shaping the relationship between capital and labour.[26] In the states mentioned, the courts can play an important role in deciding whether revising the Treaties infringes the principle of the social state or not, instead of leaving the issue solely to the discretion of parliamentarians or the electorate.

The jurisprudence of the German Federal Constitutional Court is widely considered to lead the way in this respect. Article 23(1) of the German

---

[23] On these issues, see further P. Craig, 'European Union Act 2011: Locks, Limits and Legality' (2011) 48 *Common Market Law Review* 1881, pp. 1901–2. Craig points to the possibility of reinterpreting parliamentary sovereignty to allow for the judicial review of the referendum requirement too.

[24] See Article 6(1) and (4) of the Constitutional Review Procedure Act of Estonia of 2002; Supreme Court of Estonia judgment 3-4-1-6 12 of 1 July 2012, paragraph 111; Besselink et al., n. 16 in this chapter, at pp. 68, 74, 78.

[25] Ibid., p. 73.

[26] See also K.E. Hain, 'Article 79(3)', in H. von Mangoldt, F. Klein, and C. Starck (eds), *Kommentar zum Grundgesetz*, Vol. 2 (Verlag Franz Vahlen, 6th edn, 2010), pp. 2261–2, who explains that the concept relates to a social order that includes questions on the economic redistribution, which balances the values of freedom and equality in a manner mindful of human dignity and social justice.

Constitution, its Europe clause, not only opens up the country's legal order by mandating the state to participate in 'a united Europe' committed to 'democratic, social and federal principles' through the transfer of sovereign powers, but also conditions such participation. The provision allows the state to participate in the EU subject to the so-called eternity clause in article 79(3) of the Constitution. The eternity clause bars any constitutional amendment affecting the values enumerated by it or those contained in articles 1 and 20 of the Constitution. In particular article 20(1) declares Germany to be a 'democratic and social federal state'. The provisions have been interpreted as codifying the fundamental principles the Constitution, also referred to as the 'constitutional identity' of the German state.[27]

Comparing the German Federal Constitutional Court's judgments on the constitutional compatibility of the Maastricht Treaty of 1992 and the Lisbon Treaty of 2007 reveals the Court's influence in matters of social integration in particular. In the case of the Maastricht Treaty, the Court adopted a radical interpretation of the inviolable safeguards of democracy protected via article 79(3) of the Constitution.[28] The provision was interpreted as granting standing to German voters in challenging the act of parliament adopting the Treaty, alleging that the Treaty affected their right to vote in a substantive way. The Court held that the Treaty did not affect the principle in this manner, but warned that the German parliament had to retain 'functions and powers of substantial import'.[29] The judgment on the Lisbon Treaty went a step further by fleshing out these parameters of German 'constitutional identity', whose transfer to the EU would violate the guarantees in article 79(3) of the Constitution. The Court held that the transfer of 'sovereign powers' had to be restricted 'particularly in central political areas' such as shaping living conditions through social policy.[30] In such areas, 'it is particularly necessary to draw the limit where the coordination of the cross-border situations is factually required'.[31] European unification, the Court also noted, 'may not be achieved in such a way that no sufficient space is left to the Member States for the political formation of the economic, cultural and social living conditions'.[32] These

---

[27] See also P. Kirchhof, 'Die Identität der Verfassung', in J. Isensee and P. Kirchhof (eds), *Handbuch des Staatsrechts der Bundesrepublik Deutschland*, Vol. 2 (C.F. Müller Verlag, 2004), p. 269.

[28] German Federal Constitutional Court, BVerfGE 89, 155 (*Maastricht*) 12 October 1993, paragraphs 63, 85.

[29] Ibid., paragraph 102.

[30] German Federal Constitutional Court, BVerfGE 123, 267 (*Lisbon*) 30 June 2009, paragraph 251.

[31] Ibid.

[32] Ibid., paragraph 249.

areas were defined a bit more, as including 'sensitive' decisions on public revenue and expenditure especially regarding social policy considerations.[33]

Whereas in the *Maastricht* judgment the Court based the necessity of its control on the fact that democracy at the European level was not yet fully developed, a point also stressed in the *Lisbon* judgment, the latter judgment linked the protection of important democratic decisions to the sovereign statehood of Germany itself.[34] In other words, the constitutional transfer of competences is not only curtailed by the lack of democratic accountability at the EU level, but also by German sovereignty as a fundamental aspect of the country's constitutional order. The Constitutional Court's impact on the transfer of social competences to the EU has been considerable to say the least. Sovereignty considerations have also emerged as a gauge for the transfer of national competences to the EU in the constitutional jurisprudence of other jurisdictions. In its judgment on the constitutionality of the Lisbon Treaty, the Czech Constitutional Court stated that although the limits to the transfer of sovereignty was essentially for parliament to decide, the Constitution would bar the transfer of powers 'to the effect that it would no longer be possible to speak of the Czech Republic as a sovereign state'.[35] A similar approach was taken by the Polish Constitutional Tribunal in its judgment on the constitutionality of the country's accession to the EU, while the French Constitutional Council held that changes to the European Treaties were acceptable provided they did not undermine the 'essential conditions for the exercise of national sovereignty'.[36]

15.4 EX POST CONSTITUTIONAL CONTROL

The national protection of a Member State constitutional order does not stop with the transfer of competences to the EU. Member States can always move to amend the Treaties to extend, modify or repatriate specific competences, or even withdraw from the EU as confirmed in article 50 TEU in order to protect their constitutional orders. These measures are cumbersome and difficult though, as the United Kingdom has come to realise with article 50 TEU in the aftermath of its referendum result to leave the EU.

---

[33] Ibid., paragraph 252.

[34] Ibid., paragraph 247; D. Grimm, 'Defending Sovereign Statehood against Transforming the European Union into a State' (2009) 5 *European Constitutional Law Review* 353.

[35] Czech Constitutional Court, Pl. ÚS 19/08 of 26 November 2008 (*Treaty of Lisbon I*), paragraph 109.

[36] Polish Constitutional Tribunal, K 18/04 of 11 May 2005 (*EU Accession*), paragraph 7; French Constitutional Council, no. 92–308 DC of 9 April 1992 (*Maastricht*), paragraph 14.

Apart from such far-reaching measures, Member States can obviously avail themselves of the political and judicial channels that the Treaties afford them in shaping EU legislation and policy. In making their voices heard, such channels include national executive participation in the Council according to the ordinary legislative procedure in article 289(1) TFEU or a special legislative procedure as described in article 289(2) TFEU, the role of national parliaments in reviewing the subsidiarity of draft EU legislative acts as outlined in Protocol 2 annexed to the Treaty of Lisbon, and obviously the preliminary ruling procedure open to national courts in article 267 TFEU.

The article 267 reference procedure could, for instance, be put to use in determining the scope of the duty in article 4(2) TEU resting on the EU to respect the 'national identities' of the Member States 'inherent in their fundamental structures, political and constitutional, inclusive of regional and local self-government'. These national identities, to which the TEU first referred in the Treaty of Maastricht, has widely come to be interpreted as encompassing or including the fundamental constitutional principles or 'constitutional identity' of each Member State's legal order.[37] The provision in article 4(2) TEU essentially allows Member States to invoke fundamental aspects of their constitutional orders to restrict the operation of EU law such as in the *Sayn-Wittgenstein* case.[38] In this matter, Austria was permitted to limit the right in article 21 TFEU to move and reside freely in Member States by refusing the registration of a surname in a manner that would conflict with the country's particular interpretation of equality based on its republican heritage. Article 4(2) TEU, though, has not featured much in the ECJ's case law, let alone been applied in the social field.

It was, however, in the social field that national parliaments made use of Protocol 2 by showing the European Commission a 'yellow card'. Where a third of national parliaments object to a draft legislative act on account of it violating subsidiarity, the Commission must reconsider the proposal; while the objection by at least a half of the parliaments results in an 'orange card', which allows the Council of the EU or the European Parliament to reject it immediately. The first 'yellow card' was used to object to the European

---

[37] See L.F.M. Besselink, 'National and Constitutional Identity Before and After Lisbon' (2010) 6 *Utrecht Law Review* 36, p. 44; A. von Bogdandy and S. Schill, 'Overcoming Absolute Primacy: Respect for National Identity under the Lisbon Treaty' (2011) 48 *Common Market Law Review* 1417, 1424–5, 1427; G. van der Schyff, 'The Constitutional Relationship between the European Union and Its Member States: The Role of National Identity in Article 4(2) TEU' (2012) 37 *European Law Review* 563, 567–9; E. Cloots, *National Identity in EU Law* (Oxford University Press, 2015), pp. 165–70.
[38] ECJ, judgment of 22 December 2010 in *Sayn-Wittgenstein*, C-208/09, EU:C:2010:806.

Commission's draft Council Regulation of 2012 'on the exercise of the right to take collective action within the context of the freedom of establishment and the freedom to provide services' (Monti II).[39] The right to strike, the topic of Monti II, was recognised as a general principle of EU law by the *Viking* and *Laval* judgments in 2007.[40] The right had already been included in article 28 of the Charter of Fundamental Rights in 2000, which became enforceable after the adoption of the Lisbon Treaty of 2009.

Mindful of the fact that article 153(5) TFEU excludes the regulation of the right to strike from the application of article 153 TFEU, the Commission argued that this did not prevent the clarification in Monti II of the general principles and EU rules applicable to the exercise of the right within the context of the internal market.[41] Various social partners were worried that Monti II would in effect codify the *Viking* and *Laval* jurisprudence of ECJ, which many commentators considered to be unsympathetic to the right when weighed against the interests of employers and cross-border economic competition.[42] This unease about the effective protection of the right to strike, especially where national labour constitutions cherish the right more than the Regulation, led to the mobilisation of enough national parliaments to make use of the mechanism in Protocol 2 in signalling their concerns. Monti II was subsequently withdrawn, even though the European Commission was not legally obliged to do so. Some commentators took the view that national parliaments had over-stepped their power of subsidiary review under the Protocol by addressing broader political concerns.[43] Whatever view one takes on the correct interpretation of Protocol 2, national parliaments clearly achieved a political victory in the social field by diverting the European Commission's course. That the Commission will not always allow this to happen was illustrated by its

[39]   COM(2012)130 *On the Exercise of the Right to Take Collective Action within the Context of the Freedom of Establishment and the Freedom to Provide Services* (Brussels, 21 March 2012); See F. Fabbrini and K. Granat, '"Yellow Card, but No Foul": The Role of the National Parliaments under the Subsidiarity Protocol and the Commission Proposal for an EU Regulation on the Right to Strike' (2013) 50 *Common Market Law Review* 115.

[40]   ECJ, judgments of 11 December 2007 in *The International Transport Workers' Federation and The Finnish Seamen's Union* ('Viking'), C-438/05, EU:C:2007:772, paragraph 42; and of 18 December 2007 in *Laval un Partneri*, C-341/05, EU:C:2007:809, paragraph 88.

[41]   Commission Explanatory Memorandum in COM(2012)130, n. 39 in this chapter, at p. 10. One of the aims of Monti II was to create an early warning system requiring Member States to notify the Commission and other Member States of strike action that might impede the cross border provision of services, see Article 4 of the Draft Regulation (ibid.).

[42]   See also Fabbrini and Granat, n. 39 in this chapter, at pp. 129, 133–4; Rödl, n. 4 in this chapter, at p. 651; Joerges and Rödl, n. 2 in this chapter, at pp. 18–19.

[43]   See also Fabbrini and Granat, n. 39 in this chapter, at pp. 142–3.

rejection of a 'yellow card' regarding an amendment proposed in 2016 to the Posted Workers Directive.[44]

Importantly, the draft Monti II Regulation was based on article 352 TFEU, known as the flexibility clause.[45] This provision allows the Council to unanimously adopt legislation deemed necessary to pursue one of the EU's objectives even though an explicit basis in the Treaties lacks, provided the European Parliament gives its consent. The potential for encroaching on national competences in this way has not passed unnoticed among those charged with protecting Member States' fundamental constitutional principles. In this regard the German Federal Constitutional Court held that the use of the provision requires ratification by both chambers of the country's parliament on the basis of article 23(1) of the Constitution, which prevents the eternity clause in article 79(3) from being violated.[46] Section 8 of the United Kingdom's European Union Act only allows a minister to support an article 352 TFEU draft decision if the decision was approved by an act of parliament and pertains to a range of 'exempted purposes' aimed at narrowing down the provision's use.[47] These examples show that Member States can require special measures in tightening controls before national assent may be given to specific EU procedures that could risk compromising national competences. In addition to such measures that in principle respect the primacy of EU law, Member States have also fashioned responses to the exercise of EU competences that stop short of recognising the primacy of EU law in its totality. Given their controversial nature, these approaches will now be considered in greater detail than the regular channels described above, such as the preliminary ruling procedure in article 267 TFEU.

According to the settled case law of the ECJ, as recognised in Declaration 17 annexed to the Treaty of Lisbon, both primary and secondary EU law prevails over all national laws including those of a constitutional nature.[48] Once transferred to the EU, the last word on interpreting such competences reverts to the ECJ as the ultimate interpreter of the Treaties, according to article 19(1) TEU. While recognising the primacy of EU law in most instances, many national jurisdictions hold the view that as competences were transferred to the EU by means of national law, the ultimate jurisdiction pertaining to the exercise of

---

[44] COM(2016)128 *Amending Directive 96/71/EC of The European Parliament and of the Council of 16 December 1996 Concerning the Posting of Workers in the Framework of the Provision of Services* (Strasbourg, 8 March 2016).

[45] Fabbrini and Granat, n. 39 in this chapter, at pp. 132–3.

[46] German Federal Constitutional Court judgment, *Lisbon*, n. 30 in this chapter, paragraph 328.

[47] See Craig, n. 23 in this chapter, at p. 1884.

[48] ECJ, judgment of 17 December 1970, in *Internationale Handelsgesellschaft mbH v Einfuhr-und Vorratsstelle für Getreide und Futtermittel*, C-11/70, EU:C:1970:114, p. 1134.

such competences remains with the Member States. In other words, the EU's constitutional bedrock remains essentially national, even though national competences, such as those designated in Title X of the TFEU on social policy, may be exercised in whole or in part by EU institutions.

In this regard, the Danish Supreme Court in its judgment on the Maastricht Treaty ruled that the EU may not be given the competence to rule on its own competence, echoed by the Polish Constitutional Tribunal in its judgment on the Lisbon Treaty that issues fundamental to the political system remain with the state as the master of the treaties.[49] These judgments fit well with the pioneering work of the German Federal Constitutional Court in developing the concepts of *Kompetenz-Kompetenz* and Member State mastery over the Treaties to encapsulate national constitutional reservations to EU integration.[50] The Supreme Court of the United Kingdom joined in the chorus in its *HS2* judgment, the gist of which was repeated quite crisply in the 2015 judgment in *Pham*:

> A domestic court faces a particular dilemma if, in the face of the clear language of a Treaty and of associated declarations and decisions, the Court of Justice reaches a decision which oversteps jurisdictional limits which Member States have clearly set at the European Treaty level and which are reflected domestically in their constitutional arrangements. But, unless the Court of Justice has had conferred upon it under domestic law unlimited as well as unappealable power to determine and expand the scope of European law, irrespective of what the Member States clearly agreed, a domestic court must ultimately decide for itself what is consistent with its own domestic constitutional arrangements, including … what jurisdictional limits exist under the European Treaties and upon the competence conferred on European institutions including the Court of Justice.[51]

Most recently, the Belgian Constitutional Court added its view, when it held that the transfer to, and subsequent exercise of national powers by an international organisation could not be allowed to violate the country's national identity inherent in its fundamental political and constitutional structures or the core values underpinning the Constitution's protection of its subjects.[52]

---

[49] Danish Supreme Court, judgment of 6 April 1998 (*Maastricht*) paragraph 9.2; Polish Constitutional Tribunal, K 32/09 of 24 November 2010 (*Lisbon*), paragraph 2.1.

[50] See German Federal Constitutional Court judgment, *Lisbon*, n. 30 in this chapter, paragraphs 233 (and the references there), 298.

[51] UK Supreme Court, *Pham v Secretary of State for the Home Department* [2015] UKSC 19, paragraph 90. See also UK Supreme Court, *R. (HS2 Action Alliance Ltd) v Secretary of State for Transport* [2014] UKSC 3, paragraphs 111, 207.

[52] Belgian Constitutional Court, judgment no. 62/2016 of 28 April 2016 (*European Fiscal Compact*), paragraph B.8.7. The judgment related to the Fiscal Stability Treaty of 2012.

The first part of the Court's formulation of the barrier to integration copies
the wording of article 4(2) TEU, although the Court attributes this barrier
to its interpretation of article 34 of the Belgian Constitution. The meaning
is clear: the Belgian Constitutional Court acts as the ultimate guardian of
the Constitution's fundamental constitutional principles and not the international organisation to which national powers are transferred.

The Dutch legal order seems to be the dissenting voice in the chorus, as
the country's Supreme Court accepted in 2004 the view long held in domestic academic literature that the doctrine of the primacy of EU law should be
accepted unreservedly.[53] The last word on the interpretation and application
of EU social laws in the Netherlands therefore rests with the EU's institutions
and ultimately the ECJ. This position is strengthened by the fact that article
5(e) of the Advisory Referendum Act, referred to earlier, does not allow referendums in respect of acts of parliament passed solely for the execution of
treaties, thereby including the TEU and TFEU and safeguarding the unim-
peded transposition of EU directives.

Many of the national avenues foreseen by Member States in qualifying the
primacy of EU law focus on the judicial function, thereby matching the central role fulfilled by the ECJ in the European constitutional space. Although
not all states have fully detailed their powers in exercising ex post constitutional controls, or adhere to similar constructs in this regard, a number of
possible lines can be sketched. A national decision can, for instance, hold that
the EU did not have the competence to act in a certain matter, such as finding that the EU in supporting and complementing the activities of Member
States in terms of article 153 TFEU regulated the right to strike or to impose
lockouts, both of which are expressly excluded from the EU's competences in
regard to the provision by article 153(5) TFEU. Alternatively, a decision can
find that although the EU did act within its range of competences, its action
cut too deeply into the national protection of the social state as a fundamental
principle of a Member State's constitutional order.

The judgments of the Danish Supreme Court on the Maastricht and Lisbon
Treaties, for instance, while not distinguishing clearly between these two possibilities, are wide enough to cover both these eventualities in protecting the
country's constitutional order.[54] The described actions do correspond though
to the German notions of *ultra vires* review, as adopted in the Constitutional
Court's *Maastricht* judgment, and 'identity review' as outlined in the *Lisbon*

[53] Dutch Supreme Court, HR 2 November 2004, NJ 2005 80 (*Rusttijden*), paragraph 3.5.
[54] Danish Supreme Court, judgment of 20 February 2013 (*Lisbon*) paragraph 3.

judgment, respectively.[55] In elaborating on its powers in this regard, the *Lisbon* judgment made it explicit that the Court may review not only the constitutionality of national competences being transferred to the EU, but their subsequent exercise too.[56] The Court continued that Germany's participation in the process of creating a social union depended in part on the EU's commitment to social principles.[57] The Court also explained that:

> [T]he essential decisions in social policy must be made by the German legislative bodies on their own responsibility. In particular the securing of the individual's livelihood, which is a responsibility of the state … must remain a primary task of the Member States, even if coordination which goes as far as gradual approximation is not ruled out. This corresponds to the legally and factually limited possibilities of the European Union to shape the structures of the social state.[58]

The last sentence would seem to imply that the national protection of the social state would decrease commensurate to the level of protection afforded by the EU in this regard. While arguably true, such congruency is not the only factor at play though. This is because the *Lisbon* judgment stressed the importance of retaining state sovereignty in the process of Europeanisation, thereby placing a limit on strengthening the social powers of the EU. When the Constitutional Court would act though to protect the German social state against the EU over-exercising its competences is not entirely clear. This is because the exact content of the social state, although seemingly fleshed out somewhat in the Court's *Lisbon* judgment, remains debateable, as it rests more on the realisation and protection of dynamic principles than clear rules.[59]

Similarly to the Danish Supreme Court, the German Federal Constitutional Court has committed itself to making use of the preliminary ruling procedure in article 267 TFEU, in order to allow the ECJ to clarify EU law, before finding that the EU overstepped its competences. In the OMT matter, the Court for the first time in its history referred a question to the ECJ.[60] While the outcome

---

[55] German Federal Constitutional Court judgment, *Maastricht*, n. 28 in this chapter, paragraph 106; German Federal Constitutional Court judgment, *Lisbon*, n. 30 in this chapter, paragraphs 228, 240–1, 332.

[56] German Federal Constitutional Court judgment, *Lisbon*, n. 30 in this chapter, paragraph 251.

[57] Ibid., paragraph 258.

[58] Ibid., paragraph 259.

[59] See also Hain, n. 26, at pp. 2262–3; B.O. Bryde, 'Article 79', in I. von Münch and P. Künig (eds), *Grundgesetz: Kommentar*, Vol. 2 (C.H. Beck, 6th ed., 2012), p. 217.

[60] German Federal Constitutional Court, 2 BvR 2661/06 (*Honeywell*) of 6 July 2010, paragraph 60. See also Danish Supreme Court judgment, n. 49 in this chapter, paragraph 9.3; German Federal Constitutional Court, BVerfG 2 BvR 2728/13 (*OMT I*) of 14 January 2014, paragraph 104; U. Di Fabio, 'Karlsruhe makes a referral' (2014) 15 *German Law Journal* 107–10.

in this matter did not result in a violation of the German Constitution, the same cannot be said of the Constitutional Court's 2015 judgment on the constitutionality of a European arrest warrant.[61] Here the Court held that a lower court's decision to extradite an American national to Italy in terms of a European arrest warrant had violated his right to human dignity, and thus the eternity clause in article 79(3) of the Constitution.[62] Clues can be garnered from the judgment as to how the Court will go about protecting article 79(3), as it made clear the exceptional nature of such review, thereby implying a high threshold.[63] This position was confirmed in the second *OMT* judgment, where it was stressed that such review had to be exercised sparingly.[64] What seems to be clear also, is that the Constitutional Court will refrain from reviewing secondary EU law against the fundamental rights in the German Constitution as a matter of course, provided that the EU's protection of such rights remained on a sufficiently high level.[65]

Applied to the social field, this means that the German Federal Constitutional Court will not easily find a violation of the principle of the social state, as guaranteed in article 20(1) of the Constitution and ultimately by the eternity clause in article 79(3). However, given that the eternity clause is just that, a provision that cannot be amended, any infringement of the values it protects by EU law will result in the latter being unconstitutional and therefore inapplicable nationally. The effect is that while a violation of the provision might not be likely, its consequences will be absolute in that the eternity clause will always trump EU law. This approach stands in contrast to the relative protection of the fundamental principles in the French Constitution, as the Constitutional Council has ruled that such elements cannot be violated by secondary EU law except with the consent of the constitutive authority, in practice both houses of parliament sitting jointly.[66] In addition, a conflict in the EU–French social

---

[61]   For the OMT matter, see German Federal Constitutional Court, 2 BvR 2728/13 (*OMT II*) of 21 June 2016.

[62]   German Federal Constitutional Court, 2 BvR 2735/14 (*European Arrest Warrant*) 15 December 2015, paragraph 51.

[63]   Ibid., paragraph 46.

[64]   German Federal Constitutional Court judgment, OMT II, n. 61 in this chapter, paragraphs 154–6. On the limits of 'identity review', see also C. Calliess, 'Der Integrationsauftrag des Grundgesetzes', in R.T. Baus, Michael Borchard, K. Gelinsky, and G. Krings (eds), *Die Finanzkrise als juristische Zeitenwende: zur Zukunft von europäischer Integration und Grundgesetz* (Konrad Adenauer Stiftung, 2012), p. 79.

[65]   German Federal Constitutional Court, BVerfGE 102, 147 (*Bananas*) of 7 June 2000, paragraphs 38–9.

[66]   French Constitutional Council, no. 2006–540 DC of 27 July 2006 (*Loi DADVSI*), paragraph 19. See generally, J.H. Reestman, 'The Franco-German Constitutional Divide: Reflections on National and Constitutional Identity' (2009) 5 *European Constitutional Law Review* 374.

field seems remoter than in the German case. This is because the French Constitution will protect those principles that are not also protected at the EU level, thereby narrowing the range of possible conflict.[67] To the extent that the 'social republic' in the preamble to the French Constitution is also protected at the EU level, national protection of this concept will not be necessary. In Germany on the other hand, the scope of the social state is defined purely with reference to the Constitution and not whittled down by comparable protection at the EU level.

That the possibility of exercising ex post controls in the social field is not only theoretical is proved by the 2012 judgment by the Czech Constitutional Court in which the ECJ was found to have acted outside the scope of its powers in the *Landtová* matter.[68] In this case the ECJ ruled that the 1971 Regulation on the application of social security schemes meant that the payment of a supplement benefit to old-age pensioners affected by the dissolution of Czechoslovakia could not apply to Czech citizens only.[69] The Constitutional Court though found that the matter had failed to come into the scope of EU law because it concerned a pure internal matter and consequently refused to apply the ECJ judgment nationally. Far from signalling a confrontational stance against the ECJ, Jan Komárek has argued that the Czech judgment was borne of frustration with the Constitutional Court's relationship with the Supreme Administrative Court, which referred the question for a preliminary ruling that led to the *Landtová* judgment.[70] Instead of simply extending the special pension increase to all qualifying EU citizens, the Czech Constitutional Court chose a potentially dangerous route to settle a case of national judicial rivalry.

15.5 THOUGHTS ON THE WAY FORWARD

Transferring national social competences to the EU is not as simple as ratifying an ordinary treaty, given the often increased political and judicial hurdles to be cleared in the process. Poland, for instance, is so protective of its constitutional order that it is easier to amend the Constitution than transfer national competences to the EU.[71] As the prospects for increasing the EU's

---

[67] French Constitutional Council, no. 2004–498 DC of 29 July 2004 (*Loi relative à la bioéthique*), paragraphs 4–7.
[68] Czech Constitutional Court, Pl. ÚS 5/12 of 31 January 2012 (*Slovak Pensions XVII*).
[69] ECJ, judgment of 22 June 2011 in *Landtová*, C-399/09, EU:C:2011:415, paragraphs 49 and 54.
[70] J. Komárek, 'Czech Constitutional Court Playing with Matches: The Czech Constitutional Court Declares a Judgment of the Court of Justice of the EU *ultra vires*; Judgment of 31 January 2012, Pl. ÚS 5/12, Slovak Pensions XVII' (2012) 8 *European Constitutional Law Review* 328.
[71] Besselink et al., n. 16 in this chapter, at p. 180.

social competences seem quite slim, bearing in mind the drawn-out and difficult experiences in the past, much will rest on how the EU exercises the
competences it already possesses in advancing the cause of a social union.
This question is discussed further by Geert De Baere and Kathleen Gutman
(Chapter 14, this volume). The missing congruence, as Florian Rödl called it,
between the EU's social competences and the range of social rights in the EU
Charter on Fundamental Rights will not be corrected any time soon.

As it emerged from the discussion, it is important to note that once transferred the national protection of social competences is not entirely excluded
from the constitutional landscape. Although Advocate General Cruz Villalón
warned against preserving the EU in its current form, if Member States were to
insist on each protecting their fundamental constitutional principles instead of
recognising the primacy of EU law in full, many states remain unperturbed.[72]
Despite the odd exception, such as the Czech Constitutional Court's ruling in
Landtová, the real prospect of conflict seems small given that little has come
of many states' posturing. Judges have undeniably deployed admirable skill in
avoiding outright conflict in the minefield that has come to characterise the
primacy of EU law. While this is certainly a contributing factor, the fact that
the national protection of a constitutional order usually is usually restricted to
its fundamental principles means that the range of possible conflict is limited
accordingly. In this regard, various national courts have recognised the exceptional nature of such conflicts and hence their rarity.[73]

Ensuring that constitutional conflict remains the exception and does not
become the norm, will depend especially on the continued willingness of
national courts to recognise the demands of the European project as a way of
overcoming Member State differences and realising common goals through
supranational action. In this regard, references to state sovereignty as a red
line worthy of protection, such as in German and Polish case law, should be
rethought as vehicles for protecting national constitutional orders.[74] Instead,
concepts such as *Europarechtsfreundlichkeit* in the case law of the German
Federal Constitutional Court, or friendliness to EU law, should be stressed
more than has already been the case.[75] A concept such as the latter can be

---

[72] Opinion of Advocate General Cruz Villalón of 14 January 2015 in *Peter Gauweiler and Others* v
Deutscher Bundestag, C-62/14, EU:C:2015:7, points 59–60 referring to 'constitutional identities'.

[73] See UK Supreme Court, *Pham*, n. 51 in this chapter, paragraph 91 (speaking of 'a very rare case
indeed'); Danish Supreme Court judgment, *Maastricht*, n. 49 in this chapter, paragraph 9.3
(speaking of 'an extraordinary situation').

[74] Also critical of state sovereignty, see Cloots, n. 37 in this chapter, at pp. 170–4, with reference
to Article 4(2) TEU.

[75] German Federal Constitutional Court judgment, *OMT II*, n. 61 in this chapter, paragraphs
120, 154–5; German Federal Constitutional Court judgment, *Lisbon*, n. 30 in this chapter,
paragraphs 225, 240.

developed further as a vehicle for expressing and practising real constitutional tolerance by factoring in not only the interests of the particular Member State or 'constitutional self', but also those of the EU and fellow Member States understood as the 'constitutional other'.[76] Member State judicial decision-making then is not about the fencing-off its fundamental constitutional principles, as a sovereignty-based approach would have it, but about evaluating such claims in this regard against the backdrop of the possibilities and needs of a shared constitutional space.

Likewise, the EU should pay more attention to the fact that it does not fully replace Member State constitutional orders. In this respect, special attention must be paid to article 4(2) TEU, which places a wide-ranging duty on the EU to respect Member States' 'national identities, inherent in their fundamental structures, political and constitutional, inclusive of regional and local self-government'. In exercising the competences conferred on the EU, this provision should guide it in factoring in the core social interests of Member States, as constitutionally defined by those States themselves. The more the EU moves to acknowledge and accommodate Member States as the 'constitutional other' the greater the chance arguably becomes that States will let their guard down to facilitate greater integration that could result in social convergence over time. In this respect, it is doubtful whether controversial ECJ judgments such as *Viking* and *Laval*, which come close to championing the perfection of the internal market as a goal in itself, create the necessary trust among Member States that sensitive aspects of their labour constitutions are in safe hands with the EU.[77] Encouragingly, recent judgments such as *Sähköalojen ammattiliitto ry* and *RegioPost* seem to signal that the ECJ is willing to approach internal market law in a manner more sensitive to social justice needs as conceived at the Member State level.[78] Although the internal market is important to the European project and is probably its most laudable achievement to date, it must be realised that this market cannot be treated as a stand-alone entity cut off from Member States and their constitutionally rooted conceptions of the social state. It is in this context that the value of

---

[76] For various discussions of the notion of constitutional tolerance, see D. Chalmers, G. Davies and G. Monti, *European Union Law* (Cambridge University Press, 3rd edn, 2014), p. 152 (see also 2nd edn 2010 pp. 194–7); J.H.H. Weiler, 'On the Power of the Word: Europe's Constitutional Iconography' (2005) 3 *International Journal of Constitutional Law* 173, 184–90; J.H.H. Weiler, 'In Defence of the Status Quo: Europe's Constitutional *Sonderweg*', in J.H.H. Weiler and M. Wind (eds), *European Constitutionalism beyond the State* (Cambridge University Press, 2003), pp. 19–22.

[77] For a critical appraisal of these earlier cited cases, see C. Barnard, 'Restricting Restrictions: Lessons for the EU from the US?' (2009) 68 *Cambridge Law Journal* 579.

[78] ECJ, judgments of 12 February 2015 in *Sähköalojen ammattiliitto*, C-396/13, EU:C:2015:86; and of 17 November 2015 in *RegioPost*, C-115/14, EU:C:2015:760.

article 4(2) TEU becomes apparent in mandating respect for Member States' 'constitutional choices', as the ECJ phrased it recently.[79] To date this provision's potential has been neglected by its sparse application, not to mention to isolated cases of debateable importance such as *Bogendorff von Wolffersdorff*.[80] The time is ripe to put article 4(2) TEU to work in the intricate European social field in striking a fair balance between capital and labour.

While the admittedly complicated constitutional relationship between the EU and its Member States sketched in this chapter might not always be ideal from the perspective of creating a strong EU-wide social union, it does capture the political and constitutional reality that must be navigated.

---

[79] ECJ, judgment of 2 June 2016 in *Bogendorff von Wolffersdorff*, C-438/14, EU:C:2016:401, paragraphs 64–5.

[80] The judgment concerned Germany's refusal to register a freely-adopted surname for containing aristocratic elements.

16

Social Rights, the Charter, and the ECHR: Caveats, Austerity, and Other Disasters

Alexander Kornezov

16.1 INTRODUCTION

The Charter of Fundamental Rights of the EU (hereinafter the 'Charter') raised hopes for enhancing the legal status and the enforceability of social rights in the EU. It had the potential of becoming the constitutional foundation of the European Social Model. Indeed, the Charter proclaimed a relatively wide range of social rights, to which a separate title, called 'Solidarity', was specifically dedicated. Moreover, since the Charter acquired the status of primary law,[1] its social rights were set to gain equal footing with other fundamental rights and Treaty provisions more generally.

Historically, social rights have been viewed with suspicion mainly for ideological and pragmatic reasons.[2] Ideologically, they have been thought to hamper the forces of free markets.[3] Pragmatically, they have been considered problematic since many of them are potentially costly to the budget.[4] For these reasons, social rights have often been regarded as 'second rate' rights, which are not really 'fundamental', as opposed to political and civil rights. As the argument goes, social rights should at best serve as guidelines for government action but should not be directly enforceable and justiciable.

The views and opinions expressed in this chapter are personal. The usual disclaimers apply.

[1] Article 6(1) TEU.
[2] See further A. Eide and A. Rosas, 'Economic, Social and Cultural Rights: A Universal Challenge', in A. Eide, C. Krause and A. Rosas (eds), *Economic, Social and Cultural Rights: A Textbook* (Nijhof, 1995), p. 15.
[3] See further P. Alston and H. Steiner, *International Human Rights in Context: Law, Politics, Morals: Text and Materials* (Oxford University Press, 2nd edn, 2000), p. 237.
[4] See further J. Kenner, 'Economic and Social Rights in the EU Legal Order', in T. Hervey and J. Kenner (eds), *Economic and Social Rights under the EU Charter of Fundamental Rights: A Legal Perspective* (Hart Publishing, 2006), p. 7.

Hailed as the most comprehensive and modern human rights catalogue in Europe,[5] the Charter has been credited with the potential of putting an end to this archaic distinction by elevating the status of social rights in the EU legal order. Since its entry into force, however, much of this hope seems to have evaporated.

Behind the solemn language often used to describe the Charter social rights, a different reality has been unfolding. The interplay of a number of factors has contributed to diminishing their effectiveness altogether. First, their incorporation in the Charter came at a price. Several important caveats seem to have been tailored specifically to rein in the Charter solidarity provisions.[6] Secondly, by deciding to deal with Europe's sovereign debt crisis mostly outside of the scope of the EU legal order, the EU Member States dealt a significant blow to the Charter's relevance in the social sphere at a time when it was most needed. Thirdly, the impossibility to enforce directives in disputes between private parties has proved a significant problem in the area of social law, where many disputes are horizontal (between employees and employers) and where EU legislation is mostly in the form of directives. Although the Court's case law offers alternative mechanisms for overcoming this problem, the Court has refused to apply the most promising of them in the context of social rights, namely the application of a Charter right, as given expression in a directive. Lastly, the European Convention of Human Rights (hereinafter the ECHR or the 'Convention'), which does not protect social rights as such, hardly offers a viable alternative capable of bridging these limitations.

The combined effect of these factors points to a general malaise surrounding the enforcement of social rights in the wider European landscape. Although in theory they were emancipated through their incorporation in the Charter, in practice they have been given a back seat in the EU legal order.

This chapter is structured as follows. First, the applicability of the Charter in the context of Europe's sovereign debt crisis will be examined (Section 16.2). Secondly, the question of whether the Charter's solidarity provisions add any normative value to the EU's existing social rights will be discussed (Section 16.3). Thirdly, the chapter will embark on the distinction between rights and principles in the meaning of Article 52(5) of the Charter and its ramifications

---

[5]   F. Hoffmeister, 'Enforcing the EU Charter of Fundamental Rights in Member States: How Far are Rome, Budapest and Bucharest from Brussels', in A. von Bogdandy and P. Sonnevend (eds), *Constitutional Crisis in the European Constitutional Area: Theory, Law and Politics in Hungary and Romania* (Hart Publishing, 2015), chapter 7.

[6]   Unless otherwise specified, the terms 'social rights', 'solidarity provisions' and 'solidarity clauses' are used interchangeably throughout this chapter to describe all the provisions contained in Title IV of the Charter.

for the latter's solidarity provisions (Section 16.4). Fourthly, the (un)enforce-ability of EU's social rights in horizontal disputes will be addressed (Section 16.5). Lastly, the chapter will examine whether the ECHR could offer an effective remedy where EU law has failed to do so (Section 16.6).

16.2 DOES THE CHARTER APPLY IN THE CONTEXT OF AUSTERITY MEASURES?

National austerity measures adopted across the EU in exchange for 'bail-outs' have wreaked havoc to the European social model. Although enacted in national law, most of these measures have in fact been taken as part of the conditionality for the loans granted. Such measures often involve significant cuts in entitlements and social benefits.

Historically, EU financial assistance for troubled Member States was first channelled through a facility established by a Council Regulation.[7] The loans were themselves authorised by a Council decision laying down in gen-eral terms the conditions attached to the loan. This was followed by the sig-nature of a Memorandum of Understanding (MoU) between the European Community and the Member State concerned which spelled out in more detail the reforms which had to be undertaken by that Member State. Later, the newly created European Financial Stabilisation Mechanism (EFSM), established by a Council Regulation,[8] took over the task and began dis-persing the necessary funds through the European Financial Stability Facility (EFSF), a *société anonyme* incorporated under Luxembourgish law. That mechanism has been replaced since 2012 by the European Stability Mechanism (ESM), a new permanent structure set up under public inter-national law to provide financial support to EU Member States in financial difficulty.

The question of the applicability of the Charter in this context has become particularly salient, given that the resulting austerity measures have affected deposits, entitlements, and social benefits. From a legal perspective, the anal-ysis depends on whether the austerity measures were adopted in the context of (1) the pre-ESM legal framework; or (2) the ESM Treaty. In addition, the question of judicial review of the acts of the Eurogroup adopted in tackling the crisis should also be examined.

---

[7] Regulation 332/2002 of 18 February 2002 establishing a facility providing medium-term finan-cial assistance for Member States' balance of payments, [2002] OJ L 53/1.

[8] Regulation 407/2010 of 11 May 2010 establishing a European financial stabilization mecha-nism, [2010] OJ L 118/1.

16.2.1 *Does the Charter Apply in the Context of Austerity Measures Adopted under the Pre-ESM Legal Framework?*

As mentioned above, in the past EC/EU financial assistance to troubled Member States was granted on the basis of EU measures (such as Council decisions) and/or through instruments set up under EU law (such as the EFSM/EFSF and its predecessors). Thus, on the one hand, the Council decisions, authorising the funds and spelling out the relevant conditions, could in principle be challenged on the basis of the Charter mostly through the preliminary ruling mechanism, given the strict standing requirements under Article 263(4) TFEU. On the other hand, national austerity measures adopted in this context could also be amenable to judicial review for their compliance with the Charter, provided that it can be shown that they sought to give effect to a Council decision. In a nutshell therefore, under the pre-ESM legal framework, which was essentially part and parcel of EU law, the Charter seemed perfectly capable of applying. This window of opportunity might, however, have been lost. Indeed, all the legal challenges to the pre-ESM measures have so far failed on formal grounds before the EU Courts.

The first cases concerned national austerity measures adopted prior to the establishment of the EFSM/EFSF. In Romania, where salaries in the public sector were cut by 25 per cent in 2010 as part of an austerity package in exchange for an EU/IMF loan, public servants argued that the reductions were contrary, in particular, to Articles 17, 20, and 21 of the Charter. When the national courts referred that question to the Court pursuant to Article 267 TFEU, they failed to explain whether the national law that imposed the pay cut was specifically adopted in order to implement the relevant Council decision[9] and/or MoU.[10] It was indeed not immediately obvious whether the conditions attached to the loan required that specific pay cut or whether the national authorities sovereignly decided to act in this manner.[11] In the absence of such explanations, it was unclear whether the Charter applied. Indeed, pursuant to Article 51(1) of the Charter, the provisions of the Charter are addressed

---

[9] Council Decision 2009/458/EC of 6 May 2009 granting mutual assistance for Romania, [2011] OJ L 150/6; and Council Decision 2009/459/EC of 6 May 2009 providing EU medium-term financial assistance for Romania, [2009] OJ L 150/8.

[10] 'Memorandum of Understanding between the European Community and Romania' (2009) available at: ec.europa.eu/economy_finance/publications/publication15409_en.pdf (accessed 18 November 2016).

[11] For example, Council Decision 2009/459/EC referred to 'reducing the public sector wage bill … by foregoing public sector wage increases … and by reducing public employment', n. 9 in this chapter, Article 3, paragraph 5(h); the MoU provided, in addition, for the 'elimination of the large majority of bonuses or rolling them into the base wage', n. 10 in this chapter, point 5b.

to the Member States 'only when they are implementing Union law'. In these circumstances, the Court dismissed summarily the references for lack of jurisdiction.[12] Another Romanian reference made in a similar context is currently pending before the Court.[13]

The second wave of challenges concerned national austerity measures adopted in the context of EFSM/EFSF funding. In Portugal, salary reductions and suspension of certain bonuses were challenged by trade unions on the basis, in particular, of Articles 20, 21(1), and 31(1) of the Charter.[14] However, when the Portuguese courts referred the matter to the Court, they also failed to explain whether these measures 'implemented Union law' in the meaning of Article 51(1) of the Charter. Here the matter was no less convoluted, given the succinctness of the orders of reference and the ambiguity of the legal framework. When told by the Court that more information was needed, the referring courts failed to fill in the gaps.[15] Indeed, a cursory look at the Council Decision granting EFSM funding to Portugal[16] and the MoU[17] was far from conclusive.[18] More evidence was clearly needed. In those circumstances, the Court could not be satisfied that the conditions set out in Article 51(1) of the Charter were met. Consequently, it dismissed summarily the three references for lack of jurisdiction.

In a separate development, in *ADEDY and Others* v *Council*, a trade union and two individuals sought the annulment of two Council decisions addressed to Greece in the context of the Greek debt crisis.[19] These decisions concerned

---

[12] ECJ, orders of 14 December 2011 in *Corpul Naţional al Poliţiştilor*, C-434/11, EU:C:2011:830; and *Cozman*, C-462/11, EU:C:2011:831.

[13] ECJ, *Florescu and Others*, C-258/14, pending.

[14] ECJ, order of 7 March 2013 in *Sindicato dos Bancários do Norte and Others*, C-128/12, EU:C:2013:149; *Sindicato Nacional dos Profissionais de Seguros e Afins*, C-264/12, EU:C:2014:2036; and of 21 October 2014 in *Sindicato Nacional dos Profissionais de Seguros e Afins*, C-665/13, EU:C:2014:2327.

[15] See ECJ order, n. 14 in this chapter, *Sindicato Nacional dos Profissionais de Seguros e Afins*, paragraphs 14–16.

[16] Council Implementing Decision 2011/344/EU of 30 May 2011 on granting Union financial assistance to Portugal, [2011] OJ L 159/88.

[17] 'Memorandum of Understanding on Specific Economic Policy Conditionality' (2011) available at: ec.europa.eu/economy_finance/eu_borrower/mou/2011-05-18-mou-portugal_en.pdf (accessed 18 October 2016).

[18] While the Council decision and the MoU did spell out a number of detailed conditions, none seems directly linked to the national measures at issue – for example Article 3(5) of the Council Decision 2011/344/EU, n. 17 in this chapter, requires in general terms 'reductions in social transfers'; the MoU, n. 18 in this chapter, requires for example wage freezes, annual decreases in the wage bill of the public sector through reduction of headcounts in the public administration.

[19] Council Decisions 2010/320/EU of 10 May 2010 addressed to Greece with a view to reinforcing and deepening fiscal surveillance and giving notice to Greece to take measures for the deficit reduction judged necessary to remedy the situation of excessive deficit, [2010] OJ 2010 L 145/

Greece's excessive deficit and provided for a number of measures to be adopted by Greece in view of reducing that deficit in exchange of financial aid granted to that Member State through an ad hoc intergovernmental mechanism. The General Court rejected the action as inadmissible on the ground that the applicants lacked standing. It held, in particular, that the Council decisions were broadly framed and required national implementing measures which would specify their content. The Greek authorities thus had 'wide discretion', provided that the final objective is pursued. It is therefore those national measures which, possibly, would directly affect the legal situation of the applicants. The General Court concluded that therefore the applicants were not directly concerned by the contested EU measures.[20]

Thus, so far, the Court has avoided examining, mostly on formal grounds, the compatibility with the Charter of austerity measures adopted under the pre-ESM legal framework.

16.2.2 Does the Charter Apply in the Context of Austerity Measures Adopted under the ESM Legal Framework?

The relationship between the ESM Treaty and EU law is perhaps one of the most complex legal matters that the Court has had to deal with over the last few years. This is mainly due to the fact that the Member States decided to set up the ESM as a structure governed by public international law, not EU law, while at the same time associating some of the EU institutions in the workings of the ESM.

Thus, from a legal perspective, the MoUs adopted jointly by the ESM and the Member State concerned are not acts of an institution, body, office, or agency of the Union within the meaning of Articles 263 TFEU. Consequently, the MoUs cannot be challenged as such under Articles 263 and 267 TFEU, including on grounds of their alleged inconsistency with the Charter.

Likewise, the national measures adopted in the context of ESM funding also, in principle, fall outside of the scope of the Charter. As the Court emphasised in *Pringle*, Member States are not implementing EU law within the meaning of Article 51(1) when they act within the context of the ESM.[21] Therefore, the Charter does not apply to national austerity measures enacted under the auspices of the ESM.[22]

---

6 (corrigendum OJ 2011 L 209/63) and 2010/486/EU of 7 September 2010 amending Decision 2010/320/EU, [2010] OJ 2010 L 241/12.

[20] EGC, order of 27 November 2012 in *ADEDY and Others v Council*, T-541/10, EU:.T:2012:626, paragraphs 70, 74, 76, 78, 84.

[21] ECJ, judgment of 27 November 2012 in *Pringle*, C-370/12, EU:C:2012:756, paragraph 180.

[22] However, see Subsection 2.4 on the possible impact of Regulation 472/2013.

Yet, the hybridity of the ESM is rather striking. Even though it is not part of EU law, the ESM Treaty entrusts the Commission and the ECB with important tasks: both EU institutions participate in the negotiations of the MoUs and the Commission is responsible for signing it on behalf of the ESM. But in *Pringle*, the Court held that the duties conferred on the Commission and the ECB within the ESM Treaty, important as they are, do not entail any power to make decisions of their own. Furthermore, the activities pursued by those two institutions within the ESM Treaty commit the ESM alone.[23]

At the same time, however, Article 13(3), second indent, of the ESM Treaty provides that the MoUs concluded by the ESM 'shall be fully consistent with the measures of economic policy coordination provided for in the [TFEU]'. In *Pringle*, the Court took a broad view of this provision, stating that the MoUs 'must be fully consistent with *European Union law*',[24] thus potentially also with the Charter. The Court also emphasised that the tasks entrusted to the Commission by the ESM treaty enable it to 'ensure that the [MoUs] concluded by the ESM are consistent with EU law'.[25] The fact remains however that formally the Commission (and the ECB) has no autonomous decision-making powers within the ESM.[26] It cannot therefore, as a matter of law, be held responsible for the acts of the ESM.

This was, in a nutshell, the legal conundrum that the Court had to solve in *Ledra*. In this case the applicants sought, on the one hand, the annulment of the MoU concluded between Cyprus and the ESM,[27] and, on the other hand, compensation for damages arising from the Commission's and the ECB's allegedly unlawful conduct in the context of negotiating and signing the MoU. Citing *Pringle*, the General Court dismissed the actions on the ground that the ESM is not an institution, body or agency of the EU and that its conduct cannot be attributed to the Union and its institutions.[28]

On appeal, the Grand Chamber of the Court confirmed that an action for annulment under Article 263 TFEU of an MoU concluded between a Member State and the ESM is inadmissible since the MoU is not an act of an institution, body, office, or agency of the Union.[29] By contrast,

---

[23] ECJ, *Pringle*, n. 21 in this chapter, paragraph 161.
[24] Ibid., paragraph 174 (emphasis added).
[25] Ibid., paragraph 164.
[26] Ibid., paragraph 161.
[27] 'Memorandum of Understanding on Specific Economic Policy Conditionality' (2013) available at: www.mof.gov.cy/mof/mof.nsf/MoU_Final_approved_13913.pdf (accessed 18 October 2016).
[28] EGC, orders of 10 November 2014 in *Ledra Advertising v Commission and ECB*, T-289/13, EU:T:2014:981; *Eleftheriou and Papachristofi v Commission and ECB*, T-291/13, EU:T:2014:978; and *Theophilou v Commission and ECB*, T-293/13, EU:T:2014:979.
[29] ECJ, judgment of 20 September 2016 in *Ledra Advertising and Others v Commission and ECB*, C-8/15 P to C-10/15 P, EU:C:2016:701, paragraph 55.

however, an action for damages under Article 268 TFEU and the second and third paragraphs of Article 340 TFEU is admissible. This is so because, according to the Court, the Charter applies to the EU institutions, including when they act outside the EU legal framework.[30] Thus, even when the Commission acts within the framework of the ESM, it remains the guardian of the Treaties by virtue of Article 17(1) TEU and must therefore observe EU law, including the Charter. Moreover, Article 13(3) and (4) of the ESM Treaty oblige the Commission to ensure that the MoU concluded by the ESM is consistent with EU law. Therefore, according to the Court, the Commission should refrain from signing an MoU whose consistency with EU law it doubts.[31] Hence, if the Commission signs a MoU which is inconsistent with EU law, including the Charter, the Union could be liable for damages.

This is an important breakthrough in the case law. It fills a gap in the legal protection of the affected parties by offering them the only possible legal remedy under EU law, namely the action for damages under Article 268 TFEU and the second and third paragraphs of Article 340 TFEU. This solution thus seeks to reconcile the non-EU legal nature of the ESM and the EU elements that are nonetheless present within its structure (notably, the involvement of the Commission and the ECB and the requirement for consistency with EU law).

On substance, however, the Court dismissed the action for damages as illfounded. According to settled case law, the EU may incur such liability only if, in particular, the alleged unlawful conduct amounts to a 'sufficiently serious breach' of EU law.[32] This sets the bar high. In *Ledra*, the Court thus found that the conversion of 37.5 per cent of Bank of Cyprus's uninsured deposits into shares with full voting and dividend rights pursued an objective of general interest, namely the stability of the banking system in the euro area, and did not constitute a disproportionate and intolerable interference impairing the very substance of appellant's property rights guaranteed by Article 17(1) of the Charter.[33] Thus, while *Ledra* marks a welcome and courageous development in the case law, it seems to suggest that actions for damages brought against the Union in the context of the ESM would only very rarely be successful on substance.

---

[30] Ibid., paragraph 67.

[31] Ibid., paragraph 59 and 60.

[32] ECJ, judgment of 4 July 2000 in *Bergaderm and Goupil* v *Commission*, C-352/98 P, EU:C:2000:361, paragraph 42, and of 10 July 2014 in *Nikolaou* v *Court of Auditors*, C-220/13 P, EU:C:2014:2057, paragraph 53.

[33] ECJ, *Ledra Advertising*, n. 29 in this chapter, paragraphs 71–5.

16.2.3 Does the Charter Apply to the Eurogroup?

The Eurogroup has been playing a particularly important role in handling the debt crisis. It is therefore no surprise that, in the context of the Cypriot bailout, affected depositors have sought the annulment of certain acts of the Eurogroup that were allegedly inconsistent with the Charter. Thus, a statement of the Eurogroup, which 'welcomed' the measures agreed with the Cypriot authorities, was challenged before the General Court.[34] That Court held that the Eurogroup is not a decision-making body, since it lacks the power to adopt legally binding measures. In any event, the contested act was merely a 'statement' that had no legal force.[35] Hence, the actions were dismissed as inadmissible.

This conclusion was confirmed by the Grand Chamber of the Court in *Mallis and Others*. The Court held, in particular, that the actions of the Eurogroup can be attributed neither to the Commission and the ECB, nor to the Council. Hence, an action for annulment of an act of the Eurogroup under Article 263 TFEU is inadmissible, because the Eurogroup is not of an institution, body, office or agency of the Union.[36]

The lack of judicial review of the actions of the Eurogroup thus remains a source of concern. It is true that the Treaties do not confer any decision-making powers to the Eurogroup, which has been conceived as an 'informal forum'.[37] The reality however shows that many decisions are *in fact* taken by the Eurogroup. Such a stark discrepancy between the legal framework and reality is inacceptable. It only adds to the overall picture of disturbing legal nebulosity, resulting in the absence of judicial control and, more generally, of accountability.

16.2.4 Conclusions

Even though the Court took an important step forward in *Ledra* by accepting to review the compatibility with the Charter of an MoU concluded by the

---

[34] EGC, orders of 16 October 2014 in *Mallis and Malli v Commission and ECB* (T-327/13, EU:T:2014:909); 16 October 2014 in *Tameio Pronoias Prosopikou Trapezis Kyprou v Commission and ECB* (T-328/13, EU:T:2014:906); 16 October 2014 in *Chatzithoma v Commission and ECB* (T-329/13, EU:T:2014:908); 16 October 2014 in *Chatziioannou v Commission and ECB* (T-330/13, EU:T:2014:904); and 16 October 2014 in *Nikolaou v Commission and ECB* (T-331/13, EU:T:2014:905).

[35] For example, ECG order, *Mallis and Malli*, n. 34 in this chapter, at paragraph 53.

[36] ECJ, judgment of 20 September 2016 in *Mallis and Others v European Commission and ECB*, C-105/15 P to C-109/15 P, EU:C:2016:702, paragraphs 57, 58, 61.

[37] Article 1 of Protocol no. 14 TFEU.

ESM and a Member State in the context of an action for damages under Articles 268 and 340 TFEU, the present status quo is far from satisfactory. This is largely due to the fact that the applicable law is so complex that, as a result, there is a general lack of clarity with regard to institutional responsibilities, accountability, and effective judicial protection. The resulting confusion is inevitably reflected in the case law: while an action for annulment against an ESM act is inadmissible, an action for damages linked to the same act is, by contrast, admissible. Likewise, while the Eurogroup's role in this context is crucial, its actions are not amenable to judicial review. If all of this makes sense from a purely legalistic perspective, it strikes one as being far removed from the reality unfolding on the ground.

Lawyers could of course look for some respite elsewhere. One such avenue might stem from Regulation 472/2013.[38] The Regulation applies, in particular, to Member States which request or receive financial assistance from, notably, the ESM.[39] It stipulates that, in applying the Regulation, the Council, the Commission and the Member States 'shall fully observe Article 152 TFEU' and 'take into account Article 28 of the Charter' (both provisions concern social dialogue and collective bargaining and action).[40] In addition, the 'draft macroeconomic adjustment programme shall fully observe' the two afore-mentioned provisions.[41] Moreover, the Commission 'shall ensure that the [MoU] signed by the Commission on behalf of the ESM or of the EFSF is fully consistent with the macroeconomic adjustment programme approved by the Council'.[42]

According to Lenaerts, it should be possible to challenge the Council decision approving the draft macroeconomic adjustment programme – which is an EU act – on the ground that it is incompatible with the Charter.[43] Moreover, private applicants might have a cause of action for damages under Articles 268 and 340 TFEU. However, as Lenaerts admits, the question whether *national* measures adopted on the basis of such macroeconomic adjustment programmes come within the scope of EU law is more complex. The matter

---

[38] Regulation 472/2013 of the European Parliament and of the Council of 21 May 2013 on the strengthening of economic and budgetary surveillance of Member States in the euro area experiencing or threatened with serious difficulties with respect to their financial stability, [2013] OJ L 140/1.

[39] Regulation 472/2013, n. 38 in this chapter, Article 1(1)(b).

[40] Ibid., Article 1(4).

[41] Ibid., Article 7(1).

[42] Ibid., Article 7(2).

[43] K. Lenaerts, 'EMU and the European Union's Constitutional Framework' (2014) 39 *European Law Review* 751. However, private applicants will most probably not have standing under Article 263(4) TFEU.

appears indeed somewhat convoluted because, pursuant to Regulation 472/ 2013, on the one hand, the Council only approves the *draft* macroeconomic adjustment programme as a matter of EU law.[44] On the other hand, the subsequent MoU, signed between the ESM and the Member State concerned, is not EU law. So, when that Member State adopts the relevant national measures, is it implementing the Council decision (EU law) or the MoU (not EU law)?

Another alternative might be the *Dzodzi* case law. There the Court accepted to interpret EU law on the basis of Article 267 TFEU in a situation not governed by EU law, if domestic law has rendered the latter applicable by expressly referring to it.[45] Might this case law also apply in a situation where a national austerity measure expressly refers to an MoU, which, in turn, must be fully consistent with EU law pursuant to Article 13(3), second indent, of the ESM Treaty, as interpreted in *Pringle*?

Such legal tinkering is, however, anything but conclusive. There is need for more clarity and legal certainty. It is fairly obvious that until the ESM is fully brought within the auspices of the EU legal order, its amenability to full judicial review, including with regard to the Charter, would remain questionable.

All of this has been forcing individuals to seek protection before national constitutional courts and/or the European Court of Human Rights (ECtHR). This is rather unfortunate. The judicial review of a purely European affair (the sovereign debt crisis), tackled mostly on a European level,[46] is thus being left to national and non-EU jurisdictions.

It is also unfortunate that, unlike other instruments of international law, signed by EU Member States in the context of the financial crisis, such as the Treaty on Stability, Coordination, and Governance in the Economic and Monetary Union (TSCG),[47] the ESM Treaty does not provide for its ultimate integration into EU law. If the European social model were ever meant to play a meaningful role in shaping Europe's fiscal and economic policy, the ESM must be converted into EU law without delay. This is the only sustainable way for solving its obvious pitfalls in terms of democratic legitimacy[48] and the

---

[44] It is unclear why the Regulation refers *only* to Articles 152 TFEU and 28 of the Charter.
[45] For example, ECJ, judgment of 18 October 1990 in *Dzodzi*, C-297/88 and C-197/89, EU:C:1990:360, paragraph 36; and of 18 October 2012 in *Nolan*, C-583/10, EU:C:2012:638, paragraph 45.
[46] With smaller contributions from the IMF and some national funds.
[47] Article 16 TSCG.
[48] Since neither the EP nor national parliaments are directly involved in its decision-making.

limited scope of judicial review.[49] The actions of the Eurogroup should also be made amenable to judicial review.

It is therefore good news – albeit somewhat overdue – that in June 2015 President Juncker openly called for the full integration of the ESM within the EU Treaties in the medium-term (between July 2017 and 2025).[50] The fear is that by the time the ESM becomes mainstream EU law, the urgency of enforcing EU social rights in the context of austerity measures might (hopefully) have abated. If nonetheless this commitment bears fruit, there might be a flicker of hope for better governance, accountability, and even some protection of social rights in the context of Europe's economic and monetary union.

I now turn to the protection of social rights within the scope of EU law and the structural caveats that condition their exercise.

16.3 SOCIAL RIGHTS IN THE CHARTER: NO ADDED VALUE?

The recognition of a wide range of social rights as fundamental rights in the Charter has been generally considered as an important symbol of the importance of the European social model. Their prominent position in the Charter in a separate Title IV, named 'Solidarity', was meant to express their newly acquired status of human rights on an equal footing with other more 'traditional' civil and political rights.

The case law already contains forceful examples of the potential impact of the Charter: from striking down EU legislative acts for violation of a Charter right[51] to a vigorous Charter-compliant interpretation of such acts.[52] But few of these robust examples concern the Charter social rights as such.[53]

---

[49] The ESM Treaty confers very limited jurisdiction on the Court of Justice of the EU, namely to adjudicate disputes between ESM Members or between them and the ESM (so not private parties) as to the interpretation and application (not the validity) of the ESM Treaty and the by-laws of the ESM. See Article 37(3) of the ESM Treaty.

[50] J.C. Juncker, 'The Five Presidents' Report: Completing Europe's Economic and Monetary Union, Report in Close Cooperation D. Tusk, J. Dijsselbloem, M. Draghi and M. Schulz' (2015), available at ec.europa.eu/priorities/sites/beta-political/files/5-presidents-report_en.pdf (accessed 18 October 2016).

[51] For example, ECJ, judgment of 9 November 2010 in *Volker und Markus Schecke and Eifert*, C-92/09 and C-93/09, EU:C:2010:662; of 1 March 2011 in *Association belge des Consommateurs Test-Achats and Others*, C-236/09, EU:C:2011:100; and of 8 April 2014 in *Digital Rights Ireland and Others*, C-293/12 and C-594/12, EU:C:2014:238.

[52] For example, ECJ, judgment of 13 May 2014 in *Google Spain and Google*, C-131/12, EU:C:2014:317; of 21 December 2011 in *N. S. and Others*, C-411/10 and C-493/10, EU:C:2011:865.

[53] One possible exception is ECJ, judgment of 24 April 2012 in *Kamberaj*, C-571/10, EU:C:2012:233, where a directive was interpreted in the light of Article 34 of the Charter. However, this case was, in essence, about discrimination, not about social rights as such.

There might be several reasons for that. A closer look at the general provisions of the Charter reveals that social rights are subject to a number of important caveats. One such caveat is to be found in Article 52(2) of the Charter, which stipulates that 'rights recognised by this Charter for which provision is made in the Treaties shall be exercised under the conditions and within the limits defined by those Treaties'. In *Delvigne*, the Grand chamber of the Court concluded, on the basis of Article 52(2) of the Charter and the Explanations relating to it,[54] that the right to vote in EP elections proclaimed in Article 39 of the Charter had the same content as the one laid down in the relevant Treaty provisions and secondary law.[55] Likewise, in *Gardella* the Court held that it was sufficient to examine the compatibility of the national measure with Articles 45 and 48 TFEU, no separate analysis with regard to Article 15(2) of the Charter being necessary since the latter 'reiterates inter alia the free movement of workers guaranteed by Article 45 TFEU, as confirmed by the explanations relating to that provision'.[56] In short, according to the Court, a fundamental right recognised by the Charter, to which the caveat of Article 52(2) applies, has the same normative content as the corresponding Treaty provision and/or secondary law.

Although Article 52(2) is, in principle, susceptible of applying to the whole Charter, social rights look particularly likely to fall within its scope. The Explanations relating to the Charter confirm this. Indeed, they indicate that many of the Charter solidarity clauses are based on or otherwise relate to a Treaty provision. This is the case with the workers' right to information and consultation (Article 27),[57] the right to fair and just working conditions (Article 31, paragraph 1),[58] the entitlement to social security benefits (Article 34, paragraph 1).[59] the right to social and housing assistance (Article 34, paragraph 3),[60] the right to health care (Article 35),[61] access to services of general economic

---

[54] Pursuant to Articles 6(1) TEU and 52(7) of the Charter, they shall be given 'due regard' when interpreting the Charter.

[55] Namely, Article 20(2)(b) TFEU, Article 14(3) TEU and Article 1(3) of the Act concerning the election of the members of the European Parliament by direct universal suffrage: ECJ, judgment of 6 October 2015 in *Delvigne*, C-650/13, EU:C:2015:648, paragraphs 40–4.

[56] ECJ, judgment of 4 July 2013 in *Gardella*, C-233/12, EU:C:2013:449, paragraph 38.

[57] The Explanations clarify in this respect that 'there is a considerable Union acquis in this field: Articles 154 and 155 TFEU'.

[58] According to the Explanations, the expression 'working conditions' is to be understood in the sense of Article 156 TFEU.

[59] According to the Explanations, this entitlement is based on Articles 153 and 156 TFEU.

[60] According to the Explanations, the Union must respect this right 'in the context of policies based on Article 153 TFEU'.

[61] According to the Explanations, this provision is based on Article 168 TFEU. Its second sentence 'takes over Article 168(1)'.

interest (Article 36),[62] environmental protection (Article 37),[63] and consumer protection (Article 38).[64]

The Explanations further indicate that some of the Charter social rights are also based on EU *legislation*. While the wording of Article 52(2) of the Charter refers only to the 'Treaties', the Explanations of Article 52(2) indicate that the Charter rights remain subject to the conditions and limits applicable to 'the *Union law* on which they are based'. The Explanations therefore imply that Article 52(2) also extends to EU *secondary* law. Moreover, the very wording of at least half of the Charter solidarity clauses stipulate explicitly that their exercise is subject to the conditions laid down in '*Union law* and national law and practices' or 'in accordance with Union law'.[65] The broad term 'Union law' here obviously refers to both EU primary and secondary law. As Peers and Prechal point out, EU legislation is clearly relevant for the purposes of interpreting and applying Article 52(2) of the Charter.[66] After all, the 'conditions' and 'limits' for the exercise of a 'Treaty' right are often laid down in EU secondary law.

The Explanations classify the following social rights as based on EU legislation: the workers' right to information and consultation (Article 27),[67] the right to protection in the event of unjustified dismissal (Article 30),[68] the right

---

[62] According to the Explanations, this article is 'fully in line' with Article 14 TFEU and 'does not create any new right'.

[63] According to the Explanations, this provision is based on Articles 3(3) TEU and 11 and 191 TFEU.

[64] According to the Explanations, this provision is based on Article 169 TFEU.

[65] Articles 27 (workers' right to information and consultation within the undertaking), 28 (right of collective bargaining and action), 30 (protection in the event of unjustified dismissal), 34 (social security and social assistance), 35 (health care) and 36 (access to services of general economic interest) (emphasis added).

[66] S. Peers and S. Prechal, 'Article 52', in S. Peers, T. Hervey, J. Kenner, and A. Ward (eds), *The EU Charter of Fundamental Rights* (Hart Publishing, Oxford, 2014), paragraph 52.97.

[67] Amongst the 'considerable Union acquis in this field', the Explanations mention Directives 2002/14/EC of the European Parliament and of the Council of 11 March 2002 establishing a general framework for informing and consulting employees in the European Community, [2002] OJ L 080/29; 98/59/EC of 20 July 1998 on the approximation of the laws of the Member States relating to collective redundancies, [1998] OJ L 225/16; 2001/23/EC of 12 March 2001 on the approximation of the laws of the Member States relating to the safeguarding of employees' rights in the event of transfers of undertakings, businesses or parts of undertakings or businesses, [2001] OJ L 82/16; and 94/45/EC of 22 September 1994 on the establishment of a European Works Council or a procedure in Community-scale undertakings and Community-scale groups of undertakings for the purposes of informing and consulting employees, [1994] OJ L 254/64.

[68] In respect of which the Explanations mention Directive 2001/23/EC, n. 67 in this chapter, and Directive 80/987/EEC of 20 October 1980 on the approximation of the laws of the Member States relating to the protection of employees in the event of the insolvency of their employer, [1980] OJ L 283/23, as amended by Directive 2002/74/EC, [2002] OJ L 270/10.

to fair and just conditions (Article 31),[69] the protection of young people at work (Article 32),[70] the right to protection from dismissal for a reason connected with maternity and the right to paid maternity leave and to parental leave (Article 33, paragraph 2),[71] and the entitlement to social security benefits and social advantages in the context of free movement (Article 34, paragraph 2).[72]

All of the above clearly shows that Article 52(2) of the Charter could have far-reaching consequences for most of the Charter social rights. These consequences can be summarised as follows. First, their incorporation into the Charter seems to have added no particular normative content to them. Indeed, Article 52(2) of the Charter claws them back to the applicable Treaty provision and/or secondary law.

The following example illustrates this. Article 31 of the Charter suggests a very broad material and personal scope of the right to fair and just working conditions: it applies to 'every worker' and covers working conditions 'which respect his or her health, safety and dignity' (paragraph 1), as well as the 'right to limitation of maximum working hours, to daily and weekly rest periods and to an annual period of paid leave' (paragraph 2). In comparison, the corresponding EU legislation upon which, according to the Explanations, Article 31 is based, provide for various limitations and derogations that circumscribe both the material and personal scope of that right.[73] The Court's case law clearly points to a certain parallelism between the content of the Charter social right and that of the corresponding directive. In *KHS* the Grand chamber held that the implementation by the competent national authorities of the entitlement of every worker to paid annual leave 'must be confined within the limits expressly laid down by Council Directive 93/104/EC, now codified

---

[69] According to the Explanations, Article 31(1) is 'based on Directive 89/391/EEC on the introduction of measures to encourage improvements in the safety and health of workers at work' ([1989] OJ L 183/1), while paragraph 2 is based on Directive 93/104/EC of 23 November 1993 concerning certain aspects of the organization of working time, [1993] OJ L 307/18.

[70] According to the Explanations, this Article is based on Directive 94/33/EC of 22 June 1994 on the protection of young people at work, [1994] OJ L 216/12.

[71] According to the Explanations, this right 'draws on' Council Directive 92/85/EEC of 19 October 1992 on the introduction of measures to encourage improvements in the safety and health at work of pregnant workers and workers who have recently given birth or are breastfeeding, [1992] OJ L 348/1; and Directive 96/34/EC of 3 June 1996 on the framework agreement on parental leave concluded by UNICE, CEEP and the ETUC, [1996] OJ L 145/4.

[72] According to the Explanations, this entitlement 'reflects' the rules arising from Regulation 1408/71 of 14 June 1971 on the application of social security schemes to employed persons and their families moving within the Community, [1971] OJ L 149/2; and Regulation 1612/68 of 15 October 1968 on freedom of movement for workers within the Community, [1968] OJ L 257/2.

[73] See for example, Articles 1(3), 17, 17a and 17b of Directive 93/104/EC, n. 69 in this chapter, concerning certain aspects of the organisation of working time.

by Directive 2003/88'.[74] Thus, a worker might not be able to claim a right to a working condition on the basis of Article 31 of the Charter, if that condition were subject to a derogation laid down in EU secondary law, unless he can show that that derogation is invalid.

Secondly, it might be particularly hard to argue that EU social legislation is invalid on the ground that it is contrary to one of the Charter's social rights. Indeed, as mentioned above, many of them are very broadly phrased and, in any event, subject to the conditions provided for by Union law. Article 52(2) of the Charter can further complicate such arguments. The case law suggests that it might be indeed very difficult to challenge an EU act for its alleged incompliance with a Charter social right, if the wording of the latter points back to the conditions laid down in Union law.[75] In any event, the judicial review in this context appears limited to manifest errors, given the legislator's large margin of appreciation in the area of social policy.[76]

All in all, while some uncertainties as to the precise reach of Article 52(2) of the Charter remain, it seems clear that this provision may play a central role in the interpretation and application of most of the Charter's social rights. This raises the question of whether their prominent place in the Charter is more of a symbolic gesture rather than a major normative improvement.

16.4 NO 'RIGHTS', JUST 'PRINCIPLES'?

The dichotomy between 'rights' and 'principles' is critical for the purpose of determining the effects of the Charter's substantive provisions. In essence, while a right can be relied upon to demand judicially enforceable positive action by the Union or by the Member States, a principle can give rise to no such action; it may be implemented on the Union or national level and becomes relevant for the courts only for the purpose of interpreting or reviewing these implementing acts.

This distinction is laid down in Article 52(5) of the Charter. It reflects the idea that while rights confer upon the individual subjective rights that are directly enforceable in a court, principles are mere programmatic guidelines

---

[74] ECJ, judgment of 22 November 2011 in *KHS*, C-214/10, EU:C:2011:761, paragraph 23.

[75] See for example, EGC, judgments of 4 December 2013 in *ETF v Schuerings*, T-107/11 P, EU:T:2013:624, paragraphs 100–1; of 4 December 2013 *ETF v Michel*, T-108/11 P, EU:T:2013:625, paragraphs 100–1; and CST, judgment of 30 June 2015 in *Petsch v Commission*, F-124/14, EU:F:2015:69, paragraphs 44–7.

[76] T. von Danwitz and K. Paraschas, 'A Fresh Start for the Charter: Fundamental Questions on the Application of the European Charter of Fundamental Rights', 35 *Fordham International Law Journal* 1396, p. 1414.

addressed to the legislator and/or the executive that can be used by the courts only as a benchmark to review their actions.

It is no secret that the Charter social rights are the primary target of this distinction. Lord Goldsmith, the UK representative at the Convention on the Charter, stated that the Charter social rights should be understood as principles.[77] The distinction served as a compromise that helped overcome fierce opposition on the part, in particular, of the UK to the incorporation of these rights in the Charter.[78] To avoid any doubt, Article 1(2) of Protocol no. 30 states that 'nothing in Title IV of the Charter creates justiciable rights applicable to Poland and the United Kingdom except in so far as Poland or the United Kingdom has provided for such rights in its national law'.[79]

The *rights* v *principles* dichotomy was thus clearly meant to limit the justiciability of the Charter social rights. This is explicitly confirmed by the Explanations relating to Article 52(5) of the Charter, which openly admit that this distinction is consistent 'with the approach of the Member States' constitutional systems to principles, *particularly in the field of social law*'.

Against this background, there is hardly any doubt that at least some of the Charter solidarity provisions are likely to fall into principles box within the meaning of Article 52(5) of the Charter. However, there is nothing to suggest that all of them should be considered as principles en bloc. Rather, each norm would have to be examined separately in the light of its wording, purpose, and nature.[80]

The Explanations provide a particularly helpful insight. Those relating to Article 52(5) indicate that Article 37 (environmental protection) contains a principle, while Articles 33 (family and professional life) and 34 (social security and social assistance) contain 'both elements of a right and a principle'. Furthermore, the Explanations relating to each of the Charter's solidarity provisions suggest that the following Articles contain principles: 35 (health care), 36 (access to services of general economic interest) and 38 (consumer protection). It thus seems that at least half of the twelve articles of the Charter's Title IV are to be considered as containing principles.

The doctrine has suggested further criteria for determining which provisions of the Charter contain rights and which contain principles. Such criteria include the degree of precision of the relevant norm (the more precise it is, the more likely it contains a right) or the reference to the conditions laid

[77] Lord Goldsmith Q.C., 'A Charter of Rights, Freedoms and Principles', 38 *Common Market Law Review* 1201, p. 1213.
[78] Peers and Prechal, n. 66 in this chapter, paragraph 52.159.
[79] See also ECJ, *N. S. and Others*, n. 52 in this chapter.
[80] Peers and Prechal, n. 66 in this chapter, paragraph 52.170.

down by Union and national law and practices (which would tend to indicate a principle).[81] Although not decisive per se, these criteria could indicate an even larger number of principles in Title IV. Indeed, on the one hand, most social rights are phrased in rather general terms. On the other hand, many of the Charter's solidarity provisions are explicitly made subject to the conditions provided for by Union law and national law and practices.[82]

This suggests that many of the solidarity provisions of the Charter are to be understood as principles within the meaning of Article 52(5) of the Charter. Consequently, their justiciability is limited. Most of them would therefore be unfit to support a direct claim for positive action by the Union or by the Member States. In addition, there is no obligation for the latter to act in order to implement them.[83] At best, the Charter solidarity clauses could be relied upon as an interpretative tool or, alternatively, to review the legality of Union or national action. While in theory this function could be rather effective, in practice it might be significantly curtailed on the basis of the caveat of Article 52(2) of the Charter, as discussed above.

16.5 NO HORIZONTALITY FOR SOCIAL RIGHTS

It is common knowledge that EU directives have no horizontal direct effect. This means that they cannot be relied upon in disputes between private parties. It is settled case law that 'a directive cannot of itself impose obligations on an individual and cannot therefore be relied on as such against an individual'.[84] Thus, even a clear, precise and unconditional provision of a directive seeking to confer rights or impose obligations on individuals cannot of itself apply in proceedings exclusively between private parties.[85] This case law is of particular importance for EU social law for at least two reasons. First, EU legislation in this domain consists almost exclusively of directives. Second, parts of social law, such as for example employment law, are mostly horizontal by nature. Hence, the lack of horizontal direct effect of EU directives has a particularly palpable impact on EU social law.

The Court has sought ways to attenuate the problem by creating alternative legal mechanisms. For instance, the Court has pioneered a particularly

[81] Peers and Prechal, n. 66 in this chapter, paragraphs 52.171 and 52.172.

[82] See n. 65 in this chapter.

[83] Pursuant to Article 52(5), the provisions of the Charter which contain principles *may* be implemented by legislative and executive acts.

[84] For example, ECJ, judgments of 26 February 1986 in *Marshall*, 152/84, EU:C:1986:84, paragraph 48; and of 14 July 1994 in *Faccini Dori*, C-91/92, EU:C:1994:292, paragraph 20.

[85] For example, ECJ, judgment of 19 January 2010 in *Kücükdeveci*, C-555/07, EU:C:2010:21, paragraph 46.

broad concept of the state (one that covers inter alia public sector employers and publicly owned undertakings),[86] in order to present many disputes as 'vertical'. The Court has also imposed on national courts the obligation to interpret national law, as far as possible, in the light of the wording and the purpose of the directive in question, in order to achieve the result prescribed thereby.[87] Nevertheless, these alternative mechanisms have their limits. For instance, the broad notion of the 'state' cannot compensate for the lack of direct horizontal effect of directives in a purely private dispute. The obligation of consistent interpretation is itself limited by general principles of law and cannot serve as the basis for an interpretation of national law *contra legem*.[88] In many cases therefore, none of these alternative mechanisms might be of use to individuals.

The Court has recently introduced a third mechanism, which, in substance, allows individuals to enforce the rights they enjoy by virtue of a directive (if, of course, sufficiently clear, precise and unconditional) against a private party. This new mechanism was inaugurated in *Mangold* and *Kücükdeveci*. In *Mangold* the Court held that, in a perfectly horizontal relationship, an individual can rely against another private party upon a general principle of EU law, which was given concrete expression in an EU directive. Concretely, the Court emphasised that the principle of non-discrimination on grounds of age must be regarded as a general principle of EU law, the observance of which cannot be conditional upon the expiry of the period prescribed for the transposition of the directive.[89]

This new mechanism was further clarified in *Kücükdeveci*.[90] The Court confirmed that the principle of non-discrimination on grounds of age is a general principle of EU law, now enshrined in Article 21(1) of the Charter, and that Directive 2000/78 'merely gives expression' to that principle.[91] Consequently, an individual can rely on a 'general principle of EU law, as given expression in a directive', in a dispute against another private party in order to set aside national legislation contrary to that principle. The Court has applied this formula in a number of cases since then.[92]

---

[86] For example, ECJ, judgment of 12 July 1990 in *Foster and Others*, C-188/89, EU:C:1990:313, paragraph 20.

[87] For example, ECJ, *Faccini Dori*, n. 84 in this chapter; and ECJ, judgment of 5 October 2004 in *Pfeiffer and Others*, C-397/01 to C-403/01, EU:C:2004:584, paragraphs 110–19.

[88] ECJ, judgment of 24 January 2012 in *Dominguez*, C-282/10, EU:C:2012:33.

[89] ECJ, judgment of 22 November 2005 in *Mangold*, C-144/04, EU:C:2005:709, paragraphs 74–6.

[90] ECJ, *Kücükdeveci*, n. 85 in this chapter.

[91] Ibid., paragraph 50.

[92] See for example, ECJ, judgments of 8 September 2011 in *Hennigs*, C-297/10 and C-298/10, EU:C:2011:560; and of 26 September 2013 in *HK Danmark*, C-476/11, EU:C:2013:590.

At first sight, the *Kücükdeveci* formula held great promise for strengthening the justiciability of EU social rights. Indeed, both *Mangold* and *Kücükdeveci* were delivered in the context of employment litigation. It thus seemed possible for individuals to rely, in a horizontal dispute, on the Charter's social rights, as given expression by the relevant EU directive. Critically, however, in both cases the Court reasoned on the basis of the prohibition of discrimination as a *general* principle of EU law and *not* on EU social rights as such.

This difference turned out to be crucial. A first warning came in *KHS*. The case concerned the right to paid annual leave in a dispute between private parties. The Court emphasised that that right was a 'particularly important principle of European Union social law', expressly laid down in Article 31(2) of the Charter and further specified in Directive 2003/88.[93] But it did not apply the *Kücükdeveci* formula, nor did it refer to it.

A second warning was delivered in *Dominguez*.[94] The case arose from a dispute between a worker and her employer about the former's right to paid annual leave. While the Court reaffirmed that that right was a particularly important principle of EU social law, it concluded that Directive 2003/88 cannot 'of itself' apply in proceedings exclusively between private parties. It made no mention of the *Kücükdeveci* formula. Instead, it directed the national court towards the two other alternative mechanisms mentioned above, namely the principle of consistent interpretation and the broad notion of the state, failing which the applicant could seek compensation for her loss on the basis of the *Francovich* case law.

In *Fenoll*, another case concerning the right to paid annual leave in a horizontal situation, the Court did not apply the *Kücükdeveci* formula either, mentioning only that Article 31(2) of the Charter was not applicable *ratione temporis* to the facts of the case.[95]

A closer look into the cases of *KHS*, *Dominguez* and *Fenoll* shows that the Court's refusal to apply the *Kücükdeveci* formula cannot be explained solely by the fact that the Charter was not applicable *ratione temporis*. Indeed, the Charter had not come into force in *Mangold* and *Kücükdeveci* either. This did not prevent the Court from referring to it and, more importantly, from introducing the formula in question. A more credible explanation should be sought in the carefully crafted wording of the Court's reasoning. In *Mangold* and *Kücükdeveci* the Court qualified the prohibition of discrimination on the ground of age as a *general* principle of EU law. By contrast, the right to paid

---

93 ECJ, *KHS*, n. 74 in this chapter, paragraphs 23, 31 and 37.
94 ECJ, *Dominguez*, n. 88 in this chapter.
95 ECJ, judgment of 26 March 2015 in *Fenoll*, C-316/13, EU:C:2015:200.

annual leave was described in *KHS* and *Dominguez* as a 'particularly important principle of EU social law'. The difference in terminology proved crucial.

All doubts were dissipated two years later in *AMS*. The case concerned a horizontal dispute seeking to enforce the workers' right to information and consultation within the undertaking, laid down in Article 27 of the Charter and Directive 2002/14. This time the Court expressly refused to apply the *Kücükdeveci* formula. It gave, in essence, two reasons for that. First, Article 27 of the Charter – unlike Article 21(1) which was applicable in *Kücükdeveci* – is not as such 'fully effective' since it must be given more specific expression in Union or national law, as its wording shows.[96] Therefore, Article 27 is not 'sufficient in itself to confer on individuals an individual right which they may invoke as such'. Hence, Article 27 cannot be invoked as such in a horizontal dispute.[97] Second, a replay of the *Kücükdeveci* formula – this time through the combination of Article 27 and Directive 2002/14 – is not possible either since none of them is capable of conferring rights on individuals which they may invoke as such.[98]

The judgment in *AMS* thus drew a crucial distinction between rights guaranteed by the Charter which are 'self-sufficient' and those which are not. The first category includes the so-called 'fully effective' rights, meaning rights which are sufficient in themselves to confer on individuals a subjective right which they may invoke as such. The *Kücükdeveci* formula would apply only to such rights.

By contrast, it would not apply to rights that are 'not self-sufficient'. In *AMS*, the Court implicitly suggested the following criterion for determining whether a given right falls within that category: if the wording of the relevant provision of the Charter makes the exercise of that right subject to the conditions provided for by Union and national law and practices, this would likely indicate that the right is not self-sufficient.[99] Given that at least half of the Charter solidarity clauses are, one way or another, subject to the conditions and limits laid down in Union law and national law and practices,[100] they are likely to fall within that category.

The conclusion thus seems quite clear: in most cases, the *Kücükdeveci* formula would not apply in the area of EU social law.[101] Consequently, most

---

[96] ECJ, judgment of 15 January 2014 in *AMS*, C-176/12, EU:C:2014:2, paragraphs 44–5.
[97] Ibid., paragraphs 47 and 48.
[98] Ibid., paragraph 49.
[99] Ibid., paragraphs 44–5.
[100] See n. 65 in this chapter.
[101] This was confirmed in the recent ECJ *AKT* judgment (of 17 March 2015, C-533/13, EU:C:2015:173), where the Court held that national courts were under no obligation to apply Directive 2008/104/EC (on temporary agency work, [2008] OJ L 327/9) in a horizontal dispute.

of the Charter social rights, even when considered in conjunction with the relevant EU directive, could not be relied upon in a horizontal relationship.

Finally, it would be wrong to view the Court's case law commented on above through the lens of the rights vs principles dichotomy. Indeed, there is no reference in the case law to Article 52(5) of the Charter. The fact that the case law historically refers to general principles of EU law or simply principles does not mean that the norm at issue should be regarded as a principle within the meaning of Article 52(5) of the Charter. Moreover, Article 27 of the Charter – at issue in *AMS* – uses the term right, while the Explanations relating to this article do not classify it as a principle. Therefore, the lack of horizontality of (most) of the Charter social rights is a separate caveat limiting their justiciability.

16.6 THE ELUSIVE PALLIATIVE OF THE ECHR

The ECHR offers only limited redress for the purpose of enforcing social rights in general and the EU solidarity provisions, in particular. There are several reasons for this. First, the ECHR's judge-made catalogue of social rights is narrower than the Charter's. Second, the scope of the ECtHR's judicial review is rather limited in the area of socioeconomic measures. Third, the ECtHR's response to Europe's austerity measures has been muted at best. Lastly, following Opinion 2/13, Union action cannot, in principle, be checked for compliance with the ECHR.

It is fairly obvious that the rights guaranteed by the Convention and the protocols to it are essentially civil and political. Indeed, the Convention does not guarantee socioeconomic rights as such.[102] Nonetheless, some of the civil and political rights that it proclaims have been interpreted as having 'implications of a social and economic nature'.[103] On this basis the ECtHR has been able to offer some degree of indirect protection for social rights through an extensive interpretation of the appropriate civil or political right enshrined in the Convention.[104]

For instance, Articles 2 (the right to life) and 3 (prohibition of torture and inhuman or degrading treatment) of the Convention can be relied upon in a small number of fairly striking circumstances, where the disregard of the absolute minimum of social standards could amount to a threat to an individual's

The Court made no mention of the *Küçükdeveci* formula, nor of Article 28 of the Charter. Compare with the opinion of Advocate General Szpunar (EU:C:2014:2392) in the same case.
[102] ECtHR, decision of 28 October 1999 in *Pancenko v Latvia*, 40772/98.
[103] ECtHR, judgment of 9 October 1979 in *Airey v Ireland*, 6289/73, paragraph 26.
[104] The following overview is only indicative.

life, to torture or to inhuman or degrading treatment. Examples from the case law include denial of health care, otherwise available to the population generally, putting at risk an individual's life,[105] failure to provide adequate care in a state-run care home resulting in death or long-term neglect and abuse,[106] or the 'wholly insufficient' amount of social benefits.[107] The right to respect for private and family life under Article 8 ECHR can also be invoked in some cases,[108] where a link can be established between a social measure and a person's private or family life (for example, dismissal for adultery[109]) or if such a measure affects the person's physical and psychological integrity, development and autonomy.[110] Article 11 ECHR (freedom of assembly and association) has been successfully used to challenge national measures interfering with trade union rights (for example, prescribing obligatory membership of a trade union,[111] prohibiting[112] or obstructing[113] such membership or general bans on strikes[114]).

The recourse to Article 1 of Protocol no. 1 of the ECHR (the right to property) in the field of social security and social assistance has been more controversial. This provision has been held to apply both to contributory[115] and

[105] ECtHR, decision of 21 March 2002 in *Nitecki v Poland*, 65653/01. The complaint was nonetheless inadmissible.

[106] ECtHR, judgments of 10 May 2001 in *Z. and Others v the United Kingdom*, 29392/95; and of 18 June 2013 in *Nencheva v Bulgaria*, 48609/06.

[107] ECtHR, decisions of 23 April 2002 in *Larioshina v Russia*, 56869/00; and of 28 October 1999 in *Pancenko v Latvia*, 40772/98. In both cases, the ECtHR found that there was no breach of Article 3.

[108] Article 8 can also be applied in conjunction with Article 14 ECHR in discrimination cases concerning, for example, child benefits (ECtHR, judgment of 25 October 2005 in *Niedzwiecki v Germany*, 58453/00) or parental leave allowances (ECtHR, judgment of 27 March 1998 in *Petrovic v Austria*, 20458/92). These cases are of less relevance for the present chapter since they relate more directly to the prohibition of discrimination rather than to social law matters as such. It must also be noted, for the sake of completeness, that since the entry into force of Protocol 12 of the ECHR, the principle of non-discrimination can be applied alone. In other words, with regard to the EU Member States which have ratified and signed the Protocol (only 8 so far), such cases would normally be solved without recourse to another 'vehicle' provision of the Convention.

[109] ECtHR, judgment of 23 September 2010 in *Schüth v Germany*, 1620/03.

[110] ECtHR judgment of 20 May 2014 in *McDonald v the United Kingdom*, 4241/12. Here the complaint was partially dismissed since the State had not exceeded its margin of appreciation. See also ECtHR, decision of 4 May 1999 in *Marzari v Italy*, 36448/97.

[111] ECtHR, judgment of 13 August 1981 in *Young, James and Webster v the United Kingdom*, 7601/76 and 7806/77. ECtHR, judgment of 11 January 2006 in *Sorensen and Rasmussen v Denmark*, 52562/99 and 52620/99.

[112] ECtHR, judgment of 12 November 2008 in *Demir and Baykara v Turkey*, 34503.

[113] ECtHR, judgment of 2 July 2002 in *Wilson, National Union of journalists and Others v the United Kingdom*, 30668/96, 30671/96 and 30678/96.

[114] ECtHR, judgment of 21 April 2009 in *Enerji Yapi-Yol Sen v Turkey*, 68959/01.

[115] ECtHR, judgment of 16 September 1996 in *Gaygusuz v Austria*, 17371/90.

non-contributory[116] social benefits. The ECtHR has however emphasised that Article 1 of Protocol No. 1 does not impose an obligation on the State to provide for social security benefits that do not exist within their legal system,[117] nor does it bestow a right to an income of a particular level.[118] It therefore poses 'no restriction on the Contracting State's freedom to decide whether or not to have in place any form of social security scheme, or to choose the type or amount of benefits to provide under any such scheme'.[119] If however national law provides for a certain social benefit, the latter must be administered in a non-discriminatory way. The case law thus seems to suggest that a claim to a social benefit based on Article 1 of Protocol 1 of the ECHR might succeed mostly in discrimination cases, where the Protocol is in fact used as a vehicle for bringing the matter within the ambit of the non-discrimination clause of Article 14 ECHR.[120] In a small number of cases, Article 1 of Protocol no. 1 could be relied upon alone: examples include a case concerning the total loss of a contributory benefit[121] or significant delays in the payment of old-age pensions.[122]

Compared to the wide range of the Charter's social rights, which include inter alia some core labour rights, the material scope of the ECHR's judge-made social rights protection is obviously narrower. It is telling that the Explanations do not list any of the Charter solidarity clauses as having the same meaning and scope as a corresponding Convention right.[123] As one author put it, the Convention received a '*sérieux coup de vieux*' from the Charter as far as social rights are concerned.[124] It therefore seems clear that, because of its narrower material scope, the Convention cannot be used as a safety net in many

---

[116] ECtHR, judgment of 6 June 2005 in *Stec and Others* v *the United Kingdom*, 65731/01 and 65900/01, where a violation of Article 1 of Protocol 1, in conjunction with Article 14 was claimed.

[117] ECtHR judgment, *Stec and Others*, n. 116 in this chapter, paragraphs 61 et seq.

[118] For example, ECtHR decision of 6 September 1995 in *Federspev* v *Italy*, 22867/93.

[119] ECtHR, judgment *Stec and Others*, n. 116 in this chapter.

[120] See for example, ECtHR judgments, *Gaygusuz* v *Austria*, n. 115 in this chapter; of 4 June 2002 in *Wessels-Bergervoet* v *the Netherlands*, 34462/97; of 11 June 2002 in *Willis* v *the United Kingdom*, 36042/97; of 30 September 2003 in *Koua Poirrez* v *France*, 40892/98; *Stec and Others*, n. 116 in this chapter.

[121] ECtHR, judgment of 12 October 2004 in *Kjartan Ásmundsson* v *Iceland*, 60669/00.

[122] ECtHR, judgment of 3 June 2004 in *Solodyuk* v *Russia*, 67099/01.

[123] Explanations relating to Article 52(3).

[124] F. Sudre, 'La protection des droits sociaux par la Cour européenne des droits de l'homme: un exerce de "jurisprudence fiction"?', in C. Grewe and F. Benoît-Rohmer (eds), *Colloque Les droits sociaux ou la démolition de quelques poncifs*, 15 et 16 juin 2001 (Presses universitaires de Strasbourg, 2001), p. 756.

cases where the Charter has failed to ensure protection of a social right for one of the reasons discussed above.[125]

Secondly, the Contracting States' margin of discretion is particularly fluid when socioeconomic policies are at issue.[126] The ECtHR's scope of judicial review thus seems limited with regard to upholding core social rights.

Thirdly, the ECtHR seems to have adopted a hands-off approach to Europe's austerity measures, sanctioning only the most extreme of cases. While admitting that Article 1 of Protocol 1 of the ECHR might apply to such measures, it has so far rejected most claims as manifestly ill-founded.[127] In doing so, it put great emphasis, on the one hand, on the Contracting States' very broad margin of appreciation in economic and social matters and on the exceptional character of the sovereign debt crisis. On the other hand, it held that a 'reasonable and commensurate reduction' of an entitlement, such as a salary or a pension, does not constitute a violation of the right to property. It was therefore manifest that the salary and/or pension cuts at issue, although significant, did not impose an excessive burden on the applicants. The only successful claim so far concerned a Hungarian tax on severance payments, which amounted to 98 per cent, if certain thresholds were exceeded. The decisive factor here, as it seems, was not so much the amount of the tax as such but its retroactive nature.[128] All in all, the protection provided by the ECHR in the context of national austerity measures seems very limited.

It follows from all of this that the ECHR's scope of intervention in the field of social law is relatively narrow. Consequently, it could hardly be regarded as a general and satisfactory palliative capable of bridging the Union's many gaps in the protection of social rights.

16.7 CONCLUSION

The much trumpeted incorporation of social rights in the Charter has been accompanied by a series of significant caveats – some visible, others disguised.

---

[125] For example, Article 27 of the Charter has no equivalent in the ECHR system. Thus, in a case like *AMS*, n. 96 in this chapter, the ECHR would be of little help. The same seems to hold true with regard to the right to paid annual leave, making it difficult for cases like *KHS*, n. 74 in this chapter, or *Dominguez*, n. 88 in this chapter, to succeed in the Strasbourg system.

[126] For example, ECtHR, decisions of 7 May 2013 in *Koufaki and Adedy* v *Greece*, 57665/12 and 57657/12, paragraph 31; and of 8 October 2013 in *Da Conceição Mateus and Santos Januário* v *Portugal*, 62235/12 and 57725/12, paragraph 22.

[127] ECtHR decisions, *Koufaki and Adedy*, n. 126 in this chapter; and *Da Conceição Mateus*, n. 126 in this chapter; and decision of 15 October 2013 in *Savickas* v *Lithuania*, 66365/09.

[128] ECtHR, judgments of 14 May 2013 in *NKM* v *Hungary*, 66529/11; of 2 July 2013 in *RSz* v *Hungary*, 41838/11.

On the one hand, many of these rights are actually not rights but principles within the meaning of Article 52(5) of the Charter. Hence, they are not fully justiciable. On the other hand, those, which might qualify as rights, have been divided into two further subcategories: self-sufficient and non-self-sufficient rights. It is doubtful whether any of the Charter social rights might actually be regarded as self-sufficient. Indeed, most of them are rather likely to fall into the category of non-self-sufficient rights. Consequently, they cannot be relied upon in a horizontal relationship. In any event, Article 52(2) of the Charter adds a further caveat capable of restricting the normative value of most of the Charter social clauses, be they principles or rights. Finally, the current legal structure of EU's bailout mechanisms has resulted in placing most socially sensitive measures outside of the scope of EU law altogether.

The ideal of a more social Europe, which underpinned the incorporation of social rights in the Charter, has thus been put into a straitjacket: it is there but it can hardly move.

17

The European Court of Justice as the Guardian of the Rule of EU Social Law

Koen Lenaerts and José A. Gutiérrez-Fons

17.1 INTRODUCTION

Originally, the Treaties provided virtually no legal basis for the adoption of EU measures in the field of social law. With the exceptions of the principle of non-discrimination on grounds of nationality, the principle of equal pay for men and women and the principle of equivalence between paid holiday schemes, policy choices relating to social justice were to remain in the hands of the national legislator.[1] This was because the authors of the Treaties used to believe that market liberalisation would by itself bring about social progress. Since workers would move from Member States where labour was cheap and plentiful to Member States in need of labour, workers who exercised their right of free movement would benefit from a rise in their wages and, thus, in their standards of living.[2]

However, it soon became clear that market forces alone could not bring about social progress. Since the 1970s, Treaty reforms, EU legislative action and the case law of the European Court of Justice (ECJ) have progressively built up a considerable body of rules that have not only corrected market forces in the name of social justice but have also contributed to promoting social rights both in a national and a transnational context. Most importantly, the evolution of 'EU social law' has given concrete expression to certain social values that are common to the Member States. Values such as equal

---

The views and opinions expressed in this chapter are personal. The usual disclaimers apply.

[1] See M. Weiss, 'Introduction to European Labour Law', in M. Schlachter (eds), *EU Labour Law: A Commentary* (Kluwer Law International, 2015), p. 3.

[2] See C. Barnard, 'EU "Social" Policy: From Employment Law to Labour Market Reform', in P. Craig and G. De Búrca (eds), *The Evolution of EU Law* (Oxford University Press, 2nd edn, 2011), p. 641. See also F. Vandenbroucke and B. Vanhercke, *A European Social Union: 10 Tough Nuts to Crack* (Friends of Europe, 2014), available at:www.friendsofeurope.org/media/uploads/2014/10/03-03-14-Report-SocialUnion-FINAL-V-2.pdf (accessed 10 October 2016).

opportunities for all, social dialogue, welfare, and solidarity provide the foundations of EU social law and define the 'European Social Model'.[3] Notably, secondary EU legislation based on Article 19 TFEU and Title IV of the Charter of Fundamental Rights of the European Union (the 'Charter') shows that EU social law has outgrown its internal market origins, to the point where it now contributes to defining the very nature of EU law itself. EU law is not only economic law, but also social law.[4]

Nonetheless, EU social law is not as all-encompassing as national social law. This is because the Member States have not transferred social policy as a whole to the EU, but only certain aspects of that policy.[5] Accordingly, important areas of social policy – such as social insurance, public assistance, health and welfare services, as well as housing – remain within the competences of the Member States.[6] What is more, even in relation to the aspects of social policy that fall within the scope of EU law, the EU legislator is not entitled to intervene in matters of pay, the right of association, the right to strike or the right to impose lock-outs.[7] In the same way, EU-level harmonisation is excluded in the field of employment.[8]

Accordingly, when called upon to uphold the rule of EU social law, the ECJ is to protect the 'social acquis', whilst ensuring compliance with the vertical and horizontal allocation of powers sought by the authors of the Treaties.[9]

---

[3] See F. Vandenbroucke, 'The Idea of a European Social Union: A Normative Introduction', Chapter 1 in this volume.

[4] See opinion of Advocate General Cruz Villalón of 7 October 2010 in *Dos Santos Palhota and Others*, C-515/08, EU:C:2010:245, point 51. ('Article 9 TFEU lays down a 'cross-cutting' social protection clause obliging the institutions 'to take into account requirements linked to the promotion of a high level of employment, the guarantee of adequate social protection, the fight against social exclusion, and a high level of education, training and protection of human health'. That requirement is laid down following the declaration in Article 3(3) TEU that the construction of the internal market is to be realised by means of policies based on 'a highly competitive social market economy, aiming at full employment and social progress'.)

[5] See G. De Baere and K. Gutman, 'The Basis in EU Constitutional Law for Further Social Integration', Chapter 14 in this volume.

[6] Barnard, n. 2 in this chapter, at p. 660.

[7] See Article 153 TFEU. Regarding matters of pay, see ECJ, judgments of 13 September 2007 in *Del Cerro Alonso*, C-307/05, EU:C:2007:509, paragraphs 40 and 46; of 15 April 2008 in *Impact*, C-268/06, EU:C:2008:223, paragraph 123; and of 10 June 2010 in *Bruno and Pettini*, C-395/08 and C-396/08, EU:C:2010:329, paragraph 36. Regarding the right to strike or the right to impose lock-outs, see ECJ, judgment of 11 December 2007 in *International Transport Workers' Federation and Finnish Seamen's Union* ('*Viking*'), C-438/05, EU:C:2007:772, paragraph 40.

[8] See Article 149 TFEU.

[9] See K. Lenaerts and J.A. Gutiérrez-Fons, 'The Constitutional Allocation of Powers and General Principles of EU law' (2010) 47 *Common Market Law Review* 1629. The term 'vertical and horizontal allocation of powers' refers to the balance of powers between the EU and its Member States and to that between the EU institutions, respectively.

In the aftermath of the financial crisis, this begs two different, albeit closely related, questions that this Chapter seeks to address. First, the scope of application of EU social law – and in particular, that of the Charter – is examined in situations where a Member State is the recipient of financial assistance.[10] Second, once a national measure falls within the scope of EU law, the difficult question of the horizontal application and justiciability of primary EU social law is addressed.[11]

17.2 THE SCOPE OF APPLICATION OF EU SOCIAL LAW IN THE CONTEXT OF THE FINANCIAL CRISIS

17.2.1 *The Constitutional Divide: EU Budgetary and Discipline Rules versus National Rules on the Redistribution of Wealth*

At the outset, a distinction should be drawn between two types of measures that a Member State may adopt with a view to finding its way out of financial turmoil.[12] On the one hand, a Member State in economic distress may pass legislation that sets limits to its annual deficit and public debt. Such a Member State may, for example, adopt measures that require Parliament to adopt a 'balanced budget' or to correct macroeconomic imbalances. In essence, those rules concern budgetary discipline and balance ('budgetary discipline and balance rules'[13]). On the other hand, in times of economic downturn, a Member State may be obliged to revisit the way in which public resources are allocated. In order to cut public spending, a Member State may decide to reform its pensions scheme and national health system, to reduce the wages of civil servants, and/or to increase taxes. Those policy decisions always involve hard choices that raise questions of redistributive justice, as they directly affect the well-being of citizens ('socioeconomic redistributive rules').[14]

From the perspective of the principle of conferral, that distinction is important given that, whilst the EU is empowered to lay down budgetary discipline

---

[10] See for example, C. Barnard, 'The Charter, the Court – and the Crisis' (2013) *University of Cambridge Faculty of Law Research Paper* no. 18/2013; C. Kilpatrick, 'Are the Bailouts Immune to EU Social Challenge Because They Are Not EU Law?' (2014) 10 *European Constitutional Law Review* 393; and A. Kornezov, 'Social Rights, the Charter and the ECHR – Caveats, Austerity and Other Disasters', Chapter 16 in this volume.

[11] Kornezov, n. 10 in this chapter.

[12] See, in this regard, A. Hinarejos, 'The Euro Area Crisis and Constitutional Limits to Fiscal Integration' (2012) 14 *Cambridge Yearbook of European Legal Studies* 243. See also A. Hinarejos, *The Euro Area Crisis in Constitutional Perspective* (Oxford University Press, 2015).

[13] Expression borrowed from Hinarejos, n. 12 in this chapter.

[14] Ibid.

and balance rules with which Member States must comply, it lacks the power to impose socioeconomic redistributive choices on them. It follows that the EU lacks the constitutional authority to adopt measures involving the redistribution of wealth. Indeed, socioeconomic redistributive rules touch upon aspects of social policy that remain within the competences of the Member States.

Although those two types of rules are different in nature, they are deeply intertwined: whilst EU budgetary discipline and balance rules lay down the fiscal objectives to be attained by the Member States, national socioeconomic redistributive rules constitute the means for implementing those objectives.[15]

This means that it is for the Member State concerned to adopt the 'specific policy actions' that are required. Thus, the role of the EU institutions is limited to determining whether the actions envisaged are sufficient to correct excessive macroeconomic imbalances. However, as some scholars have pointed out, conflicts with the principle of conferral may arise where, with a view to rendering EU oversight more effective, the EU institutions make recommendations that also 'require certain specific reforms to attain those objectives'.[16] In that case, those excessively detailed recommendations would involve socioeconomic redistributive choices and thus potentially encroach upon the competences of national parliaments.

It is thus for national parliaments to decide how to cut public spending and how to increase public revenue. The autonomous capacity to make those choices is, nonetheless, significantly reduced – if not forgone – when a Member State no longer has access to the financial markets. In that case, such a Member State is caught on the horns of a dilemma: either to seek financial assistance at international level (accepting the strings attached to such assistance) or to face the crippling economic and financial consequences arising from a sovereign debt default.

In the euro area, a Member State in financial difficulties may not ask the EU for financial assistance, as Article 125 TFEU expressly prevents the EU from bailing out such a Member State (the so called no-bailout clause). However, in the seminal *Pringle* case,[17] the ECJ held that Article 125 TFEU does not oppose the establishment of an international financial institution – such as the European Stability Mechanism (ESM) – that aims to safeguard the stability of the euro area as a whole, provided that the three following cumulative conditions are fulfilled: (1) the financial assistance provided by the

---

[15] See Hinarejos, n. 12 in this chapter.
[16] A. Hinarejos, 'Fiscal Federalism in the European Union: Evolution and Future Choices for EMU' (2013) 50 *Common Market Law Review* 1621.
[17] ECJ, judgment of 27 November 2012 in *Pringle*, C-370/12, EU:C:2012:756.

ESM must operate as an incentive encouraging that Member State to adopt a sound budgetary policy,[18] (2) the Member State concerned must remain liable to its creditor,[19] and (3) such assistance must be limited to cases where the stability of the euro area as a whole is put at risk.[20] Thus, compliance with the no-bailout clause requires the grant of ESM financial assistance to be subject to strict conditionality.

In that regard, the ESM Treaty provides that the ESM shall entrust 'the European Commission – in liaison with the ECB and, wherever possible, together with the International Monetary Fund (IMF) – with the task of negotiating, with the ESM Member concerned, a memorandum of understanding (MoU) detailing the conditionality attached to the financial assistance facility'.[21] It also states that 'the conditionality attached to the ESM loans shall be contained in a macroeconomic adjustment programme detailed in the MoU'.[22]

17.2.2 *The ESM Treaty: Beyond the EU Principle of Conferral but Consistent with EU Law*

The ESM Treaty gives expression to a new mode of operation that may be qualified as a 'semi-intergovernmental method'.[23] On the one hand, as the ESM sits outside the EU legal order, it is not bound by the principle of conferral under Article 5(2) TEU. This means, in essence, that the conditions attached to the granting of ESM financial assistance may provide for measures that fall outside the scope of EU law. Those conditions may involve not only the adoption of budgetary discipline and balance rules, but also the implementation of broad socioeconomic reforms for which the EU lacks competence. Those reforms may, for example, focus on the adoption of measures that aim to reform the labour market and to guarantee the sustainability of social welfare.[24] They may, for example, provide for a reduction in salary payments to civil servants and pensioners as well as an increase of the statutory

---

[18] Ibid., paragraphs 111, 121, 137, and 143.
[19] Ibid., paragraphs 137 to 141.
[20] Ibid., paragraph 142.
[21] See Article 13(3) of the ESM Treaty.
[22] See Article 16(2) of the ESM Treaty.
[23] J.-P. Keppenne, 'Institutional Report', in U. Neergaard, C. Jacqueson, and J. Hartig Danielsen (eds), *The Economic and Monetary Union: Constitutional and Institutional Aspects of the Economic Governance within the EU: The XXVI FIDE Congress in Copenhagen* (DJOF Publishing, 2014) p. 179, at p. 203. See also K. Lenaerts, 'EMU and the EU's Constitutional Framework' (2014) 39 *European Law Review* 753.
[24] See C. Barnard, 'The Financial Crisis and the Euro Plus Pact: A Labour Lawyer's Perspective' (2012) 41 *Industrial Law Journal* 98, and Z. Adams and S. Deakin, 'Structural Adjustment, Economic Governance and Social Policy in a Regional Context: the Case of the Eurozone

retirement age. They may also compel the Member State that has requested financial assistance to align severance payments under open-ended employment contracts with those applicable under fixed-term contracts and to make provision for the dismissal of a worker on grounds of his or her unsuitability. As to social welfare and healthcare, those reforms may, among other austerity measures, provide that public expenditure on social housing is to be reduced or that priority should be given to generic rather than branded drugs.

Furthermore, the ESM Treaty is to be distinguished from the 'Community method' in that it does not reproduce the EU decision-making process.[25] Neither does that Treaty offer the same level of judicial protection as that guaranteed by EU law. This is so because the jurisdiction of the ECJ is based on Article 273 TFEU. Consequently, the ECJ may only exercise its jurisdiction in disputes between Member States that relate to the subject matter of the ESM Treaty and that are submitted to it under that Treaty. Accordingly, it may only adjudicate on disputes between ESM Members (i.e. Member States whose currency is the euro), and on disputes between the latter and the ESM. Moreover, as the ECJ made clear in the *Pringle* judgment, the Charter does not apply to the ESM's activities, given that, when Member States participate in it, they are not implementing EU law.[26] In addition, despite the fact that the ESM Treaty allocates to the Commission the tasks of negotiating and signing the MoU on behalf of the ESM, those tasks do not entail any decision-making powers, as the activities pursued by the Commission within the ESM Treaty commit only the ESM.[27] This implies, as the ECJ held in the recent *Ledra* case,[28] that the MoU is not an EU measure.[29]

On the other hand, the ESM Treaty is linked to EU law, making its application and that of EU law on the European Monetary Union ('EMU') interdependent. This is because, although the ESM is not an EU institution, the

Crisis', in A. Blackett and A. Trebilcock (eds), *Handbook of Transnational Labour Law* (Edward Elgar, 2015), p. 111.

[25] 'As a general rule, EU decisions are taken by means of the 'Community' method involving the use of the ordinary legislative procedure, as defined in Article 294 TFEU. The Community Method is characterised by the sole right of the European Commission to initiate legislation; the co-decision power between the Council and the European Parliament, and the use of qualified majority voting in Council.' See Glossary of summaries, at eur-lex.europa.eu/summary/glossary/community_intergovernmental_methods.html (accessed 10 October 2016).

[26] ECJ, *Pringle*, n. 17 in this chapter, paragraph 180.

[27] Ibid., paragraph 161.

[28] ECJ, judgment of 20 September 2016 in *Ledra Advertising and Others v Commission and ECB*, C-8 to 10/15 P, EU:C:2016:701, paragraphs 54 and 55.

[29] See also M. Schwarz, 'A Memorandum of Misunderstanding – The Doomed Road of the European Stability Mechanism and a Possible Way Out: Enhanced Cooperation' (2014) 51 *Common Market Law Review* 389, at pp. 398–9.

ESM Treaty expressly provides that the conditions attached to the granting of financial assistance must comply with EU law. As the ECJ held in *Pringle*, '[u]nder Article 13(3) of the ESM Treaty, the MoU which is to be negotiated with the Member State requesting stability support must be fully consistent with [EU] law and, in particular, with the measures taken by the [EU] in the area of coordination of the economic policies of the Member States'. 'Accordingly', the ECJ wrote, 'the conditions to be attached to the granting of such support to a Member State are, at least in part, determined by European Union law'.[30] In the light of that provision of the ESM Treaty, consistency with EU law is not limited to the Treaty provisions and secondary EU legislation relating to EMU, but also to the entire body of EU law, meaning the substantive law of the EU, including EU social law.

It is true that at the start of the financial crisis there was no EU legislative framework that guaranteed full consistency between the EU multilateral surveillance framework established by the TFEU and the socioeconomic policy conditions attached to the grant of ESM financial assistance. However, that regulatory lacuna was filled with the adoption of Regulation 472/2013 (sometimes referred to as the 'Two-Pack') that lays down the rules for the approval of the macroeconomic adjustment programme contained in the MoU.[31] In particular, Article 7 of that Regulation provides that a Member State that requests financial assistance from the ESM is to prepare,[32] in agreement with the Commission, a draft macroeconomic adjustment programme. The Council, on a proposal from the Commission, is to approve such draft macroeconomic adjustment programme. In addition, Article 7 states that 'the draft macroeconomic adjustment programme shall fully observe Article 152 TFEU and Article 28 of the [Charter]'. Most importantly, '[t]he Commission shall ensure

---

[30] ECJ, *Pringle*, n. 17 in this chapter, paragraph 174.

[31] Regulation 472/2013 of the European Parliament and of the Council of 21 May 2013 on the strengthening of economic and budgetary surveillance of Member States in the euro area experiencing or threatened with serious difficulties with respect to their financial stability, [2013] OJ L 140/1. See, in this regard, Staff of the Directorate General for Economic and Financial Affairs, European Commission, 'The Two-Pack on Economic Governance: Establishing an EU Framework for Dealing with Threats to Financial Stability in Euro Area Member States' (2013) *European Economy Occasional Papers*, available at: ec.europa.eu/economy_finance/publications/occasional_paper/2013/pdf/ocp147_en.pdf (accessed 10 October 2016); and M. Ioannidis, 'EU Financial Assistance Conditionality after "Two Pack"' (2014) 74 *Zeitschrift für ausländisches öffentliches Recht und Völkerrecht* 62.

[32] Regulation 472/2013 also applies to Member States whose currency is the euro that request or receive financial assistance from one or several other Member States or third countries, the European Financial Stabilisation Mechanism, the European Financial Stability Facility, or another relevant international financial institution such as the IMF.

that the [MoU] is fully consistent with the macroeconomic adjustment pro-gramme approved by the Council'.

In our view, the adoption of Regulation 472/2013 is a positive development, as it guarantees, albeit indirectly, the consistency of the MoU with EU law, in general, and with the fundamental right of collective bargaining and action, in particular.[33] The ECJ may interpret both Regulation 472/2013 and the Council decision approving the draft macroeconomic adjustment programme, like any other EU measure. In the same way, since the Council decision approving the draft macroeconomic adjustment programme is an EU measure, it may be challenged (either directly before the EU Courts or indirectly before the national courts) on the ground that it is incompatible with the Charter.[34]

Moreover, one may ask whether private applicants might bring legal action against the Commission on the grounds that the latter signed an MoU that was, in their view, inconsistent with EU law. The European General Court (EGC), at first instance, and the ECJ, on appeal, were confronted with that very question in *Ledra Advertising* v *the Commission and ECB*, *Eleftheriou and Papachristofi* v *Commission and ECB*, and *Theophilou* v *Commission and ECB*.[35] Those cases involved depositors of two large Cypriot banks who suffered significant losses as a result of a resolution and restructuring plan adopted by Cyprus.[36] Whilst the plan was set out in a Cypriot decree that predated the MoU signed by the ESM and Cyprus, the MoU subsequently

---

[33] See Lenaerts, n. 23 in this chapter, at p. 754, and Kilpatrick, n. 10 in this chapter, at pp. 412–13. See also opinion of Advocate General Wathelet of 21 April 2016 in *Mallis and Others* v *Commission and ECB*, C-105/15 P to C-109/15 P, EU:C:2016:294, points 92 et seq.

[34] However, regarding natural and legal persons within the meaning of Article 263 TFEU, see Kilpatrick, n. 10 in this chapter, at pp. 415–16; Adams and Deakin, n. 24 in this chapter, at p. 115, and EGC, orders of 27 November 2012 in *ADEDY and Others* v *Council*, T-541/10, EU:T:2012:626; and *ADEDY and Others* v *Council*, T-215/11, EU:T:2012:627. In those cases, the EGC dismissed as inadmissible two actions for annulment brought by private applicants against three Council decisions that were adopted on the basis of Article 126(9) TFEU and Article 136 TFEU and addressed to Greece in the context of an excessive deficit procedure. The EGC found that those decisions were of no concern to the applicants, since they required national implementing measures which would specify their content and gave Greece a wide margin of discretion. Thus, in view of the EGC, it was not the Council decisions but the national measures implementing them that would directly affect the legal situation of the applicants. See also opinion of Advocate General Wathelet in *Mallis and Others*, n. 33 in this chapter, point 90.

[35] EGC, orders of 10 November 2014 in *Ledra Advertising* v *Commission and ECB*, T-289/13, EU:T:2014:981; *Eleftheriou and Papachristofi* v *Commission and ECB*, T-291/13, EU:T:2014:978; and *Theophilou* v *Commission and ECB*, T-293/13, EU:T:2014:979. ECJ, *Ledra Advertising*, n. 28 in this chapter.

[36] Those two banks were the Bank of Cyprus (BoC) and the Cyprus Popular Bank (Laïki). The plan stated that BoC was to take over the Cypriot assets of Laïki at fair value. It also provided for the conversion of 37,5 per cent of uninsured deposits in BoC into shares.

endorsed it. Applicants sought the annulment of the relevant paragraphs of the MoU and brought an action for damages against the EU. However, the action for annulment was dismissed as inadmissible by the EGC on the basis that the MoU was not a challengeable act under Article 263 TFEU.[37] In their action for damages, the applicants argued that the MoU gave rise to a violation of their right to property as enshrined in Article 17 of the Charter. In that regard, the EGC held that, since the adoption of the MoU did not originate with the Commission or the ECB, it lacked jurisdiction to examine the action for damages in so far as it was based on the illegality of certain paragraphs of the MoU.[38]

However, the ECJ took a different view. Whilst concurring with the EGC in that an MoU is not an EU act and as such, cannot be challenged under Article 263 TFEU,[39] the ECJ held that that finding does not rule out the possibility of bringing an action for damages based on the Commission's unlawful behaviour during the adoption of the MoU. This is because that EU institution must, in accordance with Article 17 TEU, always act in its capacity as 'guardian of the Treaties' even if its actions take place in the context of the ESM Treaty. This means, in essence, that the Commission must abstain from signing the MoU where doubts arise as to its consistency with EU law, and notably with the fundamental rights recognised in the Charter.[40] As a result, finding the appeals well-founded on this point, the ECJ quashed the orders of the EGC.

Next, the ECJ decided to give final judgment in the matter itself, as the state of the proceedings so permitted. It thus went on to examine whether the conditions governing the EU's non-contractual liability were met in the case at hand.[41] As to the first condition – the establishment of a sufficiently serious breach of a rule of law intended to confer rights on individuals –, the ECJ observed that Article 17 of the Charter which enshrines the right to property constituted such a rule of law. In so doing, the ECJ took the opportunity to draw an important distinction regarding the scope of the Charter *ratione personae*. Whilst the Charter is addressed to the Member States *only* when they

---

[37] EGC, *Ledra Advertising*, n. 35 in this chapter, paragraph 58; *Eleftheriou and Papachristofi*, n. 35 in this chapter, paragraph 58, and *Theophilou*, n. 35 in this chapter, paragraph 58.

[38] EGC, *Ledra Advertising*, n, 35 in this chapter, paragraph 47; *Eleftheriou and Papachristofi*, n. 35 in this chapter, paragraph 47, and *Theophilou*, n. 35 in this chapter, paragraph 47.

[39] ECJ, *Ledra Advertising*, n. 28 in this chapter, paragraphs 54 and 55.

[40] Ibid., paragraphs 59 and 67.

[41] Those conditions are: (1) the unlawfulness of the conduct alleged against the EU institution, (2) the fact of damage, and (3) the existence of a causal link between the conduct of the institution and the damage complained of. See for example, ECJ, judgment of 14 October 2014 in *Giordano v Commission*, C-611/12 P, EU:C:2014:2282, paragraph 35 and case law cited.

are implementing EU law, the same does not hold true for the EU institutions for which the Charter applies even if they act outside the EU legal framework. Accordingly, since the Member States are not implementing EU law when they participate in the ESM's activities, the Charter does not apply to them. Conversely, when adopting the MoU, the Commission must ensure that the MoU is fully consistent with the Charter.[42]

As to the question whether the Commission had contributed to a serious breach of the appellants' right to property when adopting the MoU, the ECJ replied in the negative. It found that the Commission had acted in compliance with Article 52(1) of the Charter, since the limitations on the exercise of the appellants' right to property corresponded to an objective of general interest[43] and did not constitute, in relation to the aim pursued, a disproportionate and intolerable interference, impairing the very substance of that right.[44] As a result, the ECJ dismissed the actions for damages brought by the depositors of the two Cypriot banks.

Three direct implications flow from the seminal judgment of the ECJ in *Ledra*. First, by holding that the Commission is always bound by EU law, that judgment strengthens the role of the Commission as 'guardian of the Treaties'. The Commission must thus honour that role even if it is called upon to act outside the scope of the EU Treaties. Second, as regards judicial remedies, the *Ledra* judgment is a positive development that complements the Two-Pack. Whilst Regulation 472/2013 provides for declaratory relief in so far as a Council decision approving the draft macroeconomic adjustment programme may be challenged under Article 263 TFEU, the Commission's failure to ensure that the MoU is fully consistent with EU law may give rise to pecuniary relief. For present purposes, where a provision of EU social law is a

---

[42] ECJ, *Ledra Advertising*, n. 28 in this chapter, paragraph 67.

[43] That objective was that of safeguarding the stability of the euro area banking system as a whole. Ibid., paragraphs 71 and 72. In that regard, the ECJ noted that 'financial services play a central role in the economy of the [EU]. Banks and credit institutions are an essential source of funding for businesses that are active in the various markets. In addition, the banks are often interconnected and a number of them operate internationally. That is why the failure of one or more banks is liable to spread rapidly to other banks, either in the Member State concerned or in other Member States. That is likely, in its turn, to produce negative spill-over effects in other sectors of the economy.' See also ECJ, judgment of 19 July 2016 in *Kotnik and Others*, C-526/14, EU:C:2016:570, paragraph 50.

[44] In that regard, the MoU stated that 37.5 per cent of uninsured deposits in BoC were to be converted into shares with full voting and dividend rights, that the remaining uninsured deposits of BoC were to be temporarily frozen, and that 'should [BoC] be found to be overcapitalised relative to [the core tier one target of 9 per cent under stress], a share-reversal process will be undertaken to refund depositors by the amount of over-capitalisation'. ECJ, *Ledra Advertising*, n. 28 in this chapter, paragraph 73.

rule of law intended to confer rights on individuals, the Commission's contribution to violating such a provision may give rise to compensation for the loss or harm suffered. This is so, provided that the other conditions governing the EU's non-contractual liability are also met. Third, that judgment is respectful of the vertical and horizontal allocation of powers sought by the authors of the Treaties, as the ECJ does not expand its jurisdiction over actions for annulment brought against the MoU.

Moreover, in order for the compatibility with the Charter of national measures adopted on the basis of the MoU to be examined, it must first be ascertained that those measures 'implement EU law' within the meaning of Article 51 of the Charter.[45] This question also raises complex issues. In the context of several references for a preliminary ruling made by Romanian and Portuguese courts,[46] the ECJ has been asked to determine whether austerity measures adopted in the context of the financial crisis could be examined in the light of the Charter.[47]

Those measures have, on occasion, included a reduction in the salaries of civil servants. This has, for example, been the case in Portugal where the 2011 State Budget Act provided that civil servants' incomes would be reduced. In *Sindicato dos Bancários do Norte*,[48] the trade union of a nationalised bank claimed that such a reduction was discriminatory as it did not apply to those working in the private sector. However, the Portuguese Constitutional Court took a different view and, by a judgment of 21 September 2011, ruled that the 2011 State Budget Act was compatible with the Portuguese Constitution. From a national perspective, employees of that bank had no choice but to accept that the reduction envisaged would take place. From an EU law perspective, the Labour Court of Porto reasoned that the compatibility of the 2011 State Budget Act with EU law could still be called into question in light of the EU principle of equality, which is enshrined in Article 20 of the Charter. Accordingly, it asked the ECJ whether that principle allowed room for such a difference in treatment. However, the ECJ ruled that it lacked jurisdiction to answer the questions referred, given that the order for reference contained no concrete evidence, nor any reasoning, capable of establishing that the 2011

[45] Kornezov, n. 10 in this chapter, at p. 3 et seq.
[46] As to the Romanian cases, see ECJ, orders of 14 December 2011 in *Corpul Naţional al Poliţiştilor*, C-434/11, EU:C:2011:830; *Cozman*, C-462/11, EU:C:2011:831; and of 10 May 2012 in *Corpul Naţional al Poliţiştilor*, C-134/12, EU:C:2012:288.
[47] See generally Neergaard et al., n. 23 in this chapter.
[48] ECJ, order of 7 March 2013 in *Sindicato dos Bancários do Norte and Others*, C-128/12, EU:C:2013:149. See also ECJ, orders *Corpul Naţional al Poliţiştilor*, *Cozman* and *Corpul Naţional al Poliţiştilor*, n. 46 in this chapter.

State Budget Act 'implemented EU law'. Subsequently, the ECJ reached the same conclusion in two other references made by Portuguese courts.[49]

Currently, there are two further such references pending before the ECJ: *Florescu* and *Associação Sindical dos Juízes Portugueses*.[50] The first case concerns a Romanian law that prohibits combining a pension with revenue from paid employment, where that pension is higher than the gross average national income. The second case involves a Portuguese law that brought about a reduction in the wages of judges. Thus, in both those cases, the ECJ will have to examine whether those national laws implement EU law within the meaning of Article 51(1) of the Charter, in other words, whether Portugal, whose currency is the euro, and Romania, whose currency is not the euro, are respectively fulfilling an obligation imposed by EU law, more particularly by the law of the EU on EMU.[51]

17.2.3 *Where Austerity Measures Implement EU Social Law*

Be that as it may, even if an austerity measure does not implement Regulation 472/2013 or any other EU measure relating to EMU, such a measure may still fall within the scope of other provisions of EU law. In that regard, EU measures adopted in the field of social policy may operate as a constraint on the conditions attached to the granting of ESM financial assistance.[52] It is true that the impact of EU social law is rather limited, as EU law does not contain rules that involve the redistribution of wealth at national level. That said, where the conditions attached to the grant of ESM financial assistance touch upon the labour market, EU social law may operate as such a constraint. For example, national measures implementing those conditions may not run counter to the mandatory provisions set out in Directive 2000/78[53] and Directive 2006/54.[54] In

---

[49] See for example, also ECJ, orders of 26 June 2014 in *Sindicato Nacional dos Profissionais de Seguros e Afins*, C-264/12, EU:C:2014:2036; and of 21 October 2014 in *Sindicato Nacional dos Profissionais de Seguros e Afins*, C-665/13, EU:C:2014:2327.

[50] ECJ, *Florescu and Others*, C-258/14, pending; and *Associação Sindical dos Juízes Portugueses*, C-64/16, pending.

[51] See, generally, K. Lenaerts and J.A. Gutiérrez–Fons, 'The Place of the Charter in the EU Constitutional Edifice', in S. Peers, T. Hervey, J. Kenner, and A. Ward (eds), *The EU Charter of Fundamental Rights: A Commentary* (Hart Publishing, 2014), p. 1557. See Kornezov, n. 10 in this chapter, at p. 8.

[52] Kilpatrick, n. 10 in this chapter, at p. 419, who argues that '[a] preliminary reference on interpretation can ask the [ECJ] how to resolve the presence of contradictory EU/bailout norms, one requiring social protection, the other demanding the opposite'.

[53] Council Directive 2000/78/EC of 27 November 2000 establishing a general framework for equal treatment in employment and occupation, [2000] OJ L 303/16.

[54] Directive 2006/54/EC of the European Parliament and of the Council of 5 July 2006 on the implementation of the principle of equal opportunities and equal treatment of men and women in matters of employment and occupation (recast), [2006] OJ L 204/23.

the same way, conditions attached to the granting of financial assistance may not adversely affect the mandatory provisions of the framework agreement on fixed-term contracts.[55]

Conversely, where Member States enjoy a margin of discretion to implement a directive in the field of social policy, the ESM may condition the grant of its financial assistance upon the Member State concerned opting for a lower level of social protection. For example, the Working Time Directive[56] provides that, without prejudice to the derogations and limitations set out therein, 'the average working time for each seven-day period, including overtime, does not exceed 48 hours'.[57] This means that a Member State is free to set the maximum working week at 40 or 35 hours.[58] If such a Member State is receiving financial assistance from the ESM, the latter may, for example, require the former to increase that limit from 35 to 40 hours. However, the Working Time Directive would oppose a national measure that, whilst implementing the conditions attached to the grant of ESM financial assistance, requires, or even just allows, all workers to work more than 48 hours per week. In the same way, that Directive provides that, without prejudice to the derogations and limitations set out therein, 'Member States shall take the measures necessary to ensure that every worker is entitled to paid annual leave of at least four weeks in accordance with the conditions for entitlement to, and granting of, such leave laid down by national legislation and/or practice.'[59] It follows that a Member State is free to grant workers a paid annual leave of five or six weeks. If such a Member State is receiving financial assistance from the ESM, the

---

[55] Council Directive 1999/70/EC of 28 June 1999 concerning the Framework Agreement on fixed-term work concluded by ETUC, UNICE, and CEEP, [1999] OJ L 175/43. Regarding other framework agreements implemented by directives, see also Council Directive 2010/18/EU of 8 March 2010 implementing the revised Framework Agreement on parental leave concluded by BUSINESSEUROPE, UEAPME, CEEP, and ETUC and repealing Directive 96/34/EC, [2010] OJ L 68/13, and Council Directive 97/81/EC of 15 December 1997 concerning the Framework Agreement on part-time work concluded by UNICE, CEEP, and the ETUC – Annex: Framework agreement on part-time work, [1998] OJ L 14/9. As to the UK and Ireland, see Council Directive 98/23/EC of 7 April 1998 on the extension of Directive 97/81/EC on the framework agreement on part-time work concluded by UNICE, CEEP and the ETUC to the United Kingdom of Great Britain and Northern Ireland, [1998] OJ L 131/10.

[56] Directive 2003/88/EC of the European Parliament and of the Council of 4 November 2003 concerning certain aspects of the organisation of working time, [2003] OJ L 299/ 9.

[57] See Article 6 of Directive 2003/88/EC, n. 56 in this chapter.

[58] See Article 15 of Directive 2003/88/EC, n. 56 in this chapter, which states that: '[t]his Directive shall not affect Member States' right to apply or introduce laws, regulations or administrative provisions more favourable to the protection of the safety and health of workers or to facilitate or permit the application of collective agreements or agreements concluded between the two sides of industry which are more favourable to the protection of the safety and health of workers'.

[59] See Article 7 of Directive 2003/88/EC, n. 56 in this chapter.

latter may require the former to reduce paid annual leave to four weeks, but never below that limit. The same findings apply in relation to the principle of non-discrimination.[60] If the ESM requires a reduction of severance payments or notice periods, any such reduction may not discriminate against workers on the grounds listed in Article 21 of the Charter.

17.3 THE HORIZONTAL APPLICATION AND JUSTICIABILITY OF PRIMARY EU SOCIAL LAW

17.3.1 *The Rationale Underpinning the Horizontal Application of the General Principle of Non-Discrimination*

EU social law contains mandatory norms that set limits on both the national legislator and the freedom of contract. When entering into an employment contract, the employer, as well as the employee, must abide by those norms. EU social law may confer rights and impose obligations on the parties to such a contract in so far as that law has horizontal direct effect. This means, for example, that an employee may rely on EU social law with a view to disapplying conflicting provisions of national law on which a contractual clause is based. In the context of socioeconomic reforms that focus on the labour market, such mandatory norms are important as they protect employees against conflicting national measures that implement the conditions attached to the grant of ESM financial assistance.

EU social law is largely composed of a body of directives. Those directives are not only limited to implementing the principles of non-discrimination in the context of employment and occupation,[61] but also seek to protect the employee. They concern, for example, certain aspects of the organisation of working time,[62] parental leave,[63] the protection of young people at work,[64] the safety and health at work of pregnant workers,[65] the protection of employees in the event of the insolvency of their employer[66] and the obligation to

---

[60] ECJ, judgment of 24 April 2012 in *Kamberaj*, C-571/10, EU:C:2012:233.
[61] Directive 2000/78/EC, n. 53 in this chapter, and Directive 2006/54/EC, n. 54 in this chapter.
[62] Directive 2003/88/EC, n. 56 in this chapter.
[63] Council Directive 2010/18/EU, n. 55 in this chapter.
[64] Council Directive 94/33/EC of 22 June 1994 on the protection of young people at work, [1994] OJ L 216/12.
[65] Council Directive 92/85/EEC of 19 October 1992 on the introduction of measures to encourage improvements in the safety and health at work of pregnant workers and workers who have recently given birth or are breastfeeding, [1992] OJ L 348/1.
[66] Council Directive 80/987/EEC of 20 October 1980 on the approximation of the laws of the Member States relating to the protection of employees in the event of the insolvency of their employer, [1980] OJ L 283/23, repealed by Directive 2008/94/EC of the European Parliament

inform employees of the conditions applicable to the contract or employment relationship.[67]

Where the employer is a public authority or company, national measures that conflict with directly effective provisions of a directive may be set aside. This is so regardless of whether those measures implement the conditions attached to the granting of ESM financial assistance. By contrast, the same does not hold true regarding private employers. Directives cannot have horizontal direct effect.[68] Time and again, the ECJ has ruled that 'even a clear, precise and unconditional provision of a directive seeking to confer rights or impose obligations on individuals cannot of itself apply in proceedings exclusively between private parties'.[69] In the context of EU social law, this means that an employee may not rely on a provision of a directive – that has not been or is wrongfully implemented – against his or her employer where the latter is a private individual.

That said, as the ECJ ruled in the *Pfeiffer and Others* case, 'the national court is bound to interpret national law, so far as possible, in the light of the wording and the purpose of the directive concerned in order to achieve the result sought by the directive'.[70] That duty of consistent interpretation 'requires the national court to consider national law as a whole in order to assess to what extent it may be applied so as not to produce a result contrary to that sought by the directive'.[71] The duty of consistent interpretation is, however, 'limited by general principles of [EU] law and it cannot serve as the basis for an interpretation of national law contra legem'.[72] Where the interpretation of national law in conformity with EU law is ruled out, 'the party injured as a result of

and of the Council of 22 October 2008 on the protection of employees in the event of the insolvency of their employer, [2008] OJ L 283/36.

[67] Council Directive 91/533/EEC of 14 October 1991 on an employer's obligation to inform employees of the conditions applicable to the contract or employment relationship, [1991] OJ L 288/32.

[68] See for example, ECJ, judgments of 26 February 1986 in *Marshall*, 152/84, EU:C:1986:84, paragraph 48; of 14 July 1994 in *Faccini Dori*, C-91/92, EU:C:1994:292, paragraph 20; of 7 January 2004 in *Wells*, C-201/02, EU:C:2004:12, paragraph 56; of 19 January 2010 in *Kücükdeveci*, C-555/07, EU:C:2010:21, paragraph 46; of 24 January 2012 in *Dominguez*, C-282/10, EU:C:2012:33, paragraph 37; of 15 January 2015 in *Ryanair*, C-30/14, EU:C:2015:10, paragraph 30; and of 19 April 2016 in *DI.*, C-441/14, EU:C:2016:278, paragraph 30.

[69] See for example, ECJ, judgment of 5 October 2004 in *Pfeiffer and Others*, C-397/01 to C-403/01, EU:C:2004:584, paragraph 109, and ECJ, *Dominguez*, n. 68 in this chapter, paragraph 42.

[70] ECJ, *Pfeiffer*, n. 69 in this chapter, paragraph 113.

[71] Ibid., paragraph 115 and ECJ, *DI.*, n. 68 in this chapter, paragraph 31.

[72] See for example, ECJ, *Impact*, n. 7 in this chapter, paragraph 100; ECJ, judgment of 23 April 2009 in *Angelidaki and Others*, C-378/07 to C-380/07, EU:C:2009:250, paragraph 199; ECJ, *Dominguez*, n. 68 in this chapter, paragraph 25, and ECJ, *DI.*, n. 68 in this chapter, paragraph 32.

domestic law not being in conformity with European Union law can none the less rely on the judgment in [*Francovich and Others*[73]] in order to obtain, if appropriate, compensation for the loss sustained'.[74]

However, the absence of horizontal direct effect of directives does not rule out the existence of directly effective mandatory norms that may be found in primary EU law. Regarding employment relations, Articles 18 TFEU,[75] 45 TFEU,[76] and 157(1) TFEU lay down such mandatory norms.[77] Those Treaty provisions relate, respectively, to the principle of non-discrimination on grounds of nationality, the free movement of workers,[78] and the principle of equal pay for male and female workers for equal work or work of equal value. It is worth noting that those three Treaty provisions give concrete expression to the principle of equality, a general principle of EU law enshrined in Article 20 of the Charter.

In the seminal *Defrenne* case, the ECJ ruled that the general principle of equal pay for equal work – grounded in ex Article 119 EEC (now Article 157 TFEU) – may have horizontal direct effect. After examining the aim, the nature and the place of the principle of equal pay for equal work in the overall scheme of the Treaty, the ECJ held that this principle is 'mandatory in nature' and, accordingly, applies to public authorities and private individuals alike.[79] By contrast, not only was Directive 75/117,[80] which sought to improve the legal protection of workers suffering from unequal pay caused by sex discrimination, irrelevant to the question whether the principle of equal pay for equal work could itself have horizontal direct effect, but, as the ECJ further pointed out, Directive 75/117 could in no way reduce the effectiveness and the temporal scope of that principle.[81]

---

[73] ECJ, judgment of 19 November 1991 in *Francovich and Others*, C-6/90 and C-9/90, EU:C:1991:428.

[74] ECJ, *Dominguez*, n. 68 in this chapter, paragraph 43.

[75] ECJ, judgment of 12 December 1974 in *Walrave and Koch*, C-36/74, EU:C:1974:140.

[76] ECJ, judgment of 6 June 2000 in *Angonese*, C-281/98, EU:C:2000:296.

[77] ECJ, judgment of 8 April 1976 in *Defrenne*, C-43/75, EU:C:1976:56.

[78] It is worth recalling that 'Article 18 TFEU, which enshrines the general principle of non-discrimination on grounds of nationality, is intended to apply independently only to situations governed by EU law in respect of which the Treaty lays down no specific prohibition of discrimination ... As it is, in respect of freedom of movement for workers ... the principle of non-discrimination is given specific effect by Articl[e] 45(2) TFEU'. See for example, ECJ, judgment of 4 September 2014 in *Schiebel Aircraft*, C-474/12, EU:C:2014:2139, paragraphs 20 and 21.

[79] ECJ, *Defrenne*, n. 77 in this chapter, paragraph 39.

[80] Council Directive 75/117/EEC of 10 February 1975 on the approximation of the laws of the Member States relating to the application of the principle of equal pay for men and women, [1975] OJ L 45/19.

[81] ECJ, *Defrenne*, n. 77 in this chapter, paragraph 60. See also ECJ, judgments of 31 March 1981 in *Jenkins*, C-96/80, EU:C:1981:80, paragraph 22 (holding that Directive 75/117 could not alter

Likewise, in *Angonese*, the ECJ observed that Regulation 1612/68[82] which implemented the principle of free movement of workers as laid down in ex Article 39 EC (now Article 45 TFEU) was not applicable to a recruitment procedure for a post organised by a private bank. This circumstance did not, however, prevent the principle of free movement of workers – a specific application of the general principle of non-discrimination on grounds of nationality – from having horizontal direct effect. The ECJ reasoned that its findings in *Defrenne* could apply, a fortiori, to the free movement of workers, since both principles are 'mandatory in nature' and seek to combat discrimination on the labour market, albeit based on different grounds.[83]

In the field of social law, could *Defrenne* support the horizontal application of other 'constitutional categories' of the principle of non-discrimination which are 'mandatory in nature' but are not laid down in a Treaty provision? In that regard, one could argue that in order to preserve the vertical and horizontal allocation of powers, only those general principles of EU law which are enshrined in a Treaty provision may have horizontal direct effect. A close reading of *Defrenne* reveals that the wording of ex Article 119 EEC did not play a major role in the reasoning of the ECJ.[84] Indeed, the ECJ did not focus on whether this Treaty provision was sufficiently precise to produce direct effect, preferring, instead, to 'identify and isolate' the general principle of equal pay for equal work.[85]

Most importantly, *Defrenne* shows that in deciding in favour of the horizontal application of the principle of equal pay for equal work, the ECJ had due regard to the prerogatives of the EU legislator and of the Member States. Indeed, the ECJ drew a distinction between situations where a 'purely legal analysis' was sufficient to identify the presence of sex discrimination and more complex situations where discrimination could not be ascertained unless legislative measures had been adopted at EU level.[86] While in relation to the former type of situation, the ECJ is in a position to hold that the general principle of equal pay for equal work has horizontal direct effect, in the latter

---

the content or scope of that general principle); and of 3 October 2006 in *Cadman*, C-17/05, EU:C:2006:633, paragraph 29.

[82] Regulation 1612/68 of the Council of 15 October 1968 on freedom of movement for workers within the Community, [1968] OJ Spec. Ed. Séries I-475.

[83] ECJ, *Angonese*, n. 76 in this chapter, paragraphs 34–5.

[84] For example, the ECJ observed that, while ex Article 119 EEC was formally addressed to the Member States, this circumstance did not exclude 'rights from being conferred on individuals' who seek to enforce the duties laid down therein. ECJ, *Defrenne*, n. 77 in this chapter, parargaph. 31.

[85] P. Craig and G. De Búrca, *EU Law: Text, Cases and Materials* (Oxford University Press, 4th edn, 2007), pp. 276–7.

[86] ECJ, *Defrenne*, n. 77 in this chapter, paragraphs 19–22.

type of situation the ECJ may not do so. Therefore, in so far as this distinction is complied with, the vertical and horizontal allocation of powers within the EU is not compromised by the horizontal application of a general principle of EU law. That is so regardless of whether the general principle is grounded in a Treaty provision. It is in that context that one should understand the *Mangold, Kücükdeveci* and *DI.* line of case law,[87] in which the ECJ held that the general principle of non-discrimination on grounds of age, now enshrined in Article 21 of the Charter, is applicable horizontally.[88]

The application of the general principle of non-discrimination on grounds of age does not require legislation to be drafted at EU level. This is because general principles of EU law 'have constitutional status'.[89] This means, in essence, that the application of a general principle does not require 'legislation to be drafted and enacted at [EU] level by a measure of secondary [EU] law'.[90] As the ECJ held in *DI.*, '[since] Directive 2000/78 does not itself lay down the general principle prohibiting discrimination on grounds of age but simply gives concrete expression to that principle in relation to employment and occupation, the scope of the protection conferred by the directive does not go beyond that afforded by that principle'.[91] Thus, Directive 2000/78 does not define the normative content of that general principle, but limits itself to 'establish[ing] a more precise framework to facilitate the practical implementation of the principle of equal treatment and, in particular, to specify various possible exceptions to that principle, circumscribing those exceptions by the use of a clearer definition of their scope'.[92]

That said, in order for a general principle to apply, the dispute before the national court must fall within the scope of application of EU law. Given that the general principles of EU law are not 'self-standing', a rule of EU law other than those principles must be applicable to the case at hand.[93] In that regard, Directive 2000/78 may serve the legal norm that brings the dispute in question within the scope of that law.

---

[87] ECJ, judgment of 22 November 2005 in *Mangold*, C-144/04, EU:C:2005:709; ECJ, *Kücükdeveci*, n. 68 in this chapter, and *DI.*, n. 68 in this chapter. See also opinion of Advocate General Sharpston of 22 May 2008 in *Bartsch*, C-427/06, EU:C:2008:297, points 82–5.

[88] ECJ, *Kücükdeveci*, n. 68 in this chapter, paragraphs 50–5.

[89] ECJ, judgment of 15 October 2009 in *Audiolux and Others*, C-101/08, EU:C:2009:626, paragraph 63.

[90] Ibid.

[91] ECJ, *DI.*, n. 68 in this chapter, paragraph 23.

[92] Ibid.

[93] ECJ, judgment of 23 September 2008 in *Bartsch*, C-427/06, EU:C:2008:517, paragraph 25, and opinion of Advocate General Sharpston in the same case, n. 87 in this chapter, point 69.

In *DI.*, the ECJ also provided two further clarifications regarding the horizontal application of the general principle of non-discrimination on grounds of age. First, it held that a national court cannot rely on the principle of the protection of legitimate expectations in order to continue to apply a rule of national law that is at odds with that general principle.[94] Second, in disputes between private parties, the principle of Member State liability to compensate the harm or loss caused by its breaching of EU law has no bearing on the obligation of the national court to disapply the national provision that is at odds with the general principle of non-discrimination on grounds of age.[95]

Most importantly, it follows from a joint reading of those cases that in order for a general principle of EU law to have horizontal direct effect two cumulative conditions must be met. First, such a principle must be mandatory in nature. Second, it must be sufficient in itself to confer on individuals a right which they may invoke as such before a national court.

17.3.2 *Beyond the Principle of Non-Discrimination*

It was the latter condition that played a decisive role in the *AMS* case.[96] In that case, the ECJ was not called upon to interpret the principle of non-discrimination, enshrined in Article 21 of the Charter, but Article 27 thereof. The latter provision, entitled 'Workers' right to information and consultation within the undertaking', states that '[w]orkers or their representatives must, at the appropriate levels, be guaranteed information and consultation in good time in the cases and under the conditions provided for by Union law and national laws and practices'. It is worth noting that Directive 2002/14 implements Article 27 of the Charter at EU level.[97] In the *AMS* case, the ECJ was asked to interpret Article 3(1) of Directive 2002/14, according to which the provisions of that directive apply to undertakings employing at least 50 employees in any one Member State. The problem was that French law implementing Directive 2002/14 excluded employees with assisted contracts (apprentices and trainees) from the calculation of the number of staff members, despite the fact that those employees fell within the scope *ratione personae* of French employment law. Such an exclusion, the ECJ found, was incompatible with Article 3(1) of Directive 2002/14. Next, it examined whether Article 27 of the

---

[94] ECJ, *DI.*, n. 68 in this chapter, paragraph 38.
[95] Ibid., paragraph 42.
[96] ECJ, judgment of 15 January 2014 in *AMS*, C-176/12, EU:C:2014:2.
[97] Directive 2002/14/EC of the European Parliament and of the Council of 11 March 2002 establishing a general framework for informing and consulting employees in the European Community, [2002] OJ L 80/29.

Charter, whether by itself or in conjunction with the provisions of Directive 2002/14, could be invoked in a dispute between individuals in order to disapply a conflicting national provision.

At the outset, the ECJ recalled its case law on the lack of horizontal direct effect of directives. In that regard, it held that, even though Article 3(1) of Directive 2002/14 is a clear, precise, and unconditional provision that fulfils all of the conditions necessary for it to have direct effect, it cannot of itself apply in proceedings exclusively between private parties.[98]

Since the national court had explicitly ruled out the possibility of interpreting the relevant provisions of French law in the light of the purpose and wording of Directive 2002/14,[99] the ECJ went on to examine whether the *Mangold-Kücükdeveci* line of case law was applicable to Article 27 of the Charter, namely whether that provision, by itself or in conjunction with the provisions of Directive 2002/14, produced horizontal direct effect.

As to the application of Article 27 of the Charter as a stand-alone provision, the ECJ began by recalling its case law on Article 51(1) of the Charter, according to which the Charter applies 'to the Member States only when they are implementing EU law'.[100] 'Since the national legislation at issue in the main proceedings was adopted to implement Directive 2002/14', the ECJ wrote, 'Article 27 of the Charter is applicable to the case in the main proceedings'.[101] However, the ECJ noted, in the light of the wording of Article 27 of the Charter, that in order 'for this article to be fully effective, it must be given more specific expression in European Union or national law'.[102] Indeed, the normative content of Article 3(1) of Directive 2002/14 could not be deduced either from the wording of Article 27 of the Charter or from the explanatory notes relating to that provision.[103] Accordingly, the facts of the case had to be distinguished from those which gave rise to *Kücükdeveci*. Unlike Article 27 of the Charter, 'the principle of non-discrimination on grounds of age at issue in that case, laid down in Article 21(1) of the Charter, is sufficient in itself to confer on individuals an individual right which they may invoke as such'.[104] Thus, the ECJ held that Article 27 of the Charter by itself may not have horizontal direct effect.

[98] ECJ, *AMS*, n. 96 in this chapter, paragraph 36.
[99] Ibid., paragraph 40.
[100] ECJ, judgment of 26 February 2013 in *Åkerberg Fransson*, C-617/10, EU:C:2013:105.
[101] ECJ, *AMS*, n. 96 in this chapter, paragraph 43.
[102] Ibid., paragraph 45.
[103] Ibid., paragraph 46.
[104] Ibid., para 47. See also ECJ, *DI.*, n. 68 in this chapter, paragraph 36.

In relation to the application of Article 27 of the Charter in conjunction with the provisions of Directive 2002/14, the same findings applied, 'since that article by itself does not suffice to confer on individuals a right which they may invoke as such, it could not be otherwise if it is considered in conjunction with that directive'.[105]

Having replied in the negative to the second question asked by the French court, the ECJ recalled its *Francovich and Others* case law, in the light of which a party that suffers harm as a result of domestic law not being in conformity with EU law can obtain, if appropriate, compensation for the loss sustained.[106]

The general principle of non-discrimination on grounds of age, now enshrined in Article 21(1) of the Charter, may have horizontal direct effect.[107] In the light of *Mangold, Kücükdeveci, DI.,* and *AMS*, the normative justification for that effect is twofold. First, that principle is mandatory in nature. It is submitted that what the ECJ held in *Defrenne* regarding the principle of equal pay for male and female workers for equal work or work of equal value is also valid with respect to the principle of non-discrimination on grounds of age, namely that the principle 'applies not only to the action of public authorities, but also extends to all agreements which are intended to regulate paid labour collectively, as well as to contracts between individuals'.[108] Second, unlike Article 27 of the Charter, that principle enshrines a directly applicable rule of law. By focusing on the direct applicability of the provision of the Charter in question, the ECJ distinguishes constitutional norms that are, as such, judicially enforceable from those that require the adoption of implementing measures either at EU or national level. Thus, since the general principle of non-discrimination on grounds of age is directly applicable, it may have horizontal direct effect without adversely affecting the constitutional allocation of powers sought by the authors of the Treaties. Since that principle 'is sufficient in itself to confer on individuals an individual right which they may invoke as such',[109] it does not encroach upon the prerogatives of the EU or, as the case may be, the national legislator. Conversely, given that in order to be

---

[105] ECJ, *AMS*, n. 96 in this chapter, paragraph 49.
[106] Ibid., paragraph 50.
[107] The same applies regarding the other forms of discrimination laid down in Article 21(1) of the Charter. As to the principle of non-discrimination on grounds of disability, see ECJ, judgment of 11 April 2013 in *HK Danmark*, C-335/11 and C-337/11, EU:C:2013:222. In relation to the principle of non-discrimination on grounds of sexual orientation, see ECJ, judgment of 12 December 2013 in *Hay*, C-267/12, EU:C:2013:823.
[108] ECJ, *Defrenne*, n. 77 in this chapter, paragraph 60. See also *Jenkins*, n. 81 in this chapter, paragraph 22 and *Cadman*, n. 81 in this chapter, paragraph 29.
[109] ECJ, *AMS*, n. 96 in this chapter, paragraph 47.

fully operational Article 27 of the Charter requires the adoption of legislative measures, it cannot have horizontal direct effect.[110] The fact that Article 27 is located under the 'Solidarity' Title of the Charter and is of a social nature had no bearing on the ECJ's reasoning. The ECJ is, in that respect, 'socially neutral'. If a provision of the Charter located under that Title is mandatory in nature and is sufficient in itself to confer on individuals a right which they may invoke as such before a national court, the ruling of the ECJ in AMS suggests that such a provision may produce horizontal direct effect.[111] In our view, it is too soon to tell whether many or few of the provisions located under the 'Solidarity' Title of the Charter fulfil those two conditions.[112]

17.4 CONCLUDING REMARKS

In accordance with Article 19 TEU, the ECJ 'shall ensure that in the interpretation and application of the Treaties the law is observed'. It follows from that Treaty provision that all EU acts must be interpreted so as to guarantee that the EU is based on the rule of law.

In the context of the financial crisis, this means that the ECJ must uphold the vertical and horizontal allocation of powers sought by the authors of the Treaties. As the EU is only empowered to adopt rules aiming at stabilising and ensuring the sustainability of public finances, it lacks the powers to adopt socioeconomic redistributive rules. The distinction between those two types of rules ensures compliance with the principle of democracy. Budgetary decisions are part and parcel of the choices that representatives of the people must make. As the EU legal order now stands, notwithstanding the fact that the EU may adopt budgetary discipline and balance rules which are binding upon the Member States, it is for national parliaments to decide how to cut public spending and how to increase public revenue. For the ECJ, this means that it lacks jurisdiction to interpret the Charter in respect of socioeconomic reforms that, whilst seeking to comply with the conditions attached to the granting of ESM financial assistance, fall outside the scope of EU law.

---

[110] See Kornezov, n. 10 in this chapter.

[111] For example, some authors argue that, in the light of ECJ, *Viking*, n. 7 in this chapter, Article 28 of the Charter, which enshrines the right of collective bargaining and action, is justiciable. See C. Barnard, 'Article 28 – The Right of Collective Bargaining and Action', in S. Peers, T. Hervey, J. Kenner, and A. Ward (eds), *The EU Charter of Fundamental Rights: A Commentary* (Hart Publishing, 2014), p. 793; and A. Hinarejos, 'Laval and Viking: The Right to Collective Action versus EU Fundamental Freedoms' (2008) 8 *Human Rights Law Review* 714, 725 (arguing that the fact that 'the right to collective action is a fully fledged right ... seems the most plausible interpretation').

[112] But see Kornezov, n. 10 in this chapter.

However, the ECJ does enjoy jurisdiction to interpret and examine the validity of a Council decision approving a macroeconomic adjustment programme provided for by Regulation 472/2013. Thus, the latter regulation is a positive development that contributes to guaranteeing, albeit indirectly, full consistency between EU law and the conditions attached to the grant of ESM financial assistance. In the same way, the ruling of the ECJ in *Ledra* enhances the role of the Commission as 'guardian of the Treaties'. That role must always be honoured even if that EU institution is called upon to act outside the EU legal framework. In the context of the ESM's activities, this means that it must ensure that the MoU is fully consistent with EU law. If it fails to ensure consistency with a rule of EU law intended to confer rights on individuals, such as a fundamental right recognised in the Charter, private parties who as a result are adversely affected may bring an action for damages. Needless to say, in order for damages to be awarded, the other conditions governing the EU's non-contractual liability must also be met.

In addition, where an austerity measure is not implementing EU measures on EMU, it may still fall within the scope of EU law, notably within that of the EU social acquis. In the context of the labour market, that acquis may operate as a limitation on the measures that a Member State may adopt in order to give effect to the conditions attached to the grant of ESM financial assistance. The smaller the margin of discretion that such a Member State enjoys under EU social law, the more protected social rights will be. This is because mandatory social EU norms are immune from austerity. Conversely, the broader such margin is, the more freedom a Member State will enjoy in adopting a level of social protection that complies with those conditions.

Moreover, in order for the ECJ not to encroach upon the prerogatives of the EU and national legislators, a Charter provision may only have horizontal direct effect where it is mandatory in nature and where that provision enshrines a directly applicable rule of law. That explains why the general principle of non-discrimination on grounds of age has horizontal direct effect, whereas Article 27 of the Charter does not. Thus, the rationale underpinning the AMS judgment has nothing to do with the 'social nature' of Article 27 of the Charter. Regardless of its civil, political, social or economic nature, any provision of the Charter must, in order to have horizontal direct effect, fulfil those two conditions.

If the adoption of EU socioeconomic redistributive rules were to be the solution settled upon to avoid future financial crises, this would inevitably entail a Treaty amendment that would transfer new powers to the EU. In this regard, Professor Habermas has argued that such transfer would have to go hand-in-hand with the democratic empowerment of the EU which would need to be transformed into a fully fledged supranational democracy that would, nevertheless, preserve the integrity of the Member States as States.[113] 'From the perspective of the constitutionally required legitimation', he posited, 'the Monetary Union would have to be expanded into a real Political Union'. Otherwise, unlike national parliaments, 'a technocracy without democratic roots would not have the motivation to accord sufficient weight to the demands of the electorate for a just distribution of income and property, for status security, public services, and collective goods when these conflicted with the systemic demands for competitiveness and economic growth'. We concur with that last contention.

Socioeconomic redistributive rules, and notably those adopted in the field of social policy, involve hard choices that affect individuals directly. If a Treaty reform should confer redistributive powers to the EU, compliance with the principle of democracy militates in favour of conferring real decision-making powers to the European Parliament, whilst not depriving national parliaments of their budgetary autonomy. Those rules would have to give expression to the EU's 'dual structure of democratic legitimacy', which comprises the body of all EU citizens collectively, on the one hand, and the various individual peoples of Europe organised in and by their national constitutions, on the other hand.[114] Democracy in a multilevel system of governance must be driven by a mutually reinforcing relationship whereby democracy at EU level does not seek to eliminate national democracies.[115] On the contrary, both sources of democratic legitimacy must complement each other.

[113] J. Habermas, 'Democracy, Solidarity and the European Crisis', Lecture delivered by Professor on 26 April 2013 in Leuven, available at: www.kuleuven.be/communicatie/evenementen/evenementen/jurgen-habermas/en/democracy-solidarity-and-the-european-crisis#_ftn8 (accessed 10 October 2016). More generally, see J. Habermas, *The Crisis of the European Union: A Response* (Polity Press, 2012).
[114] K. Lenaerts, 'Demoicracy, Constitutional Pluralism and the Court of Justice of the European Union', in L. van Middelaar and P. Van Parijs (eds), *After The Storm: How to Save Democracy in Europe* (Lannoo Publishers, 2015), p. 109.
[115] Notably, this means that Member States must remain free to accede to and, as the case may be, to withdraw from the EU. See K. Nicolaïdis, 'European Demoicracy and Its Crisis', at pp. 362–3, who observes that '[p]eoples as [S]tates must have the de jure right, but also de facto capacity, to choose to enter or exit the Union … Member [S]tates must remain masters of the treaties'.

PART IV

Politics

18

The European Social Union and EU Legislative Politics

Dorte Sindbjerg Martinsen

18.1 INTRODUCTION

The process of integration towards a European Social Union consists of both past achievements and current deficits. It has developed on a delicate balance between on the one hand constitutive community principles of free movement and non-discrimination and on the other hand Member State jealously guarding their welfare competences. Despite national concerns, EU social integration has occurred. Primary and secondary social legislation has been adopted through the years, building up a Community social dimension with coordination of social security across borders, equal pay and treatment between gender, health, and safety at the work place, employment law, regulation regarding insolvency, the posting of workers, the social dialogue, etc. In addition, the open methods of coordination address a wider range of social issues, however, without being binding on the Member States. On the other hand, European integration challenges social protection. The more recent economic governance of the European Union constrains national welfare policies. Convergence criteria, the stability and growth pact, and the European Semester strain contemporary social and fiscal policies in the Member States. The crises and austerity measures work severely against social policies both at the European and national level as various contributions in this volume demonstrate.

The current movement towards a European Social Union thus consists of fragmented and contradictory dynamics, which on balance have negative implications for welfare policies. Such implications may be severe indeed. Ferrera compares nowadays socioeconomic challenges with the ones faced 100 years ago, where local social communities were dissolved and replaced by national standards. Ferrera argues that it's the same kind of economic fusion we see today, and it requires pan-European responses in order to prevent social conflicts.

> As was the case one hundred years ago at the domestic level, the Europeanisation ('fusion') of national markets through freedom of movement and competition rules is (already has been) a tremendous trigger for growth and job creation in the EU's economy, enhancing life chances and welfare for European citizens. But it is also a source of social and spatial disruptions. Again economic 'fusion' requires the introduction of some common social standards, rights and obligations through a socially friendly institutional re-articulation of the novel Europeanised space of interaction.[1]

Such a social space of interaction appears to have a long way to go. The Juncker Commission has admitted to a certain need for social initiatives in the midst of crises, but it remains unclear where sufficient political entrepreneurship should come from. Vandenbroucke notes in his contribution to this volume that a European Social Union needs instruments.[2] It needs supranational devices and common standards. A Social Union cannot come into being or address the full scope of European social challenges by means of soft law, recommendation or a flexible European Semester. It needs binding measures and it needs politics.[3]

This chapter examines the legislative politics of a Union social policy. It traces its development over time and its political mandate. The chapter first examines how binding EU social policies have developed over time. It thus examines the evolvement of the regulatory field as well as by which institutions the devices were decided (Section 18.2). Secondly, the chapter turns to the more substantive side of EU social regulation, the content and main achievements of the EU social dimension (Section 18.3) and takes us up to current challenges and increased politicisation of EU social integration (Sections 18.4 and 18.5). Thirdly, in order to capture the legislative politics and conflict lines of Social Europe in a post-Lisbon setting, the decision-making process on the regulation of posted workers is analysed (Section 18.6). Finally, the chapter concludes that the recent adoption of an enforcement directive for the posting of workers demonstrates that EU legislative politics can still deliver binding measures – even in the difficult political setting of EU28 (Section 18.7). At the same time, however, political conflict lines of a European Social Union

---

[1] M. Ferrera, 'Modest Beginnings, Timid Progresses: What's Next for Social Europe?', in B. Cantillon, H. Verschueren, and P. Ploscar (eds), *Social Inclusion and Social Protection in the EU: Interactions between Law and Policy* (Intersentia Publishing), p. 18.

[2] F. Vandenbroucke, 'The Idea of a European Social Union: A Normative Introduction', Chapter 1 in this volume.

[3] Ibid.

are clearly marked and non-majoritarian decisions affects the legitimacy of decisions taken.

18.2 THE DEVELOPMENT OF EU LEGISLATIVE POLICIES

To adopt binding EU social measures is a difficult task. Institutionally the decision-making process is framed by the three legislative institutions of the European Union; the European Commission, the Council and the European Parliament (EP). The European Commission has the monopoly to propose legislation. Furthermore, it decides on Commission regulations and delegated acts. Internally, different Directorates Generals (DGs) may disagree on the aims of community policies as may the Commissioners. The Commissioner for internal market is unlikely to agree fully with the Commissioner for employment and social affairs on what should be the exact balance between internal market principles and social protection. The policy positions thus have to be coordinated internally in the Commission, which often times involves conflicts and compromises.[4] In the Council of the European Union sits the Member States. The Member States have to agree, unanimously or by qualified majority. Now counting 28 governments with different ideological positions and socioeconomic legacies, establishing a qualified majority certainly faces many obstacles. The EP may be co-legislator in the decision-making process. The EP has to establish a majority between its 751 members and different political groups. Its internal dynamics are conditioned by which committee and which rapporteur are in charge of a dossier. Finally when co-legislating, the Council and the EP has to establish a compromise between them.

There are thus reasons to assume that the EU legislative process is hindered by institutional and political rivalry and that only few pieces of secondary legislation within EU social policy are adopted. When examining the development of social policy secondary legislation between 1971 and up to the time of writing May 2016, we find that 234 directives and regulations have been adopted.[5]

---

[4] M. Hartlapp, J. Metz, and C. Rauh, *Which Policy for Europe?: Power and Conflict inside the European Commission* (Oxford University Press, 2014).

[5] The time period was set as 1971–2016 in order to begin from the year where one of the main pieces of EU social regulation was adopted, namely Regulation (EEC) no. 1408/71 of the Council of 14 June 1971 on the application of social security schemes to employed persons and their families moving within the Community. The examination was carried out by means of the EUR-LEX database on consolidated legislation with the following search code; Consolidated legislation; directory of European Union consolidated legislation; 05 Freedom

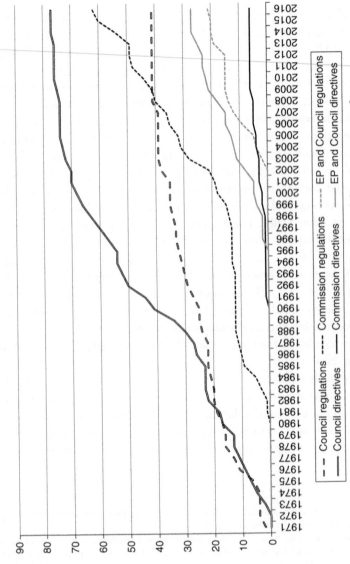

FIGURE 18.1: The development of EU social policy regulations and directives 1971–2016.

Legend:
- - - Council regulations ---- Commission regulations ---- EP and Council regulations
—— Council directives —— Commission directives —— EP and Council directives

Author's compilation. Source: EUR-LEX directory on consolidated legislation, including legislation in force and not in force.

Figure 18.1 presents the accumulated adoption of EU social policy regulations and directives for an extensive time period.[6] The type of regulatory act was manually sorted out for each year of adoption that contains important information. We see that the main type of regulatory act over time comprises Council directives, second Commission regulations, and third Council regulations. Compared hereto regulations and directives adopted by the Council *and* the EP are modest.

The examination over time may surprise the reader for two reasons. First, the Commission has a considerable importance as decision-maker. The amount of regulations adopted by the non-majoritarian institution stands out. Second, although now a co-legislator in many areas, the role of the EP when it comes to the adoption of secondary legislation is still modest.

18.3 A EUROPEAN SOCIAL UNION — ACHIEVEMENTS AND CHALLENGES

However, Figure 18.1 also demonstrates that the EU legislative institutions produce binding, and thus enforceable, social regulation and continue to do so over time. Although welfare policies are formally regarded national competence, the European Union has gradually institutionalised an advanced form of social regulation.

One of the first regulations of the European Community was Regulation no. 3 adopted in 1958, which granted migrant workers moving between the Member States the right to access the social security schemes of a hosting Member State and export already earned social security rights. In 1971, the original regulation was reformed into Regulation 1408/71.[7] In 2004, Regulation 1408/71 became Regulation 883/2004,[8] which covers not only

---

of movement for workers and social policy; 05.20 social policy; number of acts. Both legislation in force and not in force were included. As noted on the webpage of EUR-LEX consolidated legislation, the database is still in an 'experimental phase' and some references may be missing. However, a compilation of social policy legislation over time gives us an insights into the evolvement and type of regulatory instruments.

[6] Regulations and directives are the two main binding legal acts in EU decision-making. A regulation shall be applied in its entirety across the EU and is directly binding, i.e. it does not have to be implemented by national law first. A directive sets outs the goals that the EU Member States must achieve, but the Member States have to adopt national legal instruments on how to reach these goals, i.e. the directive has to be implemented by national law first.

[7] Regulation 1408/71, n. 5 in this chapter.

[8] Regulation (EC) 883/2004 of the European Parliament and of the Council of 29 April 2004 on the coordination of social security systems.

workers and self-employed individuals but all EU citizens and their family members. Also in the early days of European integration, Regulation 1612/68[9] was adopted, granting migrant workers the right to the social advantages of a hosting Member State. Both Regulations constitute major interventions in the organising principles of the welfare states, which have traditionally been based on demarcating principles of territoriality, residence and/or national citizenship.[10] In essence they build up a system of transnational solidarity where Member States are obliged to protect one another's citizens against social risks if they come to work and reside. Rights are, however, subject to certain conditions which have continuously been negotiated and interpreted by the European institutions and within the Member States. Important here is the Residence Directive 2004/38 which sets out the link between the right to reside and access to welfare benefits for the European migrant.[11] The directive lays down that one has the right to reside as long as one is not an 'unreasonable burden' on the social system of a hosting Member State.[12] However, the Directive does not define 'unreasonable burden'. As noted by Thym, the EU legislature is likely to have deliberately left the specific 'unreasonable burden' provision open and ambiguous as to allow for discrepancy.[13]

Setting the personal scope of a European Social Union, we can identify an expansive phase in EU politics, running approximately from the introduction of Union citizenship with the Maastricht Treaty in 1993 and peaking with the 2004 adoption of the Residence Directive and Regulation 883/2004 and the grand enlargement of that year. Shortly after, new political tunes sound increasingly loud. The no votes in France and the Netherlands to the constitutional Treaty expressed public concerns with the service

---

[9] Now Regulation (EU) 492/2011 of the European Parliament and of the Council of 5 April 2011 on freedom of movement for workers within the Union.

[10] R. Cornelissen, 'The Principle of Territoriality and the Community Regulations on Social Security (Regulations 1408/71 and 574/72)' (1996) 33 *Common Market Law Review* 439; R. Cornelissen, '25 Years of Regulation (EEC) No. 1408/71. Its Achievements and Its Limits.', in Swedish National Social Insurance Board (ed.), *25 Years of Regulation (EEC) No. 1408/71 for Migrant Workers – Past Experiences, Present Problems and Future Perspectives* (Swedish National Social Insurance Board); A. Christensen and M. Malmstedt, 'Lex Loci Laboris versus Lex Loci Domicilii-An Inquiry into the Normative Foundations of European Social Security Law' (2000) 2 *European Journal of Social Security* 69; D.S. Martinsen, 'The Europeanization of Welfare – The Domestic Impact of Intra-European Social Security' (2005) 43 *Journal of Common Market Studies* 1027.

[11] Directive 2004/38/EC of the European Parliament and of the Council of 29 April 2004 on the right of citizens of the Union and their family members to move and reside freely within the territory of the Member States.

[12] As stated in the Directive's Article 7 (1) b and Article 14 (1).

[13] D. Thym, 'The Elusive Limits of Solidarity: Residence Rights of and Social Benefits for Economically Inactive Union Citizens' (2015) 52 *Common Market Law Review* 17, p. 26.

directive's social impact, personalised as the 'Polish plumber' and the political campaigns 'the resurgence of nationalist and welfare chauvinist sentiments'.[14] A free movement–welfare cleavage between old and new Member States has become increasingly expressed, with political positions against 'welfare tourism' expressed in EU-15, viewed in the new Member States as 'irrational', 'short-sighted', and protectionist.[15] The situation came to a peak just before summer 2016 when the UK decided to leave the EU and thus cast the European Community into its most severe crisis ever. Free movement of persons and the right to cross-border welfare were debated fiercely in the UK, and have been pointed out as a main reason for why the UK voted to leave.[16] The scope and limits of Social Europe has become high politics. The course of legal integration suggests a similar turn from an expansive reading of Union citizenship to a more restrictive approach. Dougan finds that between 1998 and 2008, the course of legal integration extended the application of Union citizenship on the basis of Treaty.[17] With the *Sala* case in 1998,[18] the Court initiated a judicial vision of Union citizenship as a fundamental status of Member State nationals.[19] The vision was further developed and extended in the *Grzelczyk*[20] and *Baumbast*[21] cases among others, granting Union citizens' rights of residence and equal treatment, as well as access to the welfare schemes of a hosting Member State, despite being economically inactive. In these cases the Court emphasised the fundamental status of Union citizenship as laid down in the primary law of the Treaty; 'a citizen of the Union enjoy a right of residence by direct application of Article 18(1) EC'.[22] From 2008 onwards the Court

---

[14] A. Hemerijck, *Changing Welfare States* (Oxford University Press, 2013), p.320.

[15] D.S. Martinsen, and H. Vollaard, 'Implementing Social Europe in Times of Crises: Re-established Boundaries of Welfare?' (2014) 37 *West European Politics* 677.

[16] V.J. Reenen, 'The Aftermath of the Brexit Vote – the Verdict from a Derided Expert' (2016) available at: blogs.lse.ac.uk/politicsandpolicy/the-aftermath-of-the-brexit-vote-a-verdict-from-those-of-those-experts-were-not-supposed-to-listen-to/ (accessed 12 October 2016).

[17] M. Dougan, 'The Bubble that Burst: Exploring the Legitimacy of the Case Law on the Free Movement of Union Citizens', in M. Adams, H. De Waele, J. Meeusen, and G. Straetmans (eds), *Judging Europes's Judges. The Legitimacy of the Case Law of the European Court of Justice* (Hart, 2013).

[18] ECJ, judgment of 12 May 1998 in *María Martínez Sala* v *Freistaat Bayern*, C-85/96, EU:C:1998:217.

[19] Dougan, n. 17 in this chapter, at p. 133.

[20] ECJ, judgment of 20 September 2001 in *Rudy Grzelczyk* v *Centre public d'aide sociale d'Ottignies-Louvain-la-Neuve*, C-184/99, EU:C:2001:458.

[21] ECJ, judgment of 17 September 2002 in *Baumbast and R* v *Secretary of State for the Home Department*, C-413/99, EU:C:2002:493.

[22] See Advocate General Geelhoed, opinion of 5 July 2001 in *Baumbast and R* v *Secretary of State for the Home Department*, C-413/99, EU:C:2001:385.

has, however, embarked on a more restrictive course. In the *Förster*[23] and *Vatsouras*[24] cases, the Court examines the more restrictive formulations of secondary law, as contained in Directive 2004/38, derogating from Union citizens' general right to equal treatment.[25] The more restrictive judicial approach has become even more notable in the recent caselaw of *Dano*, *Alimanovic* and *García-Nieto*.[26] In the *Dano* case, the Court apparently took further note of political concerns, when ruling that an economically inactive citizen like Ms Dano was not entitled to equal treatment, did not have the right to non-contributory cash benefits under German law and did not have a right to reside under Directive 2004/38. The *Alimanovic* case follows the same line. Here, the Court ruled that jobcentre Neukölnn was right in terminating the imbursement of social assistance to Ms Alimanovic and her daughter after six months unemployment. It is striking that here the Court based its restrictive reading of the right to equal treatment on secondary law, whereas the fundamental status of Union citizenship as stated in primary law recedes into the background. Also the later case *García-Nieto and Others* continues the restrictive interpretation of EU citizens' access to social assistance despite being family members of an EU worker, hereby adding 'another dimension to the realisation that the heyday of a justice-driven EU social citizenship is behind us'.[27]

A more restrictive phase in political and judicial terms is thus identifiable in the evolvement of a European Social Union and its core features, meaning the free movement of persons, the right to cross-border welfare and equal treatment.[28] The Court and the Commission have proven rather responsive to

---

[23] ECJ, judgment of 18 November 2008 in *Jacqueline Förster v Hoofddirectie van de Informatie Beheer Groep*, C-158/07, EU:C:2008:630.

[24] ECJ, judgment of 4 June 2009 in *Athanasios Vatsouras v Arbeitsgemeinschaft* (ARGE), C-22/08, EU:C:2009:344.

[25] Dougan, n. 17 in this chapter, at p. 140.

[26] ECJ, judgments of 11 November 2014 in *Elisabeta Dano and Florin Dano v Jobcenter Leipzig*, C-333/13, EU:C:2014:2358; of 26 March 2015 in *Jobcenter Berlin Neukölln v Nazifa Alimanovic and Others*, C-67/14, EU:C:2015:210; and of 25 February 2016 in *Vestische Arbeit Jobcenter Kreis Recklinghausen v Jovanna García-Nieto and Others*, C-299/14, EU:C:2016:114.

[27] D. Kramer, 'Short-term Residence, Social Benefits and the Family; an Analysis of Case C-299/14 (*García-Nieto and Others*)' (2016) available at: europeanlawblog.eu/?p=3120 (accessed 12 October 2016).

[28] See Dougan, n. 17 in this chapter; E. Spaventa, 'Earned Citizenship – Understanding Union Citizenship through Its Scope', in D. Kochenov (ed.), *EU Citizenship and Federalism: the Role of Rights* (Cambridge University Press, 2015); N.N. Shuibhne, 'Limits Rising, Duties Ascending: The Changing Legal Shape of Union Citizenship' (2015) 52 *Common Market Law Review* 889; and H. Verschueren, 'Preventing "Benefit Tourism" in the EU: A Narrow or Broad Interpretation of the Possibilities Offered by the ECJ in Dano?' (2015) 52 *Common Market Law Review* 363.

public and political concerns, former visions for European citizenship have been shaken and rights have become more complex and differentiated. At the same time, EU politics has moved 'permissive consensus' to 'constraining dissensus'.[29] Specifically, as notable from public opinion, politicisation of EU citizens' rights to welfare in a hosting Member State has been on the rise.[30]

18.4 LEGISLATING POSTING OF WORKERS

Regulating posting of workers has historically been and still is a politically conflictual part of Social Europe.[31] As cross-border welfare, regulating posting of workers intersects the internal market and social policy. The politics of regulating workers posted in another Member State dates back to the 1980s when the relation between public procurement regulation and the internal market was first debated.[32] The trade unions in the construction sector demanded a social clause in the public procurement regulations. The unions wanted the clause to be in line with the ILO Convention 94, meaning that posting firms would comply with the working conditions and collective agreements of hosting countries. But at that time, the Council was not ready to adopt a mandatory social clause.

The European Commission had, however, noted the concerns of the construction sector and in its 1991 social action programme, it stated that it would propose a separate directive on the posting of workers.[33] In the social action programme, the Commission also stated that it would propose a principle of chain liability to guard the social rights of posted workers in subcontracting. In its proposal for the posting of workers directive, chain liability was, however,

---

[29] L. Hooghe, and G. Marks, 'A Postfunctionalist Theory of European Integration: From Permissive Consensus to Constraining Dissensus' (2009) 39 *British Journal of Political Science* 1.

[30] M. Blauberger, A. Heindlmaier, D. Kramer, D.S. Martinsen, J.S. Thierry, A. Schenk, and B. Werner, 'ECJ Judges Read the Morning Papers. Explaining the Turnaround of European Citizenship Jurisprudence', Miami EUSA conference paper 4–6 May 2017 (on file with the author).

[31] The empirics of this section is based on chapter 6 of D.S. Martinsen, *An Ever More Powerful Court? The Political Constraints of Legal Integration in the European Union* (Oxford University Press, 2015).

[32] J. Cremers, J.E. Dølvik, and G. Bosch, 'Posting of Workers in the Single Market: Attempts to Prevent Social Dumping and Regime Competition in the EU' (2007) 38 *Industrial Relations Journal* 6.

[33] E. Kolehmainen, 'The Directive Concerning the Posting of Workers: Synchronization of the Functions of National Legal Systems' (1998) 20 *Comparative Labour Law and Policy Journal* 71; Martinsen, n. 31 in this chapter.

taken out.[34] Apparently, the Commission assessed back then that a principle of chain liability was not feasible.

The Commission's proposal was negotiated for no less than five years and marked by deep conflicts internally in the Council but also between Council members and the Commission. Fierce disagreements were thus notable between internal market and social preferences, between posting and hosting Member States, between EU regulation and national law and practices and along more ideological lines between left and right. In addition posting of workers regulation has been marked by fierce political reactions against the judicial interpretations of the ECJ and the EU legislature.

When the original posting of workers directive was negotiated, the *Rush Portuguesa* case[35] from 1990 was a crucial reference point. Back then the Court had concluded that Community law did not preclude Member States from applying national labour law or collective agreements onto posting firms. Hosting Member States thus used the case as a justification for enacting national labour law onto posted workers.[36] The Commission took a different position, aiming to modify the impact of the case law, which the Commission found to work against the internal market principles.

In its original proposal, the Commission proposed an article 3.2 according to which workers posted for less than three months, would be subject to the home Member State's labour laws.[37] Political negotiations came to centre on the scope of Article 3. The EP was until 1993 only involved through the cooperation procedure. With the Maastricht Treaty it, however, gained co-legislator status. However, the EP still influenced early negotiations. The EP argued that the three months period where home Member State's legislation should be applicable was unacceptable in social terms and should be reduced to one month. The Commission accepted this view and presented a new proposal June 1993,[38] reducing the period to one month.[39]

The new proposal was, however, not welcomed by the majority of Council's members. In the finally adopted version, the period of which home Member State's legislation would be applicable was reduced from one month to eight days. Furthermore, in particular Finland, Germany, Austria, Luxembourg,

---

[34] COM(91)230 *Proposal for a Council Directive Concerning the Posting of Workers in the Framework of the Provision of Services* (Brussels, 1 August 1991).

[35] ECJ, judgment of 27 March 1990 in *Rush Portuguesa*, C–113/89, EU:C:1990:142.

[36] P. Davies, 'The Posted Workers Directive and the EC Treaty' (2002) 31 *Industrial Law Journal* 98, p. 300.

[37] See article 3.2 of the original proposal COM(91)230, n. 34 in this chapter, at p. 22.

[38] COM(93)225, *Amended Proposal for a Council Directive Concerning the Posting of Workers in the Framework of the Provision of Services* (Brussels, 15 June 1993).

[39] Martinsen, n. 31 in this chapter, at p. 192.

and France pushed for a wider application of the host country's national labour laws or their collective agreements.[40] This led to a fundamental change of the Directive's Article 3. Article 3(1) established which laws of the host Member State should be applied to posted workers, particularly those regarding minimum wages, working time, and paid annual leave. The Council majority added another 8 subparagraphs to the 3.1 and 3.2 originally part of the Commission's proposal. Article 3.1 came to set out the floor of protection – and the other subparagraphs added on. In particular article 3.7, 3.8, and 3.10 were important. Article 3.7 established that the floor of protection in Article 3.1 'shall not prevent application of terms and conditions of employment which are more favourable to workers'. Article 3.8 added that rights could also be derived from collective agreements' not only from legislation. Finally, Article 3.10 allowed the hosting Member State to take further measures in relation to posted workers than those laid down in article 3.1. Article 3.10 has been regarded as the article which made Article 3.1 a non-exhaustive, open list of measures.[41]

In December 1996, the posting of workers directive was adopted.[42] As a result of a political battle between internal market principles and social protection, it can be argued that the adopted directive foremost focused on the latter. The directive can thus be regarded as a major achievement for Social Europe, but one which relies much on justifying and protecting national schemes in an internal market.

A decade later, this agreement on where to strike the balance between internal market and national social protection was severely challenged by the ECJ.

18.5 LEGAL CHALLENGES AND POLITICAL RESPONSES

Known as the 'Laval quartet', the famous four cases *Viking, Laval, Rüffert,* and *Commission v Luxembourg* were ruled between the late 2007 and the summer of 2008.[43] In the cases, the European Court gave more consideration to the free movement principles against national labour regulation. In the *Viking* case, the Court ruled that the right to strike can only be exercised within

---

[40] See Kolehmainen, n. 33 in this chapter.
[41] Kolehmainen, n. 33 in this chapter, at p. 86.
[42] Directive 96/71/EC of the European Parliament and the Council of 16 December 1996 concerning the posting of workers in the framework of the provision of services [1996] OJ L 018.
[43] ECJ, judgments of 11 December 2007 in *The International Transport Workers' Federation and The Finish Seamen's Union ('Viking')*, C-438/05, EU:C:2007:772; of 18 December 2007 in *Laval un Partneri*, C-341/05, EU:C:2007:809; of 3 April 2008 in *Rüffert*, C-346/06, EU:C:2008:189; and of 19 June 2008 in *Commission v Luxembourg*, C-319/06, EU:C:2008:350.

certain limits. In the *Laval* case, the Court followed suit and concluded that the Treaty's Article 49 (now Article 56 TFEU) and Article 3 of the posting of workers' directive meant that a trade union could not force a posting firm to sign a collective agreement more favourable than the minimum conditions set in the posting of workers directive. The *Rüffert* case laid down that the public procurement act in Lower Saxony was against Community law. And in the last case *Commission v Luxembourg*, the Commission found that Luxembourg had not transposed Articles 3.1 and 3.10 of the posting of workers directive correctly, having imposed too many national standards on posting firms. The Court had its own view on Article 3.10, laying down that since the article constituted a derogation from principle of freedom to provide services, it had to be interpreted in a strict manner, which Luxembourg had not.[44]

The Laval quartet thus tipped the balance towards the internal market. Political responses, however, came forcefully and from different institutions. First, the European Trade Union Confederation (ETUC) and national trade unions responded with fierce criticism. ETUC proclaimed that the Court 'had confirmed a hierarchy of norms, with market freedoms highest in the hierarchy and the fundamental rights of collective bargaining and action in second place'.[45] The European social partners wanted the European legislators to respond by unambiguously clarify that economic freedoms must respect fundamental social rights.

Secondly, the EP took a strong position against the rulings and became a leading force in demanding political action. When Jose Manuel Barroso ran for his second term as President of the European Commission, the left wing of the EP demanded that in order to support him, he should promise to propose a revision of the posting of workers' directive and bring a solution to the 'case law problem'.

44 For a more detailed examination of the cases, see for example, A.C.L. Davies, 'One Step Forward, Two Steps Back? The Viking and Laval Cases in the ECJ' (2008) 37 *Industrial Law Journal* 126; C. Kilpatrick, 'Laval's Regulatory Conundrum: Collective Standard-setting and the Court's New Approach to Posted Workers' (2009) 34 *European Law Review* 844; C. Joerges, and F. Rödl, 'Informal Politics, Formalised Law and the "Social Deficit" of European Integration: Reflections after the Judgements of the ECJ in Viking and Laval' (2009) 15 *European Law Journal* 1; J. Malmberg, 'The Impact of the ECJ Judgements on Viking, Laval, Rüffert and Luxembourg on the Practice of Collective Bargaining and the Effectiveness of Social Action' (2010) *Directorate General for Internal Policies Study*, PE 440.275; M. Blauberger, 'With Luxembourg in Mind ... the Remaking of National Policies in the Face of ECJ Jurisprudence' (2012) 19 *Journal of European Public Policy* 109; C. Barnard, 'EU Employment Law and the European Social Model: The Past, the Present and the Future' (2014) 67 *Current Legal Problems* 199; D. Seikel, 'Class Struggle in the Shadow of Luxembourg. The Domestic Impact of the European Court of Justice's Case Law on the Regulation of Working Conditions' (2015) 22 *Journal of European Public Policy* 1166.
45 European Social Partners, 'ETUC Position Paper' (2010).

In September 2009, standing before the EP, Barroso thus committed himself to deliver on the case law problem.[46]

18.6 LEGISLATIVE POLITICS IN A POST-LISBON SETTING

Despite the declared commitment from the Commission's president, it took another 2.5 years for the Commission to present its new proposals. It proved difficult to form a common position internally in the Commission. Due to the salience of the issue, the college of Commissioners' was involved, as was the President. Furthermore, DG Internal Market, Industry, Entrepreneurship and SMEs and DG Employment, Social Affairs and Inclusion disagreed on the content of the proposal. Also the European social partners tried to influence the agenda-setting of the proposal.[47]

On 21 March 2012, the Commission was, however, finally ready to present two documents: (1) a proposal for the so-called Monti II Regulation,[48] and (2) a proposal for an enforcement directive on the posting of workers.[49]

The Monti II proposal was a regulatory response to the *Viking* and *Laval* case law and aimed to clarify under which conditions the right to collective action could be exercised within the internal market. The proposal, however, proved to be short-lived. The Lisbon Treaty had empowered the national parliaments with an Early Warning Mechanism (EWM).[50] The mechanism gives parliaments the competence to issue reasoned opinions within eight weeks after a new proposal has been presented by the Commission. If one-third of the national parliaments raise an objection against a proposal and reason this objection in the principle of subsidiarity, the Commission have to reconsider the proposal and decide whether to withdraw it, change it or maintain it.

Although the national parliaments have many times issued reasoned opinions, the Monti II proposal was the first time they managed to pass the one-third threshold and do so within the eight week deadline. It was thus the

---

[46] European Parliament 'Minutes of the Meeting of 14 June 2010' (2010) available at: www.europarl.europa.eu/RegData/organes/bureau/proces_verbal/2010/06-14/BUR_PV(2010)06-14_EN.pdf (accessed 13 October 2016).

[47] Martinsen, n. 31 in this chapter, at p. 200.

[48] COM(2012)130 *Proposal for a Council Regulation on the Exercise of the Right to Take Collective Action within the Context of the Freedom of Establishment and the Freedom to Provide Services* (Brussels, 23 March 2012), which is named after the former commissioner and former Italian prime minister Mario Monti.

[49] COM(2012)131 *Proposal for a Directive of the European Parliament and of the Council on the Enforcement of Directive 96/71/EC Concerning the Posting of Workers in the Framework of the Provision of Services* (Brussels, 21 March 2012).

[50] For the EWM mechanism, see Article 12 of the Lisbon Treaty and the Protocol (no. 2) on the application of the principles of subsidiarity and proportionality, articles 6 and 7.

first time that the national parliaments threw the 'yellow card'. Although the Commission did not officially agree that its proposal was in conflict with subsidiarity, it decided to withdraw its proposal on 12 September 2012. Monti II was out of the picture.

The EU legislators were thus left with the proposal for an enforcement directive. Although it had been important for the Commission not to open up for a full revision of the posting of workers directive, the enforcement proposal proved to be conflictual. Especially two provisions in the proposal divided the Member States and the Members of the EP: Article 9 dealt with the list of national control measures that a host Member State can take to secure that a posting firm complies with national rules and agreements. The Commission here proposed a closed list of control measures. Article 12 put chain liability onto the Community negotiation table: the Commission proposed a principle, termed as 'joint and several liability'. According to this principle the main contractor would be responsible for the first subcontractor regarding the pay of minimum wages, social security contributions, and taxes. Joint liability should apply to the construction sector only.

Long and difficult negotiations followed. The Polish member of the European Peoples Party Danuta Jazlowiecka became EP rapporteur on the proposal. Her position was that Article 9 should be maintained as a closed list, but Article 12 should be deleted. Jazlowiecka's draft report was opposed to by the majority of the Employment and Social Affairs committee, which was responsible for the dossier and also faced considerable opposition within the EP as a whole. In particular, the Socialists and Democrats (S&D) group was against the rapporteur's approach, wanting an open list of control measures and binding rule of joint and several liability across sectors, meaning measures that are not limited to the construction sector.

Also in the Council of Ministers disagreements loomed large. A conflict line was drawn mainly between hosting and posting states. On one side, the majority of old Member States assumed the position of hosting Member States and defended their right to control posting companies. On the other side, the Eastern European Member States and the UK defended the internal market; favouring Article 9 as proposed by the Commission but opposing Article 12 on joint and several liability regardless of the sector.

Fierce negotiations were held within and between the EU legislators, crystallising different views on the balance between economic freedoms and social protection. Up until the Council's Employment, Social Policy, Health, and Consumer Affairs configuration meeting in October 2013, the emerging common position seemed to be a non-exhaustive list of control measures combined with either a voluntary principle or no principle of joint liability.

However, in particular France kept insisting on a binding principle of joint liability, whereas Poland and the UK took a firm position against.

The special relationship formed between Poland and the UK was suddenly harmed. Late November 2013, Cameron came out with his featured article 'Free movement within Europe needs to be less free'.[51] Although Cameron addressed social security for migrant workers and not posting of workers as such, Poland found the article inappropriate and it came to influence the negotiations on the posting of workers. Cameron's statements influenced Council decision making on the enforcement directive, and in this late stage of negotiations Poland shifted side over to France, away from the UK. France had convinced Poland of the importance to signal unity for a Social Europe.[52] With the Polish change of position, a compromise could be established in the Council and with the EP. On 15 May 2014 the Enforcement Directive of the posting of workers was adopted, with a non-exhaustive list of control measures and a binding principles of joint and several liability for the first subcontractor in the construction sector.[53] The adopted Article 12 also lays down that chain responsibility may be adopted for all other sectors. An important exemption is however also part of the provision. If the contractor has shown due diligence as defined by national law, the Member State may decide not to hold the contractor liable.

The enforcement directive for the posting of workers is thus the latest legislative result within Social Europe. The Juncker Commission has in its 2016 work programme promised new initiatives and the current President has launched a more social agenda, where posted workers should be ensured 'the same pay for the same job at the same place'.[54] Thus, the Commission announced a 'labour mobility package' was under way. However, key parts hereof have been paralysed by political developments. The revision of Regulation 883/2004 was postponed to after the British referendum on UK EU membership and was presented by the Commission on 13 December 2016. On 8 March 2016, the Commission presented a proposal for revising the posting of workers directive.[55]

---

[51] D. Cameron, 'Free Movement within Europe Needs to be Less Free', *Financial Times*, 26 November 2016, available at: www.ft.com/content/add36222-56be-11e3-ab12-00144feabdc0 (accessed 13 October 2016).

[52] Martinsen, n. 31 in this chapter, at p. 216.

[53] Directive 2014/67/EU of the European Parliament and of the Council of 15 May 2014 on the Enforcement of Directive 96/71/EC Concerning the Posting of Workers in the Framework of the Provision of Services and Amending Regulation (EU) No 1024/2012 on Administrative Cooperation through the Internal Market Information System [2015] OJ L 159/11.

[54] Quoted in A. Eriksson 'Eastern EU States Lose Battle on Workers' Pay', *EU Observer*, 20 July 2016, available at: euobserver.com/economic/134433 (accessed 13 October 2016).

[55] COM(2016)128 *Directive of the European Parliament and of the Council Amending Directive 96/71/EC of The European Parliament and of the Council of 16 December 1996 Concerning the Posting of Workers in the Framework of the Provision of Services* (Brussels 8 March 2016).

However, 13 parliamentary chambers[56] submitted a reasoned opinion to the Commission, finding its proposal against the principle of subsidiarity. Together these reasoned opinions constituted another yellow card for the Commission to consider. However, in contrast to the Monti II proposal, the Commission this time decided to maintain its proposal, which is currently under negotiations. The Commission insisted on the need to re-regulate posting of workers, and this time its proposal is clearer in its social content than the 2012 proposals. Also this time, the proposal is supported both by ETUC and the S&D group of the EP. When explaining the decision to maintain the proposal despite the yellow card, the Social Affairs Commissioner Thyssen emphasised the need to 'build bridges' between EU workers and that the UK exit had taught the Commission the need to provide more social protection in the internal market in order to address many Europeans fear of globalisation.[57] A more social turn in the Commission's position is thus noted. It remains to be seen how a compromise can be established between hosting and sending Member States in the Council as well as with the EP.

18.7 CONCLUSION

The European Union has over time developed a social side to it in a delicate balance between internal market and social protection, between supranational and national competences. In setting the de facto scope and limits of Social Europe, legislative politics play a key role. First because it has the capacity to adopt binding measures, which the Member States are obliged to implement and the European Union can enforce. Secondly, because they are the venue through which political agreements can be adopted by the EU majoritarian institutions. This is crucial when we consider the legitimacy of a European Social Union. Building up a European Social Union not only needs supranational devices,[58] it also needs a political mandate to ensure legitimacy.

The social implications of the internal market and the economic governance of the European Union stands out – also to the voters. EU social regulations is increasingly politicised. As demonstrated by the case of posting of workers regulation, also EU legislative politics has its clear conflict lines. However, when looking at the development of EU social legislation over

---

[56] A reasoned opinion was submitted by: Bulgaria National Assembly, the Czech Republic Chamber of Deputies and the Senate, Denmark Folketinget, Estonia Riigikogu, Croatia Hrvatski sabor, Hungary National Assembly, Lithuania Saeima, Letland Seimas, Poland Sejm and Senate, Rumania Chamber of Deputies and Senate.

[57] Quoted in Eriksson, n. 54 in this chapter.

[58] Vandenbroucke, n. 2 in this chapter.

time it becomes clear that most decisions are taken without the EP. Also the European Commission has a decisive regulatory role.

As other contributions to this volume have pointed out, the major decisions on the scope and limits of a European Social Union are not taken by means of the classic Community Method and its majoritarian institutions. This fact calls a set of fundamental challenges and asymmetries to the fore, which constitute considerable obstacles not only to a European Social Union but also to the European Union itself:

(1) Decisions are sometimes taken by non-majoritarian institutions, by the few, by the experts. A European Social Union cannot emerge out of Brussels talking to Brussels. It cannot be imposed by a technocratic logic. The European Central Bank has appeared on the scene with a major say on national welfare policies. At the same time the European parliament and the national parliaments are not involved in main decisions taken, but as the posting of workers case demonstrates they will make noise where they can if not included.

(2) As a result of decisions taken by the few, we see a process sometimes remote from the electorates but at the same time the impact of decisions taken fall onto the many. In particular as a result of the new tools of economic governance, European integration has become even more asymmetric in that decisions are taken by the heads of states in the European Council and empower the European Commission to evaluate the fiscal policies of Member States[59] but without ensuring parliamentary accountability through the national parliaments or the EP.

(3) What about the European Court then? Can it not be a driver of social rights? The European judiciary has been argued to be a successful driver of social rights, compensating for the inabilities of EU legislative politics.[60] However, in recent judgements the Court has continued the restrictive interpretations of Union citizens right to cross-border welfare, no longer referring to the fundamental status of Union citizenship as set out in the Treaty but instead to the more restrictive content of secondary legislation, meaning directive 2004/38. As the chapter by Kornezov shows,[61] the Court lost the opportunity to apply the charter against the austerity measures. In addition, the Laval quartet was seen as a severe

[59] K. Anderson, *Social Policy in the European Union* (Palgrave Macmillan, 2015).

[60] J.A. Caporaso, and S. Tarrow, 'Polanyi in Brussels: Supranational Institutions and the Transnational Embedding of Markets' (2009) 63 *International Organization* 593.

[61] A. Kornezov, 'Social Rights, the Charter and the ECHR – Caveats, Austerity and Other Disasters', Chapter 16 in this volume.

non-social move by stating internal market principles above national labour law. In addition, the Court is a non-majoritarian institution and as such it does not have democratic legitimacy as decision-maker. The ability of legislative politics to speak back to the Court and adjust secondary legislation in line with the political majority is therefore important from a democratic and legitimacy point of view.

To conclude, for a European Social Union to turn into reality it inarguably needs a political mandate and political ownership. It needs to progress in a politically accountable manner. It cannot happen without political voice – but if disregarding its need for a political mandate, political voice against it may come to sound increasingly loud.

19

(B)Remains of the Day: Brexit and EU Social Policy

Catherine Barnard

Democracy is something for a bygone era. The world is far too complicated a place now for universal suffrage and such like ... The man in the street can't be expected to know enough about politics, economics, world commerce and what have you. And why should he?

— Lord Darlington, *Remains of the Day*.[1]

19.1 INTRODUCTION

On 23 June 2016 52 per cent of voters took the momentous decision for the UK to leave the European Union. Brexit it was. While many issues influenced the British (English) voters, immigration – or rather the inability of the UK to control its borders – was a key factor.[2] Many workers in low-skilled, low paid work blamed migrants for keeping their wages low. Those without work resented migrant workers doing jobs that they might have been able to do. There was anger, too, about the fact that migrants were able to claim benefits on the same terms as British nationals, and that the children of migrants could go to school in classrooms which were already full, speaking a language which was not English.

Fears about migration, fanned by a Eurosceptic press that willingly conflated EU and non-EU migration, provided a focus for what in fact were more indeterminate, but nevertheless very real, concerns about the increasing precarity

---

[1] K. Ishiguro, *The Remains of the Day* (Faber & Faber, 2005 edn., 1989), pp. 208–209.
[2] Ashcroft found that approximately 80 per cent of those who thought that immigration as mostly a force for good voted to Remain, while a similar proportion of those who thought of it as a force for ill voted to Leave, see lordashcroftpolls.com/2016/06/how-the-united-kingdom-voted-and-why/ (accessed 13 December 2016). Scotland regularly claims it needs migration to help build its population.

of the lives of many people,[3]. This precarity takes two main forms: financial and social. *Financial precarity* concerns a lack of guaranteed income, a lack of certainty over what work will be provided and when, and an inability to save for old age, all exacerbated by a rise in zero hours contracts and false self-employment with the resulting uncertain income. *Social precarity* involves lack of protection against the vicissitudes of life such as ill health, unemployment, and pregnancy. This precarity has, for many, resulted in a lack of a sense of security and self-worth.[4] The Brexit vote was therefore, for many, a vote of protest and frustration about their personal situation.

Thus, it was a fundamental pillar of the construction of the EU – free movement of persons – and its corollary, the principle of equal treatment, which led, at least in part, to the decision to vote to leave the EU. Migration provided the focus of public dissatisfaction, a vector for their anger often about other matters such as precarity. The EU's failure to respond to public concerns about migration, in particular at the Brussels summit in February 2016, provided a further cause for resentment. But the focus on migration was largely a distraction, diverting attention away from the real problems generated by decades of under-investment in public services, especially in the declining regions.

What has this got to do with the EU? I will argue that the EU, while aware of some of the issues about precarious work and precarious lives, couldn't (due to lack of competence) and wouldn't (due to a lack of political will) respond. When it came to the crunch, the language of EU 'social policy' proved hollow. For some the emperor's new clothes were seen for what they were. For others the EU had failed to deal with their concerns: EU (social) policy was at best an irrelevance, at worst the epitome of all that was bad about the EU (interfering, bureaucratic, incomplete). Time had come to 'take back control'. Seventeen million people voted to leave the EU.

The chapter begins with assessing *what has been*: the economic and social situation in the UK and the rights given by the EU and the limits to those rights. It then considers the (limited) role social rights played in the referendum (Section 19.2). Next, the chapter looks at *what might have been*: what might and might not have made a difference to the outcome of the referendum campaign (Section 19.3). The chapter concludes with a consideration of *what the future holds* (Section 19.4).

---

[3] See generally G. Standing, *The Precariat: The New Dangerous Class* (Bloomsbury, 2014); see also Z. Adams and S. Deakin, 'Institutional Solutions to Precariousness and Inequality in Labour Markets' (2014) *CBR Working Paper Series*, 463.

[4] J. Popma, 'The Janus Face of the "New Ways of Work": Rise, Risks and Regulation of Nomadic Work' (2013) ETUI Working Paper, 7.

In adopting this structure, I have drawn inspiration from Kazuo Ishiguro's novel *The Remains of the Day*.[5] It tells the story of Stevens, an English butler who dedicated his life to the service of Lord Darlington, a gentleman amateur politician and an increasing Nazi sympathiser, in the interwar years. The novel opens with Stevens receiving a letter from a former colleague, the housekeeper Miss Kenton, describing her married life to another man. The letter prompts Stevens to contemplate the meaning and value of his service to Lord Darlington ('what has been') and the lost opportunities with Miss Kenton ('what might have been'). At the end of the novel, Stevens focuses on the 'remains of [his] day', namely his future service with his new employer and what is left of his own life in an evolving master/servant relationship. As some of the quotes used at the start of each section of this chapter show, this story has contemporary resonance and a relevance for a chapter which argues that a failure to respond to social change eventually causes a political earthquake.

Drawing on Ishiguro's novel may seem somewhat pretentious but, I would argue, it is relevant for the story of this chapter. Ishiguro himself railed against the outcome of the referendum in a piece for the *Financial Times* entitled 'The remains of the UK'.[6] The novel also, unwittingly, shines light on the addition of a new word to the lexicon. During the referendum campaign the term 'Brexit' became common parlance. The Remain campaign struggled to come up with an equivalent; the uncatchy 'B(R)emain' was the best it could do (hence the title of this contribution).[7]

19.2 WHAT HAS BEEN

In this age of electricity and modern heating systems, there is no need at all to employ the sorts of numbers [of servants] necessary even a generation ago.

– Stevens, *Remains of the Day*.[8]

---

[5] Ishiguro, n. 1 in this chapter.

[6] K. Ishiguro, 'Kazuo Ishiguro on His Fears for Britain after Brexit', *Financial Times*, 2 July 2016, available at: www.ft.com/content/7877a0a6-3e11-11e6-9f2c-36b487ebd80a (accessed 13 December 2016).

[7] To this, post-referendum, has been added to its even uglier cousin, 'Bremoaner', a pejorative term describing those who object to Brexit or who point out difficulties with the process of leaving the EU.

[8] Ishiguro, n. 1 in this chapter, at p. 8.

19.2.1 INTRODUCTION

Social policy has long been used as an important tool to connect the public with the state. The development of education, health, and welfare policies form the core of the social contract between the state and its citizens. The EU, too, has tried to build a bridge between itself and EU citizens through the enactment of social rights – but so far only in the narrow field of employment law. In this section, I wish to argue that the broader context of precariousness in the UK was a major explanation for the Leave vote. Migration became the focus for these concerns, especially in those communities which witnessed a rapid increase in numbers of migrants (Section 19.2.2 below). Faced by these social forces, the EU's response seemed weak, even misplaced and inconsequential. The enactment of employment rights, while useful to many, diverted attention away from deep-seated social problems which in fact the EU lacked competence to deal with (Section 9.2.4).

19.2.2 THE UK LEVEL

19.2.2.1 *Financial Precarity*

With the benefit of hindsight, the seeds of the Leave vote had been sown years before the start of the referendum campaign. For some they were sown with the onset of austerity following the financial crisis beginning in 2008; for others it could be traced back to the mine closures precipitated by Conservative government policy in the 1980s, and the abandonment of some parts of the north. Whatever the origins, it is clear that the referendum took place in unhappy domestic circumstances. Consider the following factors.

First, there has been a significant decline in blue collar jobs. As Dillow puts it:

> In the last ten years we've seen big rises in 'professional occupations' and in managers, directors and senior officials – up by 23.3 per cent and 15.5 per cent respectively. But we have seen falls in secretarial and skilled jobs. And within the 'unskilled' occupations, there's been a shift from machine workers to care workers; this is partly due to the 3.5 per cent drop in manufacturing output during this period.[9]

---

[9] C. Dillow, 'On Job Polarization', *Stumbling and Mumbling*, 18 August 2016, available at: stumblingandmumbling.typepad.com/stumbling_and_mumbling/2016/08/on-job-polarization.html (accessed 13 December 2016).

Second, those in employment have witnessed a major increase in precarity: the rise in zero hours contracts (that is contracts which do not guarantee a minimum number of hours),[10] a shift from employee to self-employed status,[11] and the 'uberisation of the workforce.[12] Those working in certain sectors, such as the hotel industry, have been particularly badly affected.[13] Meanwhile, well-known employers have been seen to operate to the disadvantage of their staff: the retail giant, Sports Direct, had been avoiding paying the minimum wage;[14] the pensioners from BHS, another familiar face on the high street, suffered cuts to their pensions[15] before the company itself went under. Those from ethnic minority backgrounds have suffered in particular.[16]

All of this has fed into a growing sense of financial precarity and a feeling of powerlessness. This precarity was exacerbated by the reduction of employment rights at domestic level, in particular by making it harder for employees to claim unfair dismissal and by imposing fees for access to Employment Tribunals. Claims have since fallen by around 70 per cent.[17] The government

[10] M. Chandler, 'Contracts that Do Not Guarantee a Minimum Number of Hours: March 2016', Office for National Statistics, 9 March 2016, available at: www.ons.gov.uk/employmentand-labourmarket/peopleinwork/earningsandworkinghours/articles/contractsthatdonotguaranteeaminimumnumberofhours/march2016 (accessed 13 December 2016).

[11] See for example D. Newman, 'Deliveroo, the "gig" economy and employment rights', A Range of Reasonable Responses, 26 July 2016, available at: darrennewman.wordpress.com/2016/07/26/deliveroo-the-gig-economy-and-employment-rights/ (accessed 13 December 2016); and J. Ashton, 'James Ashton: Self-employed Are on the Rise but Pay the Price in Work Rights', *Evening Standard*, 15 September 2016, available at: www.standard.co.uk/comment/comment/james-ashton-selfemployed-are-on-the-rise-but-pay-the-price-in-work-rights-a3345826.html (accessed 13 December 2016).

[12] G. Jericho, 'The Dark Side of Uber: Why the Sharing Economy Needs Tougher Rules', *The Guardian*, 18 April 2016, available at: www.theguardian.com/business/grogonomics/2016/apr/18/uber-airbnb-sharing-economy-tougher-rules-australia (accessed 13 December 2016).

[13] Unite, 'Unethical London' (2016), available at: www.unitetheunion.org/campaigning/hotel-workers-deserve-a-living-wage/ (accessed 13 December 2016).

[14] S. Goodley and G. Ruddick, 'Sports Direct's Mike Ashley Admits Paying Staff Less than Minimum Wage', *The Guardian*, 7 June 2016, available at: www.theguardian.com/business/2016/jun/07/sports-direct-agrees-back-pay-deal-with-hmrc-minimum-wage (accessed 13 December 2016).

[15] S. Butler, 'BHS Pensioners Face Cuts to Payouts as Struggling Chain Goes into Insolvency', *The Guardian*, 9 March 2016, available at: www.theguardian.com/business/2016/mar/09/bhs-pensioners-face-cuts-to-payouts-insolvency (accessed 13 December 2016).

[16] Equality and Humans Rights Commission, 'Healing a Divided Britain: The Need for a Comprehensive Race Equality Strategy' (2016), available at: www.equalityhumanrights.com/sites/default/files/healing_a_divided_britain_-_the_need_for_a_comprehensive_race_equality_strategy_final.pdf (accessed 13 December 2016).

[17] Commons Select Committee, 'Access to Justice Damaged by courts and tribunals fees changes', Parliament, 17 June 2016, available at: www.parliament.uk/business/committees/committees-a-z/commons-select/justice-committee/news-parliament-2015/courts-and-tribunals-fees-report-published-16-17/.

has cut the financial support for those wishing to try other avenues of assistance. Take the case of the Employment Agency Standards Inspectorate. Its budget has been cut by 50 per cent since 2010, even as complaints rose by 21 per cent. With the Inspectorate's staff reduced to just two people, it failed to bring a single prosecution in 2016.[18]

The one area where the UK has improved employment protection – the introduction of the national living wage for the over 25s[19] – in fact risked exacerbating the situation because it may have created the perception that this would attract more EU migrants to the UK to the detriment of low-skilled British workers.

19.2.2.2 *Social Precarity*

More importantly, still, for the outcome of the referendum, the UK had been experiencing six years of austerity, leading to cuts in public services provided to the most vulnerable. The social consequences of this have been acute, especially for traditional labour voters, many of whom voted to leave the EU. The National Health Service – the closest that the UK comes to religion – is struggling under the burden of increasing demand.[20] A failure to deal with the chronic shortage of housing, both social housing and affordable homes,[21] has led many families to feel they are losers in a system which conspires to operate against their interests. Those on benefits have also suffered. The much publicised move to Universal Credit created real concerns that there would be losers.[22] The invasive testing for those on disability benefits

[18] European Public Service Union, 'Cuts at Agency Workers' Rights Inspectorate', Epsu.org, August 2016, available at: www.epsu.org/epsucob/2016-august-epsucobnews-10/cuts-agency-workers-rights-inspectorate (accessed 13 December 2016).

[19] In his 2015 budget, the Chancellor of the Exchequer announced a 'national living wage' – a 50p increase in the statutory minimum pay rate for the over-25s from April 2016, to £7.20 an hour (introduced through amendment to the NMW Regulations 2015), followed by a series of stepped increases expected to take the rate above £9 an hour by 2020.

[20] A. Grice, 'Theresa May's Biggest Challenge Will Come when People Realise Brexit Isn't Going to Save the NHS', *The Independent*, 10 August 2016, available at: www.independent.co.uk/voices/brexit-nhs-theresa-may-savings-health-350m-leave-biggest-challenge-managing-expectations-a7183146.html (accessed 13 December 2016); see also fullfact.org/health/accident-and-emergency-attendances-and-performance/ (accessed 13 December 2016).

[21] H. Agerholm, 'Government to Miss New Homes Target by 250,000 Shortfall, Charity Warns', *The Independent*, 24 August 2016, available at: www.independent.co.uk/news/uk/home-news/government-to-miss-their-new-homes-target-by-more-than-250000-shelter-warns-a7208146.html (accessed 13 December 2016); L. Judge, 'Can We Fix It? Solving Britain's Housing Crisis', Resolution Foundation, 26 Arpil 2016, available at: www.resolutionfoundation.org/publications/can-we-fix-it-solving-britains-housing-crisis/ (accessed 13 December 2016).

[22] P. Butler, DWP 'Punishing' Low-Paid Full-Time Workers under New Benefits Rule, *The Guardian*, 14 Arpil 2016, available at: www.theguardian.com/society/2016/apr/14/dwp-punishing-low-paid-full-time-workers-under-new-benefits-rule (accessed 13 December 2016). See also

has created fear.[23] Actually claiming the benefits is hard,[24] especially when faced with companies, employed to combat fraud on the benefits system, mis-applying the rules.[25] The numbers of people applying to food banks for help is at record levels.[26] Meanwhile, those seen as the cause of the crisis – the bankers – appeared untouched. None of this has anything to do with the EU, but the perception is that the 'state', that is to say, 'them', is failing the most vulnerable. Individuals felt worried, afraid, and let down. Migration became a convenient scapegoat: immigrants taking jobs, immigrants taking benefits. And, as we shall see below, for those living in areas which experienced a rapid increase in immigration their concerns about the pressure that immigration was putting on public services may well have been justified. Governments too often took the easy route, (subtly) blaming immigration as a way of avoid-ing admitting their own responsibility for decades of failure to invest in these declining areas.

Austerity has been the watchword of the Coalition government and then the Conservative government prior to 23 June 2016. The poor feel they have suffered the most. The fact the EU has also urged austerity, all well publicised on the British media, causing real hardship, particularly in Greece, has linked austerity measures in the UK with those in the EU.

N. Timmins, 'Universal Credit: from Disaster to Recovery' (2016), available at: www.institutefor-government.org.uk/sites/default/files/publications/5064%20IFG%20-%20Universal%20Credit%20 Publication%20WEB%20AW.pdf (accessed 13 December 2016).

[23] S. Malik, 'Minister Looking at Making It Harder for Sick and Disabled to Claim Benefits', *The Guardian*, 30 September 2013, available at: www.theguardian.com/society/2013/sep/30/iain-duncan-smith-sick-disabled-benefits (accessed 13 December 2016); F. Ryan, 'The Government Is Skewing Benefits Appeals against Disabled People', *The Guardian*, 17 May 2016, available at: www.theguardian.com/society/2016/may/17/government-skewing-benefits-appeals-process-against-disabled-people (accessed 13 December 2016).

[24] Anonymous, 'I'm a DWP Call Handler and Have No Time to Care about Your Disability Claim', *The Guardian*, 20 August 2016, available at: www.theguardian.com/public-leaders-network/2016/aug/20/work-pensions-disability-claim-call-handler-benefits-dwp (accessed 13 December 2016). See also N. Bloomer, 'The tactics the DWP uses to stack the odds against benefit claimants', politics.co.uk, 12 Aug. 2012, available at: www.politics.co.uk/comment-analysis/2016/08/12/how-the-dwp-stacks-the-odds-against-benefit-claimants (accessed 13 December 2016).

[25] A. Asthana, ''Reign of Terror' Tax Credit Company Loses HMRC Contract', *The Guardian*, 13 September 2016, available at: www.theguardian.com/money/2016/sep/13/reign-of-terror-tax-credit-company-loses-hmrc-contract (accessed 13 December 2016).

[26] The Trussel Trust, 'Foodbank Use Remains at Record High, Press Release of 15 April 2016, available at: www.trusselltrust.org/2016/04/15/foodbank-use-remains-record-high/ (accessed 13 December 2016); A. Chakrabortty, 'Life after Community Death: This Food Bank Has a Lesson for Labour', *The Guardian*, 30 August 2016, available at: www.theguardian.com/ commentisfree/2016/aug/30/life-after-community-death-food-bank-lesson-labour (accessed 13 December 2016).

The EU and the UK were connected in another way too. Both the UK and the EU have put increasing faith in the market to deliver. Unions and others on the left have complained bitterly about the marketisation of the NHS;[27] EU law, too, is seen to favour the market over the state. The much vaunted EU single *market* seems to confirm this. As O'Rourke has argued, 'Too much market and too little state invites a backlash.'[28] He concluded that the UK referendum campaign ended up becoming, to a very large extent, a debate about globalisation in its local, European manifestation. He added:

> Opponents of the treaty pointed to the outsourcing of jobs to cheap labour competitors in Eastern Europe, and to the famous Polish plumber. Predictably enough, professionals voted overwhelmingly in favour of the treaty, while blue-collar workers, clerical workers and farmers rejected it. The net result was a clear rejection of the Treaty.[29]

19.2.3 THE PROFILE OF THE LEAVE VOTER

The referendum – where every vote counted – gave those who felt left behind by deindustrialisation and globalisation an opportunity to be heard. These voters formed an unwitting coalition with social conservatives in places like Essex who objected to recent Conservative social reforms like the introduction of gay marriage,[30] and 'liberal leavers' who wanted to restore the UK's position as a global player.[31] Together these diverse groups delivered the most profound shock the European Union has ever felt. However, in this chapter I want to

---

[27] See for example B. Cooper, 'NHS Reform and the Hollow Marketisation Myth', *New Statesman*, 30 October 2014, available at: www.newstatesman.com/politics/2014/10/nhs-reform-and-hollow-marketisation-myth (accessed 13 December 2016).

[28] K. O'Rourke, 'The Lesson from Brexit Is That Too Much Market and Too Little State Invites a Backlash', Socialeurope.eu, 24 August 2016, available at: www.socialeurope.eu/2016/08/lesson-brexit-much-market-little-state-invites-backlash/ (accessed 13 December 2016). For an example of a decision to vote Leave because the EU is 'moving in an increasingly free market direction', see L. Elliott, 'Brexit Armageddon Was a Terrifying Vision – But It Simply Hasn't Happened', *The Guardian*, 20 August 2016, available at: www.theguardian.com/commentisfree/2016/aug/20/brexit-eu-referendum-economy-project-fear (accessed 13 December 2016).

[29] K. O'Rourke, 'The Lesson from Brexit Is that Too Much Market and Too Little State Invites a Backlash', Socialeurope.eu, 24 August 2016, available at: www.socialeurope.eu/2016/08/lesson-brexit-much-market-little-state-invites-backlash/ (accessed 13 December 2016).

[30] See also Bagehot, 'The new J-curve', *The Economist*, 11 June 2016, p. 34, available at: www.economist.com/news/britain/21700407-britains-flirtation-brexit-more-complicated-anti-globalisation-vote-new (accessed 13 December 2016), who argues that Leave voters included the lower middle class who feel economically safe enough to challenge the globalised establishment but not rich enough to be part of it.

[31] See EU Referendum: The Result in Maps and Charts, BBC News (June 24, 2016), available at: www.bbc.com/news/uk-politics-36616028 (accessed 13 December 2016).

focus on the first group: those who have been left behind. Matthew Goodwin puts it this way:

> Brexit ... owed less to the personal charisma of Boris Johnson [a leading Leave campaigner], the failings of [the then Prime Minister] David Cameron or the ambivalence of Jeremy Corbyn [Leader of the Opposition Labour party] than to a much deeper sense of angst, alienation and resentment among more financially disadvantaged, less well-educated and older Britons who are often only one financial crisis away from disaster. They are the voters of former industrial strongholds, like the northern towns of Barnsley, Mansfield, Stoke and Doncaster, Welsh towns like Merthyr Tydfil that once fuelled the industrial revolution, fading coastal towns such as Blackpool, Great Yarmouth and Castle Point, or blue-collar but aspirational places like Basildon, Havering and Thurrock.[32]

Goodwin contrasted two communities, Boston, a small, east coast port where 76 per cent voted to leave the EU, and Lambeth in London, the area that returned the strongest vote for Remain (79 per cent).[33] Boston, which has experienced significant migration from Central and Eastern Europe, is 'noticeable for economic deprivation. The median income in Boston is less than £17,000 and one in three people have no formal qualifications at all.' It is also 'filled with disadvantaged, working-class Britons who do not feel as though they have been winning from European integration, immigration, and globalization'. Life is remarkably different in Lambeth: 'Compared to Boston, there are more than twice as many professionals, nearly twice as many 18–30-year-olds and fewer than half as many working-class voters, pensioners and people with no qualifications. The average voter in Lambeth earns nearly £10,000 more each year than the average voter in Boston.'[34]

What has this got to do with the EU? Well everything and almost nothing.[35] The referendum was on the UK's continued membership of the EU but in

---

[32] M. Goodwin, 'Inequality, Not Personalities Drove Britain to Brexit', Politico.eu, 28 June 2016, available at: www.politico.eu/article/inequality-not-personalities-drove-britain-to-brexit/ (accessed 13 December 2016).

[33] Ibid.

[34] Ibid. See also Persaud, n. 63 in this chapter: the data reveal that there was an 'unusually positive correlation (+0.60) between the percentage of those who voted to leave in a Local Authority and the percentage of non-graduates in that Local Authority' and that 'The much-touted correlation between age and the Brexit vote was also positive, but more modestly so at +0.15. Young graduates voted heavily to remain and elder workers who didn't go to university voted heavily to leave.'

[35] On the more general question of whether the EU was to blame, see S. Deakin, 'Brexit, Labour Rights and Migration: Why Wisbech Matters to Brussels' (2016) 17 *German Law Journal* (Brexit Supplement) 14: 'deindustrialisation is largely something that the UK has brought

fact it had very little actually to do with the EU and quite a lot to do with decades of failures of UK government policy. Nevertheless, it might be asked why the EU's much vaunted social policy, introduced to help legitimise the EU in the eyes of its citizens, failed to respond to these social concerns. It is to this question that we now turn.

19.2.4 EU LEVEL

19.2.4.1 *The Rights*

It is certainly the case that the number and range of rights given to workers by EU law since 1957 has risen dramatically.[36] When the original Treaty was drafted, workers, as a factor of production, enjoyed free movement under Article 45 TFEU. The rights of free movement were seen as a safety valve: workers could move from one state where unemployment was high to work in another Member State where unemployment was much lower. They would benefit from the right of equal treatment. The Spaak report, accompanying the Treaty of Rome, envisaged migration could, however, be subject to some form of emergency brake; this was not taken up in the final version of the Treaty.

While the rights of migrant workers were clearly identified by the original Treaty, the position of *non*-migrant workers was little more than a footnote in the Treaty of Rome. Yes, the creation of the common, now single, market would enable them to enjoy an increase in the standard of living and greater prosperity, but, with the exception of equal pay, the original Treaty did not actually provide them with specific employment rights. However, by the early 1970s it became apparent that workers were disengaged from the EU project. The EU's response was to give them social rights. This led to the enactment of key directives in fields as diverse as mass redundancies (the right to be informed and consulted),[37] transfer of undertakings[38] (the right to maintain

---

upon itself, but which EU rules have done nothing to prevent, and have probably, on balance, exacerbated'.

[36] See further J. Kenner, *EU Employment Law from Rome to Amsterdam and Beyond* (Hart Publishing, 2002)

[37] Council Directive 75/129/EEC of 17 February 1975 on the approximation of the laws of the Member States relating to collective redundancies, [1975] OJ L 48/29, now consolidated as Council Directive 98/59/EC of 20 July 1998 on the approximation of the laws of the Member States relating to collective redundancies, [1998] OJ L 225/16.

[38] See for example Council Directive 77/187/EEC of 14 February 1977 on the approximation of the laws of the Member States relating to the safeguarding of employees' rights in the event of transfers of undertakings, businesses or parts of businesses, [1977] OJ L 61/26, now codified as Council Directive 2001/23/EC of 12 March 2001 on the approximation of the laws of the

employment rights in, for example, outsourcing cases) and more rights for women at work.[39] But it was not until Jacques Delors became President of the European Commission that there was a true flowering of EU employment rights in the late 1980s and early 1990s: more than twenty directives on all aspects of health and safety, together with directives on rights for pregnant workers 92/85/EEC,[40] and, most controversially, the Working Time Directive 93/104 (repealed and replaced by Directive 2003/88),[41] were adopted.

With the increased powers given to the social partners by the Maastricht Treaty in 1992, they negotiated further directives focused on the rights of atypical workers, namely part-time workers[42] and fixed term workers.[43] These directives built on the principles found in the earlier directives on gender equality, which had, in turn been subject to a broad, generous reading by the Court of Justice, improving the position for women in respect of maternity protection,[44] lifting the ceiling on compensation when discrimination has been established,[45] and ensuring equality for men in respect of occupational pension age.[46] Perhaps, most importantly, the EU has expanded the range of

Member States relating to the safeguarding of employees' rights in the event of transfers of undertakings, businesses or parts of undertakings or businesses, [2001] OJ L 82/16.

[39] See for example Council Directive 75/117/EEC on the Approximation of the Laws of the Member States Relating to the Application of the Principle of Equal Pay for Men and Women, [1995] OJ L 45/19; Council Directive 76/207/EEC of 9 February 1976 on the Implementation of the Principle of Equal Treatment for Men and Women as Regards Access to Employment, Vocational Training and Promotion, and Working Conditions [1976] OJ L 39/40. These are now consolidated into Directive 2006/54/EC of the European Parliament and of the Council of 5 July 2006 on the Implementation of the Principle of Equal Opportunities and Equal Treatment of Men and Women in Matters of Employment and Occupation (recast), [2006] OJ L 204/23.

[40] Council Directive 92/85/EEC of 19 October 1992 on the Introduction of Measures to Encourage Improvements in the Safety and Health at Work of Pregnant Workers and Workers Who Have Recently Given Birth or Are Breastfeeding, [1992] OJ L 348/1.

[41] Council Directive 93/104/EC Concerning Certain Aspects of the Organization of Working Time, [1993] OJ L 307/18, now codified as Directive 2003/88/EC of the European Parliament and of the Council of 4 November 2003 Concerning Certain Aspects of the Organization of Working Time, [2003] OJ L 299/9.

[42] Council Directive 97/81/EC of 15 December 1997 Concerning the Framework Agreement on Part-time Work Concluded by UNICE, CEEP, and the ETUC, [1998] OJ L 14/9.

[43] Council Directive 1999/70/EC of 28 June 1999 Concerning the Framework Agreement on Fixed-term Work Concluded by ETUC, UNICE, and CEEP, [1999] OJ L 175/43.

[44] ECJ, judgment of 8 November 1990 in *Dekker v Stichting Vormingscentrum voor Jong Volwassenen (VJV-Centrum) Plus*, C-177/88, EU:C:1990:383.

[45] ECJ, judgment of 2 August 1993 in *Helen Marshall v Southampton and South-West Hampshire Area Health Authority*, Case C-271/91, EU:C:1993:335.

[46] ECJ, judgment of 17 May 1990 in *Barber v Guardian Royal Exchange Assurance Group*, C-262/88, EU:C:1990:209.

'protected characteristics'.[47] So it is due to EU law that discrimination on the grounds of sexual orientation, age, religion, and belief has been prohibited.

But from the perspective of UK workers the EU story has not been unadulterated good news. Particularly serious from a trade union point of view has been the spectre of the four freedoms being used successfully by employers to challenge national rules on employment rights, as the *Viking* and *Laval* litigation shows.[48] The UK has the strictest strike laws in Europe; for trade unions *Viking* and *Laval* imposed additional requirements and made it harder still to go on strike.[49]

Even the Charter of Fundamental Rights seemed more of a threat to workers than a balm: the Court of Justice's decision in *Alemo-Herron*,[50] a reference from the UK courts about the interpretation of the UK's more generous implementation of the Transfer of Undertakings Directive, showed that the Article 16 right to conduct a business could be used to challenge and remove

---

[47] Council Directive 2000/43/EC of 29 June 2000 Implementing the Principle of Equal Treatment between Persons Irrespective of Racial or Ethnic Origin, [2000] OJ L 180/22; and Council Directive 2000/78/EC of 27 November 2000 Establishing a General Framework for Equal Treatment in Employment and Occupation, [2000] OJ L 303/16.

[48] ECJ, judgment of 11 December 2007 in *International Transport Workers' Federation and Finnish Seamen's Union* ('*Viking*'), C-438/05, EU:C:2007:772; and ECJ, judgment of 18 December 2007 in *Laval un Partneri*, C-341/05, EU:C:2007:809. See S. Feenstra, 'How Can the Viking/Laval Conundrum Be Resolved? Balancing the Economic and the Social: One Bed for Two Dreams?', Chapter 13 in this volume.

[49] K. Apps, 'Damages Claims against Trade Unions after *Viking* and *Laval*' (2009) 34 *European Law Review* 141. The ILO's committee is critical of the EU's position: ILO, '2010 Report of the Committee of Experts on the Application of Conventions and Recommendations' (2010), available at: www.ilo.org/global/standards/WCMS_123515/lang–en/index.htm (accessed 8 September 2015). See also K. Ewing, *Fighting Back: Resisting 'Union Busting' and 'Strike Breaking' in the BA Dispute* (The Institute of Employment Rights, 2011). More generally, see J. Malmberg, 'Trade Union Liability for EU-unlawful Collective Action' (2012) 3 *European Labour Law Review* 5.

[50] ECJ, judgment 18 July 2013 in *Alemo-Herron and Others v Parkwood Leisure Ltd*, C-426/11, EU:C:2013:521, paragraphs 31–5: 'the interpretation of Article 3 of Directive 2001/23 must in any event comply with Article 16 of the Charter, laying down the freedom to conduct a business ... In the light of Article 3 of Directive 2001/23, it is apparent that, by reason of the freedom to conduct a business, the transferee must be able to assert its interests effectively in a contractual process to which it is party and to negotiate the aspects determining changes in the working conditions of its employees with a view to its future economic activity. However, the transferee in the main proceedings is unable to participate in the collective bargaining body at issue. In those circumstances, the transferee can neither assert its interests effectively in a contractual process nor negotiate the aspects determining changes in working conditions for its employees with a view to its future economic activity ... In those circumstances, the transferee's contractual freedom is seriously reduced to the point that such a limitation is liable to adversely affect the very essence of its freedom to conduct a business.'

that higher protection since it was deemed to interfere with the employer's managerial freedom. These decisions shook the faith of (UK) trade unions in the benign influence of the Court of Justice and EU law more generally. Their support for the EU project was therefore more equivocal than might have otherwise been (although the main unions did eventually come out in support of the Remain campaign).

The Leave campaign saw the Court of Justice as the root of all ills.[51] For employers, some of the decisions of the Court of Justice have caused real practical and economic problems, especially its interpretation of the Working Time Directive. The Court of Justice's broad definition of 'on-call time' (to include time spent asleep but at the employer's premises) has made the Directive difficult and expensive to apply, especially in the healthcare sector.[52] Likewise, the Court's interpretation of the rules on rolled-up holiday pay has caused difficulties for employers hiring staff on short-term contracts. Employers were already a constituency with a potential grudge against the EU.

19.2.4.2 *The Limited Nature of EU Social Rights*

Even within the narrow field of employment law, the rights conferred on workers by EU law are selective and partial; a threadbare patchwork quilt, not an enveloping duvet. Not only do EU rules not cover pay, strikes, and lockouts, but they also do not cover unfair dismissal and redundancy. This is because the relationship between EU workers' rights and national law is complex and multi-layered. This has always been both the strength and weakness of the EU system: strength because the EU cannot and does not seek to replicate the national social system; weakness because the EU system contains obvious gaps while at the same time, in the rules it does have, must try to accommodate the diversity of industrial relations through a range of opt-outs, derogations, and other forms of flexibility which already dilute the substance of the rights.

---

[51] 'The European court will still be in charge of our laws. It already overrules us on everything from how much tax we pay, to who we can let in and out of the country and on what terms', see www.voteleavetakecontrol.org/why_vote_leave.html (accessed 13 December 2016). See also: 'Our courts would have the final say over those laws. When Britain joined the EEC in 1972, Parliament accepted that European law could have primacy over UK law. That law is ultimately overseen by the European Court of Justice in Luxembourg', Daily Telegraph Editorial, '20 Reasons You Should Vote to Leave the European Union', 22 June 2016, available at: www.telegraph.co.uk/news/2016/06/22/20-reasons-you-should-vote-to-leave-the-european-union/ (accessed 13 December 2016).
[52] ECJ, judgment of the Court of 9 September 2003 in *Landeshauptstadt Kiel v Norbert Jaeger*, C-151/02, EU:C:2003:437.

However, the main reason for the limited content of EU social policy is competence.[53] The EU's Member States have not given the EU the power to legislate in all areas traditionally considered part of employment law, let alone social policy more generally. Most notably, the reason why the EU has no rules in the sensitive fields of pay, strikes, or lockouts, is because, under Article 153(5) TFEU, the EU cannot legislate in these areas, thus creating a lacuna after the *Viking* decision.[54] More generally, the EU has no competence in respect of any of the key aspects of the welfare state. These are merely 'complementary' competences. Member States still cling firmly to the idea, embedded in the original Treaty settlement, that delivery of the welfare state, including employment law matters, is mainly for the domestic system. This means that even where the EU has competence, the Member States are reluctant to let it use it. This is fine so long as the national systems are able to function and respond to the needs of their people. But when (EU imposed) austerity measures and/ or national policies fail to deliver there is nothing the EU can do about it. And states are quick to blame the EU for their own failings.[55]

A further reason why the EU has not legislated as completely as might have been expected is the principle of subsidiarity. As Pochet and Degryse have shown in this volume, subsidiarity has been the friend and enemy of EU employment law. In essence the subsidiarity question asks whether social matters can be better achieved by the EU than the Member States. Often the answer to this question is a resounding no, as the yellow cards submitted in response to the Monti II proposal on strike action and the more recent proposal on posted workers (considered further in Chapter 13) have demonstrated. Not only does this show the continued lack of will for action by the EU in the field of employment law, but it also raises the question – never satisfactorily resolved – as to what function EU social policy is actually there to achieve. Is it about creating a level playing field of social rights and thus avoid social dumping, in which case EU employment law should be more

[53] For further details, see G. De Baere and K. Gutman, 'The Basis in EU Constitutional Law for Further Social Integration', Chapter 14 in this volume.

[54] See for example the saga of the Monti II Regulation: COM(2012)130 *Proposal for a Council Regulation on the Exercise of the Right to Take Collective Action within the Context of the Freedom of Establishment and the Freedom to Provide Services* (Brussels, 23 March 2012), discussed by The Adoptive Parents, 'The Life of a Death Foretold', in M. Freedland and J. Prassl (eds), *Viking, Laval and Beyond* (Hart Publishing 2015). See also De Baere and Gutman, n. 53 in this chapter.

[55] 'As Davies succinctly puts it: there have been 'years and years of opportunistic government rhetoric, in which everything short of a rainy summer was blamed on 'Europe' G. Davies, 'Could It All Have Been Avoided? Brexit and Treaty-permitted Restrictions on the Freedom of Workers', European Law Blog, 18 August 2016, available at: europeanlawblog.eu/?p=3294 (accessed 13 December 2016).

comprehensive than it actually is, or should the EU act only where there is a cross-border dimension to the issue (such as regulating the rights of employees in cross-border situations), in which case it should be less comprehensive than it is? The (now defunct) Brussels new settlement agreement of February 2016 suggested the latter, at least in the case of trade matters;[56] the Commission's Communication on the social pillar suggested the former.[57]

19.2.5 THE ROLE OF EU SOCIAL POLICY DURING THE CAMPAIGN

To what extent, did these EU employment rights, however patchy and partial, have a role to play in the referendum campaign? The pitch by the Remain camp was mainly about jobs: membership of the EU, and access to the single market was about creating wealth and thus employment.[58] As something of an afterthought, the StrongerIN campaign, the lead campaigning body for Remain, made a pitch for workers' votes based on the benefits they gain from EU employment rights:

> EU laws protect you in the workplace, meaning no government can scrap your rights.
>
> Being in the EU gives you the right to paid holiday leave, maximum working hours, equal treatment for men and women, rights for part-time workers, health and safety standards at work, parental leave and protection against discrimination based on sex, race, religion, age, disability and sexual orientation.
>
> If we left the EU, your workers' rights would be up for debate and vulnerable to being scrapped. There could be years of uncertainty for you and your employers.[59]

However, as the campaign progressed and canvassers for the Labour party, traditionally the party of working men and women, reported that many of

---

[56] 'The choice of the right level of action therefore depends, inter alia, on whether the issue under consideration has transnational aspects which cannot be satisfactorily regulated by action by Member States and on whether action at Union level would produce clear benefits by reason of its scale or effects compared with actions at the level of Member States', Council of the European Union, 'Council Conclusions on a New Settlement for the UK within the EU. They Also Discussed Migration and the Situation in Syria and Libya' of 18–19 February 2016, available at: www.consilium.europa.eu/en/press/press-releases/2016/02/19-euco-conclusions/ (accessed 13 December 2016).

[57] COM(2016)127 *Launching a Consultation on a European Pillar of Social Rights* (Strasbourg, 8 March 2016), p. 3.

[58] See www.strongerin.co.uk/#HoVuoKJQwp4LdSqi.97 (accessed 13 December 2016).

[59] See www.strongerin.co.uk/get_the_facts#scjSOEpa1HEBuASD.97 (accessed 13 December 2016).

their natural supporters were proposing to vote Leave,[60] the Remain campaign gave higher priority to making the case to stay in the EU based on protection of workers' rights. The trade union movement joined the calls. For example, Francis O'Grady, TUC General Secretary, said:

> Leave the EU and lose your rights at work – that's the message that even Leave campaigners like Priti Patel are now giving. But which rights would go – your right to paid holidays, your right to parental leave, maybe protections for pregnant workers? The EU guarantees all these rights and more, and it's why Brexit is such a big risk for working people.[61]

A letter by 10 trade union leaders encouraged workers to vote to remain, for the same reasons.[62] Even Jeremy Corbyn, the leader of the Labour party, finally found himself able to get behind the Remain campaign through promoting the cause of workers' rights. But it was too little, too late.

Further, very few of these rights in fact responded to the very real concerns of working – and non-working – people: job security, lack of affordable housing, lack of public services. All the talk of an EU social policy rang hollow. The EU didn't actually have one. The emperor had no clothes. This caused considerable difficulties for the Remain campaign. A potential goods news story – 'The EU is good for workers' – was in fact only a partially good news story, and a complicated one too – 'The EU is pretty good for workers in certain circumstances'. The Remain campaign was already struggling with a failure to address concerns about migration and specifically EU free movement rules. Since 2004 at least two million EU migrants, probably more, had come to the UK. The Leave campaign recognised the disquiet felt by sections of the public over this. They responded with the powerful and effective message 'Take back control', including of borders. And it worked. As Persaud points out:

[60] As Goodwin has pointed out: 'the vote for Brexit is also rooted strongly in Labour's working-class heartlands, revealing once again the sharp disconnect between labour and its more traditional supporters. One of the big stories of the night was the sheer level of public support for Brexit in Wales which … was once an area that the Labour party could rely on for tribal loyalty', see M. Goodwin, 'Brexit: Identity Trumps Economics in Revolt against Elites', *Financial Times*, 23 June 2016, available at: www.ft.com/cms/s/0/b6da366a-39ca-11e6-a780-b48ed7b6126f.html#axzz4Hh8k3jJN (accessed 13 December 2016).

[61] TUC, 'Priti Patel Reveals Leave Campaign Agenda to Reduce Workers' Rights, Says TUC', press release of 17 May 2016, available at: www.tuc.org.uk/international-issues/europe/eu-referendum/workplace-issues/priti-patel-reveals-leave-campaign-agenda (accessed 13 December 2016).

[62] L. McCluskey et al., 'Trade Union Members Should Vote to Stay in the EU', *The Guardian*, 5 June 2016, available at: www.theguardian.com/politics/2016/jun/05/trade-union-members-should-vote-to-stay-in-the-eu (accessed 13 December 2016).

The adjustment costs from trade liberalisation are borne most prevalently by the same group as those that voted to leave the EU: less-skilled and older workers. Brexit was not an irrational vote of the ignorant, but a highly rational vote by the same losers from trade as everywhere else ... [T]rade liberalisation increases the relative supply of people with your skills. The consequence for those for which it does is that their wages and conditions worsen.[63]

Potential leave voters needed to be convinced that there was a comprehensive social policy in place that would give them education, support, and an adequate social safety net. Domestic social policy was failing to deliver on this. As we have seen, due to lack of competence and political will, EU social policy, confined as it was to *employment* law, failed there too. So telling these Leave voters, faced with a range of socioeconomic difficulties, that the EU can give them some employment law rights was like offering them a torn umbrella in the face of a monsoon.

19.3   WHAT MIGHT HAVE BEEN?

But then, I suppose, when with the benefit of hindsight one begins to search one's past for such 'turning points', one is apt to start seeing them everywhere.

– Stevens, *Remains of the Day*.[64]

19.3.1   INTRODUCTION

The story told about the UK is probably not so different from that experienced in a number of states.[65] All Western countries have witnessed a decline in traditional jobs;[66] artificial intelligence is likely to make matters

---

[63] A. Persaud, 'Brexit and Other Harbingers of a Return to the Dangers of the 1930s', Vox, 26 August 2016, available at: voxeu.org/article/brexit-and-other-harbingers-return-dangers-1930s (accessed 13 December 2016).

[64] Ishiguro, n. 1 in this chapter, at p. 185.

[65] B. Jopson, 'Gig Economy Poses Tough Questions for US', *Financial Times*, 23 August 2016, available at: www.ft.com/content/605e1678-68e9-11e6-a0b1-d87a9fea034f (accessed 13 December 2016); Unison, 'Stronger Together: A UNISON Guide to Influencing the New NHS' (2012), available at: www.unison.org.uk/content/uploads/2013/07/PoliciesInfluencing-the-new-NHS3.pdf (accessed 13 December 2016).

[66] See for example The Economist, 'In with the New', *The Economist*, 28 June 2014, available at: www.economist.com/news/special-report/21604686-traditional-industries-are-declining-outsourcing-offshoring-and-subcontracting-are (accessed 13 December 2016); and 'The

worse.[67] Yet the UK Brexit vote was not the first. In 1992 the Danes rejected the Maastricht Treaty; in 2005, the French and the Dutch rejected the Constitutional Treaty; and in 2008 the Irish initially rejected the Lisbon Treaty. The EU had been warned. What more could the EU have done? Hindsight is of course a wonderful thing and the question of what might have been takes no account of the major crises the EU has been facing since 2008, notably the financial crisis of 2008–09 and the near collapse of the Eurozone, the migrant crisis of 2014–, and the ever-growing scourge of terrorism.

However, I would like to argue that there are three things the EU could have done – and two more that would probably have made no difference.

19.3.2 WHAT WOULD HAVE MADE NO DIFFERENCE

The EU has a well-established cohesion policy, mainly intended to assist new Member States to develop their infrastructure. Spain, Portugal, Greece, and the EU-8 states have been major beneficiaries. But so has the UK. Take the case of Cornwall. As the local authority's own website says:

> Europe impacts considerably on the work of Cornwall Council, through all departments and areas, and the Council has long recognised the importance of the EU for the County ...
>
> The Cornwall and Isles of Scilly Growth Programme is the European economic regeneration programme for the region. Running from 2014–2020 it will contribute to the EU ambition to deliver smart, sustainable and inclusive growth.
>
> The Cornwall and the Isles of Scilly Growth Programme is worth €603,706,864 (excluding technical assistance) and is made up of two main funding streams:
>
> - European Regional Development Fund (ERDF) – The ERDF Programme is worth €437,472,735.
> - European Social Fund (ESF) – The ESF Programme is worth €166,234,129.[68]

As the Leave-supporting *Daily Telegraph* pointed out, 'Between 2014 and 2020, both Cornwall and West Wales will receive over €1000 (£800) per person from

Weaker Sex', *The Economist*, 20 May 2015, available at: www.economist.com/news/leaders/21652323-blue-collar-men-rich-countries-are-trouble-they-must-learn-adapt-weaker-sex/comments?page=1 (accessed 13 December 2016).

[67] The Economist, 'Rise of the Machines', *The Economist*, 6 May 2015, available at: www.economist.com/news/briefing/21650526-artificial-intelligence-scares-peopleexcessively-so-so-rise-machines (accessed 13 December 2016).

[68] See www.cornwall.gov.uk/business/europe/ (accessed 13 December 2016).

the EU Structural and Investment Fund – similar to that received by Romania and Bulgaria,'[69] But as the *FT* succinctly put it, 'Cornwall's Brexit backers show that money cannot buy EU love':[70] its population of 530,000 people voted by 56.52 per cent to leave the EU. Cornwall has now asked for the UK government to step in to plug the funding gap.[71] So, throwing money at the problem, in and of itself, would not have helped.

Second, more workers' rights, particularly for those in the 'gig' economy (meaning those working on short-term contracts who are often described as self-employed), may have formed a brick in constructing the argument that the EU was committed to supporting workers. However, it probably would have made little difference to the outcome of the referendum. The EU is aware of the position of precarious workers. The Brussels-funded European Foundation for the Improvement of Living and Working Conditions has done some good work in mapping the diverse new forms of working arrangements;[72] the Commision's Directorate General for Employment, Social Affairs and Inclusion has funded various conferences on the issue.[73] However, the EU's limited legal competence on a matter which goes to the core of domestic labour law, namely the question of personal scope, combined with the absence of political will, has meant nothing has been done. Even a call to codify the meaning of the term 'worker', as developed in the Court's case law, has come to nothing.

19.3.3 WHAT MIGHT HAVE MADE A DIFFERENCE

19.3.3.1 *A Deal on Migration*

Three things might have made a difference to the outcome of the referendum. First, and most importantly, would have been a more robust deal on

---

[69] D. Dunford, 'Mapped: Where in the UK Receives Most EU Funding and How Does This Compare with the Rest of Europe?', *Daily Telegraph*, 1 June 2016, available at: www.telegraph.co.uk/news/2016/06/01/mapped-where-in-the-uk-receives-most-eu-funding-and-how-does-thi/ (accessed 13 December 2016).

[70] J. Chaffin, 'Cornwall's Brexit Backers Show that Money Cannot Buy EU love', *Financial Times*, 17 May 2016, available at: www.ft.com/content/9b881406-1b46-11e6-b286-cddde55ca122 (accessed 13 December 2016).

[71] W. Worley, 'Cornwall Issues Plea to Keep EU Funding after Voting for Brexit', *The Independent*, 24 June 2016, available at: www.independent.co.uk/news/uk/home-news/brexit-cornwall-issues-plea-for-funding-protection-after-county-overwhelmingly-votes-in-favour-of-a7101311.html/ (accessed 13 December 2016).

[72] See for example R. Pedersini and D. Coletto, *Self-employed Workers: Industrial Relations and Working Conditions* (Eurofound, 2010).

[73] See for example European Labour Law Network, 'New Forms of Employment and EU Law' (2014) *Seminar Report*, 2014.

migration. From his much-heralded Brussels negotiations in February 2016, David Cameron came back with a promise for an amendment to the Citizens' Rights Directive 2004/38 for essentially a complex emergency brake on the payment of in-work benefits to EU migrants. This, together with the uncertainty surrounding the precise legal status of the deal, proved insufficient to many UK voters (although a large concession from the EU). In some circles it was even counterproductive: it demonstrated how weak the UK was and how its concerns over immigration had not been listened to. Migration Watch, an 'independent and non-political think tank chaired by Lord Green of Deddington, a former Ambassador', came up with the stark but eye-catching figure that 'Under the official "high" migration scenario the [UK's] population is projected to rise by around 500,000 a year – the equivalent to a new city the size of Liverpool every year.'[74] These figures take no account of the benefits of migration to the UK economy. But the image of a new Liverpool every year was powerful, especially in areas with, paradoxically, low levels of migration (areas with the highest levels of immigration – notably London – were often among those most likely to vote to Remain).

Had David Cameron, the then British Prime Minister, come back from his negotiations in Brussels with a clear statement that he had secured the possibility of an emergency brake on free movement (or at least a postdated cheque that this would have been allowed even if only in respect of areas suffering particular social difficulties[75]), then the million plus voters who made a difference to the outcome of the referendum might have changed their mind. While some have argued that such a brake was already possible, even within the framework of the existing Treaty rules,[76] many thought it would have required a Treaty amendment. In fact, there was some recognition of the need to curb

---

[74] See www.migrationwatchuk.org/key-topics/population/ (accessed 13 December 2016).

[75] For an interesting early parallel, see Art. 115 EEC 'In order to ensure that the execution of measures of commercial policy taken in accordance with this Treaty by any Member State is not obstructed by deflection of trade, or where differences between such measures lead to economic difficulties in one or more of the Member States, the Commission shall recommend the methods for the *requisite co-operation between Member States*. Failing this, the Commission shall authorise Member States to take the *necessary protective measures*, the conditions and details of which it shall determine. In case of urgency during the transitional period, Member States may themselves take the necessary measures and shall notify them to the other Member States and to the Commission, which may decide that the States concerned shall amend or abolish such measures. In the selection of such measures, priority shall be given to those which cause *the least disturbance* to the functioning of the common market and which take into account the need to expedite, as far as possible, the introduction of the common customs tariff.'

[76] Davies, n. 55 in this chapter.

migration in the Brussels agreement[77] but strangely David Cameron put little emphasis on it in his subsequent public pronouncements.

An emergency brake on migration might have helped to show that, despite the problems this would cause to the integrity of the integration project, the EU understood the concerns of those communities where the numbers of migrants have increased rapidly in a short space of time, areas which voted resoundingly to leave. As the *Economist* notes, where foreign-born populations increased by more than 200 per cent between 2001 and 2014, a Leave vote followed in 94 per cent of cases.[78] The proportion of migrants may be relatively low in Leave strongholds such as Boston in Lincolnshire (where 15.4 per cent of the population are foreign-born). But it has grown precipitously in a short period of time (by 479 per cent, in Boston's case). The *Economist* concludes: 'High levels of immigration don't seem to bother Britons; high rates of change do.'[79] This suggests that it was the sudden (and unplanned?) influx of migrants, creating pressure on public services (such as access to schools, doctors' surgeries and housing), that may have been the reason why these groups voted to leave.[80] Allocation of public funds is a matter for domestic, not EU, government. And it is here that EU migration rules and domestic social policy collide. EU migration created pressure on domestic provision. Domestic policy let down the local population; EU social policy did not – and could not – respond.

19.3.3.2 THE EUROPEAN SEMESTER

Making the European semester work properly is the second way which might have made a difference to the outcome of the referendum if it had been able

---

[77] C. Barnard, 'The Day the Clock Stopped on EU Citizenship', in P. Koutrakos and J. Snell (eds), *Research Handbook on the Internal Market* (Edward Elgar, 2017).

[78] The Economist, 'Explaining Brexit: Britain's Immigration Paradox', *The Economist*, 8 July 2016, available at: www.economist.com/news/britain/21701950-areas-lots-migrants-voted-mainly-remain-or-did-they-britains-immigration-paradox (accessed 16 December 2016).

[79] Ibid.

[80] There are also issues about identity – that the rapid arrival of so many migrants – challenged the identity of local people. By contrast in Scotland, as Deakin argues, which has also undergone significant deindustrialisation in the same period, the protest found an outlet in the rise of nationalism and the election to office of the predominantly social democratic Scottish National Party, which has held a controlling bloc of seats in the Scottish Parliament continuously since 2011. Every Scottish region voted by a majority for Remain and the overall vote in Scotland was over 60% for rejecting Brexit, see S. Deakin, 'Brexit, Labour Rights and Migration: Why Wisbech Matters to Brussels' (2016) 17 *German Law Journal* 13.

to deliver on its promise. Little known and certainly little loved in the UK (and elsewhere), the European semester is the successor of the Luxembourg and then the Lisbon strategy. Since the late 1990s, the EU has been advocating the need for greater inclusion of those disadvantaged in the labour market (such as older workers and the disabled), better policies to encourage early school leavers to stay in education or training, and reforms to the benefits systems to encourage people into work and to ensure these systems are sustainable. However, the lack of EU competence in these key areas has significantly hindered the EU's capacity for effective action. Further, the EU's need to resort to the opaque Open Method of Coordination (OMC), has meant that any positives resulting from the European semester may not get credited to the EU. Outside the specialist literature, the European semester receives almost no coverage. The mainstream press is certainly not interested. Successive UK governments have also not been enthusiastic supporters of the semester; the Westminster Parliament has not been extensively involved. And yet, had (some) of the policy changes proposed by the European semester been introduced – for example about helping some of the most marginalised in society, ensuring better provision for training – been delivered, they might have created a more positive climate in the UK, albeit not one that is necessarily appreciative of the EU. The mood music might, however, have been better.

19.3.3.3 GREATER POLICY COMPETENCE

This brings us to the third way which might have made a difference. More effective policy response in key areas might have shown the EU as capable and a competent organisation, one that it was worth belonging to. As it was, the EU's perceived failure to deal effectively with the Eurozone crisis, and then the migration crisis, enabled the leaders of the Leave campaign to ventilate the argument that the UK should not be tethered to a sinking ship or as the President of the European Commission put it, 'trying to keep a burning plane in the air while repairing it'.[81] Those in favour of Leave were able to say that by 'taking back control' the UK will 'not have to keep bailing out the Euro'.[82]

Some of these policy 'failures' are, once again, due to the question of the division of competence between the EU and the Member States. However much the EU might have liked to order Member States to sort out their budgets or accept transfer of refugees, it lacked the powers to deliver this. For

[81] BBC, 'MEPs Elect Jean-Claude Juncker to Head EU Commission', BBC.com, 15 July 2014, available at: www.bbc.com/news/world-europe-28299335/ (accessed 13 December 2016).
[82] See www.voteleavetakecontrol.org/why_vote_leave.html/ (accessed 13 December 2016).

some this is a strength of the EU; for the UK, ultimately it turned out to be a weakness.

19.4 WHAT THE FUTURE MIGHT HOLD: THE REMAINS OF THE DAY

Perhaps, then, there is something to his advice that I should cease looking back so much, that I should adopt a more positive outlook and try to make the best of what remains of my day.

– Stevens, *Remains of the Day*.[83]

19.4.1 FOR THE UK AND FOR THE EU

So what, then, is going to happen following the referendum? One scenario is that the UK leaves the EU but joins the European Economic Area, which includes continuing unrestricted access to the four freedoms. The price for full access to the single market means some form of free movement of persons, albeit perhaps subject to an emergency brake. In this case EU social law will continue to apply, as will the judgments of the Court of Justice and the EFTA Court. At the moment the government appears to have ruled out this possibility.

Another possibility is a special association agreement for the UK that allows some form of access to the single market, with the UK being required to continue to respect EU employment rules to help to ensure a level playing field. A third possibility is some sort of free trade arrangement, as the EU has with Canada, where employment law plays no part. That said, in the draft EU Council Guidelines the EU has been clear: any future trade agreement must 'ensure a level playing field in terms of competition and state aid, and must encompass safeguards against unfair competitive advantages through, inter alia, fiscal, social and environmental dumping'. This suggests that the UK will have to continue to respect some EU social rules.

A fourth possibility is a hard Brexit: the UK leaves the EU and no alternative special relationship is put in its place. For many voting leave, this is apparently what they had in mind. They want to repeal the Working Time and Agency Work Regulations and a number of other rules. However, the Prime Minister has suggested that this is precipitous. In her party conference speech in October 2016 she said:

---

[83] Ishiguro, n. 1 in this chapter, at p. 256.

As we repeal the European Communities Act, we will convert the 'acquis' – that is, the body of existing EU law – into British law. When the Great Repeal Bill is given Royal Assent, Parliament will be free – subject to international agreements and treaties with other countries and the EU on matters such as trade – to amend, repeal and improve any law it chooses. But by converting the acquis into British law, we will give businesses and workers maximum certainty as we leave the European Union. The same rules and laws will apply to them after Brexit as they did before ... And let me be absolutely clear: existing workers' legal rights will continue to be guaranteed in law – and they will be guaranteed as long as I am Prime Minister.[84]

The Minister for Brexit, David Davis, explained this position: 'The great British industrial working classes voted overwhelmingly for Brexit. I am not at all attracted by the idea of rewarding them by cutting their rights.'

In the absence of the UK, will the other Member States proceed with alacrity to develop a full employment acquis at EU level? Current politics makes this unlikely. There is a deep cleavage between the Western and Eastern European states, with the Western states pushing for more, the Eastern states for less. This schism can be seen with the proposed Posted Workers Directive, which aims to allow host states to imposed greater rights and obligations on posted workers. The Eastern states see this as a form of disguised protectionism, with EU law operating to remove their competitive advantage.

The Social Pillar, designed to develop a fuller social dimension for the Eurozone states, is the most recent attempt by the EU 'to take account of the changing realities of Europe's societies and the world of work ... and which can serve as a compass for the renewed convergence within the euro area'.[85] As Deakin in Chapter 8 of this volume shows, it is a serious attempt to identify principles that might guide EU social policy forward but it contains a note of warning: 'The Social Pillar should contain a much clearer commitment to policies which could help build inclusive and sustainable growth inside the Eurozone, in particular legal support for centralised (sector-level and national) wage determination, and non-discriminatory employment protection laws ... What is at stake is not simply the issue of a just and equitable EMU, but whether EMU is sustainable.'

[84] T. May, 'Brexit Speech', speech at the Conservative Party Conference, 2 October 2016, available at: www.independent.co.uk/news/uk/politics/theresa-may-conference-speech-article-50-brexit-eu-a7341926.html (accessed 16 December 2016).

[85] European Commission, 'Towards a European Pillar of Social Rights', Commission Website, available at: ec.europa.eu/priorities/deeper-and-fairer-economic-and-monetary-union/towards-european-pillar-social-rights_en/ (accessed 13 December 2016).

19.5　CONCLUSIONS

One of the recurrent themes in Ishiguro's novel *Remains of the Day* is dignity and what 'dignity' actually means.[86] EU employment rights have helped to improve the position of EU workers but not sufficiently, in the case of those voting to leave, to overcome their concerns about the EU. With a government engaged full steam ahead to deliver Brexit, migration will be controlled in some form. Once migration is 'controlled', and the UK is no longer a member of the EU, who will there to be to blame for the position that many in deprived regions of the United Kingdom find themselves in? With a reduction in tax receipts and the costs of Brexit, there will be little money to provide for extensive regeneration projects. Paradoxically, many people who have voted to Leave, may find their personal situation deteriorating due to job losses brought about by recession and large employers relocating to the rest of the EU. A multilevel regional/national/EU identity may be replaced by a more precarious British identity. This is not the rosy future promised by the Leave campaign. The dignity brought about by taking back control has its own price. Across the Channel, the situation appears little brighter. A divided Europe has been a recipe for disaster in the past. The Remains of the Day are currently looking somewhat bleak.

---

[86] 'Dignity isn't just something gentleman have. Dignity's something every man and woman in the country can strive for and get.' (A local man speaking to Stevens, *Remains of the Day*, Ishiguro, n. 1 in this chapter, at p. 195.)

Index